A HISTORY OF THE

GYPSIES

OF EASTERN EUROPE AND RUSSIA

ALSO BY DAVID M. CROWE

THE HOLOCAUST:
Roots, History, and Aftermath

OSKAR SCHINDLER:
The Untold Account of His Life, Wartime Activities, and the
True Story Behind the List

THE BALTIC STATES AND THE GREAT POWERS:
Foreign Relations, 1938–1940

THE GYPSIES OF EASTERN EUROPE
(*with John Kolsti*)

A HISTORY OF THE

GYPSIES

OF EASTERN EUROPE AND RUSSIA

DAVID M. CROWE

palgrave
macmillan

To Rebecca and John

A HISTORY OF THE GYPSIES OF EASTERN EUROPE AND RUSSIA
Second edition copyright © 2007 by David M. Crowe.
First edition copyright © 1994, 1996 by David M. Crowe.

First ST. MARTIN'S PRESS hardcover edition: 1994
First ST. MARTIN'S PRESS paperback edition: 1996
First PALGRAVE MACMILLAN paperback edition: April 2007
175 Fifth Avenue, New York, N.Y. 10010 and
Houndmills, Basingstoke, Hampshire, England RG21 6XS.
Companies and representatives throughout the world.

PALGRAVE MACMILLAN is the global academic imprint of the Palgrave Macmillan division of St. Martin's Press, LLC and of Palgrave Macmillan Ltd. Macmillan® is a registered trademark in the United States, United Kingdom and other countries. Palgrave is a registered trademark in the European Union and other countries.

ISBN-13: 978–1–4039–8009–0 (second edition)
ISBN-10: 1–4039–8009–8 (second edition)

Library of Congress Cataloging-in-Publication Data is available from the Library of Congress.

A catalogue record of the book is available from the British Library.

Design by Newgen Imaging Systems (P) Ltd., Chennai, India.

10 9 8 7 6 5 4 3 2 1

Printed in the United States of America.

C·O·N·T·E·N·T·S

P·R·E·F·A·C·E
TO
S·E·C·O·N·D E·D·I·T·I·O·N

Earlier this year, Alessandra Bastagli, my editor at Palgrave Macmillan, approached me about the prospect of doing a second edition of the current book. Given its ongoing success and the fact that it has already been translated into Japanese and Russian, I thought it was time to update it, particularly in light of the dramatic changes that have swept Eastern Europe and Russia since the first edition came out in 1994. Fortunately, I have remained very active in the field of Roma studies and felt comfortable tackling this new project. There are, I suppose, many ways to approach a new edition of a book. Generally speaking, I felt, based on my work with Roma scholars in Europe and North America, that the original edition had stood the test of time well. Consequently, I decided to focus my energies on a new chapter that would address the many changes that have taken place in the region since the mid-1990s. Though I have been quite involved, both as a scholar and a bit of an activist, on Roma issues in Europe and North America during that period, I was not prepared for the dismal conditions I found there. In most instances, as the reader will see in the final chapter, most Roma are worse off today than they were in the mid-1990s and few have benefited from the more positive societal changes in the region.

One of those changes deals with the new countries that have emerged, particularly in the former Yugoslavia. One of the challenges I faced in writing the new post-1994 chapter was how to deal with the new states in the region or the ones that I did not cover in the first edition. I finally decided to approach this chapter in the same way I did the earlier edition—nation by nation. The result is that the new chapter deals with the Roma in fifteen countries— Albania, Bosnia and Herzegovina, Bulgaria, Croatia, the Czech Republic and Slovakia, Hungary, Kosovo, Macedonia, Poland, Romania, Russia, Serbia and Montenegro, and Ukraine. Though a discussion of the history of the Roma in most of these countries was included within the broader context of the original six countries covered in the first edition, I did add a little more historical background to my sections on Albania and Kosovo.

I have to admit that I approach my work on the Roma with love and commitment. It is rare that a scholar can contribute in even the most modest way to societal change, and I would like to think that my two decades of work in this field has in some way helped change ideas and policies about the Roma. I hope this new edition will further our knowledge about the plight of the Roma in Eastern Europe and Russia and in turn stimulate others to reach out to this group.

I would like to thank my wife, Kathryn, for her loving support of my work. The Associate Director of the University of North Carolina at Greensboro's Walter Clinton Jackson Library, she has not only encouraged and supported my work, she has, at times, also enjoyed time together with our Roma friends in Europe. She has also helped me locate some of the rather obscure resources I have used in this and others works on the Roma. This edition, like the first, is dedicated to my children, Rebecca and John. I also hope that in some small way it will also stimulate my four grandchildren, Sarah, Reeves, Ivy, and Courtney, to do what they can to create a more loving, peaceful, caring world.

David M. Crowe
Greensboro, North Carolina
October 31, 2006

F·O·R·E·W·O·R·D

Much has changed for the Gypsies of Eastern Europe and Russia and much has also remained the same since David Crowe published the first edition of this book in 1994. This new edition may therefore be welcomed as offering readers an update on the Gypsy condition over the long last decade as well as allowing them to measure recent developments against the historical past so well covered in the book.

The first and most striking change in scholarship and public discourse over the last decade has been the widespread abandonment of the term "Gypsy" in favor of the name "Roma." David Crowe has kept the original title of his book for bibliographical continuity and perhaps also because "Gypsy" remains the most familiar designation of the people with whom we are concerned. The newly popular plural eponym "Roma" borrows from the self-ascriptive singular term, "Rom," meaning originally a married Gypsy man.[1] The adjective "Romani," referring to the language known by its speakers as "Romanes" and now spoken or once spoken by a widely dispersed population, covers the broadest spectrum and it is also sometimes used as a noun. One encounters the variant "Romany" with the plural "Romanies," but also "Romanichels," the latter referring usually to these same people living in the English-speaking world.

The name "Roma" is a preferable alternative to "Gypsy" since the latter is considered derogatory and also historically misconceived as it suggests etymologically that "Egypt" is the ancestral home of the Roma.[2] Although the prevailing thesis of the Indian origins of the Roma has been nuanced by scholars who maintain that Romani speech and ethnic identity only emerged after the populations concerned had left India, the idea of an Egyptian origin is fantasy.[3] Even as "Roma" is fast becoming the recognized name for all people earlier referred to as Gypsies, it may still be misleading since it covers some who do not consider themselves Roma (though they would acknowledge themselves as Romani/y people) and have their own very specific ethnonyms, such as the Sinti of Germany or the Manush of France, or those whose relationship to the Roma properly speaking is under investigation, such as the Domaris of the Middle East, or the Lom once associated with Armenia. Ironically, therefore, "Roma," invoked to replace the exonym "Gypsy," itself still serves as an exonym referring to a variety of groups.

Broadly speaking, the basis for identifying a given group as Roma is linguistic since the designation is supposed to encompass all those who speak

Romanes or a variant thereof, as well as those who once spoke it or are thought to have spoken it but no longer do, such as the Spanish Gitanos. To underline the complexity of accurate and acceptable nomenclature, let us note as an example that some Hungarian Roma subscribe to the usually pejorative terms "Cigans" or "Ciganyok," presumably to underscore their distinctiveness from purported kin outside Hungary.[4] These Ciganyok, by the way, often speak only Hungarian. One may speculate as to whether the term Gypsy will ever make it back into politically correct vocabulary, as once banned terms such as "Black" or "Negro" are being resuscitated by some of their designees as a matter of pride.

In the search for a proper designation of the people with whom we are concerned here, a novel and credible variant is the double-r "Rroma."[5] Linguistically more accurate than the single-r, the term "Rroma" has been picked up recently in Romania, though it is not clear on whose initiative, as a demarcater between the majority Romanian population and the Roma/Rroma community. Though scholars may gravitate towards "Rroma," it is unlikely that political discourse and public opinion could countenance yet another change of name so soon after having been weaned away from "Gypsy" to "Roma." Finally, let us note that within the broad category of Roma/Rroma themselves or its sub-groups, often the most meaningful eponyms are those originating in specific trade-defined groups, such as Romanian Rudari or miners or Bulgarian Ursari or bear trainers.

Names may change but the Roma's historical condition remains that of victims of discrimination, as David Crowe has shown in the historical part of his book as well as in the update. This is indeed a constant but it may be argued that the condition of the Roma has actually worsened during the period of post-communism transition.[6] This is the message that one draws from David Crowe's description of the appalling material conditions of the Roma or of attitudes and policies towards Roma, including in the Czech Republic where one might have expected better from the land of Vaclav Havel. This deterioration can be partly explained in structural terms not directly related to the Roma situation. The transition has inflicted traumatic shocks on state institutions whose crash has left gaping lacunae, particularly in the social safety net. The totalitarian or quasi-totalitarian state with its heavy handed and paternalistic Communist era regulation has given way to the vacuum of the weak or inadequate state.[7]

The fall of communism has created new social and economic structures and norms that bypass the Roma altogether. There is no room for traditional Roma roles and ethos within a system that rests upon a logic of market profitability, capitalist efficiency and technological modernity. Beyond ever acuter marginalization, the only social role that appears left to the Roma is that of scapegoats for some of the miseries of transition; in this respect, Roma are picking up a position previously occupied by other minorities, such as the Jews, in the process of modernization.[8] The fact that post-communist civil society has evolved in the direction of corruption, mafioso networks and law-lessness—the sorts of ills conventionally imputed to Roma—suggests that Roma stereotypes convey a troubling alter-image of these societies' own self-perceptions and orientations.

Roma have lost whatever social entitlements they possessed in the communist era—cheap food, unattractive employment, indifferent health care; wretched but standardized housing and schooling—and they have not gained economic opportunities or greater consideration on the part of their own societies. Roma have, however, benefited from the rise of a new sensibility and a new activism originating outside the post-communist area. Indeed, concern for the plight of the Roma is becoming a measure of commitment to European values, in some ways comparable to Europe's post-Holocaust commitment to vigilance against anti-semitism. A growing number of non-governmental organizations, mostly in Western Europe and America, backed by international organizations as well as anxious governments, have focused upon the Roma's conditions of life and the discrimination they are suffering. The result has been the launching of numerous initiatives dedicated to improving the lot of the Roma. Among the most significant programs is the Decade of Roma Inclusion, a multilateral plan of Roma development elaborated by the World Bank, Soros' Open Society Institute and other international and European funding sponsors in cooperation with some post-communist states.[9] Among the highest profile institutions is the European Roma Rights Center in Budapest, also Soros sponsored, that con-centrates on legal advocacy and what it calls strategic litigation.[10]

The approach to Roma issues generated by this new sensibility is therefore two-pronged, consisting of both developmental or socio-economic integration schemes and human or minority rights promotion. Each approach poses different problems. Development schemes are vitiated by the fact that the post-communist states, after having taken a decade or more to return to their pre-transition level of output and of living standards, are being subjected to new policies of aus-terity. To their credit, Roma development programs have not relied on a general rise in economic indicators at the national level to better the condition of the Roma. It is, however, a particular challenge to improve this condition within a general context of retrenchment. Moreover, the nature of the integration sought is not clearly defined. As for the strategy of rights promotion, it relies on an American-inspired paradigm from the civil rights era. This is an approach that judicializes issues, taking advantage of national and international anti-discrimination legislation and norms. Even if the success rate of such an approach, as measured by the number of court cases won, were higher one wonders what impact such activity has on popular mentalities and pervasive social discrimination. Indeed, one may ask to what extent such an approach is counter-productive in hardening attitudes towards both Roma and the law.

Some Roma-related programs could, undoubtedly, be better conceived but many Roma activists would argue that the fundamental problem today is not program conception but program implementation.[11] Well designed programs lack the technical and material resources or the human skills required to make them function. Programs compete with each other or falter as they move from the international to the national and local level (or, sometimes, as they move in the opposite direction). The last fifteen years may yet be remembered as the period during which the principles of a Roma policy were established in Central and Eastern Europe. It would be too facile to suggest though that the coming years will be the ones when these principles will become effective.

In reflecting on the distance covered with respect to Roma issues in Russia and Eastern Europe since the early 1990s when the first edition of this book was published, one cannot overlook the enormous part played by external institutional actors. Among the earliest such actors has been the Council of Europe, an organization founded in 1949 that now numbers some forty-five members, including former communist states, and that functions as a pan-European human rights watchdog. The Council of Europe has recently reaffirmed its role with respect to Roma issues throughout Europe as a whole with the establishment of the European Roma and Travellers' Forum. The Organization for Security and Cooperation in Europe (OSCE), an even more broadly based organization that includes the USA, Canada and the Central Asian Republics, maintains a Roma and Sinti contact point in its Office for Democratic Institutions and Human Rights (ODIHR). Transnational but non-state civil society actors, such as various Christian Churches, have turned their attention to the Roma.

The prime external actor, however, has been the European Union and the prospect of EU accession has underpinned all discussions of Roma issues (as of so many other matters) in the post-communist countries. The concerns of the EU have been both principled and pragmatic. As a community of interests and values, the European Union has been troubled by the anomaly of a radically disadvantaged population living next door, or soon to be part of the Union or even, since 2004 and 2007, within the Union. The fact that this population is seen as potentially highly mobile—the dominant though erroneous image of the Central and East European Roma is that of nomads—only aggravates the perceived implications of this situation for the social stability and prosperity of the EU as a whole. During the period of candidacy, the European Union evaluated (and in the case of those countries that remain in the waiting line, still evaluates) the readiness of Central and East European countries for membership in terms of respect for minority rights; treatment of Roma stands foremost among such benchmarks. In this field as in others, "conditionality" has been Brussels' most important transformative instrument. With accession, this instrument disappears and one can only speculate about the effectiveness of alternative instruments, such as the targeting of structural and regional development funds and other redistribution policies. It is probably not unduly pessimistic to predict that the post-communist member states of the EU will be less responsive to pressure on behalf of their Roma populations that they were as EU candidate states.

It is an irreversible fact, however, that the Roma have acquired a robust organizational presence on the European and international level.[12] This is the case in spite of sometimes intense competition among Roma organizations representing various groups and interests, such as the International Romani Union and the Roma National Congress. The significant novelty today is that Roma from the "old" and the "new" Europe are participating and combining their strengths. Whatever the tensions and dissonance this engenders within the Roma movement, the result is the emergence of a trans-national Roma elite committed to its community.[13] As David Crowe points out, though Roma parties have not done well in national politics and Roma politicians are subject to criticism within their own community, Roma now sit in the European Parliament, as national MEPs—from mainstream parties, to be sure, but also as Roma activists.

The situation of the Roma throughout the post-communist area has enough similarities to warrant generalization but among the many merits of David Crowe's book, both in its original and in its revised edition, is its attention to the particular historical and contemporary circumstances of Roma in each of the countries concerned. As one follows these accounts, one is prompted to inquire to what extent the often cited distinction between a post-Habsburg and a post-Ottoman Eastern Europe is relevant to the situation of the Roma. Perhaps paradoxically, one is led to suggest on the basis of the information here that Roma may be more marginalized in the more modern post-Habsburg countries than they are in the less modern post-Ottoman states. This situation is partly due to historical circumstances; for instance, most Roma in the Czech Republic originate from Slovakia, now a foreign country, the native Roma of Bohemia and Moravia having perished in the Pořajmos or Gypsy Holocaust. In contrast,

Bulgarian Roma, for example, consider themselves part of the traditional national landscape, having long resided in these parts well before Bulgaria became an independent state a century ago and one that never encountered the modernization campaigns waged by the enlightened Austrian emperor Joseph II.

Since publication of the first edition of this book, the monographic literature on the Gypsies of Eastern Europe and Russia has expanded by leaps and bounds. However, David Crowe's book maintains its leading position within this literature, not only a path-breaking work of scholarship but also as a clear, concise and now again up to date survey of a subject of considerable historical fascination and great contemporary relevance.

Andre Liebich

Geneva, November 2006

Notes

1. Ian Hancock, "A note on names," in *We are the Romani people/Ame sam e Rromane džene*, N.P.: Centre de recherches tsiganes/University of Hertfordshire Press, 2002, p. xix.
2. David Crowe discusses in this book the myth of an Egyptian origin for the Gypsies/Roma which turns up at different times and places. A variant to this myth is reference to "Little Egypt," situated either on the Adriatic Coast or in the Eastern Mediterranean, where the presence of Gypsies/Roma was noted. In a particular twist to this story of mistaken origins, some Gypsies/Roma in Macedonia and Kosovo have enthusiastically adopted the name "Egyptians" to distinguish themselves from their kinfolk. See Ger Duijzings, "The Making of Egyptians in Kosovo and Macedonia," in Cora Covers and Hans Vermeulen, editors, *The Politics of Ethnic Consciousness*, New York: St. Martin's Press, 1997, pp. 194–222.
3. The battle between the Indianists and their critics, and even within each of the camps, is raging. Though founded in linguistics, the divergences are highly political. For a recent assessment see Yaron Matras, "The Role of Language in Mystifying and Demystifying Gypsy Identity," in The *Role of the Romanies: Images and Counter-Images of 'Gypsies'/ Romanies in European Cultures*, edited by Nicholas Saul and Susan Tebbutt, Liverpool UP, 2004, pp. 53–78.
4. Note, for example, the political party that calls itself the Democratic Alliance of Hungarian Gypsies or Magyartorszagi Ciganyok Demokratikus Szovetse.
5. Let us note the recent monumental work by Lev Tcherenkov and Stéphane Laederich, *The Rroma: Otherwise known as Gypsies, Gitanos, Γύφτοι, Tsiganes, Ţigani, çinfnw, Zigeuner, Bohémiens, Travellers, Fahrende, etc.* vol. 1: *History, Language*, and Groups; vol. 2: *Traditions and Texts*. Basel: Schwabe, 2004. The back cover of the book lists no fewer than sixty-four ethnonyms (other than those in the title).
6. International economic institutions focussing on Europe, such as the UN Economic Commission for Europe (ECE) or the European Bank for Reconstruction and Development (EBRD), have been less involved in monitoring the Roma condition (perhaps because of an implicit state-level orientation of analysis) than has the World Bank that has produced several influential reports, both acclaimed and criticized by Roma activists. Dena Ringold, *Roma and the Transition in Central and Eastern Europe: Trends*

and Challenges. Washington, D.C.: The World Bank, 2000; Ama Revenga, Dena Ringold, William Martin Tracy, *Poverty and Ethnicity: A Cross-Country Study of Roma Poverty in Central Europe*, World Bank Technical Paper no. 531, Washington, D.C.: World Bank, 2002; Dena Ringold, Mitchell A. Orenstein, and Erika Wilkens, *Roma in an Expanding Europe: Breaking the Poverty Cycle*, Washington, D.C.: World Bank, 2005 (also on the World Bank website, *web.worldbank.org* as are other relevant publications). For contrasting assessments of this last publication see reviews by Ian Hancock, *SAIS Review of International Affairs*, Summer/Fall 2005, pp. 1–6, and Michael Stewart, *Slavic Review* vol. 65 nr. 3 (Fall 2006) pp. 571–573.

7. For critical views of the transition see Branko Milanovic, *Income, Inequality and Poverty during the Transition from Planned to Market Economy*. Washington, D.C.: World Bank, 1998 and I. Szelenyi and R. Emigh (eds.) *Poverty, Ethnicity and Gender in Eastern Europe during the Market Transition*, Westport: Greenwood Press, 2000.

8. Among the first to draw attention to this phenomenon was Katherine Verdery, "Comment: Hobsbawn in the East," *Anthropology Today* vol. 8, nr. 1 (February 1992) pp. 8–10.

9. *www.romadecade.org*. The program runs from 2005 to 2015. It was spurred by the World Bank study cited above, *Roma in an Expanding Europe: Breaking the Poverty Cycle*.

10. *www.errc.org*. The Center has been active since 1996. The Open Society Justice Initiative, *www.justiceinitiative.org*, is also heavily involved in Roma legal advocacy.

11. *Romani Politics Present and Future. Poiana Brasov, Romania, May 12–14, 2005*. N. P [Princeton, N.J.] Project on Ethnic Relations, 2006. This is the published summary of unattributed remarks from a meeting held under the auspices of the Project on Ethnic Relations with a number of Roma activists.

12. See Ilona Klimovà-Alexander, *The Romani Voice in World Politics: The United Nations and Non-State Actors*, Aldershot: Ashgate, 2005 and Peter Vermeersch, *The Romani Movement: Minority Politics and Ethnic Mobilization in Contemporary Central Europe*, New York: Berghahn, 2006.

13. On this process and its tensions see Katrin Simhandl, " 'Western Gypsies and Trevellers'—'Eastern Roma': The Creation of Political Objects by the Institutions of the European Union," *Nations and Nationalism* vol. 12 nr. 1 (2006) pp. 97–115.

I·N·T·R·O·D·U·C·T·I·O·N

The Gypsies, or Roma, entered Eastern Europe and parts of the former Russian Empire and the Soviet Union during the Middle Ages from northern India. There are some legends, though, that place Gypsies in Central Asia as early as the fifth century A.D., while some Macedonian Roma folk legends trace their roots back to Alexander the Great in the fourth century B.C. A number of specialists note references to Gypsies in Eastern Europe as early as the eleventh century, though it is not until the following century that substantiated historical documents underscore a Roma presence in the region.

The most detailed allusions to Gypsies during this period come from the Republic of Ragusa, now the Croatian city of Dubrovnik, and from Hungarian Slovak records. Ragusan files suggest a rich Gypsy life in the republic, while the *Book of Executions of the Lords of Rožmberk,* from Ruzomberok, in Slovakia, has the first mention of Roma in purely Hungarian accounts. Over the next quarter of a century, official Hungarian records note a growing movement of Roma through Central Europe. Moldavian-Wallachian documents from this era center around transactions involving Gypsy slaves, or *robi,* though most Gypsies in Eastern Europe at this time were free and worked as skilled metal craftsmen, musicians, and soldiers. Gypsy smiths and soldiers were an integral part of the military forces in Hungary and Slovakia during this period, while Lithuanian officials saw them as useful citizens. However, with the growing threat of Turkey during this period in the region, and the upheavals brought about by the Protestant Reformation in the sixteenth century, attitudes toward Gypsies began to change.

The Ottoman move into the Balkans and parts of Central Europe was gradual, though the Turkish defeat of the Hungarians at Mohács in 1526 seemed to be something of a watershed in terms of public attitudes towards the Roma in Hungary and Slovakia. In 1541–1542, three separate kingdoms emerged in the former Hungarian empire. Royal Hungary, centered in Slovakia, was under Hungarian control, while two new provinces in central Hungary and Transylvania emerged under Ottoman control. In Royal Hungary, Gypsies were increasingly seen as spies and something of a Turkish fifth column, which caused them to be increasingly subjected to restrictions on their lifestyle and trade. Though still valued for their smithing skills, particularly by the military, these efforts to regulate the Roma eventually forced them to adopt a nomadic way of life. In Bulgaria, which had come under Ottoman control somewhat earlier, the Turks relegated Gypsies to the lowest social ranking, and differentiated between the predominantly nomadic Muslim Roma and the settled Christian Gypsies. The Ottoman conquest of Wallachia and Moldavia, which took place somewhat earlier than the conquest of Hungary, resulted in a series of laws and regulations that governed Gypsy *robi*.

The plight of the Gypsies in Wallachia and Moldavia is the worst example of mistreatment of this group since their entrance into the region. Implemented centuries earlier to ensure the ready availability of their unique skills, the practice of Gypsy slavery evolved into an abusive system that treated the Roma as no more than cattle. An active, illegal slave trade developed in the sixteenth and seventeenth centuries, though by the eighteenth century, there were growing hints of some concern over some aspects of Gypsy enslavement. Though local *hospodars* (governors) legally reconfirmed Rom slave status at this time, one prominent *hospodar,* Constantin Mavrocordato, tried to prevent the sale of Roma children separate from their parents. In addition, Wallachian Gypsies who had married non-Roma were emancipated. On the other hand, intermarriages between Gypsies and non-Gypsies were outlawed in Moldavia. The Russian occupation of Wallachia and Moldavia between 1829 and 1834 paved the way for the discussion of emancipation, though it took the efforts and writings of visionaries such as Mihail Kogălniceanu and Alexander Ghica to move the provinces towards Gypsy freedom. Between 1842 and 1847, church and state slaves were freed in both provinces, while revolutionary events in 1848 created an atmosphere conducive to more complete Gypsy emancipation. The Russian reoccupation of Wallachia and Moldavia just before the outbreak of the Crimean War set the stage for Ghica's decision to free all of the Gypsy slaves in Moldavia on December 10, 1855, followed by a similar act in Wallachia two months later. Full Roma emancipation came eight years later with the acquisition of full liberty for all peasants in the new union of Wallachia and Moldavia.

Gypsies under Austrian Habsburg control in Hungary, Slovakia, and the Czech lands of Bohemia and Moravia followed a different course. Hungarian Slovakia had proven to be something of a haven for Czech Roma in the seventeenth century as they fled the region to escape the upheavals triggered by the Thirty Years War. For the next century, Habsburg policies were particularly harsh towards foreign, nomadic Gypsies. However, by the time that Empress Maria Theresa came to power in 1740, Austrian policies had begun to change, and more enlightened, humane efforts arose to deal with Roma throughout Habsburg domains. In many instances, the methods devised by the Austrians to deal with their Gypsies were remarkably similar to efforts used throughout Eastern Europe and Russia over the next two centuries. Central to Habsburg policies were attempts to force an end to Gypsy nomadism, coupled with artificial efforts to force Roma to become good Austrians or Hungarians. Gypsy children, for example, were kidnapped and placed in Christian foster homes. Local officials were increasingly empowered to see that a growing body of detailed, restrictive legislation was enforced. These efforts faded quickly after the death of Maria Theresa's son and successor, Joseph II, in 1790. The empire's Gypsies now returned to their traditional lifestyle, or went elsewhere.

Gypsies in the diverse, large Russian Empire suffered from similar, though less aggressive, sedentarization policies at this time. Though Gypsies had entered Central Asia and Ukraine at a much earlier date, they did not begin to arrive in significant numbers in European Russia until the seventeenth and eighteenth centuries. In Poland, much of which was acquired by Catherine the Great in the second half of the eighteenth century, the Roma presence was significant enough to prompt the Polish crown to appoint a king of the Gypsies a century earlier to gain more control over the country's Roma. In Russia proper, a unique Roma culture began to emerge that had a powerful impact on Russian music and literature. The first hint of this special Gypsy influence began with the creation of a Roma choir by Count Aleksei Orlov, a nobleman close to Catherine the Great. In time, Gypsy choirs became a fad among the Russian nobility, and no significant social occasion was complete without a Roma chorus. This powerful Gypsy tradition quickly spread beyond the confines of the estates and soirées of the nobility and resulted in the emergence of three distinct Gypsy musical styles that deeply affected Russian music. The first style was original Roma folk music performed by individuals or choirs. The second style was choral, road house music that was more elaborate than Gypsy folk music. The last type of Russian Gypsy music was the Gypsy romance. It was not Roma music at all, but music composed by Russians with hints of Gypsy influence.

The growing Rom musical presence soon spilled over into literature, particularly after the publication of Alexander Pushkin's "The Gypsies" in the late 1820s. Another Russian literary giant, Lev Tolstoi, was equally fascinated by Roma, particularly Roma women. Gypsy influence on literature and music was not limited to Russia. Franz Liszt, who was deeply affected by their music and culture, saw the Gypsies as the creators of Hungarian national music.

Unfortunately, Roma contributions to the cultures of Eastern Europe and Russia did not earn them any significant societal respect, and Gypsies continued to be relegated to each nation's lowest socioeconomic rung. Furthermore, those Roma who had marketable skills and used them to create successful, assimilated lifestyles soon became a caste unto themselves often far removed from the harsh lifestyles of their poorer kinsmen. These differences became particularly evident in the second half of the nineteenth century as more and more demographic evidence underscored the sad plight of Eastern Europe and Russia's large, diverse Roma communities. Yet the political upheavals that swept the region during this period and through the end of World War I offered some hope that the plight of the Roma would improve once democracy took hold in the new nations and political systems of Eastern Europe and Russia.

Initially, this seemed to be the case. The 1920s saw something of a Gypsy renaissance take root in Eastern Europe and Russia as Roma intellectuals struggled to carve out a niche for the Gypsies in the new nations. Though their efforts to create organizations and publish works in Romany were admirable, they were crippled by inexperience and lack of financial support as well as centuries-old prejudice and indifference. The most remarkable, lasting gains for Roma came in the new Soviet Russian state. Seen as a means of integrating the Roma more fully into the fabric of Soviet society, the government encouraged Roma publications and in 1931 helped open the Moscow Theatre "Romen". Though the Kremlin ended most of these efforts over the next few years, the activities of the Theatre "Romen" remained a unique cultural beacon for Russia's Gypsies in the dark years ahead.

Whatever the Roma of Eastern Europe and Russia had suffered earlier, nothing prepared them for the horrors of the Pořajmos or Gypsy holocaust between 1933 and 1945. The driving force behind this tragedy was Adolph Hitler and his Nazi henchmen both within and outside of the Third Reich. Soon, most of the countries of Eastern Europe found themselves enveloped by that peculiar fascist-Nazi paranoia that became so much a part of the region's landscape during this period. As the Nazi threat of war loomed larger on the horizon in the late 1930s, most of the countries of Eastern Europe found that unless they wanted to suffer the fate of Czechoslovakia, which was carved up out of existence in a six month period in 1938–1939, or Yugoslavia, which suffered the same fate two years later, they had to enter the Nazi camp as allies. Once war came in the fall of 1939, pressure was gradually brought to bear on each nation in Eastern Europe not under direct German control to implement growingly harsh policies against the Gypsies. While initial efforts centered around registration and restrictions on nomadism, the German assault on the Soviet Union in the summer of 1941 brought new efforts that paralleled the Nazi Final Solution for the Jews. By 1942, racial laws similar to those in the Third Reich were in place throughout Eastern Europe, and genocidal policies of mass murder were underway. The success of these efforts, however, varied from country to country. In Bulgaria, which also controlled Macedonia, Gypsies and Jews were protected by the government of King Boris III and thus suffered few losses. Roma in Hungary and the rump state of Slovakia were spared from the worst genocidal indignities until Germany occupied both countries in 1944. The Roma in the Protectorate of Bohemia and Moravia, Romania, the Independent State of Croatia, and the Soviet Union suffered horrifying losses, while Gypsy deaths in Serbia were moderately high.

Any dreams of postwar healing were dashed by the gradual Soviet takeover of Eastern Europe in the immediate years after the end of World War II. Initially, some of the region's new communist rulers offered some hope that they would be sensitive to Gypsy mistreatment. Something of a mild, short-lived Roma cultural-political renaissance took hold in Yugoslavia, Romania, and Bulgaria, but was quickly replaced by Stalinistic attitudes that discouraged strong ethnic identity and sentiments. Yet it would be too simplistic to conclude that Eastern Europe now mimicked the Kremlin's ethnic policies towards the Roma, though there is no doubt that after the death of Stalin in 1953, and the rise of Nikita Khrushchev, there developed a certain community of feeling about Gypsies throughout the communist bloc.

What emerged during this period was a collective, growing sense of deep concern about the ongoing, independent lifestyle of some nomadic Rom, coupled with the appallingly low social, economic, and educational status of the Gypsies. While leaders throughout Eastern Europe put the blame for the Roma's plight on pre-communist governments, the fact remained that the growing number of Gypsies in each country remained a problem that tested each nation's commitment to bring the fruits of socialist transformation to all segments of society. Initial efforts in the 1950s to try to force settlement as a vehicle for Gypsy assimilation failed, and by the 1960s, attempts were undertaken throughout Eastern Europe to address the Roma's serious problems by improved housing and educational programs. Unfortunately, efforts to provide a quickfix for centuries-old dilemmas proved futile, particularly in the face of ongoing resentment and prejudice toward the Roma. Yet there were remarkable, though sometimes flawed, achievements during this period that at least marked a starting point for the complex process of socioeconomic assimilation of the Gypsies. Unfortunately, these efforts paid little regard to the rich traditions of the Roma and were undertaken in a manner that created more ill feeling toward the Gypsies.

These virulent sentiments exploded as the communist regimes of Eastern Europe and the Soviet Union collapsed between 1989 and 1991. Gypsies were now viewed as the symbol of all gone awry in the new democracies of Eastern Europe, and, to a lesser degree in Russia. These feelings were compounded by decade-old fears of Gypsy population growth rates, which far outpaced national averages. Furthermore, crime, long an insignificant concern, was viewed as a threatening social problem that centered around Gypsies. Yet the new democracies in Eastern Europe and Russia have offered the Gypsies more than just renewed heartache. A new Roma awakening has emerged that has seen a flurry of political, social, and cultural organizations develop that offer the Gypsies new choices for the first time in the history of Eastern Europe and Russia. Those who choose to follow the path of assimilation can follow it without the complete abandonment of age-old culture and traditions. For others, there is the opportunity to reembrace a rich, more simple lifestyle. Though this latter path is strewn with difficulties, it is, hopefully, a viable option.

EASTERN EUROPE AND RUSSIA

.1.

BULGARIA

The origin of the Gypsies in Bulgaria is tied directly to their early migration from India via Persia into Europe. Though the Bulgarian Gypsy newspaper *Romano-Esi* (Gypsy Voice), claimed in 1948 that "our minority has lived in Bulgaria since the seventh century," led by the "leader of the Gypsies throughout the world, Berko," most specialists trace Gypsy roots in Bulgaria to a much later date.[1] Some Bulgarian Gypsies have even tried to promote the idea that they are descended from ancient Lydians or Ligurians.[2] The reality, however, is somewhat different and theoretical. In all probability, the Gypsies began to migrate from India in the early Middle Ages and reached Persia sometime in the ninth century. By the eleventh century, they had moved into the Byzantine Empire from Armenia and had been referred to in a Georgian account, *Life of Saint George the Athonite.* According to this medieval text, Emperor Constantine Monomachus asked the Adsincani to get rid of the wild animals that were preying on the animals in his royal hunting preserve.[3] The name, Adsincani, used by the Byzantine chronicler to refer to the Gypsies, "is the Georgian form of the Greek *Atsínganoi* or *Atzínganoi*," and is the root word from which the various names for Gypsies are derived.[4] The Atsínganoi are mentioned again in Byzantine records in the early thirteenth century as ne'er-do-well fortunetellers, "'ventriloquists and wizards' . . . who are inspired satanically and pretend to predict the unknown. . . ."[5]

During the same period, the Byzantines conquered the independent Bulgarian empire, which stretched from the Black Sea to parts of the Adriatic, and made it a satellite kingdom from 1019 to 1185. The Greek roots of the term Atsínganoi were echoed by the strong policy of Hellenization imposed upon Bulgaria by its Byzantine rulers. The relationship between the Byzantines and the Bulgarians was troublesome, and periodic forays were made by Constantinople's troops into its new territory to put down Bulgarian uprisings. There is some evidence that Bulgarian Gypsies picked up at least one important linguistic term from descendants of Armenian troops sent in to quell the unrest.[6]

Byzantine references to Gypsies continued to crop up over the next few centuries even as Byzantine political and territorial fortunes gave way to those of the region's new power, the Ottoman Turks. These later sources refer to the Gypsies as Egyptians, a geographic misnomer that stuck nevertheless.[7] Several areas settled by Gypsies in Cyprus and Greece were dubbed "Little Egypt" by local rulers in the late fourteenth century.[8]

Bulgaria threw off Byzantine rule in 1185 and established the Second Empire. This lasted until the last quarter of the fourteenth century, when the Turks began a successful campaign of conquest that brought Bulgaria completely under their control by 1396.[9] The absorption of Bulgaria marked a high point in the first phase of Ottoman Turkish rule, which was followed by a second phase of conquest from 1413 to 1481.[10] The expansion of Turkish power in the Balkans during this period saw a wave of Gypsy migration into the region.[11]

It was also at this time that Bulgarian references to the Gypsies began to emerge. A fourteenth-century Bulgarian text, the *Life of Saint Barbarus*, alludes to Egyptians "living in large numbers" along the Albanian coast. In 1378, Tsar Ivan Shishman (r. 1371–1393) gave the Rila Monastery a number of villages in which some Agoupti (or Gupti) Gypsies lived. These villagers were among the first Gypsy groups to settle in Bulgaria.[12] Throughout Bulgaria, the Turks relegated the Gypsies to the lowest rung of the Ottoman social ladder because they "had no visible permanent professional affiliation." Ottoman officials pressured Gypsies and others who fell into this category to "move away or to settle into 'useful' occupations." On the other hand, it was felt that they were "needed to carry loads and perform some of the most demeaning labor." In Bulgarian urban areas, they had no *mahalles*, or special quarters, of their own, and each night, after working in the cities, they "returned to whatever type of housing they were able to erect beyond the city limits."[13]

The Turks divided the Gypsies into nomadic Moslems and settled Christians, which prompted some Gypsies to convert to Islam "to raise their own status and become equal to the ruling neighboring population."[14] Compared to others in parts of Europe at the time, however, the Turks were reasonably tolerant of those who followed other faiths, particularly Christians and Jews, whom they considered *zimmis*, or "people of the book." In the second half of the seventeenth century, however, the Turks began to initiate mass conversions of Bulgarians in the Rhodope region of southern Bulgaria. While it is difficult to gauge the significance and effect of these conversions on the Gypsies in Bulgaria, they did have an impact on the Romani language, particularly the non-Vlach or non-Greek dialects, which the Gypsies now call the Moslem dialects.[15]

Despite the prejudice toward them, the Roma (Gypsies) were a strong presence in Bulgarian towns and villages. Ottoman statistics for this period show that there were 33 Gypsy households in Filibe/Plovdiv in 1489–1490, consisting of 5 families a piece, out of a total household population of 907. This figure increased to 175 Roma households in 1516, out of a total household population of 1,000–1,100. A decade later, Turkish officials identified 283 Gypsy households in the city, 90 of which were Muslim, and 193 of which were registered as Christians. Another important Bulgarian town, the Thracian city of Yambol, had 7 Gypsy households out of 529 households in 1595. The Thracian district of Eski Zagra boasted 61 Gypsy families out of 2,450 in 1526–1528, although 40 years later this number dropped to 21 households. Another town with high Gypsy settlement was Pleven, which had 11 Gypsy households in 1516, 36 households by 1550, and 44 in 1579.[16] Although the Ottoman statistics may not be entirely accurate, they do provide a glimpse of the steady presence of Gypsies in Bulgaria during this period.

The steady presence of Gypsies in Bulgarian towns and cities made them liable for Ottoman taxes. The Turks traditionally collected, among other levies, a *cizye*, or head tax, on non-Muslims in return for the guarantee of state protection of their lives and property and exemption from military service. This tax was so important to Ottoman finances that it served as a brake on Turkish interest in converting non-Muslims to their faith. In 1610, the *kadi* (Muslim religious judge) in Sofia responsible for the administration of the *sancak* (provincial district) received a *berat* (imperial decree) to strengthen his ability to collect the *cizye* from the Gypsies. Christian Gypsies were to pay 250 *akçes* (100 *açkes* was equal to one Austrian gold Ducat in 1684) and Muslim Gypsies, 180 *akçes*. Everyone else in the Bulgarian capital had to pay 200 *akçes*. According to Peter F. Sugar, "All that these figures could mean is that while the Gypsies were considered such low people that even Muslims could be taxed illegally, their religion was still worth a 70 *akçe* tax discount."[17] These levies were identical to those collected from Muslim and Christian Gypsies five years earlier in Albania and western Greece. In 1684, *kadis* in the Balkans were ordered to impose new taxes on the Gypsies. Each Muslim Roma was to pay 650 *akçes*, while his Christian counterpart was to pay 720 *akçes*. These were considered "poll and pork taxes." Only one official was appointed to collect all of the taxes from the Gypsies, since "the Gypsy race lives separately and is numerically limited, but is free in every respect." The decree insisted that no other officials "interfere in the affairs of the Gypsies" nor inflict "any injustice or oppression upon them by demanding more than this my Imperial decree specifies." Another decree, issued ten years later, required Muslim Gypsies to pay an annual tax of five piastres, the new Ottoman currency, and the Christian Gypsies to pay six piastres.[18]

The end of the seventeenth and the entire eighteenth century in Bulgaria was marked by the decline of Ottoman influence and the rebirth of Bulgarian national consciousness. Periodic revolts against the Turks became frequent, and some Bulgarian refugees fled westward after the Austro-Russian War against Turkey from 1736 to 1739. The Turks responded with an era of "dreadful repression and virtual slavery" that Bulgarians referred to as the *Cherno Teglo* ("black weight"). As a result of the combination of decay and repression, "a massive exodus from the towns" of Bulgaria took place. Some Bulgarians joined bands of *Haiduti* or *hadjuks*, bandit groups of 10 or 20 men later worshipped as "national heroes and forerunners of the successful revolutionaries of the nineteenth century." While interpretations vary about the role of the *Haiduti* in Bulgarian history, their presence represents the decay and frustration that bedeviled Turkish rule in Bulgaria during the second half of the eighteenth century. Two unsuccessful wars with Russia in 1768–1774 and 1787–1791, which saw Russian forces enter Bulgaria, and Bulgarian volunteers fight with them against the Turks, brought further chaos and hardship to the region. This was compounded by the appearance of the *kurdjaliistvo*, roving armed bands of ex-Turkish soldiers and others, the *Kurdzhali* or *daalii*, who "ran riot throughout Bulgaria, burning and plundering." If the historical traditions of the Balkans and Eastern Europe held true in Bulgaria at this time, the Gypsies suffered most from the upheavals that swept this part of the Ottoman Empire.[19]

The chaos in Bulgaria mirrored serious political, military, and economic problems in the Ottoman Empire that were compounded by European threats to Turkish holdings in southeastern Europe, particularly during the Napoleonic Wars. The growing loss of control over various parts of his distant empire prompted the new sultan, Selim III (r. 1789–1807), to initiate reforms to regain control of his vast holdings. These reforms were only partially successful because of inattention to forward reaching changes and ideas as well as opposition by local officials in the Balkans and elsewhere, which ensured that Bulgaria would remain in chaos a while longer.[20]

The accession of Mahmut II (r. 1808–1839) promised new changes in the Ottoman Empire, though much of the new sultan's early reign was taken up by war, serious difficulties in Greece, and the revolt of the Janissaries, once the elite of the sultan's army and now "the chief source of the rot at its core." Their bloody destruction in 1826 paved the way for new reforms, particularly in 1832, though designed to bring the troubled regions of the empire back under the sultan's direct control through the destruction of provincial autonomy, often had no effect on social and economic problems in Bulgaria because they were rarely enforced. At the same time, the spirit of an imperial decree of 1839 that promised to "guarantee his subjects' security of life, honor, and property," regardless of their faith or ethnic background, introduced a new era in Bulgarian history that had a deep effect on everyone, Gypsy and non-Gypsy alike. However, instead of "pacifying the subject people," the 1839 decree "acted as a spur to increased agitation and struggle on the part of the Bulgars."[21]

One aspect of the new Ottoman reform program that would have such an impact on the Gypsies in Bulgaria centered around changes in the administration of the provinces that was designed "to establish a just system of rule and taxation." Taxes would now be assessed according to the "individual ability to pay" and were anchored by an empire-wide census between 1831 and 1838. These efforts were complicated, however, by the uneven enforcement of the 1834 land reform program, which triggered major, and oftentimes chaotic, social, economic, political, and cultural changes in Bulgaria "that dismantled the existing social structure without having any concept of what was to replace it." The instability that followed in the "1840s and 1850s were indeed largely the result of the inadequacies of the reforms."[22]

These problems were compounded by serious labor shortages in certain regions of the country caused by earlier wars and social upheavals. Seasonal migrant labor became the norm in many parts of Bulgaria, though it did not always resolve the labor shortage problem. These difficulties enhanced the prospects of land ownership, and, with the exception of those in the northwestern part of the country, most peasants were able to acquire land. The ready availability of land helped temper any serious "social tension within the Bulgarian villages." However, to the landless Gypsy, Bulgarian tolerance had limits.[23]

In an incisive description of Gypsy life in the Christian village of Derekuoi near the Black Sea port of Varna in 1868, the British authors S. G. B. St. Clair and Charles A. Brophy, who lived in the village for a number of years, wrote of how the Roma of Derekuoi's *Chinguine Mahalli* (Gypsy quarter) lived a life typical of Gypsies in Bulgaria at this time. Though formally Muslims, "they never enter a mosque, and otherwise observe but a few precepts enjoined by the Koran." The Gypsy women of Derekuoi, they noted, refused to wear the Muslim *yashmak* (veil). They spoke both Romani and Turkish, while their homes, similar to but smaller than those of their Bulgarian neighbors, were, though "squalid in outward appearance," a study in "neatness and cleanliness" on the inside, particularly when compared to those of their Bulgarian neighbors. Their chief occupations were "begging, basketmaking, tinkering, and forging iron." St. Clair and Brophy discounted Bulgarian claims that the Gypsies of Derekuoi were thieves, finding the Gypsies "to be as honest" as their Bulgarian neighbors.[24]

The Gypsy women of Derekuoi spent their days buying, bartering, or begging for food, aided in part by superstitious villagers who often gave them what they asked for because of their fear of the Gypsy women, who they felt had the "power to cast spells, cause rain, and other beneficent or maleficent attributes." The "men remained at home mending pots and pans, tinning copper vessels, and doing all the iron work required by the village, whilst the children blow the bellows, or accompany the cattle to their pasturage."[25]

The Bulgarians would not, however, allow the Gypsies to remain in Derekuoi for more than three or four years, though Muslim villagers tended to be more tolerant of the Roma than Christian Bulgarians. St. Clair and Brophy found local attitudes toward Gypsies quite unfair, since they earned their "living by harder labour" than the Christians, who hated the Roma more than the Muslims. The authors found village attitudes towards the Roma rather hypocritical, and "roguery [was] a rule, honesty the exception" among the Christian Bulgarians in Derekuoi. The villagers consistently overcharged the Gypsies for food and other items, for example, or exacted excessive labor from them when they could not pay in cash. They allowed the Gypsies to live in Derekuoi during the winter when they "were a positive pecuniary advantage to the villagers;" however, when spring came and the Roma had milk and butter to sell from their cattle, Derekuoi's leaders decided to force them to move on, since the Gypsies were "not paying for the privilege" of grazing their cattle on village land. Instead of ordering the Gypsies to leave, the village elders had the huts in the Gypsy quarter burned to the ground. The following winter, they invited a new colony of Gypsies to settle in the village. When St. Clair and Brophy later informed the governor of Varna about the incident, he told them that "he could do nothing, having received standing orders from Constantinople to favour the Rayahs [peasants non-Muslim Bulgarians) in every possible manner."[26]

The Bulgaria of the 1860s was beset by serious political and social upheavals brought about by a long era of Ottoman misrule. This was underscored during the years of Bulgarian nationalistic revival that blossomed from the 1830s through the 1860s. A series of peasant rebellions had rocked the northwestern part of the country in the first few decades of the Bulgarian national renaissance and had led to harsh Turkish reprisals. Though conditions in Bulgaria were no worse than elsewhere in the Ottoman Empire, continued misrule by local aristocrats in the northwest, the spirit of Turkish reforms, friction over Greek domination of the Orthodox Church in Bulgaria, and the general atmosphere of nationalistic fervor throughout southeastern Europe kept tensions high. Hand in hand with this atmosphere was the growing importance of Bulgarian trade throughout the Empire. This was enhanced after the Crimean War with the arrival of Western money and technology that sought to tap Bulgarian resources. These changes brought an economic boom to the country, but they also intensified "the process of class differentiation within Bulgarian society."[27]

This social upheaval was exacerbated, at least in regard to the Gypsies, by the struggle for control of the Orthodox Church in Bulgaria. This battle, which had accompanied other aspects of the Bulgarian national revival since the 1820s, had the indirect support of Istanbul, which felt it was "advantageous to encourage enmity between the Greeks and the Bulgars" because it would weaken the Orthodox Church, which would, in turn, hinder any "strong link between the Balkan Christians and the Russians." In 1849, the Sultan granted the Bulgarians a *firman* (royal decree) to build a Bulgarian church in Istanbul, while after the Crimean War (1853–1856), the Bulgarians in the Turkish capital asked for the right "to elect a supreme Bulgarian Church leader in whose work neither Christian nor non-Christian should interfere, and a supreme civil leader who would assist the Sultan to choose suitable Bulgars to act as judges, officials, etc., in Bulgaria." Because of strong Western, Russian, and Greek opposition to the Bulgarian request, however, the Porte did nothing, forcing the Bulgarian people to take matters into their own hands. A series of Church councils that met at Ottoman insistence could not arrive at a solution, while locally the Orthodox Church was gradually being Bulgarized. The Greek rebellion of 1866–1869 revived Turkish fear of Greek expansionism and prompted greater leniency on the part of the Turks and the Greek religious leaders toward the Bulgarian church, and in 1870 the Sultan ordered the creation of an autonomous Bulgarian Exarchate. It took two more years before his decree was enforced; for Bulgarians it meant "the recognition of Bulgaria as a separate nation," and the creation of "religious and cultural self-determination."[28]

These intense struggles strengthened the growing sense of Bulgarian national and religious identity and were quickly used to institutionalize traditional prejudices against Gypsies, particularly those that were Muslim. In the 1860s, some of the new Bulgarian Orthodox bishops, possibly in response to the wave of Gypsy immigration from Romania, decreed that it was "a great sin to give alms to a gipsy or an 'infidel.'"[29]

Despite the effect it had on the Gypsies, the acquisition of religious autonomy opened the door to Bulgarian independence. The seeds for this drive, however, had been sown much earlier, spurred by the growing impoverishment of many peasants and small craftsmen. Well-organized Bulgarian revolutionaries, aided by a number of new, economically devastating Ottoman taxes, planned a series of uprisings to encourage Bulgarian nationhood. Collectively known as the April Uprising of 1876, the brutal, successful Turkish crackdown that resulted in many deaths aroused sympathy for the Bulgarians throughout Europe.[30]

The rebellion, which began in the central Bulgarian town of Koprivshtitsa on April 19, was intended to be a national rebellion that involved "the whole people." The rebel leaders had "decided to concentrate all their forces in a few armed camps in the mountains to which the entire population would withdraw, having set fire to their villages." They would then defend these strongholds for as long as possible. In Koprivshtitsa, the local Gypsies "had been disarmed" and seemed to be in support of the rebels. However, when revolutionary leaders heard that Roma in the village of Klisura, just to the north of Koprivshtitsa, "had been among the first to set fire to the village," they decided to search Gypsy homes for evidence of similar intentions. They found "arms, cans of paraffin and a *zaptieh* (policeman)" in the Gypsy homes, while some of the Roma "admitted that it had been their intention to set fire to the town and to seek arms and help from nearby Turkish villages." Rebel leaders executed the Gypsies suspected of involvement in the plot as well as a number of armed Turks.[31]

The failed uprising and the horrible massacres that followed, as well as the outbreak of war between Serbia and Turkey on June 19, 1876, triggered deep concern throughout Europe about the Balkans. Tsar Alexander II (r. 1855–1881), under strong pressure from Russian Pan Slavists to come to the aid of the Bulgarians and the Serbs, vowed in Moscow on November 11, 1876, that if the major powers, who were about to meet in Constantinople (Istanbul) to discuss the Balkan crises, could not "bring about by peaceful means a real improvement in the lot of all the Christian inhabitants of the Balkan peninsular," then Russia was "determined to act independently." The European powers drew up a plan, which the sultan ultimately rejected, that would have divided Bulgaria "into two Autonomous Regions, an Eastern Part centered on Tŭrnovo and a Western Part centred on Sofia, each with a Christian governor, not necessarily a Bulgarian, appointed by Turkey with the agreement of the Great Powers." Tsar Alexander II, who had already mobilized Russian forces in November, responded with a declaration of war against Turkey on April 24, 1877.[32]

Some Bulgarians rallied to the side of the Russians as they entered the country, while both Muslim and Christian Gypsies joined the Bulgarian-Russian ranks against the Turks. Gypsies, for example, took part in the decisive, bloody battle of Shipka Pass from August 9 to 14, 1877, and were counted among the 3,773 Bulgarian and Russian casualties. Their presence is particularly impressive, at least from the Russian perspective, given the lack of Bulgarian enthusiasm for the Russian war effort. Russian soldiers, who thought they were fighting the infidel to free their Slavic brothers, quickly "found themselves in a foreign land among a close-fisted peasantry who, in most cases, seemed to show little spontaneous joy at their 'liberation.'" Part of the reason could have been the Russian mistreatment of the volunteers after Shipka, which prompted many of the Bulgarian volunteers to leave Russian service. Within six months, after some staunch Turkish resistance, Ottoman opposition ended as Russian forces reached the outskirts of Istanbul. Both sides concluded an armistice on January 31, 1878.[33]

The collapse of the Turkish effort against the Russians and the latter's quick drive toward Istanbul and the Straits of the Bosporus created serious concern throughout the major capitals of Europe. The threat of possible military action by Great Britain and Austria tempered further Russian moves. On March 3, 1878, Russia and Turkey signed the Treaty of San Stefano (Yeşilköy) near Istanbul. The agreement, which for Bulgarians marked the end of five centuries of Turkish rule, brought together the two sections of Bulgaria initially envisioned at the Istanbul Conference, creating a large Bulgarian state that "extended on the south from the Black Sea to the Aegean, and embraced the whole of Macedonia and a part of Serbia on the west." Though independent, the new Bulgarian state was technically "an autonomous, tributary Principality" of the Ottoman Empire, with a "prince elected by the people" who was "to rule over this new state with the assistance of a national militia and a national Assembly." A Russian force of no more than 50,000 troops would occupy the country, which measured 160,000 sq. km., for two years.[34]

Unfortunately, Austrian and British fears that "the concessions exacted by the Russians were considered shockingly extensive," and that Bulgaria would be a mere satellite of the Russian Empire, prompted immediate calls for a revision before the treaty could be ratified. The result was the formation of the Congress of Berlin (June 13–July 13, 1878), which completely reworked the Treaty of San Stefano and created a new accord, the Treaty of Berlin. The new Bulgarian kingdom "was narrowed and divided into a vassal principality and a semi-autonomous province, leaving Turkey a direct path to her western provinces and a strong frontier on the north." Turkey regained control of Macedonia and southern Thrace, while northern Bulgaria became an autonomous "vassal principality" of the Turks. The southern portion of Bulgaria, Eastern Rumelia, became "an Autonomous Province of Turkey, with a Christian Governor to be nominated by the Sultan every five years, and its capital at Plovdiv." Russia's administration of Bulgaria was to end in nine months. In addition, the "way was barred to the according of any special commercial favours to Russia." Unfortunately, these Western efforts to weaken Russian influence in Bulgaria ultimately backfired; The new agreement, which, in the eyes of Bulgarians, "brutally dismembered" the new country, "confirmed the Bulgarian conviction that Russia and Russia alone had Bulgaria's interests at heart." This strengthened the Bulgarian feeling that "nothing could or should be done without the approval of the Tsar," and "played a very important role in Bulgarian politics during the years immediately following the liberation."[35]

The division of Bulgaria and the loss of Macedonia was met with derision and public outcry. Political instability became the norm in the rump portion of Bulgaria and Eastern Rumelia, while unrest was widespread among Macedonia's Bulgarians, who made up 28 percent of the population. Northern Bulgaria's new ruler, Tsar Alexander II's favorite nephew, Prince Alexander of Battenberg (r. 1878–1886), quickly became engaged in a power struggle with Bulgarian liberals over constitutional changes that would restrict basic political freedoms, and got Russian backing from the new tsar, Alexander III (r. 1881–1894), whose father had recently been assassinated. But conflicting, uncoordinated, heavy-handed Russian interference in Bulgaria's military, political, and economic affairs undercut tsarist influence over the next few years and united Bulgaria's leaders against the Russians. By 1883, Prince Alexander had revoked the earlier constitutional changes, and within a year, liberals were in control of the government. Once political stability had been achieved in the north, Eastern Rumelian interest in uniting with the north materialized. Former radicals created a Bulgarian Secret Central Revolutionary Committee to work for unification through a mass uprising, although they quickly laid aside the idea of bringing Macedonia and Thrace into this union because of unsuccessful revolutionary activities earlier in Macedonia. On September 18, 1885, a coordinated military uprising approved by Prince Alexander took control of Plovdiv, and two days later the prince announced his recognition of the union. There was Serbian opposition in the form of a brief war, but this only united the Bulgarians against a common enemy. Further chaos came in 1886 with the army's overthrow of Prince Alexander, which was followed by eight years of heavy-handed rule known as the "*Stambolovshtina.*"[36]

The political upheaval in Bulgaria prompted some Gypsies to leave the country for places as distant as Great Britain and the United States. *Kopanari* (Romanian-speaking Bulgarian Christian Gypsies) began to arrive in the United States in the early 1880s; others emigrated to England in 1886.[37] Other Gypsies, however, disregarded the unrest and began to play an active role in the new societies. Male and female Roma found work in one of Bulgaria's first factories, a textile mill in Sliven, which already had a Gypsy quarter and boasted 1,074 Roma in 1874.[38] New laws, however, began to restrict some aspects of the Roma's cultural and historical uniqueness. In 1882, the *mahala* (or *mahalles*), self-contained ethnic quarters, became illegal, though some continued to exist in Varna, Sofia, and elsewhere. More damaging were two laws passed after the reunification of Bulgaria in 1886 that were designed to combat Gypsy nomadism and to stop Gypsies from entering Bulgaria from other countries. This brought particular "hardship and separation to families whose members were scattered throughout the Balkans and depended upon freedom of movement for their occupations." Additionally, the new laws undercut efforts by Gypsy families to enter the country from disparate parts of Greater Bulgaria, regions left out of the new kingdom.[39]

Data on Gypsies in Bulgaria during this period is somewhat difficult to come by, and what little demographic information exists is not completely reliable. This is further complicated by the fact that the country's Muslims, who made up one-half to three-quarters of Bulgaria's Roma population, chose to register as Ottoman citizens in the 1880 census "to avoid conscription in the Bulgaria army." These Muslims could later buy their release from the draft for a heavy fee, though few could afford the sum until authorities allowed the payment to be spread out over 20 years in 1910. An 1870 estimate, which did not include Eastern Rumelia, showed 20,000 to 25,000 Roma in Bulgaria. An 1877 survey, which included Bulgaria, Macedonia, and Thrace, suggested that there were 10,762 Christian Roma in these three areas and 120,000 Muslim Gypsies. The European part of the Ottoman Empire had about 200,000 Roma at this time. Official estimates for 1880 show 57,000 Gypsies in Bulgaria, while census figures from Bulgaria and Eastern Rumelia in 1881 shows 64,790 in the country. While the census of 1888 shows a Roma population of only 50,291, this decline can be explained by the emigration of Gypsies from Bulgaria after the Treaty of Berlin. The number rose slightly in 1893 to 52,132 and reached 54,557 in 1900. A decade later, though, estimates rose dramatically to 122,296, a 114.5 percent increase over 1880 figures. These estimates do not include the Bulgarian Gypsies in Turkey, who numbered 7,614 in 1906.[40]

An analysis of individual census records for some of Bulgaria's more prominent towns from 1884 to 1910 shows the impact of domestic upheavals, the 1886 nomadic and foreign Gypsy restrictions, and the maturing of ethnic policies in the young Bulgarian nation on the ebb and flow of the Gypsy population during this period. Though a few towns such as Burgas and Chirpan saw their Gypsy populations decline significantly from 1884 to 1887, many Bulgarian towns and villages saw a considerable increase in the number of Gypsies resident there. In 1880 a number of cities, such as Pleven, Razgrad, Rusé, Samokov, Shumen, Sofia, Tŭrnovo, Varna, Vidin, and Vratsa had no officially recorded Gypsy populations. In the following years there was a sudden rise in the number of people claiming to be Roma. The number of Gypsies in Pleven grew to 249 during this period, while Samokov's Gypsy population mysteriously rose to 404 during the same period. Sofia's Roma population grew to 1,231 during this time, while that of Varna and Vidin rose to 618 and to 329 respectively from 1880 to 1887. Interestingly, once the immediate spirit of the 1886 regulations waned, and the policies of the new Bulgarian kingdom towards its minorities proved to be rather temperate, these figures began to drop, an indication that some Roma had resumed their nomadic lifestyles. Plovdiv's Gypsy population, for example, which had grown from 112 to 348 from 1884 to 1887, dipped to 237 five years later. Towns with smaller Gypsy populations, such as Rusé, Tŭrnovo, and Varna saw similar declines during this period. On the other hand, urban areas that would become primary Gypsy centers throughout the country experienced steady Roma population growth in the years before the outbreak of the chaotic Balkan Wars (1912–1913). Pleven's Roma population grew to 563, or 2.44 percent of the total population, from 1884 to 1910, while that of Plovdiv blossomed from 112 to 3,534, or 7.34 percent of the total population during the same period. Similar growth took place in Burgas, Razgrad, Rusé, Samokov, Shumen, Silistria, Stara Zagor, Vratsa, and Yambol. Between 1884 and 1910, for example, Sliven's Roma population doubled, and Gypsies made up 10.41 percent of the population. Sofia's Gypsies continued to thrive during the same period, and by 1910 they numbered 2,360, or 2.30 percent of the city's total population. Equally impressive were figures for Varna, where Roma made up 5.47 percent of the population on the eve of the Balkan Wars.[41]

The political and social situation in Bulgaria from the end of the *Stambolovshtina* until the outbreak of the Balkan Wars in 1912 was uneven, with periods of stability alternating with times of domestic unrest and political uncertainty. The impact of these developments on Bulgaria's large minority population, particularly the Gypsies, does not appear to have been particularly severe. Significant ethnic and religious protection for Bulgaria's minorities were included in articles 4 and 5 of the Treaty of Berlin and were repeated in the Bulgarian Constitution of 1879. Beyond this were traditions of tolerance that Bulgarians proudly traced back to the seventh century A.D. On the other hand, the significant decline in the strength of the Turkish and Greek populations (the Turkish portion of the total population declined from 24.81 percent of the total to 11.63 percent from 1880–4 to 1910, and that of the Greeks from 1.80 percent to 1.17 percent), the anti-Greek riots of 1905–1906, and the political disenfranchisement of the Gypsies in the early part of the twentieth century, blur this image of Bulgaria as a perfect haven for Balkan minorities. Regardless, the steady growth of Bulgaria's Roma population in the first three decades of its existence says something about the atmosphere of tolerance in the country. It was enough to stimulate Ramadan Ali, the *tsaribaši* of the Bulgarian Gypsies, to bring together representatives from different Roma clans in Bulgaria on June 1, 1906. The gathering of Roma leaders drew up a petition that Ali forwarded to the Bulgarian parliament, which demanded equal rights for the country's Gypsies. The legislature, however, refused to consider it.[42]

Two of the measures of a nation's policies toward its minorities are education and literacy. The Bulgarian renaissance that had preceded independence had been rooted in the creation of a Bulgarian educational system that by the 1870s could boast several thousand schools. The Constitution of 1879 addressed national primary education, while a law in 1885 "provided that all settlements, whatever their size, should have at least one school." Six years later, another act, designed to weaken Greek influence in some schools, "allowed only non-Christian children to be educated in their mother tongue," though not at government expense. One Bulgarian source, which might have erred on the side of national pride, indicated that there were three primary schools for Gypsies in 1910 for the country's 121,600 Roma. Comparatively, however, this ratio was far less than that for Turks, Pomaks (Bulgarian Muslims), Jews, Armenians and other minorities. As a result, there was a serious problem with Gypsy literacy during this period, a difficulty also shared by Turks and Pomaks. In 1905, for example, only 3 percent of Bulgaria's Roma were literate, compared to 4 percent of the Pomaks, 6 percent of the Turks, and 47 percent of Bulgarians. These low figures, at least in regard to the Turks, were due not to "the hostility of the authorities but the backwardness, the remoteness, and the cultural exclusiveness of many Turkish communities." Added to this, at least for Gypsies, was the innate prejudice in the Balkans toward the Roma, their traditions of nomadism, and their suspicion of the *gadje* (non-Gypsies). Gypsy literacy tripled over the next two decades because of improved government settlement and education policies.[43]

During the early part of this era, Bulgaria was affected by urban disorder spurred by similar outbursts as occurred during the 1905 Revolution in Russia as well as domestic Bulgarian anger over Greek activities in Macedonia. As these difficulties faded, the Young Turk rebellion against Sultan Abdulhamit II (r. 1876–1909) in 1908 and the reforms that followed prompted Austria-Hungary to annex Bosnia-Hercegovina on October 5, 1908. Bulgaria quickly followed suit with a declaration of independence from Turkey, and Prince Ferdinand (r. 1908–1918) became its monarch. In the treaty concluded between Bulgaria and Turkey the following year, Bulgaria's Muslims were assured ample religious and educational guarantees.[44]

The joy of complete independence from Ottoman rule was short-lived, however, since within three years Bulgaria and its Balkan League allies— Serbia, Greece, and Montenegro—found themselves involved in the First Balkan War against Turkey in the fall of 1912. Bulgarian forces bore the brunt of the fighting against the Turks, particularly in Thrace; Bulgaria acquired Adrianople for its trouble in the Treaty of London the following spring. Greek and Serbian disillusionment with this accord (which planted the seed for the creating of an independent Albania several months later instead of dividing it among the victors) as well as problems over Macedonia and other areas that affected the balance of power in the Balkans, prompted Serbia and Greece to sign a secret alliance that dealt with these questions and made them allies in the event of a war. Bulgaria responded with an attack against both countries on June 29–30, 1913 and quickly discovered itself engaged in the Second Balkan War against Turkey, Montenegro, and Romania as well. The Bulgarian move was a disaster, and King Ferdinand was forced to sue for peace within a month. In addition to heavy war casualties, Bulgaria also lost much of what it had gained in the First Balkan War in the treaties of Bucharest (August 10, 1913) and Constantinople (October 13, 1913). For some, the Second Balkan War resulted "in the second partition of Bulgaria," with territorial losses "far more damaging than that agreed at Berlin in 1878."[45]

The impact of the Balkan Wars on the Gypsies was connected to the casualties and transfer of other minorities who were caught up in the territorial exchanges that took place as a result of both conflicts. In the first war, Turkish sources indicate that "60,000 Albanians, 40,000 Turks, and 100,000 Moslems were killed by occupying Bulgarian troops." While these figures are possibly inflated, there is no doubt that Gypsies were trapped when Bulgarian forces "began a campaign of slaughtering thousands of Turkish peasants in Thrace" in early 1913. Afterward, 48,570 Muslims left Bulgarian Thrace for Turkey, while 46,764 Bulgarians entered Bulgaria from Turkish Thrace. Further movements took place in the months before the outbreak of World War I in 1914 as Bulgaria and other Balkan countries initiated a campaign designed "to persuade the Turkish minorities . . . to emigrate to Turkey." Those that remained in Bulgaria, including Muslim Gypsies, fell prey to Bulgarization efforts by the Bulgarian Orthodox Church during Bulgaria's brief occupation of Ottoman territory. One Gypsy tribe, the Grebenáris, ("comb makers") reputed at the time to be "the most thievish tribe in Bulgaria," took the upheavals in stride and humorously adopted the Bulgarian military term "*requisitsia* (requisition) . . . to describe thefts from the peasantry. 'Only,' they say, 'we do not give receipts, as do the military authorities, because we canot write!'" The Grebenáris and the sedentary Gypsy Drindaris, or Calgidjis, who lived in Bulgarian Dobrudja, were affected by the loss of this region to Romania after the Second Balkan War.[46]

Within a year after the end of the Second Balkan War, Bulgaria again found itself confronted with the possibility of engaging in a conflict—World War I. During the first year of the war, Bulgaria remained on the sidelines, carefully weighing the pros and cons of entrance on the side of the Allied powers, led by Great Britain, France, and Russia, or on the side of the German-Austrian Central Powers. Particularly enticing was the latter coalition's promise to Bulgaria of "those parts of Macedonia to which it had an 'historic and ethnic' claim," plus "any additional areas in Macedonia which its armies might occupy." Since Britain, France, and Russia offered fewer incentives, and their military position was weaker in the summer of 1915, King Ferdinand's government decided to enter the war as a German ally on October 11, 1915, with an attack on Serbia. Though Bulgarian forces enjoyed success in Macedonia and Romania, growing domestic opposition to the debilitating war, in part stimulated by news of the collapse of tsarism in Russia in the early spring of 1917, seriously affected national spirit. As disaffection swept through the military, a burgeoning peace movement at home further undercut the will to fight. By September 1918, Anglo-French forces began to move into Bulgaria, and on September 29, 1918, Bulgaria was the first Central Power to sign an armistice with the Allies.[47]

Bulgaria paid dearly for its support of Germany and Austria in the Treaty of Neuilly of November 27, 1919. It lost southern Dobrudja to Romania, and much of Macedonia to Serbia, while Greece acquired "all Western Thrace, except for a narrow strip in the Rhodope Mountains." In addition, section IV of the agreement had a number of clauses that dealt with minorities. Under these terms Bulgaria agreed "to assure full and complete protection of life and liberty to all inhabitants of Bulgaria without distinction of birth, nationality, language, race or religion." It defined Bulgarian nationals as those "who are habitually resident within Bulgarian territory" at the time that the Treaty of

Neuilly came into force and assured them full "civil and political rights" regardless of "race, language or religion." It also guaranteed Bulgarian nationals full use of their language in all governmental, business, and private settings and gave them the right to open their own schools or other institutions for the free practice of their language or religion. In areas where there were considerable minority populations, instruction in primary schools could be in their own language.[48]

Gypsies responded to the Neuilly terms with a request to the Ministry of Justice of the new government of Alexandŭr Stamboliiski "for the restoration of political rights taken from them early in the century." Roma and other minorities also benefited from the educational reforms of this era, which made secondary schooling compulsory and significantly added to the number of elementary schools and pro-gymnasia (secondary school that emphasized classical education) in rural parts of the country. Literacy rates rose appreciably for Gypsies and other groups during this period. The census of 1926, for example, showed that Roma literacy rates had almost tripled, to 8 percent, since 1905, while those of the Turks had doubled. Bulgarian literacy rates had only increased 7 percent during the same period, while those of Pomaks had increased by 2.5 percent. Unfortunately, there were few minority schools available for the Roma in Bulgaria, who officially numbered 134,844 in the 1926 census. Official statistics for the 1930–1931 school year stated that there were only two primary schools for Gypsies in Bulgaria, one fewer than before World War I. Each school had only one teacher, with 53 Gypsy students between the two.[49]

A hint of Gypsy activism began to take root in Bulgaria in the early 1920s. An early Gypsy activist was Shakir Pashov, who edited Roma Gypsy publications and organized Gypsies from 1923 to 1934. Some of the Roma groups formed during this period included the Egypt Society and Future. Other Gypsies involved in choral, theatrical, political, and educational activities during this period included Nikola Terzobaliev, Petko Zhelezchev, Ivan Kostov, and Kurti Krustev. Their efforts in politics, however, were sometimes met with derision and prejudice. In local elections in Turkish areas of the country in 1929, for example, some Turks complained that "Moslem Gypsies were also included in the council elections, as a result of which the pious foundations of Turks . . . were being entrusted to irresponsible Gypsies." Furthermore, though tolerated as one of Bulgaria's "traditional minorities," Gypsies remained at the bottom of the country's social pecking order and were assigned the "lowest-status occupations." Most of Bulgaria's road-sweepers and hangmen, for example, were Roma, positions also held by Gypsies earlier during the Ottoman era.[50]

The political environment in Bulgaria throughout the 1920s helped breed this type of antagonism toward Gypsies. A coup on June 9, 1923, had severely weakened rural voting strength and made "the army and the crown . . . the chief arbiters of the nation's political life." Though there was some restoration of political freedoms over the next few years, the 1929 depression undercut these gains, and on May 19, 1934, the army again seized control of the government and began a purge of the country's political parties and newspapers and began to transform Bulgaria along Italian fascist lines. Many of these changes came under the aegis of the new Law for the Defense of the State, which outlawed "all anti-state organizations." Included in the ban were the Gypsy groups the Egypt Society and Future.[51]

Demographic figures for Bulgarian Roma during this period showed a continued increase in population. Estimates for 1930 were 147,000 Roma, though the 1934 census listed only 80,532 "by native tongue." However, it is estimated that "more than one-third of the Gypsies were linguistically assimilated, and spoke Bulgarian and Turkish," a fact that complicated efforts to gauge the level of Turkish linguistic assimilation in Bulgaria.[52] The dramatic change in Gypsy demographic figures from 1926 to 1934 reflects the Romas' need to bury their identity in the new fascist atmosphere after the coup earlier that spring. Though some aspects of the new dictatorship were tempered in early 1935 with the overthrow of the military government, the new dictatorship under King Boris III (1918–1943) retained those aspects of their reforms that strengthened his hold on power. Though he did restore the parliament in 1938, its powers were limited, although it did manage periodically to serve as a brake on monarchial authority.[53]

Like most other nations in Eastern Europe, Bulgaria was deeply affected by the rise of Nazism in Germany. The Reich quickly became Bulgaria's principal trading partner, and fascist and Nazi-type political and paramilitary movements began to crop up throughout the country. As Europe moved closer to war in 1939, Bulgaria found itself drawn more and more into the German orbit, though it eventually chose to remain neutral when World War II broke out on September 1, 1939. Despite this pull toward the German-Italian camp, King Boris's principal interest in any alliance centered around the reacquisition of territory lost in the Second Balkan War and World War I. Consequently, when it appeared in the summer of 1940 that Stalin might offer Bulgaria southern Dobrudja, Hitler intervened and arranged for Rumania to cede the province to Bulgaria in the Vienna Award of September 7, 1940. Though Bulgaria still remained technically neutral, it found itself under increasing pressure from the Reich to join the Axis. This pressure intensified as Hitler began to make concrete plans for the invasion of the Soviet Union and, later, Greece in 1941.

Bulgaria was seen as an important avenue for German forces into both countries, and on March 1, 1941, Bulgaria finally joined the Axis when it signed the Three Power Pact. Now an active German ally, Bulgaria began an uncomfortable, three-year relationship with Hitler's Reich.[54]

Bulgaria's new relationship with Germany brought it southern Dobrudja in 1940, plus Macedonia and western Thrace after it joined Hitler's invasion of Yugoslavia and Greece in March 1941. Bulgaria acquired about 8,000–12,000 Romanian Gypsies when it acquired southern Dobrudja, while most of Macedonia's Roma came under Sofia's jurisdiction in 1941. Initially, Bulgarian authorities "felt disinclined to take severe measures [toward Gypsies]" in these areas despite German pressure, though, in time, "German security police became active in the region and some Gypsies fell into the net." Gypsies who joined Macedonian partisan movements "were dealt with summarily as any others." The Germans, however, never brought up the question of the deportation of Bulgaria's Roma, though there "were a few laws and decrees limiting their freedom."[55] In early 1941, for example, King Boris put into force the Law for the Protection of the Nation, modeled after the anti-Semitic German Nuremburg laws of 1935. Though the Roma were not mentioned specifically in the new act, its Nazi-inspired spirit, which placed Gypsies in the same racially inferior category as the Jews, made the Roma subject to increased acts of discrimination.[56] In May 1942, authorities issued a decree "which provided for the employment of Gypsies for compulsory labor, mainly in public works." Further anti-Jewish legislation that summer incited a wave of attacks on the Gypsies, while Article 24 of the Decree-Law of August 26, 1942, outlawed marriages between Gypsies and Bulgarians. Another decree insisted that Gypsies receive fewer rations than other Bulgarians. In addition, the press complained "that the control and police supervision of Gypsies had cost the state 500,000,000 Leva (about £2,500,000) and that this was a waste of money." Some forced conversions of Muslim Roma also took place during this period.[57]

One of the aims of the August 26 Decree-Law had been to pave the way for the deportation of Bulgaria's Jews to death camps in Poland. In early 1943, King Boris agreed "to surrender all Jews in the Macedonian and Thracian areas acquired by Bulgaria earlier." As the deportations began, Gypsies, themselves fearful of similar treatment, tried to help the Jews. When the first trainload of Thracian Jews arrived in Lom for transfer eastward, Gypsies helped a Bulgarian nurse distribute food and other items to the Jews. However, Slavi Puntev, the local representative for the Bulgarian Commissariat for Jewish Questions and the Red Cross, seized items from the Jews and sold them to Bulgarian peasants and Gypsies.[58]

In May 1943, possibly because the 1942 Gypsy compulsory labor decree had not been "applied with the necessary stringency," the "government announced that all Gypsies between the age of seventeen and fifty found idle would be mobilized for the harvest." In August, the Sofia newspapers *Dnes* (Today) and *Dnevnik* (Diary) reported that the police had searched Sofia and other large towns for "idlers," and had made raids of "restaurants, coffeehouses, sweetshops, and taverns. . . . All Gypsies unable to prove employment of one kind or another, were deported out of the city to do compulsory harvesting or work on roads, railways, and other public utilities." On August 14, *Dnes* noted "that thousands of Gypsies had already been deported from the capital and many more would follow." King Boris, however, did not intend for the transfers to go beyond the confines of Bulgaria, and on August 25, the Ministry of the Interior ordered local authorities throughout the country to "restrict the movement of Gypsies out of twelve regions," including Sofia, "under the pretext that Gypsies were spreading infectious diseases, especially spotted typhus." One of the offshoots of these transfers was the creation of a new subgroup of Gypsies, the Žuti, who arose through the intermarriage of poor Jews and Gypsies settled "in common places in the country during the Second World War." Since neither community would accept them, they created their own "specific closed community."[59]

In time, the Germans rationalized that it would be unwise to press the Bulgarians on the matter of deportation. Adolph-Heinz Beckerle, the German ambassador to Bulgaria, told Berlin on June 7, 1943, that the reason for the Bulgarian refusal to deport Jews to Poland was "the Bulgarian mentality—its lack of ideological strength—and in particular the fact that since the Bulgarians had grown up with Armenians, Greeks, and Gypsies, they had no innate prejudice against the Jews as did the people of northern Europe."[60]

By the end of 1943, Bulgarian officials were able to ease some of these regulations, and within eight months, all anti-Jewish and other restrictive legislation was nullified. Later, Gypsies credited King Boris for "saving Gypsies who were Bulgarian citizens from Nazi concentration camps during World War II." A Gypsy survivor of that era said that "Hitler wanted to kill all the Gypsies, but Boris wouldn't let him, and this is why we love Boris." Though it is difficult to gauge how many Bulgarian Roma survived World War II and the Poŕajmos (Gypsy Holocaust), estimates are that 5,000 Bulgarian Gypsies died during the Holocaust, one of the lowest rates of Gypsy death in Eastern Europe during this period.[61]

Part of Bulgaria's reason for saving its Jews and Gypsies centered around a desire to prepare for an easy surrender to the Allies at the end of the war. The collapse of Romanian resistance to the Soviet army on August 23, 1944, brought Stalin's troops quickly to Bulgaria's doorstep, and on September 5, 1944, Moscow declared war on Bulgaria. Within four days, Sofia's last wartime government was replaced by a Soviet-sponsored coalition government, the Fatherland Front. For the next 45 years, September 9, 1944, would be celebrated as Bulgaria's national liberation day. For the Gypsies, this date marked the beginning of a four–year renaissance.[62]

While the few communists in the early Fatherland Front used their positions in the government to begin a campaign of legal terror against fascists and potential opponents, the Gypsies took advantage of the supportive atmosphere to create in 1946 the Kulturno-prosvetna organizacija na ciganskoto malcinstvo v Bălgarija (Cultural Enlightenment Organization of the Gypsy Minority in Bulgaria), a national Gypsy organization with over 200 local clubs and a "Theatre Romen in Sofia [that] had a repertoire including Cervantes and Pushkin." Gypsy leaders also established a four page newspaper, *Romano-Esi* (The Gypsy Voice), which was replaced in 1949 by *Nevo Drom* (The New Way). By 1948, all Gypsies had to subscribe to *Romano-Esi*.[63]

As the pace of Bulgaria's communization quickened between 1946 and 1948, the Roma found the support they received from the country's increasingly powerful rulers to be quite fruitful. An increasing number of Gypsies, including the activist Shakir Pashov, acquired seats in the communist-dominated Subranie (national legislature), and were appointed as Communist Party secretaries throughout the country. A Gypsy school opened in Sofia in 1948 with 40 students and within four years had 500 pupils enrolled in classes. Officially, Bulgaria's new rulers castigated the fascists for "neglecting them [the Gypsies] completely," and promised tremendous improvements in the quality of Roma life. According to a 1947 article in the *Samokov Tribune*, the goal of the Fatherland Front was "to make every effort to change the life of the Gypsies for the better, and to weld them into the political and social and economic life of the Bulgarian People's Republic." An article in *Romano-Esi* the following year admonished all Roma

> who until now have been ashamed to call themselves Gypsies, and who have gone over to the Turkish minority, or who have been baptised as Christians, to tear off the mask from their faces, to lift up their heads, and to show that they are Gypsies . . . All Gypsies to a man must become members of the organization and subscribe to the only Gypsy newspaper, *Romano Esi*.[64]

This reference to Gypsy ties to Turkish Muslims was particularly significant, since the country's leaders were about to initiate a campaign against religion, which they considered "a key factor inhibiting loyalty to the communist government."[65]

The real shift began in 1947 with the adoption of a new constitution modeled closely on Stalin's 1936 Soviet constitution. Though the document provided adequate protection for the country's minorities and promised them "the right 'to be educated in their vernacular,' [the protections] tended to be meaningless."[66] Over the next two years, all remaining political opposition was eliminated or suffered "self-liquidation," and by 1949, the Fatherland Front remained the only political party in the country. Bulgaria's Communist Party was now ready to communize the country completely. An assault on private property had begun almost as soon as Soviet tanks had rolled into Bulgaria, while the depoliticization of the country took a bit longer.[67]

The last major source of possible trouble for the Fatherland Front was religion, which was dealt by the Law on Religious Denominations of March 1, 1949. This act "subjected all religious orders to direct state control" and prompted the government to begin a policy of forced emigration of Turks and Jews. Caught up in this net were Muslim Gypsies, who were forced into Turkey during the 17 month campaign during 1950–1951. The Bulgarian goal "was to thin out the Turkish areas and rid themselves of the most religious and recalcitrant Turks by planning to resettle within three months 250,000, or more than one-third of the minority, in Turkey." In actuality, the program took much longer and resulted in the forced exodus of 154,393 Turks, or 12 percent of the total Turkish population in Bulgaria. The program stopped when the Turkish government discovered a troubling number of Gypsies among the Turkish immigrants.[68]

The incident that led to Turkey's decision to seal its frontier with Bulgaria came on October 6, 1951. Though Turkish officials had already warned Bulgarian authorities about trying to include Gypsies among the Turks, and briefly closed the border in protest, 97 Gypsies were included on a trainload of Turks on that date. Since the Roma "had no Turkish entry visas, nor could claim Turkish ethnic origin . . . they were returned to Bulgaria." According to Turkish foreign minister Mehmet Fuat Köprülü, the border would "remain closed until the Bulgarian authorities realize that they will not succeed in their plan to smuggle into Turkey persons who are not of Turkish origin." Furthermore, Istanbul intended to keep the frontier closed "until the Sofia regime should see fit to permit the gypsies to return to Bulgaria." This had little impact on Bulgaria's communist rulers, who "continued to force thousands of Turks and Gypsies across isolated areas." Estimates are that 5,000 Bulgarian Gypsies were forced into Turkey during this period.[69]

Despite the hardship it caused, the effort to force Gypsies to leave Bulgaria heralded a new era for this minority. It developed just as Bulgaria's leaders began to undo some of the more onerous aspects of the police state system after the death of Joseph Stalin on March 5, 1953. Over the next year, authorities implemented a program "to settle the nomadic Roma, often in the northern plain below the Danube," and began to encourage Muslim Gypsies to change their names. In time, "20,000 families . . . received plots of land and low-interest loans to build their own houses and numerous settlements have been created on collective farms." During the same period, several new Roma schools were opened to educate the new influx of Gypsy children. This resettlement program saw the creation of Roma ghettos throughout the country. According to an "internal communist party report . . . there were segregated Roma sections in 160 of Bulgaria's 237 cities and in 3,000 of its 5,846 villages."[70]

At the same time, authorities closed the Gypsy theatre in Sofia and slowly began to develop policies designed to destroy Gypsy self-identity. After the census of 1956, which showed 197,865 Roma in the country, "gypsies disappeared entirely from official statistics."[71] Two years later, the government issued Decree No. 258, which prohibited Gypsy nomadism. On November 5, 1958, a month before the government issued the new restrictions, *Otechestven Front*, the organ of the Fatherland Front, "stated that Front activity must be 'doubled and trebled' in order to do away once and for all with the harmful residue of the past in the consciousness of all Turks, Jews and Gypsies." On December 30, 1958, the official newspaper *Izvestia* stated that "all Gypsies without regular jobs will be ordered to work in State industrial or agricultural enterprises."[72]

Party leaders followed up the decree with a letter on June 16, 1959, to regional, city, and district committees of the Communist Party. Decree No. 258, it explained, was intended to do away with "travelling and begging in our country," to settle Roma, and to positively reorganize their "way of life, raising of the culture, and incorporation of that population to the construction of a socialist society." It admitted that Gypsy underdevelopment was linked to "neglect and discrimination towards this population in the past on the part of the Bulgarian bourgeoise," an era in which they "could not find permanent jobs . . . and were doomed to lead a pitiful existence. . . . Starvation forced them to wander all over the country, and a large number of them were forced to steal and beg." Their children were unable to attend school, and this forced them into a life of "illiteracy, ignorance and poverty." The stereotype of the Gypsy as "lazy, incapable of working . . . lacking culture" was created by the "bourgeoisie and its policies of exploitation."[73]

After September 9, 1944, the letter continued, things began to change, and a "large part of the Gypsy population joined in the socialist material and spiritual culture of the Bulgarian people," which significantly lessened the gap between the Roma and the other people of Bulgaria. Gypsies could now be successfully found in all walks of Bulgarian life, while some "have turned into wealthy members of cooperative farms, and conscientious constructors of socialism." There were 3,500 Roma in the Communist Party and "tens of thousands" in the Fatherland Front, the Komsomol, and other Party groups. Unfortunately, there were also about 14,000 nomadic Gypsies, who were homeless and practiced "begging, fortune telling, stealing, etc." This group was "the most backward part of the Gypsy population." While their behavior was understandable before 1944, the letter continued, it is "harmful and disgraceful" in today's "conditions of socialism."[74]

The letter also explained that one of the barriers to change for this group was negative attitudes, on the part of both some Roma and others, about Gypsy ideas about work. Such prejudice had no basis in Marxist-Leninist ideology and had to change. The Gypsies, like other minorities in the country, had their "destiny with the destiny of the Bulgarian people." The "tendencies of part of the Gypsy population to affiliate with the Turks, to send their children to Turkish schools, etc., are wrong." Furthermore, the "isolation of the Gypsy population in separate districts and quarters is incorrect" and had to be changed. To overcome these problems, "groups of activists among Gypsy communists" should begin to work among nomadic and isolated Gypsies to find them gainful employment. Factory and cooperative farm managers should do the same thing and teach the Gypsies proper work habits. Party leaders were responsible for their political education, while communist youth leaders were obligated to "work systematically for their [Gypsy] communist and labor education." Finally, the letter ordered that all "children of Gypsy descent must study on common grounds in the Bulgarian schools."[75]

What followed was a policy of dispersal that moved Roma from their "compact . . . communities" into Bulgarian areas. Gypsies were "offered new apartments in Bulgarian neighborhoods," with one or two families "put into each apartment entranceway." Though the new regulations initially shocked the nomadic Roma, they accepted the new housing eagerly, and Gypsy leaders later acknowledged "the beneficial effects of the decrees."[76] Over the next four years, efforts were begun to force Gypsies and non-Turkish Bulgarian Muslims (Pomaks) to Bulgarize their names, while in 1960 authorities forced the Turks to begin to abandon their separate schools and attend schools with Bulgarian children.[77]

On April 5, 1962, the Communist Party's Central Committee issued Decree A101, which expressed concern over the fact that despite considerable improvement in the quality of Gypsy and Turkish life since 1944, "some negative tendencies" had arisen because a "considerable part of the Gypsies" and other ethnic groups tended "to affiliate with the Turks" and adopted Islam as well as Turkish and Arabic names. Consequently, over 130,000 Roma and others had registered themselves as Turks, while their children attended school with Turks and learned their language. Similar bonds were formed in military units and labor groups, which had "a harmful effect on their national and patriotic education."[78]

Consequently, to stop the Turkish assimilation trend among some Gypsies and other ethnic groups, the government of Todor Zhikov ordered all Party and state organs in areas with significant Gypsy, Tatar, and Pomak populations to "take as one of the major tasks in their political and ideological work among this population" the

> gradual overcoming of the tendency to affiliate with the Turks by leading a systematic ideological and political struggle against the Turkish religious and chauvinistic propaganda and its pan-Turkish and pan-Islamic aims and aspirations.

In addition, the Ministry of Justice and other government organs were responsible for informing local officials that "religion and personal names are not criteria for nationality." In addition, "intermarriage does not lead to change of nationality of the spouses," but the children of such unions could be voluntarily registered as Bulgarians. Furthermore, name changes for citizens of non-Bulgarian descent could be done through a simple written application to their local people's councils. These efforts had to be backed up by "large and systematic popular persuasions," but without violence or administrative force. This "large campaign of public persuasion" was aimed at the Tatars, Gypsies, and Bulgarian Muslims who were registered as Turks. In addition, authorities were to stop Pomaks and Gypsies from moving to "villages or towns with compact Turkish populations," while Turkish was not to be taught to the children of Gypsies, Tatars, and Bulgarian Muslims. Efforts had to be made to ensure that Turkish instructors did not teach in schools with significant Roma, Pomak, or Tatar pupils and that students from these groups were not allowed to study with Turkish children.[79]

Military and labor officials were responsible for the "correct education of the young Bulgarian Muslims, Gypsies or Tatars" to "strengthen . . . national awareness" of "communist and patriotic education," particularly among those who affiliated with the Turks. Officials in the Bulgarian Orthodox Church and in the Ministry of Foreign Affairs were to ensure that Turkish Muslim clerics did not spread propaganda advocating "affiliation with the Turks, especially through religious services," and should not allow the "appointment of Turkish clergymen in the villages with compact Gypsy and Tatar populations and among Bulgarian Muslims." Finally, the Bulgarian Academy of Sciences should send out expeditions of specialists to study the "ethnic origin and the national peculiarities of Turks, Tatars, and Gypsies who live in Bulgaria." They were to "make further discoveries about the historical truth about the results of the assimilation policies of the Turkish oppressors, about the mass and individual conversions to Islam."[80]

To deal with the Turkicization of some of the 20,000 Roma school children in Bulgaria, the government began to open special boarding schools for them in 1964. Officials also began to eliminate Gypsy cultural organizations, though Roma students in Lom created an illegal Gypsy discussion group and a soccer club. Authorities warned the soccer club members about having separate Gypsy teams and added that the teams shouldn't have Gypsy names. Later, team members were forced to change the names of the squads to Botev, Levski, etc. (all Bulgarian national heroes). However, the Bulgarian secret police said that Gypsy teams should not bear the names of Bulgarian heroes and ordered each team to have five Bulgarian members. Consequently, the Gypsy members disbanded the soccer clubs.[81]

The practical implication of these policies was the destruction of Roma self-identity through continued forced integration and Bulgarization. These policies, however, conflicted with the new Bulgarian constitution of May 18, 1971, which promised no "privileges or limitations of rights based on ethnic belonging, origin [or] creed." In fact, within several years after the promulgation of the new constitution, Bulgarian officials began to talk of a "unified Bulgarian socialist nation," which one newspaper claimed was "almost completely one ethnic type, and is moving toward complete national homogeneity."[82] Furthermore, the country's leader, Todor Zhikov, noted in 1979 that the people had solved Bulgaria's "national question," and that there were "no internal problems" tied to it. His long range goal was to make Bulgaria "the Japan of the Balkans."[83] Bulgarian Gypsies, however, found ways around some of the new restrictions. They officially adopted Bulgarian names, which they used for documents and school, but continued to use their Gypsy names at home and in the Gypsy community. In addition, when they chose Bulgarian names, they often picked those of famous politicians, composers, or music stars.[84]

As the government proclaimed the end of the "national question," it began to abandon its dual policy of special and integrated schools for Gypsy children and move toward a program solely of segregation. In 1962, there were only 20,000 Gypsy children enrolled in Bulgarian schools, which prompted officials to create a system of special schools two years later for Roma "drawn from the poorest families or where there is a 'bad social atmosphere.'" In time, the government opened 145 special schools for these students, while many others attended integrated Bulgarian schools. By 1967, government statistics claimed that there were 55,000 Gypsy children enrolled in Bulgarian schools. Of this number, 8,000 lived in boarding schools, a figure that rose to 10,000 by the early 1970s. Estimates showed 450 Gypsies with college degrees at this time. The government was particularly proud of this figure, since Gypsies and other minorities had been given "preference for admission to higher education" since the 1950s. In addition, in 1969, the government "opened special schools in Gypsy districts to teach students special skills." Roma students in grades one through eight received certain professional training and graduated with a certificate that said that they had technical skills.[85]

However, officials began to abandon the integration efforts in the late 1970s because of problems they had with Gypsy children. In time, 70 to 80 percent of the country's Gypsies had attended the segregated schools, while "more than 50 per cent of the children of gypsies in Bulgaria lived in children's homes," which officials described as "kindergartens which provided young children, ethnic Bulgarian as well as gypsy, with a wide range of opportunities." The official reason for the shift to segregated schools centered around the small number of Gypsy children who finished school. According to a 1978 Central Committee report, only 30 percent of Gypsy children completed primary school, while the number who finished secondary school was negligible. In addition, the report claimed that "more than fifty percent of Gypsies above the age of thirty were illiterate." From the government's perspective, the segregation experiment was successful and prompted 25 to 30 percent of the Roma children to attend the new technical secondary schools. Unfortunately, the intense segregation worked against efforts at assimilation, since the "ghetto schools" were attended almost exclusively by Roma children who had weak Bulgarian language skills. Though efforts have since been made to offer younger Gypsy children Bulgarian preparatory classes before they enter primary school, they have only been partly successful in providing Roma children with the academic background necessary to compete successfully in Bulgarian schools. These problems in turn have enforced the stereotype of Gypsy inferiority, which has not been helped by a national Gypsy literacy rate of 8.2 percent.[86]

The abandonment of integrated education as a vehicle for Gypsy assimilation did not stop government efforts to create a unitary Bulgarian state. In 1984, the government began to forbid the performance of Gypsy music throughout the country, and initiated a two-year campaign designed to erase the last vestiges of ethnic identity among the largest ethnic minority in Bulgaria—the Turks. This effort also had serious implications for Muslim Gypsies who still lived in Turkish areas. The campaign began with an effort in December 1984 to force Turks to Bulgarize their names. In addition, officials closed some mosques and outlawed Muslim religious holidays. Their efforts met with strong public resistance from the Turkish community, which Bulgarian officials met with violence. Estimates are that 300 to 1,500 Turks died during the 1984–1985 campaign. A strong international outcry against Sofia's anti-Turkish policies neutralized the effectiveness of some aspects of the campaign and helped create the atmosphere of unrest that helped to bring down the Zhikov regime in 1989. These efforts also soured relations between Gypsies and Bulgarians.[87]

The assimilation campaign against the Turks heightened prejudice toward Gypsies, and signs began to appear in some railway stations that warned travelers of Roma pickpockets, while "nomadic Roma [were] regularly refused entrance to cafes and restaurants."[88] The aftermath of the November 10, 1989, collapse of the Zhikov regime saw an increase in hostility towards the Gypsies. The "loosening of previous constraints on freedom of expression transformed more subtle forms of discrimination against the Roma into open racial hatred and violence."[89] Many Bulgarians now blamed the Gypsies for the country's dramatic increase in crime. An article in the newspaper *Duma* (Word) in February 1991 said that "between 13% and 16% of all criminal acts in Sofia were carried out by Roma." In a public opinion survey undertaken by the National Institute of Youth Studies later that spring, "Gypsies were described by 89% of respondents as thieves, by 76% as bullies, by 75% as black marketers, by 70% as liars, and by 67% as drifters." This strong anti-Gypsy sentiment contrasted sharply with attitudes toward other minorities. An extensive *Times-Mirror* survey conducted during the same period showed that 52 percent of the Bulgarian respondents had favorable attitudes towards Turks, 62 percent had positive feelings about Pomaks, and 63 percent viewed Jews favorably.[90] The Bulgarian press published the first two surveys, and state-owned television and radio helped perpetuate the image of Roma as "responsible for the country's black market." At the end of 1990, the Bulgarian parliament passed a strict anti-black market law aimed principally at Gypsies, who officials felt dominated it.[91] According to Mihail Ivanov, President Zhelyn Zhelev's adviser on ethnic policies, "25–28% of the crimes (aside from economic crimes) committed in Bulgaria can be traced to the Roma." According to other figures, 80 percent of the inmates in Bulgaria's prisons were Gypsies. This new image of the Gypsy has created hatred that has resulted in violence toward the Roma. Bulgarians burned a portion of the Gypsy quarter in Podem, while 12 Bulgarians in Plovdiv staged a hunger strike to protest living among Gypsies. On June 29, 1992, police raided a Rom neighborhood in Pazardshik and "violently attacked" its inhabitants. The police "conducted abusive house searches, damaged Gypsies' property and confiscated money and property."

Roma who considered filing a complaint were warned of recurrence if they did. President Zhelev ordered an Interior Ministry probe of the incident, which concluded that the police had done everything by the book. Several new, anti-Gypsy organizations, including *Basta* (Italian for "enough") and *Vazrazhdane*, have cropped up, while other reports tell of Roma being "chased like dogs in the street."[92]

Despite this atmosphere, the Gypsies have made great strides in post-1989 Bulgaria, and a number of new Roma organizations have emerged to give Gypsies a greater voice in Bulgarian politics and society. The spirit for the revitalization of the Roma community was provided by the new leader of the post November 10, 1989, Bulgarian government, Petûr Mladenov. At the end of December 1989, he told a group of Pomaks and Turks outside the National Assembly in Sofia that their oppression was over and that "everyone in Bulgaria will be able to choose his name, religion, and language freely."[93] This atmosphere, plus the realization that Bulgaria's large Gypsy population, which the Ministry of the Interior estimated to be 576,927 in May 1989 and the Democratic Union of Gypsies—ROMA, created the following spring, claimed numbered between 800,000 and 1,000,000, had the potential to be a strong political force in a nation with a total population of slightly less than 9 million, provided a powerful boost for Gypsy leaders.[94]

What has emerged is a plethora of Gypsy political, cultural, and business organizations. One of the first was the Independent Democratic Socialist Association of Gypsies of Bulgaria, which was formed in Sliven on January 7, 1990. Bulgaria's most significant Gypsy group, the Democratic Union of Gypsies—ROMA (ROMA) represented about 50,000 Gypsies and was originally headed by Bulgaria's most prominent Gypsy leader, Manush Romanov. Romanov won a seat in parliament in the June 1990 elections through the party list of the Union of Democratic Forces. In addition, Muslim Roma also had representatives in the ethnic Turkish Party for Rights and Freedom (PRF). During the national elections on June 17, 1990, there were efforts to try to force some Roma to vote for the former Bulgarian Communist Party, renamed the Bulgarian Socialist Party (BSP). The BSP's winning of only 47.15 percent of the popular vote prompted a Sofia municipal court to declare as valid the government's Law on Political Parties, which denied ROMA, the PRF, and other minority parties "the status of a political party on the grounds that this would violate the constitutional prohibition on parties with a racial, ethnic, or religious basis."[95] Though the Bulgarian Supreme Court later overturned this ruling in time for the November 1991 elections, the Gypsies' political fortunes had already waned, particularly when Romanov lost his parliamentary seat and was removed as head of ROMA. Though Romanov later regained control of his party, a number of new Gypsy political organizations had since arisen, shattering any hope of Gypsy unity.[96]

By the spring of 1992, three separate Roma political organizations had evolved, and five more represented Gypsy cultural interests. Unfortunately, they were "fragmented and poorly organized," which meant that "Bulgaria's Roma population has thus far been unable to establish a politically powerful interest group." The reasons for these weaknesses stemmed from a number of things, in particular the earlier success of the Zhikov regime "in destroying the Roma's cultural and social organizations." In addition, the Gypsies were unable to develop any political muscle, particularly after they were denied the opportunity to form political parties in 1990. Another problem was that Bulgaria's large Roma population did "not speak with a unified voice" and was "divided along political, social, and cultural lines." This was partly caused by the Muslim-Christian split in the Roma community as well as by cultural and linguistic differences. Bulgaria's large Gypsy Muslim population traditionally had ties with the Turkish Muslim community and, after the PRF's strong showing in the 1991 elections, were receptive to the PRF's appeals for support and alliance. In addition, the fact that there are at least fifty Romani dialects in Bulgaria has created barriers that have impeded a strong, unitary consciousness among the country's Roma. Regardless, Bulgaria's Roma have struggled to overcome these problems, and on October 17–18, 1992, leaders from some of the country's Gypsy organizations held a congress and formed a national lobby called the United Roma Federation. It selected as its chairman Vasil Chaprasov, an educator from Sliven, who declared after his selection that the United Roma Federation "was independent and politically unaffiliated."[97]

Fourteen months later, a number of important Roma groups met in Sliven to request the government to put a "ban on all fascist parties and organizations." Of particular concern to Gypsy leaders were the speeches and activities of Father Gelemenov and his *Vazrazhdane* organization. In a letter to the government on December 30, 1993, the United Roma Federation, the Democratic Union of Gypsies—ROMA, and the Rom Intellectuals called Father Gelemenov's ideas "extremely dangerous." They pointed to an interview given the day before in *Trud* (labor), where Father Gelemenov admitted that though he had "abandoned traditional nationalism for the Nazi ideology," he felt Bulgaria should be "'subordinating' the country's Gypsy and Turkish minorities." The Roma groups also criticized the "Bulgarian media, including state television," for constantly giving "Gelemenov opportunities to air his extremist views."[98]

Yet it would be a mistake to place the blame for the plight of Bulgaria's Roma solely on the Gypsies themselves. Their strong association with clan or linguistic groups comes from centuries of discrimination that always placed them outside Bulgarian society. Their inability to integrate more fully into the normal social fabric of the country, particularly under the communists, can be traced to the lack of mature, sophisticated programs that addressed their special educational needs and helped them to integrate into Bulgarian society. When faced with apparent failure, the Zhikov regime resorted to segregationist policies that merely fortified the image, both within the Gypsy community and without, of Roma separateness, long the source of the stereotypes that have persecuted them throughout history. Until the Bulgarian government decides to adopt policies designed to address the special needs of the Gypsy community that demonstrate respect for their unique traditions and a serious campaign to combat prejudice against them, Bulgarian Roma will find it difficult to play a larger part in this new democracy. In the meantime, therefore, they will have to develop their own devices to handle the complex problems they face in the new Bulgaria.

.2.

CZECHOSLOVAKIA

The Gypsies entered the Czech lands of Bohemia and Moravia and the Slovak portion of the Arpad Hungarian kingdom during the late Middle Ages. The independent Bohemian or Czech state consisted of Bohemia, Moravia, and later Silesia and Lusatia. It came close to extinction as a result of the socioreligious Hussite Wars of 1420–1436 but was revitalized by the election of Władyslaw II (r. 1471–1516), eldest son of Polish king Kazimierz Jagiellończyk, to the Bohemian throne in 1471. Nineteen years later, Władyslaw became king of Hungary. The Bohemian state also had ties to the Holy Roman Empire, and since the early thirteenth century the "Bohemian king exercised the role of the first elector" in the Empire.[1]

The date for the migration of Gypsies into the Czech lands and Hungarian Slovakia is difficult to pinpoint. Robert H. Vickers asserted in his *History of Bohemia* that Bohemia's King, Břetislav II (r. 1092–1100), issued a decree soon after he took the throne in 1092 that expelled "the unwelcome people described as 'soothsayers, sorcerers, and cheats,' who had acquired much influence over the simple folk by pretended divining arts in groves and woods. They were expelled from the country; and their haunts burned." Vickers speculated that those driven from Bohemia were "probably a tribe of gypsies who had associated their practices of stealing and fortune telling with the remnants of the old paganism." He is, however, incorrect; Břetislav's decrees were not aimed at Gypsies, since it is doubtful that there were any in this part of Europe at that time, but at pagans and Orthodox Christians in his kingdom.[2]

A prominent Slovak gypsiologist, Emília Horváthová, suggested in her *Cigáni na Slovensku* (Gypsies in Slovakia) that Gypsies first entered Bohemia via Hungary with the army of King Andrew II (r. 1205–1235) after he returned from his Crusade in the Holy Lands in 1217–1218. When the Tatars or Mongols invaded Hungary in 1241 and butchered the population east and north of the Danube after their victory over King Bela IV at Muhi, the Gypsies fled into Bohemia to escape. While there is no question that Mongol extermination tactics forced many to flee in anticipation, it is difficult to prove Horváthová's assertion that there were Rom in this region. On the other hand, it is possible that there were Gypsies with Kubla Khan's armies, since the Mongols had swept through Central Asia a number of years earlier at the height of the Rom migration from India into Central Asia.[3] Two decades later, the Bohemian king Ottokar II (r. 1251–1276) wrote Pope Adrian IV about his victory over Bela IV and mentioned that among the Hungarian monarch's forces were *Cingari* (Gypsies).[4]

There was significant settling of the Slovak lands in fourteenth-century Hungary by Ruthenian, Polish, and German settlers who "created numerous villages on newly cleared land." There is some evidence to suggest that Gypsies began to appear in the region at this time in what was still regarded as a backward, "archaic," and "empty" part of Europe. The "commonest early settlement-pattern in fourteenth century Slovakia was around feudal castles," and it is possible that some Rom had encamped around Spišský (Zips) Castle as early as 1322. Officials often saw the Gypsies "as useful and from their first appearance [they] were permitted, encouraged and even forced to settle." However, they became "vulnerable to manipulation by their protectors, a situation which feudal lords were not slow to exploit." The "deeply religious inhabitants" respected the Rom because of the "Egyptian legend they recounted, according to which they played the role of religious exiles, condemned as a penance to wander around the world. They had the trust not only of the common people but of temporal and spiritual governing representatives, who even provided them with safe conduct permits ('*glejty*')." [5] During the second half of the fourteenth century, there was an increase in references to Gypsies in local records in the Slovakian areas of Hungary. A Gypsy village, Ciganvaja, existed in Szolnok County as early as 1388, and a number of families residing there began to use the surname Cigany or Cigan.[6]

It is during what would become an ongoing, four-century effort to settle this region of Europe that the "first undisputed reference to Roms in the Czechs lands (1399)" and Slovakia appears. In the *Book of Executions of the Lords of Rožmberk* (or Ruzomberok) in Slovakia, "it is mentioned that apart from several Germans in a robber band in S. Bohemia, there was a certain Gypsy, the groom of Andrew."[7] Eighteen years later, further reference is made to a large group of Gypsies that passed through Bohemia on the way to different parts of western Europe. The group was remarkable for its "numbers, novelty, and apparent nobility of their leaders," who carried safe-conduct passes from King Sigismund of Hungary (r. 1387–1437), who was also *de facto* Holy Roman Emperor, and Pope Martin V. Though at least one Czech gypsiologist speculated that this group came directly from Asia Minor with the Turks, Emília Horváthová has argued that the Gypsy band was too sophisticated to have been a mere "primitive nomadic tribe practicing their traditional occupations." Over the next six years, Pope Martin V and King Sigismund issued further travel permits to Gypsies moving through the region. On April 17, 1423, King Sigismund, resident at Spišský Castle, issued a special, detailed travel permit to the Rom leader Ladislaus.

> Came into our presence our faithful Ladislaus waynoda Ciganorum [voivode (leader) of the Gypsies] with others pertaining to him, who presented their very humble supplications to us, here in Zips in our presence. . . . In consequence we, being persuaded by their supplication, have thought proper to grant them this privilege: each time that the said voivode Ladislaus and his people shall come into our said possessions, be it free cities or fortified towns, from that time we strictly entrust and order to your present fidelities that you may favour and keep without any hindrance or trouble the said voivode Ladislaus and the Cigani who are subject to him; and by all means preserve them from any impediments and vexations. If any variance or trouble should occur among themselves, then neither you nor any other of you, but the same voivode Ladislaus, should have the power of judging and absolving. . . .[8]

The sedentary Rom settlers in Slovakia worked as castle musicians and metal workers, while an increasing number served in the armies of Hungary's monarchs. Gypsy smiths during the reign of Bohemian king Vladislas II (r. 1471–1516) "were sufficiently well established as metal workers to be entrusted with the making of weapons and other warlike material," and made the torture instruments used on the peasant rebel leader Dózsa (György Székely) after his defeat and capture by Ján Zápolský (Janos Zápolyai), the *voevod* of Transylvania, in 1514. According to one account, Dózsa was forcibly seated on a "throne of red-hot iron and crowned with a red-hot crown" purportedly made by Rom craftsmen, while "a starving mob of gipsies was then encouraged to carve cutlets from his living flesh." There are a number of positive comments about Gypsy troops during the latter part of the fifteenth century in imperial Hungarian records, and on a number of occasions, Rom troops were used in conflicts that swept Slovakia throughout the next century. In 1534, Zápolský, a frustrated contender for the Hungarian throne, used Rom soldiers to burn four eastern Slovakian towns that supported his Habsburg opponent, Ferdinand I (r. 1526–1564). Some of the captured Gypsy soldiers confessed that they had orders to burn a further nine Slovak towns. Rom troops were also prominent in the defence of the castle at Velká Ida in 1557.[9]

It was in this atmosphere, enhanced by the chaos that beset Slovakia after the Turkish defeat of the Hungarians near Mohács on August 28, 1526, and a civil war that engulfed the region over the next 13 years, that strong anti-Gypsy policies began to emerge. Some indication of this change in attitude had begun to surface in the previous century, centered around the idea that Slovakian Rom were "indifferent to religion." Some Slovaks no longer regarded them as "martyrs but spies who were preparing conditions for the Tartar invasion." Fear of the Turks, who had taken over central Hungary in 1541, created a new basis for anti-Gypsy sentiment, since some Gypsies were now viewed as "incendiaries, soldiers or spies." Sedentary and nomadic Rom were increasingly isolated from Slovak and Hungarian peasants, and new Gypsy settlers were restricted to the periphery of towns and villages. Rom craftsmen were now only allowed to make "simple implements for local farmers, weapons for nightwatchmen, etc.," while non-Gypsies dominated the "larger scale and more profitable metalworking."[10] The Turkish conquest of central Hungary and the creation of three separate kingdoms in 1541–1542 created a peculiar environment for the Rom. Royal Habsburg Hungary was now centered in Slovakia, while central "Magyar" Hungary was under direct Ottoman control. The Turks created a puppet state, Transylvania, under Janos II (r. 1556–1571), the infant son of Ján Zápolský, and his mother, Isabella. Slovakian Gypsies in Royal Hungary suffered from uneven policies of expulsion, since "some lords obeyed, [and] some were more concerned to preserve the skills of Gypsies as smiths, musicians and soldiers."[11]

Gypsy policies in the Czech lands were also uneven. The first anti-Gypsy legislation was issued in Moravia in 1538, and three years later, King Ferdinand I ordered Gypsies in his realm expelled after a series of fires in Prague that were blamed on the Rom, who were accused of being in the service of the Turks. Seven years later, the German Diet at Augsburg decided that "whosoever kills a Gypsy, will be guilty of no murder."[12] Some of the motivation for the anti-Gypsy legislation in this part of Europe was a growing fear of Turkey and the destabilizing atmosphere brought about by the wars of the Protestant Reformation. Indications are that some of the government's decrees against the Gypsies were passed "largely as a sop to public fears," since they were constantly reissued—a sign of inadequate enforcement. When public sentiment toward the Rom got out of hand in 1556, the government stepped in "to forbid the drowning of Rom women and children." At the same time, local records show that "alms and letters of recommendation" were "granted to Roms by town councils," and "others continued to travel the Czech lands supplying their usual services of horse-trading, fortune-telling and the like."[13]

The difficulties that beset the Czech lands and Slovakian Hungary worsened in the seventeenth century with the outbreak of the Thirty Years War (1618–1648), which became a time of increased prejudice toward and restriction for Gypsies. This complex series of wars began in Bohemia with the Defenestration of Prague of May 23, 1618, where Bohemian Protestant noblemen, angered over the closing of several Protestant churches, threw three representatives of King Ferdinand out the window of Hradčany Castle. This deed, which the king's delegates miraculously survived, triggered a revolt in which the "whole of Bohemia seemed to go Protestant."[14] For the next two years, the Protestant tide swept Bohemia, and the country's Diet deposed Archduke Ferdinand (r. 1617–1619), who became the Austrian emperor in 1619. In his place, the Czechs selected Frederick I (r. 1619–1620), the son-in-law of James I of England. Little Protestant support arrived from the rest of Europe, and an alliance of Catholic forces invaded Bohemia, defeating the Protestant forces at the symbolic battle of White Mountain on November 8, 1620, just outside of Prague. The political and religious changes that followed marked the "beginning of the end of Bohemian independence." Bohemia and Moravia were struck particularly hard by the "re-Catholicization" policies of Ferdinand II (r. 1619–1637), though Silesia and Lusatia "escaped punishment altogether." Over the next century, "Bohemia was swallowed up in the wider fate of the Habsburg monarchy and of Germany itself," and the Germanization that accompanied these developments saw a "precipitous decline in the public use of the Czech language," long the symbol of Czech national identity. Though the Czech regions of the empire—Bohemia, Moravia, and Silesia—were on "equal footing with one another and the Austrian provinces," the "term Kingdom of Bohemia . . . lost all practical meaning."[15]

Slovakia's fate during this period was linked to that of Royal Hungary and Transylvania, which briefly flirted with its own independence movement in 1620–1621. When it became apparent to Gabor Bethlen (r. 1613–1629), the Transylvanian ruler recently elected king of Hungary by the rebels, that he could not defeat Ferdinand II, he concluded the Peace of Nikolsburg on December 31, 1621, which granted full amnesty to the rebellious nobles, reconfirmed Hungary's religious freedom, and granted Transylvania full sovereignty, including recently conquered northern Hungary, which remained under Bethlen's control.[16]

Bohemia and Moravia were devastated by the upheavals of the Thirty Years War and suffered significant population losses. Both areas were also affected by famine, epidemics, and flight. The first two conditions forced Gypsies from the Czech lands and other parts of Europe into Slovakia, where "regulations began to be passed which legitimized the hounding of Gypsies from the towns and villages." The new restrictions, which, though aimed at all Rom, "were usually only enforced against 'foreign' nomadic groups," forced Slovak Gypsies "to lead a nomadic life and in isolated cases to make a living by parasitism"—defined as "fortune telling, magical healing, and theft." The tragedy of these policies was that "while prohibiting nomadism, the laws provided Gypsies with no realistic conditions for settling and earning an honest living."[17]

Conditions throughout the Austrian Empire remained unstable in the second half of the seventeenth century as the region continued to be plagued by threats from Turkey and independence efforts in Hungary. A French-Turkish-Hungarian alliance in 1682 triggered a Turkish effort to expel the Hapsburgs from Hungary and to capture Vienna a year later. An alliance of Austrian, German, and Polish forces drove the Turks from Vienna in the fall of 1683, which signaled the beginning of "the long Ottoman retreat from Europe, which did not end until the conclusion of the Balkans Wars in 1913." Over the next four years, Leopold I (r. 1657–1705), the Austrian emperor, pushed the Turks out of the bulk of Hungary and began to integrate Turkish Hungary and Transylvania into the Habsburg Empire.[18]

The social and economic instability that followed these complex series of wars, and a new anti-Habsburg rebellion in Hungary in 1707, prompted new efforts to assert imperial power in the Czech lands and Hungarian Slovakia. One aspect of these efforts was an attempt to halt the wandering

> of deserters or dismissed soldiers, peasants chased away from their farms, which had been pillaged and set on fire, itinerant quacks, adventurers and wandering Jews ("smoussen"), "ordinary" criminals such as those, for instance, who were condemned to banishment after an offense (as often happened), burglars, and finally . . . our well-known Gypsies.

In 1697 and again in 1701, Leopold I decreed that "Gypsies 'shall be declared outlaws ("vogelfrei") by letters patent, and that if they enter the country again they are to be treated with all possible severity both as regards body and property.'" This was followed nine years later by a more comprehensive law issued in Prague by the new emperor, Joseph I, and applied throughout Bohemia. The edict ordered "that all adult males [Gypsies] were to be hanged without trial, whereas women and young males were to be flogged and banished forever." In addition, "they were to have their right ear cut off in the kingdom of Bohemia, in the county of Mähren [Moravia] on the contrary the left ear." In other parts of Austria they would be "branded on the back with a branding-iron, representing the gallows." These mutilations enabled authorities to identify Gypsies on their second arrest.[19]

Since arrested Gypsies argued ignorance of the decree because of illiteracy, Austrian authorities adapted a system of warning-placards that was used in other German states. These boards were placed at all border-crossing points and "along . . . [the] secret paths of the Gypsies, at the cost of the local jurisdictions." Designed for the illiterate Rom,

> they depicted the horrible scene of an adult Gypsy, swinging from the gallows with next to him a young lad and a woman being flogged till the blood flowed, or having their ears cut off. Underneath such atrocious pictures a caption in the Bohemian and German language had to be fixed, saying: "This is the punishment for intruding Gypsies."

Joseph I's decree strongly encouraged local officials to hunt down Rom in their areas by levying a fine of 100 Reichsthaler for those that failed to do so. Anyone who helped Gypsies "was to be punished by half a year's forced labour." The result was "mass killings" of Rom, while "whole groups were hanged, shot or drowned and to discourage further immigration scores of Rom bodies hung from trees along frontier roads." These harsh punishments evidently did not stop Gypsies from entering the Austrian Empire, however, and on October 26, 1717, another emperor, Charles VI, "issued a third mandate forbidding Gypsies to enter his territory and repeating the order to erect 'tafelln' [warning-placards] at the boundaries of Bohemia and Silesia." In 1721, he amended this decree to include the execution of adult female Rom, while Gypsy children were "to be put in hospitals for education." Five years later, Charles VI issued a new edict that followed Joseph I's 1710 strictures, ordering that Rom women and children who reentered Bohemia be executed.[20]

The harshness of these policies began to change during this period, perhaps in response to the imperial reforms in Hungary after the Treaty of Szatmár of April 29, 1711. According to this agreement, the Hungarian nobility

> accepted Charles VI [Charles III in Hungary] as hereditary king, and he solemnly confirmed the Hungarian constitution; that is, in return for the unconditional acceptance of the Hapsburg dynasty he gave the Hungarian nobility a free hand to run the internal affairs of Hungary as they best saw fit.

Eleven years later, Charles VI began his reform of the administrative structure of Hungary, while a major colonization effort was undertaken to deal with a serious decline in Hungary's population. An estimated 400,000 immigrants swept into Hungary, many from the Slovak areas of northern Hungary, and others into the old Ottoman territories in the southeast. The Hungarian Court Chancellery, which would later initiate a new series of regulations on the Rom problem, was located in Bratislava (Pozsony), now the capital of Slovakia. As part of the reforms, which continued the traditional tax exemptions for the Hungarian nobility, the peasantry, including the Gypsies, were faced with new tax burdens. Gypsy censuses began to be initiated throughout Hungary, and in 1737, Hungarian officials in one district decreed that any Rom with a tent plus a wagon and horses had to pay twice the tax as a Gypsy without them. Annual taxes were now collected from all Rom throughout Hungary on their moveable possessions.[21]

Authorities continued to clamp down on Gypsies during the early years of the reign of the Austrian empire's new ruler, Maria Theresa (r. 1740–1780). Policies were particularly harsh in Bohemia, which briefly came under Franco-Bavarian control during the early days of the War of Austrian Succession (1740–1748). Before the outbreak of this immense war, the new empress decreed that anyone who gave food to Rom would be punished, and over the next decade she issued further edicts that reaffirmed earlier Gypsy deportation policies. If a Rom returned to the Austrian Empire, he would be flogged on the first offense and executed if he reentered the country again. On December 1, 1749, Maria Theresa issued a new Gypsy patent aimed at "driving Gypsies, nomads and foreign beggars from the land." Rom native to specific areas in the empire were to be held there by authorities. Nine years later, the Austrian Imperial Council "made local Diets of gentry responsible for Roms in their area, reserving a co-ordinating function for itself."[22]

A year after the outbreak of Maria Theresa's second major European conflict, the Seven Years' War (1756–1763), the empress issued a new Gypsy patent aimed principally at the Slovak regions of Hungary. Local noble councils became responsible for Gypsies in their area, and Gypsies were to settle and be subject to taxes and to compulsory service for the lord of the manor; they could not own horses and wagons and would need special permission to leave their villages.[23] In 1761, Maria Theresa "outlawed use of the word *Cigány* and decreed that Gypsies in the future be called 'new citizens,' 'new peasants,' or 'new Hungarians.'" Rom males over sixteen were now eligible for the draft, and "12- to 16-year-olds [were] to be taught a craft." Other Gypsy decrees issued throughout her reign were designed to force the Roma to settle and assimilate throughout her Habsburg domains.[24]

Maria's Theresa's son, Emperor Joseph II (r. 1780–1790), continued his mother's Gypsy policies, with an emphasis on the creation of Rom settlements, census taking, and the placement of children in foster homes, schools, or jobs. These efforts seemed to enflame some local hatred toward the Rom, and in 1782, authorities in present-day Hont County, Slovakia, accused 151 Gypsies of "roasting and eating several dozen Hungarian peasants." County officials brutally executed 41 of the Rom after torturing the entire group. A shocked Joseph II ordered a special commission to investigate the incident to determine the fate of the Gypsies still alive. The imperial body found that the Rom were "guilty of no more than theft and were released after a beating."[25] A year after the Hont County incident, Joseph II issued a new Gypsy patent for Hungary and extended it to Transylvania that placed new restrictions on the Roma. Other regulations issued during the era of these "Enlightened Despots" dictated that Gypsy slums on the outskirts of towns and villages be torn down and required local authorities to build new homes, where men and women were to sleep apart. Gypsies in the new settlements were under the watchful eye of the local sheriff, who made weekly checks on the Rom. The Gypsies could not leave the village without the sheriff's permission. The Rom in Slovakia and other parts of Hungary were, like other citizens, subject to all taxes and were obligated to serve in the military.[26]

Rom census data from 1780 to 1783 provides some clues about the impact of Joseph II's early policies toward the Gypsies. Married women were not included in the data. In 1780, there were 43,609 Rom in Slovakia and other parts of Hungary. This figure dropped to 38,312 in 1781 but rose to 43,778 in 1782. These dramatic changes in Hungarian Rom population figures reflect Gypsy reaction to the policies of Joseph II.[27] Gypsies in the Czech lands obliquely benefited from the spirit of emancipation embedded in Joseph II's Serfdom Patent of November 1, 1781, which

> abolished the condition of personal bondage and substituted a "moderate subjection" (Unterthanigkeit) corresponding to the peasants' legal status in Lower and Upper Austria. The peasants were now free to migrate, marry without permission, to have their children educated or apprenticed in towns, to dispose of or mortgage their land. They still owed economic obligations to their seigneurs . . .

The Serfdom Patent "transformed the serfs from subjects of the lords into subjects of the state, in theory, at least, equal before the law." Slovak peasants acquired similar privileges four years later, though employment and educational limitations in the region meant that the new freedoms did not "have the same effect on social mobility as, for instance, in the Bohemian Lands."[28]

These reforms were met with some frustration in Hungary and helped breed a new spirit of rebellion among the nobility. Consequently, on the eve of his death in early 1790, Joseph II revoked everything except his Toleration Patent that granted limited religious freedom for Protestants and the Greek Orthodox and his Serfdom Patent.[29]

In reality, what insured the abandonment of the "enlightened" Gypsy policies in Slovakia, the Czech lands, and other parts of the Austrian Empire was the course of European events triggered by the French Revolution in 1789. Over the next quarter of a century, Habsburg energies were caught up in the devastating wars brought about by these events. Information on Gypsies in the Czech lands and Slovakia during the next fifty years is almost nonexistent. Regardless, the momentous developments that swept Europe and the Habsburg Empire during this period had a profound impact on the Rom. The period from the end of the European wars with France in 1815 until the Revolutions of 1848 was an era of "reactionary police absolutism" in the Czech lands accompanied by the revitalization of Czech national identity. The Slovaks began to develop a sense of national consciousness, though its maturation suffered from Hungarian insistence "that a single state in Hungary presupposed a single political nation, the language of which could be no other than Magyar."[30]

The Revolutions of 1848 in the Austrian Empire saw the Czech lands explode briefly, while Hungary fought an unsuccessful War of Independence against Austria between 1848 and 1849. Habsburg "neo-absolutism" was introduced into the Czech lands and Hungarian Slovakia once the revolutionary threat ended, despite the fact that there had been some Slovak support for Austria against the Hungarian rebels. One of the positive developments that came out of this era in Slovakia and other parts of Hungary was the full emancipation of the serfs, which had an impact on the Gypsies.[31] Several years after the 1848–1849 revolutions, Vienna decreed that "all national cultures were to be allowed equal and complete freedom of non-political development." Consequently, some attempts were made to educate Slovakia's Gypsies, who were almost totally illiterate. In 1856, a school was opened for Gypsy children in Nových Zámkoch by the local priest, Ferdinand Farkás, which initially enrolled 43 girls. Bishop Johann Ham soon opened a second Rom school at Satmari.[32]

Unfortunately, what small gains were made during this period were severely weakened in the years after the *Ausgleich* (Compromise) of 1867, which saw the creation of a coequal Austro-Hungarian Empire. Magyarization became the dominant theme in Hungary, and the new state refused to "recognize the existence of separate nationalities and did not grant them collective national rights or political institutions." The Hungarians were particularly hard on the

Slovaks, and the use of the Slovak language in education disappeared. Estimates are that between 1869 and 1911, the number of Slovak primary schools declined from 1,921 to 440. The special Gypsy schools were caught up in the intensity of Magyarization, and conditions for both the Rom and the Slovak peasant became, according to Anna I. Duirchova, "appalling," because of "poverty everywhere and further suppression of education and discrimination in employment."[33]

Statistical data on the Slovakian Rom is hard to come by during this period, though there is some available from Hungarian censuses in the second half of the nineteenth century. A general Hungarian census in 1880 included statistics for the Gypsy population in many counties in the Slovakian portions of Hungary, broken down according to gender. Though not totally complete, the 1880 census provides some clue about the general areas of Rom concentration in Slovakia, particularly when used in conjunction with the more comprehensive, all-Gypsy census of 1893. The areas with the largest Rom populations in 1880 were Nítra, Spiš, and Zemplin, which also had large Gypsy settlements 13 years later. Almost all regions included in both the 1880 and 1893 censuses enjoyed substantial increases in their Gypsy population during this period, despite an 1887 policy "of official registration and harassment" of Slovak Roma. Nítra, for example, saw its Gypsy population grow from 1,271 to 4,304 between 1880 and 1893, while Bratislava's Rom community grew from 722 to 4,173 during the same period. Sariš enjoyed similar growth (1,121 to 3,261), as did Zemplin (1,428 to 3,081), and Spiš (1,372 to 2,792) between 1880 and 1893. Gemer had the largest Gypsy community, 5,552, in Slovakia in 1893.[34]

The 1893 census provided the first solid glimpse of Slovakian Rom in the nineteenth century. Statistics were broken down along regional and gender lines and provided specific data for nomadic, seminomadic, and sedentary Rom. It also had detailed information on Gypsy occupations, employment, marital status, and literacy rates. According to the 1893 data, there were 36,231 Slovakian Rom and 7,734 other Gypsies in this part of Hungary. Almost all the Slovak Gypsies (33,655) were settled, while 1,973 were partially sedentary, and 609 were nomadic. Over half of those employed, 4,598, worked in traditional Gypsy trades as blacksmiths, kettlemakers, and locksmiths, while 4,062 were musicians. There were 2,896 Rom employed as bricklayers; rope-, cord-, and brushmakers; and common laborers. There were also 600 Rom who, according to the census, were employed in traditional "female" occupations as weavers and laundresses. The census indicated that there were 3,154 Gypsies over the age of 15 who were without work. There was also a separate, detailed category for the 3,904 Gypsies who were involved in unsavory "occupations" as beggars, thieves, petty criminals, hobos, and bear handlers, who worked as wandering entertainers. The section on literacy showed that over 92 percent of Slovakia's Rom could not read or write. A little more than 90 percent of the Gypsies in this area were Roman Catholic, while the rest were Greek Catholics or members of the two branches of the Evangelical Church.[35]

The settled nature of the Slovakian Rom at the end of the nineteenth century did not translate into any significant move for them up the socioeconomic ladders of the region, particularly in light of the low "living standards of all of the inhabitants of the territory of present day Slovakia."[36] The only group of Slovak Gypsies to rise above the low Rom status were the professional musicians, who had "won favour at noblemen's courts and in recognition of their skill received the first permission (during the second half of the nineteenth century and at the start of the twentieth century) to settle permanently in their own houses, which usually became the basis for a Gypsy settlement." Rom craftsmen, particularly tinkers, cauldron-, chain-, and trough-makers enjoyed a better material and social position. The bulk of Slovakia's Gypsies, though, "lived not only in economic backwardness without regular income, but in illiteracy and with a completely unenlightened outlook, supported only by old traditions, customs, and superstitions." Many lived in isolated Gypsy settlements in *zemljanky* (strange burrow-like dwellings) and one roomed huts.[37] Information on Czech Gypsies remains scant during this period, though a *Zigeuner-Buch* (Gypsy book or register) compiled in 1905 in Munich showed that 20 percent of the Rom who entered Bavaria and other parts of Germany in the early part of the twentieth century came from the Czech lands and Austria, while an insignificant number came from Hungary and other parts of the Austro-Hungarian Empire.[38]

The outbreak of World War I in the summer of 1914 found the Czech lands and Slovakia unenthusiastically caught up in the military efforts of the Central Powers of Germany, Austria-Hungary, Bulgaria, and Turkey. To the Slavs of the Austro-Hungarian Empire, war with Russia and Serbia was as "repugnant as an outrage upon Slav solidarity." Large-scale Czech and Slovak defections and mass surrenders forced imperial authorities "to reorganize the regiments of the Joint Army [of Austria-Hungary] on a mixed racial basis, setting one race against another. . . ." Austrian officials arrested "thousands of Czech civilians . . . as 'political suspects,'" and almost 5,000 Czechs were sentenced to death by military tribunals. Overall, though, "most of the soldiers, no matter what their nationality, simply did their duty as citizens of the state." While the bulk of these policies were hard on the Czechs, the Slovaks suffered because of their ties with Hungary, which carried an inordinately heavy burden in the Austro-Hungarian war effort.[39] Gypsy troops in the Austrian and Hungarian armies, which became increasingly enmeshed with German forces, suffered heavy losses. The growing chaos and dislocation of the war also prompted the Hungarian government in 1916 to develop a policy to deal with homeless Gypsy children.[40]

The Central Powers enjoyed tremendous success in 1915–1916, though by 1917, Austria-Hungary's new emperor, Charles I, sought peace for his empire. The Czechs and the Slovaks demanded the union of their territories into a single democratic political unit within the Austro-Hungarian Empire.[41] Spurred by a Czech-led unity movement abroad, the concept of a completely independent Czechoslovakian nation gained steam as Central Power fortunes waned throughout 1917 and 1918. As Austria struggled to separate itself from Germany at the close of the war in the fall of 1918, an internationally blessed Czechoslovak independence was declared in Prague on October 28, 1918, followed two days later by a separate Slovak statement that "endorsed the principle of Czechoslovak unity."[42]

Over the next year and a half, the Czechs and the Slovaks struggled with a variety of complex political, economic, and social issues as they worked to create their new country. Each side brought with it the traditions of its Austrian or Hungarian past. Most striking in Slovakia was the "widespread poverty, lower educational achievements among the Slovak masses, and the heritage of the Magyar feudal-aristocratic traditions," as a result of which the "Slovak population suffered from sociological retardation and underdevelopment prior to 1918." Postwar Slovakia was industrially and agriculturally behind the Czech lands and was regarded as "an economically underdeveloped country." Efforts to rectify these inequities were undertaken throughout the 21-year history of the independent Czechoslovak state, though some Slovaks felt that Slovakia and Ruthenia, where the bulk of Czechoslovakia's Gypsies lived, "were left undeveloped and in general 'were regarded more or less like colonies' during the First Czechoslovak Republic (1918–39)."[43]

Gypsies made considerable gains as a result of the Czechoslovak Constitution of February 29, 1920, which, through linkage to the postwar Treaty of St. Germain, gave "to all inhabitants of Czechoslovakia of German, Hungarian, or other nationality, who were residents in the confines of the Republic on its inception, Czechoslovak nationality *ipso facto,* although the right of option is carefully safeguarded for specific purposes." The last segment of the six-part Czechoslovakian constitution was a Bill of Rights for National Minorities, which guaranteed all "nationals of the Czechoslovak Republic . . . absolute equality in the eye of the law, [to] enjoy the same civil and political rights without distinction of race, language, or religion." All national minorities, including the Gypsies, were also guaranteed full economic and employment rights, as well as the "free use of any language" within the confines "laid down by general legislation." The constitution also included educational guarantees for instruction in a language other than Czechoslovak in areas where a minority made up over 20 percent of the population. Finally, the constitution decreed that any "acts discriminatory toward any nationality, or tending to denationalize persons by force, [were] explicitly forbidden and regarded as criminal acts."[44]

The number of Gypsies affected by this new status was small, at least according to the 1921 Czechoslovak census, which showed 61 Rom in the Czech portions of the new republic and 7,967 in Slovakia. Most specialists agreed, however, that this figure, which was only based on those who spoke the "mother tongue," woefully underrepresented the number of Gypsies in Czechoslovakia in 1921. Figures for 1924 showed that the Košice region had the largest Rom concentration in Slovakia, 18,257, followed by the Bratislava area with 11,066. A Slovak Rom census two years later indicated that there were 60,315 sedentary Rom in this part of Czechoslovakia and 1,877 nomadic Gypsies. The 1930 national census showed 31,415 Rom throughout the country, with 31,188 in Slovakia. Of this number, "26,956 acknowledged Gypsy 'nationality,' of whom 13,211 were in the territory of today's E. Slovakian region." Gypsiologist Dr. Eva Davidova, considered these latter figures to be "extremely unreliable." She concluded:

> When we examine for example the results of the census on the 1st [of] December 1930, which give the precise numbers of Gypsy huts *(zemljanky)* and dwellings with the numbers of their occupants, and similarly also the lists of moveable dwellings, the real state of affairs can be reconstructed. According to these figures in what is now E. Slovakia lived 16,773 Gypsies in 2,754 Gypsy dwellings, and there were 182 nomads in 34 moveable dwellings. Apart from these, 4,921 citizens acknowledged "Gypsy nationality," who did not live in "Gypsy dwellings"; and because of this it is necessary to correct the total number of Gypsies to 21,876, living in 488 communities in E. Slovakia.[45]

Even with the wide variance in Rom statistics, it is clear that the Gypsies made up an insignificant part of Czechoslovakia's post–World War I population. The country had 13,374,364 inhabitants in 1921 and 14,479,565 a decade later. There were 8,760,937 Czechoslovaks (65.5 percent of the population) in the country in 1921, and 9,688,770 (66.91 percent) in 1931. The Germans were the largest minority with 3,123,568 (23.36 percent of the population) in 1921, and 3,231,688 (22.32 percent) in 1931. Magyars made up the next largest minority, with 745,431 (5.57 percent) in 1921 and 691,223 (4.77 percent) in 1931, followed by Ukrainians and Russians with 461,849 (3.45 percent) in 1921 and 549,169 (3.79 percent) in 1931. There were also 180,855 Jews (1.35 percent) listed in the 1921 census and 186,642 (1.29 percent) a decade later, as well as 75,853 Poles (0.57 percent) in 1921 and 81,738 (0.56 percent) in 1931.[46]

Consequently, despite their minority status, the Rom in interwar Czechoslovakia were not in sufficiently strong numbers to prompt any significant type of reform program to upgrade their low status. Furthermore, the bulk of the Gypsies was in Slovakia, where any solution to the "Gypsy problem" was often linked to efforts to improve the quality of life of the Slovak peasant, whose economic plight was often not much better than that of the Gypsies. This meant that Slovak Rom were "still left without almost any means of livelihood; the society of those days put up with them as a necessary evil and resisted any real mixing with them." Consequently, "the majority of them were forced to continue living parasitically and make a living only with occasional work." In 1924, a local official in Slovakia observed that "The penalty of imprisonment has no effect on them, because imprisonment only improves their living conditions. It often happens that a Gypsy without resources commits a crime only to escape the pangs of hunger." The same year, 19 Moldavian Rom were tried for cannibalism in Košice. The trial, which lasted for five years, centered around claims that a Gypsy bandit group led by Sandor Filek, murdered and cannibalized a number of victims in the region. Though the charges appeared to be trumped up, they served as a catalyst for Law No. 117 of July 19, 1927, which tried to place controls on "itinerant pedlars [*sic*] and craftsmen," the nomadic Olašsti Rom, and "nomads living in Gypsy style." It "was based on the old 1887 regulations and required all officially permited [*sic*] nomads to be registered and carry a nomad's pass, which could be withdrawn at any time." All Rom 14 years of age and over had to have a Gypsy identity card, which included his fingerprints. Children under 14 were registered in the identification of the person with whom they lived, while each family of wandering Gypsies also had to have a special license for wandering that listed members of the family and their animals. Those that did not register were subject to arrest. Over the next 13 years, officials issued 39,696 Gypsy identity cards in Czechoslovakia. Law No. 117 also required Rom to get permission from the local mayor to stay in a community, which usually only lasted for a week. The mayor was required to record his decision in a special registration book. The 1927 legislation also prohibited Gypsies "from entering whole regions, and individual communities, particularly the spa and holiday resorts."[47]

The 1924–1929 trial in Košice inflamed public opinion against the Rom, and on October 1, 1928, a pogrom took place in Pobedim, Slovakia, where peasants killed 6 Gypsies, 2 of them children, and injured 18, for pilfering crops. The attackers received only mild punishments, and the influential newspaper *Slovak* explained that the "Pobedim case can be characterized as a citizen's revolt against Gypsy life. In this there are the roots of democracy." The following year, another group of Rom were accused of "murder and cannibalism." The latter charge was dropped, "but not before the press had inflamed public opinion with sensational and inaccurate coverage."[48] Despite this atmosphere, efforts were made in Czechoslovakia during this period to help the Gypsies. In 1925, Rom schools were opened in several communities in Ruthenia and eastern Slovakia. Four years later, a group of physicians in Košice created the League for the Cultural Advancement of Gypsies, which was renamed the Society for Studying the Solution of the Gypsy Question in 1930. The group was initially concerned with Roma health problems, but soon expanded its interests and support to include education and cultural activities. The Society opened Gypsy schools in Užhorod, Košice, Hummené, and Levoča and also helped to form Rom "theatrical and musical groups" that performed throughout Slovakia. The Society inspired the creation of the SK ROMA soccer club, which gained some fame in other parts of Europe. The Society's physicians published some of their medical studies on Slovakian Rom in regional medical journals, and also "in special pamphlets, which were issued for a short time."[49]

What few improvements occurred in the lives of Czechoslovakia's Gypsies in the 1920s became mired in the economic and social difficulties of the Depression in the following decade. Slovakia was hit particularly hard, and it is estimated that during the peak of this economic disaster in 1932–1933, "about one third of Slovakia's population had no regular income."[50] Yet there are indications that despite these problems, there were some areas of positive improvement for the Rom, particularly in education. An article appeared in the liberal Czech newspaper *Lidové noviny* (People's Newspaper) on January 27, 1933, that described the history of the Gypsy school at Užhorod in eastern Slovakia. The unnamed author of the article claimed that the school, which was opened in 1926, was the center of "a Gypsy revival" and "the only educational institution for Gypsies in the world." It was not only "of educational importance for Gypsy youth of school age, but it is [sic] also became a culture centre for the Gypsies settled in Užhorod generally." The school's founder, Pavel Feodor, approached the local city council for funding in 1923 but was rejected because of opposition from "Jewish and Hungarian members" of the council. A regional school inspector, Mr. Šimek, allied with another government official, Mr. Hrbek, in 1925, and the two were able to convince officials in Užhorod to permit the construction of a Rom school after the Gypsies "promised they would carry out the work and furnish the materials" to build it. The school, which opened in November 1926, was described as "a pleasant, clean-looking building, with a large, well-lighted classroom for 55 pupils, a changing room, and a house for the teacher. An open playground surrounded with trees serves as a gymnasium."[51]

The Gypsies' teacher, Mr. Hegedüš, oversaw a five-part curriculum, with instruction in Slovak. Attendance was quite high, except for the spring, "when parents work in town or in the countryside near by, and the older children must stay at home to look after the little ones, of whom there is always a surplus." The school was a source of great pride for the Rom community in Užhorod:

> Even the Gypsy camp has greatly changed since the school has been in existence. Horrid insanitary rubbish-tips have disappeared, the row of cottages is well decorated, with chimneyed roofs and large windows, and the fronts of the houses are kept clean. In an open space which was once an evil-smelling marsh, there is now a football-ground where both young and old play from morning to night. The teachers have an able helper in the mayor, whom the Gypsies call biro. He enjoys the confidence of his small community. The members of the Gypsy colony are, even in these days, in regular employment as workmen, craftsmen (there is a model tailoring establishment), or as musicians. Mr. Hegedüs trained some of them last year for the Gypsy Academy, when they performed three one-act plays in the Uzhorod theatre. These were actual scenes from Gypsy life with the school as its centre. This was a great achievement when it is remembered that the actors were largely illiterate . . .
>
> As proof of the interest aroused by the Gypsy School, there are some hundreds of teachers, reporters and others visiting the place from all parts of the world, including Australia. Their visits are recorded by signature or card in the school chronicle, of which the kindhearted Mr. Hegedüs, whose motto is "The Gypsy is also human," is justly proud. The Gypsy school was a happy experiment, but the best thing about it is that the principle of equality has triumphed in it.[52]

Other Rom schools also flourished during this period. In 1937, the Gypsy school in Košice had an enrollment of 117 Gypsy children.[53]

Unfortunately, all of these achievements would begin to disappear with the dismemberment of Czechoslovakia in 1938 and its conquest by Hitler's Germany the following year. The story of the international crisis that swirled around Czechoslovakia during the Sudeten crisis in the summer and fall of 1938 has been well documented. Less well known, at least from the perspective of the Gypsies, were the Czechoslovakian territorial losses as a result of the Vienna Award of November 2, 1938. An Italian-German-brokered settlement of Hungarian territorial claims against Czechoslovakia, the Vienna Award gave Hungary 4,570 square miles of territory with 972,092 inhabitants (census of 1930) of whom 53.9 percent were Magyars. Particularly important for the Slovakian Rom were the towns of Košice and Užhorod, both of which now became parts of Hungary.[54]

The loss of a quarter of its population and almost a third of its territory as a result of these international decisions set the stage for a more tragic event in the spring of 1939—the complete German occupation of the remaining portions of Czechoslovakia. On the eve of the Nazi conquest, a German-orchestrated "independent" state of Slovakia was proclaimed, and on March 15, 1939, the remaining portions of Czechoslovakia were occupied by the Third Reich. On March 16, Hitler declared that the Czech areas would come under Nazi control as the Protectorate of Bohemia and Moravia. Several days later, Hungary annexed Ruthenia in eastern Slovakia.[55] A 1981 study by Ctibor Nečas on the Rom of Czechoslovakia during the Pořajmos (Gypsy Holocaust) indicates that there were 3,000 to 4,000 Rom in the Sudetenland in 1938, 6,000 in Bohemia, and 8,000 in Moravia. Another 8,000 came under Hungarian control. Several thousand Czech Rom fled to the more tolerant atmosphere of rump Slovakia over the next two years, and in 1940, Protectorate records showed a Gypsy population of 6,540. Though official accounts showed only 37,102 Gypsies in rump Slovakia in 1940, estimates are that the real figure was closer to 60,000 and would swell to 100,000 by the end of the war.[56]

The status of the Gypsies in the Protectorate of Bohemia and Moravia mirrored that of the Jews: Though both groups were permitted to live in freedom until the fall of 1941, they became outcasts in the Protectorate through the implementation of German legislation. Within weeks after the German creation of the Protectorate, the Reich Protector, the former German chancellor Constantin von Neurath, issued decrees in the name of the Protectorate's new Czech puppet government that ordered those over 18 years of age without steady employment be sent to "correctional labor camps." Later that year, police officials throughout the Protectorate were asked their opinion on a special law to control the Gypsies, which was issued on January 31, 1940. It ordered the Rom "to settle down under penalty of 'preventive' imprisonment." Those that did not were arrested, and between September 1, 1940, and December 1, 1941, authorities shipped 290 Rom to a new labor camp at Léty and 442 to a new camp at Hodonín.[57]

On December 4, 1941, authorities issued a "protective custody" regulation designed "to protect the community from all harmful persons." It was directed at anyone who, without being a professional or habitual criminal, endangers the public through his asocial behavior, beggars, vagabonds, Gypsies and persons travelling as Gypsies, prostitutes, persons with infectious diseases who do not follow the regulations of the Health Police . . . and work-shy persons.

Those placed under "protective custody" would be sent to the camps at Léty or Holodín or to prisons in Ruzyně Pardubice, Brno or Olšovec. If these were too crowded, the prisoners would be shipped to similar facilities in Germany or Auschwitz. The law had special clauses for the Protectorate's Rom:

1. Gypsies were forbidden to leave their place of residence without previous permission from Police headquarters.
2. The distribution of licenses to travel is to be transferred to the Criminal Police Headquarters.
3. The previous agreement of the Criminal Police Headquarters is necessary before permits or licenses are issued for Gypsies to carry on nomadic trades.

These regulations came on the heels of a new policy of Jewish ghettoization in the Thereisenstadt, issued by the new Reich Protector, Reinhard Heydrich, the primary architect of the most destructive phase of the Holocaust, and Adolph Eichmann, who was to oversee the transfers.[58]

In July 1942, Protectorate officials began to construct new buildings at Hodonín, and on August 1, 1942, a new decree transformed Hodonín and Léty into "concentration camps for Gypsy families." According to the new regulations, the concentration camps were

to exclude from society Gypsies, Gypsy half-breeds *(Zigeunermisch-linge)* and persons leading a wandering way of life in Gypsy fashion, and to educate them for work, order, and discipline. All men who were not engaged in regular and useful work were to be placed in these concentration camps together with their wives and children.

Between August 1942 and April 1943, 7,980 Gypsies were sent to the camp at Léty and 7,329 to Hodonín. It was during this period that German authorities began to ship Protectorate and other Gypsies to Auschwitz. Though the mass transfer of Rom to the Reich's primary death camp did not come until Heinrich Himmler's decree of December 16, 1942, scattered shipments of Gypsies had begun to arrive at Auschwitz earlier from throughout Nazi-occupied Europe. On December 3, 1942, 94 Gypsies were sent from Léty to Auschwitz, followed four days later by 75 Rom from Hodonín.[59]

Thirteen days later, Himmler issued Decree No. 1–2652/42, which set the stage for the most destructive stage of the Pořajmos by ordering "that persons of mixed Gypsy blood be sent to Auschwitz."[60] By early spring 1943, Rudolf Höss, the Auschwitz commandant, had opened a special Gypsy Family Camp at Auschwitz II—Birkenau that consisted of "40 wooden barrack blocks where they were kept in family groups in an attempt to avoid trouble until the final moment came." The first transports from the Protectorate to Auschwitz II began on March 7, 1943, and continued through late January 1944. Authorities closed the Gypsy camp at Holodín on December 1, 1943, and the last transport of Protectorate Rom, made up of 31 sick "asocials," left for Auschwitz II on January 28, 1944. By the time Höss liquidated the Gypsy Family Camp on August 2, 1944, about 21,000 out of 23,000 Gypsy inmates had perished in Birkenau's gas chambers. Of the 23,000 inmates, 4,531 were from the Protectorate.[61] According to Höss, who regarded the Rom as his "favorite prisoners,"

> By August 1944 there were only about four thousand gypsies left, and these had to go into the gas chambers. Until that time they did not know what fate was in store for them. Only as they were marched barrack after barrack to Crematory I did they figure out what was going on. It was not easy to get them into the gas chamber.

Höss, who also felt the Rom "were as trusting as children," actually gassed 2,897 Gypsies on August 2.[62]

Gypsies had also been sent to Auschwitz II from other camps in the Protectorate, though the majority of the Czech Gypsies who died in the Pořajmos met their fate at Auschwitz II. Protectorate Rom were also sent to the Buchenwald death camp in central Germany and the Ravensbruck women's camp north of Berlin. The majority of the 6,000 to 8,000 Czech Gypsies who died in the Holocaust, however, met their fate in Auschwitz II.[63] One Czech Gypsy survivor of Auschwitz, Barbara Richter, vividly described her ordeal during the Pořajmos.

> At the beginning of the war my family were in Bohemia. My father had sold his caravan and taken a house. The Czech police came and took us to Lettig [Léty]. There were eighteen to twenty families there, all Gypsies. We were kept in barracks and not allowed to go out. This was in March or April 1941. In May I escaped. When I arrived in Prague a ticket-inspector gave me clothes and a hat to hide the fact that my hair had been shaved off.

I was kept six weeks at the police station and then sent to Auschwitz (arriving there March 11th, 1943). Two Gypsies tried to escape but were caught, beaten and hanged. Later my family was released from Lettig because the Richters were a well-established family in Bohemia. My mother came to Auschwitz voluntarily. Once I was given twenty-five blows with a whip because I had given some bread to a new arrival. One day I saw Elisabeth Koch kill four Gypsy children because they had eaten the remains of some food. Another time we stood for two hours in front of the crematorium but at the last moment were sent back to the barracks. I was given lashes a second time for taking bread from a dead prisoner. Three times they took blood from me. Dr. Mengele injected me with malaria. I was then in the sick bay with my uncle. Some Gypsies carried me to another block just before all the patients in the sick bay, including my uncle, were killed.[64]

The Gypsies of Slovakia were much more fortunate than their Czech counterparts. Part of the reason for Slovakia's comparatively mild treatment of its Gypsies centered around Germany's desire for Slovakia to be "a propaganda showpiece in Southeastern Europe." Consequently, the army, Church, economy, parliament, and party enjoyed semi-autonomy. Germany's desire to Nazify this valuable economic ally was opposed by Father Jozef Tiso, the Slovak head of state, who was "dead set against the nazification and germanization of Slovak life." In time, Reich officials came to realize that the only way they could achieve their goals was through "indoctrination and political pressure with a program of continuous propaganda and education." Anything else would hamper Slovakia's remarkable contribution to the German war effort. Almost all of Slovakia's Gypsies survived the war because of this decision. This did not mean, however, that the Slovak government left its Rom population at ease, even though the Slovak constitution of July 21, 1939, granted some protection to the country's minorities. Within months after the creation of Slovakia in the spring of 1939, the Tiso government ordered nomadic Gypsies "to return to their respective legal domicile" and made it illegal for them to do any horse trading. On September 25, 1939, Jews were deprived of their Slovak citizenship, while Gypsies who were born in Slovakia and wanted Slovak citizenship had to prove that only if they

> lived an orderly way of life; had a steady place of residence and employment; and were honorable citizens as reflected in their education, their moral and political trustworthiness, and their activity in their community, could they be included in the Slovak national community. If they did not fulfill the aforementioned conditions, or

if they fulfilled them only partially—if they worked only occasion-
ally, if they spoke the Gypsy language among themselves, if their
moral and political trustworthiness was doubtful, etc.—they could
not be considered members of the Slovak national community. In
other words, wandering Gypsies did not qualify for citizenship.[65]

Four months later, Ferdinand D'určanský, Slovakia's minister of the interior, ordered that Gypsies and Jews were to serve in special labor units as alter-
natives to military service for a period was later set "at two terms of two
months twice annually." D'určanský defined a Gypsy in Law No. 130/1940
of June 18, 1940, as someone who had two Rom parents and lived as a nomad,
or a sedentary Gypsy who avoided work. Other regulations issued during
this period made it illegal for Gypsies "to enter parks, cafés and restaurants
or to use public transport." As Germany intensified pressure on the Slovaks
to increase its contribution to the war effort, the Tiso government created seasonal labor camps in 1941 where Gypsies often made up over half of the population. Conditions "in the labor units were bad. Inmates suffered increasingly
from inadequate clothing and shoes, cold, infestation with lice and bedbugs,
hunger, and disease, especially trachoma and typhus." Many practiced self-
mutilation in order to be released. In 1943, one member of the Slovak Diet,
Hut'ka, criticized the conditions of the camps at Bystré and Topl'ou. Hut'ka
felt that the original mission of the labor camps was "to re-educate the asocial elements, not . . . to torture people and bring them into an even worse
moral degradation."[66]
    On April 20, 1941, nomadic Rom were ordered to return to their homes or
local villages within eight days. Once there, they were put "under police surveillance and would be allowed to leave only with special permission. They
were to sell their wagons and horses within two weeks." Rom houses located
near public roads had to be torn down and reconstructed at a new site assigned
to them. A Gypsy representative was to work with the local mayor to ensure
that local ordinances were followed. Rom were also prohibited from keeping
dogs. These regulations evidently did not curb all Gypsy nomadism, and officials explained when they opened a new labor camp in Krupina in the summer of 1941 that "wandering Gypsies were to be placed there by force" to
teach them "to get accustomed to liv[ing] in one place and to [doing] intensive, productive self-supporting work." These efforts still did not stop Rom
nomadism, however, and on June 21, 1943, the government again ordered "the
removal of Gypsy dwellings away from busy roads."[67]
    Each Slovak community dealt with its Rom in a different manner. The 500
Gypsies in the village of Smižany were "well-integrated and [there] no one

was sent to perform forced labour." When Hlinka Guards, the Slovakian paramilitary group that modeled itself on the Italian Black Shirts and the German SA, arrived to take Gypsies from the village of Letanovce, the mayor only agreed to send two Gypsies, "both men with a bad reputation for drinking and anti-social behavior." Both Rom returned to Letanovce at the end of the war.[68] This atmosphere changed drastically, however, during the summer of 1944. In June, a Slovak law accused the Rom of spreading typhoid through the country, and forbade Gypsies to ride trains unless they had a special travel permit backed by a physician's certificate that showed them free of typhoid. The "travel permit was valid only for the outward journey and the whole procedure had to be gone through again for the return." The following month, the Interior Ministry informed its regional offices that there were still Gypsies in some of the country's towns and villages. It ordered local officials to move all Rom "away from roads" and said that if any Gypsies refused to comply, they would be executed. The decree added that "arrangements for concentration working camps for Gypsies are being prepared."[69]

The climate for the Gypsies got considerably worse with the German occupation of Slovakia on September 29, 1944. As a result of the Slovak National Insurrection of August 29–October 27, 1944, the Germans clamped down harshly on the Slovaks, including the Gypsies, for actively supporting the uprising. One Rom leader, Tomáš Farkás, led a mixed group of Gypsies and Slovaks that momentarily held up German forces near Tisovec as they moved toward Banska Bystrica, the military center of the rebellion. When Banska Bystrica eventually fell to the Germans, authorities arrested Farkás's son and sent him to a concentration camp. Tisovec, in fact, had become a center for Gypsy partisan activities earlier in the war. When the main partisan unit retreated in the face of the German advance in the fall of 1944, the Rom stayed behind to protect their families, armed with "heavy weapons and machines-guns hidden near the Gypsy camp." After the rebellion's collapse, a German intelligence officer tricked the Rom into revealing details about their weapons cache. Hlinka Guards executed the Rom partisans "in front of their families and then killed the women and children. The bodies were thrown in a lime quarry."[70]

Similar massacres took place in other parts of Slovakia as retribution for the Gypsies' role in the Slovak National Insurrection. On November 14, 1944, 65 Rom were burned to death in two huts in Čierny Balog "after being forced to carry the cans of petrol." Other Gypsies were forced to dig a grave for the dead. Hlinka Guards murdered an entire community of 111 Gypsies in Ilija eight days later, and on November 23, they butchered as many Rom as they could find in Slatina. Only three Gypsies escaped the massacre. A similar tragedy took place at Neresnice, where only two families survived.[71]

Atrocities also took place at the labor camp at Dubnica nad Vahom. On September 29, 1944, German authorities in Trenčin, just to the south of Dubnica nad Vahom, ordered that all male Rom from this region be sent to the labor camp at Dubnica. Once the camp became full two weeks later, the Gypsy transfers stopped. On November 2, 1944, Dubnica nad Vahom was transformed into a detention camp to hold all Gypsies regardless of their sex and age. To make room for the Rom, authorities released all of the camp's non-Gypsy inmates. After a typhus epidemic ravaged the camp in mid-December, authorities began to ship Gypsies from Ustie nad Oravou to Dubnica nad Vahom after the former camp was closed later that month. Before the arrival of the new prisoners, there were 729 Rom at Dubnica nad Vahom, 250 of them children. The only recorded atrocity at the camp took place on January 17, 1945, when 16 sick Gypsy prisoners were taken from the camp under the pretense of being taken to the hospital at Trenčin. Instead, they were driven in military trucks to a wooded area, forced into a pit, and executed. The camp was closed on the eve of its capture by Soviet forces on April 8, 1945. Despite the tragedies of the camps, the Gypsy survival rate was quite high in Slovakia, and estimates are that only a few hundred of Slovakia's 100,000 Rom died in the Porajmos.[72]

The liberation of Czechoslovakia in the spring of 1945 found the country traumatized by the human and economic devastation of the war and, at least in the case of the Czech lands, deeply embittered toward the Germans. These feelings were exacerbated by a more subtle threat from the Soviet Union, which helped engineer the creation of a National Front government in early 1945 that gave Czech and Slovak communists eight important seats in the cabinet of a new government under President Edvard Beneš. As the National Front struggled to rebuild a country that suffered 250,000 dead and losses of $2,400 per person in the Czech lands, and $4,900 per person in Slovakia, a national expulsion and expropriation campaign began, aimed primarily at the Germans in the Czech portions of the country, but also at the Magyars of Slovakia. The official campaign forced 1,859,541 Germans and 68,407 Magyars to leave Czechoslovakia by the end of 1946. The land expropriated by the government during this period included 270,000 farms and 6.24 million acres, much of it in the Sudeten borderland.[73]

Over the next three years, 1.5 million people, including some Gypsies, would move into the former Sudetenland from other parts of Czechoslovakia. As the Germans left Czechoslovakia, many Slovak Gypsies were sent to camps in northern Bohemia and Moravia where they worked as unskilled laborers. These transfers were intended not only to help the country cope with a severe labor shortage but also as a way of "exacting social and labor conformity from Gypsies." Not all Slovak Gypsies remained in the Czech lands, however; some returned to Slovakia "where conditions began to improve dramatically as migrants invested their earnings in new, brick-built family houses." In addition, "an estimated 6,000 nomadic Olach [Olašsti] Roms . . . still traveled the republic with horses, carts and tents." While the goals of the transfer were applied gingerly under the first National Front government of 1945–1946, the strong communist showing in the May 26, 1946, elections, saw the new minister of the interior, Vaclav Nosek, and others, push "for the application of not only harsh but restrictive measures toward the Gypsies." Nosek and his supporters argued that the Roms' "claim to Czechoslovak citizenship was tenuous at best."[74]

Efforts by Evzan Erban, the minister of labor and social welfare, to continue to send Slovak Gypsies to camps in the Czech lands were stopped by the noncommunist minister of justice, Prokop Drtina, on May 19, 1947. Drtina was unable, however, to do anything about a census of the country's entire Rom population that was directed toward "all wandering Gypsies and other work-shy vagabonds." According to the census, there were 84,438 Rom in Slovakia, and 16,752 in the Czech lands. The successful communist coup of late February 1948, brought a change in Rom fortunes: the party in power had stated a year earlier "that its ultimate goal in ministering to the needs of the Gypsies in Czechoslovakia was their integration with the rest of the population, and the raising of their economic, social, and cultural levels to those of the Slavic society."[75]

The year after the communist takeover, the government of Klement Gottwald created "an inter-ministry commission . . . to examine the social and labor aspects of the 'so-called Gypsy Question.'" The new commission sponsored a detailed study of Czechoslovakia's Gypsies, which appeared in 1950 as *Zarazovani osob cikánského puvodu do trvalého pracovniho procesu* (Position of Individuals of Gypsy Origin in the Work Process). The study was partly integrated into another report two years later by the Ministry of Labor and Social Welfare, titled *Uprava pomeru osob cikánského puvodu* (Report About the Life of the Gypsies in Czechoslovakia). *Uprava pomeru* blamed earlier governments and societies for the Rom's low social and economic status and promised that the new People's Democratic State would "successfully solve the Gypsy Question" if the Rom "willingly and quickly [became] accustomed to conscientious work, they adopt[ed] trades, they [took] part in socialist competition, they [became] shock-workers [workers highly committed to the communist party], members and functionaries of the Czechoslovak Communist Party and the Revolutionary Trade-Union Movement." These reports, however, were not a call to action, and for the next eight years, the communist leaders of Czechoslovakia did little to help the Gypsies improve their quality of life.[76]

Decrees issued by national authorities on Gypsies to various government agencies in the 1950s had little impact on the Roma, while regional and local authorities concentrated on Gypsy health care and housing needs. All of these efforts were aimed at "re-shaping Gypsy behavior," which the 1952 edition of the *Dictionary of the Czech Language* helped to define: "*gypsy*—a member of a wandering nation, a symbol of mendacity, theft, wandering . . . jokers, liars, imposters, and cheaters." [77] Communist Party propaganda, however, underscored Rom "achievement in school attendance, literacy courses for adults, devotion to hard work, and assimilation in general." However, by the mid-1950s, this congratulatory tone started to change as the reality of the Gypsy's plight and demographic growth began to concern the country's leadership. In 1956, authorities spoke of a Gypsy crisis in Czechoslovakia that was linked to their continued nomadism. According to an article in *Zemedelske Noviny* (Agricultural Newspaper) in 1957, only "40 percent of the Gypsy population has settled down to work in industry and agriculture." Their lifestyle exacerbated public feelings toward them, which the Slovak journal *Smena* (Direction) "likened . . . to the discrimination against the Negro in the United States."[78]

These problems and attitudes, coupled with the size of the Rom community, which Radio Bratislava would later estimate to be 150,000 on September 1, 1958, prompted the Communist Party to approve a resolution on April 8, 1958, that demanded an "unconditional solution [to] the Gypsy Question." Similar to new policies throughout the Soviet bloc at that time, the resolution called for a "mass campaign addressed to both the Gypsies and white bigots, for lifting the Gypsies' 'extraterritorial immunities' and punishment of nomadism." Czechoslovakia's Gypsies were now divided into three categories—nomads, semi-nomads, and completely sedentary—in anticipation of Law No. 74, of October 17, 1958, Act on Permanent Settlement of Nomadic People. The law instructed local officials to work with any nomads, whom it defined as an individual who "in groups or individually, wanders from place to place, shuns honest work or obtains his livelihood by iniquitous means even though he may be registered in some community as its permanent resident." If this person continued this lifestyle despite the offer of help, he would "be punished by deprivation of liberty for from six months to three years." Two other parts of Law No. 74 gave the minister of the interior the right "to issue executive orders to this effect, including registration of the nomads." Though the new regulations never mentioned the Rom specifically, they were its only target, particularly the country's 6,000 nomadic Olach Gypsies. Official estimates indicated that there were from 11,280 to 40,000 nomadic Rom in the country.[79]

Gypsies also acquired the status of a socio-ethnic group to avoid a "charge of racism" against the government. Unfortunately, Czechoslovak authorities did not anticipate the complex economic and social problems that would accompany its efforts to force the complete integration of the nation's Gypsies. Many nomadic Rom found ways to avoid punishment for continued nomadism, while local efforts to force settlement through the assignment of precious housing to Gypsies created growing resentment against a group that some came to see as privileged. Many Czechoslovaks now viewed the Rom as "a special caste . . . which recognized their rights but no duties." The public complained that the Gypsies were measured by a "different yardstick," and took advantage of their unique status. More important, the policy did little to upgrade the low socio-economic status of the Rom and perhaps made it worse for the newly settled Gypsies, who, located principally in Slovakia, "continued to live in shanties with no plumbing or sanitation facilities or in the slums of towns."[80]

Consequently, in 1965, the Communist Party asked local officials "to obtain background data regarding the Gypsy population and to prepare what was called a 'universal, long-range assimilation plan.'" The result was Ordinance No. 502 of June 1965, which centered around "full-employment of able-bodied Gypsies as the precondition of a decent living standard; and liquidation of Gypsy hamlets and dispersal (*rozptyl*) of these people throughout Czechoslovakia." The Academy of Sciences was asked to do "a thorough scholarly analysis of the Gypsy life," while the state-controlled media were "to combat the all too apparent racial bias in the country." A new government body, the National Council for Questions of the Gypsy Population, which had no Rom members, was created as a watchdog for the program. It produced three position papers before it was phased out of existence in 1968. [81]

At the center of this new program was the destruction of substandard Gypsy housing and settlements, primarily in Slovakia, and the forced resettlement and employment of their Rom inhabitants. Officials estimated that "of the 153,000 Gypsies in Slovakia, 103,000, i.e. 67.3%, lived in such settlements 'under conditions which are not fit for human living.'" The government pinpointed 1,266 Rom settlements in Slovakia for destruction, which would have involved the transfer of 64,096 Gypsies. Once the Rom settlements were razed, their tenants would be moved to the Czech lands, where local governments, aided by national subsidies, would be responsible not only for the Gypsies' housing but for their employment. The resettlement program was voluntary. Once a Rom family had been convinced of the wisdom of such a move, the government gave it an indemnification in a frozen account, which, together with a 25–30 percent subsidy and low-cost government loan, would be used to purchase a new home in the Czech lands. Inadequate funding (only 75 million Crowns annually [$10 million] was allotted for all aspects of the program), coupled with growing resentment towards the new Rom presence in the Czech regions of the country, and the unwillingness of some Rom to remain in Bohemia and Moravia, undercut the success of the program. Between 1965 and 1968, the government was only able to eliminate one-third of the Rom settlements targeted for destruction.[82]

As authorities struggled with the mixed results of this new transfer and employment program, Czechoslovakia was turned inside out by the events of the Prague Spring in 1968. Spawned by the on-again, off-again spirit of deStalinization that swept throughout the Soviet bloc between 1956 and 1963 and the inability of the regime of Antonín Novotny to deal with Czechoslovakia's growing economic crisis and an upsurge in Slovak nationalism, a major struggle within the Communist Party over reform at the end of 1967 saw the leader of the Slovak Communist Party, Alexander Dubček, replace Novotny as Czechoslovakia's leader on January 5, 1968. Eight months later, Dubček, originally blessed by the Soviet leadership before his accession to power, would feel the brunt of its military strength. The reason for Moscow's change of heart was the Prague Spring, Dubček's effort "to combine socialism with democracy and economic security with civil liberties." The atmosphere that emerged in the midst of this bold domestic experiment boded well for Czechoslovakia's Rom.[83]

On the eve of the Prague Spring, Czechoslovakia had one of the largest Rom populations in the Soviet bloc. Official data from the end of 1967 showed a Gypsy population of 223,993, with 164,526 in Slovakia, and 59,467 in the Czech lands. In 1968, the Rom in Slovakia were allowed to form their first official organization, the Union of Gypsy-Romanies (Zvaz Cikanov-Romov; in Romani, Romano Jekhetániben), which was followed by a similar Czech organization in 1969. Later that year, the two joined together into one organization, although they maintained separate Slovak and Czech branches. The stimulus for the creation of the new Rom organization came from Slovak intellectuals such as Dr. Anton Facuna. The Union of Gypsy-Romanies received funds from the National Front and maintained offices in each region and county. Its goals were to elevate "the social and economic levels of the Gypsies in the country" and to improve "the majority population's awareness and understanding of Gypsy culture." It also sought nationality status for the Rom, which stimulated an engaging debate among Gypsy and non-Gypsy intellectuals about the entire "Gypsy Question." Central to the debate was Jaroslav Sus's 1963 study, *Cikánská otázka v ČSSR* (The Gypsy Question in the CSSR), which described the Rom "way of life as [an] undesirable combination of 'nomadism, tribalism . . . and blood feuds,' and the Romani language as . . . unworthy of preservation." Consequently, Sus felt that "unconditional assimilation [was] . . . the only solution for the question." In the new spirit of openness that swept Czechoslovakia, Elena Hübschmannová, long an advocate of Rom nationality status, led the attack on Sus's ideas. Hübschmannová shifted responsibility for some aspects of the "Gypsy Question" to the shoulders of the government, as did the August 1969 *Programme of the Founding Congress of the Czech Gypsy-Rom Association [Union]*, whose authors felt that "fears of the results of granting rights to the Gypsies as a nationality" lay at the heart of the question. As this debate raged, plans for a Rom journal emerged, and the Gypsy-Romanies organization's membership rolls swelled to 20,000 over the next three years. A brief Gypsy renaissance, anchored by "200 Romani musical groups . . . and thirty local football clubs," swept Czechoslovakia, and the media began to refer to the country's Rom as "citizens of Gypsy origin." Unfortunately, after the Soviet invasion of Czechoslovakia on August 21, 1968, the new government of Gustav Husak introduced an era of "normalization" that gradually chipped away at many of the gains achieved in the Prague Spring. A purge of the Communist Party in 1970 was followed by the "reimposition of censorship and other restrictive controls" a year later. In April 1973, the government kicked the Union of Gypsy-Romanies out of the National Front and outlawed other Gypsy organizations because they had "failed to fulfill their integrative function."[84]

What followed was a renewed effort to force Rom integration and assimilation, coupled with a new scheme of sterilization designed to reduce Gypsy births. Census figures for 1970 showed a Rom population of 219,554, a slight drop from 1968, when officials counted 226,467 Gypsies in Czechoslovakia. Other estimates, though, put the 1970 Rom figures at over 300,000. The 60,279 Rom in the Czech Republic in 1970 made up 0.61 percent of its population, while Slovakia's 159,275 Gypsies accounted for 3.51 percent of its population. Rom growth rates in Slovakia averaged 3.71 percent from 1970 to 1980, compared to 0.73 percent for Gypsies in the Czech republic. However, since they still only made up 1.53 percent of the country's total population, the government's policies toward the Gypsies arose as much from fear of the complex social and economic problems that accompanied such Rom increases rather than the actual numerical threat of Gypsy population growth. The gradual increase in the size of the Rom population during this period also seemed more threatening because of the newness of the demographic statistics, since Gypsies had not been listed in any national census data prior to 1965. Finally, the upsurge in Rom activism between 1968 and 1971 highlighted the Rom presence in Czechoslovakia on a scale never experienced before in the country.[85]

One of the darker sides of the Husak government's assimilation campaign was the effort to promote the sterilization of Gypsy women. The idea for this plan grew out of the February 29, 1972, Ministry of Health's "Decree on Sterilization." Though "designed to safeguard against arbitrary or ill-informed sterilization of all Czechoslovak citizens," the decree was used

> to encourage the sterilization of Romany women in order to reduce the "high unhealthy" Romany population and, as a result, a dispro-portionately high number of Romany women were sterilized, often in violation of the existing safeguards and of their rights to non-dis-crimination on the basis of ethnicity or sex.[86]

According to a Slovak document released in 1979 by Charter 77, a Czechoslovak dissident group, the Slovak government had already begun a program, centered around financial incentives, to get Gypsy women to be sterilized because of earlier, unsuccessful government efforts "to control the 'high unhealthy' Romany population through family planning and contraception." Local health workers offered some prospective sterilization candidates as much as 5,000 Crowns to undergo the procedure. As pressure intensified to get more Gypsy women to agree to sterilization, some health workers often made unfulfilled offers as high as 30,000 Crowns. Charter 77 protested this practice in 1979, claiming that it violated Article No. 259 of the state penal code, which dealt with genocide. On a broader scale, the group also decried government practices aimed at halting nomadism and encouraging integration and assimilation, since all of the policies denied "Gypsy ethnicity." According to Charter 77, the collective impact of the policies was to set into motion "a process of social disintegration which has no comparison in the history of the Gypsies. This fact is substantiated by an ever increasing number of Gypsies who are sentenced to loss of freedom."[87]

While it is difficult to gauge the impact of the 1979 Charter 77 report on the Gypsies, population data from the national census the following year did spur further government action toward the Gypsies. The national Rom population grew from 219,554 in 1970 to 288,440 in 1980, a 31.4 percent increase, while the general population grew by only 6 percent. The Gypsy population in the Czech Republic grew by 47 percent between 1970 and 1980, while Slovakia's rise was 25.5 percent. Even these figures, though, are misleading, since arbitrary counting methods showed a discrepancy between national census figures and those recorded in local "Gypsy Registers," which showed 306,246 Rom in Czechoslovakia in 1980. The absolute rise in Gypsy population was less troubling to the government than the national and Rom childbirth rate. The overall Czechoslovak childbirth rate was on the decline, and by 1982 it was "below the level of biological reproduction." The average number of live births for a Czechoslovak woman was 2.4 in the 1970s, while that of a Gypsy woman was 6.4.[88]

Part of the reason for the dramatic increases in the size of the Czech Rom population was continued government efforts to destroy substandard housing in Slovakia and the forced movement of Gypsies to the Czech Republic. Other Gypsies moved to the Czech regions of the country during this period because of better job opportunities and a higher standard of living. Between 1972 and 1980, officials destroyed 4,000 Rom dwellings in Slovakia and moved 4,850 Gypsies elsewhere. Though Rom housing standards improved appreciably during this period, there were still 5.6 persons in the average Rom apartment or house, while the national average was 3.1 persons. A little more than 70 percent of the Rom population lived in apartments by 1980, though 10 percent of the Rom population still "lived in primitive camps scheduled to be razed by 1990." The number in extremely unfit housing had dropped from 80.7 percent in 1970 to 49 percent a decade later.[89]

Another part of the assimilation campaign centered around attempts to force more Gypsy children into the public schools. In 1971, only 10 percent of the eligible Rom children in Czechoslovakia attended kindergarten, a figure that rose to 58.5 percent in 1980. During the same period, the number of Rom children that finished public school rose from 16.6 percent to 25.6 percent, while the number enrolled in colleges and universities increased from 39 to 191. Nationwide, literacy rates rose to 90 percent among Rom adults. On the other hand, Gypsy school dropout rates in Slovakia increased substantially as Rom pupils moved from grade to grade. In 1983–1984, 72.2 percent of the Slovak students who failed to go into the second grade were Gypsies, and almost a third of the Rom who went to second grade had "not acquired the minimal skills," a figure that jumped to 50 percent for Gypsy 4th-graders. Many Gypsies entered the school system with a knowledge of only 200 Czech or Slovak words and were often assigned to "Special Schools (*zvláštní školy*), a euphemistic label for institutions catering to the needs of the mentally retarded." Only a third of Gypsy children finished eighth grade in 1983–1984, and only 4 percent went on to university or college.[90]

Gypsy employment figures for this period were also a mixture of success and failure. Though 1981 data showed a 87.7 percent employment rate for male Gypsy workers that was close to the national average of 91.9 percent for all adult males, the 54.95 percent employment rate for Rom female workers was well below the national average of 87.7 percent for all women. In addition, over three-quarters of all Gypsies employed held low-paying, non-skilled jobs. The overall impact of the employment, educational, and housing data

found Czechoslovakia's Rom on a socioeconomic plateau that proved difficult to transcend. According to Imrich Farkas, the official responsible for
Gypsy matters in Slovakia, the government felt that it would be harder to
improve the quality of Gypsy life "because increasingly left for solution are
those socially and culturally backward families."[91] The government tried to put
the best light on its assimilation efforts by publicizing some Rom success stories. Bratislava *Pravda* reported that 435 Rom had been elected to predominantly low-level positions such as "Deputies of Peoples Committees," and that
one Gypsy, Emil Rigo, had briefly been a member of the Politburo in 1968.
Officials also used successful Gypsies to counter efforts to acquire nationality status for the Rom. In 1986, *Rudé Právo* (The Red Right; official Czech
Communist Party organ) responded to the World Romany Congress' appeal
for nationality status for Czechoslovakia's Rom partially with a statement by
Miroslav Zajda, "an assimilated Gypsy, worker, student, Party member, and
soccer referee," who told the newspaper that he was "happy."[92]

The lack of nationality status for Czechoslovakia's Rom, who were officially referred to as citizens "of Gypsy origin," robbed them of the special
rights and support afforded officially recognized minorities and put them in
a limbo, where they were forced to identify with other ethnic groups. Not all
Gypsies, though, suffered from lack of nationality status on the same scale, and
there were a number of instances, particularly in Slovakia, where local officials encouraged Rom ethnicity. Regardless, the plight of all Roma was compounded by the growing body of prejudice that accompanied their increasing
numbers and official attention. To many Czechoslovakians, Gypsies were
the *tmaví kluci* (dark boys), a term that automatically identified one as a Rom.
According to the Czech-American gypsiologist Otto Ulč, post-1968
Czechoslovakia became a society that was "less tolerant, more impatient,
and egotistic." Increasingly, he observed, the public saw Gypsies as "benefi-
ciaries of a host of privileges on their path to the less-than-cherished goal of
integration." Furthermore, Czechoslovaks became "thoroughly uninhibited
about making racial slurs and expressing racist prejudice of the old-fashioned
vintage." They saw the Rom as "'dirty,' 'lazy,' 'dishonest,' 'primitive,' 'parasitic,' and 'inferior.'"[93]

Government efforts to counter this prejudice met with mixed results, since
the press used stories that gave explicit details about instances of unfair treatment of Gypsies with others that detailed Rom crime. Bratislava *Pravda,* for
example, claimed in 1983 that the Gypsies, who made up 4 percent of
Slovakia's population, "accounted for 24 percent of the charges of parasitism,
50 percent of robberies, 60 percent of petty thefts, 75 percent of charges for
endangering the morals of youth, and 20 percent of all crimes committed." The

overall impact of these efforts was to create a very unwelcome, suspicious climate for Czechoslovakia's growing Rom population that worsened as the country and its leadership drifted toward the collapse of the system that had dominated the nation since 1948.[94]

The seeds for the Velvet Revolution of 1989 can be traced back to the post-1968 decision by the new Husak regime to "preserve the status quo" at all costs and the implementation of its uninnovative "*intensification*" campaign to shore up the country's stagnating economy. As the Gorbachev phenomenon increasingly infected Czechoslovakia and its neighbors, gradual, though dramatic, political and social changes swept the country. Husak, who headed the Communist Party and served as Czechoslovakia's president, resigned his Party position in December 1987. Over the next 18 months, there was growing "interaction between increasing societal militancy and growing regime nervousness" that culminated in the event that triggered the beginning of the Velvet Revolution on November 17, 1989—the brutal, government-instigated police attack on peaceful student demonstrators in the center of Prague. What followed was a remarkable series of events that ended on December 29, 1989, with the election of Václav Havel, the head of the new Civic Forum (Občanske Fórum), Czechoslovakia's "umbrella for various dissident groups," as the nation's president. At his side was the newly elected head of the Federal Assembly, Alexander Dubček, the Party head during the Prague Spring. Havel had made Dubček's election a condition of his agreement to become president of Czechoslovakia.[95]

What evolved in this highly charged atmosphere was a plethora of political parties and other organizations. Within three months of the Velvet Revolution, 58 new political parties and 334 associations were registered. A number of Gypsy parties emerged during this period, including the Party of the Democratic Romany Union and the Party of the Integration of the Romany People in Slovakia. The most important was the Romany Civic Initiative (Romská obcanská iniciativa), or ROI, which had close links to Civic Forum. It quickly attracted a membership of over 70,000 and held its first national meeting in the spring of 1990 in Prague. One of its first decisions was to vote to erect a monument in Bratislava to the Rom victims of the Holocaust. The ROI congress elected Emil Ščuka, a lawyer and playwright, to head the organization.[96]

Yet the very democracy that gave Czechoslovakia's Rom the opportunity to form their own political and cultural organizations also created a new atmosphere for open, virulent expressions of prejudice toward the Rom, whose numbers continued to increase dramatically in spite of the imperceptible growth of the general population. In 1988, the government estimated that there were 391,000 Rom in Czechoslovakia, a 35.6 percent increase over 1980 figures. Other estimates ranged as high as 700,000–800,000, with 470,000 a more practical number. Some perceived these figures to be a new threat, and the newspaper *Express* warned in an article on July 2, 1990, "that the Gypsy fertility may mean a 'tragedy,' that within a century the country may well have to be renamed the *Romská republika*."[97]

These fears combined with the deep-rooted, traditional prejudices toward the Rom and prompted some people to depict the Gypsies as new symbols of everything gone awry in Czechoslovakia. At the forefront of this new assault on the Rom were renewed charges of criminality. Dramatic increases in crime had plagued the country since the early 1980s, particularly in Prague and Bratislava. In a society accustomed to traditionally low crime rates, crime reached epidemic proportions by 1990. The Czech Republic reported a 52 percent increase over 1989 figures, while Prague's crime rate rose 181 percent during this period. Slovakia experienced a 17.7 percent rise in crime between 1988 and 1989. Much of this increase was attributed to Gypsies, who as early as 1987 had been blamed by Czechoslovakian television for 38 percent of Bratislava's crimes and 40 percent of those committed in eastern Slovakia. Gypsy youth 18 years of age and younger were accused of being "involved in 44.2% of all criminal activities" throughout Czechoslovakia in 1989. Clearer heads proved that many of these statistics were exaggerated and that the Rom were responsible for no more than 7.5-11 percent of the crime in the country during this period. Though these figures were out of proportion to the number of Gypsies in Czechoslovakia, they were directly tied to post-1989 Gypsy unemployment rates that reached as high as 50 percent in certain areas.[98]

Whatever the true numbers, Czechoslovakia's Rom paid a dear price for the accusations against them. Skinhead attacks, sometimes quietly encouraged by onlookers, mounted dangerously against Gypsies and the 35,000 Vietnamese workers in Czechoslovakia throughout 1990. On April 26, Prime Minister Petr Pithart "called for 'peaceful coexistence with our fellow citizens of Gypsy origin,'" while Deputy Prime Minister Jan Carnogursky demanded "tougher action against those skinheads who had attacked the Gypsies." On May 3, 1990, Romany Civic Initiative "appealed to all political parties, social organizations, and churches in Czechoslovakia to condemn 'racist' incidents aimed 'mainly at Gypsies and foreigners.'" Four days later, Charter 77 and the Czechoslovak Helsinki Committee condemned such attacks on the Vietnamese and Gypsies, and said they

> constitute attacks on all of us. They are attacks on the most basic
> principles of ethics and humanism, attacks on the state based on law
> that is being born, attacks contradicting the ideals of our democra-

tic revolution. The fact that we silently tolerate such attacks makes us accomplices.

We call on all citizens to stop being indifferent to the manifestations of violence and intolerance. We appeal to our executive bodies to put a final stop to these attacks. Let us make the people who for years have been working in our country feel that they live in a society in which it is possible to have their basic human rights protected.

Václav Havel detailed the wrongs done Gypsies in public statements on May 2 and in an address on July 27, 1990, to the First World Romany Festival in Brno. Though admirable, particularly when coupled with the new rights acquired by the Rom over the next year, they did not prevent the racially motivated deaths of 26 Rom before the breakup of Czechoslovakia on January 1, 1993.[99]

Both the federal and individual Czechoslovak republics granted the Rom full minority status, rights, and protection in 1990–1991. Over 30 Gypsy cultural organizations arose during this period, anchored by the Union of Romany Writers and numerous newspapers and magazines. Programs in Romani Studies were opened at Charles University in Prague and at the Pedagogical Faculty in Nítra. Unfortunately, these developments were overshadowed by a new set of problems that accompanied the breakup of Czechoslovakia on January 1, 1993. Before the formal separation, Slovakia had an estimated Gypsy population of 400,000, and the Czech lands, 150,000. In anticipation of the breakup, a number of Slovak Rom began to move to the Czech lands because they felt the political and social atmosphere would be more tolerant there, and economic conditions better. The sudden increase in "unemployed Romanies, often unassimilated families from Romany villages in eastern Slovakia," stunned many Czechs, who soon pointed to a sharp increase in crime, with claims that 90 percent of it was committed by the new Gypsies. Led by individual community actions throughout the Czech Republic, the new state's prosecutor-general "proposed to the Czech parliament a draft Law on Extraordinary Measures as a means of dealing 'with unrest caused by undisciplined groups of migrants.'" Though condemned by human rights groups and the Romany Democratic Congress, which represented 19 Gypsy groups in the Czech Republic, the law had surprising support from conservatives and local officials. Though never passed, the debate that surrounded the Law on Extraordinary Measures brought to the surface traditionally strong prejudice toward the Rom.[100]

These feelings were also expressed in several public opinion surveys conducted before and after the breakup of Czechoslovakia that showed almost universal hatred and distrust toward Gypsies, particularly among young Czechs and Slovaks. In fact, the level of anti-Rom sentiments was higher in

Czechoslovakia than in any other country in Eastern Europe. Officials in both countries have remained critical of the Rom. One Czech official claimed in the summer of 1993 that the Gypsies remained "a problem . . . because most of them are criminals who are getting rich through thievery and prostitution." Slovak Premier Vladimir Meciar, who lost his post in mid-March 1994, partly because of his immoderation, created an uproar on September 4, 1993, in a speech he made in Spiš, where Gypsies made up 13 percent of the population. The premier felt it "was necessary to curtail the 'extended reproduction of the socially unadaptable and mentally backward population' by decreasing family allowances," a reference to the country's Gypsies. Famed Nazi hunter and human rights advocate Simon Wiesenthal said that Meciar "has adopted the thinking and diction of Nazism." Meciar sued the newspaperman who originally wrote about his speech, while the Slovak government threatened to sue "any newspaper, radio or television station which refused to apologize for reporting it." Slovak authorities explained that the media had distorted Meciar's speech and reported it "out of context." It then released an official translation of his talk, part of which read:

> They [gypsies] should be perceived as a problem group that is growing in size. . . . This means that if we do not deal with them now, they will deal with us later. . . . Another thing we have to consider is extended reproduction of socially inadequate population.[101]

Several months later, Monika Nemcokov, the press secretary for the Slovak embassy in Washington, D.C., wrote to *The New York Times* to complain about distortions in an article by Henry Kamm, titled "In Slovak Gypsy Ghetto, Hovels and Plea for Jobs." Kamm's article centered on Gypsies in the Slovak village of Svinia, their poor living conditions, and their high unemployment. According to a parish priest in the village of Medzev, the Rom "don't want to work," and were satisfied subsisting on government welfare. The mayor of Medzev said the only solution to Slovakia's Gypsy problem was "to shoot them all," though, after a few moments, he added, "I'm no racist . . . But some Gypsies you would have to shoot." Nemcokov said such attitudes were "not based on racial intolerance, but on a significant difference in life styles and standards." She added that almost 40 percent of all crimes in Slovakia were committed by Roma, with a range of 40 to 50 percent for all "youth cases in Slovakia." The press secretary felt that the monthly Rom stipend of $71 a month was adequate "to sustain a moderate life style in Slovakia," though she admitted it was less than half the average monthly salary of a worker. Nemcokov strongly disagreed with Kamm's assertion that there were 400,000 Roma in Slovakia and put the figure at 250,000. She noted that the government spent 70 million Crowns annually to help the Roma, which was "used for improving living standards in Gypsy villages, education and children's summer camps, including 3.6 million Crowns for Gypsy periodicals, and 10.7 million Crowns for Gypsy cultural activities."[102]

A week and a half later, *The New York Times* published another article by Kamm on the plight of Czech Roma, "Gypsies and the Czechs: Poverty, Not a Welcome," that underscored some of the same problems in the Czech community of Usti nad Labem. Rom unemployment rates were at the 60–70 percent level, while the "housing situation is desperate." One Gypsy leader, Geza Grajcar, admitted that "90 percent of the Roma are involved in smuggling . . . as well as prostitution and petty crime," which he attributed to "social insecurity." Refreshingly, Václav Havel said in an interview several days later that "the Gypsy problem is a litmus test not of democracy but of a civil society," and that "one is unthinkable without the other." Such enlightened leadership and vision is necessary to prevent Gypsies from becoming prisoners of their pasts in the Czech and Slovak republics. Until such thought and leadership is brought to bear on the complex problems faced by the Roma in both countries, the Gypsies will remain stigmatized by prejudices and traditions that will neutralize any significant gains or contributions they have or will make in either nation.[103]

.3.

HUNGARY

O fficial Hungarian documents show that the Roma settled in Hungary at the end of the Middle Ages. One Slovak scholar, Emília Horváthová, has speculated that Gypsies fled through Hungary in 1241 to escape the invading Mongols.[1] Some scholars have pointed to a letter in 1260 from Ottokar II (r. 1253–1278), the king of Bohemia, to Pope Alexander IV (r. 1254–1261), in which the Bohemian ruler mentions *Cingari* in the army of Bela IV (r. 1235–1270) of Hungary, whom Ottokar II had defeated earlier in the year in a struggle for Styria. Angus Fraser concludes in his masterful *The Gypsies* (1992) that on closer inspection "a better reading of his letter replaces *Cingarorum* by *Bulgarorum*." During the fourteenth century, Roma began to settle in the Slovak portions of Hungary, particularly around castles in the region. Initially, the Gypsies were welcomed into this part of Hungary because of the area's sparse population. The local nobility and peasants treated the Rom with respect and believed them to be religious exiles from Egypt, the mythical place of Gypsy origin to many East Europeans at that time.[2]

New references to Gypsies crop up throughout this period, and in 1378 official documents in Zagreb, the capital of Croatia (which in 1102 became part of Hungary through the joint linkage of both thrones), refer specifically to Roma. Four years later, court records in Zagreb make references to butchers with the names of "Cigan or Cygan, Chickan or Czyganychyn," though it is not certain if these names referred to Gypsies. One scholar has suggested that Sigismund of Luxemburg, who would gain the throne of Hungary in 1387, granted "a group called the *Sincani* the right to choose their own leaders," while the first specific mention of Gypsies in Hungarian Slovak accounts was in 1399, when the *Book of Executions of the Lords of Rozmberk* notes "a certain Gypsy, the groom of Andrew."[3] Hungarian records indicate that in 1416 people in the Transylvanian town of Brassó (Brasov), which is now located in Romania, "provided 'lord Emaus of Egypt and his 120 companions' with food and money." A year later, a large group of Roma traveled through Transylvania and the Slovak portions of Hungary with the permission of King Sigismund (1387–1437), who, as Holy Roman Emperor, had gathered secular and Catholic Church leaders together in Constance, Italy, to resolve a crisis in the church over the papacy. Sigismund granted the Gypsies travel privileges after significant diplomatic negotiations because the Rom, who had spent some time in the Ottoman Empire, possessed important military information on the Turks. In 1423, Sigismund granted the Gypsy leader Ladislaus and his followers a detailed travel permit that brought large numbers of Roma into Hungary. The new Gypsy settlers worked as "castle musicians and metal workers" and were so highly regarded for these latter skills "and the manufacture of weapons that they were declared royal servants, for whose settlement and employment on private estates the consent of the king was necessary." Consequently, when the residents of Hermannstadt (Sibiu) in Transylvania wanted to have Gypsies work for them, they had to get the approval of King Matthias I (r. 1458–1490). His successor, the Jagiellonian Ulászló II (r. 1490–1516), gave the Rom leader Tamás Polgár, the "*vayvodam Pharaonum*" (voivode of 'Pharoah's People'), a travel permit that allowed Polgár and his Rom followers "to move and settle wherever he pleased in the country with his 25 tents of Gypsy smiths." Polgár's smiths provided the Bishop of Pécs, among others, with musket and cannon balls as well as other military hardware. A large number of Roma also served in the Hungarian army and were highly regarded by the Hungarians, especially for their ferocity. Gypsy smiths made the torture instruments used by a frustrated contender for the Hungarian throne, Janos Zápolyai (Ján Zápolský), against the rebel leader Dózsa (Gyorgy Székely) in 1514. Zápolyai, who took the throne in 1528 with Ottoman support, used Gypsy troops to burn a number of villages in Hungarian eastern Slovakia. During his struggle to acquire power, Zápolyai's opponents impaled a band of his Gypsy supporters to death after forcing them to admit to "incendiarism [a charge] (later withdrawn) wrung from them on the rack." The new monarch rewarded his Rom loyalists with the renewal of the "ancient Gypsy liberties (*antiquis libertatibus*)."[4]

Hungarian rulers also appointed for the first time "a chief of the Gypsies" who was given the title of *egregius* (distinguished). He was served by subordinate Rom leaders or *voivode* in each county who "acted as judges in Gypsy matters."[5] Hungarian Roma also began to distinguish themselves as musicians; records show that in 1489, Gypsies were paid to perform for Queen Beatrix (r. 1475–1490), the wife of Matthias I, at Csepel Island, while another monarch, Louis II (r. 1506–1526), paid *pharaones* to perform for the court in the spring of 1525. A second document seven years later refers to Gypsy *cytharedos* (minstrels), while in 1543, Queen Isabella, wife of Janos Zápolyai and daughter of Sigismund I Jagiello of Poland, marveled at Rom musicians. She wrote that at the court in the newly created Principality of Transylvania, which she began to rule with her son in 1541, "the most excellent Egyptian musicians play, the descendants of the Pharoahs."[6]

Hungarian attitudes toward the Rom changed as the country faced the growing threat of the Ottoman Turks in the sixteenth century. After the Hungarian defeat at Mohács on August 28, 1526, Gypsies began to be viewed as "incendiaries, soldiers or spies," particularly after the Turks occupied central Hungary in 1541. Hungary was then divided into three separate states. Royal Habsburg Hungary was centered in much of modern Slovakia, while the predominantly Magyar part of the nation, centered at Buda, was under Ottoman control. In 1541, the Turks also created a third state, the Principality of Transylvania, under Isabella and her infant son, János II (r. 1540/ 1556–1571).[7] Many Rom who remained in central Hungary "became smiths for the Turkish army; others were musicians, barbers, messengers or executioners." Scattered Turkish census data from Buda in 1546 showed that there were 56 Rom in Buda, the majority of them Catholics. Those that were Muslims were named Abdullah, a name given to Muslim converts. The number of Gypsies in Buda increased to 90 over the next 30 years; most of the Rom were now Muslims.[8] Many Gypsies, though, found themselves more and more isolated from the Hungarian population, and new Rom settlers were forced by local residents to live on the edge of villages and towns. Gypsy trades were also restricted, though there were some noblemen, particularly in Royal Hungary, the portion of Hungary under Habsburg control after 1541–1542, that tried to "preserve the skills of Gypsies as smiths, musicians and soldiers."[9]

Nevertheless, the plight of the Gypsies in Royal Hungary would continue to deteriorate, particularly after the outbreak of the Thirty Years War (1618–1648). However, one Hungarian nobleman, Gyorgy Thurzó, the royal governor of Habsburg Hungary, issued a special travel permit to the Gypsy *voivode* Franciscus and his company. What is remarkable about the document, particularly in light of the fact that Thurzó only four years earlier had issued strong anti-Gypsy legislation, is its plea for understanding of the harsh Rom life.

> While the birds of the sky have their nests, foxes their earths, wolves
> their lairs, and lions and bears their dens, and all animals have their
> own place of habitation, the truly wretched Egyptian race, which we
> call *Czingaros,* is assuredly to be pitied, although it is not known
> whether this was caused by the tyranny of the cruel Pharoah or the
> dictate of fate. In accordance with their ancient custom they are
> used to leading a very hard life, in fields and meadows outside the
> towns, under ragged tents. Thus have old and young, boys and chil-
> dren of this race learned, unprotected by walls, to bear with rain, cold
> and intense heat; they have no inherited goods on this earth, they do
> not seek cities, strongholds, towns or princely dwellings, but wan-
> der constantly with no sure resting place, knowing no riches or
> ambitions, but, day by day and hour by hour, looking in the open air
> only for food and clothing by the labour of their hands, using anvils,
> bellows, hammers and tongs.

Thurzó then asked officials to allow Franciscus and his Rom "to settle in their lands, [and] erect tents and practise their smithery, and to protect them against those who would do them harm." Reimer Gilsenbach adds that the Gypsies were protected by Thurzó not because of any "humanitarian motives" but because of their "military importance," since the travel permit also included the "gipsies in military service, together with their children, families, tents, anvils, bellows and all their goods."[10]

Regardless, conditions for Gypsies continued to worsen over the next century as large numbers of Rom fled into various parts of Hungary because of wartime devastation elsewhere. New restrictions were put in force that strengthened the ability of Hungarian officials to harass Gypsies. Though these laws were aimed at foreign, nomadic Gypsies, they affected all Roma in Royal Hungary and forced them to adopt a nomadic lifestyle, since the new regulations "provided Gypsies with no realistic conditions for settling and earning an honest living."[11]

The situation remained unstable throughout the rest of the seventeenth century as the Habsburgs tried to force the Turks out of Hungary. Between 1683 and 1687, the Austrian emperor Leopold I (r. 1657–1705) pushed the Turks out of the bulk of Hungary and began to integrate Turkish Hungary and Transylvania into his empire. An anti-Habsburg uprising in Hungary prompted new anti-Gypsy legislation in 1697 and 1701. Leopold I declared the Rom outlaws and threatened them with severe punishment if they tried to enter Habsburg domains. A similar regulation in 1706 ordered the erection in public places and along major thoroughfares of *taffeln* (warning placards) to inform Gypsies of these regulations. Four years later, Leopold's successor, Joseph I (r. 1705–1711), ordered that Gypsies who entered Hungary illegally were to be branded to enable authorities to identify those who had violated the new restrictions. Since illiterate Roma claimed that they could not read the taffeln, new taffeln with vivid pictures of mutilated Gypsies were erected for Rom who could not read. The 1710 ordinance added that any official who failed to hunt down Gypsies was to be fined severely, while anyone who harbored them "was to be punished by half a year's forced labour." These efforts failed to stop Gypsies from entering the Empire, however, and in 1717 Charles VI reaffirmed the earlier anti-Gypsy legislation.[12]

In 1711, the Hungarian nobility agreed to accept Charles VI (Charles III of Hungary) as their ruler in return for almost total control over their own domestic affairs. Charles VI soon began to try to rebuild Hungary, which was weakened and severely depopulated by years of war. Over 400,000 immigrants entered Hungary during this period, some of them Balkan Gypsies who had entered Hungary via Wallachia in Romania. In 1724, Charles VI issued a new Gypsy decree dealing with nomadic Roma.

> For the second time all those gipsies who do not have a landlord proved, and all their companions who have a wandering, stealing and thievish way of life, together with their wives and children have to be registered all over Hungary and the connected parts 3 months from now, so in your county as well, Sir, as in all counties of the country with the special condition that should any of them resist with gun or cudgel then he should be killed, and those captured have to be registered in order to state their number without any further proceedings.

The decree added that any Rom "who apply for a job and want to settle their name, age and physique should be registered," while county officials were required to make periodic reports to the "royal governor council" detailing "the reformation of these persons." In turn, governors had to send a report to Charles VI on the Gypsies in their region "in order to be able to provide for the public quietness in this kingdom, as well as in other kingdoms and regions." These regulations were to be announced and "spiked on boards along royal roads, in order that this instruction should be explained to everyone." Roma living in Hungary also had to pay new taxes on their moveable possessions, and Gypsy censuses were initiated to aid in their collection.[13]

By the early 1740s, Austria's new ruler, Maria Theresa (r. 1740–1780), had implemented more restrictions against the Rom. They promised punishment to anyone who gave Gypsies food and renewed earlier threats of deportation. Any Rom who reentered the empire would be flogged on the first offense and executed if caught again. In 1749, Maria Theresa issued a new anti-Gypsy decree that ordered that nomadic Gypsies, "vagrants and foreign beggars" were to be forced out of the Austrian Empire. This legislation did not affect sedentary Roma, "some of whom enjoyed considerable favour in high places as musicians." In 1751, Count Ferenc Eszterházy, a member of one of Hungary's powerful noble families, gave five Gypsies—Ferencz, János Bakos, László Bakos, László Boroni, and László Tinka—"litteras privilegiales," which made them "Free Court Musicians and exempt from taxes."[14] Seven years later, Maria Theresa made the local nobility throughout the empire responsible for the Gypsies in their districts, though the Austrian Imperial Council retained "a co-ordinating function for itself."[15]

She also ordered Hungary's Roma to halt their nomadic ways, settle, and "be subject to taxes and to compulsory service for the lord of the manor." To strengthen the new regulations, Gypsies were no longer allowed to own horses or wagons and could not leave their villages without the permission of local officials. The local nobility were unenthusiastic about these reforms because they had to bear the costs of enforcing them.[16] In 1761, Maria Theresa decreed that Hungarian Gypsies would no longer be referred to as *Cigany* but instead would be called "'new citizens,'(*Ujlakosok*) 'new peasants,' or 'new Hungarians'" (*Ujmagyar*). All Hungarian Rom males over sixteen years of age would now be eligible for military service, while twelve- to sixteen-year-old Gypsies would be taught a trade. Efforts to draft Gypsies into the army were met with resistance by Hungarian officers, while "workers were no more enthusiastic about taking them on as apprentices."[17]

In 1767, Maria Theresa, who had begun to share her throne two years earlier with her son, the future Joseph II (r. 1780–1790), issued her *Urbarium* (Urbarial Patent). Motivated by "humanitarian and economic considerations," the *Urbarium* was designed to force the Hungarian nobility to come to grips with the terrible plight of the country's oppressed peasantry. She issued a new Gypsy decree for Hungary the same year that took the Rom out of the jurisdiction of the region's governors and made the Gypsies subject to the ordinary judicial system. Another decree in 1769 dealt with Gypsy registration.

> For the first time: As we have ordered to you, Sir, as well as to all counties and towns in our instruction of December 10th, we ask you to register all the gipsy families till the end of next February, indicating their wives, children, their sex and age, their craft—if they have any—their religion in accordance with the true facts, so that even the absent and alien persons should be indicated individually, mentioning the reason of residence according to blood-relation. Finally, these break-down records should be submitted as soon as possible to the royal governor council in order to submit it to her holy Majesty.

The Empress also ordered that Roma could no longer "set themselves apart in dress, speech or occupation, and each village was to carry out a census of Gypsies."[18] When these measures failed to bring the proper results, she issued a new ordinance in 1774 that forbade marriage between Gypsies. Furthermore, when a Rom woman married a non-Gypsy, she "had to produce proof of industrious household service and familiarity of Catholic tenets." A male Rom who married a non-Gypsy "had to prove ability to support a wife and children." Finally, "Gypsy children over the age of five were to be taken away and brought up in non-Gypsy families" to insure a Roman Catholic upbringing. Other Gypsy regulations surfacing during this period encouraged the creation of Rom settlements and ordered that Gypsy men be given regular employment. Rom children in the new settlements were to attend school regularly. When Gypsy children became ten, they had to find a useful occupation or trade. To discourage continued nomadism, Roma could only own horses if they farmed with them, though authorities preferred them to use oxen.[19]

Maria Theresa's efforts to settle and Magyarize Hungary's Rom prompted over 40 unsigned articles in the *Weiner Anzeigen,* a Hungarian journal in German. In one of them, a unique look at the Gypsies of Hungary and Transylvania, the author noted that despite appearances, there were numerous, distinct Rom groups in the region. Nomadic Gypsies lived in tents but wintered in hillside caves. Conditions for sedentary Roma who had only the barest of necessities were not much better. They primarily ate meat and starchy food, which they prepared with limited cooking and kitchen utensils. Hungarian Gypsies begged for bread and "were passionately fond of alcohol and tobacco." They had little clothing, and Roma women "obtained clothes by begging or stealing" and adorned them with jewelry.[20]

The author of the *Wiener Anzeigen* article observed that Gypsy smiths sat "crosslegged on the ground" when working, while the women worked the bellows. The smiths "were quick and dexterous, but erratic," since family members often disturbed the routine "to peddle their small wares." Roma horse traders were equally adept and excellent horsemen. They were also good at making "a sick nag look healthy." Gypsy musicians were talented and able to cater to the different musical tastes of their audience. Some Roma had evolved past the creation of traditional crafts such as "the flaying of animal carcasses and the making of sieves and wooden implements" and only did these things part-time. Others, such as the *Aurari* (gold-washers) in Transylvania and the Banat, had separated themselves from the rest of Hungary's Rom and were known to be hardworking and independent.[21]

The article's author felt Hungary's Gypsies had little "honour and shame," but plenty of pride. He noted that they "adopted the religion of their environment, without belief" and did not appear to have any special "ceremonies or customs." He felt that Gypsy behavior was "contrary to the rule of every organized society" and pointed to the way they raised their children as the cause. Though Rom parents "loved their children inordinately," he felt they failed to provide them with any education, which meant they had "no chance of changing their ways" once they became adults. He observed that Hungary's Gypsies could, if adequately educated, be productive farmers, craftsmen, or soldiers. The best thing to do for the Roma of Hungary, he concluded, "was to 'strive as far as possible to turn Gypsies into human beings and Christians and then to keep them within the state as useful subjects,'" a task that "would demand much patience and effort." The conclusions reached by the anonymous author of the articles in the *Weiner Anzeigen* were supported by Hermann Grellmann in his 1783 study, *Die Zigeuner.* Grellmann felt that efforts by Maria Theresa and her son, Joseph, were on the right track and that "education was the road leading towards the eradication of non-conformity" for Hungarian Rom.[22]

When he succeeded his mother in 1780, Joseph II undertook a massive reform campaign designed to create a "perfectly uniform state." There would no longer exist the traditional Austro-Hungarian dualism, since Joseph intended to fully integrate Hungary into the empire. In addition to efforts to create a unitary kingdom, Joseph II sought to eradicate religious intolerance with his 1781 Patent of Toleration, which gave some rights to Protestants and the Greek Orthodox. His Serfdom Patent of November 1781 was of limited significance to Gypsies and other peasants, since the peasants got no land in the deal and had "to continue to provide the lords labor or pay rents," they remained "far from equal in practice." The Serfdom Patent was not extended into Transylvania until 1783, where it was ignored by the Hungarian nobility. In frustration, Joseph II emancipated all of Hungary's serfs two years later.[23]

Joseph II also continued efforts to integrate Gypsies into the fabric of Hungarian society. In 1783, the emperor issued a new Gypsy decree for Hungary that again outlawed nomadism, forbade Roma to change their names, required local officials to write monthly reports on Gypsy activities, prevented Rom from taking part in local fairs, banned Gypsy smiths from plying their crafts except in times of special need, limited the number of Roma musicians, outlawed panhandling, required Gypsy settlers to serve others, and ordered that all Rom children age four and above be sent away every two years to neighboring districts.[24] Other regulations ordered the destruction of Gypsy slums in Hungary and required Rom men and women to sleep apart in newly constructed housing projects. Sheriffs in Hungary were to keep a close watch on all Gypsies, who had to have the sheriff's permission to travel. Despite this, Hungary's Roma still had to pay taxes and serve in the army.[25]

To give the government a better idea about the numbers affected by these regulations, annual Gypsy censuses were initiated between 1780 and 1783. Officially, there were 43,609 Rom (excluding married women) in Hungary in 1780 which included Croatia-Slavonia but excluded Transylvania. The census listed 20,629 "Neu-Bauern" (New Peasants) or newly settled Rom, and 22,567 children. There were 8,388 Gypsy youths in foster homes, while 8,982 lived with their parents. Only 481 Gypsy children were in school, while 4,716 had jobs or served in the military. Gypsy population figures dropped to 38,312 in 1781, with 11,459 listed as "Neu-Bauern." The total number of Gypsy children rose to 26,206, while those in school increased to 1,111. There were 6,059 Rom children in foster care, and 13,235 at home. Another 5,801 Gypsy youths had jobs. Gypsy registration figures from 1781 showed that there were 1,291 Gypsy families occupied as Aurari (gold-washers), 1,239 tax-paying Rom families divided into voivodships (tax districts under local governors), and 12,686 Rom families "belonging to rural communities." Of this number, 8,598 families were sedentary, and 4,088 were nomads. The Hungarian Gypsy population climbed to 43,778 in 1782, though "Neu-Bauern" rose only to 12,847. Census takers counted 32,584 children in Hungary in 1782. Over two-thirds of the Rom youngsters, 20,851, lived with their parents. There were only 809 Gypsy children in school, 5,053 in foster homes, and 5,871 Rom youths with jobs. The 1783 census recorded 30,251 Gypsies in Hungary; the number of "Neu-Bauern" dropped to 7,647. It also showed 24,613 children, with 15,306 at home, 1,056 in school, 3,515 in foster care, and 4,736 with jobs. Total Roma population estimates for the "Lands of the Hungarian Crown," which included Croatia and Slavonia, were 135,000 at this time.[26]

The dramatic change in various Rom statistics during this period gives some indication of the Gypsies' response to Joseph II's policies. Those that remained in Hungary found ways around the emperor's Rom decrees and moved from areas "where the policy was more vigorously enforced to those which were more lax." Gypsies that "did settle left their box-like houses empty and lived in shelters of their own construction; children were prone to fleeing back to their parents; and if Gypsies could not legally marry among themselves," they fell back upon their own marriage ceremonies to wed other Roma. In time, most of the Gypsy children ran away from the schools or the foster homes. Their efforts were not strongly resisted by the Hungarian nobility, who were unenthusiastic about the Rom policies because they had to bear the brunt of the costs of the education, housing, and job-training programs designed to help Gypsies assimilate into Hungarian society. (Their exaggerated reports to Maria Theresa and Joseph II about the Roma added to the statistical uncertainty of the early successes of the two monarchs' policies.)

After the death of Joseph II in 1790, efforts to assimilate the Roma in this part of the Austrian Empire waned, and many Gypsies returned to their traditional nomadic lifestyle.[27]

Joseph II had been quite sensitive to the general opposition to his Gypsy and other policies in Hungary, and on January 30, 1790, he "revoked all of his reforms in Hungary except for the Toleration Patent and the Serfdom Patent." Before he died three weeks later, he "suggested as his own epitaph: 'Here lies Joseph II, who failed in all his enterprises.'"[28] His death ended an important period in Hungarian Gypsy history. European events soon enveloped the country, and Habsburg energies were increasingly caught up in the conflicts with France and Napoleon that did not end until 1815. While there is no question that the Gypsies in Hungary were deeply affected by these events, as were Rom throughout Europe, little precise information is available on them. Statistical data indicates a Rom population in Hungary, excluding Transylvania, of 40,000 in 1809, a figure that dropped to 30,000 two decades later. However, a government report in 1805 concluded "that so far as the gipsies would not be settled generally, it was impossible to have an accurate registration."[29]

Gypsies did begin to achieve some musical notoriety during the first half of the nineteenth century because of the efforts of Ferenc (Franz) Liszt, Hungary's "greatest son," before the Revolutions of 1848. Since his youth, Liszt had always had a deep fascination with the Rom and once remarked that he was "a mixture of gipsy and Franciscan." He was particularly influenced by János Bihari, a Gypsy whom Liszt called in his *Bohemiens et le leur musique en Hongrie* (Gypsies and Their Music in Hungary, 1859), one of the nation's "most celebrated violinists." According to Liszt, Bihari became so highly sought after that "no marriage or festival of any importance, public or private, could be allowed to pass without his being invited." Bihari played regularly for the gathered courts of Europe at the Congress of Vienna in 1814–1815, where he attracted the fancies of several prominent women from some of Europe's most powerful royal families. Bihari responded by bringing his young Rom wife to court, where she dazzled the gathered nobility. Liszt also celebrated the talents of two other Gypsy violinists, János Lavotta and Antál Czermak, though there is some question if they were Gypsies.[30]

Liszt's fondness for Rom was so strong that he adopted a Gypsy child, Josi Sárai, and raised him with his other children. Sárai eventually returned to his Gypsy clan, married, and became part of a Rom ensemble in Debreczin. Sárai named his son Ferenc after Liszt, who became the child's godfather. Yet despite his support of Gypsy musicians,

Liszt's interest in Gypsy music cannot be explained on artistic grounds alone. He was drawn to the Gypsy race—to its origins, its migration patterns, its folklore, its contribution to Western culture; his interest in its music was a symptom of this absorption. Liszt admired the independence of the Zigeuner, who had survived unimaginable persecutions across the centuries, had been driven out of practically every 'civilized' country in Europe—save Hungary, where the Gypsies have always been tolerated—and yet somehow managed to preserve his cultural identity intact. Liszt marvelled at the musicality of the Zigeuner, whose intuitive grasp of the art called for an explanation. Here was a nomad, with a history stretching back into antiquity, who actively shunned all formal education. Yet, without the benefit of conservatory teaching, music sprang up spontaneously within him and gushed forth like a fountain. The typical Zigeuner could not even read music notation; yet his repertoire was all-embracing. . . . The Zigeuner transformed everything he touched, and his melodies were decorated with exotic ornamentation. Through music he expressed all his joys and sorrows.[31]

Liszt's fascination with Gypsies offended some Hungarian musicologists, particularly after he published his "Hungarian Rhapsodies" in 1851–1853 (which were inspired by Rom music) and his *Bohemiens et le leur musique en Hongrie* in 1859, which placed the soul of Hungarian music at the feet of the Gypsies.[32] Though the controversy surrounding Liszt's efforts to make the Roma the creators of Hungarian national music raged throughout his lifetime, it reached new heights after Béla Bartók and Zoltan Kodály began their monumental field work on Hungarian peasant music in 1905. In his 1924 study, *A Magyar népdal* (The Hungarian Folk Song), Bartók concluded that Rom music was rather shallow, "with an excess of *rubato* and ornaments. Their repertory is not particularly extensive; it is, indeed, mostly restricted to the tunes in fashion at the moment." Though he admitted that some Rom musicians such as Bihari had created their own works, Bartók felt "the so-called 'Gipsy music' is not Gipsy music at all, but Hungarian music, from miscellaneous sources, performed by Gipsies." Yet Bartók admitted that his work centered around the study of "Hungarian peasant music only" and left the "investigation of the music of other classes to those who are interested in that music."[33]

According to one of Liszt's biographers, Alan Walker, "the Gypsies had no real creative tradition of their own. They took music wherever they found it and fashioned it in their own image." Earlier, a nineteenth-century Italian criminologist, Cesare Lombroso, disparaged Hungarian Gypsy music "as simply 'a new proof of the genius that, mixed with atavism, is to be found in the criminal.'" Walker admitted, though, that the controversy over the influence of

Gypsies on Hungarian music missed the essence of the question for Liszt and his music. To Hungary's "national son," the Gypsy proved that "music was God-given, part of a divine plan."[34]

Liszt's efforts to give Hungarian Gypsies a greater role as the creators of Hungarian music also ran counter to the growing spirit of Magyarization that had infected that part of the Austrian Empire since the 1790s. This spirit accompanied an upsurge in Hungarian national feeling that had exploded after Joseph II had done away with most of his regressive policies in Hungary in 1790 and was designed to counter similar nationalistic tendencies among Hungary's other ethnic groups. This rebirth of Hungarian national spirit continued to grow and flourish throughout the nineteenth century and fueled one of the most dramatic events in modern Hungarian history, the 18-month, unsuccessful War of Independence in 1848–1849.[35] István Deak sees this event less as an act of revolution than as a "spontaneous effort to achieve modernization," since Hungary was "a kingdom under the Habsburg scepter," which, even after its defeat in 1849, saw the "liberal economic and social reforms adopted by the Hungarian Diet in March and April 1848" left intact and in some cases extended.[36]

The seeds for the Hungarian revolutionary crisis of 1848–1849 lie in the previous years of resurgent national sentiment and efforts by some liberal Hungarian nationalists such as Lajos (Louis) Kossuth, Hungary's leader during the revolution, to gain full equality and national autonomy for Hungary within the Austrian Empire. Of primary concern to all Hungarian leaders at this time, whether it was Kossuth or his nemesis, the romantic nationalist István Széchenyi, was the question of nationalities. Greater prerevolutionary Hungary, which encompassed Croatia-Slavonia and Transylvania, was less than 40 percent Magyar. None of the major ethnic groups except the Croats or the Germans in Transylvania "were recognized by the Hungarian constitutional tradition as having corporate autonomy." Hungarian nationalists embraced Magyar preeminence during this era as a means of combating the Germanization policies of the Viennese court, while the 1847 "liberal Opposition Manifesto," written by Kossuth and Ferenc Deák, "did not mention non-Magyars' ethnic rights" specifically, though it did call for "the civil rights of all including non-Magyars."[37]

Hungary's leaders also omitted minority rights in their April Laws, or constitution, once the revolution got under way in March 1848, despite the fact that, if Transylvania was joined to Hungary, as many hoped, there would be more non-Magyars in the new state than Hungarians. This omission was based on the fear "that granting special rights to the minorities would help restore the despicable feudal system of local or corporate privilege" and the insistence by liberals that the new Hungary must be "one nation in one state."[38] Though these discussions had little impact on the Rom, who were not considered one of Hungary's national minorities, many of them backed the revolution once it got underway in the spring of 1848. Some Gypsies chose to support it through traditional means, while others, according to Angus Fraser, "took part with their instruments in the abortive revolution," and, once it began to be put down "by a series of Hungarian defeats at the hands of the Austrians, and more rarely, the Russians," consoled the nation with their music.[39]

A bloody crackdown followed the end of the War of Independence, with the Hungarians losing their "historic rights, their centuries old constitution, and their special status." They did, however, retain many of the social and economic reforms adopted by the Hungarian legislature in the early months of the revolution.[40] Perhaps the most important of these reforms was the emancipation of the serfs, a move supported by Hungary's Diet in late 1847 and made part of the April Laws several months later. This legislation dramatically changed the social and economic structure of Hungary, since, unlike Joseph II's Serfdom Patent 67 years earlier, the peasants, including some Gypsies, received land with their new freedom. Sadly, the peasant remained poor, since over half of the land in the country remained in the hands of a quarter of the population.[41]

Post-1849 Habsburg officialdom sought "to rebuild a centralized empire, of which Hungary was to become an integral part." What developed was an attempt to create a strong, centralized, Germanic kingdom blending reaction and reform. Hungarians uniformly opposed these policies and chose to resist them passively until the political climate changed. To the peasants, some of them Gypsies, Kossuth, now in exile, achieved "mythical status as the protector of the peasantry." While abroad, he advocated liberal freedoms for Hungary's minorities, such as "free use of languages on the county level" and "total political autonomy."[42] The outbreak of the Franco-Austrian War in 1859 prompted new plans for a Hungarian uprising, backed by France. Efforts were made to get Hungary's distant minorities to support Kossuth's liberal plans for them, but with the defeat of Austrian forces at Solferina on June 24, 1859, France's emperor, Napoleon III, quickly withdrew his support for the Hungarian rebellion. The Habsburg defeat and the specter of further domestic unrest prompted Vienna to revive Hungary's legislature, with limits, which it soon overrode with the creation of an Empire-wide Imperial Council in February 1861. The country's major ethnic minorities hoped the new Hungarian legislature would recognize their existence as independent nations and accept the fact that "the common fatherland was inhabited by several nations." Instead, the Hungarian parliament's nationalities subcommittee told the minorities' representatives that "all citizens of Hungary, irrespective of their native language, comprise in the political sense only one nation, the Hungarian nation, which is one and indivisible in accordance with the historical concept of the Hungarian state."[43]

Vienna dealt with the conflict of competing national and Hungarian legislatures by dissolving the latter in August 1861. Abroad, Kossuth counseled reason and advocated the creation of a Danubian Confederation that would embrace Hungary, Translyvania, Wallachia, Moldavia, Croatia, and perhaps even Serbia. Kossuth's promise of broad, sweeping ethnic autonomy caused many Hungarians to oppose his ideas, while others sought to find ways to bring about change within the context of the Austrian Empire. The experiment of the Imperial Council failed by 1863, and, in late 1865, the Hungarian parliament was called back into session to search for a solution to the growing differences with Vienna. Spurred by renewed domestic unrest in Hungary and the unsettling military setback against Prussia in the War of 1866, Vienna began to search for a compromise with the Hungarians to restore domestic peace to the Habsburg Empire. The result was the *Ausgleich* (Compromise) of 1867, which created two separate, internally sovereign kingdoms, Austria and Hungary, which shared a common ruler and the "joint management" of "foreign policy, defense, and the finances needed for these."[44]

Unfortunately, the *Ausgleich* "ended the nationalities' hope of a federative reorganization of the empire and left them defenseless in the face of Hungarian hegemonist ambitions. For this reason, Hungary's non-Magyar nationalities were unanimously opposed to the Compromise." While the agreement was being negotiated between Austrian and Habsburg officials, the major nationalities demanded equal rights, which was opposed by some Hungarians, who felt it gave them too many rights. Consequently, the minorities' legislation that was finally approved by the Hungarian legislature in 1868 "did not recognize the existence of separate nationalities and did not grant them collective national rights or political institutions," though it did allow them liberal language privileges.[45]

The Hungary that emerged after the *Ausgleich* was to be "a unitary Hungarian national state" where the ideas of state and nation were to be equal. Initially, this translated neither into forced Magyarization nor "linguistic and ethnic assimilation," but rather a policy of "grammatical Magyarization" that centered around educational efforts "to turn the intellectuals of the nationalities into Hungarians." In the midst of these efforts, which would become much more aggressive in the mid-1880s, some scholarly work began in Hungary on the Romani language. The seed of Hungarian interest in the Gypsy language can be traced back to the pioneering work a century earlier of István Váli, a Hungarian minister, who identified a link between the

Romani spoken by the Gypsies in Györ, Hungary and the language of three students from Ceylon (now Sri Lanka) whom he had interviewed in 1753–1754 at the University of Leiden. The new work was undertaken by Archduke Josef Karl Ludwig, a Habsburg with distant ties to the throne and a resident of Hungary. The archduke was "an enthusiastic student of Romani and Gypsy ways" and had a lifelong passion for Rom music. In 1888, he published *Cigány Nyelvtan* (The Gypsy Language), "a comprehensive Romani grammar, based on several European dialects." Archduke Josef, who spoke fluent Hungarian, also set up a large Rom settlement at his estate at Alcsúth and founded similar Gypsy settlements at four other sites throughout Hungary. The archduke built homes for the Roma at each settlement, taught them to farm, and opened a special school for Gypsy youth at Alcsúth. After he died in 1905, the five Roma settlements fell into disarray.[46]

The only other glimpses of Rom life in Hungary during the second half of the nineteenth century come from the various censuses taken during this period. Austrian records estimate a Gypsy population of 93,000 in 1846, while a census in 1851 indicated that there were 30,304 Gypsies in Hungary, which included 11,440 in Hungarian Vojvodina-Banat. There were another 53,465 Gypsies in Transylvania, including 800 serving in the military. According to a study done by Dr. Sádor Konek in 1868, there were an estimated 143,150 Rom in Hungary in 1857, and 155,700 seven years later. A breakdown of this latter figure showed there were 67,610 Rom in Hungary proper, 1,760 in Croatia, 86,300 in Transylvania, and 30 in the military borderland Frontier District to the south. Konek and others attributed part of the Gypsy population increase to the emancipation of slaves in Wallachia and Moldavia during this period. A census taken in Hungarian-controlled territory in 1867 showed 33,000 Rom in Hungary proper, 58,000 in Translyvania, 4,500 in Croatia-Slavonia, and 4,500 in the Frontier District, out of a total population of 15,500,000. A special Rom census in 1873 showed 214,000 Gypsies in Hungary and Transylvania, while the more detailed census of 1880, which was the first to use language as an indirect criteria for nationality, listed 75,911 Gypsies by native language in Hungary and Transylvania (37,764 women and 38,147 men), 1,499 in Croatia-Slavonia, and 1,983 in the Frontier District. According to the analysis of this census by Hungarian demographer Károly Keleti, another 15,010 Gypsies listed Romani as their secondary language. Keleti found it impossible to determine the language status of another 2,800 Roma. The 1880 census also gave a detailed breakdown of greater Hungary's Rom population geographically, and now included women for the first time. It listed 64 settlement areas for Gypsies in Hungary and Transylvania, 8 for Croatia-Slavonia, and 6 for the Frontier District. The census of 1890, which again used language as one of the criteria for nationality, showed 91,603 Gypsies in Hungary and Translyvania who declared Romani as their primary language. Of this number, only 5.4 percent of those over the age of six could read or write, compared to a national average of 53 percent.[47]

A new, more thorough Gypsy census in 1893 indicated a Rom population of 274,940 in Hungary and Transylvania. Over 89 percent of Hungary's Rom lived in established settlements, while 7.5 percent were seminomadic, and 3.3 percent were completely nomadic. (Of the 274,940 Roma, 2,164 were in the army, police, or imprisoned, and thus not included in the residence percentages). The sedentary Gypsies lived in 7,220 settlements throughout the country, while the seminomadic Rom periodically resided in 2,399 settlements. The Gypsy nomads identified 811 separate villages as temporary homes. A little over half of the sedentary Rom lived segregated from the native population, while 40 percent lived together with non-Gypsies. Only about half of the children attended school, though over two-thirds of those who did go to school "had obtained satisfactory results in education." Two-thirds of the settled Rom lived in Gypsy houses, while the rest resided in "hovels and cabins." Census takers observed that the majority of the settled Gypsies' homes were "well managed, clean and do not differ too much from the houses of other inhabitants," conclusions that later Hungarian investigators of this data found as "too favourable." The 1893 census also looked at public attitudes toward the Rom and found that in two-thirds of the 6,000 villages surveyed, "the conduct of the gipsies was blameless." Only 5 percent of the villages investigated reported serious difficulties with the Rom. Nomadic Gypsies were viewed more unfavorably.[48]

Over 30 percent of Hungary's Rom listed Magyar as their primary language, while slightly less than 30 percent listed Romani as their native tongue. Over 62 percent of the nomadic Gypsies used Romani as their primary language. Almost a quarter of Hungary's Gypsies principally spoke Romanian, while 3.6 percent spoke Slovak. Less than half of Hungary's Gypsies were comfortable with Magyar as a second language, and even fewer used Romani as a second language, though this varied from group to group. Data on education, which was considered the "most important means of culture and social development at the time," indicated that only 5.7 percent of Hungary's Rom could read or write, while only 12,000 of 52,000 settled Rom children between the ages of six and fourteen went to school. In a survey of 6,332 settlements where Roma lived (out of a total of 7,220), two-thirds of the settlements reported that enrolled Gypsy children never went to school, while the remaining one-third reported solid Rom school attendance.[49]

Almost 60 percent of Hungary's Gypsies had a trade and earned steady income from it. Of these, 64,000 Rom declared themselves unskilled laborers, while 14,700 Gypsies worked as smiths, and 13,000 did construction work. There were also 2,000 Rom spoon makers, 3,000 wood-trough carvers, and 1,000 copper craftsmen. Almost 17,000 Gypsies declared themselves musicians. Though there were few Rom farmers, 5,600 said they worked in the countryside as servants, herdsmen, and so forth. Another 4,400 were employed as "horse-dealers, ragmen, second-hand dealers" or in other occupations. There were 32 Rom whose work fell into the category of "intellectual profession," which included 22 midwives. Another 152 Gypsies were listed as people performing "intellectual services," meaning "village drummers, school porters, mail-carriers, etc." However, census analysts agreed that these figures did not adequately reflect the true number of Rom in "intellectual professions," since, despite their lack of education, many who did acquire an education and a profession often tried to assimilate and thus chose not to identify themselves as Gypsies.[50]

In 1910, Hungary's next and last census before the breakup of the Austro-Hungarian Empire at the end of World War I, showed 147,599 Rom in Hungary, a decline of over 46 percent from 1893 figures. This decrease in Gypsy population figures was tied more directly to a series of complex economic, social, and demographic changes that took place in Hungary during this period than to any effort to drive the Rom from the country. Politically and socially, the 1890s was a period of intensified nationalistic spirit in Hungary that increasingly tried to force Magyarization on the country's scattered minorities through education and other means. Though this process was quite successful among some groups, such as the Jews and the Gypsies, other ethnic groups strongly resisted, so that according to the 1910 census, only one-fifth of the country's 8.3 million non-Hungarians knew Magyar. Regardless, estimates are that a large number of Gypsies, Jews, Germans, Slovaks, and other groups that had assimilated had done so because of "economic transformation, urbanization, and 'embourgeoisement.'" These changes, however, were countered by a wave of emigration that saw over 2 million people leave Hungary during this period, triggered by economic difficulties and the powerful force of Magyarization.[51]

Since almost 70 percent of the Hungarian Roma spoke Magyar, Romanian, or other (non-Romani) languages, and, from an official perspective, had no historically identifiable ethnic traditions of their own, the Hungarian government refused to grant them official minority status. Consequently, Gypsies were expected to become good Hungarians. Anchored by an outpouring of books and articles on the social transformation of the Rom, speakers at a 1909 conference on Gypsies suggested that they "should have their horses and wagons confiscated, together with any weapons they possessed." One participant also argued that "every Gypsy should be branded so as to assist identification." There is no question that these feelings found a wider audience throughout Hungary, and, combined with other things that affected population change in the country, helped bring about the dramatic decline in Gypsy population figures in the 1910 census. On the other hand, the conference stimulated an educational project for Hungary's Roma that continued until the outbreak of World War I and was resumed after it ended.[52]

World War I brought more dramatic changes in the Gypsy population in Hungary. Austro-Hungarian forces suffered 1.25 million deaths and almost 5.8 million wounded. Hungary "supplied proportionately more soldiers than the other half of the monarchy and, therefore, suffered heavier losses in dead, wounded, and prisoners." Though all elements of Hungarian society initially supported the war effort, enthusiasm for the war waned by 1917 as the country began to collapse from the economic and social strain produced by this deadly conflict of attrition. Hungary's minorities now saw advantages in the complete dissolution of the Austrian-Hungarian state. On October 2, 1918, the empire asked for an armistice as a prelude to peace talks, while three and a half weeks later, the Czechs, Slovaks, Croats, and Ruthenians of eastern Slovakia began to declare their independence. The Allied victors separated the Austrian and Hungarian kingdoms in the peace talks and forced Hungary to conclude the Treaty of Trianon of June 14, 1920. Delayed by the abortive, Soviet-supported coup of Bela Kun in 1919, the accord forced Hungary to give up "70 percent of her territory, and 60 percent of her total population, including 28 percent of the Hungarian speakers." Hungary's population dropped from 20.9 million in 1910 to 7.6 million in 1920. It now became almost a purely Magyar state, with only 833,475 people claiming a native tongue other than Hungarian.[53]

The harshness of the Treaty of Trianon dashed whatever hopes Hungary's remaining nationalities had for a truly innovative minorities policy, since an "irate Hungarian public pinpointed concessions to the nationalities as the major cause for the Trianon Treaty and the country's dismemberment." Instead, what emerged under the government of Count Istvan Bethlen from 1921 to 1931 was a nationalities policy that *purportedly* "provided for the full equality of all Hungarian citizens, irrespective of language, religion, or descent," but was compromised by a subtle, ongoing campaign of Magyarization. In 1923, the government created three types of schools that allowed primary teaching in the native languages. By 1928, there were 607 of these schools, 467 of them for the large German community. Native languages were also allowed to be used in government and legal matters in areas where at least 20 percent of the population belonged to the same linguistic group. In 1927, Kúno Kubelsberg, the minister of education, changed the *numerus clausus* law of 1920 that had created limits on the number of Jews who could enter higher education, and thus had made "anti-Semitism constitutional for the first time in the history of modern Hungary." Kubelsberg's changes did away with "racial and nationality considerations" as a barrier to higher education and tried to insure "that the young of all classes got a chance" to attend university.[54]

As a result of this atmosphere, some prewar educational work with Gypsies was revived, and in 1935, a Rom school was opened. Unfortunately, these efforts, though promising, could not overcome the powerful force of Magyarization that insisted that to achieve "completely equal membership in Hungarian supremacy," one had "to accept the Hungarian way of life." This spirit partly explains the extremely low Gypsy population figures in the census of 1930. Though Hungarian minority specialist Gábor Kemény later estimated that there were probably 100,000 Rom in Hungary in 1930 (out of a total population of 8,688,319), only 14,473 Gypsies officially showed up in the census that year.[55] These figures are doubly significant in light of the dramatic increase in native language identification among Hungary's other minorities the same year. Whatever atmosphere emboldened Hungary's other ethnic groups to be more open soon changed as the Depression swept into Hungary. Growing dissatisfaction with the policies of the Bethlen government forced its collapse in 1931. It was followed by a transition government under Count Gyula Károlyi, which fell the following year under the weight of growing labor unrest and continued economic chaos. A hesitant Admiral Miklós Horthy, Hungary's regent and chief of state, chose his old ally, Gyula Gömbös, to serve as prime minister with the proviso that Gömbös would "maintain the existing governmental system and refrain from propagating racist ideas." Instead, Gömbös set immediately to work on the creation of a "fascist state system."[56]

Gömbös's initial efforts to transform the face of Hungarian politics were ultimately unsuccessful, as were his attempts to seek closer ties with fascist Italy and Nazi Germany. His Party of National Unity handily won control of the parliament in 1935 in elections that were considered to be the "most corrupt and violent in Hungary's history." Afterwards, Gömbös boasted to Adolf Hitler's heir-apparent, Hermann Göring, and others, "that a one-party regime would be set up in Hungary within the following two years."[57] Despite this victory for "Right-Radicalism," Gömbös's death on October 6, 1936, enabled Horthy to appoint someone "who would reestablish the old order in politics," keep a lid on the Right and the Left, and stop efforts to draw closer to Germany and Italy. His choice, Kálmán Darányi, dismantled "Gömbös's political machine," but succumbed to mounting Nazi-fascist pressure at home, strengthened by the German takeover of Austria in the spring of 1938. Horthy, who began to play a more important role in day-to-day Hungarian politics, became increasingly doubtful of Darányi's ability to maintain "unity between the existing factions of the government in the event of an external threat or of stemming the danger from the extreme Right." Of particular concern to Horthy was Ferenc Szálasi's Party of the National Will. Szálasi's party was banned in 1937 after his arrest for antigovernment activities, though Szálasi later had a hand in creating a new party, the Hungarian National Socialist Party (*Magyar Nemzeti Szocialistista Párt*), which was banned in early 1938. Szálasi created a new party, the National Socialist Hungarian Party—Hungarian Movement (*Nemzeti Szocialista Magyar Párt—Hungarista Mozgalom*), in the spring of 1939, and the following year organized the infamous Arrow Cross Party—Hungarist Movement (*Nyilaskerezstes Párt—Hungarista Mozgalom*), which had strong anti-Semitic ideological foundations. In national elections in the spring of 1939, Arrow Cross won 25 percent of the vote, and, in league with similar political factions, acquired an influential voice in Hungarian politics. Darányi's inability to curb the growing influence of Szálasi's and other extremist movements led to Darányi's dismissal as prime minister on May 13, 1938. It was during this period that legislative attention was also drawn to the Gypsies. During one legislative debate in 1938, Gyozo Dródy noted that Hungary now had a Rom population of 130,000 to 150,000, possibly an exaggerated estimate designed to make the Gypsy threat appear greater.[58]

Darányi's successor, Béla Imrédy, initially struck out harshly against right-wing extremists and had Szálasi imprisoned. However, by early fall, Imrédy turned rightward "in one of the most startling turnabouts in Hungarian history," a move that ultimately cost him Horthy's support. Before his downfall in early 1939, Hungary acquired 12,009 square kilometers of territory with 1 million inhabitants in the German-Italian First Vienna Award. Afterward, he pushed through Hungary's Second Jewish Law, which tightened "economic, professional and racial restrictions on the Jews." Imrédy's replacement, Pál Teleki, continued Hungary's pro-Nazi drift, which saw it join Hitler's Anti-Comintern Pact in early 1939 and withdraw from the League of Nations later that spring. After Germany's occupation of rump Czechoslovakia in March 1939, Hungary occupied, at German insistence, Ruthenian eastern Slovakia, acquiring 11,085 additional kilometers of territory and over one-half million new citizens. About 8,000 Slovakian Gypsies now came under Hungarian jurisdiction, which gave Hungary a Roma population of about 100,000. Hungary acquired further territory from the Third Reich in the Second Vienna Award in the summer of 1940. Designed to keep Hungary from seizing Transylvania, the Award gave Hungary an additional 2.5 million people and 43,104 square kilometers of land in northern Transylvania. Berlin now began to take a more direct role in Hungarian politics with the creation of a new, pro-German party, the Hungarian Revival and National Socialist Alliance. Teleki concluded afterward that the only way he could curb Germany's new influence and growing right wing extremism was to out-Nazi the Nazis by adopting "increasingly right-wing policies."[59]

Yet Teleki hesitated to move completely into the German camp in World War II, a move that seriously undercut his position in the government. Before his death in 1941, Teleki tried to shore up his ties with Germany by releasing Szálasi from prison, promising further anti-Jewish legislation, and making Hungary a member of the German-Italian-Japanese Tripartite Pact on November 20, 1940. In February 1941, his government "made plans to intern in work-camps all Gypsies who had no profession," a move applauded by the newspaper *Esti Újság* (Evening News), one of the official organs of Teleki's *Magyar Élet Pátja* (MÉP or Party of Hungarian Life). Pressured to side with the Reich after its invasion of Yugoslavia later that spring, Teleki committed suicide on the night of April 2, 1941, after failing to convince Horthy and the military to honor Hungary's friendship accord with Yugoslavia and remain a non-belligerent. His successor, László Bárdossy, Teleki's foreign minister, who supposedly had little use for the Nazis, quickly sided with the Germans and ordered Hungarian troops to invade Yugoslavia, "occupying the Báska and parts of the Vojvodina" [Délvidék] a week after he took office. Hungary acquired 11,000 square kilometers of new territory as a result of this move.[60]

Bárdossy's government quickly "implemented new measures of coercion and magyarization against the national minorities, whose proportion of the total population had now grown to more than a quarter." After the occupation of the Délvidék, Hungarian authorities ordered all Gypsies who had not been resident in Hungary before October 31, 1918, to leave the newly acquired territory. The Roma were allowed to take "personal belongings and enough money for the journey." Hungary's declaration of war on the Soviet Union five days after Hitler's June 22, 1941, invasion of that country placed Hungary fully in the Nazi camp and brought an increase in German pressure to deal more firmly with Hungary's Gypsy and Jewish populations. (According to 1941 census figures, there were 57,372 Rom [as defined by language], and 76,209 Rom [by nationality] in Hungary out of a total population of 14,679,573.)[61] The result of this pressure was the Third Jewish Law, which was in part "the expression of Hungary's indebtedness to the Reich for the reoccupation of Northern Transylvania and the Délvidék." The Third Jewish Law outlawed marriage between Jews and Christians and excluded Jewish employment in state government or involvement in Hungarian economic life. Other regulations at this time created special auxiliary service battalions for

Jews and forbade Jewish service in the remainder of the armed forces.[62] Hungarian reactionaries then turned their attention to Gypsies and promoted the theme of "After the Jews the Gypsies." The Hungarian press bemoaned the fact that "the handling and supervision of the 300,000 Gypsies cost the Government seventy-five million pengoes ($22,207,000) yearly—equal to the amount spent on diplomatic representation." Some "leading Magyar personalities" were "horrified and scandalized" by the fact that the Rom were intermarrying with lower-class Hungarians, "creating a large and dangerous stratum of half castes." Consequently, in the summer of 1942, the "Budapest Chamber of Agriculture petitioned the Government to introduce wholesale sterilization of all male Gypsies." *Esti Újság* "also urged labor camps as a 'radical solution of the Gypsy problem.'"[63]

However, Horthy's new prime minister, Miklós Kállay, had "reservations about National Socialism" and tried to steer the country away from its dependency on the Third Reich. Several months before Kállay entered office, Nazi officials had finalized plans for the eradication of Europe's Gypsies and the Final Solution against the Jews. Berlin began to pressure Kállay and Horthy to extend these programs into Hungary. Some anti-Semitic atrocities had already been committed by German forces at Kamenets-Podolsk in Hungarian-occupied Carpatho-Ukraine on August 27–28, 1941. Four months later, German and Hungarian troops were involved in the massacre of Jews in Novi Sad in the Délvidék, which outraged the Hungarian public. In the spring of 1943, Hitler demanded that "Hungary's Jews be sent to concentration camps or liquidated in the mass extermination camps in Poland" and began to work with pro-German factions in the country to pave the way for the Final Solution. However, the fall of Mussolini several months later prompted Horthy and Kállay to intensify "their efforts to create the preconditions for Hungary to get out of the war at the earliest opportunity," and by the early fall of 1943 they began to pull Hungarian forces back from the Eastern Front. Germany's disillusionment with Hungarian policies forced Kállay's dismissal on March 17, 1944, and two days later the Reich occupied Hungary. The new government of Lt.-General Döme Sztójay was dominated by members of the pro-Nazi National Socialist Party Alliance, who quickly began to implement pro-German policies. Aided by Hungarian gendarmes, Arrow Cross, and other paramilitary organizations, the government also began genocidal policies toward Hungary's Gypsies and Jews.[64]

Some Hungarian Gypsies had already been sent to the Gypsy Camp at Auschwitz-Birkenau on March 16, 1943, as part of a larger shipment of Austrian Rom. Of the Hungarian Gypsies, 14 men were members of the Petermann family (camp register numbers 3632–3639, 3649) and the Strauss family (register numbers 3628, 3640–3643). Most were executed within a few months of their arrival, though a few survived until 1944.[65] Nazi officials were initially occupied with the roundup of the country's 825,000 Jews and did not begin to deal with the Gypsies until the fall of 1944. In the interim, Horthy dismissed Sztójay and replaced him with General Géza Lakatos. After the Red Army invaded Hungary on September 23, Hungary entered secret negotiations with the Soviets in Moscow that would turn Hungarian forces against the Wehrmacht. When Horthy ordered the Hungarian army to stop fighting on October 15, the Germans kidnapped his son and forced Horthy to appoint Szálasi as prime minister. Gypsies now began to be rounded up by gendarmes and Arrow Cross and sent to special internment or transport camps as a reign of terror swept the country. According to the Hungarian War Victims Association, 28,000 Rom were shipped out of Hungary, and only 3,000 returned after the war. Donald Kenrick and Gratton Puxon estimate that 31,000 Hungarian Gypsies were deported by the Nazis. After World War II, 5,000 of the Roma who had been deported applied for special compensation. Other specialists estimate that 32,000 Hungarian Roma died during the Porajmos. Although there is much information on the remarkable efforts of Raoul Wallenberg, the Swedish diplomat, to save the lives of thousands of Hungarian Jews during this period, there is nothing to indicate that Wallenberg did anything to aid Hungary's Gypsies.[66]

Russian forces took Budapest on February 13, 1945, and on April 4, 1945, drove the last German troops out of the country. Hungary was now under Soviet military occupation. Backed by the Red Army and Stalin's blessings, Hungary's communist leader, Mátyás Rákosi, returned from Soviet exile to take control of Hungary's Communist Party and move the country along the path of full communization. Undeterred by a weak showing in elections on November 7, 1945, and April 31, 1947, Rákosi was able to orchestrate the slow transformation of the country into a Soviet satellite by 1948. He was aided by the transfer of over 600,000 former civil servants and military personnel "for reconstruction work" in the Soviet Union, and the forced expulsion of over 250,000 ethnic Germans and a large number of Slovaks in 1946–1947. This assault on the country's "ethnic fabric," combined with a growing emphasis on "Stalinist internationalism that branded emphasis on ethnic identity as a form of 'bourgeois ideology,'" discouraged Gypsies and other minorities from voicing ethnic preferences once the communists took power. Consequently, despite the new communist leadership's promise of support for full minority rights, few took them seriously. In Hungary's first postwar census in 1949, only 21,387 Gypsies chose Romani as their native tongue, though 31,000 chose Gypsy nationality out of a total population of 9,204,799.

Estimates are that there were probably at least 6,000 more Rom in Hungary at this time who chose not to identify themselves as Gypsies. Given the strong anti-minorities spirit in Hungary at the time, these figures were not out of line with statistics for other minorities. Over 98 percent of Hungary's population declared themselves ethnic Hungarians in this census.[67]

Authorities did give lip-service to minority needs, driven by the spirit of "automation, the expectation of the automatic elimination of the problem of nationalities through the erection of socialism." Special language schools were started, for example, that balanced classes in Hungarian and in the minority language, as well as and special teachers' colleges. (Germans were not provided with secondary schools until 1952, however, and teachers had no colleges until four years later.) The Gypsy question, however, was not addressed, and the Roma "were not seen as a 'national minority' but as a group 'excluded from capitalist society.'" It was presumed that in time, Gypsies, "along with other oppressed groups would disappear in the cauldron of the People's Republic."[68]

The death of Joseph Stalin in 1953, and the subsequent revolution in Hungary in 1956 after Nikita Khrushchev's attack on Stalin earlier that year, forced a new approach to minority questions under Hungary's new leader, János Kádár. On October 7, 1958, the ruling Hungarian Socialist Workers Party (*Magyar Szocialista Munkaspart* or MSzMP) decreed that "workers of nationality background, including university graduates, should be employed in areas inhabited by the same native speakers." Linked to growing concern over the plight of Hungarian minorities in neighboring countries, this statement signaled a new commitment to "a policy of active, legal support for the development of minority culture and education, and emphasized the importance of each minority's national organization in these efforts."[69]

On October 20, 1957, *Népakarat* (Popular Will) announced the creation of a Cigányszövetség (Gypsy Council), which disappeared two years later. In a census in 1960, only 25,633 Gypsies identified Romani as their native language, while another 14,230 Gypsies identified Rom as their nationality. Those who chose Roma identity almost always chose Magyar as their native tongue. Unofficial sources, though, estimated there were actually 180,000 to 200,000 Roma in Hungary at the time. One clue to the inaccuracy of these figures was enrollment statistics for Gypsy school children in 1957–1958, which showed 27,606 Rom attending public school throughout the country. Estimates are that about 60,000 of Hungary's Rom were assimilated or settled at this time, while a similar number were partly assimilated, and about 80,000 continued to live as nomads. If unofficial estimates were correct, then Hungary's Rom made up 2 percent of the country's population of 9,961,044.[70]

A resolution of the MSzMP's Central Committee on June 20, 1961, under-scored official concern over the growing Gypsy population and its problems. It noted that

> Although our laws do not contain provisions that could serve as the basis of discrimination against the gypsy population, they, especially in rural areas, are still up against the phalanx of prejudice. It is, for instance, a widely held belief that most gypsies are criminals, whereas criminal statistics show that the ratio of criminals among them is only slightly higher than among the non-gypsy population. The great majority of people still feel an almost irrational aversion to the gypsies. [According to the resolution (No. 2,014/1964),] the Political Committee establishes that ending the isolation of the gypsy population and its assimilation into our society are important social tasks made still more urgent by the size and grave backwardness of this group. Our policy must rest on the principle that despite certain ethnological traits, the gypsy population does not constitute a national minority. In order to help solve their problems, we must take their special social position into consideration. We must ensure the enforcement of their full rights and duties under the Constitution and must provide the political, economic and cultural conditions necessary to their implementation. The stand still taken by the population at large must be combated, for it impedes the assimilation, social, economic and cultural advancement of the gypsies.[71]

In fact, the government had been actively engaged for some time in an effort to counter the growing prejudice against the Rom. A 1958 article in *Népszabadság* (Peoples' Freedom), the official newspaper of the MSzMP, said that rural prejudice toward Gypsies often made it difficult for them to find proper homes, which was exacerbated by official grassroots dislike for the Roma. In 1959, *Népszabadság* decried anti-Gypsy feelings among Hungary's working class, saying it arose because of "discredited, inhuman racial theory." The current plight of the Gypsies, *Népszabadság* argued, arose because of "their centuries-old oppression and exclusion from society, which makes them live, still today, on the fringes of society." Other articles also condemned discriminatory hiring practices that created apartheid conditions for those whom many regarded as the "Brown Hungarians."[72]

The government also tried to improve the lot of the Gypsies through a housing program created in 1964 to destroy the most primitive Rom settlements in Hungary and make improvements in less objectionable homes "until they could be eliminated." Officials also set up a special interdepartmental committee to oversee "measures designed to improve the condition of the gypsy population." Razed Gypsy housing was replaced by homes built with low-interest government loans. Between 1965 and 1970, these funds were used to construct 2,500 new homes for the Roma, while between 1964 and 1975, the government "extended credit worth 700 million forints to the gypsy population to help them break away from the colonies." Unfortunately, there was still a great deal of substandard Rom housing in Hungary throughout its 2,100 Roma settlements. According to Secretary of State Lajos Papp, only about half of the homes in these "shanty towns" had a well, and two-thirds had no electricity. Furthermore, Gypsy homes were usually much smaller than non-Gypsy dwellings. Over 41 percent of Hungary's Roma lived in two-room homes, compared to 28.4 percent of the population nationally. Furthermore, 49.9 percent of Hungarians lived in three-room houses, compared to only 33.6 percent of the Gypsies. About two-thirds of Hungary's Rom lived in Gypsy settlements in the early 1970s, and about 40 percent of them lived in "poor shacks and wooden huts."[73] Authorities also opened 3,000 apartments for Roma throughout Hungary, but stopped Gypsy settlement in Budapest, whose Rom population had grown to between 40,000 and 50,000 by the early 1970s. By 1974, Budapest's Gypsy population had grown to 65,000, "many of whom lived in primitive quarters on the outskirts." About half of Budapest's Roma had "relatively acceptable accommodation," though city officials admitted that there were "2,350 [Gypsy] homes without running water and 1,500 without electricity."[74]

Hungarian novelist Menyhért Lakatos vividly described life for Budapest's Rom in a 1973 article in the journal *Forrás* (Source).

> Larger gypsy colonies within the administrative boundaries of the capital are clustered chiefly around the peripheral districts. There is substantial difference in the living conditions of those occupying overcrowded basements or converted shop premises in the outlying districts of the capital and those living downtown. The life-style of gypsies with grass roots in Budapest's downtown section is harmonious, they have good or acceptable standard of housing. They send their children to school, and we find many skilled workers and white-collar workers among them. Over 30 per cent have some sort of secondary education, and their standard of living equals the general level attained by the non-gypsy population. Nevertheless, they are immersed in permanent isolation. As regards their racial nature, external influences do not interrupt their everyday life; these people do not hide their gypsy background, though they do not boast about it either. These are the people who smile when praised and who do not fight against prejudice. Feeling at home in both worlds, they are reluctant to break with either. Their sole purpose in life is to create a petit-bourgeois existence for themselves.[75]

The government took a more positive view of its accomplishments and applauded efforts to eradicate substandard Rom housing. In a roundtable discussion on the Gypsy question published in *The New Hungarian Quarterly* in 1979, Papp boasted that the number of Rom living in "shanty towns" had dropped from 126,000 to 28,000 between 1969 and 1979. However, Andras Balint disagreed with this view in a 1983 article in *Heti Vilaggazdasag*. He felt that the program had failed, since by 1975 "only 18,000 of 55,000 Gypsy families had been able to improve their housing conditions." He did not put the blame for the failure totally on government shoulders but felt that the refusal of some older Gypsies to leave their "hovels" had also contributed to the program's failure. However, according to Gypsy expert Grattan Puxon, there were 100,000 Roma still living in "shanty" housing in the mid-1980s.[76]

Of equal concern to Hungarian officials were Gypsy educational deficiencies. When the government began its housing program in 1964, 30 percent of the Rom population was illiterate; seven years later, "39 per cent of gypsies past school-age were illiterate." In addition, "70 per cent of gypsies over the age of 59 had never gone to school, while the same is true of 50 per cent of the gypsies in the 35 to 39 age group." However, by the late 1970s, only 14 percent of the Gypsies born between 1953 and 1957 had not gone to school, a figure that dropped to 10 percent for those born between 1958 and 1963.[77] The reason for the decline in Gypsy illiteracy was an aggressive educational program initiated by the government in the 1960s that centered around the creation of "special classes that had been set up within the national school system for retarded or difficult children." This, however, amounted to "systematic segregation," which often led "to Gypsy withdrawal from school." Other Rom children were sent to boarding schools, where some did fairly well. In the 1970s, authorities began "to step up the pressure on the Gypsies through child-abduction on a considerable scale." As a result, almost 25 percent of the children in "special educational institutions," traditionally "for retarded or difficult children," were Gypsies in 1974–1975, and 11.7 percent of all Rom school children were in schools for the handicapped. These figures rose to 36 percent and 15.2 percent respectively over the next decade.[78]

In 1988, Hungarian sociologist L. Laki looked at the relationship between school attendance and educational attainment figures for Gypsy and non-Gypsy school children between 1970 and 1980. During this period, 23 percent of the students

> who had not completed general school by the age of fourteen were gypsies, [while] 42.9 per cent of gypsy fathers and 50.9 per cent of gypsy mothers had received no schooling whatsoever, compared with 12.1 per cent and 11.9 per cent respectively for non-gypsy fathers and mothers.

According to László Siklós, about 89 percent of the Gypsy children entering Hungarian schools during this period were Vlach Rom and had little knowledge of Hungarian. Some teachers felt that "the six-year old Gypsy child is equivalent to a 3, 4 or 5 year-old Hungarian child. From the first day at school he is at a disadvantage with the other six-year olds." The new Rom first grader often began school with a knowledge of "only about 30 to 40 Hungarian words." With 25 to 35 students in each class, Hungarian teachers had "no opportunity to teach the Hungarian language to the odd four or five Gypsy children." These deficiencies made the Gypsy children the brunt of their peers' criticism, while Hungarian parents complained that teachers spent too much time with their Roma pupils. This atmosphere, plus lack of family support, resulted in initial Gypsy dropout rates of 50 to 60 percent.[79]

In response, officials began to create special classes for Gypsies and opened a school for Rom children in Ráckeve. This reflected a growing conviction among Hungarian educators "that by providing appropriate social conditions at an early age, the effects of the handicaps can be decreased, halted or prevented." In addition, communities pitched in to make Gypsy children feel more at home in their new schools. In Kajdacs, "the local council allocated money for clothes," and several children got free day-care. Elsewhere, local community organizations gave Roma children

> shoes and clothing since with the first rain or during the winter the children could not go to school otherwise. They were also given textbooks, notebooks and pens and pencils, because Gypsy parents cannot buy them and without them school would have no meaning.

Yet, according to Andras Balint, even when Gypsy children got school supplies, they could not be taken home, since "they [were] immediately pounced upon and 'confiscated' and destroyed by his small brothers and sisters." In Szentetornya, Rom children received hot lunches, and an afterschool program was set up. These efforts were particularly important, since most "Gypsy children attend[ed] normal primary schools with normal curricula and their teachers [did] not receive any special training."[80]

Given the steady increase in Gypsy school enrollment (from 5.3 percent of Hungarian student totals in 1970–1971 to 6.2 percent nine years later), the Hungarian government could boast of some significant achievements in terms of retention and graduation for Roma students. By 1979, 71 percent more Gypsy children reached eighth grade than in 1970–71. Yet, according to Janos Gosztonyi, an under secretary in the Ministry of Education in 1979, "the ratio of Gypsy pupils in need of care in institutions for handicapped children is 28.5 per cent, that of mentally defective Gypsy children is 31 per cent."

Gosztonyi added that "half of the children accommodated in welfare centres are Gypsies." In addition, an article by Ferenc Partos in the journal *Szociologia* in 1980 showed that 39 percent of Gypsies over 14 were still illiterate, and only "21% of those 15 to 19 years old graduated from primary school, the remainder having dropped out."[81]

Unfortunately, efforts to improve the quality of Gypsy life in Hungary through better housing and educational programs had their limits. Authorities suppressed a commissioned study on Roma by the Hungarian Academy of Sciences in 1971 because of what its conclusions "revealed about the Gypsies' social conditions." One Hungarian specialist on the Gypsies, István Kemény, concluded that though the Roma had "in a certain sense been integrated by the early 1970s, [it] had taken place at the very bottom of the social hierarchy." Primarily concentrated in three counties of eastern Hungary, the Gypsies consistently lived in the worst housing and had the lowest educational achievement scores and salaries. The average size of the Roma family was 4.58, compared to the general national average family size of 3.18. Kemény noted that almost 25 percent of Hungary's Gypsy families were made up of 5 or more people versus only 6.6 percent of non-Gypsy Hungarian families. The average number of dependents per 100 was 224 for Gypsies and 82 for non-Gypsies. Low Roma salaries compounded these problems. Over 16 percent of Hungary's Rom families had annual salaries of 40,000–50,000 forints, compared to 6.4 percent of the non-Gypsy families nationally. Slightly over 28 percent of the country's Roma families had salaries in the 50,000–75,000 forint range, versus 26.4 percent of non-Gypsy families nationally, and 19.7 percent of Hungary's Roma families had salaries in the 75,000–100,000 forint range, 6.7 percent less than non-Gypsies families. According to an analysis by Nigel Swain of several recent studies on Rom in the Hungarian labor force, Gypsies were "found above all in the harder and dirtier jobs." They were also "disproportionately concentrated in cleaning jobs, in the construction industry and in the worst paid jobs on state farms." At a local parquet factory in Harangos,

> [Gypsy] workers stood in wood dust all day with no protective breathing equipment. At the slaughterhouse, a gypsy brigade did the foulest of disembowelling. In all these places gypsy labour constituted some 15–18 per cent of all manual labour, compared with 1.7 per cent of manual labour at the pleasantly situated lung clinic in the hills above the town. Average figures for the steel vat factory in Harangos . . . indicated that gypsies earned some 760 forints (that is, about one-fifth of the total wage) less per month than their Hungarian colleagues.

Swain concluded that "for all the reduction in inequality, unskilled workers, women, and gypsies were not highly prioritized in the new socialist system."[82]

Elsewhere, about 30 percent of Hungary's Rom had jobs as unskilled construction laborers, while 18–20 percent worked in "the agricultural sector" on state farms. Few gypsies were employed in the country's "agricultural producer co-operatives because 'the co-operatives often refuse to engage them [because] prejudice has deeper roots in the countryside and it is more difficult for them to integrate with the population.'"[83] According to Andras Balint, about three-quarters of Hungary's Roma were employed. He estimated that 70–85 percent of male Gypsies, and 25–40 percent of the women had steady work. About 75 percent of Gypsy laborers worked in industrial areas, though no more than 2–3 percent had skilled positions.[84] According to Mrs. Istvan Kozak, who was the head of the Council Office of the Council of Ministers and secretary of its interdepartmental committee on Gypsies, 8 percent of the Gypsies were skilled laborers in 1985 versus 30 percent of the country's non-Roma. About half of Hungary's Gypsies remained unskilled workers, compared to 12 percent nationally.[85] Consequently, by the early 1980s, at least 10 percent of the Roma population continued to live as nomads, while about 50 percent had stopped their wandering and settled in "Gypsy colonies or slums," although they were not fully assimilated into Hungarian society. Yet, according to *Heti Vilaggazdasag,* almost 40 percent of the country's Rom were fully integrated into society, meaning they did not "live in slums or colonies anymore; they have jobs; and their income reaches or at times exceeds the subsistence level of 2,700 forints per month."[86]

These problems were compounded by a Gypsy population whose growth was dramatically outpacing the growth of the general Hungarian population. According to the 1970 census, as defined by language, there were 34,957 Gypsies in Hungary, out of a total population of 10,322,099. However, a sociological survey a year later put the Rom population at 320,000, or 3.2 percent of the total population.[87] In 1977, officials estimated that Roma would make up 10 percent of Hungary's population by the year 2000. In 1980, there were approximately 340,000–360,000 Gypsies in Hungary, a figure that the author of a 1978 article in *Munkaugyi Szemle* (Review of Labor Affairs) thought would increase to 450,000–500,000 by 1990. What concerned many Hungarians about these figures were the tremendous Gypsy growth rates vis à vis the static or declining birth rates of the general Hungarian population, particularly in the 1980s.[88] Between 1984 and 1987, Hungary's population dropped slightly, from 10.7 million to 10.6 million, while Rom birth rates were doubling every 20 to 30 years. A concerned Imre Pozsgay, head of the MSzMP's Patriotic Peoples' Front (PPF), told a PPF gathering in late 1985 that though Hungary had an exemplary minorities' policy, it had to do more to integrate the Roma into Hungarian society and "halt the decline in Hungary's population."[89]

As part of this effort, the government realized in 1974 that it had to do more to organize the Rom along the lines of other minorities. It created a consultative *Cigányszövetség* (Gypsy Council) that year, though the only impact of the new Gypsy council was to "draw more attention to the plight of Hungarian Rom." In early 1978, the Politburo passed a resolution "to promote the fullest possible equality of the minorities through the consistent implementation of a Leninist line." While this pronouncement was aimed at the country's official national minorities, its spirit also affected Roma. According to an article that year in the journal *Kritika,*

> a suitable minorities policy should never strive for forced assimilation but for integration in society, in the course of which minorities can retain their characteristics, language, and culture. One should create a natural situation in which minorities can remain minorities.

As in the past, the thrust of this commitment to an equitable minorities' policy was an attempt

> to follow an optimal nationality policy and practice at the very center of the Danube Basin, which could serve as a model for the neighboring socialist countries in promoting the development of friendly relations and improving the lot of the Hungarian minorities living there.

Not all Hungarians, though, supported these policies, and some argued that "over the borders, they are far from being so generous toward the Hungarian ethnic minorities."[90]

The following year, the Council of Ministers' Resolution No. 1,019/1979 granted ethnic group status to the Roma. According to the newspaper *Magyar Hirlap,* the new status was, in "international terminology identical with a nationality group." The government's refusal to grant Gypsies full minority status was based officially on the fact that "75% of them speak only Hungarian." This decision deprived the Rom of the "advantages of this status as provided in the constitution," which, among other things, would enable them to have their own publications and organizations fully recognized by the government. In May 1985, the government created a new Gypsy organization, the Országos Cigánytanács (National Gypsy Council or NGC) to work in an advisory capacity with the PPF, a move spurred in part by a panel discussion at the UN several months earlier on the plight of the Roma in Hungary. The 35-member NGC was headed by poet Joszef Daroczi, while Agnes Bujdos, a physician, was selected as one of the NGC's vice chairpersons. Unfortunately, the NGC was only an advisory body working with the equally politicized PPF and had no legal authority to represent the country's Rom, another argument for full minority status.[91]

Among Daroczi's immediate goals was to organize handicraft associations to promote traditional Gypsy skills and the creation of a Rom newspaper. He felt this was particularly important, since the only other media outlet that dealt regularly with the Roma was "Blue Light," a television public-information show about solved and unsolved crimes, which treated Gypsies in a "one-sided" manner. Daroczi felt the Rom needed their own national organization linked to full minority status. He noted that when Gypsy delegates had been asked to a conference of Hungary's national minorities, the non-Rom delegates "walked out, asking 'what are the Gypsies doing here?'"[92] These actions spurred the government to further efforts regarding Gypsies. In April 1985, a cultural and advisory center was opened for Roma in Budapest's Thirteenth District. It helped organize programs on folklore, helped children of disadvantaged families prepare for school, and assisted educators working with adult Gypsies. Rom "literary evenings" were organized in other parts of the country with uneven success. A Gypsy festival was held in Budapest from May 28 to June 1, 1985, at the Istvan Pataki Cultural Center, which highlighted Gypsy culture and music performed by Roma. The event was so successful that plans were made to have "National Gypsy Artistic Days" in 1986. On July 18, 1985, Radio Budapest announced a new government resolution "on the improvement of the employment and professional training of the Gypsy population," spurred by a new study on the "Gypsies' situation."[93] Several years later, Gypsy intellectuals helped form the Tudományos Ismeretterjesztö Társulat (Hungarian Society for the Dissemination of Knowledge), which had as one of its goals better educational conditions for Rom children. In the spring of 1985, with substantial financial backing, authorities created the Romane Kulturake Ekipe (Rom Cultural Association) to oversee the country's burgeoning Gypsy cultural and artistic groups.[94]

In time, these efforts began to have a backlash effect that strengthened prejudice against Gypsies and subjected them to even more discrimination. Hungarians had long resented the heavy investment in Gypsy housing, education, and welfare and were particularly sensitive to these renewed efforts in the 1980s as the nation struggled to cope with the ravages of rising inflation and growing disillusionment with the policies and government of Janos Kádár. Of particular concern to public and government alike were Rom crime statistics. According to a 1985 article in *Heti Vilaggazdasag*, 7,000 to 8,000 Roma committed crimes each year, while *Borsod Szemle* (Borsod Review) reported that Gypsies "committed '40% of all burglaries, 60–65% of the thefts, half of all instances of rowdyism and rape, and 30–40% of homicides and attempted homicides'" in Borsod-Abunj-Zemplen County. These statistics plus television shows such as "Blue Light" fortified traditional stereotypes of Gypsies.[95]

A 1985 survey by Endre Hann showed that there had "been no improvement in public perceptions of Gypsies," while "being different in our society is regarded with a lot less tolerance than is desirable." He pointed to the case of a female visitor from Chile who, because people thought she was a Gypsy, "was the subject of insults, was spit at, and had to endure countless humiliations." Hann's study indicated that 28 percent of those surveyed "gave criminal behavior (violence, rowdyism, theft, and fraud)" as their reasons for disliking Rom, while 21 percent said they felt strongly against Gypsies because of their "exploitation of society, parasitism, begging, prodigality, and taking advantage of their situation." Another 11 percent of Hann's respondents cited Roma alcoholism as the root of their dislike of Gypsies. Hann felt that an irresponsible Hungarian media had helped create part of this negative public image and that while Gypsy crime rates were "out of proportion to their share of the population; when the crime rate of the disadvantaged strata as a whole was examined, it became not a Gypsy problem but one of society as a whole."[96]

Articles in *Napjaink* and *Magyar Ifjusag* (Hungarian Youth) in 1986 underscored the question of perceived Gypsy criminality. *Napjaink* informed its readers that "two-thirds of the inmates of the Tokol juvenile penitentiary" were Roma, while the National Police Headquarters said that Gypsy crime statistics were "twice as high" as their "share of the population." National Police figures claimed that Rom were responsible for "almost all of the robberies in the countryside and from 60–70% of robberies in cities and towns." Police officials also blamed the Gypsies for "about three-quarters of all cases of rowdyism."[97]

Hungary's belated political transformation in the late 1980s saw Kádár removed as head of the MSzMP in May 1988 and the gradual evolution toward a multiparty political system the following year.[98] In this atmosphere, a new sense of Rom national awareness began to be translated into political opportunism. In the summer of 1989, the National Gypsy Council, which was beset by infighting and corruption, asked the government to appoint a "commissioner to mediate among the organization's competing factions." At the same time, a number of new Gypsy organizations and political factions that represented Rom interests began to emerge throughout the country. One, Phralipe (Brotherhood), was formed in the spring of 1989 by Gypsy intellectuals who were uncomfortable with government policies toward the Roma and demanded "the observation of Gypsies' rights in the workplace and in their dealings with authorities." Phralipe also emphasized "the common destiny of Gypsies and Hungarians."[99]

Another Rom group, the Democratic Alliance of Hungarian Gypsies, was created in early 1989. Among its goals was the creation of Gypsy settlements throughout Hungary similar to "Israeli kibbutzim on large tracts of uncultivated land." Unfortunately, after the Alliance received a 3 million forint government subsidy to use in the December 1989 elections, "money corrupted some of the alliances's leaders," and intrigues and infighting became commonplace. Also formed in 1989 was the Hungarian Gypsy Party (HGP), which hoped to promote candidates in the spring 1990 elections, and the Hungarian Gypsies' Social Democratic Party (HGSDP), which had a membership of 15,000 by early 1990.[100] Hungary's first postcommunist national elections in the spring of 1990 gave several of the Rom parties their first taste of democratic politics. Unfortunately, preelection polls indicated that the largest Gypsy party, the HGP, had the support of only 1 percent of the respondents. What little influence the Roma parties did enjoy during this period came about because of ties with Hungary's new, mainstream political groups. Initially, the HGSDP linked up with the Hungarian Social Democratic Party (HSDP), but the two split in late March 1990 after the Gypsies accused the HSDP's leader, Anna Petrasovits, of breaking her promise to put Gypsy candidates on the HSDP's election list. The HGSDP also said, "Petrasovits had treated them offensively and only wanted to take advantage of the 'sister party.'" The short-lived alliance was of no consequence to the HSDP, which failed to win any seats in the Hungarian legislature.[101]

The Association of Free Democrats (AFD), which emerged after the March 25, 1990, elections as the second most important party in the country, allied with several Rom groups and "took the Hungarian Gypsies situation seriously in its program." The AFD "promised nationality status and government aid to the Gypsies," which garnered it some Rom support. On the eve of the second round of elections on April 8, the AFD supported the candidacy of four Gypsies for parliament. Two public school teachers, Antonia Haga and Aladár Horváth, were elected AFD representatives to the new legislature. The country's largest party, the Hungarian Democratic Forum (HDF), was also supportive of Gypsy issues, though "the public's perception of the HDF as a nationalist party probably did not increase its support among Gypsy voters." The HDF's minority program discussed the Gypsy problem at some length, though it was wrapped more in "idealistic statements" than in practical solutions.[102]

The Roma's new political voice and greater social presence created some problems. Antonia Haga said that one of the questions most frequently asked by Gypsies during her 1990 election campaign was how could they "defend themselves against violence." As early as 1986, a punk-rock *oi* group had surfaced that performed a song with the following words:

> The flamethrower is the only weapon I need to win, All Gypsy adults and children we'll exterminate, We can kill all of them at once in unison, When it's done we can advertise: Gypsy-free zone.

In Budapest, walls were sometimes spray-painted with the slogan "KTG" (Kill the Gypsy). Local elections in the fall of 1990 were marred by threats and violence against the Gypsies. These actions were buffeted by public attitudes measured in a Los Angeles *Times-Mirror* poll in 1991 that showed a 5 to 1 general dislike of Gypsies. The survey also showed that "anti-Gypsy sentiment was stronger among supporters of change (84% vs. 77%) and among those with higher (82%) and average (80%) levels of education." Another poll the same year by Freedom House and The American Jewish Committee indicated that 76 percent of its Hungarian respondents preferred not to have any Gypsies living in their neighborhoods, while 25 percent of those questioned felt Roma had too much influence in society. Almost 70 percent of the Hungarians questioned said that Gypsies behaved in a manner that provoked hostility.[103]

The new wave of violence against the Gypsies was linked to the perception that "a disproportionate share of convicted criminals" were Roma, a feeling of particular concern to a nation that saw its crime rate almost double between 1988 and 1990.[104] According to *Der Spiegel,* much of the crime committed by Roma merely fed existing stereotypes of them, particularly scenes of "begging women with whimpering babies in downtown Budapest; gypsies in the black market; young gypsy women offering their bodies to westerners near the big hotels along the Danube." Furthermore, Budapest police estimated in 1990 that "80 percent of all burglaries and 95 percent of all pocket pickings are committed by gypsies," figures that Roma legislator Antonia Haga said were probably true. Yet the reason for such statistics, she argued, was ongoing Gypsy poverty. The Ministry of Welfare reported that an extremely disproportionate number of the country's homeless population were Gypsies, while national Gypsy unemployment rates reached 40 to 45 percent by the latter part of 1993, almost triple the national unemployment rate of 14 percent. In the Hungarian town of Òzd, almost 90 percent of its Roma were unemployed. According to the head of Ozd's Council on Minorities, "People are stealing because they are hungry."[105]

While Gypsy leaders like Antonia Haga blamed Roma crime on economic and social inequities, other Gypsy leaders such as Géza Reményi, the president of the Hungarian Gypsies' Justice Union, blamed it on Vlach Roma. Reményi claimed that this group made up only 28.1 percent of the country's total Rom population, the rest being assimilated Hungarian Gypsies. He added that Hungary's prisons were full of Vlach Roma, who were "all thieves and robbers" and responsible for the bad reputation of other Gypsies in Hungary. Reményi was also critical of "those protecting Gypsy criminals in the name of humanitarian slogans: 'a murderer is a murderer, no matter what ethnic group he belongs to. Let the hand of justice clamp down on him.'"[106] Rom difficulties were also exacerbated by the large influx of foreigners from other parts of Eastern Europe after 1989, particularly Romania and the former Yugoslavia. Though most new immigrants were law-abiding, some, including Gypsies, were "involved in underground activities or dubious business deals." In 1991–1992, there were 131,000 legal aliens in Hungary and another 50,000 illegal residents. In 1991, 33 million foreigners entered Hungary, many as tourists, while in the first six months of 1992, border officials turned 500,000 foreigners away.[107]

As the government struggled with ways to tighten its entry requirements, a number of extremist groups began to deal with the tremendous influx of foreigners in their own way. In Budapest, for example, there were about 450 hardcore skinheads, with some 1,000 sympathizers, while nationwide, there were about 2,500 skinheads. Police attributed most cases of racial violence to these individuals and groups but emphasized that their "primary target is not foreigners but Gypsies living in Hungary." In the fall of 1990, skinhead gangs of 80 to 100 members attacked Rom ghettos in Eger and Miskolc. They beat innocent pregnant women, children, and elderly people and ransacked apartments in the Gypsy settlements. In September 1992, the homes of two Rom families in Kétegyhaza were firebombed and their inhabitants beaten by local peasants. Two months later, a Gypsy was beaten to death by street thugs, while a farmer shot two Gypsies for stealing pears. This atmosphere was not helped by statements in August 1992 by Istvan Csurka, the vice president of the Hungarian Democratic Forum, that blamed some of the country's difficulties on "genetic reasons," a statement viewed by some as "an allusion to Gypsies." The following month, Aladár Horváth responded to the violence in a speech before parliament. Horváth said that the government "completely disregards the interests of the Roma minority" and that "its policies have openly deepened the Roma people's misery." Horváth demanded full minority rights for Hungary's Gypsies and said the Roma still had faith in the Hungarian people's "sense of justice." He also hoped "the Hungarian Republic does not further increase the deprivation, misery, defenselessness, and humiliation of our people. We have no other choice but to help each other." The rising violence against Gypsies and others saw a number of foreign students transferring to safer universities in Czechoslovakia, Romania, and Russia or simply going home. The following summer, in Eger, more than a thousand Gypsies and their supporters demonstrated peacefully against racism and fascism. The group's leaders said that Hungary's "fledgling democracy could only be secure when the country rejected such extremism." Officials had already intensified efforts to crack down on these hate groups, and in late 1992, 48 skinheads were imprisoned for their attacks. On February 2, 1994, the government initiated criminal proceedings against two members of one organization, the World National Popular Rule, and requested its dissolution, since it had "violated the constitution by inciting hatred against minorities," particularly against Gypsies and Jews.[108]

In addition to intensified crackdowns on racial extremists, Hungarian authorities had also been working since independence to strengthen minority rights for all groups. Constitutional changes in the summer of 1990 declared that the country's "national and ethnic minorities living in Hungary 'share[d] in the power of the people and [were] constituent elements.'" The constitution now insured full protection for these groups as well as their "collective participation in public life, the cultivation of their own culture, the use and instruction of their mother tongue, and the use of names in their original ethnic form." The changes also allowed minorities to set up their own local and national organizations and called for the creation of a special legislative committee to deal with ethnic questions. In early 1991, the parliament granted 200 million forints to aid all new minority organizations, with over 40 percent of these funds going to Roma groups. The result was an explosion of Gypsy organizations that totaled almost 1,000 by 1993, though only 200 of them were officially registered with authorities. Unfortunately, Horváth noted, some of these groups were made up of no more than "two or three members" and were created solely "to receive funds from the state."[109]

On July 7, 1993, the Hungarian parliament passed a new Law on the Rights of National and Ethnic Minorities, which specifically mentioned the Roma among the groups that had lived in Hungary for at least a century. The new law was based on the 1990 constitutional changes and outlawed "every form of discrimination against minorities." It guaranteed "equal opportunity" for minorities and said that they had the right to use their "mother tongue in the parliament, in government agencies, and in the courts." In areas with significant ethnic concentrations, officials had to speak "the language of these minorities" and permit the erection of "bilingual street signs." It also stipulated that special self-governing groups could be set up in areas where over 30 percent of the population belonged to a particular ethnic group. Once established, these groups had the right to set up their own schools and other institutions. The new legislation recognized the special needs of Gypsies and talked of "aims to compensate them for their social disadvantages." However, according to Zsolt Csalog of the Raoul Wallenberg Society, the new law "would not go far enough to protect gipsies, who often find police unwilling to investigate crimes against them." While no single piece of legislation can correct centuries of abuse and socioeconomic dislocation, Hungary's new minority law has finally granted Roma their long-cherished official minority status. This, combined with the emergence of a new generation of Rom politicians, should at least keep the complex issues facing Hungary's large Gypsy population on the nation's political, social, and economic front burners, a prerequisite for any long-range solution to the problems that face this ethnic community. Perhaps the greatest issue, though, is the mutual fear and distrust that clouds relations between Hungary's Gypsies and non-Gypsies, a problem that lies beyond the scope of any legislative solution.[110]

.4.

ROMANIA

There is some disagreement over when Gypsies began to enter Romania, though most evidence supports Nicolae Gheorghe's contention that they arrived in Wallachia in the twelfth century and later in Moldavia. Their presence in the region predates the creation of Wallachia in the early fourteenth century by Voivode Basarab, as well as that of Moldavia in the mid-1300s. Known to Hungarian rulers as Cumania, Wallachia and Moldavia initially served as Hungarian outposts against incursions by the Crimean Tatars, successors to the Mongols. The Mongol invasion of southeastern Europe via Russia in 1241–1242 had temporarily halted Hungary's move into Transylvania and stimulated efforts by Wallachia's voivode (princes) to assert their independence from Hungary. Moldavia found itself threatened by the Crimean Tatars and by Poland, which desired Moldavia's strategic trade outlets. Both principalities found themselves increasingly threatened by the region's new power, Ottoman Turkey, by the end of the fourteenth century, while Wallachia continued to guard against Hungarian incursions. It was in this atmosphere that the earliest concrete evidence of Romanian Gypsies surfaces. On October 3, 1385, a document issued by Voivode [Prince] Dan I (r. 1385–1386) to the Monastery of the Virgin Mary at Tismana confirmed an earlier gift of 40 Roma families to the Monastery of St. Anthony at Vodita from his uncle, Voivode Vladislav.[1]

Three years later, Voivode Mircea the Elder made a gift of 300 Roma families to the Cozia Monastery, and in 1428, Voivode Alexander the Good gave "31 tents of *tsigani* [Gypsies] and 13 tents of Tatars" to the monastery at

Bistrita. The Gypsies given to these monasteries were slaves, a condition unique to the Gypsies and the Crimean Tatars of Wallachia and Moldavia. Their plight came about as a result of war, as Roma captured during Tatar raids were enslaved by Romanian princes. In time, the practice became more widespread as Gypsies filled a void between the social classes, becoming, in essence, the Romanian working class. Gypsy skills were absolutely essential to the transport business of Wallachia and Moldavia, which ended under the Turks in the sixteenth century. Gypsy slaves (*robi*) were at the bottom of the Romanian social pyramid, which centered around free peasants or serfs. Free Wallachian and Moldavian peasants had "inherited their land as a family group from a common ancestor," and only owed the local prince a *djima* (tithe). Serfs owed feudal dues, which consisted of one-third to one-half of the crops they grew on land leased by the landlord as well as "statute labor, mainly carting work." The Gypsy *robi* worked primarily as craftsmen or blacksmiths for princely courts or large monasteries, while Tatar slaves functioned as farm hands. Tatar slaves had no rights and could be sold as ordinary property.[2]

By the 15th century, Gypsy slavery had become widespread throughout the Romanian provinces. In 1445, Vlad Dracul (the Devil), the father of Vlad Tepeş (the Impaler), the historic Dracula, forcibly brought back to Wallachia "11,000–12,000 persons, without luggage and animal, who looked like Egyptians," from successful campaigns in Bulgaria against the Turks. Romanian Gypsy specialist Nicolae Gheorghe concluded that Dracul's prisoners were Roma. Vlad Tepes supposedly enjoyed mistreating Gypsy slaves. According to one apocryphal story befitting the Dracula myth

> He invited them [Gypsy slaves] to a festival, made them all drunk, and threw them into the fire. Another amusement of his was the construction of an enormous cauldron, into which he thrust his victims. Then, filling it with water, he made it boil, and took pleasure in the anguish of the sufferers. When the people whom he impaled writhed in agony, he had their hands and feet nailed to the posts. Some were compelled to eat [a] man roasted.

In 1471, Prince Stephen the Great of Moldavia invaded Wallachia to replace its ruler, Radu the Handsome, who had fallen under Ottoman influence. Stephen routed Radu's forces, forced him from the Wallachian throne, and replaced him with his own candidate, Basarab Laiota. Stephen then returned to Moldavia with "over 17,000 *Tsigani* (Gypsies) in order to use their labour forces." Gheorghe feels, however, that "these large numbers of captives might have been an exaggeration in order to demonstrate Romanian victories."[3]

By the early sixteenth century, Wallachia and Moldavia, which had resisted Ottoman vassal status for over a hundred years, succumbed to Turkish pressure and became Ottoman tributary states. This required both kingdoms to pay a yearly tribute to the Porte and supply the empire with exports, namely foodstuffs. In return, Wallachia and Moldavia retained full control over their internal affairs. The Romanian peasant, whose lot had already been reduced in the fifteenth century to semi-serf status, saw his position decline further under the Romanian boyars over the next century. According to P. N. Panaitescu, from "this time forward the destiny of the Tziganes is so closely allied with that of the peasants that it is impossible to speak of the enslaved Gypsies without mentioning at the same time the enslaved peasants."[4]

The Roma in Wallachia and Moldavia retained their positions as craftsmen and monopolized the smith trade. Referred to in early documents as "*sclavi, scindromi*, or *robie*," in time they were broken down into distinct occupational categories. According to Ian Hancock, there were two main groups of Romanian *robi*: "house slaves (*ţigani de casaţi*) and field slaves (*ţigani de ogor*)." The state's domestic *robi* were "the *sclavi domneşti* (noblemen), *sclavi curte* (court) and *sclavi gospody* (householders)." The nobility's field slaves were known as *sclavi coevesţi*, while those of small farmers were called *sclavi de mosii*. The Crown owned three types of *robi*, the "*rudari* (or *aurari*) or goldwasher," the "*ursari* or beartrainer," and the "*lingurari* or carver of wooden spoons." Some Gypsy slaves, the *laieşi*, had a little freedom of movement because of their varied occupations, particularly the "*lautari* or musicians (properly 'fiddlers')." The *sclavi monastiveşti* owned by the Orthodox Church's monasteries included "*vatraşi*, who were grooms, coachmen, cooks and petty merchants, and numbers of *laieşi*." The various skills of the "*laişei*" have supplied the names of some of the *vici*, or clans, found among the contemporary Vlax (i.e. 'Wallachian' or Danubian) Gypsies: *kirpači* 'basket-makers', *kovači* 'blacksmiths', *zlatari* 'goldwashers', *čurari* 'sieve-makers', *chivuţe* 'whitewashers' and so on."[5]

More restrictive laws were passed during this period to strengthen the institution of Gypsy slavery. By the end of the 15th century, any non-Gypsy who got a Rom woman pregnant, and then chose to marry her, had to become a slave. Equally demeaning was the castration of certain *sclavi domneţti*, the *skopici*, "who had been castrated as boys and whose job it was to drive the coaches of the women of the aristocracy without their being in fear of molestation." As the value of Gypsy *robi* increased, a steady trade in kidnapped Roma slaves developed "on the frontier areas in the Balkans and Central Europe." Raids by *ghazis* (or *akindjis*, or raiders) prompted one Wallachian *voivode* to protest these activities to the Porte in 1560. He hoped royal intervention "would stop the leakage [of kidnapped Gypsy slaves] across the Danube," since it deprived the *voivode* of property and potential revenue.[6]

Over the next century, new laws were passed that strengthened the boyars' control over their Rom slaves. In 1652, a Moldavian prince, Vasile Lupu (Basil the Wolf), had a number of laws on Gypsies in his 40 article *Pravila cea Mare* (Great Code):

> If the Gypsy slave of a boyard or any other proprietor, his woman or one of their children steal once, twice or thrice a chicken, a goose or any other trifle, they shall be pardoned; but if they steal something more valuable, they shall be punished like robbers.
>
> A slave who rapes a woman shall be condemned to be burnt alive.[7]

The status of Roma worsened in the eighteenth century as Wallachia and Moldavia lost much of their earlier autonomy to a new, Phanariot line of Ottoman-appointed rulers. Totally subservient to Istanbul, Romania's new *hospodars* (governors or lords) introduced an era of ongoing political instability in both provinces during the Phanariot era (1711–1821). It was also a period of tremendous suffering for the peasants, who were "plunged into utter misery" by greedy Phanariots, noblemen, the Orthodox Church, and others who tried to exact as much profit as possible from peasant labor. Between 1741 and 1746, over 52 percent of Wallachia's peasant families fled the province to escape economic oppression.[8]

Some efforts were taken to ameliorate the plight of the peasants during this period. In 1726, Hospodar Mihai Rakovit of Moldavia outlawed the taxation of Gypsies as being "of no benefit to the country," while two decades later, between 1744 and 1749, Constantin Mavrocordato, who was *hospodar* of Moldavia on four occasions and ruled Wallachia five times, issued decrees in both provinces that tried to improve conditions for the peasantry by reducing their tax burdens and outlawing serfdom. Peasant conditions had deteriorated so much that the "'vecini' ('neighbors,' villagers who had originally been prisoners of war, and were tied to the soil)," were "in fact treated on the same footing as the 'robi'—a class of veritable slaves recruited from among the gipsies." Mavrocordato's April 6, 1749, *Act pentru desrobire teranilor in Moldavia* ordered that the emancipated *vecini* were not to be treated as *robi*, and thus "not be separated from their homesteads and family." Furthermore, they were only obligated to pay the "tithe and to do twenty-four days service annually." On the other hand, Mavrocordato reconfirmed the status of the Gypsy slaves in his Uricariul (Charter) of 1749, which stated that

> Les tziganes sont complètement asservis et doivent avec femmes et
> enfants servir d'une manière permanente leurs maîtres.

Furthermore, Mavrocordato's successor, Grigore Ioan, declared in his charter of July 3, 1753, that any vagrant Rom who did not belong to a boyar or to the Church automatically became "the property of the State," a condition not without benefits, since state *robi* "had a certain degree of liberty," though they had to pay taxes. When Mavrocordato returned to power in Moldavia in 1756, he sponsored legislation stating that Roma children "could no longer be sold without their parents." Unfortunately, these reforms proved to be illusory because of Mavrocordato's limited power over the Church and the nobility, who strongly resisted them.[9]

To maintain control over Roma slaves, officials kept constant watch over their activities and personal habits. On January 25, 1766, Wallachian *hospodar* Alexander Ghica emancipated Gypsies married to Moldavians but declared that the husband, "and any of their children over seven years of age, would have to continue to work for their previous owner." The same year, Moldavian *hospodar* Constantin Moruz outlawed marriages between Gypsies and non-Gypsies. Any priest who married such couples would be removed from the priesthood and fined. If such marriages continued to occur, the couple would be forced to divorce. All priests in Moldavia had to sign a pledge that they had read the *hospodar*'s decree, and after June 18, 1766, Moldavians who had married Roma were to inform authorities of these marriages. In return, they would "obtain mercy . . . and justice." Nineteen years later, officials reaffirmed the illegality of mixed marriages, because they were "causing individuals with Rumanian blood to become slaves."[10]

The unchanged status of Romanian Gypsy slaves centered around the boyars' total dependency on their talents:

> The Gypsy slaves were almost the only artisans. The Boyard had everything he needed on his estate: cooks, bakers, postilions, gardeners, masons, shoemakers, blacksmiths, musicians, labourers, other classes of workers—and all of them were Tziganes. The Gypsy women helped the mistress of the house with her work, and they were on such good terms that they were even allowed to assist in the beautiful embroidery done by the young Rumanian women which is admired throughout the world.

Other accounts detail a boyar life of genteel, self-contained isolation sustained by Gypsy slave labor. If the boyar

> thought it necessary [he] could close his gates and live for months
> at a time with his family, his women servants and his men—80 to
> 100 of them (Tziganes)—without having the slightest need of those
> who lived outside . . . in those quarters where the Gypsies lived were
> expert bakers, tailors, shoemakers, etc.

Consequently, any significant alteration in the status of Wallachia's and Moldavia's Gypsy populations would have to be part of even greater changes in the two principalities.[11]

The dramatic upheavals that swept the region during the Napoleonic Wars and afterward provided such an atmosphere. Oddly enough, it was Russia, already handicapped by its own oppressive serf system, that provided the impetus for a change in the plight of Romania's Gypsies. Tsar Alexander I (r. 1801–1825) had occupied and "devoured" Wallachia and Moldavia from 1808 to 1812, while his younger brother, Nicholas I (r. 1825–1855), took control of the provinces in 1829 after a successful war against Turkey. Russian forces were to remain in the area until the Turks had completely paid the war reparations laid out in the Treaty of Adrianople of September 14, 1829. Russia's Plenipotentiary of the Divans of Wallachia and Moldavia, Pavel D. Kiselev, found the provinces in a deplorable condition eight years after the collapse of the Phanariot dynasty and was "sickened by the concept of slavery on moral grounds." According to an account a decade earlier by British diplomat William Wilkinson,

> There does not perhaps exist a people labouring under a greater
> degree of oppression from the effect of despotic power, and more
> heavily burdened with impositions and taxes than the peasants of
> Wallachia and Moldavia, nor any who would bear half their weight
> with the same patience and seeming resignation. The habitual
> depression of their minds has become a sort of natural stupor and
> apathy, which renders them equally indifferent to the enjoyments of
> life and insensible to happiness.

Wilkinson, who included a lengthy section on Gypsies in his *An Account of the Principalities of Wallachia and Moldavia* (1820), expressed disgust at their plight. Boyar kitchen slaves, for example, were forced to work in conditions "not less disgusting than the common receptacles of swine," while recalcitrant Gypsies were punished with the *bastinado,* which was "applied to the naked soles of the feet," or by

> passing the culprit's head through a kind of iron helmet, with two
> immense horns of the same metal, and locking it under the chin in

such a manner as to render it extremely troublesome to the bearer, and to keep him from eating or drinking.

Though Gypsies made up "a necessary part of the community," Wilkinson noted, they "were held in the greatest contempt by the other inhabitants, who, indeed, treat them little better than brutes."[12]

Pavel Kiselev, who had his own ideas about Rom slavery, "was initially quite determined to see it abolished." However, opposition from local boyars and the transitory nature of Russia's presence in Wallachia and Moldavia convinced him instead to try to counter the plight of the peasants and *robi* with a program that would "construct a social base of support for Russian power among the peasants." It centered around reforms that would "eliminate the most offensive abuses which local officials inflicted upon the peasants." As early as 1816, Kiselev had written Alexander I that the "absolute and arbitrary power which the landlords wielded over their serfs must be curtailed by the precise definition of the obligations which lord and peasant had to each other." His Reglement Organique of 1831–1832 followed these guidelines and emphasized the right of the nobility "to retain full title to all their lands," while the peasantry could "leave their masters if they wished." The result of this spirit was to create "the slavery of labour service" for the peasants. The *Reglement*'s Gypsy clauses were laid out along the same lines, and better defined the status of the Gypsies, and "strengthened their owners' control over them." It also set up a "fund for redeeming the Tsigans from vagrancy, and obliging them to build houses and dwell in them." According to Ian Hancock, some Gypsy *robi* were so moved by Kiselev's efforts that

> they promised him as much gold as a horse could carry if he would abolish slavery. Kisselef, however, reacted with anger; He accused the Gypsies not only of trying to bribe him, but of stealing some of the gold they had washed from the rivers. Because of this, he said, they would have to remain slaves forever.

Kiselev's attitudes reflected the gradualist approach to emancipation of Nicholas I.[13]

In 1833, a year before Russia ended its occupation of Wallachia and Moldavia, Kiselev enacted a new Penal Code with Gypsy slave clauses. The Moldavian code said:

> Legal unions cannot take place between free persons and slaves.

> Marriage between slaves cannot take place without their owner's consent.

> The price of a slave must be fixed by the Tribunal, according to his age, condition and profession.
>
> If anyone has taken a female slave as a concubine she will become free after his death. If he has had children by her, they will also become free.

Special provisions were laid out in the new criminal laws for the Netoci, nomadic Rom feared by Gypsy and non-Gypsy alike. Described as "half savage, half naked, living by theft and rapine, feeding in times of want upon cats, dogs and mice," they were to be captured and "distributed between the landowners and the state."[14]

This general condition of degradation was shared in varying degrees by all Wallachian and Moldavian Roma. Most demeaning were the slave auctions. One 1834 scene described the horror that stimulated some Romanians to begin to reconsider the institution. Barbu Ştirbei, a wealthy landowner, needed funds to redo his palace and thus auctioned 3,000 Gypsy slaves in Bucharest to pay for the renovations. At the auction,

> passers-by quicken[ed] their steps and lower[ed] their eyes so that they [didn't] have to look at the men and women tearing at their rags in anguish. Dishevilled, dark-skinned, these are Gypsies. You can't escape the entreaties of the mothers whose children are being torn from them, nor their sobs and screams of fear, nor their curses; you can't escape the cracking of the whips breaking down their stubborn resistance to the separations inevitably to come.

It is interesting that one of the first proponents of Gypsy slave emancipation was Ştirbei. An important member of the committee that wrote the Reglement Organique, he was so disturbed by public reaction to the sale of his *robi* that he "hurriedly suggested abolition as a means of regaining face—but this was at once overridden by the boyars."[15]

In some ways, Gypsy slavery had come to symbolize the backwardness of Moldavia and Wallachia, while efforts to eradicate it indicated broader changes in the provinces' political, social, and economic landscapes. In 1837, Mihail Kogălniceanu, the liberal writer, social critic, and later one of the architects of Romanian nationhood, described his childhood memories of *robi*:

> I saw human beings wearing chains on their arms and legs, others with iron clamps around their foreheads, and still others with metal collars about their necks. Cruel beatings, and other punishments such as starvation, being hung over smoking fires, solitary imprisonment

and being thrown naked into the snow or the frozen rivers, such was the fate of the wretched Gypsy.

The same year, Alexander Ghica, the vain, ineffective governor of Wallachia from 1834 to 1842, freed his state slaves and "granted them equal status with the white peasants who worked for him." He also permitted his former *robi* to practice their customs and speak Romani. Some were "settled in villages, where the boyars were charged with giving them work as peasants." Though there is some disagreement over the number of Roma slaves affected by Ghica's efforts, it was a significant beginning. Wilkinson said there were 150,000 Gypsy slaves in the provinces in 1820, while Kogălniceanu estimated there to be 200,000 *robi* in 1837. According to Tihomir Gjorgjević, there were 3,851 Rom slave families in Moldavia and 33,000 *robi* families in Wallachia. Of this latter number, 14,158 Wallachian Rom were servants, while 5,635 were state slaves who worked as gold-gatherers.[16]

In 1842, Mihail Sturdza, the *hospodar* of Moldavia and a strong admirer of Tsar Nicholas I, emancipated state *robi* as part of a reform effort "to lift Moldavia from the slough of primitive stagnation and instil modern ideas of government." Two years later, Sturdza freed Moldavia's Church slaves, an act duplicated three years later by Gheorghe Bibescu, the Paris-educated, romantically nationalistic *hospodar* of Wallachia. In some ways, these efforts mirrored the spirit of Russian attitudes on serf emancipation. Kiselev's occupation of Moldavia and Wallachia ended with the Convention of St. Petersburg in early 1834, which forced Turkey to acknowledge the Reglement Organique, and made Russia the "spokesman on behalf of the Principalities." In the future, any significant reforms in the principalities came under the watchful eyes of Russia's consuls.[17]

When Kiselev returned to Russia, Nicholas I immediately sought his "views on serfdom." In 1836, Kiselev became Nicholas I's chief of staff for Peasant Affairs, and, a year later, his minister of State Domains. The tsar charged Kiselev with drafting legislation to lessen the plight of Russia's serf population. And although Nicholas I admitted in 1842 that serfdom was "evil," and "palpable," he felt "to touch it *now* would be still a more disastrous evil." The Russian emperor, however, had no difficulty encouraging emancipation in Wallachia and Moldavia, as long as it was done in the spirit of the Reglement Organique. Russia's heavy-handed presence in the principalities stimulated the budding Romanian opposition movement, which centered around concern over "Russian interference and princely subservience." The only common ground between the provinces' Russophiles and the new opposition was concern over the plight of the Gypsies.[18]

A year after Bibescu freed Wallachia's Church *robi,* the revolutionary fervor enveloping Europe swept into the principalities. In Moldavia, reform-minded leaders such as Kogălniceanu and Alexander Cuza, who later became prince of Moldavia, petitioned Sturdza to initiate individual liberties and other reforms "taken from the French model." Nothing was mentioned in the request about the Gypsies, "peasants, nor independence or union of the provinces." Sturdza responded by ordering the arrest of Cuza and others, which quickly brought unrest in Moldavia to an end.[19] Revolutionary events in Wallachia were more complex and threatening. Stimulated by liberals just returned from Paris, where the French king, Louis Philippe, had been toppled and replaced by a provisional government, a Wallachian revolutionary committee developed a program similar to the one in Moldavia, with additional provisions for peasant emancipation and land redistribution. On June 21, 1848, the Wallachian revolution began with the public reading of a declaration in Islaz, which added, in addition to previous demands, an end to being a foreign protectorate, the election of a prince for five years, a representative assembly, and the emancipation of the Jews and Gypsies. Its statement on Rom emancipation declared, "The Rumanian nation shakes off the inhumanity and disgrace of slave-holding and proclaims the freedom of privately-owned Gypsies." On June 23, Gheorghe Bibescu, who had initially hoped to arrest the coup's leaders, accepted the Islaz Declaration and created a revolutionary cabinet. He then fled to Transylvania. The new government immediately pledged its loyalty to the Turks and sought European support "for their 'interest and mediation in the work of regeneration.'"[20]

The growing threat of Turkish and Russian intervention prompted efforts to negotiate with Turkey. Suleiman Pasha, the Turkish commissioner sent to deal with the Wallachians, was so impressed with his reception that he told one official that there "was only one thing still wanting—the union of the two Principalities. That would be a stake in the entrails of Russia." Nicholas I responded with criticism of Wallachia's revolution and the idea of unification. On September 25, 1848, Turkish forces took Bucharest. Two days later 45,000 Russian troops entered Wallachia and Moldavia.[21] The joint occupation of Wallachia brought the revolution to an end as its leaders fled into exile. Russia and Turkey declared the reestablishment of the Reglement Organique, and on May 1, 1849, they concluded a new agreement on the two provinces at Balta Liman. The accord provided for the joint appointment of new *hospodars* as "high functionaries" of Wallachia and Moldavia for seven years. The new *hospodars* would appoint Divan Ad Hoc with extremely limited powers to replace the representative assemblies. Grigore Alexandru Ghica became the new prince of Moldavia, and Barbu Ştirbei was named to rule Wallachia.[22]

Transylvania was infected by the same revolutionary spirit in the spring of 1848, and on March 24, Romanian nationalists in Transylvania demanded the "recognition of the Romanians as a 'nation' alongside the other three traditional 'nations,' and the abolition of serfdom." Conflicts soon arose between Romanian and Hungarian nationalist aspirations, while peasants became disillusioned with the pace of serf emancipation. The Romanians took matters into their own hands on May 15–17, 1848, with a gathering later termed the Blaj National Assembly. Simeon Bărnuţiu, an educator from Blaj, addressed the delegates first, saying that Romanians would only join a Hungarian state if all of its people were granted "the same rights whatever their racial group." This was followed by a petition that, among other things, abolished serfdom without compensation. Hungarian leaders rejected the demands of Transylvania's Romanians, which forced Romanian nationalists into the arms of the Austrians. As a result, Romanian units joined Habsburg forces to destroy Hungarian power in Transylvania. This was only accomplished, however, in the summer of 1850 after a desperate appeal by Austria's new, young emperor Francis Joseph (r. 1848–1916) to Tsar Nicholas I, who responded by sending 40,000 soldiers into Transylvania and 100,000 into the Carpathians via Galicia. Within a few months, more than 350,000 Russian troops had entered Hungary and Transylvania. Afterwards, Transylvania was detached from Hungary and given Grand Principality status, though the Austrians did not emancipate the serfs as they had done in Hungary. The province's 70,000 Gypsies used their new freedom "to move, and many did, to swell the Gypsy colonies in the towns."[23]

The Russo-Turkish occupation of Wallachia and Moldavia ended in 1851, the same year as a highly publicized sale of Moldavian Gypsy slaves by the estate of Aleku Sturdza, the former Moldavian minister of finance. The sale of 104 Gypsy families, which consisted of 349 individuals, symbolized the prevalence of Rom slavery in Wallachia and Moldavia despite the earlier emancipation of state and Church slaves. The *robi* auctioned at the Sturdza sale were primarily Lăieši, whose occupations were listed as "Ferariu and its Moldavian equivalent Herariu, 'smith,' Kantarąiu, 'weigher,' Kobzariu, 'goldsmith,' . . . Ciurariu 'sieve-maker' . . . and Pădureanu 'forester.'"[24] In some way, the continuing existence of privately owned slaves reflected the continued "hold by 'landowners' on their dependent peasants" implemented by Ştirbei and Ghica in their new agrarian laws of 1851. The dependent peasants were now called farmers, and had to give their masters twenty-four days of work instead of twelve, whereas the Lăieši sold by the estate of Aleku Sturdza were obligated to pay tribute to their owner. Gypsy slaves, of course, were also the personal property of the owners.[25]

Within two years, the fate of Wallachia and Moldavia once again entered the international arena when Nicholas I reoccupied the provinces in the early stages of a dispute with the Turks that was initially over control of Christian religious shrines in the Holy Lands. The tsar, who considered the "Principalities an independent state under [his] protection," had, at least in concerned British eyes, grand designs on Europe's "Sick Man," the Ottoman Empire. Russia's occupation of Wallachia and Moldavia on June 26, 1853, came after Turkey refused to agree to "a formal guarantee of Russia's right to protect some twelve million Orthodox Christians in the Ottoman Empire." Ştirbei and Ghica fled to Vienna, while Turkey responded with a declaration of war against Russia on October 4, 1853, and was joined by Britain and France on March 28, 1854. Nicholas I now found himself pitted against this triumvirate in the Crimean War.[26] The war served as a boon for Romanian nationalists such as Mihail Kogălniceanu, who published a newspaper, *The Star of the Danube*, with readers in France as well as Belgium. In the meantime, Nicholas I, fearful of Austria's entrance into the war, evacuated the principalities at Austrian insistence in the summer of 1854, a void quickly filled by Austrian troops. Ghica and Ştirbei were restored to their thrones that fell under the protective eye of the Austrians, whose unpopular military presence did not end until 1857. The Crimean War ended with the Treaty of Paris of March 30, 1856, which left Wallachia and Moldavia divided and under Turkish control. The peacemakers agreed to revise the Reglement Organique, though Russia lost its protective rights in the provinces. Southern Bessarabia was added to Moldavia.[27]

As the war ground to a halt at the end of 1855, emancipation efforts were initiated in Moldavia and Wallachia. Moldavia's *hospodar*, Ghica, ruled a more stable province and used "the services of many progressives" in his government. In addition, he was "a man of high character and genuinely zealous for reform," though he lacked good judgment and was "incapable of sustained effort." Consequently, though he abhorred slavery, Ghica "hesitated to take any actions." He did pass a law early in his reign that forbade the separation of Gypsy slave children from their parents, but hesitated to do more. However, at the urging of one of his advisers, Edward Grenier, and Ghica's daughter, Natalia Balsch, "who had already liberated her own slaves and who had already persuaded eight other households to follow her example," Ghica finally decided to act. He broached the subject with his *Divan* Ad Hoc ("small aristocratic caucus") and told them that for

> many years, slavery has been abolished in all the civilized states of the old world; only the principalities of Moldavia and Wallachia retain this humiliating vestige of a barbaric society. It is a social disgrace.

His advisory council agreed totally, and on December 10, 1855, the ownership of private Gypsy slaves became illegal in Moldavia, with compensation
for the former owners. Boyars would receive "eight ducats in respect of
Linguari and *Vatraşi* and four for *Lăieşi* whether male or female, but nothing
was to be paid in respect of suckling children and the infirm." On February
8, 1856, Stirbei followed suit in Wallachia and freed its private Gypsy *robi*.[28]

Freedom for Wallachia and Moldavia followed on the heels of Gypsy
emancipation. Elections for *Divans* Ad Hoc in Moldavia were held in July
1857, but the results were questioned by the Turks. Pressure from Great
Britain, France, Russia, and Prussia forced Constantinople to allow new elections in Moldavia and Wallachia. The new legislatures were dominated by
nationalists such as Kogălniceanu, who "put forward a proposal for the union
of the two principalities into a single state to be called Romania, which would
be ruled by a foreign prince chosen from a reigning European family." The
new state would be a constitutional monarchy whose "independence would be
guaranteed by the seven great powers." Kogălniceanu's proposal was approved
by Moldavia's legislature 81 to 2, while the Wallachian *Divan* Ad Hoc
approved the concept unanimously. Since the terms of these proposals ran
counter to the 1856 Treaty of Paris, France's emperor, Napoleon III, brought
the other powers concerned together to write the Convention of Paris of 1858,
which created the United Principalities of Moldavia and Wallachia. The convention stated that each nation would have a separate prince and legislature,
though they would share a common court of justice. The boyars would lose
their traditional privileges and a new statute for the peasants was drawn. The
Porte would retain sovereign powers over the United Principalities and had "to
approve the election of the prince who was elected by a special assembly." Of
particular significance to Gypsy slaves was a clause dealing with "the equality of all citizens before the law." This would pave the way for final, complete
Rom emancipation six years later.[29]

Frustrated Romanian nationalists in Wallachia's and Moldavia's new legislatures responded to their continued separation by electing the same prince,
Colonel Alexandru Ioan Cuza, to head both principalities in early 1859. Most
of the major powers accepted the unified leadership of Cuza within a few
months, with the proviso that it applied only to Alexandru Cuza and not to his
successors. The Porte agreed to accept Cuza's singular leadership later that
year, and followed this up with a *firman* (decree) on December 2, 1861, that
"recognized administrative and political union, but only for the duration of
Cuza's reign."[30] During his years in power, Cuza implemented reforms that
"laid the political, economic, and cultural foundations of modern Romania."
On February 5, 1862, he got both legislatures to approve the Permanent

Union of the Principalities, with the capital in Bucharest and a single parliament. After frustrated attempts to deal with conservative large estate owners, who initially controlled the new Romanian parliament and opposed his land-reform efforts, Cuza turned to Mihail Kogălniceanu's and the Liberals, reform-minded small landowners, state officials, and professionals, to initiate his reforms. When the Conservatives rejected Cuza and Kogălniceanu's land reform package, Cuza dissolved the legislature and held a national referendum on "constitutional reform giving wider powers to the prince and increasing the electoral basis." With 99 percent of the voters approving, Cuza pushed through agrarian reforms by decree on August 26, 1864. It granted Romania's peasants full personal liberty, freed them from all feudal dues and tithes, and removed all restrictions on their movements. Peasants could now buy the land they farmed in installments from the state, which immediately compensated the boyars for their lost property. The acquisition of total freedom by Romania's peasants included the Gypsies, whose emancipation was now complete.[31]

The end of Gypsy slavery in Romania was applauded throughout Europe and later celebrated in several poems published by Adriano Colocci in his *Gli Zingari* (The Gypsies, 1889).

> Come running, beloved brothers all—
> Today, come running all;
> For freed we are, by the Rumanian prince.
> Let us cry out with full voice,
> So be it!
>
> God; Earth; Sun; Moon;
> Dawn; Forest; Humanity—
> In chorus they honor Tot
> For the goodness of Moldavia
>
> Everyone!
> The old, the grown,
> young men, babes yet in arms,
> and children! They have
> broken off
> our irons
> The Prince, and all
> his citizens.
>
> Great God, and all your stars
> which give to us the light,

Love all Rumanian people,
For breaking our bonds
of slavery.

Be glad, ye nobles sons of Rom,
In all whose breasts do beat
the hearts of men.
No longer slaves!
The Good Word has come down.
Happy he must be who first among us said
    "Rejoice at this, Moldavians!
    Our holy altars now are washed clean!
    Our Church has slaves no more!"
Honor to he who freed them!
For each had a heart, and each had a soul,
Each had God as his master,
and each was born of woman—
Still, each was clamped into the iron yoke.
Honor!
Honor to you who freed them![32]

In 1870, Alexander Paspati, a specialist on Gypsy linguistics, joined this chorus of praise, predicting "This people, so long oppressed, enslaved in body and mind, will probably, in a short time, as they rise in wealth and learning, under the fostering hand of freedom attain to some yet higher consideration."[33] Unfortunately, the end of Gypsy slavery triggered an unparalleled Rom exodus out of the new Romanian kingdom that continued in various waves through the early twentieth century. Stimulated initially by fear of reenslavement after the second round of emancipation decrees in late 1855 and 1856, the next wave of Gypsy migration followed general peasant emancipation eight years later. Other important Gypsy migrations from the region came in the aftermath of periodic difficulties that plagued Romania over the next half-century. It is important to note, however, that the traditional explanation for these great Gypsy migrations was recently challenged by Angus Fraser, who felt that "the apparent chronology and pattern of the migrations and the social organization of the Rom" undercuts this explanation, since "recorded antecedents of particular Rom, Ursari and Rudari families who came west point to an extensive sojourn in countries other than Moldo-Wallachia."[34]

All indications are that the plight of Romania's Gypsies improved little because of emancipation. Like other peasants, who suffered from growing land shortages exacerbated by continued boyar control of the best land, Gypsies remained deeply impoverished social outcasts. Many Rom, "with no money or possessions, and having nowhere to go, offered themselves for resale to their previous owners." Charles Boner said in 1865 that Gypsies in the Tîrgu-Mures region of Romania saw those "gipsies living on the estate of a noble, as a sort of appendage not to be got rid of," while Konrad Bercovici felt that a postemancipation government ban on nomadism forced many Rom to return to their traditional estates, where "they begged the boyar to retain them in his employ." He cited as an example the former Gypsy *robi* on the estate of Prince Bibesco, who told him "You are our boyar, prince. You must take care of us." J. W. Ozanne noted in his detailed account of life in Romania a few years later that most servants in Bucharest were still Gypsies or Szekelers (Magyarized Turks), the servant positions traditionally held by Gypsy *robi*, who were known as Vatras. Such developments helped determine "the patterns of distribution of the Romani population in Rumania" at least until the eve of World War II. According to Ian Hancock, Gypsies who lived in Romania "stayed mainly in the areas in which they had been traditionally located," which meant that large Roma settlements were "found around the monasteries, which had owned many of the slaves." Ozanne's study, which was influenced by local prejudices, provided an in-depth glance of Gypsy life in the new country. While some Roma had now begun to farm, most, according to Ozanne, preferred "a wandering mode of life." He saw Gypsies as little more than children, who, if humored, "are easily led." Ozanne felt that nomadic Romanian Gypsies were "always studying how to exist without performing their daily round of work," while employers paid them in food for fear they would spend real wages on alcohol. In fairness, Ozanne noted in a separate section of his book that the non-Gypsy Romanian peasant usually "worked half the week," after which he stopped working, with "nothing [to] induce him to return until the following Monday." He felt the lot of the Rom was "improving every day," though they were still intensely looked down upon by other Romanians. He concluded that "gradual intermarriages with the native population may, however, finally place the more steady-going among them in the position to which they aspire."[35]

Tihomir Gjorgjević agreed with Ozanne's assessment about improvement of the quality of Rom life after emancipation. He felt that Gypsy freedom "was attended by excellent results" and accepted Mihail Kogălniceanu's idealistic observations, in his 1891 *Desrobicea Tsiganiloru* (The Enslavement of Gypsies), that within a decade after emancipation, Roma had begun to emerge in Romania as "business men, artists, admirable officers and surgeons, and even parliamentary speakers." In time, Kogălniceanu claimed, only two of Romania's traditional Gypsy tribes, the Lăieši, or truly vagrant Gypsies, and the Ursari, the blacksmiths and tinkers, had not fully assimilated into

Romanian society. The Lingurari (spoonmakers), who also worked as skilled wood craftsmen, "charcoal burners, or cattle drovers and dealers," and the Rudari (miners) or Aurari (goldsmiths or gold washers), plus the *robi,* had been "assimilated by the native population, and are only to be distinguished from it by their dark Asiatic complexion and the liveliness of imagination."[36]

Many Gypsies continued their traditional lifestyle, particularly the Laješi (Lăieši) and the Ursari. Gypsy nomads lived in tents during the summer and "in winter in underground cabins or shelters which they dug in the forest near villages, so that they might obtain fuel, also work for the peasants, and have opportunities for stealing." Traveling Gypsy groups were usually made up of 1 to 15 families (*salas*), headed by a *jude* (leader). The *judes* from various *salas* were led by a *buljubaša* or *voivode,* who was usually elected from a family "in which there had already been *buljubašas.*" This "Gypsy king" was required "to dress better than the rest; to be of mature age and to have an imposing appearance." The *buljubaša* was elected "in the open sky" and afterwards was "raised aloft three times amid joyful exclamations." The *judes* and the *buljubašas* almost always rode horses, could "grow a beard, wear a long purple cloak, yellow or red top-boots, a lambskin bonnet similar in shape to the Phrygian cap (*subara*), and to carry in their hand the triple-thronged whip with which they punished the Gypsies for stealing." The *buljubašas* wielded immense political and judicial power and "received two percent of the Gypsy tribute," which was determined and collected by the Grand *voivode* of the Crown Gypsies. The *buljubašas* were intermediaries between the Rom and local officials, while the "Grand *voivode* communicated to the Gypsies the orders of the Government" and served as the Gypsies' "supreme court of appeal."[37]

Charles Boner painted another image of Rom life in the Tîrgu-Mures region of north-central Romania during this period. The area's postemancipation Gypsies were

> particularly wretched. Though cold and frosty, children of ten or twelve years of age stood outside the huts without a particle of clothing. In that state they will often sit on a piece of ice, and with feet drawn together, slide thus down a frozen slope. Many die, however, from exposure and privation; but the first years once over, their hardened frames bear every clemency. These people can support heat and cold; everything, in short, except wind. Of that the gipsy has a thorough horror; it completely incapacitates him for everything; he shrinks before it helpless.

Boner also disagreed with the image of the Rom as lazy. He felt that the Gypsy was a "better labourer than the Wallack; he is much quicker, and more expert."

He did think that Gypsy workers had to be supervised more carefully than non-but that they were quite adept at threshing, particularly when paid in grain. Gypsy farm hands were also good at hoeing and reaping, but not at mowing or haymaking. Rom women, Boner observed, were much better at hemp work than Wallachian women, while the men excelled at "earth work, making embankments and trenches." Gypsies were also the best farriers, and blacksmiths in the region, and had a genius for ironwork and music. Boner found something of a social pecking order among the Rom, who were regarded by non-Gypsies as "the lowest in the social scale." There were distinctions among Gypsies from various villages, which often prompted Rom from one community to refuse to drink from the same glass or pitcher as a Gypsy from another village. In addition, Roma also "do not intermarry, as one says the other is unclean." On the other hand, Boner found that the Gypsies in the Kokel region of Transylvania intermarried freely with Hungarians and Wallachians.[38] He also did a study of Gypsy criminals at a prison in Transylvania and found that violent crime rates were much higher among Hungarian, Szekeler, and Romanian prisoners, while Gypsies were more likely to commit less serious crimes. Prison officials also noted that Gypsy prisoners were somewhat easier to deal with than the Hungarians and Szekelers.[39]

In some ways, Boner's description of the Rom's "particularly wretched" condition in the years immediately after emancipation bore some resemblance to comments made by Mihail Kogălniceanu in a speech before the Romanian Academy on April 9, 1891, commemorating Gypsy emancipation. The scenes he described, drawn from his own childhood and published in his 1837 work, *Esquisse sur l'histoire, les moeurs et la langue des Cigains,* painted a horrible picture of Rom enslavement and mistreatment.[40] Though Romania's Gypsies were much better off after emancipation, their low status on the Romanian social ladder made them particularly prey to the serious economic and social inequalities that so deeply impoverished other members of Romania's peasant and lower classes. Aided in part by an ongoing series of political crises that haunted the country in the years after independence, Romania's large-estate owners gradually regained control of so much land that by 1895, "6,500 people owned half of the total agricultural land, that is to say as much as was owned by over a million peasant families." Approximately 20 percent of the population, many of them Gypsies, were without land and desperate. A large number of Romania's large estate owners did not live on their plantations and farmed for the international export market, which produced serious food shortages in the countryside. Peasant unrest exploded in a major uprising in 1888 that saw "mayors' offices sacked, grain reserves pillaged, and an attempt to cut up the large fields." A new land law the following year tried to address some peasant grievances but fell far short of expected gains when newly redistributed lands fell into the wrong hands. According to R. W. Seton-Watson, "the decades that followed were the Golden Age of irresponsible landlordism, and in some respects the peasant found himself as much exploited, as fatally tied to the soil, as in the vanished days of serfdom."[41] Romania's Gypsy population, which one estimate placed at 300,000 in 1900, was deeply affected by continued unrest in the countryside. In 1904, Professor Basilescu warned that the "volcano is trembling at our feet" and that "a day will come when fire will devour the palaces, the granaries and all the property of those who exploit the peasantry." Three years later, his fears came true in the Great Peasant Rising of March 1907, which resulted in 10,000–12,000 deaths. The uprising broke out rather suddenly near Botosani, and soon peasant mobs began to ransack the homes of Jews and large landowners throughout Moldavia. The government, in league with King Charles, initiated some reforms to still the tide of peasant unrest and launched major military campaigns that butchered many peasants and destroyed entire villages. Once the rebellion was put down, further reforms were undertaken to deal with some of the worst abuses in the countryside. Unfortunately, the government "remained aloof, even hostile, vis à vis peasants, and the prevailing political currents shied away from any significant reform." This was also a period of "unexampled prosperity and commercial development for Romania," in which, sadly, few peasants shared.[42] It was perhaps appropriate that six years after the Great Peasant Rising, the Gypsies celebrated the erection of a statue to Mihail Kogălniceanu at Piatră Neamţ in northeast Romania. His son, Vasile, a recognized advocate of peasant education, had been arrested in the 1907 rebellion. On June 14, 1913, *Near East* magazine reported that two days after Kogălniceanu's statue was publicly dedicated,

> a vast concourse of gipsies arrived at Piatră Neamtz and proceeded to the monument. Before the statue they placed a wreath of oak leaves and wild flowers, and then, to the weird accompaniment of a gipsy band, the whole party joined in a national dance round the statue of their liberator.[43]

A year later, Europe drifted into World War I. Initially, Romania remained aloof, though pro-Allied feelings gradually took root among the government and general public. By the summer of 1916, Romania had held secret talks with Great Britain, France, Italy, and Russia that resulted in an accord that promised Bucharest Austro-Hungarian territories with a Romanian population at war's end. On August 14, 1916, Romania declared war on the Habsburg Empire, and three days later, Germany responded with a similar declaration against

Romania. An initial Romanian thrust into Transylvania brought charges of atrocities from both sides, while Austrian and German forces soon drove the Romanian army out of the region and occupied Wallachia. On November 23, 1916, Central Power (Germany and Austria-Hungary) troops entered Bucharest, while Russian intervention in early 1917 split Romania into two parts. The Romanian government, which had fled to Iaşi, was now in control of only one-third of the country, principally Moldavia. To counter the growing threat of pacifism and revolutionary ideas, particularly after the February Revolution in Russia that had helped to topple Tsar Nicholas II (r. 1894–1918), King Ferdinand I promised in late March that once peace returned, new land redistribution and political reforms would be initiated.[44]

A failed Russo-Romanian offensive in the summer of 1917, followed by the Russian withdrawal from the war after the October Revolution later that year, forced the Romanian government to seek armistice terms from the Central Powers. The Treaty of Bucharest on April 23, 1918, saw southern Dobrudja ceded to Bulgaria and 5,600 square kilometers with 150,000 residents transferred to Austria-Hungary. The treaty gave the Central Powers special claims to Romanian agricultural and industrial goods as well as its oil. Wallachia was to remain under Central Power occupation until World War I ended. Romania, now "no more than a German protectorate," was allowed to double the size of Moldavia with the occupation of Bessarabia, a future bone of contention with Lenin's new Soviet state.[45]

As World War I ground to a halt in the early fall of 1918, Romanian nationalists in Transylvania voted to join the Romanian state, while the government sought ways to delay ratification of the Treaty of Bucharest. On November 10, 1918, Romania resumed military operations against the Central Powers, followed three days later by an armistice. Romania's new government under King Ferdinand I fully expected the Allied Powers to abide by the terms of the secret 1916 treaty that brought Romania into the war. To promote his country's claims, the king officially "endorsed union between Transylvania, Banat, and part of Hungary and the old Kingdom" on December 11, 1918, and set up provisional governments for each region. The major powers, however, decided to treat Romania as a secondary Allied Power at the Paris peace talks and reneged on some of the promises made in the 1916 accord. Regardless, Romania gained Bukovina, southern Dobrudja, Transylvania, Crisana, Maramures, and the northern Banat in the various treaties signed at Paris in 1919–1920. The Allied Powers required Romania to accept significant minorities' guarantees in these accords, while signature of the Treaty of Trianon with Hungary was delayed until June 4, 1920, because of Romania's involvement in Bela Kun's abortive Soviet revolution in Hungary.[46]

The new, postwar Romania saw its territory and population increase significantly because of its new acquisitions. According to 1912 estimates, there
were 7.2 million residents in Romania, with only 8 percent of them non-
Romanian. The Romanian demographic register of 1920 provided a glimpse
of the country's ethnic makeup, though its figures are highly debatable.
Consequently, two analysts, Elemér Illyés and Joseph Roucek, have come up
with totally different conclusions about the country's total population in 1920
and the size of its Gypsy community. Illyés estimated Romania's population
to be a little over 16 million in 1920, with 28.1 percent of it non-Romanian.
Of this number, he said there were 133,000 Gypsies, who made up 0.8 percent of the total population. Roucek, however, claimed Romania had a population of 16.9 million in 1920, with 60,000 Rom in the newly acquired
territories, and 225,000 Gypsies in the Regat, or prewar Romanian lands, for
a total 1920 Roma population of 285,000 (1.7 percent of the country's population). Romania's first official census a decade later is more revealing. It
showed a total population of slightly over 18 million, with 262,501 Gypsies
by national origin. About 38 percent of the Rom surveyed (101,015) chose
Romani as their primary language. A further breakdown of these statistics
showed that there were 107,202 Gypsies in Transylvania who identified themselves as such by national origin, while 40 percent (43,000) chose Romani as
their native tongue.[47]

The Paris Minorities Treaty of December 9, 1919, forced Bucharest to recognize the rights of postwar Romania's minorities. It "guaranteed the minorities protection through the League of Nations, the constitution and a promise
to implement rights of minorities." Specifically, all national minorities were
to be "guaranteed equal rights and religious freedom as well as schools in their
mother tongue." Jewish rights were dealt with in a separate part of the
agreement. Not all of these guarantees, however, were included in the 1923
Romanian constitution, and their uneven enforcement became a serious hand-
icap for the nation.[48] According to Joseph Rothschild, the "ethnic minorities,
whether those who had been indigenous since medieval times (Magyars,
Saxons) or more modern immigrants (Jews, Russians, Ukrainians), were
regarded as foreigners." Particularly disliked were the Magyars and the Jews
because of the former's "political prowess" and the latter's "hegemony over
trade and finance." Romania's other ethnic groups were not as affected by the
"principled discrimination" aimed at the Jews and the Magyars. The Gypsies,
forever at the bottom of the ethnic social order, quietly took advantage of this
new era in Romania's political history to continue their traditional lifestyles
or to work their way up Romania's complex ethnic and social ladders.[49]
Consequently, the picture that emerged of Romanian Gypsies in the first

decade or so after the end of World War I was a mixture of significant social and economic change blended with a tendency to cling to old ways. Traditional prejudices toward the Rom found fertile ground in Romania, particularly among the peasants, who, hurt by the continued "economic weaknesses of Romanian agriculture or the social problems of rural backwardness," resented the acquisition of land by Gypsies and others who were not cultivators during the great land-redistribution programs of this era.[50]

Gypsy life in interwar Romania varied greatly according to region and lifestyle. T. Oakes Hirst, for example, found the Gypsies in Bukovina in 1922 to be principally nomadic, though some "had settled down in some of the villages and [had] begun to till the ground." Rom nomads traveled throughout the region in caravans of six to ten families and lived in crude huts. Hirst noted that Bukovina's Gypsies were "adept at stealing, cheating, and disguising the appearance of animals they have stolen." He was complimentary of their colorful appearance and described Bukovinan Rom males as excellent blacksmiths. In some areas, settled Gypsies became official village blacksmiths. They were also "skilled farriers, their horses as often as not being stolen from their rightful owners and disguised by the extraction of teeth, docking of tails and similar methods." Bukovina's Rom were also good musicians and better educated than other Gypsies in the region. Bukovinan Rom women worked as fortune tellers and sold herbs and drugs to the local peasantry.[51]

At the other side of the social spectrum were the sedentary and semi-sedentary Gypsies of the Regat. While some continued to live their traditional lifestyles, those lifestyles differed from those of pre-1914. The *buljubaša* , for example, no longer had official power, though among the Gypsy clans he remained deeply revered, and "his decisions [were] law." The country's largest Rom community was found in Braila, a little over a hundred miles northeast of Bucharest. According to Konrad Bercovici, the town supplied Romania with some of its best musicians, "many of whom have won distinction the world over." Music had become an important avenue of success for some Romanian Gypsies, and Bercovici praised the accomplishments of Tenasi, "the greatest violinist of Romania," and Dinicu, who earlier had become director of the Conservatory of Bucharest. Braila's Rom musicians, such as "Barbu Lantaru, Coshima and Barleaza, [became] as legendary as the country's heroes" and were able to command concert fees that compared "favorably with that of the best-paid performers in Europe and even America." Sedentary Gypsy settlements, centered around the families of Rom musicians, were found on the outskirts of Bucharest, Jassy, Galati, Craiova, and Braila. Rom children in these ghettos attended school, though "neither teacher nor schoolmate ever forgets to put the Gypsy in his place by reminding him of the fact that he is a Pharon." Bercovici felt that settled Roma were "like caged sparrows; like pheasants in a chicken-coop. Every epidemic hits them first." Much like Liszt and Hungarian Gypsies, Bercovici linked the soul of Romanian folk culture to its Roma. If not for the Gypsies, Bercovici argued, "Roumanian folklore would have perished before anyone had thought of fixing it upon paper."[52]

It was from among the settled Romanian Gypsies that a new sense of Rom self-awareness began to emerge. In 1926, intellectuals founded the General Union of Rumanian Romi, which began a journal, *Neamul Tiganesc* (The Gypsy Family), in 1930. Three years later, this group sponsored an international Gypsy conference in Bucharest that drew delegates from throughout Europe. The conference had as its slogan "United Gypsies of Europe" and adopted as its initial goals the rejuvenation of national consciousness and the struggle for Gypsy civil rights. It also adopted a national Romani flag, consisting of two horizontal bars, the lower green and the upper blue. At its opening session, M. G. Lazaresco told the delegates that "modern inventions and professions were ruining his brethren" and said that "something had to be done to counter these trends." Afterwards, Romanian Gypsies founded the General Association of Gypsies (Tziganes) of Romania and elected Lazaresco as its acting president. The goals of the new association, which opened its offices in Bucharest on November 16, 1933, were designed to counter the destruction of traditional Rom culture and traditions, yet also help the Gypsies to function better in Romanian society. The General Association wanted to organize conferences and art shows to revive traditional Rom skills. To protect native Gypsy craftsmen, the association wanted officials to stop the influx of foreign workers, who took jobs away from skilled Gypsy workers. It also wanted special concessions for Rom "flower-sellers . . . boot-blacks, and peddlars who wished to earn their living rather than increase the number of unemployed." Gypsy women dominated newspaper and flower sales in cities like Bucharest. The association also wanted Rom musicians to have the right to register as artisans so that they could receive government "benefits for sickness, old age and death." The Gypsy organization also asked for land for "a large garden for Tzigane children, a library, a maternity hospital, and office for the settlement of claims, a dispensary, and a place of refuge for those who had come to Bucharest temporarily or those who are being persecuted."[53]

The association was also concerned about the plight of nomadic Rom and wanted legal permission for them to begin settling near towns and villages. According to the organization's statutes, the abandonment of the "vagabond life" would enable Gypsies to "cease to indulge in the thefts that dishonour our race." Rom leaders were quite sensitive to the general prejudice toward Gypsies in Romania and demanded "complete equality for Gypsy citizens, so that they be no longer exposed to mockerey and contempt." They noted that Gypsies were loyal citizens of the Romanian state and "aloof from all extreme parties." To underscore their Romanianness, the association's statutes urged its members, whether Gypsy or non-Gypsy, to "fight the cause of our orthodox Church" and noted that the "Holy Patriarch will name a church where the Gypsies may attend services on Saint Mary's Day, August 15." The association placed great emphasis on education and wanted land for a Rom school. It also asked the government to open two Rom summer schools for Gypsy children and wanted talented, young Rom musicians to be allowed into academies or to receive scholarships to pursue their education abroad.[54]

Finally, the new Gypsy organization wanted the government to help finance travel to international Gypsy conferences and grant railway passes to two members of its Central Committee to enable them to visit Gypsy colonies and give them advice. It also asked for travel discounts for Roma throughout the country to come to the capital to attend religious ceremonies, cultural meetings and congresses. On July 1, 1934, the Gypsy association sponsored a nationwide, eightieth anniversary celebration of Rom emancipation and hoped this would serve as a model for an "annual Romani holiday commemorating emancipation from slavery." Small ceremonies were held in Gypsy communities throughout Romania, while a major gathering was held in Bucharest. Gheorge Nicolescu, the "Voivode of all the sedentary Gypsies in Rumania," told the Roma:

> So long as we travel the paths of justice, honour and duty, no one and nothing can turn us from our goal, because we have at our side a devoted and honourable ally—suffering. The road to emancipation is free; those who love us will be loved by us in return. Let us march forwards together, ever forwards.

At the end of the Bucharest meeting, it was decided to "erect a monument in grateful memory of Prince Ghica, and to place it in surroundings most densely populated by Gypsies." The Roma association also began to publish two newspapers, *Glasul Romilor* (The Voice of the Roma) and *O Rom,* which later failed. *Glasul Romilor* was edited by N. Nicolescu and was preceded by two earlier Rom newspapers, *Timpal* (The Time) and *Neamul Ciganese* (The Gypsy People).[55]

The Gypsy association formally ceased to exist in 1938, although it was revived between 1946 and 1954. Looking back on this era on the eve of World War II, George Potra, a student of P. N. Panaitescu, discussed the gains the Gypsies had made over the past twenty years:

In the last few decades, the number of nomadic Gypsies has decreased since they started to settle down. There are Gypsies working in agriculture, some of whom have become excellent farmers and sent their children to school. [These children] have grown up and become professors, lawyers, priests, doctors, military officers, etc. Nevertheless, the majority of Gypsies stayed in cities and in market areas, doing all sorts of jobs.[56]

At the very moment that Romania's Gypsies seemed to have achieved an extraordinary sense of ethnic self-awareness, the country was struggling under the weight of the monarchial dictatorship of King Carol II (r. 1930–1940) and his premier, Gheorghe Tătărescu. The country had suffered from a sad political malaise since the end of World War I, colored by periods of martial law and censorship. In 1928, the Liberal Party, which had dominated the country for a decade, was replaced by the National-Peasants, who tried initially to return some normalcy to the country's political system. Two years later, Crown Prince Carol, who had been forced in 1926 to give up his claim to the throne in favor of his son, Michael (Mihai), returned to Romania and had himself declared monarch on June 8, 1930. The National-Peasants acceded to Carol's move and entered a political alliance with him over the next three years. Though King Carol II "had irredeemably broken" the back of the National-Peasant Party by the end of 1933, one of its premiers, Nicolae Iorga, had established an undersecretaryship for minorities and created chairs for ethnic studies at some of the country's prominent universities. These reforms soon went the way of the National-Peasants, but they did herald a brief period of national sensitivity toward minority questions.[57] For the next four years, Tătărescu's Liberals governed by martial law, while King Carol increasingly relied on Corneliu Zelea Codreanu's fascist Iron Guard to defend against the country's other political parties. The Iron Guard blended some of the traditional tenets of fascism with a revived anti-Semitism anchored by "Orthodox religiosity." Codreanu valued "organization . . . dedication . . . discipline and martyrdom," and wanted "honesty, stamina, and stoicism" to replace Romania's "conventional mendacity, sloth, and verbosity." In late 1933, efforts by King Carol's first Liberal premier, Ion Duca, to crush the Iron Guard resulted in Duca's murder by the fascist group and "suggested police, and possibly royal, complicity." The growing power of the Iron Guard particularly appealed to the country's peasant masses, who made up almost 80 percent of Romania's population and suffered from "acute misery" exacerbated by the Depression.[58]

By early 1938, King Carol had worked his destructive political magic on the Liberals, and on February 10, 1938, he suspended the constitution and announced his own royal dictatorship. He chose as his puppet premier the "vain and hypernationalist Orthodox Patriarch Miron Cristea" but used Armand Călinescu as his "reliable agent within the cabinet." The king sealed his dictatorship with a new, corporatist constitution, disbanded all political parties, and quickly brought the courts and the universities under his control. He tried to counter the influence of the Iron Guard with a "pseudo-radical, semi-fascist burlesque" that gloried in "organic nationalism, family, church, and the gospel of work," anchored by the king's new party, the Front of National Resistance. Carol II bankrolled his regime with the country's abundant oil reserves and tried initially to maintain balanced relations with the major powers. However, like the region's other nations, Romania soon found itself swept up in the Third Reich's autarkic economic net, and by the summer of 1940, Romania had entered the German camp.[59]

King Carol's drift into the Nazi fold also provided the seeds for his undoing. With Hitler's approval, the monarch ceded Bessarabia and northern Bukovina to the Soviet Union on June 28, 1940, in response to Soviet demands for the territories. Carol's move opened up a territorial Pandora's box, and Hungary and Bulgaria soon asked for the return of Transylvania and southern Dobrudja respectively. Bulgaria received the latter region, while Hungary was able to acquire only about two-fifths of Transylvania in the Second Vienna Award of August 30, 1940. A week later, an Iron Guard-military alliance forced King Carol II to flee into exile, replaced by his son, Michael I (Mihai), who shared power with "an army-Iron Guard duumvirate led by General Ion Antonescu and Horia Sima." On September 14, 1940, the Iron Guard became the country's only legal party, and two months later it celebrated its accession to power with "a sustained rampage, slaughtering scores of political opponents . . . [and] massacring Jews" and others. The Iron Guard's obscene, indiscriminate violence prompted a response from Hitler, who, preparing for his 1941 attack on the Soviet Union, needed a disciplined, stable Romania. Consequently, Hitler allowed Antonescu to "suppress" the Iron Guard on January 21–23, 1941. Antonescu replaced the National Legionary State with his own brand of military authoritarianism and a new relationship with the Third Reich that made Romania "Hitler's favorite ally."[60]

Antonescu's regime was initially quite popular, particularly after his reacquisition of Bessarabia and northern Bukovina in the early days of the assault on the Soviet Union. Strong ties with Germany also brought some mimicking of Nazi racial policies and ideology. In March 1941, the Antonescu regime began to implement an array of anti-Semitic decrees that gradually removed Jews from the fabric of Romanian society. Three months later, Romania joined the German invasion of the Soviet Union. Antonescu, now in personal command of the armed forces, committed 15 divisions to the Nazi cause and began to move into Bessarabia, northern Bukovina, and southern Ukraine. Italian journalist Curzio Malaparte, who traveled in the region as German-Romanian forces occupied these territories, said that after authorities had rounded up some of the area's Jews and sent them to camps in Bessarabia, he came upon a group of Gypsies and peasants stripping the corpses in the village of Poduloea. According to a local rabbi, "It can't be helped. It is the custom. They will come to us tomorrow to sell the clothing stolen from the dead and we shall have to buy it—what else can we do?"[61]

In a speech on July 8, 1941, Antonescu talked about the elimination of national minorities, which one Romanian captain supported when he said, "Mice, rats, crows, Gypsies, vagabonds and Jews don't need any documents." Romania's Gypsy population, which the *Anuarul Statistic* in 1939-1940 said still numbered 262,501, now became the target of an array of anti-Roma actions. According to Antonescu during his war crimes trial, the Gypsies were rounded up because "the public appealed to me to protect them because [the Gypsies] were breaking into houses at night." Police investigations, Antonescu claimed, "determined that armed Gypsies, many with war weapons," were responsible for the burglaries. King Michael said in 1991 that "nomadic or semi-nomadic" Rom were viewed officially as "antisocial." They were particularly vulnerable to mistreatment because they "had no defence or protectors outside of Romania," and were "easy targets due to their lack of papers and documentation." Those who suffered most were the Gypsies in the new, Romanian-occupied areas of Russia renamed Transnistria, which became an important dumping ground for Gypsies and Jews. During the first year of the German-Soviet war, "25,000 Gypsies from the Bucharest areas were transported across the Dnieper to the Stalingrad region."[62]

According to one Rom survivor, Petre Radita, the Gypsies were shipped

> from Bucharest in cattle trucks, the journey took some weeks and because of the cold nights, lack of blankets and inadequate food supply, many died of hunger and exposure before arriving at the River Bug in the Ukraine. Those that had survived were lodged in huts and made to work digging trenches. Those found with gold teeth had them pulled out. Two children caught carrying messages to the partisans were executed in front of their parents.[63]

Some German officials were concerned over the movement of Roma into Ukraine, and in August 1942, Erich Koch, the Reichskommissar Ukraine, wrote to Alfred Rosenberg, the Reich Minister for the Eastern Occupied

Territories (Ostministerum), complaining about the shipment of Roma into his province. On September 11, 1942, Rosenberg sent a letter to Joachim Ribbentrop, the minister of foreign affairs, "pointing out the danger that these Gypsies would try to settle on the east bank of the Bug and would then be a bad influence on the Ukrainian population." Rosenberg added that the region was "populated by ethnic Germans" and asked Ribbentrop to do what he could to discourage the Antonescu government from sending Roma there in the future.[64] According to Donald Kenrick and Grattan Puxon, Romanian authorities also shipped the entire Gypsy village of Buda-Ursari to Nikoleav in Transnistria, where many "women and children died on the way." One Roma, Bogdan Nikulaje, lost his entire family in the transfer.[65]

Five days after Rosenberg sent his letter to Berlin, Constantin Brătianu, a former leader of the defunct Liberal Party, wrote to Antonescu to question the shipment of Roma to Transnistria. He felt the Gypsies were

> Orthodox and have an important role in the economy, being good handicraftsmen, such as farriers, blacksmiths, brick layers, farmers, and unskilled day laborers. Many are small merchants, small landowners, milkmen, etc. Almost all fiddlers in our country are Gypsies, and there is no holiday where people can enjoy themselves without their music.

Now, Brătianu noted, Gypsies were being forced to leave Romania, a "country for which they shed their blood (due to army enrollment)." These transfers were particularly difficult since winter was approaching, with "aged people, women and children being forced over the frontier into unknown regions where their lives have no meaning." Brătianu wondered if the country could afford to "sacrifice such a large number of citizens" with skills as "handicraftsmen and workers." He felt that these transfers were being initiated without Antonescu's knowledge, and asked the *conducător al statuliu* (führer or duce) "to stop these persecutions," since they "would take us a few centuries back in world history."[66]

The Romanian newspaper *Eroica* (Heroic) explained in October 1942 that "the Gypsy question was as important as the Jewish" one and "mourned the 'prevailing dangerous opinion that Gypsies were part of the Rumanian race.'" Because of mixed marriages, *Eroica* claimed there were 600,000 Roma "half-castes" in the country. It demanded that marriages between "Gypsies, half-castes and Rumanian women be prohibited" and felt that Gypsies had to be "eliminated from any part they played in the social life of the state." One solution, *Eroica* argued, was to put all Rom nomads in labor camps. According to the report of the Romanian War Crimes Commission at the end of World War II,

Tens of thousands of defenseless Gypsies were herded together in Transnistria. Over half of them were struck by the typhus epidemics. The gendarmerie practiced unprecedented terror; everybody's life was uncertain; tortures were cruel; the commanders lived in debauchery with beautiful Gypsy women and maintained personal harems. Approximately 36,000 Gypsies fell victim to Antonescu's Fascist regime.[67]

Most of Romania's Gypsies escaped capture, though according to one Rom, "during the war it was much better not to be a Gypsy." Frightful rumors made Gypsies particularly watchful, while some told stories of late-night escapes to avoid detection. Those who were not sent to Transnistria "remained free and [were] comparatively unaffected by the war."[68] Mihai Dimitriscu, for example, was in the ninth Romanian Division's cavalry regiment but was captured in 1942. He was beaten twice by his officers for refusing to cut his long hair. Another Gypsy, Pirvan Regalie, served with the Third and Fourth Romanian armies in the battle of Stalingrad from July 1942 to February 1943.[69]

After the Stalingrad debacle, efforts were made to patch up relations with the Allied Powers, in hopes of getting a separate Anglo-American peace with Romania that would keep the Red Army at bay and allow "Romania to regain the provinces lost in June, even August 1940." The Allied Powers responded that Romania would actively have to change sides in the war and would only get northern Transylvania in return. An air raid that destroyed the center of Bucharest on April 4, 1944, underscored Western resolve against the Antonescu regime. In the meantime, King Michael I initiated an alliance with the communist underground, and on August 23, 1944, he arrested Antonescu and set up a coalition government under General Constantin Sanatescu. Romanian forces now allied themselves with Red Army units to drive the Wehrmacht out of Romania, a process that was not completed until October 25, 1944. The king asked General Nicolae Radescu to form a new government six weeks later and immediately began to do away with Antonescu's anti-Gypsy and anti-Semitic legislation. On February 6, 1945, the Radescu government issued its Statute for National Minorities, which "gave complete equality to all Romanian citizens, without prejudice towards nationality, language, or religion."[70]

Eighteen days after the announcement of Radescu's minorities statute, a communist-provoked crisis led to the collapse of Radescu's government. Andrei Vyshinsky, the architect of a 1940 Soviet takeover of Latvia, arrived in Bucharest and forced King Michael to accept a new coalition government under Petru Groza, head of the Ploughman's Front, on March 6, 1945. Though the communists held only four cabinet positions, they dominated Groza's new National Front coalition since representatives of other parties were "designated by the Soviets rather than the parties themselves." Groza's position was strengthened by the return of northern Transylvania and the huge growth of the Romanian Communist Party, whose ranks were swollen as "hundreds of thousands of Romanians recognized the permanence of Soviet domination." Gypsies were particularly encouraged to join "local and regional administrative political elites," since they were seen as "the most disadvantaged of the exploited classes." Some Roma followed this path because they saw opportunities "for upward mobility and equal treatment under the law."[71]

The conclusion of an Allied-Romanian peace treaty on February 10, 1947, which formally ended World War II for Bucharest, included modest protection against discrimination for the country's minorities and stimulated the "pace of Sovietization" of Romania, which was declared a People's Republic on December 30, 1947. All opposition parties were abolished and replaced by the Romanian Workers' Party, which became totally subordinate to Moscow under the leadership of Gheorghe Gheorghiu-Dej. Over the next five years, the Gheorghiu-Dej regime adopted two new constitutions modeled closely on the 1936 Soviet Stalin constitution. Though both documents gave lip service to basic educational, linguistic, and cultural rights for the country's "national" and "cohabiting nationalities," a secret, "anti-nationality system began to develop." It put Romanians in upper and mid-level positions of power in regions throughout the country inhabited by the national minorities. Increasingly, what gains the country's major ethnic groups had made since 1944 were compromised by "an awakening spirit of Romanian nationalism." Yet the government also continued to maintain "a certain amount of tolerance for the needs and wishes of the ethnic minorities."[72]

This shift toward a greater emphasis on Romanian national identity is reflected in the 1948 census, which showed that 87.4 percent of the population of 15,872,624, chose Romanian as their primary language, compared to 73 percent in the 1930 census. The 1948 census showed a Roma population of only 53,425 Gypsies by native language, versus 101,015 in the 1930 census. This was a 47 percent drop in Roma figures from 1930 to 1948, compared with a 12 percent decline in total population statistics for the same period. The Gypsies, who now officially made up 0.3 percent of the population compared to 0.6 percent 18 years earlier, were located primarily in the countryside. It was presumed that most of the Gypsies listed in the 1948 census were nomads, while the 14 percent that lived in Romania's urban areas were settled or semi-nomads.[73]

The continued existence of Gypsy nomads had troubled communist leaders since 1946, and efforts were made to force them to settle. Initial policies centered around the confiscation of horses and wagons, which was vividly described by a Roma from Brasov:

> The police came and took my horse. Others, my brother-in-law, many others, lost wagons. It was my way of making a living, but no one cared. They just wanted us to stay in one place. It was a shock. I could never understand why.

When these efforts proved ineffective, the Interior Ministry began a new program in 1951 designed to break up small groups of Roma so that "they could be more easily monitored by the police." Some Gypsies were forced to settle on the edge of villages, where they were often unwelcome and later mistreated by the peasants. These efforts coincided with similar forced transfers of 30,000-40,000 Swabians in Romanian Banat who had protested the forced collectivization of agriculture that had begun in 1948. According to Sam Beck, official concern over Rom nomadism centered around an historic Romanian aversion to nomads. These feelings had deep roots and centered on the idea that "nomads deter development and threaten civilization." Romanians, Beck felt, implicitly saw the Gypsy "as genetically inferior, or culturally conservative and unable to change."[74]

The 1956 census in Romania provided the first real glimpse of the Gypsies since the creation of the People's Republic nine years earlier. It indicated a total Rom population of 104,216, with 46.15 percent of the Gypsies indicating Romani as their native tongue, compared to a little over 45 percent of the registered Gypsies selecting Romanian as their primary language. About 8.6 percent of the country's Rom chose Hungarian as their principal language. The census also showed that 17.3 percent of Romania's Gypsies had settled permanently in the nation's urban areas. A little over 40 percent of the Roma in the 1956 census declared themselves to be workers, 0.58 percent as "Functionaries," or "engineers, technicians, and specialized personnel," 6.73 percent as "Collective Farmers," 16.35 percent as "Individual Farmers," and 2.88 percent as "Liber Professionisti," a category that included "lawyers . . . physicians and sanitary personnel, artists . . . actors and instrumental performers, as well as others not employed in an institution or enterprise for pay." (This category was removed from the 1966 census.) Almost three-quarters of Romania's Gypsies were over 8 years old, and about 43 percent of this number were enrolled in primary schools. The level of Gypsy school enrollment beyond this level was negligible, which helped explain the group's 37.7 percent illiteracy rate. Comparatively, the country's Romanians had a 10.9 percent illiteracy rate, the Hungarians, 3.1 percent, the Germans, 1.1 percent, and the Jews, 3.1 percent. (Officials eliminated the illiteracy category from the 1966 census.) Trond

Gilberg concluded from his analysis of the 1956 census's educational data that the country's Roma were "marginally touched by modernization."[75]

These figures took on greater significance when compared to 1966 census data. The decade in between was an era when "the large ethnic minorities continued to enjoy a certain amount of religious, social, and even economic autonomy." The total Gypsy population recorded in the 1966 census dropped by over 38 percent, though the number of Gypsies who declared Romani to be their native tongue declined by only 21.2 percent during the same period. Over 65 percent of the country's urban Gypsies selected Romani as their primary language, compared to 57.62 percent of the Rom who lived in the countryside. According to Gilberg, the decline in Gypsy identity during this period came about because of a "tendency among many in this ethnic group to simply abandon the 'Gypsy' label altogether and instead declare themselves Romanian." This assumption is borne out by the fact that Gypsy urbanization rates rose from 17.3 percent to 26.5 percent between 1956 and 1966, while the number who declared Romanian to be their primary language declined by almost 42 percent. Gypsy urbanization increases also reflected the massive urbanization trend nationwide during this period. [76]

The 1966 census showed that over 47 percent of the country's Roma declared themselves "Workers," while the percentage of those listed in the "Functionaries" category dropped slightly. The number of Roma "Collective Farmers" increased from 7,037 to 19,501 between 1956 and 1966, while the number of "Individual [Roma] Farmers" declined from 17,278 to 1,670 during the same period. The demise of the Gypsy private farmer came about because of the "completion of agricultural socialization" or collectivization in 1962 and the decision of some Gypsies to move "from non-agricultural occupations into collectivized agriculture." According to Gilberg, Roma left "'traditional' Gypsy occupations such as handicrafts, small trading, or simply nomadism . . . into a more settled existence in collective farms."[77]

Roma continued to be woefully underrepresented in the country's educational system above the primary grades, and the 1966 census indicated that only one Gypsy was officially enrolled at the university level. These figures underscore the difficulties faced by the Gheorghiu-Dej regime as it tried significantly to address high Gypsy illiteracy rates between 1956 and 1966. Gilberg concluded that it would take a long time before the Gypsies were able to catch up with the educational attainment levels of the country's other nationalities. He felt that the other minorities' educational successes could widen the gap between the Roma and these groups and that "assimilation through education" could very well become an "elite phenomenon" that would be "limited to individual Gypsies who leave their area of residence and cultural background and subsequently accept Romanian culture and language."[78]

The death of Gheorghiu-Dej in 1965 heralded a new era in minorities policy under Romania's new dictator, Nicolae Ceauşescu. Ceauşescu put less emphasis on forced assimilation and emphasized the idea "that Romania is the fatherland of all ethnic groups within its borders, where all nationalities can and must live together in fraternal relations in the common quest for socialism and under the common leadership of the RCP [Romanian Communist Party]." Ceauşescu, ever the Romanian nationalist, emphasized the need for "ideological orthodoxy, greater political control of all aspects of societal life, and the elimination of all group autonomy." His evolving, personal brand of Romanian "chauvinism spelled increasing trouble for the ethnic minorities, since the Ceauşescu vision was heavily colored by a rather unsophisticated notion of Romanian history."[79]

According to Helsinki Watch, by the early 1970s the "official policy was simply to ignore the existence of the Gypsies," while in 1972 the Romanian government announced that the minorities question was resolved. However, the huge increase in Roma population according to the 1977 census forced the government to rethink its policies toward the Gypsies. The Roma population now officially stood at 227,398, or 1.05 percent of the total population (21.6 million), a 80.2 percent increase over 1966 figures. Several government agencies, however, estimated the Rom population to be at least 540,000 (2.5 percent of the total population) at this time, figures that matched earlier, non-Romanian estimates of the country's Gypsy population. Estimates were that 72 percent of this number lived in the countryside, and over 70 percent lived in Transylvania. About 7 percent of Romania's Gypsies lived in Bucharest. Of particular concern were Roma unemployment levels, which stood at 32.7 percent for Gypsy men and 48 percent for women. Among the country's 66,500 nomadic and semi-sedentary Rom, unemployment rates were over 84 percent. Consequently, the government decided in 1977 to do more to integrate the Gypsies into Romanian society. The year before, authorities had created a Commission on Demography, which formed "local committees . . . to study the problems of integrating Gyspies." These groups were made up of "educators, health officials, and representatives from the RCP and the police" and worked primarily on gathering statistics.[80]

According to an extensive report on Roma integration prepared by the Propaganda Section of the Central Committee of the RCP in 1983, the work of the committees prompted a number of efforts to help nomadic and semi-nomadic Gypsies to settle. In counties with large Roma concentrations, Gypsies were given land and other help to build homes. Local committees set up for this purpose also worked to persuade Gypsies "to take jobs in fields of activity such as agriculture, industry, handicrafts, service rendering, and sociocultural areas." The 1983 study indicated that other measures were taken to encourage better school enrollment for Gypsy children and the adoption of better health and hygiene habits. The results, according to the 1983 report, were that many Gypsies "gave up their parasitic way of life and gradually settled down to activities that benefit[ed] society."[81]

Yet officials felt these gains were unsatisfactory, since a number of Gypsies "persist[ed] in retrograde traditions and mentalities, tend[ed] to lead a parasitic way of life, refused to go to work, and live[d] in precarious conditions, and refused to take part in activities for the welfare of society." Gypsy unemployment figures were not higher than in 1977, although nomadic and semi-nomadic Rom mostly had "temporary jobs, and only about 900 were skilled." Linked to unemployment were high Gypsy crime rates, which translated into Rom prison inmate rates of 2 percent of national totals in 1979, and 3.3 percent in 1982. Statistics were even higher for "crimes such as murder, theft, the dollar black market, prostitution, and procurers." The use of children to commit many of these crimes affected school attendance: county school officials reported that 3,500 Gypsy children did not go to school in 1982-1983, while the Ministry of Education estimated the number to be much higher.[82]

The 1983 study found many Rom adults illiterate or semi-illiterate, which also affected their attitudes toward their children's education. As a result of "weak attendance, poor material conditions, and backwardness at home," many Rom children had to repeat grades or simply stopped going to school. High Gypsy unemployment translated into extremely bad housing conditions without adequate sanitation. When Roma were given proper housing in government apartment complexes, they often "destroyed many of them, making them 'unlivable.'" Officials were also concerned over the lack of good health and hygiene among the country's Roma and noted that they had high rates of infant mortality, venereal disease, typhoid fever, and tuberculosis. The 1983 report was also critical of Gypsies' refusal to abide by local and national laws, family disorganization, and the misuse of government subsidies for large families. Consequently, the report made a number of suggestions to force greater integration and sedentarization upon Romania's unsettled Gypsy population.[83]

Nationwide, local officials were to do a detailed gathering of statistics on the Rom's "numerical situation" and "social status." Gypsies who had not registered with authorities were required to get official government identification, while the Ministry of the Interior was to ensure that Roma abided by "the laws referring to private identity and housing." This agency was also responsible for making sure that Gypsies lived and worked only in the places described on their identification papers. The Ministry of Transport and Telecommunication was to establish strict regulations "for harness and horse transport by rail to prevent the Gypsy families from further migration." In addition, the Ministry of Education was to work with local officials to ensure rigorous Gypsy school attendance, and, in areas with large Rom concentrations, to "organize a full day of education activities (including lunch)." In instances "where scholarship pupils exist, the money shall be used to ensure food supplies." Handicapped Gypsy children were to attend special schools, while special intensive courses were to be set up for all Roma who had not completed the eighth grade.[84]

Similar efforts were to be undertaken to deal with Gypsy unemployment, anchored by the provisions of Law 25/1976, which dealt with "the placement of all people fit to work in a useful work place." Emphasis was to be put on finding jobs for Roma in construction and agriculture. Gypsies who had special trades were to be given licenses that only allowed them to practice their skills in their resident county. County officials with state support, were to work with Gypsies to build homes with and develop plans "to do away with the dilapidated households and Gypsy caravans" and homes not located "on authorized building ground." State and local health officials were to locate all dilapidated houses in which "families have been infected with tuberculosis and other contagious diseases," as well as those housing "families with parasites." Infected housing was to be destroyed. Health authorities were to immunize Gypsies and to conduct monthly health and hygenic check-ups in areas with large Rom concentrations. The ministries of Health and Labor were to study the decree adopted by the Central Committee on June 14, 1980, that placed restrictions on families with more than five children and ensure that if government subsidies were paid for large families, that "one of the parents is employed in a useful social activity and that the children attend compulsory classes." The Ministry of Education was also to develop better means to ensure that Rom children from poor, large families could "benefit from a proper education." All three ministries were responsible for placing "abandoned Gypsy children, beggars or vagabonds in special social assistance units."[85]

State and local organizations were also to do more to "systematically execute special cultural and educational activities" in parts of the country with significant Roma populations, particularly in the areas of "political education and sanitary and moral education." Officials were to emphasize "learning about and respecting laws, Party decisions and documents." Gypsy groups were to be part of the national Celebration of Romania, with an eye toward "creating an appreciation for authentic [Gypsy] folklore." To ensure the success of these efforts, "well organized, respected and well looked upon" Gypsy families were to "be used to influence the behavior and way of life of the rest of the Gypsies." Roma "with a high civic consciousness and a positive attitude towards work" were to be promoted and elected throughout government and Party organizations nationwide. The 1977 local and state commissions created to look into better ways to integrate Gypsies into Romanian society were to be revived in order to study means to put into action the suggestions contained in the 1983 report.[86]

Unfortunately, most of these goals were not achieved. Some efforts were made between 1983 and 1985 to create a Gypsy cultural/neighborhood association. A Gypsy folk festival was held in Sibiu in the fall of 1984. However, when the Rom organizers tried to get permission to hold a second Gypsy festival the following year, the Propaganda Section of the Central Committee turned them down. This coincided with the growing emphasis by Ceauşescu on Romanian nationalism and the organic society, which "relegated all others to a position of secondary or tertiary rank." Linked to this was Ceauşescu's growing paranoia and megalomania, which caused a significant degeneration in the "intellectual and emotional climate of interethnic relations." Over time, government policies toward minorities, linked with the economy's decline, "made the physical and psychological conditions of the minorities intolerable."[87]

Ceauşescu's post-1983 housing and employment efforts for Roma met with mixed success. The housing goals were part of his "systematization" scheme, which centered around "a massive program of reorganization of the countryside" and was seen by some as directly discriminatory. Though the "systematization" program was not set up specifically to destroy Rom housing, entire Roma neighborhoods were razed, and Gypsies were forcibly settled in large apartment buildings. According to Nicolae Gheorghe, these new tenements were often "in urban ghettos" that caused "a deterioration of social life" for Gypsies. Roma were often given the housing of other minorities, particularly Hungarians and Germans, who had left Romania because of Ceauşescu's policies. Consequently, officials were unable to stop Gypsy nomadism, and Roma were able to get around the restrictions "by paying fines and bribes to the police." Brian Hall vividly described his encounter with destitute Romanian Gypsy nomads during his travels in the region at this time:

> I passed a Gypsy encampment just as the sun was setting. Three cat-like dogs came screaming up the road, but kept their teeth to themselves. The men and boys of the camp called out, as the Gypsies always do, for me to stop, but I pushed on. I remember the camp as a scene of pastoral squalor in the highest degree. The dogs were mangy and quarrelsome, the two horses thin and dispirited; horse manure and empty cans littered the ground; old clothes and discol-

ored blankets fluttered in the wind from tree branches and low bushes; filthy, torn plastic sheets made up most of the walls of the shacks; and garbage of all sorts lay, like crusted snow, in the creases of the earth.

Early the next morning, Hall was awakened by the "sound of hooves, the slap of reins. The Gypsies were on the move." Hall concluded that though some Roma continued to live as nomads, "Ceauşescu's government had made it clear that they would have to learn, sooner or later, how to be socialist citizens."[88]

Efforts for the dramatic improvements of Gypsy education and employment proved equally problematic, particularly in light of the country's growing impoverishment. According to Nestor Ratesh, by the end of the 1980s, Romania had become the "Ethiopia of Europe." The country's economic, social, and political impoverishment led to the violent overthrow of the regime of Nicolae and Elena Ceauşescu on December 22, 1989, which was fueled by the week of unrest that began in Hungarian communities in Transylvania. Three days after their capture, the Ceauşescus were violently executed after a makeshift kangaroo court convicted them of genocide.[89] In the violent days after the Ceauşescus' arrest, Gypsy children carried "water and food under fire exchanges to soldiers" who had joined the revolution against Ceauşescu's dreaded Securitate (secret police).[90]

The void left by the collapse of the Ceauşescu regime was filled quickly by the National Salvation Front (NSF or Frontul Salvării Naţionale), led by Ion Iliescu. Iliescu, a communist with outstanding credentials, had fallen into disfavor with Ceauşescu years earlier and had become identified within the Romanian Communist Party as an opponent of Ceauşescu. Almost immediately after taking power, the NSF proclaimed new democratic freedoms, including recognition of "the rights and freedoms of national minorities and their full equality with Romanians." Though the NSF was viewed initially as a provisional government, its decision on February 6, 1990, to register as one of the country's new political parties for elections later that spring triggered a wave of mass protests that severely undermined the NSF's credibility. On February 19, the government shipped 5,000 miners to Bucharest from the Jiu Valley to intimidate the protestors. The miners explained that their move was in response to unrest "perpetuated by 'hooligans and unemployed gypsies,'" while some demonstrators earlier had blamed violence within their own ranks on the Roma.[91]

Dissatisfaction with the NSF's political monopoly had already forced it to agree to share power until the May elections with an array of new political parties on a provisional, 180-member Council of National Unity. Seats were provided on the Council for "members of ethnic minorities," which allowed the Gypsies' new organization, the Democratic Union of the Romanies in Romania (DURR), to acquire observer and then permanent status for its representatives. The NSF, which also "had sought to give better treatment to the ethnic Hungarians and 13 other minorities in the country," also called upon Gypsy leaders such as Ion Cioaba, the chief of the nomadic and kettle smith Gypsies since 1971, to help restore order. Cioaba took his responsibilities quite seriously, and in mid-January 1990, he went on Bucharest radio to ask the Roma "to cease immediately all actions that create disorder and panic." A month later, he asked his radio listeners "to contribute to the country's economic recovery and to respect the achievements of the revolution." After Cioaba's talk, the radio announcer added: "Beautiful words! Let us hope that the deeds will match them!" Cioaba claimed during this period that "under the Ceauşescu regime Roma were detained and tortured and their prosperity, including the gold jewelry of the women, was forcibly taken by government officials."[92]

While official policy statements on minorities were aimed at Romania's traditionally more vocal ethnic groups, such as the Hungarians, more and more demographic evidence pointed to the Gypsies as one of the country's largest minorities. In 1987, the Minority Rights Group in London estimated that there were 760,000 Gypsies in Romania out of a total population of 22,683,000, though more generous estimates put the figure between 1 and 2 million. In 1992, Andre Liebich estimated that 760,000 was the highest credible figure, though Gypsy leaders claimed on the eve of Romania's 1992 census that the Gypsy population stood at 2.3 million out of an estimated 1991 population of 23.2 million.[93] According to one prominent Romanian demographer, Vasile Ghetan, the best way for the Roma to answer questions about their actual numbers was to persuade Gypsies "to declare their [true] nationality at the next census," something they had been hesitant to do in the past. Ghetan felt the recently created DURR could play an important role in getting more Gypsies to declare themselves Roma.[94]

In fact, there had been a frenzy of Gypsy political activity since the overthrow of the Ceauşescu dictatorship. Initially, most Roma had declared themselves supporters of the NSF, though in time more and more independent Gypsy organizations began to crop up. The DURR was the most prominent. Founded in Bucharest in mid-February 1990, it served as an umbrella organization for Roma throughout the country, including Bucharest Gypsies; "the nomads and the kettle smiths, with headquarters in Sibiu; the settled Gypsies and the fiddlers, with headquarters in Tirgu-Jiu; and the Hungarian-speaking and the 'silk' Gypsies, with headquarters in Cluj." The DURR supported Ion Iliescu in his bid for the country's presidency in elections on May 20, 1990, and sent representatives to the Fourth World Romani Congress in Poland earlier that spring. Among the more prominent Romanian delegates were Ion Cioaba, who represented the NSF and the DURR, and Octavia Stoica, a delegate for the Democratic Romani Alliance. Divisions among the Romanians at the Congress caused a bit of a stir, though Nicolae Gheorghe, who was appointed to the Congress's Encyclopedia Commission, gained the delegates' respect because of his struggle with Romania's National Minority Commission over categorizing national minorities. A number of other Gypsy political parties also surfaced during this period, including the United Democratic Party of the Romanies, the Fiddlers and Wood Carvers of Romania, the Tinsmith Romanies' Progressive Party, the Free Romanies' Democratic Party, the Gypsies' Party of Romania, the Free Democratic Union of Romanies, and the Christian Democratic Party of Romanies. Equally interesting was the Voluntary College of the Gypsy Elders' Council, whose representative appealed to his fellow Roma "'to halt any act of indiscipline' and overcome tribal dissension." Gheorghe Răducanu, representing the Romanies' (Gypsy) Democratic Forum, was given a seat in the Assembly of Deputies after the May 20 elections because of a law that insured "a representative for each minority unable to win representation through elections" to the lower house.[95]

Romania's Gypsies also took advantage of this highly charged atmosphere to begin a number of publications. Some, such as *O Glaso el Romengo/Glasul Romilor* (The Romanies' Voice), seemed to have links to the past. Others, such as *Citadela* (The Citadel), *Aven Amentza/Ventli Cu Noi* (Come with Us), *Neo Drom* (New Road), *Satra Libera* (The Free Gypsy Camp), and *Fruncea Tiganilor* (The Gypsy Elite), represented regional or tribal interests. Equally important were the creation of "'a Gypsy-language theater company in Timisoara,'" and efforts to publish the Bible in Romani.[96]

Unfortunately, this growing body of Gypsy political, literary, and cultural activities fed a growing wave of anti-Roma sentiment that continues to haunt Romania's Gypsies. It has manifested itself not only in increasing physical violence toward Gypsies but also in press accounts of the Roma. Within a month after the collapse of the Ceauşescu dictatorship, one Romanian newspaper accused Ceauşescu of being "of Tatar-Gypsy extraction," and said his wife, Elena, was also of Gypsy origin. Prominent Roma intellectual Nicolae Gheorghe felt the press was "resorting to an exotic scapegoat as a means of exorcizing their past," while Ion Cioaba noted that "[Ceauşescu] was no Gypsy." Cioaba added, "Whatever is no good, every reject, is left at the Gypsies' door."[97]

More tragic than these ridiculous charges were the growing acts of physical violence against the Roma. Bombarded by general feelings that the "Gypsies were 'a social sore,'" and "inclined at birth to larceny, fraud, robbery, [violent] crime, and so on," the Gypsies became the national scapegoats for Romania's immense problems. In 1991, Helsinki Watch reported 17 assaults on Gypsy communities since late 1989 and five Roma deaths attributed to mob violence. Equally troubling, said Helsinki Watch, was the failure of the Romanian police and the Romanian government to respond effectively and appropriately to these assaults. The collective impact of these attacks was "devastating for Romanian citizens of Gypsy ethnic origin."[98]

Government complicity in anti-Rom violence was particularly evident in the June 1990 pro-government, officially inspired miners' riot in Bucharest. The riots were in response to ongoing, peaceful demonstrations and protests that began in April 1990 against the continued presence of Ceauşescu operatives in high positions in government. On June 12, several weeks after the National Salvation Front had secured control of Romania's parliament and executive branch, President Iliescu decided to bring the demonstrations to an end. After police efforts proved ineffective, the government unleased 10,000 burly miners from Jiu Valley on the city. After wreaking havoc at the city's center, some of the miners then moved into Bucharest's Gypsy quarters, where they "ransacked their homes, stole their belongings, and severely beat many of the inhabitants." Other Roma were indiscriminately attacked on the streets merely for being Gypsies, while other Gypsies were arrested by the police. Romanian television proved quite supportive of the crackdown, creating an image of the protestors as Roma "dregs of society" who "camped out in the middle of Romania's capital, profiting from illegal activities." On June 13, Emanoil Valeriu, the head of Romanian state television, claimed in a broadcast that "the television studios had been attacked and destroyed by Gypsies" and asked the public "to protect and defend the institution." Later, Nicolae Gheorghe and Vasile Ionescu, representing the new Ethnic Federation of Gypsies, filed a legal complaint against Valeriu for "nationalistic and chauvinist propaganda, public instigation, [and] calumny."[99]

On May 31, 1991, the International Helsinki Federation for Human Rights protested "Pogroms against Gypsies in Romania," while six days later the International Labor Organization (ILO) decried continuing ethnic violence against the Roma and Hungarians. The ILO's report also zeroed in on the other problems facing the Gypsies of Romania:

> The situation of members of the Rom minority was characterised by both direct and indirect discrimination. Direct discrimination was based on presumed physical or moral characteristics, such as, for example, Gypsies don't like work. These generalisations have a racist character. They take on concrete form in the field of employment, in

the allocation of Roma to the most arduous jobs with the lowest social status, in wage differentiation and difficulties in respect to promotion. Indirect discrimination occurs in training and access to employment: certain Roma are marginalised because of their low incomes; consequently, their children are unable to receive the technical or vocational training provided by the educational system. The result is that these children encounter difficulties in respect of access to skilled jobs and are reduced to a marginal status which tends to repeat the pattern set by the previous generation.[100]

The violence, combined with the Roma's "extreme poverty, the prejudice and discrimination they are subject to, their traditional inclination to a nomadic way of life, and even their seemingly innate ability to cross frontiers illegally," triggered a "massive gypsy emigration from Romania." According to one Rom intellectual,

> the risks involved in being a Gypsy in Romania in 1990 persuade all those offered the opportunity to take refuge abroad; perhaps it is no better there, but at least you can nourish the hope that it is up to you alone to maintain your dignity.

Many of the Rom emigrants fled to Germany, a country increasingly troubled by the social and economic costs of reunification and a growing, non-German immigrant population. Almost 130,000 Romanians legally fled abroad in 1990, though Radio Bucharest claimed "that more than 800,000 people had emigrated in the first eight months of 1990." German authorities reported that over half of the 35,345 Romanians who entered Germany in 1990 were Gypsies, while in 1992, 33,600 Romanian Gypsies reached that country. The new arrivals were soon subjected to an upsurge of neo-Nazi and right-wing violence that resulted in a growing number of Roma deaths. On September 23, 1992, a month after riots against foreigners forced authorities in Rostock to evacuate 200 Romanian Gypsies from a hostel, German and Romanian officials signed an accord in Bucharest that gave "about $20 million to reintegrate Romanian citizens being deported from Germany." Estimates were that most of the 50,000 Romanians affected by the treaty, which went into effect on November 1, 1992, were Gypsies. The agreement, which was aimed at illegal Romanian refugees without proper documentation, did little to stem the tide of anti-Gypsy violence in Germany, with new outbursts in Rostock on the eve of the deportations. On December 6, 1992, the German parliament passed new legislation that made it more difficult for political refugees to enter the country.[101]

The Romanian Gypsy refugees in Germany reacted with horror to the news. George Petra felt the Roma were "automatically blamed for everything," and saw it as "a plan to exterminate us. It's a Nazi mentality." Natalia Muntean said she feared for the lives of her family if they were forced to return to Romania, while the International Romani Union said that Berlin was "sending thousands of people to hell." Romanian Gypsy leaders doubted if the money allotted for the reintegration of the emigrant Roma would be spent for such purposes. Costel Vasile, for example, pointed to the Iliescu government's failure to turn over a building promised to the Bucharest Rom community, while others said that the government had excluded Gypsies "from claiming land when the plots of state agricultural cooperatives were divided among farmers after the fall of communism." Gypsy leaders felt that the deported Roma would return to a community deeply affected by housing shortages and rising unemployment. Nicolae Stafanescu-Draganesti, the head of the Romanian League for the Defense of Human Rights, predicted that "with no jobs and no houses, the number of wrongdoers among them will only increase."[102]

One of the most tragic manifestations of Gypsy impoverishment in Romania centered around the plight of Gypsy orphans. Once the shroud of communist dictatorship fell in 1989, it was discovered that Romanian orphanages were filled with over 100,000 children abandoned by their parents in response to Ceaușescu's 1966 decree banning abortions for women "under 45 who had not yet produced four children." Westerners flocked to Romania in 1990 and 1991 legally or illegally to adopt or buy these orphans, which forced the Iliescu government to pass legislation in the summer of 1991 that made "selling babies a crime punishable by up to five years in prison" and outlawed the adoption of children "abandoned for less than five months." The law also created a Romanian Adoption Committee that would screen all requests by foreigners to adopt Romanian children. Sadly, a few Gypsies were identified in the Romanian press and elsewhere as prime movers in the Romanian "Baby Bazaar," though Romanian orphanage directors later reported that children of "mixed Gypsy and Romanian blood or full-blooded Gypsies" were "considered unadoptable—thoroughly undesirable."[103]

Such developments only strengthened negative Romanian images of the Gypsies. A report published by the National Police in July 1990 claimed that "11 percent of major crimes are committed by Gypsies," while a survey by the Romanian Institute of Public Opinion the following year found that "41% of those surveyed thought that Gypsies should be poorly treated." In October 1993, a Budapest daily, *Curierul National,* published another survey in which one respondent, Olivia D., said, "I'm sorry I don't have the power—I would exterminate them all." Nicolae Gheorghe, who in 1991 became head of the General Union of Romanies, which supplanted the DURR, felt that the Iliescu government was indifferent to the plight of the Roma and that it tolerated and justified violence against Gypsies. Human rights advocate Smaranda Enache added in the fall of 1993, "Gypsies 'are generally persecuted by the police, humiliated by local authorities and made to live on the margin.'" She also noted that there "is a large campaign to present Gypsies all the time as criminals, in the press and television, and this is perpetuated by teachers." This, Enache felt, "is a tragedy of our schools." Parliament member Gheorghe Raducanu pointed to educational failures of the Ceauşescu era as part of the reason for the low literacy rates of Gypsies, which Nicolae Gheorghe said were "'dramatically low'—less than half the Romany population." Gypsy parents felt that the quality of their childrens' education had degenerated since the 1989 revolution because of mounting prejudice. The Iliescu government did initiate a program in 1990–1991 "to train future teachers who will be more sensitive to the cultural and educational needs of Gypsy children." The new teachers under this program were also supposed to be able to "communicate with them in Romani." However, Gypsy parental suspicions about the program inhibited some of its early development.[104]

And here lies the barrier to a solution of the differences that confront Gypsies and non-Gypsies in Romania: suspicion and mistrust. Until these feelings are addressed, it will be difficult to overcome the complex social, educational, and economic issues facing not only Gypsies, but Romanian society as a whole. In the interim, the country's Roma will continue to live as scapegoats and outcasts.

.5.

RUSSIA

The Gypsies of Russia occupy a unique place in the history of European Rom. Relative latecomers to Russian parts of the burgeoning tsarist empire, Gypsy musicians—and a Rom mystique—captured the imaginations of the Russian public in the eighteenth and nineteenth centuries and became an integral part of Russian music, literature, and theater.

However, Gypsies entered future portions of the Russian Empire at a much earlier date. Central Asian Gypsies (the Liuli) began to move into that area in the tenth century to escape Muslim assaults in northern India, the original home of the Rom. Some legends, though, point to a migration of Gypsies into Central Asia from India as early as the fifth century. Kh. Kh. Nazarov, for example, who draws his work from A. P. Barannikov's pioneering study, *Tsygane SSSR* (1931), points to the legend told by the Persian poet Firdousi about 12,000 Indian Luri performing artists invited to the court of the Persian king, Bahram Gura, as entertainers in the fifth century A.D. This tale, which is also referred to by some Indian historians, would, according to Nazarov, "appear to coincide with historical reality." Angus Fraser notes in his *The Gypsies* (1992) that "*luli* or *Luri* are still Persian names for 'Gypsy.'"[1]

Gypsies moved into Ukraine, which later came under Russian control, from the Balkans as early as 1428. To the north, Rom in the future Polish and Lithuanian segments of tsarist Russia began to migrate along the southeastern Baltic littoral at the end of the fifteenth century, entering Poland to escape persecution in Germany. As their numbers dramatically increased, Polish officials called for their punishment and expulsion. In 1533, one Polish writer, Przyluski, "condemned Polish hospitality, and said that they [Gypsies] should be put in irons and sent to forced labour as convicts." In 1557, the city of Warsaw declared, "Gypsies, or people who are unnecessary, we will drive out from these lands and thereafter they are not to be received back into them." Eight years later, the city of Piotrków in western Poland ordered the expulsion of Gypsies. Both decrees were not adequately enforced, however, and in 1578, King Stephan Bathóry "threatened sanctions against people who harboured Gypsies on their lands—who were to be punished as accomplices of outlaws." Initially, some Rom moved into the Lithuanian portions of the new Polish-Lithuanian kingdom, where Lithuanian regulations were more moderate and designed "to try to make useful citizens of the Gypsies by providing special facilities and reliefs for them." In 1501, for example, Lithuanian officials gave Gypsies the "right to live according to privileges and customs granted earlier." New Lithuanian decrees in 1564–1566 declared that any Rom who wanted to remain in the country had to settle "under good lords" or risk expulsion. Gypsies were also allowed to serve in the Lithuanian army during time of war. Unfortunately, Lithuanian policies began to become more restrictive over the next twenty years while Gypsies were banned from Poland.[2]

Gypsies also entered Ukraine during this period from Wallachia, and by the end of the sixteenth century they were scattered throughout the region.[3] The Rom continued their migration into Ukraine via Germany and Poland throughout the seventeenth century in response to intensified persecution. Though the mistreatment of Rom was particularly harsh in some of the German states, the Gypsies also found themselves increasingly unwelcome in Poland. The only exception was in Podlesie in eastern Poland bordering Belorussia, where Rom blacksmiths were a vital part of the economy. Officials in Podlesie protested Poland's strict anti-Gypsy legislation, which prompted the Sejm in Warsaw to modify some of it in 1601 and 1607. As a result, "Podlesie ceased to fall within the jurisdiction of the harsh legislation covering the rest of the country, and thus provided a refuge for large numbers of Gypsies who fled here from other areas."[4]

The growing domestic and international friction that beset Poland during this period saw the government's anti-Gypsy measures fall into disuse. In fact, because of the military needs of Poland's dominant class, the magnates, and efforts to gain more control over Poland's growing Gypsy population, the Rom acquired some stature with the creation of the official position of the king of the Gypsies. Created between 1624 and 1652, the Polish crown saw it as a way to stop Gypsy "lawlessness and criminality, and force Gypsies to pay taxes." Though its first appointees were Rom, King Jan Kazimierz Vasa made John

Nawrotynski, a non-Gypsy, the Rom monarch in 1668. The position would continue to be held by Polish noblemen until 1780, when King Stanislaus Augustus Poniatowksi appointed a Polish nobleman, Jakub Znamierowski, "headman for the area of the Grand Duchy of Lithuania only." In 1795, Znamierowski died, the same year that Poland disappeared as a nation, a victim of three partitions of Poland in 1772, 1793, and 1795 by Russia, Austria, and Prussia. The Polish Gypsy throne remained vacant until the reemergence of an independent Polish state after World War I.[5]

The Gypsy migration along the southeastern Baltic littoral continued during this period. A Latvian Rom legend, "May Rose," is drawn from a similar Latvian tale about events that took place in the early seventeenth century. Rom also began to move into Moldavia at this time, while Gypsies are mentioned in a document published in Moscow in 1660. Thirty-six years later, a Gypsy named Jacob was captured by Peter the Great's forces after his victory at Azov on July 22, 1696. The tsar (r. 1682–1725) had Jacob "carted in the triumphal entry of the Czar into Moscow on a cart in which tall gallows took the place of the cover, with a crescent on his breast and the hangmen by him, and [had him] executed as a traitor to the faith and the Czar." The speculation was that Jacob had been sent by Peter I to spy on the Turks, but had "deserted to the other side and then betrayed secrets."[6]

By the early eighteenth century, Ukraine had a mixed Rom population of nomads and sedentary Gypsies. According to M. Plokhinsky, both groups dealt "in horses and bartering horses, as well as farriery, smithcraft, and stealing; women practised fortune-telling, conjuring, etc. In food and dress they did not differ much from the Ukrainians." Plokhinsky adds:

> The Gypsies of the Ukraine living on the left bank of the Dnieper were divided, as well as the Little Russians [Ukrainians], into ten regiments; at the head of each regiment stood a Gypsy chieftan. As long as lease existed, the Gypsy chieftans were appointed by the leaseholders, although with the assent of the administration; when the lease was annulled, the chieftan was named by the General Office of the Army. The gypsies had the right to ask for the appointment of one or another chieftan, and this chieftan, in his turn, named the chief of the regiments. To the Gypsies of Little Russia were joined in the 18th century the Gypsies of Wallachia who were governed by their own chieftans. The principle duty of the chieftans consisted in ruling the Gypsy population subject to them; as long as lease existed, they were obliged to collect taxes from the Gypsies.[7]

Gypsies continued to migrate into Russia during this period along the southeastern Baltic coast, in central Russia, and into western Siberia. In 1721, mention is made of Gypsies in Tobolsk, the administrative center of the region and a "mighty fur-collecting city."[8] On June 7 and July 5, 1733, Empress Anne Ivanova (r. 1730–1740) ordered Gypsies to pay taxes to help form a new military regiment. Several months later, the Russian Senate, created by Peter the Great to oversee provincial administration and the collection of taxes and to be the country's highest judicial authority, decreed that Gypsies could live in Ingermanland, or Ingria, the area that encompassed St. Petersburg, and could engage in horsetrading.[9]

One Soviet gypsiologist, L. N. Cherenkov, suggested that some Rom had begun to move into the Crimea by the mid-eighteenth century, though another, V. I. Naulko, felt that the Gypsies did not enter the region until the end of that century.[10] In Ukraine, Rom leaders "were given the right of dispensing justice among the members of the Gypsy population" after 1757 and were responsible for keeping the Rom "from unpleasantness." The Rom in Ukraine were regarded as a group that was "inferior to the common people" and were required to pay "a fixed tax into the Military Treaty of Little Russia ('Boiskoboi Malorossiskii Skap.')."[11]

Complaints about the growing Rom presence in the Russian capital, St. Petersburg, prompted Empress Elizabeth (r. 1741–1762) to issue a decree on August 16, 1759, that forbade Gypsies from entering the city and its environs. (Elizabeth's decree would not be repealed until 1917).[12] On March 1, 1766, the Senate enacted new legislation that imposed a 70-kopek tax on Gypsies and ordered that after the beginning of 1767, unsettled Rom would be restricted to the *guberniyas* (provinces) of Slobodska Ukraine around Kharkov, Moscow, Voronezh, Astrakhan, and Kazan. A census done in the Belgorod *guberniya* north of Kharkov from 1763 to 1767 showed that of the 4,441 Rom settled in the region, "there were only 11 families who chose a permanent settlement for themselves." The Gypsy chieftan, Minenku, collected taxes from the Belgorod Rom community totaling 591 rubles, 58.25 kopeks during this period. The only other statistics available on Gypsies are from the midst of the Russo-Turkish War of 1768–1774, when "456 Rom families with five chieftans were forced to move from Bendery to Novorossiya." Bendery, in Moldavia, was taken after a two-month siege by the Russians on September 16, 1770. Novorossiya (New Russia) was a new *guberniya* created by Catherine the Great (r. 1762–1796) in 1764 that included parts of central and southern Ukraine.[13]

It was during this period that Count Aleksei Grigor'evich Orlov, a court favorite of Catherine the Great's and brother of one of her lovers, Grigorii Orlov, organized Russia's first private chapel Gypsy choir, drawing both male and female singers from the serf population of the village of Pushkino near

Moscow. Orlov's Gypsy choir became "very much in vogue in its day and could often be heard at the soirées given by Catherine the Great's favourites, such as Prince Potemkin, Zubov and Zorich." In time, "a Gypsy chorus and a good orchestra were indispensable adornments in the home of every important member of the nobility." Certain literary and musical circles became entranced with the Rom, which prompted an interesting poetic dialogue between two of the more innovative poets of Catherine the Great's era, Gavrila Derzhavin and Ivan Dmitriev. In 1788, a short, two-act operetta called *The Gypsy* was produced in Moscow with Roma playing the three principal parts. Rom music was also used in "several plays and vaudevilles arranged with Gypsy songs by the talented conductor Koshinsky" during this period.[14]

Catherine the Great's oblique interest in Gypsies made her a favorite subject of Rom folk legends. According to one story, the Empress

> once watched a tall, dirty, bedraggled, bearded Gypsy passing up and down below her windows. She ordered Prince Potemkin to bring that Gypsy to her apartments.
>
> An hour later, the Gypsy was ushered into her presence. But he had been bathed, perfumed, and his beard had been shaven. Instead of his rags, he wore beautiful garments. Catherine was furious. 'I wanted him as he was, and not as he is,' she cried out.
>
> The Gypsy looked at her steadily, and then, recalling to Catherine her humble origin under which he had known her, he said: 'And I, too, have wanted you as you were and not as you are.'
>
> Incensed by the remark of the Gypsy, Catherine ordered that he be stripped nude and made to stay outdoors overnight, chained to a warmly dressed soldier. It was forty degrees below zero. In the morning, Catherine went to see what had happened. The soldier was dead, frozen stiff, while the naked Gypsy was snoring peacefully beside him.[15]

Catherine's mythical fascination with the Rom did not prevent her from addressing problems of Gypsy idleness and nomadism, particularly when it related to the collection of state taxes. On December 31, 1783, the Senate tried to halt the mobility of the Rom and other unregistered peasants by limiting their ability to "negotiate [the] departure from one landowner in order to move to another." Gypsies were regarded as state peasants (*gosudarstvennyye krest'yane*), a group that made up 26.25 percent of the total peasant population in the census of 1762–1764. State peasants were found primarily "in northeast Russia and Siberia, along the old military lines in the south, and in Left Bank Ukraine, and New Russia." The state peasant's status was much better than that of a serf since he had some freedom of movement and occupation.

At the same time, the state peasant had some labor and financial obligations to the state. Peter the Great ordered in 1724 that the free peasants pay a poll tax of 70 kopeks, plus a tax or obrok (quitrent) of 40 kopeks, a regulation that was extended to "Little Ukraine, Slobodska Ukraine, the Baltic Provinces and Finland, and the newly acquired Polish provinces" in 1770. The 1783 decree brought the spirit of the 1770 regulation to complete fruition. Officials hoped that the nomadic Gypsies would end their idle ways and begin to live productive, settled lives.[16] The Senate followed up the 1783 decree with new ones on January 24 and November 4, 1784. The first enabled Count George Browne, the governor-general of Livonia (Latvia) and Estonia, regions acquired from Sweden during the Great Northern War (1700–1721), to place wandering Gypsies from neighboring districts under surveillance and then to return them to their appropriate region. As a result of a report from Moscow's tax collector, the decree of November 4 stipulated that Gypsies without a passport would not be able to travel outside Riga or Revel (Tallinn). To obtain travel documents, Rom would have to register with city officials, which would make them subject to government taxes.[17]

Gypsies were also mentioned in a decree of the procurator general of May 28, 1792, that dealt with the collection of taxes in the Ekaterinoslav *guberniya*. Theoretically, the procurator general "was the link between the Senate and the sovereign" and wielded vast authority through local procurators who served as the monarch's eyes and ears throughout the country. The May 28 decree levied a tax of 14,451 rubles and 7.5 kopeks on the *guberniya*'s Rom and warned them not to do anything to hinder the collection of the poll tax.[18] The Ekaterinoslav *guberniya* had been created after the formal Russian acquisition of the Crimea from Turkey in 1783 and was part of the southern Russian "empire" of Grigory A. Potemkin, one of the most important figures in Catherine the Great's reign until his death in 1791. The *guberniya* was centered at Ekaterinoslav, which was named by Potemkin for his former lover, the empress, in 1778. From Ekaterinoslav, Potemkin also ruled the *guberniyas* of New Russia and Azov, and the Crimea. As these areas were underpopulated, Potemkin invited settlers from throughout Europe to his "empire." Earlier efforts to increase the size of the Rom population in the area were unsuccessful. The 456 Gypsy families sent to Novorossiya in 1768–1774 had dwindled to only 255 men and a smaller number of women by 1794. According to government officials, the Rom in the Ekaterinoslav guberniya "wandered from town to town and presented something of a plague for the population of Novorossiya."[19] Captain Sergei Pleschev made a similar observation in his 1792 account, *Survey of the Russian Empire*:

About the Don, as well as in almost every part of Russia, from time to time are found gipsies, a race well known every where by their cheating and pilfering. They have no fixed residence, but wander continually from one place to another, and exercise the trades of blacksmiths and farriers and horse-dealers, which last they generally do by exchanging instead of selling their horses. In order to collect the poll-tax with more certainty, the greatest part of them are put under the inspection of different masters, of whom they are obliged to take their passports before they can go upon their peregrinations.[20]

To the far north, similar feelings were expressed in Lithuania in 1787, an area which was soon to come under Russian control during Catherine the Great's final Partition of Poland in 1795. A minister there felt that "Gypsies in a well-ordered state are like vermin on an animal's body."[21] The clergyman best described Lithuania's forest Rom, who were so poor that "even in severe frosts they go out covered in sheets, carry their babies in bags hanging from their backs." Other Lithuanian Rom groups, such as the Golden Horde, Lithuania's richest Gypsies, were better off, and linked to Jakub Znamierowski, the headman of Lithuanian Roma. The collapse of the Polish kingdom in 1795 saw a "mass exodus of the Gypsies from Lithuania." Those that remained in Russia soon drew the attention of its new ruler, Paul I (r. 1796–1801), the son of Catherine the Great. On February 2, 1799, he issued an imperial ukase that declared that Gypsies who had previously wandered free in Lithuania now came under the umbrella of the Senate decree of December 31, 1783, and were thus state peasants of the Russian Empire, with all of the obligations that accompanied this status.[22]

Paul followed up this decree with a more restrictive Senate ukase on July 16, 1800, that ordered the registration of Gypsies throughout the empire wherever they were located. Motivated by a desire to undo what he felt were the disastrous reforms of his mother, Paul worked to reestablish Russian absolutism and bring tranquility and order to his country. He sought to rule the country with military efficiency and insisted that "each segment of society, from the great nobility to the peasant serfs, was confirmed and reinforced in its traditional role and status." The July 16 ukase laid out the difficulties of collecting taxes from Gypsies in different parts of the country. In some areas, officials had successfully collected taxes from settled Rom involved in farming or business, though they found it difficult to collect revenue from heavily impoverished Gypsies, particularly those who refused to work on state lands as peasant laborers or who were unfamiliar with farming. In some instances, Gypsies who continued to wander were often allowed to settle with their families on local estates for a small fee.[23]

Paul's son and successor, Alexander I (r. 1801–1825), followed this up with a Senate ukase on June 17, 1803, that was based upon the recommendation of Viktor P. Kochubei, the head of the new Ministry of the Interior. Concerned about the disorderliness and impudence of some Rom, the ukase decreed that the Gypsies should be gathered together in small groups and settled in government villages. Once settled, the Rom would be deprived of their passports to prevent them from leaving the area. The ukase mentioned the difficulty that one official in Nizhegorodsk in the Crimea had with local Gypsies and warned against the unfair treatment of Rom.[24]

Two years later, an imperial name-day ukase gave a group of Russians in the Saratov region on the lower Volga permission to move to an area on the Uzen River that had a small Gypsy population. The ukase noted that the Rom lived in villages in the region and worked as petty tradesmen and cattle drovers.[25] Officials continued to watch the Rom and remained concerned about their continual wanderings. A report from the Senate prompted a new government decree on April 20, 1809, that reinforced earlier policies and reemphasized the need for Gypsies to settle and register with officials in villages and towns throughout the country. The ukase noted that the adoption of a sedentary lifestyle by the Rom would improve their lot.[26] The following year, the newly created Ministry of Police, charged with protecting "the life and property of individuals as well as maintaining the internal security of the State," became responsible for overseeing Gypsies in Russia. Armed with a new watchdog agency, on September 28, 1811, the Senate ordered the registration of Gypsies throughout the country by January 1, 1812, and in Siberia by July 1, 1812. Those who failed to register with police officials by this date would be regarded as vagrants and slackers. Such registration allowed for the better collection of taxes from the Rom, as evidenced by the imposition of a two-ruble head tax on Gypsies in the Taurida *guberniya* in the Crimea on February 20, 1812. Seven years later, Alexander I abolished the police agency amidst charges that its operatives had "not been confining themselves to gathering information, [but rather had] been seeking to incite crimes and suspicions." The Ministry of the Interior subsequently took over the functions of the Ministry of Police.[27]

Russia acquired more Gypsies after Alexander I signed the Treaty of Bucharest with Turkey on May 16, 1812, which ended the six-year Russo-Turkish War and ceded Bessarabia to Russia. Occupied by Russia during most of the war, the southern part of Bessarabia

> was virtually depopulated as a result of the Russian expulsion of the Turks and Tatars living there during the 1806–1812 war. During the

war Russian schismatics, runaway serfs and outlaws moved into the region and their presence was tolerated by the Tsarist authorities. After the war they were joined by state peasants, Germans, Bulgarians, Swiss and Romanians in officially sponsored immigration.

Among the new settlers in Bessarabia were Gypsies, who were included in a series of decrees that accompanied the charter granted the region by Alexander I in 1818. The tsar gave the region "a considerable degree of self-government" and left the "Romanians' social, governmental, tax and legal systems virtually intact." (Serfdom was never introduced into Bessarabia by the Russians.)[28] The rights and privileges of Gypsies were laid out in the new charter, and some Rom were initially attracted to the region because of its liberal immigration laws. However, over the next decade, Russian officials phased out most of the local privileges, which were almost completely eliminated in a new charter in 1828. In 1824, Gypsies were included in a regulation that defined the rights of guilds in Bessarabia, although in paragraph 4 of the new Bessarabian charter of 1828, the Rom became the serfs of Bessarabian or Russian landlords. The following year, another decree forbade Bessarabian Gypsies from working on state lands, while an official statement in 1831 noted that the sale of Gypsies in Bessarabia without land was not an act of emancipation. By 1836, 752 Gypsy families had settled on 9,902 *dessiatines* of land (1 *dessiatine* equals 2.7 acres) in Bessarabia. There were now two Rom villages in the province: Kair with 141 huts and Faraonovka with 146 huts.[29]

In the new Russian-controlled Polish kingdom created at the Congress of Vienna in 1815, Gypsies found themselves subject to equally harsh tsarist policies. On May 11, 1816, the government issued an "Order of the Government Commission for Internal Affairs and Police," that gave Rom six months to settle if they wanted to stay in Poland.

> The local district, municipal and parish authorities were obliged to record the personal particulars of Gypsies on special forms provided for the purpose; these data were to include also information on the place which the Gypsies had chosen for permanent settlement. On receipt of this information, the local authorities were to provide the Gypsies with certificates which would enable them to travel to the place that they had chosen for settlement.

The decree had provisions that allowed Gypsies who "maintain[ed] themselves from their labour or from an honest and useful craft" the right to acquire a travel permit, though local officials were instructed "to record the time spent in the place and their employment there." Polish authorities soon withdrew these liberal privileges because of difficulties with nomadic Rom and ultimately gave travel certificates only to permanently settled, single, male Gypsies who could travel in search of jobs. Local authorities often had difficulty interpreting the new regulations and periodically questioned officials in Warsaw about them. The prefect in Radom department, south of Warsaw, who had recently arrested and questioned a band of 40 Gypsies, asked what to do with "Gypsies against whom no offence had been proved, but 'from their way of life there is no profit.'" In 1819, authorities in the Mazoiva region near Warsaw asked the government for directions on handling 24 Gypsy Ursari (bear leaders or trainers). On July 13, they were told that the Ursari could have a passport for a year to move to any district they chose to stay with their bears but that they had to settle permanently in their area of choice. If they failed to do this, "they would be punished as 'breaking the law of the country.'" The Ursari never stopped wandering, however, and used the passports "to move on from place to place." Polish officials punished "the village headmen for granting 'visas' to Gypsies 'who engaged in vagabondage' and imposed a fine for this of six Polish zlotys." Local authorities took the fine to heart and on July 20, 1820, arrested 15 Gypsy families for "lazy vagabondage" because they "had suddenly descended upon the inn at Rzyszew and behaved very noisily."[30]

In Russia proper, a caring paternalism toward the Gypsies seems to have surfaced during this period. One document in late 1832 noted the exemption from military service and taxes (plus arrears of 427 rubles and 95 kopeks) of 54 northern Caucasian Gypsies in the village of Nizhnepodgorni in the Pyatigorsk *okrug* (district). This exemption, which was given for five years, was compensation for deaths, kidnappings, and other losses suffered at the hands of robbers. (Gypsy financial losses in the raids totalled 13,659 rubles and 60 kopeks, with 6 Rom dead and 22 captured by the bandits.) The same year, northern Caucasian Gypsies in the Stavropol region were exempted from service in the Volga Cossack regiment for five years: the exemption was extended in 1838.[31]

However, three months later, Gypsies in the Crimean region of Taurida were ordered to form two military work companies and two correctional companies for state labor. This represented a renewed effort to make Gypsies useful members of the Russian nation. On April 29, 1839, a decree ordered all Gypsies throughout the Russian empire to settle on or before January 1, 1841. Gypsies now came under the jurisdiction of Pavel D. Kiselev, head of the recently created Ministry of State Domains and architect of a reform program designed to improve the administration and plight of the country's 20 million state peasants. Efforts to free them from the "tyranny of the petty provincial bureaucrats" failed, however, because the new system placed them under another "tyrannical, rigid, corrupt-ridden bureaucracy." In Finland, which enjoyed an autonomous status directly under the tsar, the sons of Gypsies in prison or without a steady livelihood were threatened with military service. Other documents point to efforts to improve the lot of Gypsies in Sevastopol through education.[32]

On December 10, 1846, Nicholas I decreed the registration of state Gypsies, while the following year, landowners in Bessarabia were forbidden to own Gypsies, who were now regarded as petty bourgeoisie. In 1848, the Senate ordered a new Gypsy census in Bessarabia, and in 1850 the Council of Ministers issued new recommendations for the control of Gypsies who belonged to the Don and Azov Cossack hordes. As friction with Turkey loomed on the horizon, efforts were made to insure Gypsy military service. On December 22, 1852, Gypsies in the Taurida region who had not registered with a Cossack horde were liable for general military conscription. By 1853, Russo-Turkish antagonism had exploded into the Crimean War, which pitted Russia against Turkey, Britain, and France, with the bulk of the fighting in the Crimea. Consequently, in late October 1855, as all sides looked for a way out of the devastating Crimean stalemate, Taurida's Gypsies were informed that they had the same military obligations as the region's Muslim Tatars. On January 9, 1856, state Gypsies throughout Russia were placed in the same military service category as everyone else in their communities.[33]

Three weeks later, the combatants signed the Protocol of Vienna, which ended the war and humiliated Russia. Russia's defeat was compounded by its tremendous human losses (over 450,000 dead) and the severe economic dislocations and indebtedness suffered throughout the tsarist empire. The peasants suffered the most, and by the end of the war, great numbers were deeply impoverished. Russia's new ruler, Alexander II (r. 1855–1881), who succeeded to the throne after the death of his father, Nicholas I, on March 2, 1855, slowly came to realize the need to address directly the country's most severe problem—serfdom. One high official in Alexander II's government called serfdom the "question of questions, the evil of evils, the first of all our misfortunes." The tsar agreed, prompted less by humanitarian feelings than by fear "that it was better to liberate the peasants from above than to wait until they freed themselves, from below." Between 1856 and 1861, great efforts were put into the creation of a complex emancipation program. Announced on March 3, 1861, it gave state and private peasants freedom with land acquired through longterm redemption payments to the government. Peasant dreams and tsarist economic reality clashed quickly as disillusionment with the terms of the emancipation surfaced. In may ways, the peasant was worse off after 1861 because of "fiscal burdens, social and economic disabilities and an uncontrollable population growth." The nobility found themselves "impoverished by

the liberation without even the consolation of increased political influence."
The country's Rom suffered the same fate as other peasants who continued to
wallow in dire poverty.[34]

In Poland, where the peasants had been free for over 50 years, nationalists
took advantage of the reformist spirit of Alexander II as he moved the rest of
Russia toward full emancipation. This changed atmosphere did little to help
Poland's Rom, who since 1849 had suffered from new regulations that encouraged police and other officials to initiate Gypsy hunts for rewards.
Unfortunately, the Polish dragnet often captured sedentary Gypsies and
arrested them on trumped up charges of "vagabondage" to obtain a reward.
Polish officials also inflated the age of Gypsies, since rewards were higher for
adults than for children, and in some instances officials claimed dead Rom
among their living victims. The plight of Poland's Gypsies was compounded
by the migration of Kalderash (tinsmiths) and Lovari Rom from Wallachia,
Moldavia, Hungary, and Transylvania into Poland in the 1860s. The
Kalderash, well-to-do by Gypsy standards, were described as "beautiful figures, well-built, with clear and piercing eyes," tried "to establish a dominant
position among the Gypsies and even to create, in the Kwiek family, a dynasty
of 'kings' of Polish Gypsies." Resented by Polish Rom, and discouraged by
Poland's own disorders, such as the January Uprising of 1863 that prompted
a harsh tsarist, anti-Polish crackdown, these new immigrants would later
make their way out of Poland into Russia and elsewhere. These moves into
Russia were later put into song and performed by Pyotr Demeter, an actor with
the Moscow "Romen" Theater: "From the country Romany which is not on
the map. From the country dispersed by an indelible wind I rode and rode on
a swift horse, and dismounted on the Russian side."[35]

The suffering of the Gypsies and other peasants during this troubling period
in Russian history did little to weaken Russian fascination with the Rom. The
Gypsy choral tradition begun by Aleksei Orlov continued to blossom, creating new professional outlets for some Russian Gypsies as it spread to Moscow,
St. Petersburg, and other parts of the empire. During the heyday of Russian
choral music between 1775 and 1825, choirs "had a profound impact upon the
status of Church music and choral musicians in Russia." The private choirs
"were the only musical establishments where vocal ensemble and choral
music was cultivated in Russia at the time." By the early nineteenth century,
the Orlov Gypsy choir was directed by the "indefatigable collector of folk-
songs," Ivan Trofimov. After his death, Trofimov was replaced by his nephew,
Ilya Sokolov, who directed the Orlov Gypsy choir through the mid-nineteenth
century and moved it to Moscow before the French invasion in 1812. Nicholas
I invited Sokolov and the Orlov choir to perform at one of the tsar's palace

concerts for Franz Liszt, an aficionado of Gypsy music, during the Hungarian composer's concert tour of Russia in 1843. The Orlov choir's music entranced him so much that he "took off his decorations and put them in his pocket, closed his eyes, leaned back and gave himself up to the delight of listening." Several days later, Liszt arrived quite late for a concert at a packed Bolshoi Theater. Once he appeared, he immediately enraptured his audience with a Gypsy tune, "You Don't Know How Charming You Are," followed by "improvised variations on the melody." During the intermission, he revealed that he had been late because he "had been visiting some Gypsies earlier in the evening and had become so engrossed in listening to them that he had forgotten all about the concert." Liszt personally invited Sokolov and the Orlov choir to his final 1843 concert in Russia. Russian Gypsies so fascinated him that he devoted an entire chapter to them, "The Gypsy Women of Moscow," in his 1859 *Bohemiéns et de leur musique en Hongrie.* Yet Liszt felt that though

> their music has 'inimitable charm,' few of the women there have beautiful voices. Too exposed to atmospheric changes, too accustomed to strong drinks, too soon fatigued by their extravagant dances and the cries with which they intersperse them; too exhausted by the weight of their children . . . the freshness in quality of their voices disappears rapidly, and is succeeded by a loss of voice before their youth can be said to have entirely passed.[36]

Over time, the original Gypsy choral repertoire spread beyond the confines of religious music and drew

> upon traditional Russian and Ukrainian folk songs as well as the poetic songs of Alexandr Sumarokov, Ivan Dmitriev, and Gavrila Derzhavin. The gypsy chorus soon transformed these songs harmonically and structurally to make them more compatible with their own folk tradition. They simplified the coloring and style, endowing the songs with a greater potential for improvisation, and inserted refrains, stripping the lyrics of their bookish quality.[37]

S. P. Zhikarev, a government official and diarist, vividly described the vibrant Gypsy dancing and music at the Orlov summer estate in his 1805–1806 journal, *Notes.* Derzhavin's 1805 "Gypsy Dance" particularly lent itself to Rom musical interpretation with its "exotic sexuality" and "hypnotically sensual twirling of a Gypsy woman."[38]

The 1812 conflict with Napoleon saw younger, emancipated members of the Gypsy choirs join Hussar and Ulan units in the army. Older Gypsies contributed a great deal of money to the war effort; the smallest amount contributed by a single member of the Orlov chorus was 500 rubles. According to an anonymous source used by Vladimir Bobri in his "Gypsies and Gypsy Choruses of Old Russia," after the war ended,

> it became the vogue among the Muscovites to have large dinner parties in the out-of-town inns, with Gypsies supplying the entertainment. All dishes (and there were usually at least a hundred) were served in the old-fashioned Russian style, in keeping with the reaction against everything French which followed the invasion. To stress further the national character of these occasions, the inn-keeper-hostess would usually officiate in the old-time Russian dress of gold brocade with a towering head-dress and quantities of pearls and turquoises. She would likewise be made up in the 18th century fashion, which, in the words of our anonymous informant, "made her look like a doll heavily rouged and whited." The guests would dine, and then would summon the chorus to perform. The Gypsies were splendidly attired. The girls were usually wrapped in rich gold-embroidered shawls hanging from one shoulder and leaving the other bare. Their earrings, bracelets and necklaces were a profusion of small gold-coins. All the men were bearded, and wore yellow, red or multi-coloured shirts with rolled-up sleeves. The savage vigour of their performance often reached the point of sheer frenzy. Their wild shouts would electrify the audience, and sometimes, says our chronicler, "it is difficult to realize that they were denizens of this planet."

Russians who frequented these *traktirs* (inns) were known as *guliaka* or "'rake[s]' ... the Russian counterpart of the *aficionado* of all things Flamenco in Spain." The *guliaka* went to the inn daily, drank heavily, and threw "large amounts of money to the Gypsy girls for their songs." Wealthier *guliaka* "would throw fistfuls of gold and silver into the midst of the Gypsy singers," and, if "particularly pleased . . . he would break the dishes and glasses, sweep everything off the table on to the floor, and smash the all the mirrors in the establishment."[39]

Three types of Gypsy music evolved during this period, with the seven-stringed Russian guitar as the favored instrument for choral accompaniment. The first, "*polevuiye tsiganskiye peisny* 'Gypsy songs of the fields,'" or "*tabornuiye* 'of the camp,'" were simple and folklorist in style. They could be performed by a choir or by a solo performer. The next style, Gypsy "Road House," music, "was exclusively choral, and harmonically more elaborate." The third type of Gypsy music, "Gypsy romances," was not Rom music at all but rather music composed "by Russians in a more or less Gypsy-like style."

Though some Gypsy musicians would later adopt some of these tunes, they were not considered authentic. This type of music was particularly popular with the educated classes of Russia, and it was a rare family "that did not possess an album of 'Gypsy' transcriptions for piano," usually "Gypsy romances."[40] One of the first serious composers in Gypsy music was Alexis N. Verstovsky, who used Rom music in some of his early compositions and who eventually became director of the Imperial Opera in Moscow. His interest in Gypsies was partly motivated by the fact that he "married a beautiful and talented young actress who had carried the public by storm in scenes from Pushkin's *The Gypsies*."[41]

The most famous Russian Gypsy singer during this period was Tanya (Tat'yana Dmitrievna Dem'yanova). Born in 1808, Tanya was a member of the Orlov chorus directed by Ilya Sokolov. Her singing "often reduced the great poet Pushkin to tears," and

> there is a story that the celebrated Italian soprano Catalani heard her sing, burst into tears, and taking from her own shoulders a magnificent cashmere shawl, presented it to the Gypsy, saying: "This shawl was given to me in token of my being a singer without peer—but I can see that you deserve it more than I do."

The novelist Boleslaw Markevich later discussed Pushkin with Tanya, particularly Pushkin's relationship with his close friend, Pavel V. Nashchokin. Nashchokin lived with a Gypsy, Olga, who bore him two children. Pushkin was a godfather to one of them, a girl, and "was an intimate of the disorderly ménage which he describes realistically." Tanya also inspired three poems by Nikolai M. Yazykov; "Vesennyaya Noch" (Spring Night), "Tat'yane Dmitrievna—Elegiya," and "Persten" (Ring Finger).[42]

Pushkin's fascination with the Rom began during his forced exile in Bessarabia and elsewhere during the early 1820s for "political radicalism." During trips

> to Akkerman and Izmail . . . he had been able to take a closer look at these proud creatures, verminous, independent, hospitable, incomprehensible. He talks to the bear trainers and the handsome, brown and supple girls who read your palm and stole your watch with an engaging smile. He had loved them. And he re-created them accurately in his poem.

These experiences inspired him to begin his masterful lyric poem "The Gypsies" in December 1823. Completed in 1826, it depicted the Rom of Bessarabia "as ideal representatives of a natural state of human society" affected by the "transitory nature of existence." At least one commentor, D. S. Mirsky, regarded it as "the most temptingly universal imaginative work in the Russian language." Its opening passages celebrated the freedom of Rom life:

> The Gypsies Bessarabia roam
> In noisy crowds . . . Above a river
> In tattered tents they make their home,
> From night's cool breeze seeking cover.
> In open air calm is their sleep;
> Like freedom glad their rest is . . . Under
> The rug-hung caravans there leap
> A fire's bright flames whose shadows wander
> And lick the wheels; close to the blaze,
> A family for supper gathered,
> Prepare their meal; a tame bear lies
> Behind the tent; nearby, untethered,
> The horses graze . . . The steppe all round
> Is full of life . . .

The poem details the tragic moral interaction of the Rom with a non-Gypsy, Aleko, who has settled among them because he feels the Gypsies were the "sole possessors of truth." Aleko marries a Rom, Zemfira, who falls in love with another. Jealousy overcomes Aleko, who murders his wife and her Gypsy lover. Zemfira's father tells Aleko:

> 'Go, proud one, leave us! We are led
> By different laws and want among us
> No murderer . . . Go where you will!
> By your black deeds and foul you wrong us
> Who do not like to wound or kill.
> Your love of freedom—how you flaunt it!
> Yet for yourself alone you want it,
> This freedom, and a stranger dwell
> Here in our midst. We're kind and humble;
> You're hard; where you dare tread, we stumble—
> So go in peace and fare you well.'[43]

"The Gypsies" appeared on the stage in 1832, but it was received with less praise than his poem, since many critics felt it "was essentially literary and not adapted to the theatre." Pushkin's lengthy poem inspired other efforts, such as Stepan P. Shevyrev's 1828 poems "Gypsy Song" and "Gypsy Dance" and Mikhail Lermontov's 1829 "The Gypsies." The following year, Koshinsky's late eighteenth-century Gypsy plays were revived, and in 1831, Pushkin's friend and contemporary Evgenii A. Baratynski published a narrative poem, "The Concubine," that was later retitled "The Gypsy Girl (Tsyganka)." Baratynski's first dramatic poem, "The Gypsy Girl" deals with "a dark beauty who kills her unfaithful lover, trying to reconquer his love by what she believes to be a love potion." Aleksei K. Tolstoi, a distant cousin of Count Lev Tolstoi and a prominent Russian historical dramatist, wrote "Gypsy Song" in the early part of his career in the 1840s. Aleksei Tolstoi's wife, Sofia, was used by Lev Tolstoi as a model for Anna in *War and Peace*. A great-uncle of the famous novelist, Fyodor Tolstoi, "married a Gypsy. This Count Tolstoi was an amusing raconteur, a much appreciated wit and great amateur of Gypsies." According to Alfred Hamill,

> His wife he stole from her tribe and after marriage surrounded her with good teachers and all the paraphernalia of conventional life for three years on his estate. Then he introduced her to Moscow society, with what effect I have not been able to learn. After his death she became extremely pious, devoting to religion all of the energy not employed in mistreating her servants. By one of these she was eventually murdered. Her daughter by Tolstoi, as a writer, achieved the favourable notice of at least one well-known critic of her time. The turn to religiosity was not unusual among Gypsy women who married Russians and was exampled again in the wife of Leo Tolstoi's brother Serge. This unconventional nobleman, less daring than his great-uncle, bought his bride from her family. The novelist loved and admired his sister-in-law, who seems to have lived most amicably with her husband. A contemporary poet Apukhtin celebrated their love and narrates that on the death of their child she returned to her tribe. So, at least, is the story of his *The Old Gypsy*.

Sergei Tolstoi's Gypsy mistress, and later his wife, Maria Shishkin, had been a singer in a Rom chorus. Sergei paid the chorus leader a steep price for her and "intended to take her to his estate at Pirogovo and break off all relations with any neighbors who dared to raise their eyebrows." Maria bore Sergei several children before he finally married her on June 7, 1867. Aleksei N. Apuktin, a friend of Peter Ilyich Tchaikovsky, wrote "The Old Gypsy" in 1870 to commemorate the love of Sergei and Maria. Some of his poetry became popular Gypsy romance songs, particularly "Sleepless Nights." Tchaikovsky also set some of Aputkin's works to music.[44]

Lev Tolstoi's interest in Gypsies preceded that of his brother, Sergei. After he left university in 1847, he returned to live and write at his family's estate at Yasnaya Polyana. Tolstoi frequently traveled to Tula on business, but he spent much of his time there "haunting the singers of the Gypsy chorus." In his diaries he noted, "No one who has known the gypsies can ever cease humming their songs over and over, in or out of tune, but always with pleasure, because they remain so sharp in his memory." In *A Holy Night* he described the Rom music that so deeply moved him to tears:

> Then there is a chord, and then the same melody, over and over, in a gentle, tender, sonorous voice with extraordinary inflections and astonishing flourishes, and the voice grows steadily stronger and more vigorous until the melody is imperceptibly transmitted to the chorus, which takes it up in a group.

In *The Living Corpse,* Tolstoi writes of how Rom music reminds him of "the steppe, they're the tenth century, not freedom, but independence. . . . How is it man can attain that ecstasy and then can't make it last inside him? Ah, Masha, Masha, how you made my guts heave."[45]

Lev Tolstoi's interest in the Rom was not just musical. During his stays in Moscow, where he had an apartment in the Arbat, the young Tolstoi had difficulty avoiding Gypsy cabarets. The model *quliaka,* he and his friends frequented "the suburban cabarets where the beautiful Bohemians with gleaming teeth were performing—the terror of fiancées, wives and mothers." In his diary accounts of December 24–29, 1850, Tolstoi castigates himself for his passion for Gypsy women. In his favorite cabaret, the Gypsy singer Katya, sitting on Tolstoi's knee, "hummed his favorite song, 'Tell Me Why,' and vowed between verses that she had never loved another man. 'That evening I believed her sly gypsy chatter with all my heart, I was in a good mood and no 'guest' came to disturb me,'" he wrote in his diary. Tolstoi forswore his Gypsy haunts for a while but discovered new ones in St. Petersburg when he moved there in 1856 after serving as an officer in the army during the Crimean War.[46]

Tolstoi's contemporary, Appolon Grigoriev, published several works with Gypsy themes that, like those of Pushkin and Tolstoi, were based on personal experiences from "the days of his carousals" in Moscow from 1847 to 1856. Grigoriev published his best poetry during this period, which was "inspired by his intimacy with the gypsy choruses." Although Grigoriev was known primarily as a literary critic, his early poetry, such as "Two Guitars," "To My Guitar," and "Hungarian Gypsy Girl," which Alexander Blok termed a "single pearl of its own kind amongst Russian lyrics," is deeply touched by Gypsy themes. Grigoriev begins "To My Guitar" asking his Gypsy instrument to "Speak to me, my seven-stringed friend!"[47] Gypsy themes had a particularly strong influence on Blok, who was deeply affected by Grigoriev's work. One scholar, Viktor Shklovskii, noted "affinities between the Gypsy romance and Blok's poetry." The "gypsy woman, as seen in 'The Stranger' (Neznakomka),

'In the Restaurant' (V restorane), and 'To My Muse' (Moei muze) represents the opposite side of Blok's celestial 'Beautiful Lady,' who figures so significantly in his poetry." In 1913, Blok dedicated his *Carmen* to Lyubov Delmas, who starred in a 1913 production of Bizet's opera in St. Petersburg.[48]

Russian Gypsies also influenced the work of Afanasy Fet, who befriended Tolstoi and Ivan Turgenev and worked closely with Grigoriev. Fet's contemporary, Fyodor I. Tyutchev, "the greatest nature poet that Russia has produced," was also inspired by the Rom. Turgenev made references to Gypsies in his 1852 *A Sportsman's Sketches* (*Notes of a Hunter*), where he described Masha, a Gypsy choral singer. Turgenev's emphasis on peasant "humanity . . . imaginativeness . . . poetical and artistic giftedness, their sense of dignity," and their intelligence echoed the romantic views of Gypsies painted earlier by other writers. The same year, O. Boethlingk included two Gypsy songs in his study of the Gypsy language in Russia.[49]

These Gypsy motifs coincided with the emergence of a number of prominent Gypsy choirs in Moscow and St. Petersburg. The most famous Gypsy choral groups in Moscow during this period were directed by Nikolai Klebnikov, Ivan Vasil'ev, and Fyodor Sokolov. Ilya Sokolov's brother, Peter, conducted one of St. Petersburg's famous Gypsy ensembles, while by the end of the century, a new group had emerged under N. E. Shishkin. Each Roma choir had its own stars, including Pasha Patnichika, Sasha Veterochek, and Olga D. Bityurova. Perhaps the most interesting was the Gypsy contralto Manya, who "made the refined Muscovites weep when she improvised a Gypsy song." Manya had a love affair with Ivan Vasil'ev, yet declared that she, a Gypsy, had no interest in being a princess.[50]

In many ways, the fascination of the Russian writer with Gypsy themes and music coincided with the height of the Gypsies' own cultural development during the nineteenth century. Their work was particularly brilliant during the reign of the Tsar Emancipator, Alexander II, whose murder in 1881 signaled the end of an era. Turgenev, who died in 1883, and Fyodor Dostoevsky, who died only weeks before the death of Alexander II, spoke at ceremonies commemorating Pushkin in Moscow in 1880. Dostoevsky's monumental talk included references to the unique literary figure found in the character of Aleko in "The Gypsies," while Turgenev praised "the simplicity, the candor, the liberating, and hence moral, power" of Pushkin's work.[51] Twelve years later, the brilliant young Sergei Rachmaninov paid his own unique tribute to Pushkin with the creation of his one-act *Aleko,* which he based on Pushkin's *The Gypsies*. Written as part of his final examination from the Moscow Conservatory, it was performed with considerable success in Moscow in 1893.[52]

Unfortunately, the romanticized Gypsy life depicted in the works of these great artists, or enjoyed by a handful of Gypsies in Moscow and St. Petersburg, was worlds away from that experienced by the bulk of tsarist Russia's Gypsies. Yet even among those in Moscow and St. Petersburg, there were still strong connections to past traditions:

> If you had visited a Gypsy household in Moscow, where most of the Gypsies were concentrated in the Gruzino quarter, you would have been aware at once of a sense of emptiness. You would have seen few of the things that occupy the average living-room, and the contrast with the clutter of the usual old-time Russian interior would have been particularly striking. The Gypsies were simply not accustomed to possessing many things. One or two stools, a broken-down table, a very large wooden bed with dozens of down pillows—these were their household possessions. Upholstered chairs and sofas were unnecessary, according to the Gypsies, and only crowded the room.[53]

The Rom urban presence was not inconsiderable during the nineteenth century. According to 1834 population estimates, which indicated a total Russian population of 60 million, there were 48,247 Gypsies throughout the empire, with 8,000, or 16.6 percent, living in urban areas, and 18,738 in Bessarabia. A quarter of a century later, G. Tkachev estimated that there were 50,000 Gypsies in Russia, with 17,000 in Bessarabia and 7,500 in the Crimea.[54] The more accurate census of 1897 showed a Rom population of 44,582, with 8,636 Gypsies in Bessarabia. Of this number, 38,031 lived in the countryside, and 6,551 lived in Russia's urban areas. There were 1,056 Gypsies in Poland, 1,750 in Estonia and Latvia, 3,003 in Lithuania and Belorussia, 3,177 in Ukraine, 14,300 in New Russia, 2,829 in the northern Caucasus, 212 in Transcaucasia, 628 in Middle (now Central) Asia, 143 in the Steppe, 6,238 in Siberia, 2,138 in the southern Volga region, 1,080 in the northern Volga area, 2,021 in northern Russia, 2,784 in central Russia, and 3,223 in the central Black Earth region. The decline in Gypsy population between 1834 and 1897 ran counter to Russia's general population growth during this period, which grew to 125.7 million. However, the 1897 census was only taken in "the 50 *guberniias* of European Russia," and excluded Finland as well as "the *guberniias* between the Black and Caspian Seas, from Ekaterinodar and Stavopol southward." If these areas were included, the total population of the Russian Empire in 1897 would have been closer to 129 million. There were also serious inconsistencies in census taking, which casts some doubt on the accuracy of the Roma statistics. A report prepared by the Finnish Committee for the Investigation of the Gypsy Question in the Country

(Finland) in 1900, and addressed to Tsar Nicholas II, estimated that there were 50,000 Gypsies in Russia at this time, plus 1,551 in Finland, 15,000 in Poland, and 10,000 in Lithuania. The last figure runs counter to other estimates, which showed only 70 Gypsy families in Lithuania in 1840 and no more than 1,500 in the country in 1923.[55]

Problems with census taking, though, only partly explain the drop in official Gypsy population estimates between 1834 and 1897. The 1890s was a period of intense social and economic dislocation throughout the Russian Empire. A famine and cholera epidemic in 1891–1892 caused 406,000 deaths, which added to deep peasant impoverishment already worsened by excessive post-emancipation land payments vis à vis declining peasant land holdings and increased population. These crises, coupled with the increasingly repressive atmosphere of the regimes of Alexander III (r. 1881–1894) and his son, Nicholas II (r. 1894–1918), also affected Rom population statistics at this time.[56]

The picture of Gypsy life in the Russian Empire at this time is rich and complex, reflecting the diversity of the vast tsarist kingdom. Most Rom in the Crimea, for example, were Muslims, settled and "engaged in definite manual trades and shopkeeping." By 1874, the Gypsy community in Simferopol "possessed a cultural club of 300 members." There were three principle Rom groups in the Crimea, the "Gurbét (horse-dealers), Elektschi (sieve-makers), and Ayuchdschi (bear-leaders, tinners, and smiths)." The Gurbét, however, considered the name Gypsy "a disgrace," and called themselves Turkmans or Tartars.[57]

Gypsies in European Russia lived an equally diverse, settled life. According to several studies by V. N. Dobrowolski on Russian Gypsies in the village of Kisilefka in the Smolensk region from 1897 to 1908, the Rom were renowned for their skills as musicians and fisherman, but lived principally as thieves. The Gypsies of Kisilefka and its surrounding villages were originally nomads but were forced to be so by decrees that prevented them from living in barns and forbade them "to leave the places where they are registered to encamp or erect temporary shelters in the form of tents or huts." The non-Gypsy population of the region viewed the Roma with a mixture of awe and fear. The Rom leader, Ivka, had gained some notoriety in the 1870s for capturing a thief, Byelyatskie, whose band had terrorized the governments of Smolensk and Mogilev. Ivka's power over the Rom was such that he regulated

> the relation of the Gypsies towards their neighbours; on whom they shall make raids and on whom not, whom they shall touch and whom not. Sometimes, at the request of neighbouring landowners or notables, Ivka directs Gypsies to return horses to a proprietor from whom they have been stolen, and he is obeyed: quite by accident, as it were, the person injured finds his property in an appointed place.

Ivka worked with local officials to control the activities of his Rom. He could, for example, guarantee

> a district inspector or a constable that during a certain time the Gypsies shall not, in such and such a district, under any pretence disturb the inhabitants by their thefts; and to bind the Gypsies to obedience Ivka exacts an oath from them. The Gypsies consider the oath a heavy one, and it makes a profound impression on them; they weep while taking it; they hold it impossible to evade; its literal sense is not to be escaped by any trickery or mental reservation, nor by any twisting, as the peasants sometimes do with their oaths; they hold the oath inviolable. Their children take part in it, for the Gypsies swear before God by their dearest possessions, their children. Moreover, the oath is that of the community, binding on all the Gypsies of the neighbourhood.

Ivka and the Gypsies also had some influence in village affairs, though much of it was negative. Most Rom in Kisilefka could not vote since they were counted among "the urban and not the village population" or had "for ever lost their electoral rights through being convicted of theft." Ivka, a frequent observer of village court activities, encouraged the Gypsies to intimidate villagers in support of a particular candidate for village head. The Rom also criticized "the clumsiness of the peasants, sometimes in trying to turn it [the peasants' clumsiness] to their own advantage." The villagers, in turn, were "very careful not to offend the Gypsies . . . not wishing to have any disputes with them, nor desiring to create dangerous enemies in the same village."⁵⁸

The texture of Russian Gypsy life began to undergo changes during the early twentieth century as Lovari Rom began to move into Russia from Germany via Poland. The new immigrants came from the Netherlands via England to the Second Reich, where they were unwelcome. In 1904, the Prussian Landtag adopted legislation "to regulate Gypsy movement and means of livelihood," while on February 17, 1906, the Prussian minister of the interior issued a special order for the police on *"Bekampfung des Zigeunerunwesens"* ('combating the Gypsy nusiance')." The regulations noted special agreements with Russia and eight other European countries designed to deal with nomadic Rom. Prussian authorities also began to keep a "special register . . . to keep a record of Gypsy activities." In southern Russia, there was some movement of Crimean Gypsies into the Caucasus.⁵⁹

The new Gypsy arrivals entered Russia at a time of growing upheaval, beginning with the outbreak of the Russo-Japanese War in 1904 and the subsequent Revolution of 1905. At a distance, these events seemed to have little impact on Russia's Gypsies. Vlas Doroshevich, a well-known journalist, and theater-lover, wrote in early 1905, "In a world shaken by revolution they [the Gypsies] alone appear to remain forever unchanged." Doroshevich, like writers and composers before him, saw the Russian Gypsies in a romantic light, enhanced by the image of Rom performers such as Varvara V. Panina. This image was kept alive by contemporary observers such as R. H. Bruce Lockhart, who called Panina "the greatest of all Gypsies," while Alexander Blok referred to him as the "Boshestvennaya Varya Panina! [the divine Varya Panina]." Russian literary fascination with the Roma remained great during this period, anchored by a growing body of scholarly studies on Gypsy language and culture.[60]

Though Gypsies had been a source of literary and musical inspiration in Russia for some time, significant scholarly works on the Rom did not begin to appear until the second half of the nineteenth century. P. Keppen's article "Chronoligicheskii ukazatel' materialov dlya istorii inorodtsev Evropeiskoi Rossii [Chronological Index of Material for the History of Aliens in European Russia]," was the first detailed glimpse of official policies toward the Rom and paved the way for a flurry of studies on them, particularly in Bessarabia. Among the more prominent Russian gypsiologists in the years after emancipation were A. Eguhov, K. Khanatskii, G. Tkachev, and A. D. Grebenkin. V. N. Drobrowol'skii begin to publish his first works on Gypsies in 1891; he published his masterful study of Kisilefka Gypsies in two parts in 1897 and 1908. K. P. Patkanov published his pioneering study "Tsygany. Neskol'sko slov o narechiyakh zakavkazskikh tsygan: Bosha i Karachi [Gypsies: Some Words on the Dialects of the Transcaucasian Gypsies: Bosha and Karachi]" in 1887 for the Imperial Academy of Sciences, followed 13 years later by his *Tsyganskii yazyk* (Gypsy Language), "a grammar of the Russian Gypsy dialect, published under the pseudonym of P. Istomin." Evgenii Sno published a number of encyclopedic works on Russian Gypsies in 1903, while Kh. F. B. Linch wrote a number of studies in 1910–1911 on Gypsy influence on Russian music and literature. Vlad Azov published similar studies over the next two years. As Russia moved toward the event that would forever transform the face of the tsarist empire—World War I—the Gypsy was securing a firm place in its culture and history.[61]

World War I, much like the Romanov dynasty's other international conflicts over the previous 60 years, underscored Russia's serious leadership and domestic problems. A war that most people supported and felt would be over in a matter of months became a lingering conflict that produced growing public disgust with the policies and leadership of Tsar Nicholas II. By early 1917, this unrest had exploded into public demonstrations against the government and ultimately led to the regime's collapse on March 15–16, 1917.

Nicholas II was replaced by a provisional government made up of members of the former Duma (legislature) that tried to "move the country towards democracy and keep Russia in the war as a loyal western ally." Unfortunately, the provisional government's refusal to deal with some of the country's most basic problems, particularly the war and land redistribution, undercut its authority and paved the way for a more radical solution to the country's ills, espoused, among others, by the leader of the Bolshevik wing of the Russian Social Democratic Labor Party—Vladimir Ilyich Ulyanov (Lenin). Within a month after Nicholas II's abdication, Lenin began to create a shadow opposition movement that challenged the authority of the provisional government and on November 6–7, 1917, seized control of the capital, Petrograd. Over the next three years, Lenin's new Bolshevik regime fought a broadening civil war against its White and other opponents for control of the country. Though the Bolsheviks ultimately won the civil war, their wartime economic policy, War Communism, which had nationalized industry and forcibly seized grain from the peasants, alienated many of their original supporters. After a dramatic, bloody uprising at the Kronstadt naval base from March 1 to March 18, 1921, Lenin adopted what was known as the New Economic Policy (NEP), which was designed to revive the economy through a blend of government "control over the 'Commanding Heights' of the economy (foreign trade, transportation, and heavy industry) while opening other sectors to limited capitalist development." Equally important, the NEP stimulated a cultural and political renaissance for many of the new Soviet state's minorities, particularly the Gypsies.[62]

Prior to 1991, Russia's Gypsies traditionally viewed the advent of Lenin's regime as "the beginning of civil rights for Roma in the USSR." However, since the demise of the Soviet Union, Gypsies have waxed romantic about the "elegance, beauty, and freedom" of the "time of the Tsars," while "old family ties with aristocracy gain[ed] fresh currency."[63] The civil rights acquired by the Rom in the first decade of post-civil war Soviet power were shared with other ethnic minorities, who were given tremendous leeway in culture, education, and literature in return for loyalty to the ideals of the ruling Bolshevik elite.[64] For Soviet Russia's Gypsies, this translated into a tremendous burst of Rom educational and cultural activity as the government, aided by Gypsy activists, tried to address some of the deeper social, economic, and educational problems that had plagued the Roma under the tsars. Hand in hand with the educational and cultural activities were programs designed to address the Gypsies' long-standing economic difficulties, which officials linked to their nomadic traditions. On October 1, 1926, the Soviet Communist Party's Central Executive Committee issued a decree, "Omerakh sodeistviya perekhody kochuyuchshakh tsygan k trudovomy i osedlomy obrazu zhizni [On Measures for Aiding the Transition of Nomadic Gypsies to a Working and Settled Way of Life]," which tried to encourage Roma to adopt a sedentary lifestyle. Some efforts were made during this period to settle Gypsies on land set aside in 1926 by each Union Republic for this purpose. Roma who had earlier settled in villages were the first to accept the new grants of land, while a group of Gypsies who had supplied the Red Army with horses during the Russian Civil War formed the first Gypsy collective farm, "Khutor Krikunovo," near Rostov in the spring of 1925. At its peak, 70 families worked at "Khutor Krikunovo," farming 4,700 acres.[65]

Many Gypsies, though, resisted the move to state land, which prompted a new decree on February 20, 1928, "O nadelenii zemlei tsygan, perekhody-achshikh k trudovomy osedlomy obrazu zhizni [On the Allotment of Land to Gypsies for the Transition to a Working and Settled Way of Life]." According to one Gypsy leader, "Our grandfathers and great-grandfathers never ploughed land, and neither shall we."[66] Gypsies near the village of Bolshaya Bykovo in Belorussia told researcher Maurice Hindus that despite Soviet pressure to force the Rom "from the fields and forest, and harassing them in the market places with fees and fines," it was difficult for the Gypsies to give up their traditional lifestyle. According to one Roma

"a *muzhik* has his land, and a Gipsy, his horse. Do you understand? Our horse is our land, our bread-box, our treasure. We are not trained to till the land, and we are not as clever as Jews; we cannot change so easily.

"My father," broke in another man, "once tamed a wolf. He fed it milk and meat, fondled it, played with it, made it his pet. But one day it got loose from its chain and dashed away into the woods. It never came back. We are like that. Try as hard as you please to domesticate us, the first chance we get we run off to the woods. It is in our blood, Stranger."

"Every bird picks up its food with its own beak," said another, "You cannot graft a hen's beak on a dove or a heron's on a goose, or a duck's on an eagle. A Gipsy has his own beak, and no other will fit him."

Regardless, it was estimated that between 1926 and 1928, "5000 Gipsies had settled in places in the Crimea, the Ukraine and the North Caucasus" out of an official 1926 Soviet Gypsy population of 61,299. Of this number, 20.9 percent lived in urban areas. At least one gypsiologist, Konrad Bercovici, disagreed with these figures. He argued that there were between one hundred and fifty and two hundred thousand Gypsies in Russia [in 1928] of which at least one-half live in settled districts outside the large cities. A hundred thousands Tziganes travel in tremendous caravans of five to six hundred souls each, led by a Tziganski Ataman, Gypsy chief, whose power over them equals that of the autocratic ruler of any country, and was, in a sense, molded on the autocratic power of the czar over his people.[67]

Though Soviet authorities were not able to force all Rom to give up their nomadic ways, they were able to stimulate a Gypsy cultural and educational renaissance. At the center of these efforts was the All-Russian Union of Gypsies (USTs) created in 1925 and headed by A. S. Taranov. The USTs's efforts were strengthened by the acquisition of Gypsy nationality status the same year.[68] The following year, work was begun on a new Gypsy Cyrillic alphabet, which led to the publication of a Gypsy magazine, *Romaní Zor'a* (Gypsy Dawn) in 1927, and "a Primer for grown up people," *Névo Drom* (New Way), which replaced *Romaní Zor'a* in 1930. After *Névo Drom* sold out, a new primer was released, *Jidí butí*. According to the prominent Soviet gypsiologist A. P. Barannikov, these publications were of great importance to Russian Gypsies, since "urban Gypsies ha[d] no special culture" and because there was "nothing of the Gypsy left in their songs save the times." The new publications addressed these problems because

> educated Gypsies [took] part in them. Besides their civilizing role, they [gave] a rich material in the contemporary Gypsy language of different spheres of life; there [were] chiefly many terms referring to conditions of life and culture. They treat[ed] of the present inclination of the Gypsies living in towns for a cultured life and of the Gypsy schools and clubs in Moscow. The Gypsy Primers [paid] much attention to the question of the Gypsies' passing over to agriculture. These editions [were] printed in Russian characters; their orthography [was] based on the same principles as that of the Russian language.[69]

Gypsy activists were quite concerned over the "linguistic denationalization" of the Roma. Only 64.2 percent of the Gypsies in the 1926 census claimed Romani as their native language versus a national average of 87.1 percent among the 79 nationalities listed in the census.[70]

Of particular importance to the revitalization of Gypsy language skills was the development of a Romani grammar to support the educational and literary activities that had begun to blossom. Several Gypsy schools were opened to teach literacy in Romani, and by the mid-1930s, there were over forty

Gypsy students in the medical school at Smolensk. These educational developments were accompanied by a flood of Gypsy publications. In 1931, after consulting with Gypsy workers, teachers, and writers, M. V. Sergievskii published his monumental *Tsyganskii yazyk* (Gypsy Language) "for the use of native Gypsy teachers and Gypsies, writing in their national tongue." Designed to replace Patkanov's outdated *Tsyganskii yazyk* (1900), it centered around the "North Russian [Gypsy] dialect, as opposed to the dialects of the Gypsies of the Ukraine." This would be supplemented seven years later by Sergievskii and Barannikov's *Tsygansko-russkii slovar* (Gypsy-Russian Dictionary). Unfortunately, this Gypsy renaissance had political overtones and though "Roma could finally be active in the political realm in Romani . . . the terms were defined by non-Roma:"

> The writers' subjects were circumscribed more by the aims of *political* literacy, and less by those of literacy in the language itself. *Nevo Drom* for example . . . included articles explaining the new land tenure system, the five year plan, how to work in artels, how to become atheist, live in houses, and go to school. The alphabet books and grammars, written in Romani by Dudarova and Pankov, tells the parable of a family who starves because their only means of subsistence is fortune-telling, until they change their ways and go to work at the factory. A lesson accompanies each letter of the alphabet: "work," "our work," "Masha works," "our Romnia (fm.pl.) [feminine plural] don't work but tell fortunes," "I want to work. . . . "[71]

Not all aspects of traditional Gypsy culture thrived during this period. One of the phenomena to emerge in the 1920s was the "*tsiganshchina* or *psevdotsiganshchina* . . . 'inauthentic' performances by urban Romani choirs" that emphasized the "so-called 'Gypsy Romance.'" This music offended "the new proletarian audiences" in the new Soviet state, who saw them as throwbacks to the tsarist era. In addition, a number of non-Gypsy groups began to imitate Roma choirs. According to Ludmilla Kafanova, these developments "discredited the very concept of genuine Gipsy art."[72] This criticism led to the gradual disappearance of the Gypsy choirs, which concerned Gypsy leaders, who felt there should be some expression of the revitalization of their traditional culture. In 1929, the State Theatre of the Ethnographic Department of the Russian Museum in Leningrad added two Gypsy companies of 40 performers each to its program. Initially, only sedentary northern Roma were included in the troupes, though by the early 1930s efforts were made to include nomadic Gypsy performers and their music. After a year of training, the new Gypsy companies began to perform and soon "achieved great success and much popularity."[73] In 1939, the director of the Roma troupes, "W. N. Wsevolojsky, wrote them a special play, *Románo Drom*, in the performance of which the Gypsies showed considerable and artistic talent." As a result, "the Federation of Gypsy writers in Moscow intend to compose a Romani play reflecting the contemporary lifestyle of the Tsiganes."[74]

The success of the Ethnographic Department's Romani choirs stimulated efforts by Ivan Rom-Lebedev and other Gypsy activists involved "in Romani literacy campaigns and setting up Romani cultural centers" to approach Anatolii V. Lunacharskii, the Commissar of Enlightenment (Minister of Culture), about opening a Gypsy theater. Lunacharksii's surprised response to Rom-Lebedev's request was "Tsygane?! Does this mean that the word of Lenin has reached even them?" Lunacharskii's dismissal in 1929 because of his opposition to new cultural policies "that emphasized class war not only in the political realm but also at the ideological and cultural fronts" did not stop dreams of a Gypsy theater. In 1930, two Gypsy clubs were formed in Moscow. One, "Loly cheren [Red Star]," played an important role in the creation of the Gypsy Theatre "Romen" in 1931. On October 4, 1930, Protocol No. 4 of the Commissariat of the Enlightenment approved the creation of the Studio Indo-Romen, which was formed on December 20, 1930 in Moscow. This was followed by the formal opening of the Gypsy Theatre "Romen" in the Soviet capital on January 24, 1931. The new theater "was created both to 'preserve a national culture' and to 'aid the assimilation, sedentarization and education of nomadic peoples.'" Roma involved in the Moscow Gypsy Theatre hoped that their efforts "would help raise standards of living through political literacy and information about opportunities for Gypsies."[75]

The creation of a Gypsy theater was more complex than the formation of choral groups. Rom leaders were aided in the effort by non-Gypsies, particularly those from the Moscow Jewish Theatre. Moshe I. Goldblatt, an actor with the Jewish Theatre, became Theatre "Romen"'s director and chief producer. A. Tishler, who also worked with the Jewish Theatre, became "Romen"'s scenic designer; using Gypsy motifs, he made a number of "new contributions to the art of theatre design." Other non-Gypsies involved in the early work of the Gypsy Theatre were S. M. Bugachevskii and two ballet specialists, Lobackov and Wolf. The real spirit of the Theatre "Romen", however, was provided by its Gypsy writers and musicians, particularly A. V. Germano and G. P. Lebedev. The theater officially opened in April 1931 and performed M. Bezlyudskii's political review "Yesterday and To-day" and Ethnological Sketches, a collection of popular songs and dances put together to convince officials at the Commissariat of the Enlightenment "that the Gypsies were a people instinctively fitted to express themselves through the medium of the theatre." Appropriately convinced, Soviet artistic officialdom decided that Theatre "Romen" should perform six months out of the year in Moscow to keep Gypsy artists close to the latest literary and theatrical developments in the Soviet Union. Their performances in the Soviet capital would help the fight against "anti-Gypsism," while the artists would spend each summer as "pedagogues of their own people. Armed with textbooks and medicinal supplies the theatre tour[ed] through the nomadic encampments, giving the improvisation of their performance round the campfires." These rural performances also helped recruit new actors and musicians for the Gypsy Theatre. Since some Roma were illiterate when they arrived in Moscow, special classes had to be organized to teach them to read and write. In between these efforts, the Theatre "Romen" would do one-week stints in Soviet cities, where they would resume "their fight against anti-Gypsism."[76]

Theatre "Romen"'s next production was Aleksandr Germano's three act play *Life on Wheels*, an exploration of the difficulties faced by nomadic Gypsies as they tried to adopt a sedentary lifestyle. The theater's second Roma play, Germano's *Between Fires*, underscored the difficulties of the nomadic Gypsy lifestyle in Siberia during the Russian Civil War. In 1933, the theater expanded its repertoire and produced "Bizet's *Carmen*, based on a short story by Prosper Mérimée," which put the theater on a new plateau and enabled it to reach a broader audience. All works now had to be performed in Russian. Plans were made to do Pushkin's *The Gypsies*, interspersed with new plays by Rom-Lebedev and Germano.[77]

However, by the mid-1930s, Soviet minority policies were undergoing dramatic changes, and the Gypsy renaissance faded quickly. The tolerant atmosphere of the NEP had lingered after the NEP ended in 1927, as the Soviet Union's new leader, Joseph Stalin, consolidated his power and initiated schemes to collectivize agriculture and dramatically build up the country's heavy industrial base. As Stalin intensified greater control over the country, particularly after strong, violent, peasant resistance to collectivization, Soviet nationality policy shifted toward a greater emphasis on assimilation, and later, Russification. As propaganda spread about "nationalist deviations," authorities began to emphasize "*sliiane* ('drawing together') which basically entailed Russification." In the mid-1930s, Stalin initiated a violent purge of the Communist Party's leadership in response to criticism of his policies. As the purge's tentacles spread, 8–9 million people entered the Stalinist prison-camp system before the purges ended in 1938. In this atmosphere, "the Romani language schools were closed and, after 1937, nothing was published in Romani until 1989." Only the Theatre "Romen" survived this cultural and educational assault and continued to perform.[78] Thousands of Roma, under increased pressure to settle and collectivize, were sent en masse to Siberia or shot. Some all-Gypsy collectives were disbanded and its members forced to integrate with non-Roma collective farms.[79]

The upheavals that plagued Russia and its Gypsies throughout the 1930s paled compared to a much more cataclysmic event—World War II. Stalin initially avoided conflict with the war's instigator, Adolph Hitler, because of the conclusion of a last-minute Nazi-Soviet accord signed on August 23, 1939, nine days before Hitler began World War II with the invasion of Poland. This nonaggression pact and secret territorial agreement made the Soviet Union an active ally of the Third Reich since it obligated Stalin to invade eastern Poland as German troops moved in from the west. It also placed Bessarabia, Estonia, Latvia, and later, Lithuania, into a secret Soviet sphere of influence. On September 17, 1939, a hesitant Joseph Stalin moved the Red Army into his half of Poland. This region, with a population of 13 million, was formally integrated into the Ukrainian and Belorussian Soviet Socialist Republics in early November 1939. The following summer, the Soviet Union invaded the Baltic states and made them the fourteenth, fifteenth, and sixteenth Soviet Socialist Republics. At the same time, Bessarabia and Bukovina became part of the Ukrainian Moldavian Autonomous Republic.[80]

The acquisition of these territories boosted the Soviet Union's Gypsy population, though the actual number of Roma in each of the newly acquired regions is difficult to gauge accurately. Donald Kenrick and Grattan Puxon state in their classic, *The Destiny of Europe's Gypsies,* that Estonia had a prewar Gypsy population of 1,000; Latvia, 5,000 Rom; and Lithuania, 1,000 Gypsies. Both authors indicate that Poland had a 1939 Roma population of 50,000 and that there were 200,000 Gypsies in the Soviet Union in 1939. These estimates, however, conflict with official census data for Poland and the Soviet Union. Michal II Kwiek, the "King of the Polish Gypsies," conducted an officially approved census of Polish Rom in the 1930s that showed only 14,000 Gypsies in Poland, though one Polish gypsiologist, Jerzy Ficowski, feels this was "only about 50% of the real numbers." The prewar 1939 census in the Soviet Union showed an official Gypsy population of 88,200. It is not known how many Gypsies were in Soviet-occupied Polish territory in 1939 or escaped to Soviet territory over the next two years to flee the Nazis.[81]

The fate of the Roma in Stalin's newly acquired Baltic and Bessarabian territories was not particularly harsh, and, according to one Latvian Gypsy, Vanya Kochanowski, "the Soviet Government treated the Gypsies well, and although we were all obliged to work hard and to attend school or university, we Tziganes were satisfied with their régime." Kochanowski felt that Soviet insistence that everyone "embrace the same ideals (a policy fatal to free thought)" prompted students "to look forward to a new 'Liberator'—the Nazis." The brutal Sovietization of the Baltic states added to this desire for a German savior. These naive longings quickly changed to horror and fear once the full weight of Operation Barbarossa—the German invasion plan of the Soviet Union—was unleashed on June 22, 1941.[82]

The nature of the German assault against the Soviet Union differed significantly from any previous German attacks in Europe, since, according to General Erich von Manstein, perhaps Hitler's best field commander, the Soviet Union was the center of the "Jewish Bolshevistic system" and had "to be exterminated once and for all." German officials used specially trained killing squads, the Einsatzgruppen (task forces), to initiate its reign of terror in Russia. The Einsatzgruppen were armed "with special tasks for the preparation of the political administration." There were four main Einsatzgruppen units of 600 to 1,000 men, each attached to major army groups. The specially trained members of the Einsatzgruppen were drawn from the SS (Schutzstaffel, or elite guard), the Sipo (Sicherheitspolizei, or Security Police), and the SD (Sicherheitsdienst, or SS Security Service). Most of the Einsatzgruppen's officers were intellectuals and professionals. Members of the SS Einsatzgruppe A, with 1,000 members, operated in the Baltic states. Einsatzgruppe B, which had about 655 men, worked in Belorussia and the Smolensk area, while Einsatzgruppe C, with 780 soldiers, operated in northern and central Ukraine. Einsatzgruppe D worked in southern Ukraine, the Crimea, and the Caucasus. Individual units within each Einsatzgruppe were the Einsatzkommando and the smaller Einsatztruppe. Also attached to the Einsatzgruppen were Sipo Sonderkommando detachments, as well as a Vorkkomando unit (with Einsatzgruppe B). About one-sixth of the Einsatzgruppen forces were drawn from Order Police Battalion 9. There was also extensive cooperation between the Einsatzgruppen and the Wehrmacht (German army). The Einsatzgruppen's primary victims were Jews, whom Hitler told his generals before the June 22 attack were "the resevoir of Bolshevism." According to Otto Ohlendorf, commander of Einsatzgruppe D, his unit's "goal was to liberate the army's rear areas by killing Jews, Gypsies and Communist activists." He added, "On the basis of orders which were given to me by former Brigadier Streckenbach . . . a number of undesirable elements composed of Russians, Gypsies and Jews and others were executed in the area detailed to me." Between June and November 1941, the Einsatzgruppen executed 500,000 Jews and an untold number of Gypsies.[83]

Though initial Einsatzgruppen reports concentrated primarily on Jewish executions, by the fall of 1941 they detailed an increasing number of Roma victims. Einsatzkommando 8, which was attached to Einsatzgruppe B, gave "special treatment" to "13 male and ten female Gypsies . . . for having terrorized the countryside and committed numerous thefts" in July 1941. Sonderkommando 4a of Einsatzgruppe A, reported the execution of Gypsy "asocials" during this period. Einsatzgruppe C's Sonderkommando 4a, which operated in the Ukraine around Kiev, reported in mid-September 1941 that it stopped "a Gypsy band of 32 persons." When the Germans searched the Roma wagons, they found German pieces of equipment. Since the Gypsies "did not have any [identification] papers, and since they did not have any explanation for the origin of the goods, they were executed." In the Crimea, the operational area of Einsatzgruppe D, officials reported, "Work with Jews is rendered much more difficult because of the Karaite/Krimchaks [non-rabbinic Jews/Crimean Jews] and Gypsy problem." Consequently, the unit intensified its executions of the Rom and reported that by December 15, 1941, 824 Gypsies had been murdered. By early January 1942, Einsatzgruppe D reported that the Gypsy problem in the Crimean city of Simferopol had been solved, meaning they had either exterminated or deported all of the city's Roma population. From February 16 to February 18, 1942, Einsatzgruppe D reported the shooting of 421 Roma, and the following month it indicated the execution of "810 asocial elements, Gypsies, mentally ill and saboteurs." In the second half of March, the unit executed "261 asocial elements, including Gypsies." By April 8, 1942, the Crimea was free of Gypsies and Jews. One German report noted that the "population did not show any particular anxiety about the fact that the Krimchaks and Gypsies were made to share the fate of the Jews." Einsatzgruppe B reported the murder of 78 Roma during the same period, while *Einsatzgruppe* A executed 71 Gypsies for "different offences and crimes."[84]

By 1942, Einsatzgruppen reports indicated a new enemy subject to liquidation: partisans. The growth of the Soviet partisan movement took the Germans by surprise during the early part of the year and prompted Joseph Goebbels, Hitler's propaganda minister, to warn forces in Russia, particularly in Belorussia and Ukraine, to be on their guard against these groups. Stalin began significantly to increase support for these units during the summer of 1942, and by 1943, their ranks had swelled. In Belorussia, for example, the area with the greatest partisan activity at the time, there were 65,000 partisans in early 1943, and 360,000 by the end of the year. Ukraine boasted 220,000 partisans by the end of 1943. Early German efforts to counter partisan activities backfired and drove many pro-German elements into Stalin's arms. On August 18, 1942, the OKW (Oberkommando der Wehrmacht or High Command of the Armed Forces) issued Führer Directive No. 46, "General Directions for the Intensified Fight Against Banditry in the East." It placed all anti-partisan activities in the civilian-controlled areas of the occupied Soviet

Union (Ostland) under the jurisdiction of Reichsführer-SS Heinrich Himmler. German forces in this region were to use all "means of politics, economics, and propaganda" as well as "all available military, SS and police units . . . against both active and passive adherents to the movement." As part of the new anti-partisan campaign, the Chiefs of the Army Field Police noted on August 25, 1942, that

> The appearance of Gypsy bands is a major threat to the pacification of the territory as their members are roaming the country as beggars and render many services to the partisans, providing them with supplies, etc. If only part of these Gypsies who are suspected or convicted of being partisan supporters were punished, the attitude of the remainder would be even more hostile towards the German forces and support the partisans even more than before. It is necessary to exterminate these bands ruthlessly.

Consequently, military and police activities against the Gypsies and the partisans intensified, guided by a November 11, 1942, OKW "Directive for Anti-partisan Warfare in the East." Partisans and "anyone who harbored, fed, concealed, or otherwise aided partisans [were] to be executed." Partisan deserters or captives "who could prove that they had been pressed into the movement and who were able to work were to be sent to punitive work details and be considered for labor service in Germany." These efforts, designed to "undermine the movement by weaning away its external support by the people and weakening it from within by granting preferential treatment to partisan deserters were . . . 'too little too late.'" In early 1943, as a result of Operation Hamburg in the Slonim area of Belorussia, "30 Gypsies were arrested inside the area," along with a large stockpile of supplies. Afterwards, 58 Gypsies were arrested during Operation Altona in western Ukraine on suspicion that they worked with the partisans. Though the fate of these Gypsies is unknown, the fact that Einsatzgruppen reports do not mention their immediate execution makes it possible that they were forced into labor units. There were, of course, Roma who joined Soviet partisan units without coercion. Others were accused by the Germans of espionage.[85]

Soviet accounts of Einsatzgruppen and other Nazi genocidal behavior between 1941 and 1945 placed Gypsy, Jewish, and other deaths in the broader context "of a larger phenomenon—the murder of civilians, whether Russians, Ukrainians, Belorussians, Gypsies, or other nationalities. It was said to be a natural consequence of racist fascism" that resulted in over 20 million Soviet deaths.

The most famous exceptions to this sentiment were Yevgeny Yevtushenko's 1961 poem, "Babi Yar," and Anatoly Kuznetsov's documentary novel, *Babi*

Yar. Babi Yar, a wooded ravine in northwest Kiev, was the site of a thirty-six hour massacre of 33,371 Jews on September 29–30, 1941. This was, however, only the beginning, for "Babi Yar served as a slaughterhouse for non-Jews as well, such as Gypsies and Soviet prisoners of war" until November 1943. The Soviet monument to the Babi Yar atrocities, which stands one mile from the actual site, commemorates the deaths of "over 100,000 citizens of Kiev and prisoners of war." Yevtushenko's poem was written to protest the failure of the monument's planners to mention its Jewish victims and to remind his countrymen of Russia's historic anti-Semitism. Though Yevtushenko makes no mention of the Gypsy victims at Babi Yar, they were not forgotten in Kuznetsov's *Babi Yar:*

> The fascists hunted Gypsies as if they were game. I have never come across anything official concerning this, yet in the Ukraine the Gypsies were subject to the same immediate extermination as the Jews.
>
> Passports had decisive importance. They were checked in the streets and during house searches. Next in importance was appearance. Persons with dark hair and eyes and long noses were better off not showing themselves in the streets. Whole tribes of Gypsies were taken to Babi Yar, and they did not seem to know what was happening to them until the last minute.

Among Ukrainians, who were encouraged by the Germans to turn in hidden "Jews, partisans or important Bolshevik officials" for rewards of 10,000 rubles, a popular saying was "Jews *kaputt,* Gypsies too; and the Ukrainians, then come for you [Yudam kaput, tsyganam tozhe, a vam, ukraintsy, pozzhe]."[86]

This fear became commonplace throughout German-occupied Russia as Nazi atrocities mounted and non-Einsatzgruppen also became involved in the crimes. SD (Sicherheitsdienst or Security Service) division 281 murdered 128 Gypsies in the Novorzhev area south of Pskov on June 7, 1942, while Sipo units killed others during the same period in Kamenets-Podolsk in southwestern Ukraine. In Klintsy, Gypsies were arrested, then murdered. They were taken "to the side of a ditch where their money and outer clothes were taken off them. Then they were shot in groups in front of those waiting their turn for execution," usually in the neck. Germany and its allies also used portions of the occupied Soviet Union as dumping grounds for Gypsies from other parts of Europe. The Romanians brought 25,000 Rom from the Bucharest area to its newly created province in the Ukraine, Transnistria, while 5,000 Gypsies were sent from Germany to ghettos in Riga, Kaunas, Minsk, and Lodz.[87]

Despite the indiscriminate murder of Gypsies, the Nazis did not adopt a firm policy on the Roma in the Soviet Union until 1943. In the fall of 1941, Heinrich Lohse, the Reich Commissioner for the Baltic states and Belorussia, had written Heinrich Himmler about problems with nomadic Gypsies. Lohse was concerned about their spreading disease and being unfit for work. Himmler, struggling with his own passion for "nomadic 'pure' Gypsies," whom he wanted to put on "special reserves" because of the "presumed 'Aryan' origin of the Gypsies," initially failed to respond to Lohse's query. The response finally came through Dr. Landgraf, the senior SS-officer and Chief of Police for the East, who told Lohse in Riga that the Roma were to be included "in the 'final solution.'" Consequently, Lohse, who had also questioned Berlin on November 15 about the wisdom of killing Jews who might be useful laborers, "issued a confidential order to the SS on December 24, 1941" on the Gypsy question.

> The Gypsies wandering around the country are a double danger.
> (i) They carry disease especially typhus.
> (ii) They are unreliable elements who cannot be put to useful work.
> Also they harm the German cause by passing on hostile news reports.
> I therefore determine that they should be treated in the same way as
> the Jews.[88]

Less than a month later (January 20, 1942), the infamous Wannsee Conference was held in Berlin, where plans for the Endlosung (Final Solution) of the Jews was discussed. Though the Gypsy question did not come up at this important meeting, they were to be part of the Final Solution, though it would take almost a year of struggle within the higher echelons of the Nazi regime to force the incredibly powerful Himmler to stop protecting a mixture of "traditional, nomadic and racially 'pure' Gypsies and the 'socially adapted' sedentary ones" from the Third Reich's more deadly regulations. In June 1942, Alfred Rosenberg, Reich Minister for the Eastern Occupied Territories, asked Lohse "for information on the Gypsies in order to establish a general policy." Lohse was also pressured by Martin Bormann, Hitler's personal secretary and the "power behind Hitler's throne," Joseph Goebbels, and others on the matter. On December 3, 1942, Bormann wrote Himmler, who still wanted to preserve the "pure" Sinti and Lalleri German Gypsies:

> Such a special treatment would mean a fundamental deviation from
> the simultaneous measures for fighting the Gypsy menace and would
> not be understood by all the population and the lower leaders of the
> party. Also the Führer would not agree to giving one section of the
> Gypsies their old freedom.

At the bottom of Bormann's letter, Himmler wrote, "Inform the Führer where Gypsies are." Two weeks later, Himmler "signed the order despatching Germany Sinti and Roma to Auschwitz. . . . The 'Final Solution' of the Gypsy question had begun."[89]

Lohse now began to work on a plan to deal with the Roma under his jurisdiction. In May 1943, he sent his scheme to Himmler, Rosenberg, and other Nazi officials. He "proposed that the Gypsies should be put in special camps and settlements. They should not however 'be treated as Jews' (be killed). No distinction was to be made between nomadic and sedentary Gypsies. Part-Gypsies should generally be treated as Gypsies." Later, he changed his proposal to exempt the sedentary Gypsies and issued his new Rom decree:

Order of November 15th 1943

(i) Sedentary Gypsies and part-Gypsies are to be treated as citizens of the country.
(ii) Nomadic Gypsies and part-Gypsies are to be placed on the same level as Jews and placed in concentration camps.
The police commanders will decide in case of doubt who is a Gypsy.

The "distinction between sedentary and nomadic Gypsies was only made in the USSR and the Baltic states." Settled Roma in occupied Russia could be "drafted to serve in labour brigades," though some were sent to concentration camps. These regulations were only applicable to the areas under Lohse's control but not to areas the military controlled such as the Crimea and the Caucasus.[90]

It is difficult to determine the number of Gypsies sent to concentration camps or to labor units. Records from the large Gypsy Camp at Auschwitz-Birkenau (Sector B.II.e, Birkenau) shows that of the 20,943 inmates there, only 49 were from the Soviet Union or the Baltic republics. Those put in labor units worked throughout Europe. Whatever the destination of their victims, the Nazi actions against the Roma in the Soviet Union had a devastating impact on Gypsy communities. The Germans almost totally annihilated Estonia and Latvia's Gypsies, while two-thirds of Poland's Rom and about half of Latvia's Gypsies died during the Porajmos. About 30,000 to 35,000 Soviet Gypsies died at the hands of the Nazis.[91]

The Soviet Union's comparatively large Gypsy survival rate came about because the Germans only occupied parts of the country and failed to take the important cities of Leningrad, Moscow, and Stalingrad, which provided a crude defensive line for the rest of the vast Soviet Union. Consequently, despite the initial ferocity of the German attack in 1941, many Rom were able to escape to Soviet-controlled territory; they subsequently supported Soviet actions against German forces. Probably no group represented Gypsy commitment to the Russian war effort better than the Theatre "Romen," which was on tour in Central Asia when the war broke out. Undeterred, the troupe crossed the Caspian Sea—as the Luftwaffe soared above—and established temporary headquarters near Rostov, where "the Gypsy actors performed for the soldiers, using trucks as platforms." After the Germans captured Rostov on November 19, 1941, the Theatre "Romen" toured throughout Siberia and the Soviet Far East for 30 months. During this time, they performed in 59 cities and gave over 600 concerts and performances for the Red Army. Some members of the Theatre "Romen" joined the Soviet armed forces. Two, Sergei Zolotaryov and Viktor Belyakov, were highly decorated for bravery in combat. The war bore heavy on the Theatre "Romen," and several of its postwar productions, including Cervantes' *La Gitanilla*, and Alexander Afinogenov's *All About You*, an adaptation of Aleksei Apukhtin's ballad written for Gypsies, reflected the impact of this tragedy on the Roma and the Soviet Union. In many ways, the Theatre "Romen"'s endurance throughout such hardship symbolized the strong will of the Russian people. More important, it was now the "cultural centre of the Gypsy people" in the Soviet Union.[92]

This role was particularly important, given the police-state atmosphere that Stalin reinstituted as the war ground to a close. Partly Stalinistic paranoia, and partly an attempt to hide the country's tremendous losses in World War II, a gradual nationwide program evolved that was designed to combat the "excess of local patriotism" and glorify the Soviet regime and the "superiority of the Russian people." By 1948, new dimensions of this antinationalist campaign struck out against "cosmopolitanism" in an effort to minimize "national sentiments" and "liquidate foreign influences." Though much of this propaganda was aimed at the Soviet Union's Jewish community, who would soon be subjected to more deadly, anti-Semitic efforts, it created an unstable atmosphere for all of the country's ethnic minorities. All surviving Roma collectives were disbanded during this period, its members forced to join non-Gypsy collectives. Some Roma, however, began to enter universities during this period and eventually helped "cut a path for some Roma to enter the Party and to build academic and professional careers." Joseph Stalin's unexpected death on March 5, 1953, brought an end to this horrific atmosphere. Oddly enough, Nikita Khrushchev, the man who would do more than any other leader to change positively the face of the Soviet state (other than Mikhail Gorbachev), adopted policies in 1956 that would begin to destroy the traditional nomadic lifestyles of many Roma throughout the Soviet Union.[93]

Khruschev set the stage for an entirely new era in Soviet history with his dramatic attack on Stalin in his secret speech before the Twentieth Communist

Party Congress in Moscow on February 24–25, 1956. In it, he accused Stalin of committing crimes against the Communist Party and the military during the Purges in the 1930s, which left the country unprepared for World War II. Khrushchev also attacked Stalin's "Cult of Personality" and criticized him for numerous domestic and international failures. The speech sent shock waves throughout the communist world and set the stage for a brief, unStalinistic, liberal atmosphere in the Soviet Union.[94]

Russia's Gypsy community was therefore shocked by the issuance of the decree "On Reconciling Vagrant Gypsies to Labor" on October 5, 1956, by the Presidium of the Supreme Soviet. The new law completely outlawed the nomadic way of life, and, according to N. G. Demeter, was the "only Soviet law which define[d] a crime on the basis of nationality," since it struck at the core of the traditional Rom way of life. Though many Soviet Gypsies had given up nomadism, many of its traditions were revered by the country's Roma.[95] The new law was unevenly enforced, however, and many Gypsies continued their nomadic ways. According to Basil I. Rakoczi, who spent time with Gypsies in the Soviet Union in the late 1950s,

> the Gypsies have now been "freed", as compulsory settlement has proved to be quite an unworkable proposition. Gypsies again travel the roads of the U.S.S.R., plying their traditional crafts and trades as they did under the Tzars. They journey vast distances, covering with ease areas bigger than Western Europe; their largest encampments are to be found in the South, in Kasak, Usbek and Turkmen, and of course in Georgia and Armenia. But not a few also are to be found playing their wild music in the towns and villages about Moscow and Minsk.

Gypsy seasonal workers also moved around as livestock traders, drovers, farm workers, and street merchants, particularly in remote areas of Siberia and Central Asia. Concern over continued nomadism surfaced in some of the works of the Theatre "Romen" during this period, albeit in a rather subtle manner. Some of its plays emphasized "the opportunities that citizenship affords" in an effort to convince nomadic Rom of "the advantages of a settled life."[96]

Many who did settle did so grudgingly and tried to do what they could to retain certain aspects of their nomadic lifestyle. Some elderly Roma showed deep "contempt toward furniture" and felt that "Furniture is sticks; people do not need it." One older Rom, V. N. Sapegin, adapted his home on the Red Dawn collective farm at Gnezdovo near Smolensk to remind him of his traditional tent. According to Soviet anthropologist I. M. Andronikova, who studied the living habits of nomadic Gypsies recently settled on the Red Dawn collective, Sapegin and other Gypsies do not sit on the chairs but use them as stands for samovars. A square table in the Sapegin home presented as a gift by the collective farm was rebuilt. The legs were sawed off at a length of twenty centimeters, and the table thus became the kind the Gypsy wanderers had. When guests come, it is put in the middle of the room, covered with a tablecloth, and the visitors are welcomed with tea. All present seat themselves around it on the floor, Gypsy fashion, crossing their legs. After the tea, the table is removed, leaving the room space unoccupied.

Not all Gypsy movement in the Soviet Union during this era came about because of preferences for a nonsedentary lifestyle. A number of Polish Gypsies trapped in Soviet-occupied Poland at the beginning of World War II and deported to areas behind the Ural Mountains, were now allowed to return to Poland. They were joined by other Polish Roma who had earlier escaped to Latvia or Belorussia.[97]

Efforts to halt Gypsy nomadism did not seem to have any impact on Rom population growth in the postwar Soviet Union, though there are indications in the 1959 census that they did affect Gypsy ethnic identity. The Soviet Union's first postwar census showed a Gypsy population of 132,014, a dramatic increase of 49.7 percent over 1939 figures. They made up 0.06 percent of the nation's total population of 208.8 million. Given the Rom losses during World War II, this increase is doubly impressive. Of this number, only 59.3 percent chose Romani as their native tongue, compared to 64.2 percent in 1926. While these figures are quite low when compared to the percentage of other minorities in the Soviet Union who chose an ethnic language as their native tongue, they compare favorably to those with no ethnic administrative region of their own. On the other hand, only 31 percent of the country's Gypsies chose Russian as their primary language, a figure that would barely change 11 years later. However, the percentage of Gypsies identifying Romani as their primary language rose to 70.8 percent in the 1970 census. The low 1959 figures are no doubt related to the lack of Romani language publications after 1937, and ongoing pressure to settle and assimilate. The RSFSR (Russian Soviet Federated Socialist Republic) had a Gypsy population of 72,000 in 1959; the Latvian SSR 4,301 Rom; the Moldavian SSR, which included most of Bessarabia, 7,265 Gypsies; the Belorussian SSR, 4,662 Roma; and Ukraine, 22,515 Gypsies. There were 7,600 Liuli (Central Asian Gypsies) in the Tadjik and Uzbek SSRs. Only 39.1 percent of the Ukrainian Gypsies listed Romani as their primary language.[98]

These figures increased significantly in the 1970 census, which showed a Soviet Rom population of 175,335, out of a total population of 241.7 million.

This represented a 32.8 percent increase over 1959 figures and was more than double the growth rate of the entire Soviet population. Gypsies now made up a little over 0.07 percent of the population. Many western and Soviet experts feel that the true Gypsy population in the Soviet Union at this time actually was two to three times this number and attributed the undercount to the fact that "being marked 'Tsygan' bears a stigma which many prefer to avoid by registering as a different nationality." This did not, however, translate into a total cultural or linguistic identification with the other nationality. According to the prominent Gypsy scholar Lajko Cherenkov:

> It is rare to meet a Rom in the USSR to-day who cannot read and write, while before the war among certain groups, for instance those in Bessarabia, nobody could. Most of the young generation to-day are finishing eighth or tenth class, and one cannot distinguish in towns between Rom and other nationalities in this respect. But they have not lost their language nor their national sentiment. This is why I doubt that the conservation of Romany nationality depends on nomadism and traditional occupations. They have given up these aspects of their life voluntarily—they being more necessary to the ethnographers than to the Rom themselves.

He added that throughout his extensive travels and correspondence with Roma in the Soviet Union, he had "not met Rom who have forgotten the language or the Romani traditions, whatever their age or level of education." These contentions are supported by the fact that 70.8 percent of the Gypsies recorded in the 1970 census chose Romani as their native tongue, while only 53 percent indicated a good knowledge of Russian as their second language. The RSFSR had the largest Roma population with 97,955; Ukraine, 30,091 Gypsies; Moldavia, 9,235 Rom; Belorussia, 6,843 Gypsies; Latvia, 5,427 Roma; and Lithuania, 1,880 Gypsies. There were 11,362 Liuli in Uzbekistan; 7,775 in Kazakstan; and smaller numbers scattered throughout the other Central Asian republics. In the RFSFR, the largest Rom populations were located in the south in the Rostov *oblast,* the Krasnodar *krai* (territory), and the Stavropol *krai,* where almost 63.4 percent lived in the countryside. In Ukraine, the heaviest Roma concentrations were also located in the south in its Transcarpathian, Voroshilovgrad, and Kherson *oblasts.* Over 72 percent of Ukrainian Rom lived in urban areas, with only 27.1 percent in the countryside.[97]

   Gypsy self-identity was also aided by the achievements of prominent Gypsy writers, musicians, artists, politicians, and other professionals. Dr. Maxim Lukyanenko achieved some fame for his work in the Bryansk area, while Yakov Iordan was twice elected to the Moldavian SSR's legislature. Ten

Gypsies belonged to the prestigious Soviet Writers Union, and one, Djordjis Cantea, "published a collection of poems [in 1970]—the first book in Romanes to appear in the Soviet Union since the war." The 1987 edition of the *Literaturnyi entsiklopedicheskii slovar'* listed a number of prominent Gypsy writers, such as G. V. Kantya in Moldavia, K. Rudevich in Latvia, Leksa Manush (A. D. Belugin) in Moscow, and Vano Romano in the Altai region. A Liuli worker, Rakhbar Kazakova, received the Order of Lenin for her labor in the late 1960s, while a number of Gypsies associated with the Theatre "Romen" such as Ivan Rom-Lebedev, Vasili Bizev, Lyudmila Yaroshenko, Boris Tashkentskii, and Irina Nekrasova, were honored as Merited Artists of their respective republics. Another Rom performer who traced his roots to the Theatre "Romen", Nikolai Slichenko, gained an international reputation as a singer and actor. He was viewed as the "most famous and popular representative of the Gypsy nationality . . . in the USSR." Vladimir S. Vysotsky, an extremely popular non-Gypsy Soviet movie star, musician, and poet, was well known for his renditions of Roma songs such as "Dark Eyes" and "One More Time." Small "collections of songs of the Russian Gypsies" also appeared during this period. The most complete was S. N. Bugachevskii's "Tsiganskie narodnye pesni i pliaski [Gypsy Folk Songs and Dance Melodies]," in 1971. In academia, Roma Vladimir Ivashchenko completed a doctoral dissertation "On the Position of Gipsies in the USSR" for the history department of Rostov State University, while G. B. Kantei published *Folkloros romano* (Gypsy Folklore) in Soviet Moldavia.[100]

This atmosphere helped spur another significant increase in the official number of Roma in the Soviet Union in the 1979 census, which showed 209,157 Gypsies in Russia, an increase of 19.3 percent over 1970 figures. Gypsy growth rates continued dramatically to outpace those of the nation, which had a total population of 262,084,634 in 1979. Roma now made up almost 0.08 percent of the Soviet population. There continued to be a significant difference between official and unofficial estimates as to the true size of the Soviet Gypsy population. Grattan Puxon put the number of Roma in the Soviet Union at 480,000 in 1980, which made it the sixth largest Gypsy population in Europe. Over half of the country's Roma, 121,000, lived in the RSFSR, while 34,500 lived in Ukraine. There were 11,000 Gypsies in the Moldavian SSR, 6,100 in Latvia, and 2,300 in Lithuania. One Soviet specialist, N. G. Nazarov, estimated the number of Liuli in Central Asia to be about 30,000 at this time. Over 74 percent of the country's Gypsies claimed Romani as their native tongue, while 59.1 percent indicated a good knowledge of Russian as a second language. Almost half of the Roma officially listed in the 1979 census were Muslim.[101]

The Soviet Union's Roma population continued to grow and thrive over the next decade, despite the country's uncertain political climate. Leonid Brezhnev, who had ruled the Soviet Union since 1964, died in late 1982, followed in quick succession by Yuri Andropov, who passed away in early 1984, and Konstantin Chernenko, who died in the spring of 1985. Chernenko's successor, Mikhail Gorbachev, would oversee the complete transformation of the Soviet state, and the breakup of Moscow's empire in Eastern Europe. A year after he came to power, Gorbachev set the tone for his six-years in power with the adoption of the policy of *glasnost* (openness), followed in 1987 with his scheme for *perestroika* (restructuring), which was designed to transform economically the face of the Soviet Union. The new, heady, liberal atmosphere that accompanied these policies stimulated a new ethnic renaissance throughout the Soviet Union.[102] Soviet Gypsy culture thrived during this period, and reached new heights of development, yet Gypsy activists longed for contacts abroad. One, Sasha Zavodny, said in the late 1980s that members of the Soviet Gypsy intelligentsia were "eagerly following the worldwide movement for the emancipation of Gypsies, their freedom of language and culture." He was sorry, though, that Soviet Rom were unable to join this movement because of continued government restrictions on such membership. His hopes were soon fulfilled when the newly formed Romani National Union established a relationship with the World Romani Union. Soviet officials allowed Gypsy delegates to attend the Fourth World Romani Congress in Warsaw from April 8 to April 12, 1990, the location a result of the fact that the Gorbachev phenomenon had swept Eastern Europe. Leksa Manush, a bibliographic researcher for the Academy of Sciences Social Sciences Institute, and member of the Congress's Presidium, was one of five Roma speakers to address the conference's opening session on April 8. He also read one of his poems about the position of the Roma. Dr. George Demeter, a professor of the history of sport from Moscow and member of a prominent family of Roma scholars, delivered a report on Soviet Gypsies on April 9. He said the Soviet delegation "had come to learn, not to teach," although he felt there was "a need to emancipate and teach about [Gypsy] culture." Demeter underscored the importance of Romani language development and felt "it was necessary to pursue and continue the work to look for a standardized [Romani] language and a literary language." He also hoped that historians would do more "to write about the life of Roma in all countries." At the end of the conference, Demeter was elected to the Congress's new 27-member Presidium.[103]

The emergence of Soviet Rom in international Gypsy affairs mirrored Roma development and growth in the Soviet Union during this period. New films, such as "Tsyganka Aza [The Gypsy Aza]," and a TV series, "Gypsies," created a new artistic genre for Soviet Rom, though they also helped perpetuate traditional stereotypes of Gypsies. A new body of Rom scholarship began to appear in the 1980s, anchored by such classics as R. S. and P. S. Demeter's *Obraztsy fol'klora tsygan-Kelderarei* (A Sample of the Folklore of the Kalderash Gypsies, 1981) and their *Tsygansko-Russkii and Russko-Tsyganskii slovar (Kelderarskii dialekt)* (Gypsy-Russian and Russian-Gypsy Dictionary, Kelderish Dialect, 1990) as well as I. Rom-Lebedev's *Ot tsyganskogo khora k teatry "Romen"* (From the Gypsy Chorus to the Theatre "Romen"). The growth of Rom ethnic consciousness was also apparent in the 1989 census, which recorded a Gypsy population of 262,015 out of a total Soviet population of 285,743,000. The Roma, who now made up over 0.09 percent of the Soviet Union's population, continued to have growth and native language identity rates far higher than the general Soviet population. The new census showed a 25.3 percent Gypsy population increase over 1979 figures, almost triple the national growth rate for the country. Furthermore, 77.4 percent of the Gypsies now chose Romani as their primary language. Once again, however, the real size of the Gypsy population of the Soviet Union remained controversial, since Grattan Puxon and the London-based Minority Rights Group placed the Soviet Rom population at 530,000 in 1987. The RSFSR continued to have the largest Roma population, with 152,939; followed by 47,917 Gypsies in Ukraine; 11,571 in Moldavia; 10,762 in Belorussia; 7,044 in Latvia; 2,718 in Lithuania; 1,774 in Georgia; 665 in Estonia; and 48 in Armenia. There were 16,397 Liuli in Uzbekistan; 7,165 in Kazakstan; 1,791 in Tajikistan; 990 in Kirghizia; 145 in Azerbaijan; and 119 in Turkmenistan.[104] The majority of the country's Roma, 64.3 percent, lived in urban areas. An even greater percentage of the Gypsies in Ukraine (70.7 percent), Belorussia (77.8 percent), Estonia (86.3 percent), Lithuania (90 percent), Latvia (80.7 percent), Moldavia (68.6 percent), Georgia (67.8 percent), and Armenia (83.8 percent) were town or city dwellers, as were most Central Asian Liuli. The only Soviet republic with a significant rural Gypsy population was Tadjikistan. About 41.6 percent of the RSFSR's Rom lived in rural areas.[105]

Public reaction to the revived presence of Gypsies in Soviet society has been mixed. A 1989 public opinion survey in Ukraine showed "a predominantly unfavorable attitude towards Gypsies," though Rom never came up as objects of prejudice in several surveys conducted by the Los Angeles *Times-Mirror* in 1991 in the Soviet Union and Ukraine. Instead, Russians and Ukrainians expressed strong dislikes for Central Asians, Armenians, and Georgians. Some ill feelings toward Gypsies have surfaced among the new generation of right-wing and nationalist groups, particularly after the collapse of the Soviet Union and the removal of Mikhail Gorbachev as Soviet leader at the end of

1991. Under Gorbachev, these groups had remained on the fringe of Soviet politics, although they have since found new life in the more open climate of his successor, Boris Yeltsin.[106]

This new outpouring of hatred gained new strength in the 1993 parliamentary election campaign. Perhaps no man better symbolized the growth of nationalist fascism in the new Russia than Vladimir Volfvovich Zhirinovsky, the head of the misnamed Liberal Democratic Party (LDP), which won 64 seats in the new Russian Duma with 22.79 percent of the popular vote on December 12, 1993. (Zhirinovsky had garnered 7 percent of the popular vote in the 1991 presidential elections where he came in third.) During his Duma campaign, Zhirinovsky said, "Jews, Central Asians, Armenians, and Azerbaijanis should be driven from positions of influence" in Russia. While on a state visit to Bulgaria in late December 1993, he "called Romania 'an artificial state' inhabited by 'Italian Gypsies.'" His remarks so angered the Bulgarians that they expelled him the next day. Radio Bucharest called his remarks "pathological," and dangerous, since "they could be transformed into 'departure points for developments with nefarious consequences' for Europe and mankind." Zhirinovsky's words were symptomatic of growing prejudice in Russia toward "'chyorniye (blacks)' or 'churki (wood chunks)'" from the Caucasus. Some Gypsies and other dark-skinned individuals have been caught up in an anticrime dragnet in Moscow and elsewhere that arose after the violent *coup* of October 3–4, 1993. These developments have been far-reaching. The Russian newspaper *Trud,* for example, reported on December 16, 1993, about a news conference held in Perm by the "Falcons," the youth wing of the LDP. In addition to uniting the Perm oblast with the Sverdlovsk oblast, the "Falcons" also proposed forcing "all Gypsies, Transcaucasians and Vietnamese" from the region. Such outpourings have gained increasing weight in the aftermath of Zhirinovsky's troubling electoral victory as well as the ongoing political, economic, and social chaos in the former Soviet Union. Such instability has historically been the breeding ground for virulent anti-Gypsy hatred and violence.[107]

.6.

YUGOSLAVIA

T he Roma of the southern Slavic lands and Albania entered the region in much the same fashion as did other Gypsy groups in the Balkans during the Middle Ages. The first recorded mention of them in the region was in Macedonia in 1289, though, like many early accounts about the presence of Gypsies in the Balkans, these tales are often shrouded in myth. The early fourteenth-century Bulgarian version of the *Life of Saint Barbarus,* for example, indicates the existence of Gypsies in Albania and in Niš, Serbia. Other claims of an early Gypsy presence in the area, particularly in Macedonia, center around speculation that Byzantine references to Egyptian acrobats who moved through Macedonia might have been Gypsies, while Macedonian Gypsy folktales trace their roots much further back, to Alexander the Great, and claim the legendary conqueror as "one of their own blood."[1] By the mid-fourteenth century, Turkish Gypsies had settled in Serbia, where they became known as the Majstori or master craftsmen, because of their talents in a wide range of skills and trades.[2]

Other southern Slavic references to Roma at this time center around stories about bridle makers and smiths, who are mentioned in Serbian records in 1348 and who are referred to as Cingarije, a word of Persian origin that means "shoemaker" in medieval Serbian. According to traditional accounts, the Cingarije were slaves or chattels of the monastery of the Archangels Michael and Gabriel at Prizren in Kosovo and were "placed under a 'Protomaster' who required them to make a payment to the monks of forty horseshoes annually.

One gypsiologist speculated that from the monks' perspective, Roma nomadism was the offshoot of their having "left the faith," which justified their enslavement as a seven-year act of penance. Though long accepted as one of the first provable instances of a Roma presence in Serbia, some scholars now feel the reference was to non-Gypsy shoemakers and had nothing to do with Gypsies.[3]

The first concrete evidence of Gypsies in the southern Slavic part of the Balkans comes in a document from the Republic of Ragusa, now the city of Dubrovnik plus several islands to the northwest in Croatia. On November 5, 1362, officials ordered a local jeweler, Radenus Bratoslauich, to return a number of silver coins to two Ragusan Roma, Vlachus and Vitanus. In the document, the two Gypsies are referred to as "Egyptiorum," or Egyptians.[4] By 1373, there is evidence of Gypsies in Zagreb, the center of the small Croatian state that had established a special relationship with the Hungarian empire in 1102, while a document dated May 7, 1378, refers specifically to Roma in the Croatian capital. Angus Fraser makes reference to court records in Zagreb four years later in *The Gypsies* (1992) that deal with brothers named "Cigan or Cygan, Chichen or Czyganychyn," though he questions whether these terms refer to Gypsies.[5]

As evidence of a growing Gypsy presence in the Republic of Ragusa (Dubrovnik) and Croatia mounted, Serbia, later a major center for the Roma in the southern Slavic region, was faced with a threat that would change the course of the history of the Balkans: the Ottoman Turks. Medieval Serbia was at its peak in the fourteenth century, encompassing "Albania, Epirus, Thessaly, Macedonia and most of the Adriatic and Ionian coasts from the mouth of the Neretva to the Gulf of Corinth." Its most prominent ruler was Stephen Dušan (r. 1331–1355), who had assigned the Cingarije to the monastery of Archangels Michael and Gabriel two years before he was crowned tsar of Serbia in Skopje, Macedonia. After his death, the Serbian kingdom fell into disarray, and, after the Turkish victory in the epic battle of Kosovo Polje (Field of the Blackbirds) on June 15, 1389, it came under Ottoman control. One of the villains in this battle, Vuk Branković, was later believed by some Montenegrans to be the ancestor of local Gypsies. One of the reasons for the significance of this battle in later Serbian myths was the fact that both the Serbian and Turkish leaders, Prince Lazar Hrebeljanović and Sultan Murad I (r. 1360–1389), died during it. The Serbian "Kosovo Epic" had it that Branković, the son-in-law of Prince Lazar, betrayed him and caused his death. The identification of Montenegran Gypsies as his descendants was a careful blend of ancient myth with contemporary prejudice designed to justify ongoing anti-Roma sentiment. The Turks soon gained control of most of Macedonia, while their efforts to subdue Albania took much longer. Ottoman control over Serbia was not secure until 1459, while Bosnia did not come under Turkish domination until 1463, and Hercegovina took another 15 years.[6]

The fifteenth century in the southern Slavic lands was a period of chaos and warfare as the Turks fought to gain full control over Serbia, Bosnia, Hercegovina, Macedonia, and Albania. One state that did not fall under Ottoman control at this time was the Republic of Ragusa. Protected by the Venetians, who controlled the central Dalmatian coast to the north, the Republic of Ragusa remained independent, though it often had to pay "an annual tribute to the Turkish sultan in order to remain free and to develop its trade." It is from the detailed records of the *Historijski archiv* in Ragusa that we get our first significant glimpse of Gypsy life in the southern Slavic area in the fourteenth and fifteenth centuries. The fifteenth-century records offer abundant references to the life of the Gypsies in the Croatian city-state. Initially, Gypsies were referred to in Latin as Egyptians ("Egiptius," "egiupach," or "jegupach") or Gypsies ("Cinganus," "Zinganus," "Cingalus," or "Azinganus"). Between 1404 and 1494, the *Historijski archiv* refers to 27 Roma, some by a single name, such as Raychus, Filippus, and Jurag, and others by their surnames. Their choice of Slavic surnames (some of the more common were Dimitrouich, Nicholich, Stepanoiich, and Giurgeuich) indicates that they had spent some time in other parts of the Balkans and probably fled to the relative safety of Ragusa to escape the Ottoman wars of expansion from the late fourteenth century onward. Though the Gypsies in Ragusa were completely free, they held the lowest rank in the Republic's social order. They lived principally in the suburbs of Ploče and Gruž and worked as servants, musicians, and craftsmen. Their principle occupation, particularly after 1460, was trade and small-scale business, although the *Historijski archiv* mentions several prominent Roma musicians, including Oliver Cinganus, a lute player who owned his own home in Dubrovnik. In fact, indications are that the Roma played an important role in certain levels of Ragusan society and did not appear to suffer from the traditional prejudice Gypsies experienced in other parts of Eastern Europe.[7]

With the gradual solidification of Turkish control over Serbia, Bosnia, Hercegovina, Macedonia, and Albania came Ottoman regulation and taxation. One of the distinctive features of the new administrative system were *millets*, organizations for non-Muslims along legal-religious lines. While this structure "strengthened the separate identity of the Orthodox and Catholic populations by giving them each a religious hierarchy with limited political jurisdiction," it did nothing for Gypsies, whether they were Muslim or Christian. In fact, Muslim Roma were looked upon as "part of the Empire's establishment." Beyond this, the Turks also imposed new, stricter urban divisions in the few towns and villages that dotted the newly conquered areas. Known as *mahalle* or "boroughs," they followed ethnic and religious patterns. The Gypsy quarters in each town or village were known as the *Ciganluk* or *Ciganska mala (mahalle)*.[8]

Other aspects of Gypsy life were also strictly organized. In 1574, for example, the empire's new sultan, Selim II, ordered Roma miners in Banja Luka, Bosnia, to elect "a chief for each group of 50." As the Gypsy population increased, particularly in the southwestern Slavic area and Albania, the Turks began to impose taxes on the Roma. In 1604–1605, Sultan Ahmed I ordered that "taxes and fines . . . be collected from the Gypsies (*Kibtian*, i.e. Egyptians) in Rumelia (Albania, Macedonia, and Thrace). The Sultan's *firman* decreed that settled Gypsies as well as nomadic Roma, who had previously "remained as free as possible from the regulations of the central government," were now required to pay Ottoman taxes, particularly the *cizye*, or head tax, traditionally required of non-Muslims based on their ability to pay. While it is difficult to determine why Muslim Roma were now required to pay a non-Muslim tax, at least one scholar has speculated that it was because the Turks viewed them as schismatics. Regardless, the 1604 to 1605 *firman*, similar to the tax decree issued for Bulgarian Roma in 1610, reveals a great deal about Turkish attitudes towards sedentary, nomadic ("dwellers in tents"), and enslaved Gypsies in Rumelia. The new taxes would be collected from all Gypsies from March 1, 1604 to March 1, 1605. The rate was to be 180 *akçes* for Muslim Gypsies and 250 *akçes* for Christian Roma. Ottoman records for this period indicate that there were 5,940 registered Gypsies in Rumelia, the bulk of them nomads, and predominantly Christian. While the official collecting the taxes was not to harass or oppress the Roma, he was also to make certain that they did not try to claim improper exemptions by saying they worked as specialized, protected occupations such as "iron workers, charcoal burners, and castle watchmen" to avoid payment of the new levies. Furthermore, the single tax collector was not to "allow them to be contumacious and obstructive." Of greater concern to Turkish officials were the nomadic Roma, who they feared would try to run away or claim temporary absence to avoid paying the new taxes. They were to be caught with all haste and forced to pay not only the 180 or 250 *akçes* levy, but also a fine of 300 *akçes*. The decree also dealt with other taxes owed by Roma from time to time, such as fines for various crimes as well as the *ispenç*, the slave tax. Ottoman regulations gave slaves the option of paying a small tax plus personal service or simply a larger amount without the personal service. Because of local prejudices against the Roma, it was presumed that Gypsy slaves probably paid the higher levies.[9]

Further Turkish regulations dealing with Roma came in 1630, when a decree was issued in the name of Sultan Murad IV (r. 1623–1640) that attempted to discourage the wanderings of the "Bijeli," or White Gypsies, in Serbia. These Roma were found in Bosnia, Hercegovina, and neighboring parts of Serbia. Placed in the non-Vlach or Turkish group of southern Slavic Gypsies, they spoke a dialect later defined as Arlija, which had few traces of Romani, the Romanian-based Vlach category of Gypsy dialects. The White Roma made up the "masses of Gypsies to be found in Macedonia and the southern parts of Serbia, and, to a lesser extent, in Northern Serbia," although a small number also lived in Vojvodina. In time, the White Gypsies would come to "deny their Gypsy origin," and began to marry with the non-Gypsy population, which paved the way for their integration into southern Slavic society. A small number also lived in Vojvodina. Efforts were also made during this period to limit the occupations of Gypsy craftsmen in Serbia. Serbian coppersmiths in Vojvodina disallowed Roma from manufacturing copper utensils throughout the seventeenth century. These were probably Karavlasi Roma, "Black Rumanians," or Lingurari Gypsies who had fled into Vojvodina to escape the growing pressures of slavery and political instability in Wallachia and Moldavia. The former group was Orthodox and made troughs, spindles, and spoons, while the latter derived its name from the Romanian for spoon-makers (*lingura*). The Lingurari in postemancipation Romania were regarded as "the wealthiest and most respected class of Gypsies" in that country.[10]

In 1669, a British physician, Dr. Edward Brown, was taken by a Gypsy guide to a Roma settlement outside of Pristina in Kosovo to avoid the plague in the city. Brown reported that he and his companions were "well accomodated" in the village. Considering that his previous lodging in Pristina had been in "a very good house . . . with Carpets and other Ornaments," the Gypsy lodging must have been equally satisfactory. He described the Roma he met in this portion of the Balkans as "stout and bold," though some of them were "noted Robbers." Most lived in "Towns" and made their living "by labour, and handy-crafts Trades." He noted that many of them colored their hands and feet with a "reddish colour of *Cnà*" because they felt it protected them from the cold. This fascination with the reddish features of Roma in this region also cropped up in Albanian folk tales, which stated that Gypsies' "red tongues . . . attracted attention."[11]

At the end of the seventeenth century, Roma in the southern Slavic region and Albania suffered from a new round of Ottoman taxes that one writer has suggested were designed to "tax them out of existence" because the Turks viewed them as nothing more than "prostitutes and . . . pimps." Regardless of the motivation, the new levies of 1684 came down hard on the Roma, particularly on the Muslim Gypsies.[12] Particularly affected were Bosnian Gypsies, who had settled near the villages of Fojnica and Olovo by 1620. The Gypsies, who were referred to as *Kiptijan tajfesi* (Egipcani) in local records later in the seventeenth century, appear in official documents in the early 1700s, which give detailed evidence of Roma activities in both villages from 1703 to 1741.[13] During the same period, Romanian Gypsies began to move steadily into Serbia as they continued to try to escape the dual ravages of slavery and political instability in Ottoman Wallachia and Moldavia. Both Romanian *gadje* (*Gadže* or non-Gypsies) and Roma found a safe haven in Serbia, which suffered its own major population loss between 1690 and 1694 after Austrian forces, which had conquered Serbia and other parts of the Balkans in 1688–1689, retreated after the outbreak of the War of the League of Augsburg in 1689. The Serbs, who had actively supported the Austrians when they entered the region, now feared Turkish reprisals. As a result, in 1690, Serbian Metropolitan Bishop (Patriarch) Arsenije III Cernojević led 200,000 Serbs (30,000–40,000 families) into Austrian territory, followed by a smaller group in 1694.[14]

In 1699, Turkey, Austria, Poland, and Venice signed the Treaty of Karlovci, which saw Croatia fall into Austrian hands. Nineteen years later, the Banat (Vojvodina) and a bit of Serbia below the Sava-Danube line came under Austrian control. It is in the Banat, which, with Bačka later formed Serbian Vojvodina, that the first significant data is available for Roma in the southern Slavic lands in the eighteenth century. Formally integrated into the Habsburg Empire after the Treaty of Belgrade in 1739, the area was placed under direct military administration until 1777, when Empress Maria Theresa (r. 1740–1780) dissolved it, with one half under civilian control and the "southern and eastern portions transformed into the Frontier 'District.'"[15]

Croatia gained a number of Slavonian districts in this reorganization, and census data from 1781 to 1783 shows a significant Gypsy presence in the newly acquired Slavonian counties. In 1781, for example, Virovitiča had a Roma population of 648, a figure that fell to 622 a year later. Kriźevčka suffered an even greater drop in Gypsy population, 102 to 26, during the same period. Požeška's Roma population dropped from 166 to 156 between 1781 and 1782, but rose to 186 the following year. Sremska had 407 Gypsies in 1781, 416 in 1782, and 471 in 1783. Svega, with Slavonia's largest Roma population, had 1,323 Gypsies in 1781. These figures fell dramatically over the next two years from to 1,220 and then to 657. While it is difficult to explain the significant drop in Roma population in some of the Slavonian counties, it was probably due to the intensification of Habsburg control over Croatia in the early 1780s, which saw Virovitiča and Sremska integrated into Hungarian counties, and the imposition of Austrian regulations on Gypsy nomadism, which stimulated a major decline in Roma population in Hungary and elsewhere.[16]

A census taken in Novi Sad in 1765, a year after the southern Banat was transformed "into a regular military border," indicated that there were 35 Roma in the city, "all of them married men and of age." Data from another census in the same city 14 years later showed that there were 30 Roma families in Novi Sad. The new census takers asked the Gypsies whether they lived in regular houses, cottages, or tents. Presumably this question was the result of the extension of Maria Theresa's policy of assimilation towards the Habsburg Empire's Gypsies, which permitted authorities in 1780 to remove Gypsy children from their homes and place them in special boarding schools. It also reflected concern over the dwindling population of this important border region, which had been weakened by Serb migrations.[17] While these statistics provide a glimpse at the Gypsy presence in the southern Slavic portions of the Habsburg Empire during this period, it is difficult to pinpoint their exact numerical strength. Estimates are that there were 43,609 Gypsies in Hungary in 1780, which included Croatia and Slavonia, a figure that dropped to 30,251 three years later. Total Roma population estimates for the "Lands of the Hungarian Crown" at this time were 135,000.[18]

This uncertainty over Gypsy population figures is linked to the instability that swept the region at this time. In early 1788, for example, Austria, attempting to take advantage of a new war between Russia and Turkey, declared war on the Ottoman Empire. Though Austrian forces under Emperor Joseph II (r. 1780–1790) did badly when the Turks moved into the Banat, a revitalized Austrian force drove the Turks south the following year and moved into Bosnia and Serbia in the fall of 1789, where once again they were welcomed by the Serbs. These gains were short-lived, however, because Joseph's successor, Leopold II (r. 1790–1792), signed a treaty with Turkey in August 1790 that restored the pre-1789 frontiers between the two countries.[19]

The new Ottoman ruler, Selim III (r. 1789–1807), adopted a conciliatory policy toward the Serbs, who had aided the Austrians in an effort to gain their support against Turkish opponents to his new reform programs that would modernize the Ottoman spirit along French lines. He felt that if his reforms were put in force, they would "establish a regime of security, tolerance, and justice, perhaps [serving] as a model for subsequent reforms elsewhere in the empire." Selim III's principal opponent in Bosnia and Serbia was Pasvanoglu Osman Paşa, a rebellious Bulgarian nobleman who had led raids into Serbia and who established close ties with Bosnian opponents of the Porte's reforms. Though Paşa (his honorary title) Pasvanoglu was momentarily subdued by one of Selim III's backers, the ongoing chaos in the region prompted more Gypsy population shifts.[20] Turkish landowners in Bosnia, for example, began to move across the Drina River into Serbia. They brought with them White (Bijeli) Gypsy musicians, blacksmiths, and horse-traders (*džambasi*). The White Roma migration from Bosnia into western Serbia took place over a period of time. Though initially thought of as Turks, the Gypsies soon began to identify themselves as Roma to avoid mistreatment as Turks, particularly after the Serbian insurrection of 1804–1806.[21]

The Serbian revolution of 1804 was fueled by Serb discontent over the revocation of reforms by Selim III that had granted the Serbs "a degree of self-government." By 1802, Serbian leaders had begun to plan for an uprising against the Turks, which took place in early 1804 after Turkish Janissary leaders began to execute scores of prominent Serbs in early 1804. Led by Karadjordje (Djordje Petrović), who appealed to Russia and Austria for support, the initial Serbian outbursts were aimed at local, rebellious Turkish rulers and not at the sultan. Selim III responded by sending his *vezir* (high Ottoman government position) of Bosnia to defeat the Janissaries. He ordered their four leaders executed and insisted that their heads be sent to Istanbul. One was lost, "carried away by the Danube whilst being washed by a gypsy in preparation for the journey." Selim III feared, however, that Karadjordje wanted more than the restoration of order and the earlier reforms and thus decided in the summer of 1805 to break the back of the Serbian rebellion. The Serbs stopped the Turkish offensive, and conquered the small *pashalik* (administrative district) of Belgrade, the nucleus of the future Serbian nation, by the end of 1806.[22]

Though the Turks now agreed to all Serbian demands, including the removal of the Janissaries and the use of Serbian troops to man local military installations, Russia seemed to promise to support the Serbs if they chose to fight for complete independence from Turkey. The Serbo-Turkish conflict resumed in 1809 with an Ottoman attack on Belgrade. The Serbs received some Russian military aid in 1810 when General Mikhail I. Kutuzov briefly took command of Serbian forces, strengthened by the infusion of Russian arms and money. Two years later the Russians, preparing for war with Napoleon, shifted gears and agreed to the "full reoccupation of Serbia by the Ottoman authority" in the Russo-Turkish Treaty of Bucharest, although its Article VIII provided for vague Serbian autonomy and amnesty. Three Turkish armies reoccupied Serbia in the summer of 1813, and Serbian leaders subsequently fled into Austrian territory.[23]

The initial Serbian victories in the first two years of the rebellion spilled over into Austrian-controlled Vojvodina (Bačka and Banat), where religious leaders secretly approached the Russians about creating a "protectorate that would

include the Serb area of southern Hungary together with Serbia and Bosnia."
In addition, Serbian Gypsies were actively involved in an uprising in the
Sremska region of eastern Slavonia. Stimulated by Serbian rebel leaders in
Šabac just to the south in Serbia, the uprising broke out against Hungarian offi-
cials on April 6, 1807. According to a letter from the chief priest in Zemun,
Mihajlo Pejić, to Metropolitan St. Stratimirović, on April 18, three nomad
Gypsies ("Gurbetdžije") arrived in the village of Pećinci and urged the peas-
ants to join the rebellion in Sremska. They asked them, "Why do you toil and
not join our company?" From there the Roma moved to the village of
Dobanovci, where they asked a crowd of peasants, "What are you waiting for,
why do you not keep pace with the people? It is time now to liberate ourselves."
When officials learned of the Roma's activities, they sent troops to capture
them. Two were arrested, shackled, and sent to the town of Sremska Mitrovica,
while the third escaped. Estimates are that another 10–12 Gypsies were also
involved in the rebellion in the Sremska region, which was finally put down
in May 1807. While the fate of the Roma insurgents is unknown, the leader of
the rebellion, T. A. Tican, was captured, "broken on a wheel . . . and finally
quartered after his death." Not all Serbs in this region supported the rebellion,
however. Many Serbian troops served loyally in the Austrian army during this
period, and a number of Serbs rose to high ranks in the Austrian army.[24]

The Turkish reoccupation of Serbia six years later was bloody. According
to one account, the

> Turkish, Albanian and Bosnian Muslims who formed the occupying
> army pillaged and looted in a reign of terror which included the killing
> of males over the age of fifteen in some areas, the enslavement of
> women and children, and the brutal torture of any Serbian leaders who
> fell into their hands. One account describes the impalement of scores
> of men on wooden stakes, where they were left to die along the side
> of the roads leading to Belgrade. Some lived for days in this pitiful
> condition, their feet gnawed by dogs, until they died in agony.[25]

After the countryside was subdued, the *pasha* of Belgrade, Suleiman Usküplü,
adopted a policy of conciliation and made *knezes* (princes) of Serbian nobles
willing to serve the Porte. A number of Serbian attacks on Turkish officials
triggered countermeasures that fueled rumors of a general massacre of the
Serbian population. Consequently, one of the princes who served the Turks,
Miloš Obrenović, agreed to lead a new rebellion against the Turks in the
spring of 1815. Obrenović's forces quickly took control of the countryside,
while the Russians, now free to pressure Turkey after the defeat of Napoleon
at Waterloo, convinced the sultan, Mahmut II (r. 1808–1839), through the

Russian ambassador to Constantinople, Andrei Y. Italinskii, to begin negotiations with Obrenović. Turkey agreed to make Obrenović the "supreme *knez* of all of Serbia, and allowed the Serbs to have their own national assembly and army." An Ottoman governor would remain in Belgrade to coordinate administration with the Serbs, while some Turkish forces would remain in the country. The Serbs would be completely free "to collect taxes, and would share judicial powers with the governor in all cases dealing with Serbian Christians."[26]

The chaos in the region after 1804 triggered some Muslim Gypsy migration into "the four Ottoman vilayets, or provinces in European Turkey that were administered for the most part by Albanian Moslems," while White Gypsies in Šabac found themselves abandoned by their Turkish masters. Though they originally identified themselves as Turks, the Gypsies felt it wise to reveal their true origins for fear of Serbian revenge. Sabac's White Gypsies had few Turkish roots, yet they suffered from the fact that the "Serbs often give the name of 'Turks' to anyone who belongs to the Moslem faith." Despite this, the Serbs were not initially "interested in the faith of the Gypsies," though this would later change.[27] Those Gypsies who remained in Serbia were responsible for paying Serbian taxes, one of the rights the Serbs gained from the Turks in 1815. Roma paid their first capitation, or head tax, in Serbia in 1818 and continued to do so for the next 20 years. According to Professor Tihomir P. Vukanović, an "adult male had to pay 21 piastres (4.20 dinars), and a child 8 piastres (1.60 dinars)."[28]

Overall Serbian revenue from the capitation tax increased significantly during this period, in part because of the large Gypsy migration from Wallachia into Serbia. Stimulated by the acquisition of virtual Serb independence in 1830 and the appalling conditions of slavery across the Danube, Romanian Gypsies began to cross into Serbian territory at Kladovo and elsewhere. Prince Miloš Obrenović, who had a Gypsy musician, Mustafa, living in court, kept close tabs on the new Rom immigrants. On October 12, 1830, he wrote Stefan Stojanović, his "headman" in Kladovo, "to send all skilled coachmen, cooks and smiths to himself personally for a decision as to their personal fate." Stojanović informed Obrenović in several letters throughout October and November 1830 that he had searched the region for Gypsies to send to Belgrade. He sent the Serbian ruler three Roma coachmen on November 9 and 30.[29]

Stojanović kept up his correspondence with Prince Miloš about the Romanian Gypsies, and on August 20, 1833, he asked his advice about claims by the *boyard* Skordin of Cernec that the Rom family of Constantin Gjumis was his property. A month later, Stojanović informed the Serbian ruler of more Gypsy arrivals. In 1836, he reported the crossing of "20 Gypsy families, numbering 61 members in all," on June 17–18, though in none of these cases was there any clue as to the prince's response. Andrew McFarlane speculates that in "all probability Miloš simply directed that these refugees should be forwarded to him if their skill rendered them valuable, since the Turkish military commander in Kladovo had been given a kind of standing order" to do so. Most Gypsies, however, were ultimately allowed "to wander or settle where they willed."[30]

Many of the Gypsies settled "in the District of Belgrade and, secondly, in the District of Kragujevac," though Roma could be found throughout the country. Gypsies were not included in the statistics for the first official Serbian censuses of 1834, 1841, and 1843, though it is estimated that there were 18,000 in Serbia in 1834, and 12,000 in 1841. The 1846 census counted settled and nomadic Rom, but they were again left out of the official counts of 1850 and 1854. An estimated 11,000 Rom lived in Serbia in 1850 and 12,000 in 1854. City records for Belgrade show that there were 251 Rom living there in 1846, yet only 151 eight years later. Overall statistics for the period from 1847 to 1859 show a 1 percent increase in Rom population. Part of the reason for the inexact figures on Gypsies in Serbia at this time was the manner in which they were counted. With the exception of the 1846 census, Gypsies were included in the category of general taxpayers, since many of them had begun to settle "permanently in villages, where they constructed their own houses" and were thus liable for a variety of taxes." The censuses of 1866, 1874, and 1880 "included all Gypsies resident in Serbia," though, "for the most part these enumerations do not record any ethnical features," with Rom usually "included in some other ethnic group, mostly among the Serbians." However, a Viennese gypsiologist, Franz Miklošič, said that there were 24,693 Gypsies in Serbia in 186; 8,396 of them kovačev or blacksmiths.[31]

The growing sedentarization of the Serbian Gypsies saw some identify more closely with Serbian national sentiments. This was particularly true in Vojvodina during the revolutions of 1848, where Serbian Gypsy folklore celebrated the exploits of the Rom leader Tasa Ivanović. Ivanović was viewed with fear and awe by the Serbian Rom—the folktales claim that "enemy bullets could never penetrate him" and that on one occasion, "a bullet that struck his head bounced off and killed three other Gypsies without hurting him." Nonmythical events in Serbia had been stirred by news of revolution in Hungary and Austria in March 1848. Serbian peasants now refused to pay their "feudal dues and services to their seignurs," while in May a Serbian National Assembly asked for the creation of "a new crownland, the Serbian Vojvodina, composed of Bačka and Baranya counties, the Banat, the (Croatian) županija (district) of Srijem, and all the adjacent military borders." In addition, "Vojvodina was to form a federal union with Croatia." The Vojvodina Serbs created a government and prepared to resist Austrian attempts to retake the region. Austrian difficulties in Hungary soon found the Serbs allied with the Austrians, and in November 1848, Vienna recognized the Serbian provisional government in Sremski Karlovici. In March 1849, Emperor Francis Joseph (r. 1848–1916) declared the creation "of the new crownland of the 'Serbian Vojvodina and the Banat of Timişoara,'" which placed 321,000 Serbs in the midst of 390,000 Romanians, 221,000 Hungarians, and 335,000 Germans. Regardless, the Serbs made significant linguistic and religious gains, which helped stop the tide of Magyarization in Vojvodina.[32]

Despite the settlement of some Serbian Rom, many still wandered the countryside as nomads. One of the earliest accounts of nomadic Gypsies in Serbia and Bosnia during this period describes the free-flowing movement of Roma across the invisible frontiers of Serbia and Bosnia. The account, ridden with deep-seated prejudice toward Gypsies and Jews, still gives an insightful glimpse of the Ursari (bear trainers) Gypsies in Serbia in the early 1850s. During a venture from Požarevac, long a winter settling place for the Ursari, a group led by a Mr. Skene, accompanied by a Gypsy coachman, came across "an extensive Gypsy camp" dominated by a chieftan "who wore a rich Albanian dress." Though Skene describes other Rom in the group to be ragged, he does say that they rode fine horses, apparently ready, he felt, "for some marauding expedition, as the robbers in this country are generally Gipsies." Skene and his companions encountered the same Gypsies several days later outside of Tuzla in Bosnia. His jaundiced eye saw individual camp-fires, each "superintended by an old hag" and watched by "half-naked brats." The colorful setting included a bear turning a spit that held a roasted lamb, watched by a "monkey in a cocked hat and feather." Despite the relaxed, care-free setting, he suspected the Rom had spent the day stealing their food, "tinkering and fortune-telling."[33]

A small group of Gypsies that Skene described as "wild-looking" greeted the Europeans "with a sort of cordiality." Among them, dressed in "tattered garments," was the Rom chieftan met earlier in Serbia. The Gypsy leader explained that he wore different clothes because in Bosnia, "the more miserable he seems, the better he will be treated," whereas in Serbia, "a man is respected only when he appears to require nothing of them." The elegant horses ridden by the Rom in Serbia had now been changed for "sorry brutes" in Bosnia. Despite the courtesy and friendliness of the Gypsies, Skene was certain they meant his group harm. He again met the Ursari chieftan at Zepče, southwest of Tuzla, where the frightened Rom took the European party for haiduks (bandits). Despite the Gypsies' relief once they learned their mistake,

Skene still saw them as "deprecatory and cringing." Later, he saw the Rom chief in Serbia and suspected him of robbing an old Jewish peddler in Bosnia. His final glimpse of the Rom leader some time later was when the chieftan was in police custody. Skene suspected that had the authorities not apprehended him, the friendly, courteous Rom chieftan and his companions would have robbed the Europeans.[34]

The Gypsy movements described by Skene became more widespread in Serbia during the second half of the nineteenth century. The migrations would usually begin on *Mitrov Dan* (St. Demetri's Day), October 26th of the old style," when men would leave their families for up to two years. In time, entire families would "wander abroad to different villages looking for a place in which to spend the winter months. As a rule the same family never spent two winters in the same village," because, according to one Serbian gypsiologist, "during a single winter the Gypsy women became too notorious among the local population for their thefts and deceits." The Rom settled in forested areas where there was ample wood "and where the harvest had been abundant and the peasants prosperous." Some families lived in a *bordaj*, a "hut dug out of the earth." Once spring arrived, they left to meet other Gypsies on *Djurdjev Dan* (St. George's Day). The Ursari were among the most prominent Rom groups to begin to migrate to other parts of Europe during this period and were considered one of "the most mobile ethnographic groups" in Europe. The Ursari, who lived in tents, were viewed by other Gypsies as "superior only to beggars," a feeling shared by *gadje* (non-Gypsies). When the Ursari showed up near a community, "the common people were always afraid of them." Such movements were linked to the more widespread upheavals in Europe at this time, though they can also be traced to specific developments such as, among others, new economic opportunities outside of the Balkans.[35]

The movement of Rom out of Serbia was not caused by harsh mistreatment, since evidence suggests that the Gypsies of Serbia suffered less from prejudice there than they did in other parts of the Balkans. In fact,

> the leveling power of Turkish rule, exerted for successive ages, had the effect of elevating the Gypsies somewhat toward the social status of the other rayahs [non-Turkish subjects]. Here, therefore, although they are still an inferior caste, and not allowed to exercise the right and powers of citizenship, the Gypsies are perhaps less widely separated from the peasantry around them than anywhere else in Europe. They fought bravely with their Servian neighbors against the Turks, and as smiths, farriers, and dealers in live stock, have many of them earned a comfortable livelihood, and proved themselves respectable members of society.[36]

Furthermore, not all Gypsies were welcome in Serbia. The Serbs expelled a number of Muslim and pro-Turkish Rom in 1862 after the Serbian conflict with the Turkish garrison in Belgrade. Triggered by "the killing of a Serbian boy by Turkish soldiers," the incident evolved into a confrontation between the Serbian army (created to fight a "war of liberation from the Turks" on the road to the creation of a Greater Serbia) and the Turkish garrison of Kalemegdan. The Turks shelled the city and killed a number of Serbs, while foreign diplomats scurried to end the feud. The sultan agreed to withdraw his forces from two less important forts at Užice and Soko Banja and, under pressure from Alexander II of Russia, agreed to withdraw all Ottoman troops from Serbia in 1867. Muslim influence in Serbia, which had been on the wane since 1830, dissipated completely after 1867.[37]

Within eight years, Serbia and Turkey were again in conflict over the uprising in Bosnia and Hercegovina. In the summer of 1875, Bosnian peasants rose up against the European Muslim aristocracy, who were "more Turkish than the Turks in outlook." Serbia and Montenegro, which saw territorial opportunities in the conflict, joined the fray the following summer. Though the Montenegran forces did well, the Turks were able to rout the Serbian army, and by the fall of 1876, only a Russian threat to attack Turkey saved Serbia from possible reconquest. Representatives of the major powers met in Istanbul in December 1876, proposing, among other things, the restoration of the prewar boundaries of both Serbia and Montenegro, plus reforms in Bosnia and Hercegovina, which would henceforth be united. The new sultan, Abdulhamit II (r. 1876–1909), countered with a new constitution for the Ottoman Empire, which allowed him to reject the Western plan. War with Russia soon followed, which resulted in a disastrous defeat for the Turks. Russia then dictated the Treaty of San Stefano of March 3, 1878, which, among other things, tripled the size of Montenegro, but gave Serbia only 150 square miles of new land. British and Austrian objections to the accord sunk it before it could be ratified. Instead, a major allied conference, the Congress of Berlin, met from June 13 to July 13, 1878, to discuss the matter. The result was the Treaty of Berlin, where Russia represented the interests of Serbia and Montenegro. Both states were declared independent and "took an obligation to maintain religious equality and freedom of worship." Serbia acquired only 50 more square miles of territory than in the San Stefano agreement, while Montenegro was reduced to about 60 percent of its San Stefano size. The combined republic of Bosnia-Hercegovina came under Austro-Hungarian control, while the *sancak* (provincial district) of Novi Pazar, which divided Serbia and Bosnia-Hercegovina, was occupied by Austrian forces.[38]

The acquisition of Serbian independence brought significant changes in the lives of the country's Gypsies, particularly in their nomadic habits. In 1879,

the government stated that "wandering was strictly forbidden," a point under-
lined in a decree of June 14, 1884, that reconfirmed this stricture and promised
to put the Rom "nominally on an equal footing with the rest of the inhabitants
of Servia." Since this regulation proved ineffective, officials "announced in
1891 that all Gypsies caught travelling on the road at the commencement of
the new year would be arrested and imprisoned." Soon after the new anti-
nomad restrictions went into force, the bishop of the Timok diocese, Melentije,
"issued a confidential mandate ordering the Serbs to make Orthodox converts
of 'irreligious' Gypsies." Over the next three years, Melentije had 2222
Gypsies baptized in his diocese.[39]

Part of the reason for this effort to sedentarize and Serbianize the Rom was
the size of the Gypsy community in the new Serbian state. While the census
of 1880 still did not list the Roma as a separate ethnic group, the census of
1890, which did, showed a Gypsy population of 37,581. The greatest Rom
concentration was in the Podunavlje region, while Belgrade had just under 400
Gypsy residents. The census of 1895 provides an even better glimpse of the
makeup of the 46,212 Rom now in Serbia. Over 81 percent lived in villages,
while 54.8 percent listed Serbian as their native tongue, 25 percent listed
Romani, 18.6 percent listed Romanian, and a little over 1 percent listed
Turkish. Gypsy urban dwellers were more likely to use Serbian and Turkish,
while those in the countryside were more apt to speak Romani and Romanian.
The urban areas of Serbia experienced the greatest Gypsy population growth,
while the overall Serbian Rom population rise between 1890 and 1895 was
attributed to increased births and the movement of Gypsies from other parts
of the Balkans into Serbia.[40] The Serbian census of December 31, 1900,
showed a slight decrease in the number of Rom in the country, with 46,148,
1.85 percent of the Serbian population at this time. Of this number, 25 percent
were Muslims. The proportion who listed Serbian as their native language rose
to 60.34 percent, as did that of those who listed Romani as their primary
tongue, 29.06 percent. The percentage of Gypsies who were Romanian primary speakers dropped to a little over 10 percent, and the number who now
listed Turkish as a native tongue was almost negligible. The figures for
Romanian Gypsies in Serbia are a little misleading, however, since they did
not "include the many Rumanian Gypsies in Serbia who have long ago forgotten their Rumanian language."[41]

The status of Gypsies in other parts of the southern Slavic region during this
period is more difficult to pin down. Demographic figures for Prizren in
Kosovo showed that city with 603 Rom households in 1853, while the
Hungarian census of 1867 noted the presence of 4,300 Rom in Croatia-Slavonia
and the Frontier District. The more detailed 1880 census listed "1499 Gypsies

whose mother-tongue at that date was Romani" in Croatia-Slavonia, and 1,983 in the Frontier District. Records from the Austro-Hungarian census of January 31, 1893, for the Slovenian parts of Carniola, Carinthia, Styria and the Littoral shows 4,073 Rom living in villages that would later be split between Slovenia and Hungary.[42] There were about 2,000 White and Karavlasi (Black) Rom in the Vlasenic region of Bosnia during this period, while Macedonia, which, though controlled by Turkey, was desired by Serbia, Greece, and Bulgaria, had a Rom population of 8,550 in 1906 and 10,000 in 1910.[43]

It was the desire of Serbia and Bulgaria for Macedonia, among other things, that triggered the Balkan Wars of 1912–1913 and provided the first significant glimpse of the dark side of Serbian attitudes toward their Rom. When the wars ended with the Treaty of Bucharest on August 10, 1913, Serbia, which "almost doubled in size," gained northern and central Macedonia and divided the *sancak* of Novi Pazar with Montenegro. Greece acquired the southern portion of Macedonia as well as other areas, while Albania again became independent.[44] Some of the area acquired by Serbia during these conflicts had Albanian Muslim inhabitants, whom Serb propaganda during and after the wars depicted as "utterly incapable of governing themselves and as the sort of element that ought to be exterminated." According to Vladan Djordjević, "a noted Serbian statesman and public health specialist," Albanians were "skinny and short, possessed of gypsy and Phoenician features—indeed, reminding him of the 'prehumans, who slept in the trees, to which they were fastened by their tails.'" While Djordjevic and other Serbian propagandists dehumanized Albanians, there were those who saw them as "lost Serbs" worthy of conversion and assimilation. The Serbian propaganda helped stimulate Serbian and Montenegran atrocities against Albanians during both Balkan Wars and afterward. According to a report later released by the Carnegie Endowment for International Peace in 1914, these people with "gypsy features" saw their homes and

> whole villages reduced to ashes, unarmed and innocent populations massacred en masse, incredible acts of violence, pillage and brutality of every kind—such were the means employed and are still being employed by the Serbo-Montenegrin soldiery, with a view to the entire transformation of the ethnic character of regions inhabited exclusively by Albanians.

A wave of Serbian and Montenegran settlers soon followed to begin the process of assimilation and occupation.[45]

This derisive view of "gypsy features" did not seem to translate into any overt Serbian outburst against its own Gypsies, who remained loyal Serbian citizens throughout World War I. The immediate events that led to war began with the murder of the Austrian heir-apparent, Franz Ferdinand, and his wife by Bosnian Serb nationalists, aided by various groups in Serbia, on Serbia's national day, June 28, in Sarajevo. On July 23, Vienna presented Belgrade with "eleven threatening demands" that "required Serbia to suppress and punish all forms of anti-Austrian sentiment . . . with the help of Austrian officials." Austria declared war on Serbia on July 28 after Belgrade qualified its acceptance of Austria's terms. Russia's mobilization in support of Serbia prompted a German declaration of war against St. Petersburg on August 1, and within a few days, most of the countries of Europe were pitted against one another in a new, horrible conflagration.[46]

Austrian forces began an immediate bombardment of Belgrade and invaded Serbia on August 11. A Serb counteroffensive drove the Austrians out of Serbia over the next two weeks, which prompted a new Austro-Hungarian drive that resulted in the capture of Belgrade on December 2, 1914. The Serbs retook their capital 13 days later, while a new enemy, typhus, ravaged the Serb population. Estimates are that 150,000 Serbs died from typhus in 1914–1915, which also spread into parts of Macedonia. A weakened Serbia was invaded by Austria, Germany, and Bulgaria, which had just entered the war on October 3, 1915, in an effort "to provide direct access to the Turks defending Gallipoli." Bulgarian forces quickly moved into Macedonia, while the Serbs were driven southeastward to Kragujević and then, to escape total destruction, fled through Kosovo and Albania to the Adriatic. From there, French ships took them to Corfu, where 120,000 Serb troops and a temporary government-in-exile took refuge. The bulk of these forces joined the Allied attack on Saloniki on September 10, 1916, which led to the Franco-Serbian occupation of Bitola in southwestern Macedonia. With the exception of this enclave, "all the lands which in 1918 were to be included in the new South Slav state were under foreign occupation" for the next two years.[47]

The Gypsies played an active role in the war in Serbia and suffered heavy losses in the conflict as a result. While no statistics are available, indications are that Rom civilian and military deaths were high. A number were captured by Austro-Hungarian forces during their drive into Serbia. These forces also sent a "group of spies, consisting of prominent engineers," into Serbia during this period disguised and trained as Gypsy bear-leaders who operated throughout Serbia before their capture at Čačak in 1915. The Serbs found "a number of plans and drawings and military objects" on the "counterfeit Gypsies" when they captured them. In Albania, rebel troops captured a supporter of King Wied in 1914 and, "to disgrace him deeply . . . made a Gypsy get on his back and ride him around Tirana." The Rom, whom one observer felt all

Albanians hated, were treated much better in Bosnia-Hercegovina and Serbia during this period. In 1916, the "Austrian government granted them ground . . . near Rogatica, and each family built itself a house and sowed vegetables for food." In Belgrade, Serbs enjoyed Gypsy music. In 1915, a bank official went overboard in his enthusiasm for "the renowned Gypsy band of Cievarić," which performed at the restaurant "Makedonija,":

> [when] he was in high spirits, he distributed all the money he had with him among the musicians, then took off and gave them his watch and his rings and, finally, presented them with his coach and horses. The next morning the Gypsy musicians drove through the streets of Belgrade in their own luxurious carriage.[48]

For the most part, though, Serbian Rom played a more serious role in the war effort. In the village of Turska Trnava, Muslim "Bijeli" Gypsies were constables who helped protect the village. Their bravery and losses on the battlefield in Serbia were recognized after the war with a two-meter-high obelisk in Belgrade that read: "In memory of Gypsy heroes who died or were killed during the War, 1914-1918." Each of the Rom victims of the war was individually listed in gold on the obelisk, as were the names of those who donated money for the erection and upkeep of the monument. Anyone who donated "200 dinars to the *Bibi* Society is entered on the list of benefactors, and his name is carved on the stone in 'letters of gold.'" The monument was "erected through the initiative of Marinko, a Belgrade musician of some renown." (The Bibi Society was founded in Belgrade after the war by local Rom and was named after a female cult figure venerated by Serbian Gypsies.) Gypsies burned candles at the monument for the souls of all the dead.[49]

    Throughout the war, several Serbian factions promoted the idea of either a Greater Serbia or a southern Slavic union of the Serbs, Croats, and Slovenes. Serbia's tremendous losses in the war and its valiant struggle against the Central Powers paved the way for Allied support of a new southern Slavic nation, which was officially proclaimed on December 1, 1918, as The Kingdom of the Serbs, Croats, and Slovenes. The new country, which had a diverse population of almost 12 million divided along ethnic and religious lines, included Serbia, Montenegro, Croatia-Slavonia, Bosnia-Hercegovina, Dalmatia, Carniola, and parts of Austrian Styria, Carinthia, and Istria as well as former portions of Hungary (Baranja, Bačka, and the western Banat). The Serbs and the Croats were the dominant groups in the country, with a combined population of almost 9 million, while there were a little over 1 million Slovenes. The 1921 census, using language as an ethnic criterion, found that Germans, Hungarians, Albanians, Romanians, Jews, Turks, Czechs, Slovaks,

Ruthenes, Poles, Russians, Italians, and other groups made up the rest of the population. There were 34,919 Gypsies who listed Romani as their mother tongue in 1921, with 16,674 Rom in Serbia, 14,489 in Kosovo and Macedonia, 3,104 in the Banat, and 652 in Bachkoj and Barani.[50]

From the outset, the new southern Slavic kingdom was beset by serious ethnic and boundary problems. Though the latter were finally resolved in 1926, the country's new constitution, proclaimed on Serbia's national day, June 28, in 1921, deemphasized "the extremely important historical and cultural, religious, and ethnic differences and diversities of the Yugoslav peoples." Instead, the themes of "common origin, similarities of language and customs, and shared historical experience of centuries of foreign overlordship" were used to create a Serb-centered political structure based on the 1903 Serbian constitution. What emerged was an extremely powerful constitutional monarchy provided by the Serbian Karadjordjevic dynasty, with the capital in Belgrade. Political power "tilted toward the executive" branch, and when the system began to come apart in 1928, "the monarch provided a rallying point for the nation" through the creation of a "temporary royal dictatorship."[51]

The new constitution provided protection for "freedom of belief and conscience" and granted "legal recognition . . . to the existing Orthodox, Roman Catholic, and Moslem confessions." Other groups were afforded "internal autonomy" and could "obtain recognition under the general terms of the law." The constitution had only one clause "devoted to the subject of the rights of minorities." It stated that "to minorities of other race or language elementary instruction shall be given under conditions which the law shall prescribe."[52]

There is little information about the new kingdom's Rom in the 1920s, so it is possible to catch only a glimpse of their lives. The chaos in the Balkans at the end of World War I saw some Turkish Gypsies, the Čergari ("tent-dwellers"), move into Serbia, while the ongoing land reform program in different parts of the kingdom deprived some Bosnian Bijeli Gypsies "of their protectors"—Turkish Muslim estate owners who owned large tracts of land redistributed to poor Christian peasants in 1923. Despite these changes, Gypsy life in the new southern Slavic state remained vibrant. In the late 1920s, King Alexander (r. 1921–1934) renamed the country Yugoslavia, dissolved the parliament, overturned the constitution, and created a new administrative structure that centered around *banovinas* (provinces), whose "boundaries were drawn with the intention of weakening or destroying traditional loyalties," yet "served to enhance Serb domination." While an accompanying crackdown drove some extremists from the country, most of the country's Gypsies, who lived primarily in Serbia and Macedonia, seemed unaffected. Rom music, for example, remained central to Serbian life and reflected, particularly in the years immediately after World War I, the relief felt by all after the war's end. In 1919,

> the Belgrade Gypsies played a composition, which they called "Viljem Telac od Verduna" (William the bullcalf, by Verdun). It was a Gypsy medley of purely Gypsy motifs and Gypsylike melodies from Verdi's Il Trovatore and from Rossini's William Tell. No wonder that they transformed the name Verdi into Verdun. This French fortress was frequently mentioned during the war, while the Gypsies did not know what Verdi meant. Of all the names of famous musicians and composers, the Yugoslav Gypsies knew best the name of Paganini (who they called "Panganini" and believed that he, too, was a Gypsy.[53]

The Rom were also affected by land reform efforts in Yugoslavia, and some began to settle (similar efforts had taken place earlier in Serbia). One Orthodox Rom family in the Serbian village of Kopljari had some financial standing in the community, which consisted of 150 Serbian and 18 Gypsy dwellings. They owned over five acres of land with a home "and by profession [were] blacksmiths, who manufacture axes, shovels, drills, nails and rakes," which they sold at village fairs in the summer. Belgrade Rom prospered to the point that the Bibi Society was able to purchase a tract of land in the suburbs at Pašino brdo for the worship of this Gypsy saint, who was honored with her own icon in 1929.[54]

Gypsies did experience difficulties in Serbian-controlled Kosovo, where they, along with the half-million Albanians living in the region, suffered "as targets of a Slav majority all too eager to 'settle accounts' with people they associated with centuries of Turkish terror." (The Serbs closely identified the Rom with the hated Albanian Muslims.) From the end of 1918 until mid-1920, Serb forces committed untold atrocities against Albanians in Kosovo and northern Albania. Over the next decade, Albanians in Yugoslavia became the country's "most oppressed national group." Nevertheless, in 1929, the Yugoslav Ministry of Foreign Affairs stated that "there are no national minorities in our southern regions."[55]

Consequently, independent Albania became a haven for Kosovan Rom, who found the positive atmosphere little changed from the Turkish era. Despite an unsuccessful attempt by the government in 1920 to stop Gypsies from dancing in public for money, most Albanian Gypsies continued to practice their traditional lifestyles. (In 1934, "the first restriction having lapsed dancers had to pay a special fee to license their performance.") Orthodox Christian Rom worshipped in the same church as the Albanian Orthodox, though Muslim

Gypsies "were still not appreciated inside the mosque or, for that matter, inside the burial grounds." Consequently, in 1923, the Rom in Durazzo built their own mosque, "a small, styleless box with a modest minaret." The Gypsies of Scutari had a mosque of their own for some time, although one located in Elbasan fell into disarray. All three mosques were located in the Rom *mahalle* (quarter) of each village. Some Rom "had intermarried with local Turks and Moslem Gypsies in the coastal lowlands" and thus forgotten their language and certain aspects of their culture. One British Albanophile, Joseph Swire, provided an interesting glimpse of Rom life in Albania's capital, Tirana, during this period. According to Swire, the Gypsy *mahalle* consisted of

> a cluster of neat white cottages. These Cigans, as they are called, being no longer nomads, have lost their language, though they still tell the tradition that their forebears came over the sea from the direction of the sun (meaning Egypt). Their type is very swarthy and quite unlike the average Albanian, but in common with nomadic Romanies (Vlachs) their physique is poor. The men, when they must work, become hamals or blacksmiths or executioners or scavengers— it is the Gypsy who drowns the stray dog and carts away the refuse— tasks to which the Albanian will not stoop. There are many of them at the ports, where they work as stevedores and boatmen and porters. These women are stocky, hardworking, far neater than the Tirana Moslems, and they are often employed for servants, for the Albanian dislikes charing. Their noses are markedly semitic. Their intelligence is average, but they keep their houses much cleaner than the lowland Albanians. Nevertheless the latter despised them, so the old official class is afraid foreigners should think them Albanian; and once the Minister of the Interior prohibited the taking of photographs of the Cigane quarter in case it should be represented as typical of Tirana![56]

Swire found this amusing, since he felt Tirana "was an untidy place." He felt that

> nomadic Romanies are well represented in Albania, too, the grammar of their language being very close to that of our British Gypsies. They believe in a supreme god (called, in Romany, Devil) and various nature gods symbolised by the sun, moon, dawn, the sea, and so forth. They live in tents—near towns in winter. Their women, as everywhere, practise fortune-telling and are most lascivious; and the men make baskets, ropes, and deal in horses like their kind in other lands.

Albanians feared the nomadic, Christian mountain Rom, whom they called *gurbati* (beggars). Another British specialist on Albania, Edith Durham, said that the real wild Balkan gypsies rarely bother about a tent, but couch in the lee of any bush or bank that is near water and fuel supply. Swarthy, scarlet-lipped, with black brilliant eyes, long heavy elf-locks of dead black hair, and unspeakably filthy, they are scorned alike by Serb and Albanian. The scorn they return tenfold, for they hold that they are the chosen of all races, and that none other knows how to enjoy the gift of life.

Though it is difficult to determine the exact number of Rom in Albania at this time, a "popular estimate gives 2,400–3,000 sedentaries at Durazzo, 1,500 at Berat, and 2,000 at Elbasan, making perhaps 20,000 for the whole country." Included in these figures were 2,000 nomadic Rom.[57]

Demographic figures for Yugoslavian Gypsies are a little easier to calculate, particularly after the March 31, 1931 census. There were 70,424 Gypsies who chose Romani as their native tongue, while 65,000 claimed Roma ethnic status. Almost 30 percent (20,688) of the Gypsies who claimed Romani as their primary language identified themselves as Orthodox, the principle faith of the Serbs, Montenegrans, and Macedonians, while 16.9 percent (11,957) called themselves Roman Catholics, the predominate faith of the Croats. Over half of the Gypsies (53.6 percent, or 37,715) identified themselves as Muslims. Gypsies made up 0.4 percent of the Yugoslavian population of 13.9 million when ethnic origin was the criteria, and 0.51 percent when language was used for minority identification. This made them one of the largest non-Slavic groups in the country.[58]

During the same year as the new census, King Alexander introduced a new constitution that provided "a fig of legitimacy to cover the crude reality of the royal dictatorship." It reworked the administrative structure of the country "to reduce separatist sentiments" and was designed to insure that political power continued to rest in Belgrade. Efforts by Croats and others to push for "democratisation . . . and . . . regional autonomy" were met by a government crackdown in 1933 that succeeded in antagonizing most of the country's important political parties, including some that supported the government. The murders of King Alexander and French Foreign Minister Louis Barthou in Marseilles on October 9, 1934, by Croatian and Macedonian separatists with Hungarian and Italian complicity, deeply added to the woes of a country already mired in the Depression.[59]

Prince Paul, the regent for the new monarch, Peter II (r. 1934–1945), struggled to keep the country together and to seek some solution to the growing friction between the Croats, who wanted greater autonomy, and the Serb-dominated government. New elections in the spring of 1935 paved the way for a prime minister committed to solving the Croat dilemma, and so

Milan Stojadinović was chosen. As Yugoslavia struggled to find its way in the tense world of European politics, Stojadinović worked to find a solution to the "Croat problem . . . before an explosion could take place in Europe, when the Croats might rebel and Yugoslavia [might] be dismembered." Croatia's desire for greater autonomy would also have to take into consideration similar demands from the country's other regions based on language, history, or ethnic background. It took a change in government at the end of 1938 and the threat of a European war in 1939 to create a settlement—the Sporazum of August 26, 1939. What emerged from the settlement was the creation of a new Croatian *banovina*, Savska, which had a population of 4.4 million, 74 percent of them Croats. The *banovina*'s newfound autonomy did little to still Croatian extremists, "who now looked to Hitler for the achievement of a mock-independent status for Croatia." Considering Prince Paul's dictatorial tilt toward the Axis powers, the fragile bond that held the nation together was about to be torn asunder by World War II.[60]

Gypsy life in Yugoslavia during this unsettling period was vibrant, while Rom intellectuals struggled to define the unique, positive characteristics of Gypsy ethnic identity. A Serbian Gypsy organization, Drustva Rom (Gypsy Society) was formed in Belgrade in 1930, though it foundered for lack of funds. Five years later, a Serb, Alexander Petrović, was instrumental in founding a newspaper, *Romano Lil* (or, in Serbo-Croatian, *Tsiganske Novine,* Gypsy Newspaper), in the Yugoslavian capital. The Gypsy community, particularly its budding intellectual class, responded with enthusiasm to the monthly publication, which quickly ran into serious financial difficulties. Government authorities agreed to allow the publication, but only as long as "the tone of the paper would be morally high." They felt that the purpose of *Romano Lil* "was to work for an improvement in the education and cultural outlook of the Gypsies, and must battle against, not condone, their criminality." The Rom involved in producing the newspaper countered with their own guidelines: *Romano Lil* would only publish news about Gypsies that was positive.

> They were tired, they complained, of having all the crimes of the land laid at their innocent doors. True, they had their black sheep; well then, let these individuals be named and denounced, but the WHOLE race of Gypsies must not be branded as liars, cheats, robbers and assasins.

The result was a Serbian Gypsy newspaper "about Gypsies and solely for Gypsies" that would print "nothing but praise of the *Roma*." Unfortunately, *Romano Lil,* survived only three months. The first issue, published in March 1935, featured an article that emphasized "a truer appreciation of Gypsies and

their good qualities." Another piece expressed Gypsy regret for the assassi-
nation of King Alexander, while a third discussed ways "to safeguard the
health of Gypsy children." The second issue, in April, continued the series on
health and education questions for Roma children and included an article on
the history of the Rom in Belgrade. The third and final edition of *Romano Lil*
discussed the "widespread fame and the policy of the paper," along with
Serbian Gypsy folktales and local news.[61]

The atmosphere that spurred the creation of *Romano Lil* and *Drustva Rom*
seemed to be one of tolerance. Rebecca West noted in *Black Lamb and Grey
Falcon* at least one positive Serbian view of the Rom:

> In the eastern parts of Yugoslavia, in Serbia and in Macedonia, the
> gipsies are proud of being gipsies, and other people, which is to say
> the peasants, for there are practically none other, honour them for
> their qualities, for their power of making beautiful music and danc-
> ing, which the peasant lacks, and envy them for being exempt from
> the necessities of toil and order which lie so heavily on the peasant.

Her Serbian companion, a Yugoslav official, went on to explain that while the
Austrians and the Germans "despise the gipsies" because of their poverty, lack
of hygiene, and questionable musical talents, the "Serbs are not bourgeois, so
none of these reasons make us hate the gipsies."[62]

West discovered other evidence of the differing views on Gypsies in
Skopje, the capital of Macedonia. According to one unofficial estimate, the
Gypsy settlement in Skopje already had "two thousand houses . . . which
means ten thousand gipsies." Considering that Skopje had only an estimated
population of 70,000 at the time, it was well on its way to becoming one of
the most important Gypsy centers in the Balkans. Most of the Rom in Skopje
were Muslim, though the women went unveiled, which Ms. West felt was "an
extreme example of the position their kind has won for itself as professionally
free from ordinary social obligations." Equally unique among Macedonia's
Rom were the Gunpowder Gypsies, who "used to collect saltpetre for the
Turkish Army" and who were known for their "beauty, their cleanliness,
their fine clothes." Yet despite these positive impressions of the Macedonian
Rom, one of West's companions, a German married to a Yugoslav, angrily
criticized Skopje's Rom as "dirty and uncivilized savages, who ought not to
be in Europe at all." These feelings reflected sentiments that would later
come to haunt the region's Gypsies.[63]

The richness and diversity of Rom life in the regions of Yugoslavia with the
greatest Gypsy concentrations—Serbia and Macedonia—would be severely
damaged by the excesses of World War II. Prior to Yugoslavia's invasion by

the Axis Powers in 1941, Prince Paul tried to maneuver his country through the complex, dangerous waters of the times in an attempt to preserve his country's neutrality. Although he was initially sympathetic to the Allied side, he finally succumbed to German pressure to join the Tripartite Pact alliance of Germany, Italy, and Japan. As Yugoslav diplomats signed the accord in Berlin on March 26, 1941, a coup took place in Belgrade that removed Prince Paul as regent. His hesitant cousin, King Peter II, assumed the throne in his own right, though not quite 18. Ten days later, a German-led coalition of Italy, Bulgaria, Hungary, and Romania invaded Yugoslavia with the goal of carving much of it up among themselves. What the invaders did not absorb was transformed into puppet Croatian and Serbian states. The new Croatian satellite became the Independent State of Croatia (Nezavism Drźava Hrvatska, NDH), which was divided into German and Italian spheres-of-influence. An Italian nobleman, the Duke of Spoleto, became its king, as Tomislav II, though he never visited Croatia. The new state was effectively ruled by Ustaša ("insurrection") leader, Ante Pavelić, whose movement had been formed on Italian soil with Mussolini's aid in 1929. An illegal, terrorist movement, Ustaša found itself increasingly relegated to isolated Italian villages after its role in the murder of King Alexander and Barthou in 1934. Ustaša's plight within Italy worsened between 1937 and 1941 as Yugoslavia, Italy, and Germany drew closer together. Regardless, Ustasa remained committed to its goal of acquiring Croatian independence at any cost; it now added genocide to its methods of maintaining it.[64]

Approximately 28,500 Rom were trapped in the NDH in 1941, which included most of Bosnia-Hercegovina, while many Gypsies who had earlier fled to Italian territory were put in detention camps in Sardinia or Puglia. Those who entered Italy after the creation of the NDH in 1941 were watched to try to keep them from reentering Croatia to help relatives. The Italians, who had no tolerance for the genocidal policies of their allies, also gave some Rom "Italian identity cards to put them further beyond the reach of the Nazis and Ustaše until 1943," while those who were "caught in the German dragnet . . . were sent to camps in Austria for extermination." The new Croatian Ustaša government in the NDH quickly adopted Nazi-type racial laws and genocidal tactics to deal with Serbs, Jews, and Gypsies, whom it termed to be "aliens outside the national community." Gypsies were forbidden to walk on sidewalks, while signs were posted in all public places and transportation that stated, "No Serbs, Jews, Nomads [Gypsies] and dogs allowed." Two decrees, "The Protection of Aryan Blood and the Honor of the Croatian People" (No. XLV–67–2–p.1941), and "Belonging to the Same Race" (No. XLV–68–2–p.1941), laid out "the rights of the 'elite' and the duties of the 'inferior races,'" and decreed that anyone who had "two or more Gypsy grandparents" was a Rom. The Ministry of the Interior's Decree No. 13–542 ordered all Gypsies to register with the police on July 22–23, 1941. Rom property was seized by the Croatian government, while most of the republic's Gypsies were arrested and sent to Ustaša concentration camps. Over the next two years, some Croatian Rom were sent to death camps in Germany and Serbia, while others were executed "in reprisal for Partisan and Četnik activities in the NDH." Estimates are that 26,000 to 28,000 Rom died in the NDH during the Poŕajmos (Gypsy Holocaust).[65]

Rump Serbia, which had a Gypsy population of no more than 40,000 in the spring of 1941, was "under the military control of the German army," aided by the puppet Government of National Salvation. Serbian Rom suffered from similar, though not as deadly, policies as their Croatian counterparts. The Gypsy quarter on the outskirts of Belgrade in Zemun had been bombed, like the rest of the Serbian capital, several days before the Germans invaded the city in early April 1941. Once it had fallen, Nazi authorities required the Rom to wear yellow armbands with "Zigeuner" printed on them. On May 31, 1941, German military authorities decreed that "Gypsies are to be treated as Jews" and defined a Rom as "a person who has at least three Gypsy grandparents." In addition, all people with one or two "Gypsy grandparents and who [were] married to Gypsy women [were] to be classed as Gypsies." Finally, all Rom were to be put on a special register. On October 23, 1941, authorities decided to open a concentration camp for Jews and Gypsies on the fairgrounds at Zemun and destroyed the Gypsy quarter that lay at its edge for health reasons. Since the area under consideration was in NDH territory, the Croatians agreed to the use of the site for a "interim mini-death camp," which became known as Semlin, as long as it "was guarded by Germans, not Serbs." Later, "jurisdiction of Zemun passed to the Croat regime, and the Ustashi guarded the camp under German Security Police command." Over the next year, about 10 percent of Belgrade's Rom were sent to the Semlin camp, where they became slave laborers, forced to dig graves for Jews killed in mobile gas vans and buried in Avala south of Belgrade. Rom were also used as hostages as part of the Reich's scheme to kill "Gypsies, Jews and other hostages at a ratio of 100:1 for every German soldier killed in Serbia." Though the Germans claimed by 1942 that Serbia was "Gypsy free," they only "effectively controlled about one-third of Serbia's Rom population." In reality, they woefully overestimated the number of Gypsies and Jews in Serbia and Belgrade. German officials initially calculated that there were 150,000 Gypsies in Serbia in the spring of 1941; on the eve of the opening of the Semlin camp in early December 1941, they expected "16000 Gypsies and Jews to be interned" at the new *Judenlager* (Jewish camp). Though records vary, it is estimated that only 6,280 Jews and Gypsies were in the camp by March 1942, with Jews making up 90 percent of the inmate population. Many Gypsies had already "fled, hid, evaded, or joined the resistance." Since Gypsies were "usually . . . not welcome among the Serbian nationalist Četniks," they often joined the communist partisan forces. Estimates are that of the 60,000 Rom in prewar Serbia, 12,000 died in the Porajmos.[66]

Macedonia, which, next to Serbia, had Yugoslavia's largest prewar Gypsy community, came primarily under Bulgarian control in 1941 and, as seen earlier in the detailed account on the plight of the Bulgarian Rom during this period, benefited greatly from Bulgarian resistance to the more deadly genocidal policies of the Nazis and their puppets elsewhere in Yugoslavia. The bulk of Macedonia's Gypsy community was able to survive the Porajmos, as did many Slovenian Rom. Slovenia, which had a small Rom community, was divided between Germany, Italy, and Hungary. The northern portion of Slovenia was integrated into the Reich, which deported 16,000 undesirable Slovenes, including Gypsies, to camps in Croatia and Serbia. The Germans then transferred 20,000 Slovene Germans and a number of Tyrolean Germans into the newly evacuated "Slovene Marches." Italy acquired Ljubljana and the rest of Slovenia, while Hungary got the Prekmurje area of eastern Slovenia. Hungarian authorities interned some Rom, and a large number were arrested and sent to death camps when Germany occupied Hungary in 1944.[67]

Albania's Gypsies benefited from Italy's conquest of the country in the spring of 1939 and its transformation into Italian Greater Albania with the addition of Kosovo in 1941. Italian and other Axis occupation forces "paid scant attention to the Gypsies[,] who made up only an 'insignificant part' of the total population." Germany's occupation of Albania after the fall of Mussolini's government in September 1943 saw an aggressive, though not terribly successful, change in policy toward the Gypsies, since the Germans, who turned local administration over to Albanian fascists, found it hard to distinguish between the country's Albanians, Turks, Gypsies, and Vlachs. Though some Albanian Gypsies were caught and sent to concentration camps in Yugoslavia and the Reich, many survived by supporting local fascist authorities or the Nazis, who Greater Albanian Rom saw as allies against a greater enemy—the Serbs, "who equated Nazi occupation with centuries of Turkish terror." After Mussolini's fall in 1943, some Albanian Gypsies joined the communist partisan forces. In relation to Gypsy losses in other parts of Yugoslavia, those in Albania, which had a prewar Rom population of 22,000, were comparatively light.[68]

The horrible conflicts that had befallen Yugoslavia from 1941–1945 resulted in the deaths of 1.75 million people, 11 percent of the country's prewar population. Over half of those killed died at the hands of other Yugoslavs. The victory of Marshal Tito's partisan forces in 1945 signaled the beginning of the process of reconstruction and communization of the country.[69] The question of ethnic identity and rights in the new Yugoslav state took its direction from the 1946 constitution, which was modeled on the 1936 Soviet "Stalin" constitution. Article 13 of the new Yugoslav document guaranteed national minorities "the right to and protection of their own cultural development and the free use of their own language," while Article 21 stated that "all citizens of the Federative People's Republic of Yugoslavia are equal before the law and enjoy equal rights regardless of nationality, race and creed." It added that it was illegal to limit or propagate "national, racial and religious hatred and discord," and the government backed this later with criminal code legislation. The 1946 constitution built its federal republic system around the major nationalities—Croat, Macedonian, Montenegran, Serb, and Slovene—which provided the nucleus for five of the country's six republics. The sixth, Bosnia and Hercegovina, had a mixed population of Croats, Serbs, and Muslims. The People's Republic of Serbia included the autonomous province of Vojvodina and the predominantly Albanian autonomous Kosovo-Metohijan region. Tito designed the new constitution to deemphasize nationality as an active force in the dynamics of the Yugoslav state by limiting the autonomy of the republics through the bicameral national legislature, the Federal Assembly, and depriving the republics of legislative authority "that was independent and different from the federal organs."[70]

The partisan victory was welcomed by many Rom, since Tito gave brief consideration to the creation of "a Gypsy autonomous area in Macedonia" in compensation for their "fanatical commitment to the partisan cause." Though this idea never bore fruit, it did pave the way for considerable Rom development in the new Yugoslav state, particularly in Macedonia.[71] A Macedonian Gypsy literary awakening began in 1946, that centered around a new generation of Roma poets whose works dealt with the plight of the Gypsies. Within a few years, Gypsy writers, with the support of the new Macedonian Roma association, Phralipe (Brotherhood), formed the literary organization, Fraternité. Phralipe also sponsored a theater company that performed throughout Europe. In 1948, Gypsies were also elected to seats on the Skopje city council.[72]

The positive atmosphere for Rom translated into impressive population gains over prewar figures from the 1948 census, particularly in light of the losses they suffered during World War II. The federal census, which was based on ethnic affiliation, showed 72,651 Rom in Yugoslavia, with 52,115 in Serbia, 19,500 in Macedonia, 405 in Croatia, 46 in Slovenia, 422 in Bosnia and Hercegovina, and 163 in Montenegro. Over 50 percent of those counted were listed as workers and apprentices, while over 18 percent considered themselves farmers and fishermen. There were 273 Gypsy professionals, while 9,728 considered themselves artisans. A little over 42 percent were under 14 years of age, and the rest were primarily between the ages of 15 and 59.[73]

The 1953 census was even more thorough. Yugoslav gypsiologists were able to break down the Rom population figures according to ethnic identity, mother tongue, and gender. There were 84,713 Gypsies in Yugoslavia by ethnic identity in 1953, with 76,379 choosing Romani as their native tongue. There were 58,800 in Serbia, and out of this number, 11,525 were in Vojvodina, and 11,904 in Kosovo-Metohija. Almost a quarter of the country's Rom, 20,462, lived in Macedonia, while 1,261 lived in Croatia, 1,663 in Slovenia, 2,297 in Bosnia and Hercegovina, and 230 in Montenegro. One Yugoslav Gypsy specialist, T. P. Vukanović, argued, however, that these figures were exceedingly low and felt that Yugoslavia probably had at least 160,000 Rom in 1953. He attributed the difference in figures "to the fact that the Gypsy population of Yugoslavia endeavors to conceal, in many cases, its real ethnical character, which is quite feasible, because in Yugoslavia everyone is allowed to determine freely his nationality, and all nationalities enjoy in our country the same rights." Pavla Štrukelj, a Slovenian gypsiologist, explained that the sharp rise in Rom figures in Slovenia between 1948 and 1953 partly came about because of the return of large numbers of Slovene Gypsies from Vojvodina. Lured to the Serb province in 1948 with the promise of land, the Gypsies returned to the Prekmurje region of eastern Slovenia because it was more familiar to them. It could also be added that the most dramatic increases in Gypsy population figures from 1948 to 1953, years when overall Rom growth far outpaced that of Yugoslavia as a whole, took place in the German or Ustaša "killing fields" of Croatia, Bosnia and Hercegovina, and Slovenia. While part of the increases in these regions could be attributed to migratory patterns, it is also possible that it took many "closet" Rom eight years after the end of World War II to feel comfortable identifying themselves as Gypsies.[74]

The 1950s were a subdued period of development for the Rom as the Yugoslav nation struggled with its new domestic and internal role as a communist maverick. Though one of Tito's early postwar goals was "to realize the Soviet vision or model of a socialist system," a 1948 split with Stalin prompted the country's leaders to rethink their ideological mimicry and discover a new Marxist approach to socialism. The result was "national communism," an independent, experimental path that emphasized decentralized worker control and talked of local administration that conformed "to the ethnic mosaic of Yugoslavia as well as to its tradition of localism." Driven "by a Yugoslav faith in its partisan resistance," the spirit of these changes was imbedded in the Fundamental Law of 1953, which tried further "to de-emphasize ethnic representation" in the national legislature, the People's Assembly. Other changes by Tito's government, spurred by the death of Stalin in 1953 and Khrushchev's deStalinization speech in 1956, resulted in more liberal economic policies and a "freer cultural atmosphere," while a sense of Yugoslavness designed to temper ethnic differences further began to emerge.[75]

For Yugoslavia's Gypsies, the somewhat contradictory period of socialist experimentation that talked of greater societal homogeneity balanced with more local control in social and economic matters was a time of uncertainty. Efforts to promise "parallel instruction in different languages" in Macedonia (which, according to Gypsy specialist Grattan Puxon, had an estimated Rom population of 140,000 in 1958) were unsuccessful. On the other hand, Gypsy music continued to thrive throughout Yugoslavia, and in 1956, Slavko Vorkapić produced a new film, *Hanka*, a Gypsy romance based on a real incident that took place in Bosnia-Hercegovina between World War I and World War II. The tale centers around the love affair of a beautiful young Gypsy, Hanka, with a charcoal-burner, Seydo, and efforts by a powerful Roma chieftan, Ahmed, to thwart the relationship between the two lovers.[76]

The spirit of "Yugoslavness" that swept the country in the 1950s carried with it a strong theme of assimilation, particularly for groups such as the Gypsies, who had no official nationality status. Consequently, in the 1961 census, only 31,674 Gypsies, many from Macedonia, chose Romany as their primary language, while others chose to identify themselves with other minorities or opted for the Yugoslav or "Other" categories in the census. Not all minorities were willing to chose alternative categories for ethnic identification. Yugoslavia's Albanians, for example, the bulk of them in Kosovo and Macedonia, had grown steadily throughout the postwar years, numbering 1,309,523 in 1971. This was only 878,477 fewer than the entire population of Albania, an almost ethnically pure nation with only 10,000 Rom in 1961.[77]

Macedonia's Rom gained some notoriety during this period as a result of the construction of what would become the world's largest Gypsy community, Šuto Orizari, in the suburbs of Skopje. Šuto Orizari began as a temporary, American-built Quonset-hut community in the aftermath of an earthquake on July 26, 1963, that destroyed three-quarters of the Macedonian capital and left 200,000 homeless. Reconstruction of the old Rom quarter, Topana, entailed "the addition of two intersecting freeways," and officials gave Gypsy leaders two choices: they could move into new, integrated neighborhoods, or they could move into their own suburb on the outskirts of Skopje. By the mid-1970s, it had rapidly mushroomed into a township with its own district council offices, cinema, shops, dance-hall and football ground. Roma who had lost their homes in the old quarter were given free building land and grants to construct new houses. Some 5000 houses have since been built, mostly by the families themselves with minimal technical and professional assistance. There are now 120 asphalted streets, and recently trees have been planted and recreational areas laid out.

Šuto Orizari, which some Rom have "half-seriously called the Romani state," became the nucleus of a Gypsy community located within a 50-mile radius of Skopje that had an estimated population of over 40,000 by 1977, with 23,000 in Šuto Orizari. These figures would swell to 80,000 by the mid-1980s. According to Abdi Faik, a Rom deputy in the Macedonian legislature, the new Rom settlement was "the only place where Gypsies aren't a minority."[78]

While Skopje was recovering from the devastation of the earthquake, the country adopted a new constitution in 1963 that strengthened each republic's control over social and economic matters. A broad economic reform package in 1965 eased restrictions "on the migration of Yugoslav workers who wished to work abroad." This triggered a wave of Gypsy migration to the West that involved Yugoslav Rom "from a variety of tribal and linguistic groups." Among the most conspicuous were the *Xoraxané Roma* ("Turkish Gypsies"), a predominantly Muslim nomadic group from Bosnia-Hercegovina, Montenegro, and Kosovo. Some of the current hostility to Rom *gastarbeiten* (guest workers) in Germany and elsewhere can be partially traced to this period in Yugoslav history. The economic reforms of the mid-1960s also brought latent economic and cultural hostilities to the surface that led to a flurry of constitutional changes in 1967 designed to appease Slovene, Croat, and Macedonian discontent over their unequal status in the Yugoslav federation. For the next four years, a national-liberal coalition of these three republics pushed for "further decentralization and 'democratization' both of the LCY [League of Communists of Yugoslavia] and of society." The culmination of this ongoing liberalization campaign, which to some was aimed at "Great Serbian assimilationism," was a series of amendments to the constitution in 1971 that "amounted to the reconstitution of Yugoslavia as a confederative republic."[79]

These changes did little to still the nationalistic passions of some Croats, which prompted a harsh response from Tito after student protesters in Zagreb demanded in November 1971 that Belgrade "stop the plunder of Croatia," among other things. The following month, the country's leadership decided "to suppress any manifestations of nationalism in the population at large." Tito struck out harshly against "nationalism and 'rotten liberalism'" in all republics and informed the LCY that he intended to return it "to the Leninist principle

of democratic centralism." He followed this up with a new, complex constitution in 1974 that gave greater autonomy to the individual republics and
provinces and created new mechanisms, including a collective presidency,
designed to enhance greater cooperation and decision making on the national
level. Unfortunately, Tito's changes did little to quell the deeper nationalistic
urges of the country's many ethnic groups. Croats saw the harsh crackdown
in 1971–1972 as a "Belgrade-led [i.e. Serbian], anti-Croatian crusade" and the
new prominence gained by the military in the 1974 constitution as a "coup of
the Serbian generals." In turn, Serbs viewed Tito's efforts to remove them
from positions in the "army and industry, to make room for minority groups"
during this period as unfair.[80]

Yugoslavia's Gypsies benefited from some of the changes put in force in
the first half of the 1970s, which enhanced their sense of ethnic identity. In the
1971 census, for example, 78,485 Gypsies chose Romani as their mother
tongue, well over twice the number recorded a decade earlier. Serbia continued to have the largest Rom community, 49,894, with 14,593 in Kosovo,
which had been upgraded to provincial status in 1968, and 7,760 in Vojvodina.
Macedonia had a Rom population of 24,505, while Bosnia-Hercegovia had
1,456; Croatia, 1,257; Montenegro, 396; and Slovenia, 977. These figures
were considered quite unrepresentative of the real size of the Yugoslav Gypsy
population, which some estimated as between 400,000 and 650,000, with
100,000 in Serbia and 100,000 in Kosovo. According to one Yugoslav magazine, *NIN*, Gypsies tended to "declare themselves as belonging to other
nations and nationalities, as a phenomenon of ethnic mimicry . . . due to their
unresolved constitutional status."[81]

The government's efforts to open doors for underrepresented minorities
brought more Gypsies into the mainstream, though they still lagged far behind
more well-established ethnic and religious minorities. There were 440 registered Gypsy members of the Serbian Communist party in 1973, a figure that
rose to 614 two years later. In Macedonia, Abdi Faik, the representative from
Šuto Orizari in the Macedonian parliament, was able to push through an
amendment to the Macedonian constitution in 1971 that upgraded the status of
the Rom to an officially recognized ethnic group. While this did not put them
on par with the republic's Albanian and Turkish nationalities, it did afford them
the use of the Romani national flag, and gave them certain cultural rights that
included "publications in Romanes and time on radio and television."[82]

The Yugoslav press also seemed more sensitive to the Gypsies and began
to honor their request to use Rom instead of *Cigan*. A biography of Tito
appeared in Romany in 1978, and two years later, "the Nasa Kniga publishing house of Skopje brought out the first Romani grammar to be entirely

written in the Romani script and orthography." The original printing of 3,000 copies sold out quickly. In 1981, "the world's largest anthology of Gypsy poetry was published in Belgrade," while Radio Tetovo in Macedonia and Radio Belgrade (Studio "B") began to do daily half-hour programs in Romani. Eighty Rom associations evolved throughout this period, while Yugoslav Gypsies such as Slobodan Berberski and Abdi Faik were prominent leaders in the World Romani Congress.[83]

These Rom achievements, which culminated with the acquisition of nationality status in 1981, were not enough to mask some of the deeper problems of the Yugoslav Gypsies, which the *Report of the Yugoslav Federal Presidency* of the same year called "a serious basic social issue." According to a 1978 report prepared by Ales Bebler, a member of the Yugoslav Federal Executive Council, the key to the Gypsies' slow integration into Yugoslav society was the low quality of life and education. He noted that the "mortality rate for children in the first year of life had been as high as 50%." Government requirements that someone have at least an elementary-school education to be employed severely hurt the Rom, since "only some 20% of Rom adults have even this minimum qualification." He added that a "majority of [Gypsy] children are growing up illiterate, either because they do not attend school or they drop out early, and local authorities have failed to show concern." Bebler proposed that Yugoslavia's Gypsies be granted nationality status, as well as recognition "as an undeveloped *narodnost*, with a position similar to undeveloped regions. They could then benefit from 'positive discrimination,' i.e. programmes against illiteracy, for housing construction and job training."[84]

There were also serious problems for Rom who had grown beyond these serious limitations, particularly the

> small number of Gypsies who are active in the administrative apparatus. One Gypsy activist from Nis (Serbia) emphasizes, for instance, that of 12,000 in Nis, they have not one delegate on the municipal assembly, on the executive bodies of political organizations and associations. "The situation is similar in many other places, and that's also how it is at the republican and federal levels." The Gypsy association in Pirot (Serbia) has a membership of some 6,000 and they do not even have a place to hold their meetings. The same situation exists in Vranjska Banja (Serbia), where 2,000 Gypsies live. Many Gypsy associations . . . operate under impossible conditions. Of the total number of Gypsies in Yugoslavia, only about a hundred are studying at the university level.

According to a study done by Trivo Indjic on the plight of the Gypsies and other minorities in Yugoslavia in the early 1980s, the government was often hiding behind "constitutional rhetoric." As an example, he pointed to the remarks of Svetozar Tadic, the president of the Council on Interethnic Relations in Serbia, who said that "there is no need to speak of a specific Gypsy question; neither is there any need for, nor can there be, any particular approach to the problem," since Gypsies in Serbia "are all equal and enjoy constitutional rights." Instead, Indjic felt that the Yugoslav government should heed the advice of Said Balic, the Yugoslav president of the World Romani Congress. Balic said that Yugoslavia's Rom could not "muster sufficient forces to effect their own complete equality in everyday life" and needed "the help of political organizations of social emancipation."[85]

The acquisition of Rom nationality status came at a difficult time for Yugoslavia, which struggled with a plethora of economic, political, and social problems that seemed particularly menacing after the death of Tito on May 4, 1980. Ridden by growing ethnic unrest, particularly in Kosovo, Gypsies found that their newly won status was not uniformly accepted throughout the country. Only Bosnia-Hercegovina and Montenegro came to recognize the Gypsies as a nationality in their republic's constitutions, while the constitutions of Yugoslavia's other four republics continued to identify them as an ethnic group. This hesitancy to grant full nationality status to one of the country's fastest growing and increasingly vocal ethnic minorities was linked to the gradual disintegration of that delicate bond that Tito had used to hold the nation together, as well as the powerful forces of ethnic identity and separateness that would come to destroy Yugoslavia a little more than a decade later.[86]

As these problems began to surface more rapidly after Tito's death, the Rom found themselves caught up in the bitter upsurge of Albanian nationalism in Macedonia, which had spilled over from Kosovo. Officials claimed that during the 1981 census, "Albanian nationalists, including Muslim clergy of Albanian extraction, had exerted pressure on Macedonian Gypsies . . . to declare themselves Albanians." This situation was doubly problematic for Macedonia's leaders, since the 1981 census showed a dramatic increase over 1971 figures in the number of Gypsies who claimed Romani status. There were now 43,223 Gypsies in Macedonia, an increase of 18,718 over 1971 figures. Similar increases in the Gypsy population were recorded throughout Yugoslavia in the 1981 census, which saw figures rise from 78,485 in 1971 to 168,197 in 1981. Serbia's overall Gypsy population increased to 57,140, with the most dramatic change in Kosovo, where figures more than doubled to 34,126. The increase in Vojvodina was even greater, which now had an official Rom population of 19,693. Bosnia-Hercegovina had 7,251 Rom, an incredible rise of almost 6,000 since 1971, while Slovenia's Gypsy population almost doubled to 1,435. Croatia's Rom community tripled in size to 3,858 during the decade, and Montenegro's Gypsies showed similar, dramatic increases between 1971 and 1981 that saw the number of Roma increase from 396 to 1,471.[87]

This dramatic growth, which, with the exception of the Albanians, was unique to the Gypsies, had less to do with an absolute increase in numbers than with a change in affiliation stimulated by the drive to acquire nationality status, which the Belgrade journal *Politika* officially announced on December 4, 1982. Furthermore, like previous censuses, the new figures woefully underestimated the true size of the Rom population in Yugoslavia. Though estimates varied, Yugoslav sources indicated that the real number of Gypsies in the country ranged from 700,000 to 1 million at this time.[88]

The upsurge in Rom ethnic identity that preceded and accompanied the acquisition of nationality status in Yugoslavia came at a time of significant political soul searching throughout the country. Initial efforts to come to grips with the country's difficulties under the existing system soon failed, and by 1984 the country's leadership looked to changes in the constitution as a solution to Yugoslavia's problems. Complex divisions quickly surfaced between those republics and autonomous provinces that sought a greater strengthening of central Yugoslav power as a solution and those such as Slovenia and Croatia, who wanted to preserve certain aspects of the 1974 "confederalist" system that had strengthened local autonomy. By 1987, the same year that Serbian nationalist Slobodan Milosević seized control of the Serbian party apparatus, discussions began on specific changes to the 1974 constitution. Slovenia reacted harshly to the proposals and felt they would be a vehicle for Serbian nationalist, centrist tendencies. In time, Milosević, who spoke of a "strong Serbia, strong Yugoslavia," alienated other republics as well, and by 1989, resistance to his efforts to strengthen the authority of the central government in Belgrade vis à vis that of the republics and autonomous provinces created a backlash that strengthened the confederalists.[89]

In the midst of these debates, efforts were made to improve the plight of Yugoslavia's Gypsies. The single greatest barrier to a better life for the country's Rom was education. Gypsy students in the educational system prior to the opening of some Romani schools in 1983 were frequently absent, and many dropped out before finishing primary school. Estimates were that most Gypsy children did "not even finish primary school, while in Serbia less than one in sixty goes on to secondary education." Dropouts were caused by the need "to help their families (begging, manual labor, menial part-time employment, etc.)," and an alien educational world that used a language unfamiliar to them.

School authorities often sent them to "preparatory or specialized departments of the school," which "separated them from other children."[90] As a result, the country's universities only enrolled between 50 and 100 Roma in the late 1970s, and there were only "a little over two hundred Roma in the professions, working as doctors, lawyers, engineers and so on, though this is double the figure twenty years ago." By 1983, ten primary schools were "using the Romani language as the teaching medium for the first four grades," though the process of education in the Gypsy language was handicapped by the lack of teachers trained to teach in Romani. The first of these schools was opened in Kosovo, "where Moslem [Albanian] Roma have had a hard time making their voice heard in the past."[91]

Unfortunately, these changes could only provide long-term solutions to immediate problems that made the Gypsies "the poorest sector of Yugoslav society." Their dilemma centered around unemployment, which was partly caused by the fact that "almost all employers demand at least an eighth-grade education" of prospective employees. When Gypsies did find work, they often held "the least remunerative jobs." *NIN* reported in 1980 that "in the town of Leskovac [Serbia] . . . of 5,180 Gypsies, only 560 are employed; in Priştina [Kosovo], of 6,740 Gypsies, only 634 work; and in Bujanovac [Serbia], of 3,500 Gypsies, only 50 hold jobs." The Serbian government viewed the Rom as "socially endangered persons," while a report on Gypsies living in Cakovec, Croatia, reported that some, who lived "in mud-covered willow hovels . . . wander en masse through the villages, scavenging food from the garbage cans, and often resorting to stealing crops, for lack of the basic means of subsistence." Their plight often subjected them to mistreatment. In 1985, authorities arrested a "gang of kidnappers, who has been abducting children from defenseless Gypsy families for sale abroad to Italians and Americans, and to be trained as thieves in Rome and Paris."[92]

Another problem that plagued the Gypsies was traditional prejudice, which worsened with the growing fractionalization of the Yugoslav state and the new assertiveness of the Rom. In 1986, Muslim residents in the Bosnian village of Novo Kasaba tried to stop Gypsy Muslims from burying their dead in the local cemetery. The police finally had to intervene to resolve the crisis. Ongoing Slovenian-Serbian friction and the Serbian annexation of Kosovo in the spring of 1989 intensified the divisiveness in Yugoslavia. This, plus the tide of democratization enveloping Eastern Europe, saw Yugoslavia "swept by a wildfire of nationalism" that manifested itself in a wave of multiparty elections in 1990. In Slovenia, officials tried to keep Gypsies from voting, while in the village of Hydej, residents refused to share voting booths with local Rom, who had to use separate booths set up for them. That summer in Kosovo, "a young

Roma woman was allegedly beaten up in the streets because of her origin and petrol sprinkled on her hair and set alight with no one attempting to help her." In Kursumlija, Serbia, the police refused to investigate the deaths of several Gypsies "under suspicious circumstances," saying that "it would do no harm if 'even more of them burned.'"[93]

This violence did not stop Rajko Djuric from presenting a petition before the Yugoslav parliament in 1989 that "proposed that a uniform status of nationality be agreed for the Roma in all republics and provinces." The legislature tabled the petition, and later Djuric received several death threats. After his home in Belgrade "was ransacked by state authorities . . . he was forced to leave Belgrade and Yugoslavia." Gypsies in Croatia were a little more successful with their political activities. As early as 1980, Croatian officials met with Gypsies from the Zagreb area and from the Federation of Rom Societies in Serbia to "discuss the position of Croatia's Rom." A decade later, Croatian Gypsies formed the Romani Party of Croatia, whose goal was "to seek recognition of the Roma nationality and rights, and to appeal to the Croatian national assembly for primary and secondary level classes and textbooks in Romanes for the now estimated 150,000 Roma in Croatia."[94]

One of the most interesting manifestations of new Rom assertiveness cropped up in Macedonia, where an "Epicani" Association of Citizens in Ohrid was founded in 1990, followed by an Association of Egyptians from Kosovo and Methohija, and, ultimately, a 15,000-member Yugoslav Egyptian Association, headed by an Albanian-Macedonian Muslim, Nazmi Arifi. Some members had tried as early as the 1981 census to claim Egyptian as a new ethnic status but were put in the "miscellaneous" category. Rajko Djuric called the group "gentrified gypsies who are trying to distance themselves from the shunned, poverty-stricken gypsies." He felt that the "Egyptian business is all an escape from reality." Rade Bozovic of Belgrade University said that the Rom Egyptians "look different from the gypsies and the Albanians . . ." Nazmi Arifi added that unlike "most Yugoslav gypsies who eke out a living as itinerant musicians, fortune tellers and unskilled laborers, the would-be Egyptians are a prosperous and educated people who have lived a sedentary life in enclaves at the center of towns."[95]

Such newfound feelings of ethnic self-awareness took place in the midst of growing friction between Croatia and Serbia over the plight of Serbs in Kninska Krajina, Croatia, where a limited civil war broke out over local Serb autonomy in August 1990. Friction between Serbs and Muslims in Bosnia and in southern Serbia added to the tension, while "Serbia, Croatia, Slovenia, and Montenegro allegedly diverted money sorely needed for economic investment into arms purchases" in preparation for a possible conflict. Last-minute efforts to resolve the complex problems facing Yugoslavia collapsed with the Croatian and Slovenian declarations of secession on June 25, 1991. Fighting erupted in Kninska krajina, and a civil war ensued between Croatia and Serbia the following month. As the European Community moved closer to the recognition of Croatian and Slovenian independence, Bosnia-Hercegovina, fearful of membership in a rump Yugoslavia dominated by a nationalist Serbia, adopted a "Memorandum on Sovereignty" on October 15, 1991. The Serbs in Bosnia, who made up 31.3 percent of the population, created a Serbian Republic of Bosnia and Hercegovina on December 21, 1991. Two months later, a Serb-boycotted referendum on Bosnian independence was overwhelmingly supported by the country's Muslims and Croats. On March 1, the day after the vote, the Serbs responded with an attack on Sarajevo. The decision of the European Community and the United States to recognize Bosnian independence on April 6–7 prompted the new Bosnian Serb republic to declare its own sovereignty. Over the next year, civil wars spread throughout the country, with separate struggles between Serbs and Croats, Serbs and Muslims, Croats and Muslims, and the symbolic, Serbian siege of multiethnic Sarajevo. Genocidal "ethnic cleansing" policies adopted by all sides failed to spur the West to do anything more than adopt diplomatic means to halt the fighting. By the summer of 1993, Bosnia-Hercegovina had almost ceased to exist, with the Serbs in control of over 70 percent of Bosnia and a portion of Croatia. Croatia controlled most of the rest of Bosnia and Hercegovina. The tables turned on the Serbs in early 1994, though they still controlled over two-thirds of Bosnia. On March 18, 1994, the Bosnian Muslims and Croats signed an accord creating a "Bosnian federation."[96]

The plight of the Rom in this modern genocidal tragedy is difficult to gauge. Even before the outbreak of civil war, Yugoslavia's Gypsies felt particularly vulnerable to growing nationalism and the deteriorating economic situation, which hit them "especially hard as the poorest of the poor." As a result, Gypsies who had the means were "leaving Yugoslavia 'by the thousands.'"[97] They became part of a larger refugee problem that saw almost two million former Yugoslavs driven from their homes as a result of the fighting in Bosnia and Hercegovina and Croatia. The fact that a large portion of former Yugoslavia's Gypsies lived in Serbia did not alleviate concerns for Serbia's Rom, since the country was ridden by virulent nationalism and economic chaos partially caused by UN sanctions.[98]

The only bright spot for Yugoslav Gypsies in this otherwise bleak picture is in Macedonia, which had an estimated Rom population of 200,000 in 1991. President Kiro Gligorov has shown some sympathy to the Rom and has "repeatedly and explicitly recognized them as full and equal citizens of the

Republic of Macedonia." Furthermore, a dialogue was opened between leaders of the Gypsy community and the Macedonian Ministry of Education about the creation of a Romani educational program throughout the country. In September 1993, "two hours a week of instruction in the Romany language" was "introduced in grades one through eight." At the same time, Skopje University opened a Department of Romany Studies "for the study and research of the Romany language, history, and culture." The principle group responsible for these gains was the Party for the Complete Emancipation of Romanies in Macedonia, headed by long-time Gypsy activist Abdi Faik. The Romany cause in Macedonia was also aided by Macedonia's desire to achieve international recognition and UN membership. Macedonia's Gypsies will also be helped by the presence of UN forces in the new country, there to thwart any southward moves by the Serbs.[99]

.7.

THE HISTORY OF THE ROMA IN EASTERN EUROPE AND RUSSIA SINCE 1994

I n the early years after the collapse of communism, the Roma of Eastern Europe and Russia quickly saw their hoped for dreams of acceptance and integration into society quickly dashed by the very prejudices that had haunted them for centuries. In fact, the new-found hatreds they faced had a particular virulence to it that harked back to the Nazi era. Much has changed in the region since the mid-1990s. The collapse of Yugoslavia into its constituent ethnic republics is now complete and the pace of European integration in Central and Eastern Europe is moving forward quickly. As is seen in this chapter, the Roma question has now moved center stage and has become something of a measure of the state of democracy in each of the region's new, postcommunist states.

Albania

Roma have lived in Albania for over six centuries. Roma religious evolution followed that of their Albanian neighbors. Though the early Albanians were primarily Roman Catholic, in time they split into four faith traditions. By the 1850s, over 50 percent of Albania's population was Sunni Muslim, while 25 percent belonged to Shiite Bektashi brotherhoods or crypto-Christian communities: Fifteen percent of Albania's population at this time was Greek Orthodox, and the rest Roman Catholic. Traditionally, the Roma adopted the faith of the majority or dominant group around them while privately maintaining or blending in their own beliefs. Consequently, depending on where they lived, there were Roma members in all of the major faith communities in Albania, though most Albanian Roma are Muslims.[1]

Though the Roma in the Balkans originally came from India, a number of unproven stories about the origin of Albanian Roma have circulated in that country for decades. Stuart Mann, for example, said that one tale brought some Albanian Roma into the country during the early nineteenth century, as part of the Egyptian intervention in the Greek revolution of 1821–1827. The Roma came as slaves in the Sultan's army, and then escaped to Albania. Another story says that some Roma followed an unnamed Spanish monarch into Italy, where they behaved so badly that the unnamed king forbade them to return to Spain. He then cursed them, saying "May you never take root anywhere!"[2]

These colorful stories are impossible to prove. The first concrete evidence we have of a Roma presence in Albania comes in 1522–1523. By this time, the Turks had conquered Albania, Bosnia, Herzegovina, Macedonia, and Serbia and introduced the sophisticated Ottoman administrative and taxation system throughout the region, which opened doors of opportunity for the Roma. A Turkish census indicated that there were 374 Roma campfires in Albania, indicating a Roma population of about 1,270.[3]

About eighty years later, an Ottoman *firman* (decree) ordered that "taxes and fines be collected from the Gypsies (*Kibtian*, i.e., Egyptians)" in the provinces of Elbasan, Valona, Delvino, and Yannina in Albania, and Aetolia-Akarnania in northwestern Greece. The decree, issued by Sultan Ahmed I (r. 1603–1617), ordered that settled Roma and nomadic Roma, who had previously "remained as free as possible from the regulations of the central government," had to pay Ottoman taxes, particularly the *cizye* or poll tax traditionally required of non-Muslims. Muslim Roma had to pay 180 *akçes* and Christian Roma 250 *akçes*. Ottoman records indicate that there were 5,940 registered Roma in this part of the Ottoman empire, mostly Christian nomads. While the official collecting the taxes was not to "harass or oppress" the Roma, he was also to make certain that they did not try to claim improper exemptions as "iron workers, charcoal burners, and castle watchmen." Furthermore, he was not to "allow them to be contumacious and obstructive." The Turks were particularly concerned about the nomadic Roma, whom they feared would try to "run away" or claim temporary absence to avoid paying the new taxes. They were to be caught quickly and forced to pay not only the 180 or 250 *akçes* levy, but also a fine of 300 *akçes*. Ahmed I's *firman* also dealt with other taxes the Roma had to pay, such as fines for various crimes as well as the *ispenç*, the slave tax. Ottoman regulations gave slaves the option of paying a small tax plus "personal service," or simply a larger amount without the "personal service." Local prejudices dictated that Roma slaves probably paid the latter tax.[4]

   M. Roques also mentioned the Roma in his *Le dictionnaire albanais de 1653*, referring to them as "Aegyptus-magiop."[5] In 1684, the Turks instituted a new tax policy that was meant to "tax them [the Roma] out of existence." According to Margaret Hasluck, the Ottomans regarded all Roma women in the empire as prostitutes and the men as their pimps. Muslim Roma were now required to pay an annual tax of 5 *piastres* (the new Ottoman currency) and Christian Roma 6 *piastres*.[6] Such efforts were ineffective. The Albanian provinces had become a refuge for Roma fleeing persecution in other parts of the Balkans and Central Europe, and who, over time, became Muslims. John Kolsti thinks that they were attracted to Albania because of its rich ethnic mix and its traditions of nomadism. It was here, he notes, that the Roma "probably came closest to finding a sense of equality with those around them."[7]

   There is little information on the Roma in Albania until the end of World War I. By then, Albania was a nation troubled by serious domestic instability and international uncertainty. Though Albania gained independence from the Ottoman Empire in 1913, only a rump Albanian state survived World War I. Threats from the new Yugoslavian kingdom saw Italy assume a protective role of Albania, while domestically Muslim *beys*, or powerful landlords, continued to dominate politics and the economy. Albania was primarily a Muslim nation, though Muslim Roma were still not viewed as true believers. Very often, they were not welcome in mosques or allowed to bury their dead in Muslim graveyards. On the other hand, Albanians still permitted Roma craftsmen to sell their goods in local markets, and nomadic Roma continued to settle on the outskirts of towns and villages. Some sedentary Muslim Roma even began to marry Turks and settled along the coastal regions of the country. Gradually, these Roma began to lose ties to their Roma past, particularly their language, Romani. In the mountains, Muslim Roma bands of *gurbati* (beggars) moved about freely and frightened Christian Albanian villagers.[8]

Many important Albanian towns had a Roma *mahalle* or quarter. Joseph Swire described the Roma quarter in Tirana, the Albanian capital, in the 1920s:

These Cigans, as they are called, being no longer nomads, have lost their language, though they still tell the tradition that their forebears came over the sea from the direction of the sun (meaning Egypt). Their type is very swarthy and quite unlike the average Albanian, but in common with nomadic Romanies (Vlachs) their physique is poor. The men, when they must work, become hamals or blacksmiths or executioners or scavengers—it is the Gypsy who drowns the stray dog and carts away the refuse—tasks to which the Albanian will not stoop. There are many of them at the ports, where they work as stevedores and boatmen and porters. These women are stocky, hardworking, far neater than the Tirana Moslems, and they are often employed as servants, for the Albanian dislikes charing. Their noses are markedly semitic. Their intelligence is average, but they keep their houses much cleaner than the lowland Albanians. Nevertheless the latter despised them, so the old official class is afraid foreigners should think them Albanian.[9]

Swire's account is similar to Margaret Hasluck's description during the interwar period. Hasluck was able to capture the rich diversity of Roma life as well as the varying attitudes toward different Roma groups. She estimated that there were probably 20,000 settled Roma in Albania in 1930 and about 2,000 nomads, who were divided into distinct substrict ethnic lines.[10]

In Berat, for example, which had a Roma population of 1500, nomadic Roma were known as *cergatarë* or *cergarë*, while the settled Roma were called *evgjit*. In Korça, the locals called the nomadic Roma *kurbetë* or *skinite* and the sedentary Roma *evgjit*. The word *cergatarë* has some Turkish roots, while *kurbetë* was Arabic for "tent." According to Marcel Courthiades, *kurbat* is also similar to the Turkish word *gurbet*, which means "emigration." This, in turn, is possibly linked to the Arabic word for "foreign land," *gorbat*, and the Persian word for "exile," *ghorbat*. In northern Albania and Kosova, Roma are generally referred to as *Magjup*, *Magjup*, or *magjypë*, which, like *eygjitë*, is derived from "Egypt." The Roma language, Romani, is referred to as *Magjupisht* or *Magjupçe*.[11]

Today, Albania's Roma are divided into two principal groups, the *Gabel* and the *Jevgjit* (*Jevg*), and four clans—the *Mećkàră* (*Meçkars*), the *Kabuzie* (*Kallbuxhi*), the *Ćergàră* (*Cekars*), and *Kurtòfã* (*Kurtovs*). Scholars doubt whether the *Jevgjit* are assimilated Roma, because of their close association with the Roma, or a separate ethnic group. Marcel Courthiades argues that the *Jevjgit* are not true Roma. Most of Albania's *Jevgjit* live in Tirana and strongly disassociate themselves from other Roma. Traditionally the *Jevgjit* earned their living from begging, though many have become successful in all levels of Albanian society. Courthiades says that they have a higher level of alcoholism than other groups in Albania, and are known for their untrustworthiness. The fact that many Albanians think that the *Jevgjit* are Roma tends to strengthen negative views of the Roma.[12] What seems most to separate the two groups is their level of assimilation. The *Jevgjit* tend to look down on the poorer Roma whom, they think, tend to be disinterested "in living normally as Albanians," while the Roma view the *Jevgjit* as inferior because they "have lost their culture."[13]

These stereotypes have long haunted the Roma in Albania, though their mistreatment seems to have been less harsh than in other parts of the Balkans. Enver Hoxha, the Stalinistic dictator of Albania from 1946 to 1985, said that "their [Roma] tragic history is but a succession of persecution over the centuries."[14] Such statements did little to alter public opinion of the Roma. Christian Albanian folk tales depicted Muslims as pigs, while Muslim Albanians questioned the commitment of Muslim Roma to some of the basic tenets of Islam.[15]

Hoxha's death in 1985 signaled an end to Albania's isolation. His successor, an old crony, Ramiz Alia, gradually tried to distance himself from Hoxha's repressive, isolationist policies. But there was little he could do to still ethnic Albanian unrest, particularly in light of Slobodan Milosević's crackdown on Kosovar autonomy in neighboring Yugoslavia. The gradual breakdown of the communist system created social and economic chaos that led to food shortages, particularly in the winters of 1990–1991 and 1991–1992, and brought the country close to collapse.[16]

Unemployment rose to 40 percent by 1991, while six years later the country, still one of the poorest in Europe, came close to economic collapse with a failed pyramid banking scheme. Since then efforts to revive the economy and strengthen its democratic institutions have been difficult. By 1999, Albania remained in desperate straits, with the northern parts of the country under the control of gangs. Its problems intensified with the flood of refugees from Kosova.[17] The situation has since improved and international observers noted that Albanian elections have been fairly open and free. In 2005, the Democratic Party was swept to power with promises of fighting corruption and improving the country's economic problems. Though the unemployment rate has dropped officially to 14.3 percent (unofficially 30 percent) since 1991, it remains a serious problem.[18]

Today, there are 80,000–150,000 Roma in Albania out of a total population of about 3.5 million. Albanians make up about 95 percent of the population. The country is about 70 percent Muslim, 20 percent Orthodox, and 10 percent Roman Catholic.[19] The vast majority of Albania's Roma are unemployed and poor. The Open Society Foundation Soros (OSFS) puts national unemployment at 18 percent. Overall Roma unemployment is 71 percent, though there are some communities where 100 percent working age Roma are without jobs. To survive, many Roma must rely on government assistance.[20] Unfortunately, "the poorest Roma are allegedly denied social assistance by state offices in a discriminatory manner."[21]

These problems are exacerbated by widespread illiteracy, which the OSFS puts at 64 percent among young Roma between ages 7 and 20. These statistics are doubly troubling in light of the fact that national literacy rates are 86.5 percent for all Albanians over age 9.[22] Part of the reason for Roma illiteracy is discrimination in the public schools. Roma parents are often hesitant to send their children to school because teachers and students often pick on them and call them " 'dirty Gypsy' or 'stupid Gypsy.' " Teachers also physically punish Roma children using " 'measures' " that are "not always applied toward the non-Roma children."[23] *Amaro Drom* has initiated a number of projects throughout Albania designed to enhance the quality of life for Roma. In Levani, for example, *Amaro Drom* and Spolu oversaw the construction of a sewer system for the 2,400 Roma living in the village. In Morava, *Amaro Drom* helped local Roma obtain a building for a school. Some parents were hesitant to send their children to a school five kilometers away because of dangerous roads. *Amaro Drom* helped find facilities for a temporary school and then worked with local officials to find a more permanent building in the village. Attendance at the new school is high and local Roma support it because they feel they own it. Elsewhere, *Amaro Drom* is involved in projects to help provide Roma with better job skills or improved housing.[24]

The Roma in Albania also suffer from other serious problems such as sex trafficking. Lack of education and poverty make Roma women and children particularly vulnerable to "trafficking," where they are forced into prostitution or sexual slavery. Impoverished Roma women, thinking they are improving the lives of their children by letting them work abroad, are often, in reality, selling their children to sexual predators. Traffickers often use the promise of marriage, employment, or a better life abroad; or, threats of violence to induce women to follow them or send their children abroad.[25]

One young Roma woman described her situation:

> It was 2002. At that time I was seventeen years old. I fell in love with a white young man. He deceived me, promising a safe future, even "marriage ceremony" and stuff like that. It didn't happen that way as I fell prey of trafficking, being sold to a friend of his from Korca.
>
> It was winter and an icy weather. We departed to Greece at night, as we had to go there illegally. I was tired and terrified by the long walk in mountainous footpaths; without being aware of what was happening to me. What I understood was that it was cold and I was missing my

family, even though I last saw them two days ago. When I reached the place of trafficking, started the long torturing and overwhelming pain. I didn't want [to]. They beat me with the pants' belt. They forced me to stay under icy water. They let me outdoors tied with a rope forcing me to exercise that profession [prostitution]. It was even more painful when I strived to leave somewhere else, but it was impossible.

They had located "protector" everywhere. I remember when one of them tore my hair so hard that he gave me a tuft of hair in my hand. In the course of time my tears became even colder. An enormous hatred started to emerge deep down [inside] myself. I sold my body for four years. I was released from this agony, if I can say so, when a client of mine not less than 25 years of age, saw in my body the signs caused by the beating with the pants' belt. He stopped the sexual intercourse immediately and swore before me that he would never have sex with a prostitute. Thanks to him I am presently free, but my freedom is cursed. That entire story left serious consequences in my life.

My body has already lost all the required energies. My mind deteriorates from time to time because of past tortures and pain. I am capable of nothing. I cannot report the persons who traffick because I am afraid of my family.

I wish only one thing: God, please don't abandon me and give me strength to overcome that situation as I feel miserable.[26]

Such tragedies, of course, underscore the deep impoverishment, economically, socially, and intellectually, faced by most Roma in Albania. A 2002 report by the Soros Foundation, the World Bank, and other international organizations highlighted these problems and prompted the government to adopt the Albanian National Strategy for the Improvement of Living Conditions of the Roma Minority (2003–2015). The Strategy involved efforts to improve every aspect of Roma life such as education, cultural identity, family, social welfare, employment, health care, and civil engagement. Nothing was said in the Strategy proposal about human rights or ways to empower the Roma politically. Moreover, some language in the Strategy seemed to "imply limiting the Roma to occupations deemed 'typically' Roma, thereby perpetuating their marginalization."[27] The government set up a special body to monitor the success of the Strategy, though it did not initially include Roma specialists.[28]

In the summer of 2006, the Foundation for Open Society in Albania-Soros (OSFA) organized a meeting to discuss the success of the Strategy. Experts from OSFA, the Albanian Helsinki Committee, the Center for Children's Protection, and representatives of the Roma community concluded that the Strategy had some serious problems. There was no attempt in the Strategy document to determine the costs of the program, and little attention was paid to issues such as "the registration of Roma population, the building of Roma awareness on such issues as education, health care, and enjoyment of their rights." There was also little coordination between government agencies involved in implementing the Strategy and little interaction between the government, NGOs, and Roma communities. Government planners had no idea about the number of children attending public school. In addition, few Roma had benefitted from the program and social protection efforts. Little had been done to improve health care for Roma, in part because government officials had no idea about the number of Roma living in Albania or their health care needs.[29]

The experts at the OSFA meeting made the following recommendations to the government. They advised the government to do a thorough examination of the Strategy "to ensure better and efficient connection among objectives, time lines, and budgets." It was essential, the experts argued, for the central government to work closely with Roma leaders, local leaders, Roma NGOs, and donor organizations to ensure that the Strategy truly meets Roma needs. The experts also thought it important that local governments design local plans that complemented national Strategy goals. They should do everything possible to inform local civil servants of Strategy goals and work with local Roma NGOs to ensure that local Roma communities were aware of Strategy programs. Local officials should also do everything possible to ensure that adequate national funds were properly transferred to ensure the success of local programs.[30]

The experts also said that Roma organizations and NGOs should do everything possible to work together with a common voice. Roma NGOs should work closely with national and local governments to learn more about operating in a civil societal environment. It was also essential for Roma organizations to monitor the success of Strategy goals and programs nationally and locally. Roma organizations should also be actively involved "with protection of human rights and civil society in general in order to ensure an efficient approach in the fight against all types of discrimination." Finally, monitoring the success and/or failure of Strategy programs should be the responsibility of the "different actors of civil society." National and local leaders should play an active role "to ensure support for capacity building of Roma organizations." Finally, fund raising organizations should create special guidelines and application procedures to enhance Roma NGO access to funds for developing civil society in Albania.[31]

Bosnia and Herzegovina

The genocidal war that swept over Bosnia and Herzegovina from 1991 to 1995 has had a traumatic impact on that country's Roma. When Serbian forces invaded Bosnia-Herzegovina to halt its secession from the Yugoslav federation, 43.7 percent of the population of 4 million was Muslim, a little over 31 percent Serbs, and 17.3 percent Croats. It is difficult to determine how many Roma lived in Bosnia at the time. Jeremy Druker estimated that there were between 35,000 and 80,000 there in 1997, but this does not take into account Rajko Djuric's claim that 300,000 Bosnian Roma were "ethnically cleansed" and forced into exile during the war. The European Roma Rights Center put this figure at 30,000. Current estimates suggest that there are between 80,000 and 120,000 Roma living in Bosnia and Herzegovina. According to Roger Thurow, 1.5 million Bosnians were "still wandering abroad or internally displaced" at the end of August 1999.[32]

When fighting broke out, Serb, Croat, and Muslim forces forced the Roma in their areas into fighting units or made them work in special labor details clearing mines and burying the dead who were murdered in ethnic cleansing campaigns. Muslim Roma, who loyally served in four special Bosnian units, were particularly vulnerable to Serb and Croat mistreatment. Serb forces made Roma in Banja Luka kill one another, while Serb forces killed 47 Muslim Roma in the massacres in Srebrenica in 1995. The Serbs forcibly displaced most of the 15,000 Muslim Roma living in the Tuzla district, then home to the majority of Bosnia's Muslim Roma community. Today, there are only about 10,000 Roma the Tuzla Canton, which is now part of one of Bosnia's two political entities, the Republika Srpska. It includes about 49 percent of the land of Bosnia and Herzegovina, and 34 percent of the population, most of whom are ethnic Serbs. The second entity, the Federacija Bosna i Hercegovina, has a population of 2.5 million, 80 percent of them Bosniak (*Bošnjaci*) Muslims.[33]

The suffering of the Roma, particularly refugees, was harsh, since relief aid was often given out along ethnic lines. According to Jud Nirenberg, who was on a Regional Roma Participation Program fact-finding mission in Bosnia in 1996, if a Catholic organization gave out aid, it was usually to Croats, even though there were also needy Roma Catholics. Nirenberg saw everyone but the Roma getting food and asked relief workers why. They told him that "we're sure the Roma got it, too; they must have sold it on the black market."[34]

Many Bosnian Roma have settled in parts of Western Europe and the United States. At one time, there were 20,000–30,000 Bosnian Roma in Germany. Those who wanted to return to Bosnia found that they were unwelcome by the Muslims, the Croats, and the Serbs. And even if they were able to return to Bosnia, many exiled Bosnian Roma found themselves stateless, since the Bosnian government refused to issue them passports. Efforts by the German government to force its Bosnian Roma refugees to leave was finally halted after the Council of Europe recommended that such efforts be stopped because of the unstable situation in Bosnia. The United States Agency for International Development has since stepped in and tried to aid the country's Roma, and an All-Bosnia Roma Union was created to help. Human Rights Watch has done everything possible to bring international attention to the plight of Bosnia's Roma, and the Council of Europe recommended that the Bosnian government recognize the Roma as an ethnic minority.[35]

Unfortunately, little has changed in Bosnia and many Roma still live there as stateless inhabitants without personal documents or full citizenship rights. This, in turn, affects the ability of many Roma to apply for basic government services such as housing, public education, health care, and voting rights. But the lack of personal documents is only part of the reason that many Bosnian Roma, the majority of them Bosniaks or Bosnian Muslims, suffer from high unemployment, low literacy rates, and severe poverty. Their situation seems more severe in the Republika Srpska, though many of these problems are Bosnian-wide. A Council of Europe fact-finding mission in 1996 concluded that most Muslim Roma from what is now the Republika Srpska felt that "the very basic conditions in the field of human rights required to enable the return of displaced persons are not met in the Republika Srpska."[36] These difficulties, in turn, are complicated by ongoing problems with police brutality and harassment. Finally, Roma women and children have fallen prey to illegal sexual predators who have forced or abducted many into Bosnia's "sex industry."[37]

With the exception of Albania, the economic, social, educational, and political environment in Bosnia and Herzegovina is probably the worst in Europe, both for the Roma and others. But the situation is much more dire for the Roma. Though statistics vary widely, unemployment in Bosnia and Herzegovina is slightly over 45 percent, though employment in the "grey economy" might reduce that figure to 25–30 percent. Reports from NGOs indicates that only about 1–1.5 percent of the Roma population have steady work, a figure considerably lower than the pre-1992 figure of 17 percent. The situation is even more severe for Roma women, many of whom are Muslim. About a fifth of the Bosnian population lives below the poverty line and another 30 percent is close to it. Yet literacy is quite high in Bosnia and Herzegovina, with about 95 percent of the adults being able to read and write. About 86 percent of the country's children attend primary school and 79 percent secondary school. This is in dire contrast to Roma attendance statistics, which indicate that 64 percent of the country's Roma never attend primary school, one of the causes of high Roma illiteracy rates.[38] The plight of the Roma in Bosnia and Herzegovina has drawn a lot of international attention since the end of the Bosnian war. In 2001, representatives from a number of Roma organizations met in Sarajevo to develop a National Platform for Roma in Bosnia and Herzegovina. Roma leaders hoped the National Platform,—which dealt with education, health care, housing, employment, politics, and refugees—would be transformed into a National Action Plan for Roma, and would include a survey in local Roma communities. The meeting also created what later became the Council of Roma (*Vijeće Roma*), which would work with the government and local Roma communities to develop Roma aid programs. In subsequent meetings, the Bosnian government's Ministry for Human rights and Refugees promised to create a national Advisory Board on Roma (*Savjetodavni odbor za romska pitanja*) made up of government officials, Roma leaders, and members of the international community. It did so a year later, making the new Advisory Board a consultative body within the Council of Ministers of Bosnia and Herzegovina. In 2002, the Advisory Board approved the first draft of its Working Plan and Programme for 2002–2006, which addressed personal documentation, health care, education, employment, social welfare, property return, refugees, and displaced persons.[39]

Later that year, the Roma Advisory Board fine-tuned the Working Plan to include "birth records; education in the Romani language; health insurance, employment, and social care, facilitating the return of prewar property to refugees and displaced persons; housing issues; the establishment of Romani media; and possibilities for being informed on the Roman language."[40] In 2003, the government pledged to do everything possible over the next four years to address Roma education, housing, and employment. In 2003, Bosnia's parliament passed the Law on the Protection of the Rights of the Members of National Minorities (*Zakon o zaštiti prava pripadnika nacionalnih man-jina*). Article 3 granted the Roma minority status, which, on paper, changed their legal status; Article 4 made it illegal to discriminate against the Roma or force them to assimilate. It also protected their right to maintain and develop their own language and culture and the right, in Article 11, to use their language publically and privately. Articles 13 and 14 allowed the Roma to set up their own schools and develop materials for public education in their own language. Article 19 gave them access to all levels of government service.[41]

Unfortunately, according to many Roma activists, the Advisory Board did not do a good job consulting Roma leaders about the minorities law. One Roma organization in Tuzla, *Sae Roma*, sponsored a round table in 2003 to discuss the draft of the minorities law and created a commission to gather and create proposals for it. The commission submitted its proposals to the government only to discover that the law was passed just a few days afterward, without even looking at the Roma proposals. Roma leaders have also criticized the law for its failure to offer minority protections to noncitizens, though there were promises to make certain changes in the law. This is an important consideration, given that many Roma forced abroad during the war have no documents and cannot prove citizenship. And few Roma know anything about this law or their minority status in Bosnia and Herzegovina.[42]

For the most part, these efforts have had little impact on the Roma, and their situation remains desperate. In fact, the United Nations' Committee on the Elimination of Racial Discrimination (CERD) concluded in 2004 that "there is a silent boycott in Bosnia and Herzegovina towards [the] Roma population."[43] Two years later, CERD conducted hearings in Geneva and noted that the Roma Advisory Board "had not been truly effective" because of limited resources and the failure of the government to consult it on matters dealing with Roma issues. Little had changed in the field of education for the Roma and many still found it difficult to regain the property lost during the Bosnian war, something "crucial to their enjoyment of fundamental rights." The same was true of the ongoing problem of "lack of identity documents."[44]

The European Roma Rights Center (ERRC) in Budapest has concluded that the Roma in Bosnia and Herzegovina lack the basic protections against various acts of discrimination. Many do not have access to the basic personal documentation "necessary for the fundamental social, economic, civil, and political rights," and few have access to adequate, safe housing. It insists that the Bosnian government should double its efforts to make the Roma a normal part of society, including effective legal protections against all forms of discrimination, and efforts to combat and eliminate Roma.[45]

Bulgaria

Like the Roma in other parts of the Balkans, the Roma in Bulgaria continue to suffer from an environment so prejudicial that it fosters Roma "poverty and despair." In some Roma communities, only 10 percent of eligible workers can find employment. Most Roma still do not attend school beyond the elementary level. The Project on Ethnic Relations says that "adequate health-care and other basic services [for the Roma] are nonexistent."[46] The fact that the Roma do not have an effective political voice does not help. Article 11 of the Bulgarian constitution forbids political organizations "formed on ethnic, racial, or religious lines" to halt the development of political parties that would "prove divisive for national unity by stirring up ethnic tension for political purposes." Court challenges have enabled the Turkish Movement for Rights and Freedoms to continue to be active, though similar political organizations for the Roma and other minorities remain prohibited.[47]

In fairness, the country's leaders have become more sensitive to the widespread prejudice against the Roma. In 1997, President Petar Stoyanov apologized to Bulgaria's Muslim community and Turkey for the Teodor Zhikov regime's efforts to "Bulgarize" Turkish names. The following year, Stoyanov condemned parliament member Roumen Vodenicharov's anti-Roma and anti-Semitic comments at Zhikov's funeral. The Zhikov family also criticized Vodenicharov, while the Bulgarian Socialist Party removed him from their election list. Unfortunately, such condemnations have done little to ameliorate the more serious problems of police and judicial mistreatment of the Roma. Attacks by skinheads and other Bulgarians against Roma continue throughout the country. The police and the courts provide little protection for the Roma since they are often the victimizers. The widespread prejudice against the Roma means that they are also discriminated against in other areas of society. Though there are now 34 all-Roma schools in Bulgaria, only half the pupils attend class regularly because of the discrimination they face in the classroom. Many of them prefer to beg on the streets to help their families.[48]

Today, there are about 800,000 Roma in Bulgaria out of a population of 7.3 million. Over 82 percent of Bulgaria's population is Orthodox and 12.2 percent Muslim. Population-wise, the Roma wield a lot of potential political clout in certain parts of the country, though it is only recently that the Bulgarian government has begun to offer the Roma the legal and other protections political activists need to begin to flex their muscles. These efforts have in large part been driven by pressure from the European Union, which will allow Bulgaria to become a member in 2007 if the government agrees to address, among other issues, the lack of legal and citizenship protections for the Roma and other minorities.[49]

In 1999, the Bulgarian government and representatives from the Roma community signed a document creating the Framework Programme for Equal Integration of Roma in Bulgarian Society. Over 70 Roma organizations throughout the country voiced their support for this initiative. What made this program different from others in the past was the involvement of major Roma leaders and organizations in drafting the document.[50] The Framework's introduction laid out the basic problems facing the Roma in Bulgaria.

> Roma in Bulgaria are the group which occupies the lowest level in the social hierarchy. They are not adequately represented in the political life and the government of the country. In the social-aspect as a whole, the status of the Roma is dramatically lower than the Bulgarian average; high unemployment rate, deplorable living conditions, bad health, high illiteracy rate, etc. These stable characteristics in the situation of the Roma community are external manifestations and direct consequences of discriminatory treatment.
>
> *The elimination of discrimination towards Roma should become one of the main political priorities of the Bulgarian State.*

The Framework then lays out eight major areas of concern that the government needs to address to ensure that the Roma enjoy the complete fruits of democracy in Bulgaria—laws to protect the Roma from discrimination, the creation of a government committee to investigate and suggest ways to prevent discrimination against the Roma, improvement in the economic status and well-being of the Roma, adequate health care, improved housing and neighborhood status, education, support for all manifestations of Roma cultural and ethnic expression, equal access to media, and equal status for Roma women in all aspects of life.[51]

Though Bulgaria has made some progress in these areas, the Council of Europe's European Commission against Racism and Intolerance reported in 2004 that there remained serious problems with police abuse of Roma. The report also noted that

> a large majority of Roma continue to face serious financial and social problems, live in very deprived neighbourhoods and are hard hit by unemployment. There is still a widespread problem of segregation of Roma children in schools, and, so far, the implementation of the Framework Programme for Equal Integration of Roma in Bulgarian Society, which the government implemented in 1999, is still in its early stages.[52]

While police violence and abuse of Roma was one of the hallmarks of life for Roma throughout Central and Eastern Europe in the immediate years after the collapse of communism, it has continued to be a sad aspect of life for the Roma in Bulgaria. In fact, the European Roma Rights Center in Budapest, which monitors various Roma abuses throughout the region, has devoted more attention to this issue in Bulgaria than to any other subject. These problems have extended into the prison system and the military.[53] One prison commandant, Lieutenant-Colonel Karpatov, admitted to the discriminatory treatment of the Roma in his prison:

> They again send me a Gypsy sentenced to serve a year and a half effectively in prison for having stolen some-thing small, like a rotten barn door, when a non-Gypsy who steals a brand new luxurious car gets away with a six month prison term, and even that term was suspended.[54]

In 2004, the European Court of Human Rights (ECHR) ruled against the Bulgarian government in the case of *Nachova and Others v. Bulgaria*, which involved the shooting of two Roma recruits by military police officers in 1996. The ECHR, sitting as a Grand Chamber, confirmed its decision a year later.

Despite ample evidence to the contrary, military authorities cleared the four officers involved in the shootings. In February 2004, the ECHR ruled that the Bulgarian government had breached the victims' "right to life" under the Council of Europe's Convention for the Protection of Humans Rights and Fundamental Freedoms "by failing to adequately regulate the use of firearms by military police, and by failing to properly investigate the young men's deaths."[55]

This landmark decision was extremely important, both domestically and internationally, since it highlighted a core problem in Bulgaria that had to be addressed before the Roma could begin to feel safe and protected in their own country. Roma activists and NGOs adopted a three-part strategy to address this problem—use of the media to highlight the problem and force Bulgarian authorities to address such abuses, legal challenges in Bulgarian courts, and meetings with police to deal with the mistreatment. The Project on Ethnic Relations and the Bulgarian Human Rights Project have met with national and local police officials to discuss racist attitudes and behavior among the police though, for the most part, these discussions seemed to have had very little impact locally, since cases of police abuse of Roma continue to this day. Part of the problem is police refusal to accept the fact that some officers are racists. Police officials found it much easier to blame such behavior on the Roma themselves and their serious social and economic problems. One police official in Lom who seemed sympathetic to the plight of the Roma said that "45 percent of the criminals in the region are of Romani origin," a common stereotype in Bulgaria and elsewhere.[56]

The Roma have been more successful attacking this and other discriminatory problems in the courts. In the fall of 2004, the Bulgarian parliament passed the Protection against Discrimination Act that included an Anti-discrimination Commission with various subcommittees to deal with racial and gender discrimination. One of the groups actively involved in writing this legislation was the Romani Baht Foundation.[57] What followed was a flurry of successful lawsuits filed by the European Roma Rights Center, the Romani Baht Foundation, and the Bulgarian Helsinki Committee that dealt with anti-Roma discrimination. These groups, individually or collectively, won five important cases in 2004, which symbolized the beginning of the transformation of the Bulgarian legal system to one more sympathetic to acts of discrimination against the Roma. Dimitrina Petrova, the Executive Director of the ERRC, said:

> We welcome the rulings. Laws are only as good as their implementation. Bulgarian courts, to their credit, have now shown this clearly. They have embraced the opportunity to apply a solid new law and in doing

so correct the injustice suffered by Romani victims of discrimination. Also, the Bulgarian example proves that breaking new legal ground does not always need to take a long period of time, once the necessary statutory tools have been made available.[58]

Such cases, of course, do not address some of the deeper problems and issues facing the Roma, which are linked to their low social and economic status. Many of these problems, of course, are linked to their lack of education, a serious issue for the Roma throughout Central and Eastern Europe. Literacy is quite high in Bulgaria, as 98.6 percent of the population aged 15 and over can read and write. About 8–16 percent of the Roma population are illiterate and only 36–46 percent have a primary school education; 8–8.5 percent have gone on to secondary school, and only 0.3–1 percent have a university education.[59]

But these figures only tell part of the story. For decades, Bulgarian authorities adopted a segregationist policy that forced Roma children to attend rundown, underfunded schools in Roma neighborhoods. About 70 percent of the country's Roma children attend these schools. Few can afford to attend kindergarten, and many often start first grade without adequate knowledge of the Bulgarian language. These deficiencies often translate into forcing Roma children into special schools for students with "mental disabilities." Ilona Tomova has estimated that while Roma children "comprise 9.7 percent of the pupils in mainstream schools, they amount to 32.1 percent in auxiliary schools [for students with 'retarded mental development'], 21.6 percent in vocational schools [for juvenile delinquents], and 29 percent in schools for children with behavioural problems."[60]

All of this translated in a dramatic drop in the number of Roma students attending public school. Khristo Kyuchukov estimated that 120,000 Roma children attended school prior to 1989. These figures dropped to 50,000 in the immediate years after the collapse of communism, even though there were more Roma children than ever in Bulgaria. He attributed this decline to the bad economic situation throughout the country, though there were deeper issues that caused Roma parents not to want to send their children to school. The government responded with several programs designed to help Roma and other students gain better knowledge of Bulgarian before they entered first grade, and published a bilingual reading book for Roma students. Authorities also introduced some Roma culture and music classes in school with large Roma student enrollment.[61]

In 2002, one Roma organization, Amalipe, in league with the Bulgarian Ministry of Education and the Open Society Foundation-Sofia, introduced optional folklore classes in 14 schools in Veliko Turnovo County. Teodora

Krumov and Deyan published a wonderful collection of folktales for teachers in the special classes, *Razkazi i Pamet* (Stories and Memories). Since then both authors, in league with Antoniya Kr'steva, have published two workbooks for Roma children—*Istorii krai ogonishcheto: Ychebno pomagalo za ychenitsi ot 2 do 4 klas* (Stories Around the Fire: A Textbook for 2–4 Class Students) and *Razkazani P'tisccha: Pomazalo za ychenitsi ot 5 do 8 klas* (Told Roads/Paths: A Textbook for 5–8 Class Students). This program was so successful that the government decided to use it in other parts of central Bulgaria in 2003. One of the goals of the project was to include non-Roma students in the classes in an effort to help them overcome their own prejudices towards Roma. Local education officials said they saw overall Roma achievement scores rise considerably because the classes stimulated increased "student activity and self-confidence." According to Teodora Krumova, who oversaw this project, there was more involved than just education. She explained that "very often, in the course of the implementation of the project, we had to solve problems that were not necessarily related to the education process but had to do with human rights, Romani emancipation and community building. It would be a limitation to assess the project only as a new course in the school curriculum. It has a more profound nature." Deyan Kolev said the program had a twofold purpose: to help the Roma promote their own culture, which in turn strengthened self-identity and helped emancipate Roma communities. This was essential to ensure Roma integration, not assimilation, into Bulgarian society.[62]

In 2002, the Ministry of Education issued its "Instruction for the Integration of Minority Children and Pupils," which proposed the integration of minority children while simultaneously preserving their sense of ethnic identity. It promised that the government would work to end public school segregation for minorities since it denied minority students equal access to quality education. It also pledged that the government would do everything possible to foster "successful socialisation of the young people from different ethnic minority communities."[63]

Unfortunately, government pledges and promises have had little impact locally, though there are exceptions. There has been a highly successful desegregation project in the Vidin public schools that took 300 Roma children out of ghetto schools in Vidin and put them in regular schools. At this time, Donka Panayotova estimated that 70 percent of Roma pupils in Bulgaria attended segregated schools. These ghetto schools suffer from ill-prepared teachers, run-down facilities, and administrators who dislike Roma. The Vidin project involved busing Roma children to schools outside of the ghetto and financial help to ensure that they had adequate school supplies. It also involved special anti-bias training for teachers. The project was run by a local Roma organization,

Organisation Drom, with financial support from the Open Society Institute's Roma Participation Program. Like the Veliko Turnovo project, the Vidin program had to deal with more than busing, student funding, and prejudicial teachers. There was also considerable community work convincing Roma parents to let their children attend nonsegregated schools, who feared for their children's mental and physical well-being in the integrated schools. Organisation Drom mounted a major publicity campaign to support the project, which helped strengthen community support for the project. Needless to say, the Vidin project was a great success and has been duplicated in other surrounding communities. Most importantly, it showed that when given patient instruction and care, Roma students could perform as well as any non-Roma students in an integrated public school, despite the fact that most Roma pupils entered the Vidin schools considerably behind the non-Roma students. But Donka Panayotova notes that the continued success of integration experiments rests on a "good government agenda directing and financing such action, as well as establishing good co-operation between the Roma non-government organization and education officials."[64]

Frustrated by the pace of integration, Romani Baht and the European Roma Rights Center filed a law suit against the Ministry of Education, the city of Sofia, and the 75th Todor Kableshkov Municipal School in Sofia in 2003, charging them with racial segregation that forced Roma children to attend inferior schools in all-Roma neighborhoods in Sofia. Though the plaintiffs lost this case, they filed a second suit a year later against the Education Ministry, the city of Sofia, and School No. 103 in Sofia on the same charges. The new antidiscrimination law strengthened their hand and prodded the district court to rule in the plaintiffs' favor. On October 25, 2005, the court declared that the segregation of the Roma in School 103 "was not the result of their free will but of circumstances beyond their control, accompanied by inaction on the part of authorities obliged to take measures to remedy this situation." The court also rejected efforts by school officials to blame the Roma children's "poor educational performance" on "irregular school attendance." It concluded that "the negative consequences for society resulting from the existing situation are tremendous."[65]

Unfortunately, such victories, while impressive, simply plug the hole in the dike of Roma inequality and discrimination in Bulgaria. At the very moment that a corner seems to have been turned in terms of addressing one area of discrimination, others crop up. This is particularly true when it comes to Roma housing and housing rights. Roma property owners often find themselves victims of urban development. Many Roma have built homes on municipal property and, lacking documents to prove ownership, find themselves facing evictions by a government that is interested in developing only the lands their homes stand on. The result is that many poor Roma find themselves homeless, despite government pledges to improve Roma housing. In the fall of 2005, the European Roma Rights Center wrote Prime Minister Serguei Stanishev of these problems, explaining that "a very significant part of the Romani community in Bulgaria lack security of tenure and live in a constant state of forced eviction from housing." It added that the failure of his government to address these problems not only violated the Framework but also prompted the ERRC to file a complaint against the government under the Revised European Social Charter (RESC). Article 31 required signatory states to promote access to "housing of an adequate standard," to eliminate homelessness, and make housing accessible to the poor. Needless to say, Bulgarian authorities throughout the country have violated the Charter time and again. On June 26, 2006, a number of international human rights organizations complained of these forced evictions, which has drawn the attention of the European Committee of Social Rights, the watchdog organization tasked with monitoring violations of the RESC.[66]

It is really difficult to find a silver lining in any of this. Armed with the backing of powerful international organizations and the threat of losing European Union membership, the Bulgarian government has made modest promises to improve the situation of the Roma. But it has failed to provide the necessary funding or spiritual backing to initiate significant change. This has been left to Roma organizations, politicians, and NGOs, who are making significant but slow progress. In 1999, Roma political parties began to enjoy some success in local elections, though the Roma had only one representative in each of the three national parliaments from 1990 to 2001. This changed modestly in 2001 when two Romani organizations, the Confederation of Roma "Europe" and the Association of Romani Foundations, linked up with the *Balgarska Socialisticeska Partija* (BSP; Bulgarian Socialist Party) in national elections, which saw several Roma elected to parliament. Unfortunately, they were viewed simply as members of the BSP and not as independent Roma politicians speaking for their kinsmen. Alliances with other Bulgarian parties such as the Turkish Movement for Rights and Freedoms (*Dvizhenie za prava i svobodi*), the Union of Democratic Forces (SDS; *Sajuzna Demokraticnite Sili*), and the National Movement "Simeon II" (*Nacionalno Dvizenie Simeon Vtori*) proved equally ineffective, given that Roma listed on these parties' tickets usually were placed in lower level positions election-wise. Efforts to form a viable coalition among Roma parties proved unsuccessful, given the lack of resources, political expertise, and the sense that some viewed the coalition's leaders, Roma businessmen, as opportunists who would use their positions to further their own personal interests.[67] In 2003, 126 Roma, representing eight Roma political parties, were elected to councilorships in 70 towns and cities throughout Bulgaria. Unfortunately, Roma electoral successes fueled some backlashes. In Samokov, for example, flyers were posted throughout the city against a mayoral candidate the flyers claimed would turn the town into a "Gypsy town" because he was so friendly with Roma. Similar claims were made in flyers distributed in Razlog and Vidin. Sadly, there has also been criticism within the Roma community about Roma political activists. Some claim they are in it for the money or do it because they cannot find work in more respected fields. But as Rumyan Russinov has noted, to be an effective figure in the complex world of Bulgarian politics, you must do it full time as a "professional politician." But the mere fact that there is such criticism is positive, given the long history of Roma political inactivity in the country.[68]

Croatia and Slovenia

Though Croatia and Slovenia have some of the smallest Roma populations (30,000 to 40,000 out of 4.5 million; 3,000 to 10,000 out of 2 million respectively) in Southeastern Europe, their small numbers have not protected the Roma in these countries from suffering the same discriminatory fate as their counterparts in other parts of the region. The situation in Croatia is unique since there is one group, the Serbs, who suffer as much as the Roma. In 2004, the Croatian government adopted a National Programme on the Roma as part of its effort to seek European Union admission. In its introduction to the Roma program, Croatian officials openly discussed the marginalization of the Roma, the deterioration in their quality of life, and the various educational, social, and health care problems the Roma face in Croatia. It recognized the inability of the Roma to "overcome the existing gap [in society] on their own," and pledged government help in seeing that the Roma enjoyed their full rights under the country's constitution. It also pledged to "eliminate all discrimination" against the Roma. The ultimate purpose of the National Programme on the Roma was "to provide systematic assistance to Roma to improve their living conditions and to include them in social life and decision-making processes in their local and wider community, while at the same time preserving their identity, culture, and traditions."[69]

Unfortunately, this document has been criticized for its failure to address the complexity of women's issues, particularly in its section on "Protection of the Family, Maternity and Youth." This is partly caused by the fact that Roma women, like most other minority females, suffer from dual discrimination both in their relationship with Roma men and the larger society. The protection of minority rights subsumes women's rights to those of the larger minority group without addressing the special needs of women vis à vis their special needs as a minority within a minority. According to Ana Bogdanović, there is, conceptually speaking, a clear "contradiction between the choice of framing the issue in these terms and any goal of Romani women's empowerment." From her perspective, the most important issue is "who is protected by group-differentiated rights of minority groups on a *de facto* level, men or women?" She thinks that gender issues should be more carefully thought out and expressed in various national plans for the improvement of the life for the Roma.[70]

The European Roma Rights Center (ERRC) also took up the issue of women's rights in its *Shadow Report* to the United Nations' Committee on Elimination of Discrimination against Women later in 2004. It was particularly critical of the fact that there was inadequate statistical data to determine Roma women's access to education, health care, employment, and other societal and political opportunities. It considered portions of the National Programme on Roma to be "contemptuous of Roma," "biased," and "paternalistic." The ERRC also took Croatian officials to task for claiming in the program's introduction that the Roma were "incapable of caring for itself," an indication that they knew little about the Roma, statistically or otherwise.[71]

Another minority within a minority are Roma children, an issue addressed by the United Nations Committee on the Right of the Child (UNCRC). In its 2004 report on Croatia, it was also critical of the failure of the Croatian government to collect reliable data on children, Roma or otherwise, under 18. This lapse hindered the efforts to analyze the problems of Roma children and others. Without such information, UNCRC said it was difficult to determine the impact of societal discrimination on Roma youths, access to quality health care and education, and the success of the National Programme on the Roma as it related to Roma youth.[72]

Slovenia's small Roma population suffers from different problems, in large part driven by what Jasminka Dedić calls Slovenian administrative efforts to ethnically "cleanse" its Roma population by dividing them into "autochthonous" and "non-autochthonous" groupings. "Autocthonous" Roma are those who have lived in Slovenia for more than a century, while "non-autocthonous" Roma are those who arrived from other parts of the former Yugoslavia, particularly since the 1970s. Essentially, use of this ill-defined term meant that many "non-autochthonous" Roma were deprived of citizenship, something Slovenian officials have since tried to clarify legally. Unfortunately, at least according to the Council of Europe's European Commission against Racism and Intolerance (ECRI), the definition, application, and use of these terms still confuses some

Roma who are unclear about its legal consequences. In its 2003 *Second Report on Slovenia*, ECRI urged Slovenian officials instead to consider using terms preferred by the Roma, "traditionally settled" and "non-traditionally settled."[73]

This ECRI report also criticized Slovenian officials for failing adequately to implement its two initiatives on the Roma, the 1995 Programme of Measures of the Protection of Roma in the Republic of Slovenia, and the 2000 Programme for the Employment of Roma in Slovenia. A third initiative, the 2004 Strategy for Education of Roma in the Republic of Slovenia, is too new to evaluate, though there are hints that there are also problems with this program. According to a report issued by the Council of Europe's Commissioner for Human Rights in 2005, one of the goals of the educational initiative in one model elementary school in Bršljin was to end segregated classes and move Roma children into integrated classes during the 2004–2005 school year. Yet by the spring of 2005, the European Roma Rights Center reported that the 80 Roma children in the school were to be moved back to segregated classes, something Dr. Milan Zver, the Ministry of Education and Sport denied. Instead, he claimed, Roma children would remain in mixed classes with other Slovene children, though Roma children who were having trouble with the standard curriculum would be taught using a special curriculum developed for their special needs.[74] What is at play here, of course, is a question of perception. Government officials interpret or misinterpret such programs and policies to fit their perception of the problems, while the Roma view this much differently. Little will change in Slovenia until both groups see eye-to-eye.

Czech Republic

Today there are approximately 300,000 Roma in the Czech Republic, out of a population of 10.2 million. Prior to the formal separation of Czechoslovakia into two nations on January 1, 1993, there were 150,000 Roma in the Czech lands and 400,000 in Slovakia. The increase in Roma population in the Czech Republic is due to the large number of Slovak Roma who fled westward to seek a better life in the Czech lands.[75]

Though the Czech Republic was distantly viewed as a model postcommunist state, its discriminatory policies toward the Roma have tarnished this image. Time and again, stories have appeared in the Western press detailing various acts of discrimination and violence against the Czech Republic's Roma. Skinhead violence has always been a problem since the collapse of communism in Czechoslovakia during the Velvet Revolution of 1989. In 1990, there were 17 "racially motivated" crimes in the Czech Republic. This figure rose to

130 in 1994 and 364 by 2000. The Association of Czechoslovak Roma in Canada reported that there had been over 30 Roma murders in the Czech Republic during this period and over 1,000 acts of violence.[76]

Stimulated in part by this growing crescendo of violence and a show on TV Nova, "Through Our Eyes," which discussed the life of Czech Roma in Canada, thousands of Roma, particularly from the Ostrava region, which had been hit hard by floods in the summer of 1997, applied for emigration to Canada. By the end of the year, thousands of Czech Roma had applied for asylum in Canada and ultimately about 3,000 were allowed to settle there. But Canadian authorities soon shut their doors to Czech Roma, fearful of a flood of Roma asylum seekers.[77]

The Canadian asylum crisis did little to still the violence against Roma in the Czech Republic. By 2001, the Czech Ministry of the Interior reported 402 cases of "racially motivated" violence, most of it aimed at the Roma. Given the penchant of government officials to downplay such crimes, we can assume that there were far more unreported crimes committed against the Roma during this period. While most of the violence was attributed to skinhead and neo-Nazi groups, many of which were registered with the Ministry of the Interior as "civic associations," some were linked to Miroslav Sladek's Republican Party, which opposed affirmative action rights for the Roma. These groups operated quite openly despite efforts by the Czech government to teach its police how to "recognize racially motivated violence and give it more attention."[78]

Unfortunately, the police were part of the problem, and there were reports of numerous acts of police abuse of Roma.[79] Public sentiment did not seem to condemn such acts. The Institute for the Investigation of Public Opinion discovered in a 1999 survey that a third of all Czechs under 19 admitted "harbouring sentiments of racial antipathy," while 63 percent of all surveyed reported that they had seen racial or ethnic incidents, most of them aimed at the Roma.[80] This atmosphere, the European Roma Rights Center in Budapest concluded in a 1999 report, found the Roma in the Czech Republic living "in general exclusion from the opportunities enjoyed by the majority community." According to the report, the Roma faced racial barriers at every social, economic, and educational turn in the road. They are segregated in an educational system that disproportionally sent a very large number of Roma children to schools for the mentally challenged.[81]

Perhaps nothing better represented this atmosphere than the "wall" crisis in Usti nad Labem in the northwestern part of the Czech Republic. It began when several Czech cities discussed building walls to separate the poorer Roma neighborhoods from the larger community. The city council in Plzen (Pilsen) approved plans to move the city's Roma to portable cabins outside of the city that would be watched 24 hours a day by the police. Though authorities agreed to delay their plans, they were never completely abandoned. These decisions were followed by skinhead attacks in Most and elsewhere. On June 17, 1999, Usti nad Labem's city council voted to build a 70 foot cement "noise barrier" to separate a Roma section of the city from a Czech neighborhood. The decision to erect the wall was met by widespread domestic and international protests.[82]

The city's Roma unsuccessfully occupied the site when construction of the wall began on October 5, 1999. City leaders were once again inundated by appeals from Czech President Vaclav Havel and the European Union to halt construction of the wall. They responded by arguing that the 70 foot cement "noise barrier" was a "symbol of law and order" and was designed to protect Czech citizens from the "noise, garbage, and crime by their Gypsy neighbors." The Roma countered that the wall reminded them of the concentration camps and ghettos of the Holocaust. Petr Uhl, the Czech government's Human Rights Commissioner, vowed that the wall would somehow be removed. Within six weeks, it was gone, and is now standing at the Usti nad Labem zoo. But the emotions it aroused did not disappear, particularly among the *gadžé* (Romani; non-Roma) in the area bordering the Roma ghetto. Some demanded that the city buy their homes and move the Roma elsewhere.[83]

In some ways, though, the "wall" incident marked a turning point for the Roma in the Czech Republic. With the support of the European Roma Rights Center in Budapest, and pressure from the European Union, the Council of Europe, various NGO organizations, and other groups, Czech Roma have gained access to the country's courts in an effort to challenge the more blatant episodes of discrimination and violence they face. But these efforts have not stopped the violence, which drew the attention of the United Nation's Committee against Torture (UNCAT). In the spring of 2004, the UNCT expressed concern about "the persistent occurrence of violence against the Roma and the alleged reluctance on the part of the police to provide adequate protection and to investigate such crimes." Though Czech officials have given considerable lip service to such efforts, what is decreed in Prague seems to have little impact on local officials.[84]

Perhaps the most important of these challenges dealt with the ongoing policy of forced sterilizations of Roma women. Begun in the 1970s in an effort to slow down the high Roma birth rates, the continuation of such practices drew the attention of the UNCAT, which in 2004 urged the Czech government to investigate such charges. While Czech officials denied that they had such a program, it admitted that there were "cases in the 1990s where sterilisation was performed in violation of binding legislation by individual doctors and hospitals."

They also later admitted that there was a "serious problem of a lack of patients rights culture in the Czech medical community." In early 2005, 25 Roma women who had been forcibly sterilized formed the Group of Women Harmed by Sterilisation. Their goal was to work collectively to seek justice for the crimes committed against their bodies. One of the group's leaders, Helena Ferenčiková, stated that the organization's goal was

> public recognition of the Czech government of our suffering. We are owed legal remedy because our fundamental rights have been systematically violated by Czech doctors and other officials. We have decided that we will not be silent anymore.[85]

They soon had gathered testimony of 70 women, most of them Roma, and submitted these affidavits to the Czech Public Defender of Rights or Ombudsperson. The Czech government had created this position to "remedy the disadvantageous status citizens with respect to the system of state administration."[86]

In the spring of 2005, Helena Ferenčiková went to court over her forced sterilization four years earlier, asking for damages of one million Czech crowns (about $45,000). Once the Roma community learned of her case, she was inundated with calls from other Roma women who had been similarly sterilized. In November 2005, the District Court in Ostrava, where Ferenčiková filed her case, indicated it would rule in her favor. A month later, the Ombudsman issued a report that concluded that the forced sterilization of Czech women continued to be a problem in Czech society. He recommended changes in the country's health care laws better to protect women from forced sterilization, including the publication of a handbook on sterilization written for the lay person. He also suggested better training for health care professionals on the legal rights of patients regarding sterilization and suggested the government set up some mechanism for giving reparations to women forcibly or ignorantly sterilized.[87] In 2006, Gender Studies, the League of Human Rights, and the ERRC issued a *Shadow Report* on the discrimination against women in the Czech Republic. It concluded that no action had been taken by the Czech government since the release of the Ombudsman's report regarding reparations or prosecution of those involved in the sterilization of Roma women.[88]

In the end, the sterilization issue symbolizes the continued marginalization of the Roma through Czech society. Laura Laubeová has drawn attention to the growing tension between Roma and non-Roma in the Czech Republic, which, when coupled with 70 percent–90 percent unemployment rates and inadequate educational and job training opportunities, have "contributed to the violence toward and criminalisation of the Roma community." This has all helped to create, she concludes, stereotypes that depict the Roma as the "most dangerous" group in Czech society. When coupled with public attitudes about Roma criminality, it is little wonder that Roma who want to be integrated into the workforce and the public education system find it so difficult to do so.[89] The European Commission against Racism and Intolerance's *Third Report on the Czech Republic* was even more critical of Czech efforts to help integrate the Roma into Czech society.

> ECRI expresses deep concern at the deplorable situation of the Roma at the local level. Roma communities continue to suffer from a culmination of social and economic disadvantage, aggravated by changing economic conditions, discrimination and a lack of willingness by local officials and communities to adopt the necessary measures to improve the situation. There have been few detectable improvements since the ECRI's second report. Instead, Roma communities are being increasingly pushed out of Czech towns into ghetto-like neighborhoods where their condition of marginalisation intensified.[90]

It went on to criticize specifically the failure of Czech authorities to deal with discrimination in housing and public education, where large numbers of Roma children were put in schools for the mentally challenged. The report was also critical of Czech efforts to take Roma children from their parents and put them in foster care homes and the harassment of Roma children by the police.[91] Needless to say, little has improved for the Roma in the Czech Republic since the collapse of communism and they seem more marginalized than ever.

Slovakia

Roma women in Slovakia have suffered from similar abuses though such mistreatment should be put in the broader category of inadequate health care not only for Roma women but for all Romani. This in turn is influenced by the widespread hatred of the Roma through much of Slovak society, which manifests itself in widespread violence and discrimination against the Roma. All of these issues combine to make Slovakia a very unhealthy place for the country's 380,000–500,000 Romani (out of a population of 5.4 million). Most of the ECRI's 2004 *Third Report on Slovakia* dealt with the continual problems faced by Roma in Slovakia. The report took Slovak officials to task for their failure to address adequately the Roma's high unemployment rates (80 percent–100 percent), housing conditions that are so bad that most Roma settlements lack even "the basic amenities such as water, sanitation, and electricity," and limited access to proper health care. It also encouraged Slovak officials to do more to empower the Roma and make them an integral part of any government initiatives designed to help their communities. More also had to be done, the report continued, to help change the very negative public climate for the Roma. It also raised the question of reports about ongoing sterilization of Roma women and continual educational problems for Roma children. In some parts of the country, up to 80 percent of Roma children are placed in special schools for the mentally challenged. They also suffer from widespread discrimination and abuse in the schools, which in large part explains why so few Roma children get beyond elementary school. It concluded that "the over-arching goal of providing the Roma with the opportunity to participate on an equal footing within an integrated society seems far from being realised."[92]

Indiscriminate violence toward the Roma has been a feature of Slovakian society since the collapse of communism. It was so widespread in the 1990s that the European Roma Rights Center titled its 1997 study on the plight of the Roma in Slovakia *Time of the Skinheads*. In some ways, this violence very much reflected the racist political climate in Slovakia under the government of Vladimir Mečiar, who was well known for his anti-Roma sentiments. But rightist politicians still feel comfortable making public racist statements about the Roma. Robert Fico, who became Slovakia's prime minister in 2006 as head of the Direction-Social Democracy Party (*Smer-sociálna demokracia*), pledged during his 2002 campaign that he would "actively effect the irresponsible growth of the Romani population." Jan Slota, whose Slovak National Party (*Slovenská národna strana*), in league with Mečiar's People's Party— Movement for A Democratic Slovakia (*L'udová strana-Hnutie za demokratické Slovensko*) and Fico's party, took control of the government in 2006, commented that year when asked about the problem of prostitutes in the country, "those hideous [people], [they are] mostly Gypsies that just stand there, they should be simply beaten."[93]

Such attitudes are widespread throughout the country. Public opinion polls indicate widespread dislike of the Roma throughout the country: 80 percent of a recent poll's respondents indicated that they would be uncomfortable having Roma living in their neighborhoods, while many expressed strong dislike for what they perceived to be the Roma's principal negative traits—"criminal activity, avoidance of legitimate jobs, poor hygiene, drinking, noisiness, and craftiness." David Z. Scheffel noted in his *Svinia in Black and White: Slovak Roma and their Neighbors* that attitudes toward the Roma in the eastern Slovakian village were based on the perception that the Roma were unable to "live up to basic standards of civilized behavior." Most of the residents of

Svinia viewed the Roma that lived in the local ghetto as, collectively, an "animalistic society that generates and adheres to customs that negate Slovak norms of propriety."[94] One shopkeeper who dealt frequently with the village's Roma said:

> They have no discipline, no character. Negative culture. Recently a kid came around, naked, without pants or anything. What then? And the way they live, I can't even talk about it, because they have sex within the family, [and then they produce] imbeciles.[95]

Prime Minister Mečiar echoed these very sentiments a decade earlier when he told a crowd in Spišská Nová, in response to growing worries about Roma population explosion.

> Another thing we ought to take into consideration is an extended reproduction of the socially unadaptable population. . . . Already children are giving birth to children—poorly adaptable mentally, badly adaptable socially, with serious health problems, who are simply a great burden to this society.[96]

It is easy to see how anti-Roma violence and prejudice has flourished in this environment. It has also helped to keep the Roma at the edge of Slovak society.

In her landmark study on the plight of the Roma in Slovakia, *On the Margins: Slovakia* Ina Zoon laid out three major areas in dire need of attention—legal standards, health care, and housing. At root, of course, is the dire poverty faced by the Roma throughout the country. According to the World Bank, a quarter of the country's Roma live on less than $2 a day ($730 annually), far less than the per capital income of $16,100. Such abject poverty forces unemployed Roma to rely on social services for survival. The racial climate of the country is the principal reason for such high Roma unemployment figures. Nothing else could explain the wide gap between national unemployment rates (11.7 percent) and Roma unemployment figures (80–100 percent).[97] One Roma NGO noted: "the color of the skin . . . [is] one of the decisive feature[s] for being accepted for a job . . . [and is] a decisive element in dismissing employees . . . and in conducting business."[98]

Housing is another serious area of concern. Ina Zoon notes that the "Romani communities of Slovakia suffer some of the most appalling living conditions that exist in Central and Eastern Europe." A third of Slovakia's Roma live in squalor just hours from Vienna. Most of these Roma communities have no electricity or running water and are disease-infested since they have no sewer systems. Conditions in many urban Roma ghettos are no better.

Instead of dealing creatively with these problems, scores of communities in eastern Slovakia began to adopt policies designed to drive the Roma out of their slums and ghettos. These policies finally drew the attention of the United Nations' Committee on the Elimination of Racial Discrimination (CERD), which found in 2005 that Slovakia had violated three provisions in the International Convention on the Elimination of all forms of Racial Discrimination (ICERD) in Dobsina after the city council cancelled plans to build inexpensive housing for the community's Roma. The Roma only turned to ICERD when local, district, and national legal authorities refused to hear their case. ICERD found that Slovakia had breached its obligations "not to engage in any act of racial discrimination," both nationally and locally, and also failed to guarantee that all of its citizens had the right of "equality before the law" when it came to equal access to housing. The Slovak legal system, ICERD concluded, also failed to seek a remedy to this problem. Despite this ruling, serious housing problems continue to exist. Officials evicted 40 homeless Roma in an abandoned apartment building in Košice in the summer of 2005 and turned off the hot water and heat in the Lunik IX Roma housing complex there that fall, leaving 5,000 Roma to face a winter without heat or hot water. By the spring of 2006, the Roma were still without public utilities, something public officials blamed on the Roma, some of who were behind in their payments.[99]

The Organization for the Security and Cooperation in Europe (OSCE) stated that inadequate access to health care as one of the main reasons the Roma continued to live in poverty in Central and Eastern Europe. Such problems were particularly acute for Roma women, "who often bear the double burden of ethnic discrimination by majority society and gender discrimination from within their communities."[100] This issue is linked to the unwillingness of officials to give or inform Roma about the legal documentation necessary to be eligible to use such state services. Such access is doubly important to Roma women, some of whom continue to suffer from the effects of state-forced sterilizations over the past four decades. Even Slovak authorities admit that there is a health care crisis among the Roma.

> Health conditions in Roman settlements are alarming. Because of poor hygiene, increased epidemics threaten many settlements. Since 1989 the incidence of bronchitis has increased and in some settlements tuberculosis has begun to spread. Frequent injuries, dermatological problems and sexual diseases confront the population. Some Romani children suffer from contagious and parasitic diseases, which no longer occur in the majority population. A great danger is the spread of meningitis.[101]

Such problems translate into considerably reduced life expectancy rates and higher infant mortality rates for the Roma vis à vis the general population. Part of the problem is legal, though much of it is rooted in the general prejudice toward the Roma throughout Slovakian society. Many health care professionals feel open hostility toward the Roma "because of their race, the color of their skin, their poverty, and their lack of education." There are a number of reported cases of health care professionals openly expressing their disgust in front of their Roma patients. One physician in a Roma ghetto told his patients, "you stink" and frequently called them "dirty dog[s]" or "idiot Gypsy," while nurses in Vitkovce constantly humiliated their Roma patients. In Košice, physicians told Roma women after they gave birth, "Well, you knew how to go to your man's bed, so now you look after yourself."[102]

These problems, of course, have further isolated the Roma and enforced public attitudes about the importance of completely isolating and segregating them from Slovakian society. Many of the problems faced by the Roma can be attributed to core racial prejudice. But this, in turn, has been influenced by the political environment and the fact that, relatively speaking, Slovakia is a poor country that spends a far smaller amount on health care per capita than many of its richer European neighbors. In many ways, Slovak authorities seemed to have left the Roma to their own devices when it comes to these problems. In some cases, their response has been dramatic, underscoring their desperation, as evidenced by the riots in 2004 in Košice, Prešov, Banska, and Bystrica counties to protest cuts in welfare payments that seriously affect large Roma families. The Slovak press collectively responded to these outbursts with headlines that read "This is War!"[103]

Hungary

In the summer of 1998, this author and several other Roma specialists testified before the United States Congress' Commission on Security and Cooperation in Europe to discuss the plight of the Roma in Central and Eastern Europe vis à vis the prospect of American funding for the upgrading of the militaries of Hungary, Poland, and the Czech Republic, which were up for NATO membership. Congressman Christopher H. Smith asked the group if there were any success stories when it came to Roma policy in Central and Eastern Europe and if we could rank countries from worst to best when it came to adoption and implementation of innovative policies toward the Roma. This author responded that "you were talking about varying degrees of bad or worse" with "Hungary being the best of the worst."[104] I think that statement holds true today.

According to Claude Cahn, Hungary considers itself "among European states," of being in the "minority avante-garde" because of its 1993 Minorities Act and other policies. Unfortunately, Cahn argues, high unemployment, poverty, and widespread discrimination have neutralized any positive effects from this legislation. He terms minority policy in Hungary as nothing more than "smoke and mirrors."[105] Éva Orsós, a Roma who headed the government's Office for National and Ethnic Minorities from 1995 to 1998, said she was surprised by the deep prejudice toward Roma she found among the staff in the minorities office. Though she was proud of the achievements there during her tenure, particularly the implementation of the government's Medium Term Strategy for Romani Issues, "which defined a set of tasks in the fields of education, culture, employment, agriculture, regional development, housing, health care, social welfare, anti-discrimination, and communication," she felt that three things were now necessary "to address the perilous situation of the Roma in Hungary—political will, a good programme, and implementation." Political will, she concluded, was essential to implementation of any government policy since, without it, policies were no better than the paper they were written on.[106]

Hungary's failure to improve the plight of the Roma using these "mid-term" goals drew the attention of the Council of Europe's Special Group on Roma/Gypsies. After a visit to several Roma communities in eastern Hungary in early 2001, Josephine Verspaget, the chair of the Special Group, wrote the Hungarian Ministry of Justice criticizing the government for failing to address a number of problems including "evictions and an increasing number of homeless Romani families, segregation of Roma pupils in remedial special schools, and the lack of communication between the government and NGOs." While the Special Group was aware of "ambitious initiatives at national and local levels," there was "a strong feeling of disappointment and distrust among Romani representatives" and a lack of communication between the government and various Roma groups and leaders.[107]

The following year, the United Nations Committee on the Elimination of Racial Discrimination (CERD) expressed dismay over the considerable problems still faced by the Roma in Hungary. Its November 1 "Concluding Observations" pointed to "persisting intolerance and discrimination" against the Roma and insisted that the Hungarian government do everything possible to speed along the writing of a "comprehensive anti-discrimination law." CERD expressed specific concerns over "allegation of ill-treatment and discrimination against the Roma and non-citizen by law enforcement officials, especially the police," high dropout rates among Roma students, "assigning Roma children to schools and classes for the mentally disabled," the high unemployment rate among Roma, housing discrimination, and discrimination in public places.[108]

Public violence toward the Roma, whether committed by police, skinheads, or others, has been a persistent problem in Hungary. Human Rights Watch considered such violence "the most immediate and serious violations of their rights," while the European Roma Rights Center in Budapest has issued scores of reports about police and skinhead anti-Roma violence. A survey of 1,530 policemen found that 80 percent of Hungary's police considered the Roma violent and "inclined to crime." Over half the number of people surveyed thought that "a criminal way of life is the key element of the Romani identity." Three quarters of the country's police officers felt that there were connections between ethnicity and crime. A third advocated the use of force in dealing with the Roma, arguing that the public expected them "to be tough on the Roma."[109]

If one presumes that such attitudes are reflective of broader societal views, then one only needs look at general public attitudes toward the Roma in Hungary to prove this. In 2000, the mayor of Csór, Dezsö Csete, told a television reporter that the Roma "have no place among human beings. Just as in the animal world, parasites must be expelled." A decade earlier, he commented that "every Gypsy should be shot with one bullet." In 2001, a middle-school teacher in Erdötelek made his Roma students write that "the Gypsies can be characterized by high rates of unemployment and by their special odour." He also taught them that Roma made up 80 percent of the country's prison population. After he complained to the town's mayor about this, Erdötelek's Roma leader, Miklós Pusoma, received death threats. One read, "Smelly Gypsy, you will die." A fifth grade textbook used throughout the country said that Roma could not "lead a European lifestyle" and that "the life of a part of the Roma is marked by crime." It also claimed that the Roma were spies for the Ottoman Turks when they conquered Hungary and were involved in the executions of prominent Hungarian historical figures at that time. The Ministry of Education later banned the use of this particular text.[110]

In 2005, Budapest's Romani radio station C filed a complaint with the police to have an Internet game, "Oláh [Wallachian] Action," removed from the Internet because it partially dealt with the murder of all Roma in Hungary. Once Hungary is completely "cleansed" of all Roma, it turns white. A telephone booth in the game had the following phrase scribbled across it: "They [the Roma] do nothing. They steal, they cheat, lie. They are a serious plague to the world, especially for this tiny European country." Efforts to convince the police to have the game removed from the Internet failed initially because police officials did not think the game, though provocative, fell within the "legal concept of incitement." Police later agreed to have the game removed from the Internet and it was no longer available in early 2006, though Hungary's National Bureau of Investigation refused to charge anyone with violations of the country's anti-Hate Speech Act and the Minorities Act, even though two Ombudsman officials declared the game in violation of both laws.[111]

But even more troubling was the 2005 statement by Bishop Andras Veres that the Hungarian Catholics' Bishop Conference agreed that white Hungarian children should not be forced to attend school with poor [Roma] children, since this would be a "setback for 'normal' children." This caused outrage throughout Hungary's Roma community, prompting a group of prominent Roma leaders and intellectuals to sign a statement objecting to the continued discrimination of Roma children throughout the public school system. Aladar Horvath, the head of the Roma Right Foundation, said that 50 percent of Roma school children are forced into classes for mentally challenged students.[112]

Troubled by such attitudes, the European Roma Rights Center filed a detailed *Shadow Report* with the United Nations Committee on the Rights of the Child complaining about the difficulty they had getting reliable data on Roma children, the forced removal of Roma children from their homes, discrimination in the adoption process in Hungary, inadequate health care for Roma children, inadequate access to decent housing for Roma families, which affects the welfare of their children, widespread school segregation, and adequate protection for abused Roma children. While the report applauded government efforts to improve life for Hungary's Roma children, it concluded that more needed to be done. Far too many Roma children still lived in poverty and some were literally starving to death. Almost 900 Roma settlements lacked a kindergarten, meaning that a fifth of the country's Roma children would be sent to public school without the linguistic skills necessary to compete with other Hungarian children. When this happened, the Roma children were often forced into schools for the mentally challenged, which deprived "them of future possibilities to get into higher education and get access to the labour market." Extremely poor Roma children are often then removed from their homes and placed in state-run facilities "which can lead to homelessness. And then the vicious circle goes around."[113]

Csaba Bader, the chairman of the RomaNet Media Foundation, a Roma internet learning center in Hungary, complained after the Hungarian Catholic Bishops' Conference issued its statement about the segregation of Roma children in the public schools, that "government in Hungary and the EU have done nothing to disperse anti-Roma behaviours and hate-speech against the Roma community."[114] Given its NATO (1999) and European Union (2004) membership, one would have expected more from Hungary, particularly in light of the traditional suffering of Hungarian minorities in other parts of Europe. But today, it would even be hard to make the case that Hungary's 450,000–600,000 Roma (out of a total population of 10.2 million) are much better off than their brethren in other parts of Central and Eastern Europe.[115]

Kosovo

Until recently, few people other than Balkan specialists knew anything about the Serbian province of Kosovo. About 88–92 percent of Kosovo's 2 million people are Albanians, most of them Muslims. The 1991 census showed a Kosovar Roma population of 43,000, though the European Roma Rights Center has said that the Roma could make up as much as 5 percent of the Kosovo's population. Shani Rafati, though, says that there were 200,000–250,000 Roma in Kosovo before the 1999 conflict.[116]

Roma are mentioned in Kosovo as early as the late fifteenth century. They were known as skilled smiths and metal workers. A census in 1520 indicated that there were 164 Roma families in Priština, 145 in Novo Brdo, and a few scattered Roma settlements in other parts of Kosovo. Only a minority of these Roma families were Muslim. During this period, the Ottoman government initiated new tax policies that saw Muslim Roma pay fewer taxes than Christian Roma. As elsewhere in the Balkans, Muslim Roma in Kosovo were highly regarded by the Turks as soldiers.[117]

Most Muslim Roma, who were known as *magjups*, were now sedentary and lived primarily in Prizren, Peś, Gjakova, and Priština. They spoke Albanian and worked as metal smiths, iron workers, or unskilled laborers on farms. Most of Kosovo's nomadic Roma were Albanian Orthodox, while the nomadic Roma in eastern Kosovo were Serbian Orthodox. There were also semi-nomadic Muslim Roma in Kosovo.[118]

There is little information on the Roma in Kosovo over the next four centuries, though the 1948 Yugoslav census indicates there were 11,000 Roma in the province.[119] It was during this period that the Serbs reasserted control over what became known as the Serbian autonomous Province of Kosovo—Methohija. The Albanians were now allowed greater use of their language and some autonomy, though the Serbs continued to hold the most important government positions. On the other hand, Kosovo's ethnic Albanians began to assume more control over the League of Communists, the police, and the security organs. Serb control over Kosovo was also affected by the drop in the number of Serbs and Montenegrins in the province. Between 1961 and 1981, the percentage of the total population dropped from 27 percent to 15 percent. By the time that the Kosovar war broke out in 1999, Serbs made up only 10 percent of it's population.[120]

Kosovar dissatisfaction with earlier Serbian police repression and bad economic conditions prompted a series of changes in the Yugoslav Federal Constitution in 1974. Kosovo became an autonomous province within Serbia along with Vojvodina, though the Serbs resented their loss of total control over

Kosovar affairs. Such attitudes worsened after Albanian Kosovar street demonstrations broke out in 1981. The demonstrators called for independence and union with Albania. Many Albanian Kosovars were frustrated by the fact that though Serbs and Montenegrins made up only 15 percent of the population, they controlled almost a third of the jobs. This resentment was compounded by the fact that Kosovo had the highest unemployment figures in Yugoslavia.[121]

Serbs and Montenegrins fled Kosovo in such large numbers after the demonstrations that by the end of 1981 they made up only 10 percent of the population. This exodus shocked the Serbs, who felt they were losing control of the cradle of Serb civilization. Slobodan Milosević, who became head of the Serbian Communist Party in 1987, used the Kosovo crisis to inflame Serb nationalism.[122] In fact, it was his speech at Kosova Polje on April 24, 1987 that helped propel him to the Serb presidency two years later. Milosević gave the talk just after a meeting with angry Kosovar Serbs who complained of mistreatment at the hands of Kosovar Albanians.

> First I want to tell you, comrades, that you should stay here. This is your country, these are your houses, your fields and gardens, your memories. You are not going to abandon your lands because life is hard, because you are oppressed by injustice and humiliation. It has never been a characteristic of the Serbian and Montenegrin people to retreat in the face of obstacles, to demobilize when they should fight, to become demoralized when things are difficult. You should stay here, both for your ancestors and your descendants. Otherwise you would shame your ancestors and disappoint your descendants. But I do not suggest you stay here suffering and enduring a situation with which you are not satisfied. On the contrary! It should be changed, together with all progressive people here, in Serbia and Yugoslavia. *Yugoslavia does not exist without Kosovo! Yugoslavia would disintegrate without Kosovo! Yugoslavia and Serbia are not going to give up Kosovo!*[123]

These words were more prophetic than Milosević ever imagined.

Over the next three years, a tide of nationalism swept the Yugoslav confederation that eventually erupted into war as Milosević tried to halt its disintegration. In Kosovo, Milosević engineered a series of changes in the Serbian constitution that took away much of Kosovo's autonomy and placed it firmly under Serb control. Kosovo became a rigidly controlled Serbian police state with numerous human rights abuses. In the summer of 1990, a young Kosovar Roma woman was beaten by Serbs. Afterward, they poured gasoline on her hair and lit it. No one tried to help her.[124]

The Serbs now tried to draw some Roma leaders into alliance with Kosovar Serbs. Many Kosovar Roma had voted for Milosević as president in 1990 because, as one Roma noted, "We thought in the beginning he was good. We did not know that he would set a trap for us."[125] The trap centered around a bargain that gave the Roma a modest role in governing Kosovo in return for their support of the province's Serbian rulers. In reality, few Roma gained from this alliance and most remained politically "mute." Claude Cahn and Tatjana Peric concluded that most Roma stayed out of politics because they felt trapped between the "exacting standards of loyalty among the Albanian community" and the "omnipresent Serbian police."[126]

Regardless, most Kosovar Albanians saw the Roma as Serbian allies. This was particularly true after the NATO air campaign in the spring of 1999 ended Serbia's brutal "ethnic cleansing" campaign in the province. According to one Kosovar Albanian, the "Albanians feel much more betrayed by the Roma than by the Serbs, who were always against them—it is much more emotionally charged. Gypsies lived predominantly with the Albanians and went to Albanian schools, but they always voted with the Serbs." What particularly angered some Kosovar Albanians, particularly in the capital, Priština, which had a large Muslim Roma population, was the fact that the Roma seemed to flaunt their pro-Serb feelings. *The New York Times*, for example, reported that at the height of the ethnic cleansing campaign, Priština's Roma organized "a parade of their own police unit."[127]

Ibrahim Makolli, the head of the Council for the Defense of Human Rights and Freedoms in Priština, partially defended some of the Roma. He said that the Serbs had drafted many of the Roma and possibly forced some of them to behave the way they did. The Serbs, he noted, often forced the Roma to do the "worst jobs" such as collecting the bodies of the dead and burying them. Regardless, he explained, many Kosovar Albanians would "find it hard to forgive the apparent alacrity with which many Roma looted, burned, and wielded weapons during the last months" of the ethnic cleansing campaign. He added that he had testimony that some Roma took part in the Serb atrocities against Kosovo's Albanians. Other Roma, he explained, "took people from refugee columns, they demanded identification papers, they took action in the same way that the Serbian forces did."[128] Mr. Makolli said that the Albanians expected such behavior from the Serbs. They did not expect the Roma to behave like Serbs.[129]

Yet who were these Roma accused of helping the Serbs? A statement by the Priština office of Rromani Baxt in August 1998 discussed the role played by some Roma in Kosova since the end of World War II. According to Rromani Baxt, some Roma groups did play the "Albanian card" to ingratiate themselves with the Serbs. They were encouraged by what Rromani Baxt called "a hand-ful of pro-Serbian politicians," some of whom were Roma. This small group, Rromani Baxt claimed, "lead a strong campaign of propaganda against the 'Albanian danger' all over Serbia." Many of the Roma who supported the Serbs were Orthodox, though there were also some pro-Serbian Muslim Roma. According to Rromani Baxt, the pro-Serbian Roma hoped to get "more help from a strong central government than from the local Albanians of their every-day life, who had disappointed them."[130] Some of the pro-Serbian Roma, Rromani Baxt claimed, were not Roma at all, but a Muslim group known as the *Ashkali*, who originally came to the Balkans from Egypt. Rromani Baxt said that the *Ashkali* were among "the most fiendish groups in Kosova and showed 'an alarming barbarian cruelty.' " Even so, Rromani Baxt noted, there was nothing to indicate that these groups had caused physical harm to anyone in Kosovo.[131]

There were many Roma, though, who did not support the Serbs and who suf-fered from Serb abuse. Some Muslim Roma were driven out of their homes throughout Kosovo by Serbian police during the NATO bombings, and there is some evidence of Serbian policemen raping Roma women before the air cam-paigns began. Roma refugees said that in some cases, the Serb police forced them to loot and burn Kosovar homes to ensure that the Roma would be blamed for some of the destruction.[132]

Yet the Serbs were not the only ones who mistreated the Roma. Roma refugees reported numerous instances of threats and murders by the Kosovo Liberation Army (UçK). UçK soldiers attacked Roma who had Serbian friends and raped Roma women. There were also cases where Albanians mistreated Roma in efforts to get them to declare that they were Albanian. Mamidije Krasiãi described the deadly world of the Muslim Roma in Kosovo.

> There was shooting everywhere around us. The Albanians from one side, the Kosovo Liberation Army, and the Serbian military and police from the other. We were abused by both sides. Roma were beaten and our lives depended on the money, food and other goods that we were forced to give to anyone who asked for it. Our lives became even worse after the beginning of the NATO air strikes. When the NATO bombing started, the Serbian police and military started to all treat us more intensively, because they considered us Albanians. So we had to run away, and we did so in April [1999]. Since we had no passports, we decided to go through the forest and to cross the Macedonian border illegally. While running through the forest we noticed Serbian military on patrol. We all lay down, so they did not see us and passed us by. So we crossed the border and now we are in Kumanovo [Macedonia].[133]

Once the fighting ended, returning Albanian Kosovars took revenge on the Serbs and Roma who remained in Kosovo. They attacked, looted, and burned any town or village with a Roma quarter. In fact, even before the Kosovars returned home, they attacked Roma in refugee camps in Albanian and Macedonia. In the Cegrane refugee camp in Stankovec, Macedonia, angry refugees assaulted a Roma family on June 5, 1999. Catholic aid workers said that if they had not rescued a 7-year-old Roma boy from his attackers, they would have torn him apart. The Albanians accused the boy's father and brother of being Serb collaborators. According to one aid worker, the Kosovars "had fire in their eyes." By the end of July 1999, there were few, if any, Roma left in Kosovo.[134]

The intensity of the attacks shocked human rights groups and Roma organizations. Soon after the NATO bombings began, the International Romani Union (IRU) in Berlin decried unsubstantiated press accounts in France, Italy, and Kosovo that pointed to Roma paramilitary attacks against Albanians. The IRU statement also criticized the use of the word *cigány* and Gypsy in the press, both words laden with prejudicial meaning. In an allusion to the Holocaust, the declaration stated:

> The Rromani Union is convinced that democratic Europe and the civilized world will not permit that genocide of our people will repeat itself. And that they will use all media to their disposal, without hesitation to block the mechanisms that lead to such a genocide.[135]

The Balkan Roma Conference on Peace and Security, which met in Sofia, Bulgaria from June 18 to 19, 1999, also drew on the Roma tragedy during the Holocaust to remind the United Nations, the Council of Europe, the European Commission, and NATO of the threat to Kosovar Roma, both in refugee camps and in Kosovo itself. On July 14, 1999, the United States' Commission on Security and Cooperation in Europe (CSCE) sent Secretary of State Madeline Albright a letter asking her "what measures the Department is seeking to ensure their [Roma] safety during this period of refugee resettlement" in Kosovo, in refugee camps, and in other countries. The CSCE also wanted to know what was being done to bring Kosovar Roma to the United States.[136]

In reality, nothing had been done to protect the Roma, since NATO had not foreseen the tremendous refugee problem in Kosovo. In fact, the United Nations' administration in Kosovo admitted that "little thought was given to protecting innocent Serbs or Gypsies from revenge." By mid-August 1999, there were only 20,000–25,000 Serbs left in Kosovo out of a population that had numbered almost 200,000 only months earlier. Almost all of Kosovo's

Roma had fled the province.[137] Those who remained did so without any hope of protection from Albanian forces, though a few Roma were elected to parliamentary seats in November 2001 elections.[138] The United Nations High Commissioner on Refugees reported on the severity of this problem in 2002.[139] These fears finally exploded in March 2004, when a wave of anti-Roma, anti-Egyptian, anti-*Ashkali*, and anti-Serb violence swept Kosovo, led by ethnic Albanians. Scores of homes and churches were destroyed in the pogrom.[140] On May 18, 2004, Kosovo's Ombudsperson sent letters to a number of European countries hosting Kosovar refugees and advised them not to return to Kosovo. He said that Roma as well as *Ashkali* and Egyptians, groups often associated with the Roma, faced "considerable risks to their personal safety" if they returned. Moreover, if they did so, this would "violate international human rights standards."[141]

Sadly, their situation has not improved. On June 27, 2005, representatives of the European Roma Rights Center (ERRC) in Budapest gave testimony before the European parliament about the plight of the Roma in Kosovo. They provided parliament members with evidence of continued human rights abuses including constant threats of violence and basic human rights protection. These were some of the reasons that many Roma feared returning to Kosovo. And for those brave enough to do so, ERRC representatives told parliament, they could find neither work nor adequate housing as most of their homes were either destroyed or stolen during the civil war.[142]

Those who remained in Kosovo have suffered unspeakable hardships. In Mitrovica, once home to one of Europe's largest and most prosperous Romani communities, some Roma have been forced to live in squalid refugee camps near a toxic waste site. In 1999, the United Nations set up three refugee camps (Cesmin Lug, Kablar, and Žitovac) in northern Kosovo after the destruction of the Roma *mahalle* in Mitorvica. Though these camps were meant to be temporary, hundreds of Roma continued to live there until late 2005. The camps, built near a toxic waste site, were so unhealthy that in 2005 the World Health Organization (WHO) considered them unfit for habitation and called for the "immediate evacuation of the children, relocation of the camps, and immediate treatment." The Roma forced to live there suffered from "high levels of lead in their blood streams, causing stunted growth, mental retardation and paralysis." Canadian relief efforts to move the Roma to a healthier French military camp in the same region offered no real solution since this site was also contaminated.[143]

In many ways, the health crisis of the Roma in the Mitrovica has come to symbolize the dreadful plight of the Roma throughout Kosovo. If, as seems possible now, Kosova gains full independence from Serbia, then "this elephant in the room [Kosovar independence]" could actually make things worse for the Roma. Most could be forced to flee to Serbia while those living as refugees in other European countries could be forced to return to Kosova, where they would be unwelcome. The Ontario Consultants for Religious Tolerance have concluded that "the Roma in Kosovo may be the most oppressed of all. They appear to be hated by both the Albanian/Muslim majority and the Serbian/Christian minority" in a country the ERRC calls a "human rights vaccum" for Roma.[144]

Macedonia

Though Macedonia did not suffer from the same dreadful upheavals of Bosnia and Kosovo in the 1990s, it is still a country with serious problems that have deeply affected the Roma. According to Judith Latham, the Roma in Macedonia have always been an "underclass," who, though not as despised as elsewhere in the Balkans, are still viewed as "dirty" and "lazy." Hugh Poulton adds that most Roma in Macedonia live well below the economic norm and face constant discrimination. He adds that few Macedonian Roma have obtained the education necessary to join the country's professional ranks, and most are employed in industrial jobs or work as farmers.[145] Despite this, Human Rights Watch concluded in a 1996 report that

> Comparatively speaking, the Roma community in Macedonia is better off than in other countries of the region. There are a number of Roma political, social, and cultural organisations functioning in Macedonia, and a Roma party is represented in parliament. Roma are recognized in the constitution as a nationality, and relations with the ethnic Macedonian population are generally good.[146]

When Macedonia sought its independence in 1991, it had a Roma population of about 200,000–220,000, though the official census that year showed only 55,580. The internationally sponsored 1994 census showed 43,707 Roma in Macedonia, though Roma leaders feel this figure should be 150,000–250,000. A 2005 study by the Untied Nations Development Programme estimated the country's Roma population to be about 135,000 out of a total population of a little over 2 million. About two-thirds of Macedonia's Roma are Muslims. According to the preamble of the 1991 Macedonian constitution, the Roma have "full equality" and "permanent coexistence" with the Macedonia people and the country's other minorities. Article 78 created a Council for Inter-Ethnic Relations that would be made up of two representatives each from the

Macedonian, Albanian, Turkish, Vlach, and "Romanies" communities and other groups.[147]

Yet, as a 1998 report by the European Roma Rights Center (ERRC) notes, these guarantees and the more positive environment for the Roma did not necessarily translate into increased rights for many of them. Roma are often pressured and bribed by other ethnic groups, particularly Albanians and Turks, to claim an ethnic identity other than their own. Moreover, in 1990, the Presidium of the Republican Committee for Nurturing the Ethnic and Cultural Traditions of Roma accused the Albanian Party for Democratic Prosperity in Macedonia of using Islam to manipulate the Roma. If this were not enough, the 1992 Citizenship of the Republic of Macedonia law created financial, residential, and other requirements that prevented many Roma immigrants who had fled abroad and returned from acquiring Macedonian citizenship.[148]

In 2005, almost 39 percent of the workforce was unemployed. Roma unemployment figures are almost twice as high.[149] Though considerable national and international efforts have been taken to increase employment opportunities for Macedonians, the Roma have benefited very little from such programs. Many require some education and literacy, which hurts Roma with little education or weak reading skills. The Roma are also not well informed about such initiatives because the publications are not written simply or in Romani. Many Roma blame these problems on the fact that they do not have leaders to "protect their economic rights" nor organizations that work together "to advocate and lobby" for their economic rights.[150]

The high rate of unemployment has also contributed to widespread anti-Roma violence, particularly from the police. In fact, according to the ERRC, such mistreatment has become "so common in Macedonia that it has become part of the Romani social landscape, an object of folk culture." Much of the trouble centers around government efforts to halt or restrict small-time street trade that the Roma had been forced to undertake because of massive unemployment.[151] According to the ERRC,

> all of the tendencies seen elsewhere in the region, from weakness as a minority up to vulnerability to racist attack and failure to achieve remedy, are present in Macedonia. Perhaps most importantly, however, Macedonia authorities are not viewing the growth of anti-Romani sentiment and anti-Romani violence in Macedonia with the gravity it merits.[152]

Macedonia's Roma have been particularly vulnerable to the country's economic problems because of their high illiteracy rates. Šemci Šajnov says that about 80 percent of Roma children never finish elementary school. Fait

Kamberovski of the Democratic Party for the Total Emancipation of Roma in Macedonia disagrees. He says that about 90 percent of the country's Roma go to first grade, but only about half of them reach fifth grade. He adds that 35–40 percent of Roma children will finish eighth grade, the last mandatory grade. Quotas and financial problems have kept Roma from attending the country's higher education institutions in significant numbers.[153]

Educational reform has been one of the principle issues promoted by Macedonia's most important Roma political parties, the Party for the Complete Emancipation of Romanies in Macedonia (PSERM) and the Democratic Progressive of Romanies (DPSR). In the spring of 1993, PRERM, which was headed by Faik Abidj, demanded that the government offer Roma students three to four lessons a week in Romani and the creation of a Department of Romani at Skopje University. The government has offered Romani classes in Skopje, though its efforts have been less successful in other parts of the country. According to Zoran Todorov of the Ministry of Foreign Affairs, government efforts to offer more Romani classes is hampered by the lack of trained teachers and the fact that there are two Macedonian Romani dialects. He added that two optional Romani language classes were opened in Skopje and Šuto Orizari in 1996. In addition, a special training program was set up for future teachers of Romani. However, the quality of instruction was suspect. Šemci Šajnov noted in 1997 that it was "particularly bad" in the two schools in Šuto Orizari and that some Roma parents had to hire private tutors to ensure that their children received an adequate education.[154]

The Macedonian Center for International Cooperation (MCIC; *Makedonski Tsentar za Megynarodna Sorabotka*) has funded 88 educational projects for Roma children since 2000 that has seen school enrollment jump from 18 percent to 23 percent between 2000 and 2005, and dropout rates fall from 61 percent to 57 percent during the same period. Its program was also able to reduce the number of Roma repeating classes from 84 percent to 34 percent. The United States Agency for International Development has funded similar programs designed to improve educational opportunities for Roma children. Its program in Kumanovo has been particularly important. Ramis Osmanovski, the director of the Roma Educational Center in Kumanovo, noted that "without the pre-school help [tutorial sessions for Roma children], many of the kids have no chance to compete with Macedonian students. We also work with the parents, because many of them are not motivated, and that has an effect on the children."[155]

Such efforts, unfortunately, are just beginning to filter down to the Roma. And though most specialists agree that the Roma in Macedonia are better off than their peers in other Central and East European countries, it will take herculean efforts to make the Roma equal partners in Macedonian society. While the Roma in Macedonia suffer from the same social, employment, abuse, and other problems of Roma in other parts of Central and Eastern Europe, their lack of a significant voice seems the greatest barrier to the improvement of their plight. Shayna Plaut and Azbija Memedova blame this on the fact that "there is still no place for Roma to learn the 'game' of ethnic politics nor have they created a new, public political alternative." The European Roma Rights Center and the National Roma Centrum argued in 2006 that recent initiatives such as the 2005 National Strategy for Roma in Macedonia and the Decade of Roma Inclusion will not be effective because the government lacks the "real political will to implement those measures."[156]

Poland

Though Poland has a small Roma population (30,000–50,000 out of a total population of 38.5 million), they suffer from the same prejudices and discrimination that haunt Roma in other parts of Central and Eastern Europe.[157] They are divided into four major groups: the *Polska* (Polish) Roma, the Lovara and Keldara Roma (who are collectively known as Vlach Roma), and the Bergitka Roma. There is also a small group of Sinti in western Poland. Traditionally, all but the Bergitka were nomads, though this began to change after World War II when Poland's new communist government adopted policies to halt Roma nomadism. The Council of Ministers' 1952 decree "On State Help in the Transition toward a Settled Way of Life" addressed this problem, hoping that Roma sedentarism would provide the basis for the "satisfactory cultural, economic and social development of the Roma, and for securing the participation of Roma in the fulfillment of the economic goals of the socialist state." Distressed over its efforts to halt Roma nomadism, the government issued much harsher restrictions in 1964 to force the Roma to settle, though it would take two more decades for Roma nomadism finally to disappear.[158]

Communist leaders saw education as one way "to subject them [the Roma] to a cultural impact" and became one of the government's principal vehicles for forcing them to assimilate. By the early 1960s, only about a quarter of Poland's Roma children attended public school, and most of these were settled Bergitka Roma. The government invested a great deal of money in educational programs for Roma children, and by 1970, 82 percent were attending public schools. Unfortunately, education did not prove to be the key to forcing the Roma to become more "Polish," since many Roma children failed to go on to the next grade. Much of this was caused by high absentee rates and inadequate preschool preparation. By 1983, almost a third of the Roma children in Polish schools were not promoted to the next grade.[159]

As Andrzej Mirga has pointed out, not all of these problems could be blamed on the schools, though efforts to force ill-prepared Roma children in integrated classrooms when they knew little formal Polish only brought ridicule from their non-Roma classmates. When coupled with the lack of enthusiasm for public education by their parents, some of whom were illiterate and still lived as seminomads, many Roma children became discouraged with the idea of attending public school. Why would any child feel comfortable in an educational environment where they were taunted by their schoolmates and struggled with the basic language of instruction? Beyond this, of course, was the fact that for "many Romani families, especially the more traditional ones which by definition were those of nomadic origins, schooling of their children and schools in general, were viewed as a threat to their Romani identity, and thus, as something to be avoided."[160]

Government efforts to improve the lot of the Roma through formal education waned after the 1981 revolution, which saw the imposition of martial law throughout Poland. Opportunities were realized for the Roma with the collapse of communism eight years later, particularly after minority affairs were transferred from the hated Interior Ministry to a new Bureau for National Minorities in the Ministry of Culture and Art. Unfortunately, the Roma benefited little from these changes. In fact, though the Roma are considered an ethnic minority, in reality they are treated as a national minority, in part because of the growth of Roma nationalism in the 1990s and the fact that most international organizations such as the Council of Europe were pushing for better treatment of the Roma throughout the region.[161]

Such efforts, unfortunately, have not had much impact on the Roma. In his 1999 report for the Helsinki Foundation for Human Rights, Dr. Sławomir Łodziński noted that the plight of the Roma had actually worsened in the years since the collapse of communism, in large part because of an atmosphere of public prejudice that continued to view a Roma as "someone who is [a] fraud or a thief." Such attitudes were the basis of a number of anti-Roma riots that took place throughout the country in the 1990s. In 2005, the Council of Europe's European Commission against Racism and Intolerance (ECRI) noted in its *Third Report on Poland* that very little had changed for the country's Roma since an earlier ECRI report had urged Polish authorities to pay "immediate attention" to the widespread discrimination they faced throughout the country. This was doubly troubling, given the fact that the government had adopted two programs, the Government Pilot Programme for the Roma Community in the Malopolska Province (2001–2003), and the 2004 Programme for the Roma Community in Poland.[162]

The Malopolska project was the first national government effort to address the problems in the Roma community and was partially driven by negative international publicity over the flight of large numbers of Roma to Great Britain and efforts to draw closer to the European community. The pilot program in Malopolska Province in the Kraków area was to address education, housing, unemployment, health, security, culture, and public knowledge of the Roma. The Polish government allotted 1.5 million zlotys ($468,750) for the first year of the program and six million zlotys ($1,875,000) for the next two years.

Roma leaders in Maloposka Province insisted on education being the first priority of the program, with an emphasis on hiring Roma assistants in the public schools, providing special help sessions for Roma students in certain subjects, free school supplies for Roma students, and special training sessions for principals, teachers, and Romani assistants. Unfortunately, Roma leaders such as Andrzej Mirga, while applauding this initial effort, were concerned over the failure of the program to address the issue of segregated Roma classes set up a decade earlier. Roma leaders felt such classes were a throwback to government policies of the 1960s and 1970s and worked "against the very interest of Romani children, since it diminishes their chances for getting a normal education and deprives them of equal educational opportunities." Mirga was also concerned over the failure of the program to introduce classes on Roma history, culture, and language. He was also critical of the fact that the government failed to appoint Roma to the program's various governmental program coordinating bodies. Finally, he argued that it also failed to address the serious issues of "discrimination and racism."[163]

Such criticism ultimately led the government to create the National Programme for the Roma Community. In its written introduction to this new plan, the Ministry of Interior woefully underestimated the size of the Roma population in Poland and blamed some of the Roma's problems on the former communist government and its assimilation policies. And while the report admitted that the Roma suffered greatly, the ministry noted that the Roma were also partially to blame for their plight. Roma cultural distrust of outsiders and their refusal to take advantage of "the rights guaranteed by the Republic of Poland and ethnical minorities," government authors explained, were part of the reason for high Roma unemployment, their growing sense of insecurity, and numerous social and health problems.[164] While there is certainly no question that Roma cultural traditions have been something of a barrier to greater integration in Polish society, such a tone only serves further to alienate a Roma community already suspicious of failed government efforts to force them to assimilate into a society that really does not seem to care for them.

Romania

Though the 2002 census only showed a Roma population of 535,250 out of 21.7 million (22.3 million in 2006), estimates are that there are about 1.8–2.5 million Roma in Romania, making it home to the largest Roma population in the world. In many ways, it could be argued that Romania is the European homeland of the Roma.[165] Given these numbers, and Romania's historic backwardness over the past half century, it is not surprising that the Roma have fallen victims to widespread discrimination and violence in the years since the collapse of communism. In its 2006 report on Romania, the Council of Europe's Commission against Racism and Intolerance (ECRI) called the plight of the Roma in Romania "disturbing." The report noted that the Roma continue to be discriminated against in education, employment, housing, health care, and are frequently denied access to public places. Though the Romanian government promised to address these issues in its decade-long Strategy for Improving the Situation of the Roma, which was adopted in 2001, the ECRI noted that the programs lacked adequate funds and "the necessary political will to ensure the success of the Strategy." What's doubly troubling about all of this is that the government feels that it has fulfilled the initial goals of the Strategy, while outside observers note just the opposite. In 2002, Prime Minister Adrian Nastase said that "the Strategy is excellent, we adopted it, everybody was satisfied, and after that we put it in the drawer."[166]

The real success of any such program, of course, is its impact on local Roma communities. Yet according to the Open Society Institute's detailed report on the impact of the Strategy in five counties with large Roma populations (Brăila, Cluj, Dolj, Jaşi, and Timiş), its impact "remains low" mainly because its objectives "have not been successfully translated to the local level." In fact, local officials are generally unaware of how to implement the Strategy's goals. This is because the "administrative structures at the central and local levels are still functioning poorly and lack financial and material resources."[167]

In many ways, such government inaction stems from the generally negative view of the Roma throughout Romanian society. Its most public expression comes in the form of public and police violence, something that has haunted the Roma in the decades since the collapse of the government of Nicolae Ceauseşcu in 1989. If anything symbolized the horror of such violence for Rom, it was the pogrom in Hădăreni in 1993 that saw the murder of three Roma males (two were beaten to death; the other burned to death) and the destruction of fourteen Roma homes. Though the Roma filed charges against 12 civilians and several police officers, they were soon dropped against all of the policemen despite subsequent trial testimony documenting their involvement. The Roma received only token payments for their losses. In 2000, after Romania's president pardoned two of the three civilians convicted of the murders, the ERRC's legal office brought the case before the Council of Europe's European Court for Human Rights (ECHR). In the fall of 2004, the ECHR advised the Romanian government to work out a "friendly" agreement with the injured Roma, resulting in a settlement of 238,000 Euros. The court ruled a year later that "the applicants' Romani ethnicity played a decisive role in the incidents of 1993 as well as in the subsequent failure of the authorities to investigate the events and provide redress to the applicants."[168] Needless to say, this case has come to symbolize, at least for the Roma in Romania, both the widespread anti-Roma prejudice in the country as well as the lack of commitment of public officials to their plight.

One of the measures of government's success in dealing with its Roma population is its treatment of Roma women, given their special role in the Roma family and community. Sadly, their plight is often submerged into the greater issue of the Roma in general, and while there are various national and European laws and policies dealing with gender equality and discrimination, there is nothing that deals specifically with Roma women.[169]

Stereotypically, Roma women in Romania are viewed as "illiterate, loud, lazy, and irresponsibly burdening the state by bearing too many children, and too often." However, the Open Society Institute's detailed study of the plight of Roma women in Romania, *Broadening the Agenda: The Status of Romani Women in Romania* (2006), demolishes this myth, showing that while Roma women are "the most deprived category of the Romanian population," they are also an astute, concerned, responsible group burdened by the double standard of discrimination they suffer in Romanian society and within their own communities.[170]

Over 63 percent of the Roma women interviewed in this study stated that they felt unequal to men within their own families and communities. Though there seemed little hope in gaining gender equality, three quarters were frustrated over their diminished role in decision making in the family and the raising of children, while almost 60 percent were frustrated over their unequal access to jobs. Part of the reason for this inequality was the fact that most Roma women married at 17 and had their first child within the first two years of their marriage. In the general population, the average marriage age for women was 24. Within the family, women had one job—housekeeping. The Roma male was considered the sole breadwinner for the family, which further limited opportunities for women. Consequently, Roma women were almost solely responsible for raising the children, though those surveyed thought it should be shared by both husband and wife.[171]

These responsibilities in turn limited educational opportunities for Roma women: 23 percent received no formal education, compared to 15 percent of the men. Only 4 percent of the women in the Romanian population have no formal education. These statistics are particularly troubling given that 97.7 percent of Romania's women over age 15 can read and write. Despite this, Roma women are expected to be involved in all aspects of their children's education. Most find this very frustrating, since almost a fifth of the country's Roma children attend segregated schools. Over 83 percent of the Roma women interviewed preferred that their children attend integrated schools. Interestingly, Roma women were quite supportive of gender-biased occupational choices when it came to their children. Females, many concluded, were best suited for teaching, medicine, and garment industry work, while they considered transportation, engineering, physicians, and legal work the best jobs for males.[172]

Health care was another concern of these women, and almost half of those interviewed felt that their health was mediocre or bad. They considered their children to be healthier than themselves though 15 percent thought their children suffered from poor health. Over a third said they never used any sort of contraceptive, while 78 percent considered abortion the best form of birth control. But it was they, not their husbands, who chose whether to get an abortion or not. Over two-thirds felt they were discriminated against by local health care professionals, which was partially based on their gender. Such discrimination manifested itself in disinterest on the part of medical staff, inaccessibility to the most readily available medical care, inexpensive drugs, and forced payments for health care that was supposed to be free.[173]

Roma women were also frustrated over what they saw as widespread discrimination at the work place, some of it gender based. It usually manifested itself in bad working conditions and low paying jobs. A third thought that men had more opportunities than women in the workforce, while almost 40 percent had not earned any money working over the past year. Those who did worked on farms or sold used goods and medicinal herbs. The majority of those who were regularly employed said they had no contractual agreement with their employers, meaning that, their work was unreported to the government.[174]

If anything most reflected Roma poverty, though, it was housing: 10 percent of the women surveyed said their homes lacked electricity, while 53 percent said they did not have a separate kitchen, meaning that their families lived and cooked in the same room. Less than 15 percent of Roma homes had a bathroom, while 84 percent of the Roma women surveyed said their homes had no running water. The result is a patch quilt of Roma slums dotting the Romanian countryside. Such conditions have often led to the forcible eviction of Roma families as individuals and communities either seek to rid themselves of Roma slums or take their land. In 2001, the mayor in Bârlad announced plans to build a separate community for the Roma on the outskirts of the town. Such a cultural "village," he argued, would attract tourists and remove the Roma from the rest of the community since they did not "live in a civilised manner," destroyed furniture, and committed "illegal acts."[175]

Forced evictions of the Roma have become a mainstay of local government policy throughout Romania. In 2002, the government expelled 300 Roma from the Piscul Crăsani neighborhood in Bucharest. Prior to the expulsion, one city official stated that "carts are not allowed in Bucharest. If they [Roma] return, I will burn their carts and make salami of their dogs." Widespread evictions also took place in other parts of the city. Such evictions are often followed by the destruction of Roma dwellings, which leaves them homeless. In the summer of 2005, a large Romanian mob destroyed several Roma houses in Seica Mare and beat an elderly man. Police dismissed the incident as a local conflict with no racial overtones.[176]

The final portion of the *Broadening the Agenda* study dealt with the role of Roma women in the country's political and civic life. There have always been considerable barriers to active Roma involvement in political life, much of it caused by poverty and illiteracy. But Cristi Mihalache, an Advocacy Officer for the European Roma Rights Center, also blames the "traditionalism" in the Roma community, particularly when it comes to female Roma voters. Revered leaders wield a lot of influence and, given the gender inequities in the Roma community and family, "a woman's desire to vote [can] be seen as jeopardizing the authority of the head of the family." Furthermore, there is also a tendency among Roma women to vote for the same candidates as their husbands. Regardless, *Broadening the Agenda* shows that 82 percent of the country's female Roma voted in the 2004 local and national elections, though only 26 percent were involved in "political, civic, or community based organizations." Many Roma women felt that there were considerable ethnic and gender barriers to such participation and yet argued that men should lead such groups. They thought that the only way to change this was to educate their daughters. And many argued that the involvement of Roma women in politics would improve things for the Roma. One group of Roma women in Bontida discussed this during one of the study's interview sessions:

"Why did you go to vote?"
"We went to get things solved."
"We went because we need supplies for our children's school and wood for winter."
"I participated so they would help us, once we elect them."
"Yes, I voted and I hope I will get some help getting gas [for cooking and heating]."

But perhaps a Roma woman in Valea Viilor best captured the essence of the democratic spirit among many Roma when she noted, "We always participate . . . for the benefit of the country and the benefit of Roma and Romanians alike. I think everyone should go to vote."[177] Perhaps this is the light at the end of the tunnel for Romania's Roma.

Russia

Given their unique history in the tsarist and Soviet state, one would have hoped that the Roma in post-Soviet Russia would have fared better than their counterparts in other parts of Central and Eastern Europe. Unfortunately, this has not been the case. Their plight has been the subject of a number of detailed reports and a hearing before the U.S. Congress' Commission on Security and Cooperation in Europe. All conclude that the plight of the Roma has deteriorated since the mid-1990s, driven in part by the growing xenophobia in Russia and the seeming unwillingness of officials to address the problem of anti-Roma prejudice. The Council of Europe's ECRI noted in its 2006 *Third Report on the Russian Federation* that "Roma in particular are victims of the deterioration of the general climate of opinion as regards racism," while the International Federation for Human Rights' (IFHR) 2004 report on Russian Roma noted that "there has been a general increase in nationalism and xenophobia, to which the Romani people directly fall victim." The European Roma Rights Center's report, *Violations of Roma Rights in the Russian Federation* (2004), said the "magnitude of the abuse is only comparable to that of the perpetrators' impunity,"[178] while its *In Search of Happy Gypsies: Persecution of Pariah Minorities in Russia* (2005) stated that:

> violence by state officials, paramilitary and nationalist-extremist groups, and discriminatory treatment of Roma in the exercise of civil, social and economic rights are aggravated by the complete absence of government action to address these problems.[179]

Each of these reports also underscored the widespread, indiscriminate violence toward Roma. What makes this environment different is that there are no international organizations, such as the European Union, using membership as a threat to help prod the government to improve conditions for the Roma. Russia remains, as it has always been, an insular state without any regard for international concern or pressure regarding its treatment of minorities. Police brutality toward the Roma has been a constant in Russian society since the collapse of communism. Much of this has been motivated by what the IFHR calls "ambient racism," the blend of nationalism and xenophobia so prevalent in Russia since Vladimir Putin assumed the presidency in 1999. In this environment, the Roma are disliked not only because of the stereotypes that traditionally depicted than as "thieves, vagabonds, filthy, saddled with a swarm of kids they cannot feed" but also new societal hatred of *chernye* (blacks). Though aimed initially at individuals from Central Asia and the Caucasus, Roma are now trapped in this new web of prejudice.[180]

Dimitrina Petrova, the executive director of the European Roma Rights Center, testified before the Helsinki Committee in 2004 that much of the current violence toward the Roma is driven by public and police perceptions that the Roma are major players in the country's illegal drug trafficking network. This has led to widespread abuse by police and other officials, much of which is unreported. Alexander Torokhov blamed a lot of this misperception on the media, which perpetuates "negative stereotypes about the life of the Roma community." Police corruption is also another factor in this abuse. Corruption is endemic in Russian society, and the police are its most abusive representatives. Most police mistreatment, Torokhov explained, took place during police security checks or raids on Roma communities. Leonid Raihman, a consultant for the Open Society Institute, testified that the government was unaware of much of this corruption and that it took place in an atmosphere of benign governmental "neglect" and indifference rather than as a "conscious policy." What concerned Raihman about all of this was that such corruption has now taken on a "racist dimension."[181]

What is surprising in all of this is that the Roma have traditionally been more accepted into Russian society than their counterparts in other parts of Europe, though this has more to do with their romantic, literary, and musical role in Russian society than anything else. Furthermore, the "historical misunderstanding of a little-known lifestyle feeds prejudice, as does the belief in the Roma's hidden wealth." Anti-Roma prejudice is widespread in the media and prompted the United Nations Committee on the Elimination of Racial Discrimination to report in 2003 that it "was disturbed by the information whereby racist documents on minority groups that perpetuate stereotypes are disseminated in the national media." ECRI noted in its 2006 report that the media has played a big role in perpetuating negative stereotypes of the Roma, particularly as they relate to crimes and drug trafficking. Such reports have "even incited . . . racial hatred, notably by reporting open calls to murder Roma, without issuing any warning or condemnation." As a result, the term *tsyganskii* has become synonymous with the term for illegal drug trafficker, *baryga*. Given official efforts to crack down on crime, life for many of the country's 182,000–1,200,000 Roma (out of 142,800,000) is made difficult by such irrational and stereotypical associations.[182]

This blatant stereotyping and mistreatment affects every aspect of Roma life in Russia. In its *In Search of Happy Gypsies*, the European Roma Rights Centre documents in detail the impact of widespread anti-Roma prejudice on Roma throughout the country. Many Roma, it noted, lived separately from the rest of the population in isolated settlements or ghettos that often lack basic sanitation, water, sewage, and electric services. And those who qualified for government housing often faced discrimination when they applied for apartments. And those who did qualify often had to live in government-sponsored slum dwellings unfit for human habitation. In Volzhskiy, Roma were forced to live in a city-owned building called the "Gypsy house" that was

> in a dilapidated condition despite the fact that the municipality had registered the building as fit for dwelling. Some windowpanes and even frames were missing. The walls inside the flats were made of cardboard and in many places were falling apart. There were mice in the flats, so children were scared to walk to the bathroom during the night. Many flats had high levels of humidity. Some Roma suffered from tuberculosis yet lived together with their family members.[183]

The government forced large families to live together in the "Gypsy house"; as a result, as many as 15 people were often forced to live in two small rooms. This was particularly hard on the disabled. The city did agree to make some repairs to the building in 2003, but most of the work they did was cosmetic. Though subsidized by the city, the Roma still had to pay rent for their apartments. And though they regularly paid their electric and gas bills, the ERRC team found that city officials had cut off the gas and electricity for the building before they visited the "Gypsy house."[184]

Though it is more difficult to gain information about the Roma in Russia than in any other country in the region with a large Roma population, the information we do have suggests that they suffer from the same depredations as their counterparts in other parts of Europe. The cycle of poverty that is so devastating to Roma elsewhere is equally prevalent in Russia. This spills over into education, access to health care, women's rights, and basic protection under the law as citizens with full human and civil rights protections. In many ways, the problems that the Roma face in Russia simply mirror those of the Roma in other parts of Central and Eastern Europe. The only difference is that Russian authorities seem impervious to any outside pressure to address the complex issues facing the Roma today. While some efforts have been made regionally by local authorities to address the numerous educational, social, and economic problems of the Roma, there is nothing in place nationally to address these issues. Criminal laws remain weak when it comes to the prosecution of racial and hate crimes, while the police continue to be a power unto themselves. Moreover, though the Roma have rights under the 1996 Federal law on National Cultural Autonomy, there is no national antidiscrimination law, meaning that the Roma lack some of the basic legal protections necessary to seek redress in the courts.[185] But given Russia's slow drift from the lofty democratic ideals in the early years of the postcommunist era, the tendency toward authoritarianism, and its continued isolation from the mainstream of European politics, it seems doubtful that there will be any dramatic changes in the near future for the life of the Roma living there.

Serbia and Montenegro

Prior to their split in 2006, Serbia and Montenegro had one of the region's largest Roma population, with estimates between 143,000 and 450,000, including Kosovo's population.[186] The Roma in Serbia and Montenegro have suffered a great deal from the social and economic upheavals caused by Slobodan Milosević's deadly adventures in Bosnia and Kosovo in the 1990s. Their problems were carefully laid out in a lengthy memorandum prepared by the UN Office of the High Commissioner for Human Rights (UNOHCHR) and the European Roma Rights Center in 2003. Their problems are complicated by the large-scale refugee problems caused by Serbia's conflicts in the former Yugoslavia.

Given the vicissitudes of politics in Serbia over the past few decades, one would expect the plight of the Roma there to be dreadful. And while one could certainly argue that point with some ease, Serbia's presence on the international stage has at least given the Roma hope of improved life in a country still trapped in something of a time warp, nationalistically speaking. But before that can happen, Serbian authorities will need to address the serious educational, economic, social, and legal problems faced by the Roma throughout the country.

Education, or lack thereof, is one of the core issues facing the Roma in Serbia today. Though statistics are hard to come by, studies in the 1980s indicate widespread illiteracy (34.8 percent) among the country's Roma, a shocking figure in light of 96 percent literacy for the country as a whole. According to a study by the Minority Rights Group International, there are over 200,000 Roma children in the public schools in Serbia and Montenegro, and they suffer from widespread discrimination and segregation in the public school system. Because many Roma children speak little Serbian at home, they quickly fall behind in the public schools, and are often forced into special schools. According to the UNOHCHR memorandum, "Romani children are reportedly particularly over-represented in classes for mildly mentally disabled children," when all they really lack are basic Serbian language skills. This, coupled with the verbal abuse and physical mistreatment they suffer at the hands of their classmates and teachers, discourages parents from sending their children to school. The fact that there are few Roma teachers in these schools or even assistants who might help Roma pupils in the classes makes matters worse.[187]

What is sad about all of this is that Roma parents want to send their children to school because they believe that this is the only way for them to improve their lives. Yet 30 percent of Roma children never attend primary school and almost 79 percent drop out before they complete their elementary education. Attendance rates are much lower for Roma females; 40 percent of Roma females never attend primary school and almost 90 percent drop out during this early stage of their education. Given all of this, it is little wonder that only 0.4 percent of Roma ever make it to university.

One of those who did make it to the university was Refika Mustafic, a Human Rights Education Coordinator for the European Roma Rights Center and founder of the Roma Education Center in Niš. Her peers and professors always considered her "strange, unusual" and presumed she would never graduate. After graduation, she miraculously got a job in a public school, though she was dismissed after the first year because parents "didn't want their children to be taught [the] Serbian language by some Gypsy." Her principal apologized for this decision, assuring Refika that he supported her, but would lose his job if he did not transfer her. Her next job was at the local "Roma school," where over half of the students were Romani. She was met with the same suspicion and distrust, even by her Roma pupils, who questioned her ability to teach them. The local school board sent a state inspector to observe her teaching the first day of class to determine if Rifika was knowledgeable enough to teach language and literature. She was often met with silence in the halls by her peers, who often complained about their Roma students, whom they thought were "dirty, stank, were messy and stupid." The faculty felt that their parents "were irresponsible, without interest, and also stinking and lacking in culture."[188]

Refika took these complaints to heart and committed herself to do everything possible to help and work with her Roma students. She spent all of her free time with them, and suggested extra classes to help them. She also thought that more had to be done to improve communication with their parents. Her principal told Refika that there were no extra rooms available for the supplementary classes even though the school was letting private groups use the school's gymnasium for money-making activities. He also told her that she could not contact the parents as a representative of the school. If she wanted to contact them as a private person, that was another matter. This environment, Refika, concluded, "creates children who did not believe in themselves, who believed they were not worth any attention and that they were stupid."[189]

The Roma and their children are also plagued by an atmosphere of violence, both in the public and private sector, that goes to the core of their lack of basic human and civil rights protections. Such violence is simply one aspect of the greater discrimination faced by Roma throughout Serbia and Montenegro. Though such violence, whether at the hands of police or private citizens such as skinheads, continues unabated, the Roma have been able to seek some redress through international bodies such as the United Nations Committee against Torture (UNCAT). On November 21, 2002, UNCAT found against the Montenegrin government in a 1995 case involving a massive race riot in Danilovgrad that resulted in the destruction of an entire Roma neighborhood. In 2003, the Montenegran government agreed to pay the 74 Roma victims 985,000 Euros as compensation for their losses.[190]

Unfortunately, this is only one instance of what seems to be a steady stream of indiscriminate violence against the Roma. In 1997, a group of skinheads in Belgrade brutally murdered Dušan Jovanovič. His case received international attention after the publication of a book, *They Killed His Eyes*, highlighted this crime. This is only one of many cases that drew the attention of the UNCAT. Another involved the arrest and torture of Danilo Dimitrijević by police in Novi Sad on suspicion of theft. Afterward, Mr. Dimitrijević filed a complaint with local authorities about his torture but received no response. In 2000, the Humanitarian Law Center and the European Roma Rights Center filed a complaint about Mr. Dimitrijević's case with UNCAT, which ruled in 2005 that Mr. Dimitrijević had indeed been the victim of torture. It also declared that Serbian and Montenegran authorities had failed to look promptly into his claim, which prevented him from seeking compensation for his mistreatment.[191]

Such violence is so widespread that it has drawn the attention of a number of other international organizations. In 2004, the World Organisation against Torture in Geneva published a detailed study of this problem, *State Violence in Serbia and Montenegro*, which focused not only on the Roma but also Serbian women and children. It blames much of this on the militant atmosphere in Serbia throughout the 1990s, particularly the crisis in Kosovo in 1998–1999. The subsequent political instability in Serbia and Montenegro has "slowed down the process of social reform and of international integration and, hence, the development of democratic institutions and mechanisms for the protection of human rights."[192] Until Serbia is politically stabilized, and begins to embrace basic human and civil rights reforms necessary to become part of the larger

European community of nations, we can expect such abuses against the Roma to continue.

Ukraine

Though Ukraine has a relatively large Roma population (over 100,000 out of 46.7 million), little was known about this understudied minority until recently. Almost a third of the country's Roma live in Transcarpathia (*Zakarpats'ka oblast'*) in the extreme western part of Ukraine, while the rest live in other oblasts in the southern and southeastern parts of the country. Most Roma live in appalling poverty. Zoltan Fedorovych Olakh, the Roma *Starosta* (leader) in the Roma *tabor* (settlement) in Mukachev, told ERRC investigators in 1997 that the Roma in his settlement were so poor that they

> are starving and they eat trash. When the Roma here die, there is no money for a coffin. We put them in sacks to bury them. Of course, absolutely anything can be arranged with money, but since we have no money, we have nothing.[193]

Matt Hagengruber, a Peace Corps volunteer, reported similar poverty in another Transcarpathian city, Uzhgorod, in an article in *The Christian Science Monitor* in 2005.

> In Uzhgorod, the Roma live hard lives, often completely off the books because they lack official documents and are wary of the government in general. They move often. Bands of kids spend their days in the center of town, begging and chasing after stray dogs.
>   I once saw a Roma kid, racing down the street with his friends, stop and check a trash bin. Inside, he found an empty yogurt cup, which he licked clean and threw back in the trash. It was a hot August day.
>   There are dozens of Roma camps in the area, rampant with contagious diseases. Illiteracy and drugs also abound.[194]

If one ever sought a laboratory to study the evils of the cycle of poverty, Ukraine might be the place to begin.

In 2003, the Chirikli Romani Women Charity Foundation and the International Renaissance Foundation, Roma of Ukraine Program, sponsored a conference in Kyiv (Kiev), "Roma Women: Double Discrimination." The conferees discussed statelessness and lack of residency permits (*Propiska*), *tabor* sanitation and housing problems, health care, and education. They were particularly upset about the latter issue and concluded that only about 2 percent of the Roma population could read and write.[195] While this figure seems a little extreme, the ERRC's 2006 CERD report noted that

> 69 percent of Roma [in Transcarpathia] could hardly read and another 68 percent had difficulties with writing and 59 percent did not know how to count properly and 25 percent could do neither of the three.[196]

Most of the problems are caused by government refusal to enroll Roma pupils in regular integrated schools and parental resistance to send their children to the inferior, segregated schools. Such schools lacked the most basic educational tools for teaching, sanitary facilities, and cafeterias. And if a Roma child was permitted to enroll in a regular integrated school, her or his parents were often afraid to send them there because of the abuse and discrimination they would face once enrolled. Another problem, at least according to Roma activist Zemfira Kondur, is that most Roma children have no access to preschool education. Part of the reason for this is lack of money or transportation and the fact that some Roma parents are not aware of the importance of preschool education in preparing their children for the elementary grades. Consequently, according to the Ukrainian Institute for Social Research, about 50 percent of Ukraine's Roma children do not attend school regularly.[197]

Yet most of the recent, detailed reports on the plight of the Roma in Ukraine deal primarily with the more blatant forms of discrimination such as public and police violence. In fact, the ERRC's 1997 study, *The Misery of Law*, dealt almost exclusively with police abuse and the unwillingness of Ukraine's judicial system to deal with these problems in Transcarpathia. In many ways, the abuse of the Roma is symptomatic of what Nina Karpachiva, the new Ukrainian Parliament Commissioner for Human Rights (Ombudsman), said in her 2000 report on human rights in Ukraine.

> Despite democratic legislation in the sphere of human rights available in Ukraine, under the conditions of social and economic crisis, decline of a general level of culture and moral in Ukraine, the efficient mechanisms to protect human rights are non-existent, which leads to massive and regular violations of human rights and freedoms, and sometimes makes their realization impossible. The situation is worsened due to poverty, which is a violation of human rights as well.[198]

The Czech-based Dženo Association, which is dedicated to furthering the well-being of Roma throughout Central and Eastern Europe, noted this widespread mistreatment in all facets of Roma life in its 2006 report on Ukraine. It stated that almost 80 percent of the Roma workforce had no full-time work, which explains in part the widespread malnutrition among the Roma. It added that only half of the Roma in Ukraine could afford to eat daily and that a third only ate a few times a week or had nothing to eat at all. This, and the terrible living conditions of most Roma, led to widespread medical and health problems. Between 10 and 40 percent of Ukraine's Roma suffer from tuberculosis.[199] Ukrainian officials principally blame the Roma for these problems, though there seems to be some hint of change after the Orange Revolution in 2005. But the desperate Roma need more than spirited gestures to avoid the human rights, health care, and educational crises they currently face in Ukraine.

.8.

CONCLUSION

The history of the Roma of Eastern Europe and Russia is a troubling story that centers around centuries of mistreatment towards this group. It is tempered only by the resiliency of the Rom themselves, and the few non-Roma who tried to ameliorate their plight. Since it is a little difficult to pinpoint when and how the Roma entered this part of Europe, it is equally hard to explain how a group that initially enjoyed a unique status as musicians and craftsmen came, in time, to be one of the most despised groups in Europe. Given the superstition and chaos of the late Middle Ages, the physical, linguistic, and cultural features that at one time made the Roma objects of interest as "Egyptians," came later to haunt them. The unsettling and frightening Turkish conquest of the Balkans, and the ongoing fear of Turkish incursions elsewhere intensified fear of outsiders, particularly if they were dark-skinned and non-Christian. While continuing to rely on Roma nomadic craftsmen for many basic metalworking and equine needs, early modern Eastern Europe kept these outsiders at a distance through the creation of an array of stereotypical myths about the Roma that became an integral part of the social fabric of the region. These images helped keep alive Roma nomadism, which arose from the unwillingness of villagers and officials to let them do more than live temporarily on the outskirts of local settlements. The nomadic life style, in turn, severely restricted economic opportunities for the Rom, and kept them deeply impoverished. Though it is important to understand that economic and social conditions varied from tribe to tribe and region to region, those Roma at the lowest rung of the social pecking order in Eastern Europe and Russia lived in conditions too gruesome and primitive to imagine. Unfortunately, their plight only served to fortify a growing body of prejudice that categorized all Romani as lazy, and untrustworthy thieves.

In some ways, such feelings said as much about the societies that created these images as it did about the Roma. One of the things not covered in this study was a comparative look at the plight of the peasants and serfs of Eastern Europe and Russia during the time of discussion. For many peasants, life was almost as hard as that of the Rom, and one suspects that part of the reason for reducing the Roma to something less than human somehow elevated the status of the backward, poor villager. Regardless, what emerged from centuries of growing distrust and suspicion of the Romani was a body of prejudice that often turned violent. The dehumanization of the Roma became an effective means of rationalizing societal behavior towards them.

Yet despite the general Eastern Europe and Russian dislike for the Roma, there was also a grudging admiration for many of their special talents and skills. Their value to the boyars of Moldavia and Wallachia helped pave the way for their enserfment, while others came to rely heavily upon their musical skills. While there is no question that Liszt and Bercovici went overboard in placing the heart and soul of Hungarian and Romanian culture at the feet of the Romani, there is no question that their talents in this area were immense and deeply influential. Sadly, even these unique contributions were viewed derisively by some in an effort continually to diminish the Roma and confirm their societal backwardness.

As Eastern Europe and Russia struggled with the new social, political, and economic challenges during the Enlightenment, some thought was given to the plight of the Roma. Given the strong spirit of nationalism that began to emerge throughout the region in the late 18th and early 19th centuries, any attempt to tackle the Romani question was coupled with the desire of central authority to assert greater control over the Roma, and to make them good Austrians, Hungarians, or Russians. Reformers saw nomadism as the core reason for Roma backwardness, and sought to restrict their movement throughout legislative and police means. There was no attempt to try to understand the nature of Rom nomadism, or to understand the culture that made it such an integral part of Roma life. While nomadism could certainly be understood in the context of centuries of East European and Russian mistreatment and ostracism towards the Roma, their nomadic culture had evolved far beyond the scope of a mere reactive institution. For many Romani, nomadism gave them a sense of freedom and superiority to the surrounding non-Roma world that has proven impossible to eradicate. The failure to understand the roots of this important Rom institution and its complexities has been one of the principle failures of reformers.

Efforts to force the Romani to give up their nomadic ways has also suffered from unimaginative attempts to force them to adopt sedentary practices in a rather hasty, superficial manner. There are striking similarities between efforts by Maria Theresa and the communist regimes of Eastern Europe after World War II. Each adopted insidious methods to force Rom settlement, including the kidnaping of children or forced sterilization of Roma women. Almost all efforts historically to force Rom sedentarization have included some educational experiments, though they have been applied with impatience. It is impossible to expect a group that has spent centuries on the periphery of society suddenly or comfortably to adapt to a completely new educational and social environment, particularly when this minority is ridden with poverty. Efforts educationally to transform the Roma communities of Eastern Europe and Russia have faltered because of the inability of respective governments to look first at the deep, complex problems of their respective Romani communities. Roma linguistic, attendance, or behavioral problems are linked directly to Roma poverty and its associated ills. While Rom educational efforts are absolutely necessary to begin the process of Romani integration, particularly in Eastern Europe, these experiments must first begin with programs designed to address Rom poverty.

This dilemma, in turn, is tied to a complex set of issues tied directly to centuries of social mistreatment and segregation. Low Rom salaries and limited employment opportunities have kept the Romani impoverished and unable to afford anything more than substandard housing. East Europeans, though, will point to numerous attempts to provide the Romani with scarce housing since World War II, and then note that the new Roma owners immediately turn these dwellings into slums. Unfortunately, as with education and labor, little attempt is ever made to understand why Romani do this. It is fruitless merely to mainstream a Roma child into a school with inadequate linguistic training or skills, or give an semi-nomadic Romani family new housing without some consideration to their traditional lifestyle or lack of knowledge of proper, modern house-keeping norms. In terms of salary and skilled employment opportunities, similar consideration must be given to lack of training and the deep prejudice in the workplace.

Another trap in exploring the history of the Roma in Russia and Eastern Europe is to dwell on the negatives without some view towards Romani accomplishments. Despite long periods of abuse, enslavement, and prejudicial treatment that at least during one era—the Holocaust—saw efforts completely to eradicate the Romani, the Roma have shown a remarkable socio-cultural resiliency. While admirers like Liszt, Tolstoi, Pushkin, and Bercovici perhaps waxed too romantic about the Romani, their culture, and their lifestyle, it would be wrong to fully dismiss these wistful idealizations. The musical and cultural presence of the Roma in the collective civilizations of Eastern Europe and Russia is a constant that has withstood the ebb and flow of numerous conquerors, governments, and dictators. Their special equine and metalworking skills are still valued, though less so than in a world once predominantly agricultural. And it is this respect for Roma culture that is the key to any effort to develop programs in Russia, Central or Eastern Europe, or elsewhere to draw the Roma more fully into society. The worst type of assimilation experiment is one that demands the full destruction of the Roma's traditional heritage and culture. Few ethnic groups in Eastern Europe or Russia have suffered as much from efforts to destroy their native culture and traditions. Lacking a traditional, protective homeland or outside, supportive community, Roma have to rely on their own local or tribal devices to preserve their core traditions and values. Romani have long demanded official minority status to acquire government support and funding to maintain and preserve their important cultural, linguistic, and historic traditions. Official unwillingness to grant this status underscored a lack of commitment to anything more than an effort to transform Roma into little Hungarians, Romanians, or Russians. What is so remarkable about this is that the region's communist rulers tended to be more nationalistic about such efforts than their predecessors.

Yet all of these experiments at Roma integration and sedentarization will have limited success until the Romani communities of Eastern Europe and Russia are fully embraced and welcomed into the fabric of each society. And this will not occur until officials and others address the deep, painful prejudice towards the Rom. Time and again throughout the history of Eastern Europe and Russia, the Romani have been convenient scapegoats for everything gone awry. Rooted in centuries of prejudice, the negative, public image of the Roma is an historical constant. Outlandish claims of excessive Romani criminality are timeless reminders that Eastern Europe and Russia have come far is some respects, yet changed little in others. Furthermore, the failure to celebrate the accomplishments of so many important Roma professionals and others clouds the history of a people who have played a unique, contributory role in the history of Russia and Eastern Europe. Until the Roma are seen in a more positive light, the deep suspicion that has plagued relationships between the Roma and the non-Rom will continue to cripple efforts to draw them more deeply into the fabric of East European and Russian society.

Unfortunately, this has not happened. Eastern Europe and Russia have gone through incredible upheavals and changes since the collapse of communism, and the Roma are more despised than ever, despite the fact that democracy seems to be maturing in the region and a number of countries have been allowed to join the European Union and NATO. Though pressure has been brought to bear on these countries or those on the eve of European inclusion to do more to address the plight of the Roma, most have responded with what appear to be fancy programs with little significant financial backing or public support.

One could argue that these countries should never have been allowed to join these "concert of Europe" organizations until they truly developed mature programs for dealing with Europe's most oppressed indigenous minority. Yet countries like the Czech Republic and Hungary, whose Roma policies are considerably lacking, have been allowed onboard united Europe's principal organizations. The thinking seems to go like this—it is easier to force member states to make significant changes than non-members. But the carrot of membership is powerful and once such countries are permitted to join the European Union or other European-wide organizations, it is hard to remove them. And despite terrible human rights reports to the contrary, Bulgaria and Romania are to become members of the European Union in 2007. While it would be wrong to suggest that united Europe has turned a blind eye to Roma problems in Eastern Europe and Russia, European leaders seem more concerned about drawing these former communist dictatorships into the fabric of greater Europe than addressing the plight of the Roma. Only time will tell if these short range gains bode well for the Roma.

But is there any light at the end of the tunnel for the Roma? Yes. But it seems to place a significant burden on the shoulders of the Roma and various human rights and NGOs to initiate significant change. If left to their own devices, local and national leaders in the region will do nothing more than give lip service to the "Roma question." What is missing in all of this is a strong public demand for change. Ideally, in democracies, the policies of national leaders should reflect the will of their constituents. But in Eastern Europe and Russia, with their immature democratic traditions, strong national leadership is often not enough to overcome local prejudices. Look, for example, at the case of Vaclav Havel in the Czech Republic.

Such an environment places a great deal of responsibility on the Roma to initiate their own changes from within. And one of the slight glimmers of hope to emerge in the two decades since the collapse of communism is a new, vibrant, small group of well educated, young Roma leaders who are committed to bringing about change in their communities. But their efforts are complicated by two struggles—one against the centuries-old, core societal prejudices that the Roma face throughout the region and the understandable suspicion that the Romani have of non-Roma. These young leaders, in league with various human rights organizations and NGOs, seem to offer the best hope for change in Eastern Europe and Russia.

Education and the courts, both national and international, offer the best hope for change. Educating new generations of Roma is an essential starting point for breaking the inhumane cycle of poverty that has haunted and crippled the Roma for centuries. This, coupled with aggressive use of domestic and international courts to force the region's new democracies to enforce the growing body of laws designed to protect Eastern Europe and Russia's minorities, are essential to improving the life of the Roma. But such changes take time, and during the interim, something needs to be done to address the basic, day-to-day poverty of the Roma. It took a dramatic civil rights movement led by Dr. Martin Luther King, Jr., really to draw attention to the poverty and discrimination faced by African Americans in the United States. Perhaps it is time for a similar movement to sweep Eastern Europe and Russia.

N·O·T·E·S

CHAPTER I

1. F. G. Ackerley, "Romano-Esi," *Journal of the Gypsy Lore Society*, Third Series, Vol. 27, Nos. 3–4 (July–October 1948), p. 158.
2. Elena Marushiakova, "Ethnic Identity Among Gypsy Groups in Bulgaria," *Journal of the Gypsy Lore Society*, Fifth Series, Vol. 2, No. 2 (August 1992), p. 110.
3. M. I. Isaev, *Sto tridtsat' ravnopravnykh* (Moskva: Izdatel'stvo "Nauka," 1970), p. 73; George C. Soulis, "The Gypsies in the Byzantine Empire and the Balkans in the Late Middle Ages," *Dumbarton Oaks Papers*, Vol. 15 (1961), pp. 144–145.
4. Angus Fraser, *The Gypsies* (Oxford: Blackwell, 1992), p. 46.
5. Soulis, "The Gypsies of the Byzantine Empire," pp. 146–147.
6. Mercia Macdermott, *A History of Bulgaria, 1393–1885* (New York: Frederick A. Praeger, 1962), pp. 18–20; B. Gilliat-Smith, "Endani 'Relatives,'" *Journal of the Gypsy Lore Society*, Third Series, Vol. 37, Nos. 3–4 (July–October 1958), p. 156.
7. Soulis, "The Gypsies in the Byzantine Empire," pp. 147–150; Kiril Kostov, "Virkhu proizkhoda na tsiganite i tekhniya ezik," *Bulgarski ezik*, Vol. VII, No. 4 (1957), p. 344; Bulgarians and Greeks were the most predominant groups enslaved by the Turks in the fourteenth century. Halil İnalcik, "Servile Labor in the Ottoman Empire," in Abraham Ascher, Tibor Halasi-Kun, and Béla K. Király, eds., *The Mutual Effects of the Islamic and Judeo-Christian Worlds: The East European Pattern* (Brooklyn, N. Y.: Brooklyn College Press, 1979), p. 38.
8. Jean-Pierre Liégéois, *Gypsies and Travellers* (Strasbourg: Council for Cultural Cooperation, 1987), p. 14.
9. Stanford Shaw, *History of the Ottoman Empire and Modern Turkey*, Volume I, *Empire of the Gazis: The Rise and Decline of the Ottoman Empire, 1280–1808* (Cambridge: Cambridge University Press, 1976), pp. 20–22; northern Bulgaria remained nominally independent until 1393, when the Turks took over Nikopol, the northern capital of Bulgaria's ruler, Tsar Ivan Shishman. Within three years, all other Bulgarian opposition leaders were overthrown, and Bulgaria passed completely into Turkish hands. Macdermott, *History of Bulgaria*, pp. 20–21.
10. Peter F. Sugar, *Southeastern Europe under Ottoman Rule, 1354–1804* (Seattle: University of Washington Press, 1977), p. 14.
11. Dr. S. S. Shashi, *Roma: The Gypsy World* (Dehli: Sundeep Prekashan, 1990), p. 21; Ian Hancock, "The Romani Diaspora," *The World and I* (March 1989), p. 615.
12. Soulis, "The Gypsies in the Byzantine Empire," pp. 160–161; Donald Kenrick and Grattan Puxon, *The Destiny of Europe's Gypsies* (New York: Basic Books, 1972), p. 15; Marushiakova, "Ethnic Identity Among Gypsy Groups in Bulgaria," p. 100; Fraser, *The Gypsies*, p. 57; Vesselin Popov, "The Gypsies and Traditional Bulgarian Culture," *Journal of the Gypsy Lore Society*, Fifth Series, Vol. 3, No. 1 (February 1993), pp. 21, 31 n. 1.
13. Sugar, *Southeastern Europe under Ottoman Rule*, pp. 77, 86.
14. Marushkiakova, "Ethnic Identity Among Gypsy Groups in Bulgaria," p. 113, n. 3; Helsinki Watch, *Destroying Ethnic Identity: The Gypsies of Bulgaria* (New York: Human Rights Watch, 1991), p. 7.

15. Shaw, *Empire of the Gazis*, p. 19; John Feffer, *Shock Waves: Eastern Europe after the Revolutions* (Boston: South End Press, 1992), p. 227; the only instances of forced conversions in the sixteenth century besides those already mentioned were of "Balkan slave boys recruited to staff the imperial household." Paul Coles, *The Ottoman Impact on Europe* (London: Harcourt, Brace, 1968), pp. 174–175. It was also during this period that mass conversions of Albanians and Montenegrins took place; "Petrulengo," "Report on the Gypsy Tribes of North-East Bulgaria," *Journal of the Gypsy Lore Society*, New Series, Vol. 9, No. 2 (1915–16), pp. 65, 69.

16. Ilhan Şahin, Feridun M. Emecen, and Yusuf Halaçolu, "Turkish Settlements in Rumelia (Bulgaria) in the 15th and 16th Centuries," in *The Turks of Bulgaria: The History, Culture and Political Fate of a Minority* ed. K. H. Karpat (Istanbul: The Isis Press, 1990), pp. 27–28; Machiel Kiel, "Urban Development in Bulgaria in the Turkish Period: The Place of Turkish Architecture in the Process," in Karpat, ed., *The Turks of Bulgaria*, pp. 87, 89, 91, 95, 106, 109. For more on the reliability of Turkish statistics, see Stephen P. Ladas, *The Exchange of Minorities: Bulgaria, Greece and Turkey* (New York: Macmillan, 1932), p. 9; One of the negative aspects of the Gypsy presence in cities such as Plovdiv and Sofia was prostitution, which Suleiman the Magnificent tried to regulate in 1530. Fraser, *The Gypsies*, p. 175.

17. Sugar, *Southeastern Europe under Ottoman Rule*, pp. 37, n.3, 46, 102-103; Shaw, *Empire of the Gazis*, pp. 19, 26.

18. George C. Soulis, "A Note on the Taxation of the Balkan Gypsies in the Seventeenth Century," *Journal of the Gypsy Lore Society*, Third Series, Vol. 38, Nos. 1–2 (January–April 1959), pp. 154–156.

19. R. J. Crampton, *A Short History of Modern Bulgaria* (Cambridge: Cambridge University Press, 1989), pp. 9–11; Macdermott, *History of Bulgaria*, pp. 43–45, 47–51, 105–107; Sugar, *Southeastern Europe under Ottoman Rule*, pp. 242–245.

20. Shaw, *Empire of the Gazis*, pp. 260–261, 264–265; Macdermott, *History of Bulgaria*, pp. 104–105.

21. Stanford J. Shaw and Ezel Kural Shaw, *History of the Ottoman Empire and Modern Turkey*, Volume II, *Reform, Revolution, and Republic: The Rise of Modern Turkey, 1808–1975* (Cambridge: Cambridge University Press, 1977), pp. 12–21, 59–61; Lord Kinross, *The Ottoman Centuries: The Rise and Fall of the Turkish Empire* (New York: Morrow, 1977), pp. 437–456; R. J. Crampton, "Bulgarian Society in the Early 19th Century," in *Balkan Society in the Age of Greek Independence*, ed. Richard Clogg (Totowa, NJ: Barnes & Noble Books, 1981), p. 157; Macdermott, *History of Bulgaria*, p. 116.

22. Shaw and Shaw, *Reform, Revolution, and Republic*, p. 40; Crampton, "Bulgarian Society," pp. 157–158.

23. Crampton, "Bulgarian Society," pp. 173–177, 180–181.

24. S. G. B. St. Clair and Charles A. Brophy, *A Residence in Bulgaria: Or Notes on the Resources and Administration of Turkey* (London: John Murray, 1869), pp. 7–8.

25. Ibid., p. 8.

26. Ibid., pp. 9–11; this word is also rendered as rayas or Reaya ("The Flock"). Originally, Rayahs were all of the "subjects of the sultan who were not members of his Ruling Class." In time, the term came to mean only the non-Muslim peoples of the Ottoman Empire. Shaw, *Empire of the Gazis*, p. 150; Sugar, *Southeastern Europe under Ottoman Rule*, p. 348; Kinross, *The Ottoman Centuries*, pp. 112–113.

27. Macdermott, *History of Bulgaria*, pp. 170–186; Shaw and Shaw, *Reform, Revolution, and Republic*, pp.. 160–161; Crampton, "Bulgarian Society," pp. 172–177, 184.

28. Macdermott, *History of Bulgaria*, pp. 144–157, 161–165, 167; Crampton, *Modern Bulgaria*, p. 17.

29. St. Clair and Brophy, *A Residence in Bulgaria*, p. 45; many Romanian Gypsies had fled Romania soon after their emancipation in 1864 because they feared "reenslave-

ment if the political system collapsed as it had in 1848." David M. Crowe, "The Gypsy Historical Experience in Romania," in *The Gypsies of Eastern Europe*, ed. David M. Crowe and John Kolsti (Armonk, NY: M.E. Sharpe, Inc., 1991), p. 67.

30. Macdermott, *History of Bulgaria*, pp. 170–186; Shaw and Shaw, *Reform, Revolution, and Republic*, pp. 160–162; Crampton, *Modern Bulgaria*, pp. 18–19.

31. Macdermott, *History of Bulgaria*, pp. 250, 254, 261.

32. W. E. Mosse, *Alexander II and the Modernization of Russia* (New York: Collier Books, 1970), pp. 130–131; Macdermott, *History of Bulgaria*, pp. 276, 283–289. Bulgarian, Western, and Turkish claims about the extent of the massacres after the April Uprising vary widely. Macdermott says that 30,000 Bulgarians were killed, while some British press reports claimed as many as 100,000 died at Turkish hands. Shaw places the number of Christian dead in Bulgaria at 4,000 but admits that far more Muslims died. Furthermore, there was "some massacre and countermassacre between Muslim and Christian villages." Shaw and Shaw, *Reform, Revolution, and Republic*, p. 162; for more on the role of the British press in the early stages of this crisis, see Ann Pottinger Saab, *Reluctant Icon: Gladstone, Bulgaria, and the Working Class, 1856–1878* (Cambridge, MA: Harvard University Press, 1991), pp. 82–90; Mihailo D. Stojanović, *The Great Powers and the Balkans, 1875–1878* (Cambridge: Cambridge University Press, 1968), pp. 130–132.

33. Bart McDowell, *Gypsies: Wanderers of the World* (Washington, DC: National Geographic Society, 1970), p. 119; B. H. Sumner, *Russia and the Balkans, 1870–1880* (Hamden, CT: Archon Books, 1962), pp. 337–338; R.W. Seton-Watson, *The Russian Empire, 1801–1917* (Oxford: Oxford University Press, 1967), pp. 453–456; Macdermott, *History of Bulgaria*, p. 296. The Turks suffered 10,000 casualties in August 1877 at Shipka Pass, at which there were several other important battles during the war. Shaw and Shaw, *Reform, Revolution and Republic*, pp. 184–186.

34. Stojanović, *Great Powers*, p. 232; Macdermott, *History of Bulgaria*, pp. 298–299; Shaw and Shaw, *Reform, Revolution and Republic*, p. 188.

35. Macdermott, *History of Bulgaria*, pp. 308–309; Stojanović, *Great Powers*, pp. 280–281; oddly enough, a peculiar Gypsy presence was felt at the Berlin talks. The British foreign secretary, the Marquis of Salisbury, later described Count Julius Andrassy, the Austro-Hungarian foreign minister, as looking "thinner and gypsyer" at the gathering. Sumner, *Russia and the Balkans*, pp. 507, 526–528; Shaw and Shaw, *Reform, Revolution and Republic*, pp. 188, 190–191; Crampton, *Modern Bulgaria*, pp. 19–20.

36. Crampton, *Modern Bulgaria*, pp. 21–31; Macdermott, *History of Bulgaria*, pp. 311–342 passim; Shaw and Shaw, *Reform, Revolution and Republic*, p. 208; Hans Rogger, *Russia in the Age of Modernisation and Revolution, 1881–1917* (London: Longman, 1983), pp. 169–171.

37. Fraser, *The Gypsies*, pp. 231, 235–236; Carol Silverman, "Bulgarian Gypsies: Adaptation in a Socialist Context," *Nomadic Peoples*, Nos. 21–22 (December 1986), p. 53.

38. Macdermott, *History of Bulgaria*, p. 321; Helsinki Watch, *Destroying Ethnic Identity* p. 24; Silverman, "Bulgarian Gypsies," p. 51.

39. R. J. Crampton, "The Turks in Bulgaria, 1878–1944," in K. H. Karpat, ed. *The Turks of Bulgaria* p. 52; Kenrick and Puxon, *Destiny of Europe's Gypsies*, p. 54.

40. R. J. Crampton, "The Turks in Bulgaria," p. 55; John Georgeoff, "Ethnic Minorities in the People's Republic of Bulgaria," in *The Politics of Ethnicity in Eastern Europe* ed. George Klein and Milan J. Reban (Boulder/New York: East European Monographs and Columbia University Press, 1981), pp. 71–73; Ministry of Foreign Affairs, *The Bulgarian Question and the Balkan States* (Sofia: State Printing Press, 1919), pp. 250–251, 260; Ministère des Affaires Étrangères et des Cultes, *La Vérité sur les accusations contre la Bulgarie* (Sofia: Imprimerie de L'état, 1919), p. 10; R. A. Scott Macfie, "Bulgarian Gypsies," *Journal of the Gypsy Lore Society*, Third Series, Vol. 3, No. 4

(1924), p. 189; Silverman, "Bulgarian Gypsies," p. 51; Reimer Gronemeyer and Georgia
A. Rakelmann, *Die Zigeuner: Reisende in Europa: Roma, Sinti, Manouches, Gitanos,
Gypsies, Kalderash, Vlach und Andere* (Köln: Dumont Buchverlag, 1988), p. 207.
41. Crampton, "The Turks in Bulgaria," pp. 72–79.
42. Crampton, "The Turks in Bulgaria," pp. 63–64, 70–71; Sumner, *Russia and the
Balkans*, p. 659; Ian Hancock, "The East European Roots of Romani Nationalism," in
Crowe and Kolsti, *Gypsies of Eastern Europe*, pp. 139–140.
43. Crampton, *Modern Bulgaria*, pp. 12, 24; Ministère des Affaires Étrangères et des
Cultes, *La Vérité sur les accusations contre la Bulgarie*, p. 10; Crampton, "The Turks
in Bulgaria," pp. 67–68.
44. Crampton, *Modern Bulgaria*, pp. 52–53; Shaw and Shaw, *Reform, Revolution, and
Republic*, pp. 266–267, 273–277; Crampton, "The Turks in Bulgaria," p. 63.
45. Barbara Jelavich, *History of the Balkans*; Volume II: *Twentieth Century* (Cambridge:
Cambridge University Press, 1988), pp. 96–100; Crampton, *Modern Bulgaria*, pp. 59–63.
46. Feffer, *Shock Waves*, p. 228; Shaw and Shaw, *Reform, Revolution, and Republic*, p. 296;
Stephen P. Ladas, *The Exchange of Minorities*, pp. 15, 20; Marin Pundeff, "Churches
and Religious Communities," in *Südosteuropa-Handbuch: Bulgarien*, ed. Klaus-
Detlev Grothusen, Band VI (Göttingen: Vandenhoeck & Ruprecht 1990), p. 562. In
1912, "the British and Foreign Bible Society published the Gospel of St. Luke in
Bulgarian Romani." B. Gilliat-Smith, Review of N. Scheitanow, "A Contribution to
the Dialect of the Sofia Gypsies," in *Journal of the Gypsy Lore Society*, Third Series,
Vol. 13, No. 3 (1934), p. 161; "Petrulengro," "Report on the Gypsy Tribes of North-
East Bulgaria," p. 31; Bernard Gilliat-Smith, "The Dialect of the Drindaris," *Journal
of the Gypsy Lore Society*, New Series, Vol. 7, No. 4 (1913–14), p. 260; Crampton,
Modern Bulgaria, p. 63.
47. Crampton, *Modern Bulgaria*, pp. 64–71.
48. Bilâl N. Şimşir, ed., *The Turks of Bulgaria in International Fora Documents*, Volume
I (Ankara: Turkish Historical Society Printing House, 1990), pp. 217–218; David M.
Crowe, *World War I and Europe in Crisis: 1914–1935* (Piscataway, NJ: Research and
Education Association, 1990), p. 46; C. A. Macartney and A. W. Palmer, *Independent
Eastern Europe* (London: Macmillan, Ltd., 1972), p. 132.
49. Crampton, "The Turks in Bulgaria," p. 70; Crampton, *Modern Bulgaria*, p. 91; G. P.
Genov, *Bulgaria and the Treaty of Neuilly* (Sofia: Hrist G. Danov & Co., 1935),
pp. 133–134.
50. Donald S. Kenrick, "The Gypsies of Bulgaria Before and After 10th of November,"
paper delivered at the 1991 Annual Meeting of the Gypsy Lore Society, pp. 2–3; Vasil
Marinov, "Nablyudeniya vurkhy bita na tsigani v Bulgariya," in *Izvestiya na etnograf-
skiya institut i muzei*, Kniga V (Sofiya: Isdatelstvo na Bulgarskata akademiya na
naukite, 1962), p. 267; Feffer, *Shock Waves*, p. 240; Helsinki Watch, *Destroying
Ethnic Identity*, p. 7; Raymond Pearson, *National Minorities in Eastern Europe,
1848–1945* (London: Macmillan, 1983), p. 175.
51. Crampton, *Modern Bulgaria*, pp. 98–99, 107–113; Helsinki Watch, *Destroying Ethnic
Identity*, p. 7.
52. Donald S. Kenrick, "Notes on the Gypsies in Bulgaria," *Journal of the Gypsy Lore
Society*, Third Series, Vol. 45, Nos. 3–4 (July–October 1966), p. 77; V. I. Kozlov,
"Changes in the Ethnic Composition of Rumania and Bulgaria," *Soviet Sociology*,
Vol. 3, No. 2 (Fall 1964), pp. 35–37; Dudley Kirk, *Europe's Population in the
Interwar Years* (Geneva: League of Nations, 1946), p. 228; Peter John Georgeoff and
David Crowe, "National Minorities in Bulgaria, 1919–1980," in *Eastern European
National Minorities, 1919–1980: A Handbook* ed. Stephen M. Horak, (Littleton, CO:
Libraries Unlimited, Inc., 1985), p. 281.
53. Frederick B. Chary, *The Bulgarian Jews and the Final Solution, 1940–1944*
(Pittsburgh: University of Pittsburgh Press, 1972), pp. 5–6, 9–10.

NOTES 303

54. Ibid., pp. 10–23; Gerhard L. Weinberg, *Germany and the Soviet Union, 1939–1941* (Leiden: E. J. Brill, 1972), pp. 99–100; Stephane Groueff, *Crown of Thorns: The Reign of King Boris III of Bulgaria, 1918–1943* (Lanham, MD: Madison Books, 1987), pp. 290–295.
55. Fred S. Pisky, "The People," in *Bulgaria* ed. L. A. D. Dellin (New York: Frederick A. Praeger, 1957), p. 76, estimates that Bulgaria acquired 8,000 Gypsies when it obtained southern Dobrudja, while V. I. Koslov, in his "Changes in the Ethnic Composition of Rumania and Bulgaria," p. 37, maintains that there were 12,000 Roma in the region at the time of its transfer; Kenrick and Puxon, *Destiny of Europe's Gypsies*, p. 119; Fraser, *The Gypsies*, p. 268; in October 1941, German officials "began a policy of executing Jewish and Gypsy men as a reprisal for acts of resistance against Yugoslavs." Chary, *The Bulgarian Jews*, pp. 120, n. 24, 195.
56. Chary, *The Bulgarian Jews*, pp. 35–41; Gabrielle Tyrnauer, *Gypsies and the Holocaust: A Bibliography and Introductory Essay*: (Montreal: Montreal Institute for Genocide Studies, 1991), p. xii; Sybil Milton, "The Context of the Holocaust," *German Studies Review*, Vol. 13, No. 2 (May 1990), pp. 270–271.
57. Chary, *The Bulgarian Jews*, p. 120, n. 24; Kenrick and Puxon *Destiny of Europe's Gypsies*, pp. 130–131; Marushiakova, "Ethnic Identity Among Gypsy Groups in Bulgaria," p. 105.
58. Georgeoff and Crowe, "National Minorities in Bulgaria," p. 283; Chary, *The Bulgarian Jews*, pp. 119–121; Hans-Joachim Hoppe, "Bulgarian Nationalities Policy in Occupied Thrace and Aegean Macedonia," *Nationalities Papers*, Vol. 14, Nos. 1–2 (Spring–Fall 1986), pp. 95–99.
59. Marushiakova, "Ethnic Identity Among Gypsies in Bulgaria," pp. 101–102; Joseph B. Schechtman, "The Gypsy Problem," *Midstream*, Vol. 12, No. 9 (November 1966), p. 57; Office of Strategic Services (Research and Analytical Branch), "Population Development of Bulgaria," in *Fifty Years Ago: Revolt Amid the Darkness* (Washington: United States Holocaust Memorial Museum, 1993), pp. 263–265; Chary, *The Bulgarian Jews*, pp. 142–143; Kenrick and Puxon, *The Destiny of Europe's Gypsies*, pp. 130–131.
60. Chary, *The Bulgarian Jews*, pp. 153–154.
61. Georgeoff and Crowe, "National Minorities in Bulgaria," p. 283; Helsinki Watch, *Destroying Ethnic Identity*, p. 8; Pearson, *National Minorities in Eastern Europe*, p. 200.
62. John D. Bell, *The Bulgarian Communist Party from Blagoev to Zhikov* (Stanford, CA: Hoover Institution Press, 1986), pp. 73–76; J. F. Brown, *Bulgaria under Communist Rule* (New York: Praeger Publishers, 1970), pp. 8–9.
63. Grothusen, *Bulgarien*, p. 482; Kenrick, "The Gypsies of Bulgaria," pp. 2–3; Bernard Gilliat-Smith, "The Gypsies in Bulgaria (1948)," *Jounral of the Gypsy Lore Society*, Third Series, Vol. 27, No.s 3–4 July–October 1948), p. 157; from 1944 to 1947, the Bulgarian Communist Party "launched minority recruitment campaigns" throughout the country. Torsten F. Baest, "Bulgaria's War at Home: The People's Republic and Its Turkish Minority (1944–1985), *Across Frontiers* (Winter 1985), p. 20.
64. Kenrick, "The Gypsies of Bulgaria," p. 3; "The Gypsies," *East Europe*, Vol. 14, No. 10 (October 1965), p. 24; Gilliat-Smith, "The Gypsies in Bulgaria," p. 157; Ackerley, "Romano-Esi," pp. 157–158.
65. The Minority Rights Group, *Minorities in the Balkans* (London: Minority Rights Group, 1989), p. 10.
66. Bell, *Bulgarian Communist Party*, p. 97; Helsinki Watch, *Destroying Ethnic Identity*, p. 35 n. 28; The Minority Rights Group, *Minorities in the Balkans*, p. 9.
67. Brown, *Bulgaria under Communist Rule*, pp. 13–16.
68. Bell, *Bulgarian Communist Party*, pp. 98–99; there were 51,500 Jews in Bulgaria in 1943, and 49,172 at war's end. Between 1948 and 1952, most were forced to emigrate, and by December 1951, only 7,676 remained in the country. Peter Meyer, "Bulgaria,"

in *The Jews in Soviet Satellites,* ed. Peter Meyer, Bernard D. Weinryb, Eugene Duschinsky, and Nicolas Sylvain (Syracuse, NY: Syracuse University Press, 1953), p. 575; Georgeoff and Crowe, "National Minorities in Bulgaria," p. 284; Grotthusen, *Bulgarien,* p. 558; Bilâl N. Şimşir, "The Turkish Minority in Bulgaria: History and Culture," in Karpat, *Turks of Bulgaria,* p. 167.

69. Joseph B. Schechtman, *Postwar Population Transfers in Europe, 1945–1955* (Philadelphia: University of Pennsylvania Press, 1962), pp. 350–351; Bell, *Bulgarian Communist Party,* p. 99; Kozlov, "Changes in the Ethnic Composition of Rumania and Bulgaria," p. 37. According to Bulgarian figures, only 15 Roma emigrated in 1950. Georgeoff, "Ethnic Minorities in the People's Republic of Bulgaria," p. 77.

70. Minority Rights Group, *World Directory of Minorities* (Chicago: St. James Press, 1989), p. 120; "The Gypsies," p. 24; Grothusen, *Bulgarien,* p. 482; Luan Troxel, "Bulgaria's Gypsies: Numerically Strong, Politically Weak," *RFE/RL Research Report,* Vol. 1, No. 1 (March 6, 1992), p. 59; see also Silverman, "Bulgarian Gypsies," p. 53, for more on the implementation of this policy in Sofia; there are indications that efforts to halt Roma nomadism were not completely successful. See Stowers Johnson's description of nomadic Gypsies in the decade after this policy was implemented in his *Gay Bulgaria* (London: Robert Hale, 1964), pp. 135–136.

71. Helsinki Watch, *Destroying Ethnic Identity,* p. 12; Kenrick, "Notes on the Gypsies in Bulgaria," p. 77; Kozlov, "Changes in the Ethnic Composition of Rumania and Bulgaria," p. 35; Ali Eminov, "There are No Turks in Bulgaria: Rewriting History by Administrative Fiat," in Karpat, *Turks of Bulgaria,* p. 212.

72. "Minorities in Eastern Europe," *East Europe,* Vol. 8, No. 3 (March 1959), p. 14; "Minorities in Eastern Europe-II," *East Europe,* Vol. 8, No. 4 (April 1959), p. 6; Helsinki Watch, *Destroying Ethnic Identity,* p. 8.

73. Helsinki Watch, *Destroying Ethnic Identity,* pp. 61–62.

74. Ibid., pp. 62–63.

75. Ibid., pp. 63–66.

76. Ibid., pp. 13, 20–21.

77. Eminov, "There are No Turks in Bulgaria," p. 206; Şimşir, "The Turkish Minority in Bulgaria," p. 168.

78. Helsinki Watch, *Destroying Ethnic Identity,* pp. 69–70.

79. Ibid., pp. 71–72.

80. Ibid., pp. 72–73.

81. Grattan Puxon, *Rom: Europe's Gypsies* (London: Minority Rights Group, 1973), p. 17; Grattan Puxon, *Rom: Europe's Gypsies* (London: Minority Rights Group, 1975), p. 13; Helsinki Watch, *Destroying Ethnic Identity,* pp. 14–15.

82. William B. Simons, ed., *The Constitutions of the Communist World* (Alphen aan den Rijn: Sijthoff & Noordhoff, 1980), pp. 45–47; Şimşir, *Turks of Bulgaria,* I, pp. 88–89.

83. Şimşir, *Turks of Bulgaria,* I, p. 89; Şimşir, *Turks of Bulgaria,* II, p. 56.

84. Silverman, "Bulgarian Gypsies," p. 58.

85. Puxon, *Rom* (1973), p. 17; Vladimir Pekelsky, "Die Zigeunerfrage in den ost-und südosteuropa staaten," *Osteuropa,* Heft 9 (September 1970), p. 616; Helsinki Watch, *Destroying Ethnic Identity,* pp. 30–32.

86. Helsinki Watch, *Destroying Ethnic Identity,* pp. 29–34; Şimşir, *Turks of Bulgaria,* II, pp. 88, 98, 103; recent statistics showed 71.3 percent literacy rate for Jews, 59.5 percent for Armenians, 54 percent for Bulgarians, 40 percent for Gagauz, 27.3 percent for Tatars, 11.9 percent for Turks, and 6.5 percent for Pomaks.

87. Hugh Poulton, *Minorities in the Balkans* (London: Minority Rights Group, 1989), pp. 12–19; Grattan Puxon, *Rom: Europe's Gypsies* (London: Minority Rights Group, 1987), p. 11; Helsinki Watch, *Destroying Ethnic Identity,* p. 49; Rada Nikolaev and G.S., "Forced Assimilation of the Turks," in *Soviet/East European Survey, 1984–1985* ed. Vojtech Mastny (Durham, NC: Duke University Press, 1986), pp. 187–192; Feffer,

Shock Waves, p. 230; Silverman, "Bulgarian Gypsies," p. 58; Carol Silverman, "Tsiganes musique et politiques en Bulgare," *Études Tsiganes,* No. 4 (1988), pp. 17, 19.

88. Puxon, *Rom* (1987), p. 11.
89. Troxel, "Bulgaria's Gypsies," p. 59.
90. Troxel, "Bulgaria's Gypsies," p. 59; *Times-Mirror* (Los Angeles), *The Pulse of Europe: A Survey of Political and Social Values and Attitudes* (Washington, DC: *Times-Mirror* Center for the People & the Press, 1991), p. 43.
91. Helsinki Watch, *Destroying Ethnic Identity,* pp. 42, 45–46.
92. Troxel, "Bulgaria's Gypsies," p. 59; "True, Tormented Pan-Europeans," *The Economist,* October 26, 1991, p. 66; Ivan Ilchev and Duncan Perry, "Bulgarian Ethnic Groups: Politics and Perceptions," *RFE/RL Research Report,* Vol. 2, No. 1 (19 March 1993), p. 39; Project on Ethnic Relations, *The Romanies in Central and Eastern Europe: Illusions and Reality* (Princeton, NJ: Project on Ethnic Relations, 1992), p. 8; Hugh Poulton, *The Balkans: Minorities and States in Conflict* (London: Minority Rights Group, 1991), p. 116; Helsinki Watch, "Bulgaria: Police Violence against Gypsies," *Helsinki Watch,* Vol. 5, No. 5 (April 2, 1993), pp. 1,7–8.
93. John D. Bell, "Bulgaria," in *Yearbook on International Communist Affairs, 1990* ed. Richard F. Staar and Margit N. Grigory (Stanford, CA: Hoover Institution Press, 1990), p. 316; Feffer, *Shock Waves,* p. 232.
94. Helsinki Watch, *Destroying Ethnic Identity,* p. 5; Troxel, "Bulgaria's Gypsies," p. 58; Bell, "Bulgaria," p. 308; after the December 1992 census, which showed a Rom population of 313,000, officials estimated that Bulgaria's Roma population was actually 550,000–600,000, while the nation as a whole had 8.47 million inhabitants. Ilchev and Perry, "Bulgarian Ethnic Groups," p. 35; Kjell Engelbrekt, "Bulgarian Gypsies Demand Ban on 'Fascist' Organizations," *RFE/RL Daily Report,* January 3, 1994, n.p.
95. Troxel, "Bulgaria's Gypsies," p. 60; Helsinki Watch, *Destroying Ethnic Identity,* pp. 43–44; Duncan M. Perry, "Bulgaria: A New Constitution and Free Elections," in *RFE/RL Research Report,* Vol. 1, No. 1 (January 3, 1992), p. 80; Manush Romanov discussed the Democratic Union of Gypsies—ROMA as well as its goals and policies in his "Chants rom de Bulgarie," in *Études Tsiganes,* No. 1 (1991), pp. 36–37; Romanov also headed the Cultural, Educational Organization for Roma in Bulgaria at the same time he took over ROMA. Poulton, *The Balkans,* pp. 116–117; André Liebich discusses the problem with Roma demographic estimates in "Minorities in Eastern Europe: Obstacles to a Reliable Count," *RFE/RL Research Report,* Vol. 1, No. 20 (May 15, 1992), pp. 38–39; the BSP admitted that some of its party activists had been somewhat overzealous in the countryside and had put "heavy pressure" on local villagers to vote for its candidates. The BSP won 47.15 percent of the vote and 211 seats in the new Grand National Assembly, the United Democratic Front 36.20 percent and 144 seats, the Agrarian National Union 8.03 percent and 16 seats, the PRF 6.03 percent and 23 seats, and other parties, 6 seats. Since any act by the new legislature required a two-thirds majority, the BSP found itself continually frustrated by the opposition. John D. Bell, "Bulgaria," in *1991 Yearbook on International Communist Affairs* ed. Richard F. Staar and Margit Grigory (Stanford, CA: Hoover Institution Press, 1991), pp. 263–264.
96. Troxel, "Bulgaria's Gypsies," p. 60; Feffer, *Shock Waves,* p. 238.
97. Troxel, "Bulgaria's Gypsies," pp. 60–61; Ilchev and Perry, "Bulgarian Ethnic Groups," p. 39, n. 10.
98. Engelbrekt, "Bulgarian Gypsies Demand Ban on 'Fascist' Organizations," n.p.

CHAPTER 2

1. Robert A. Kann and Zdeněk V. David, *The Peoples of the Eastern Hapsburg Lands, 1526–1918* (Seattle: University of Washington Press, 1984), p. 23; Norman Davieěs,

God's Playground: A History of Poland, Vol. I (New York: Columbia University Press, 1982), p. 138.

2. Robert H. Vickers, *History of Bohemia* (Chicago: Charles H. Şergel, 1894), p. 125; Will S. Monroe, *Bohemia and the Čechs* (Boston: L. C. Page and Company, 1910), p. 27.

3. Emília Horváthová, *Cigáni na Slovensku* (Gypsies in Slovakia) (Bratislava: Vytadel'stvo Slovenskej Akademie Vied, 1964), p. 33; S. E. Mann, "Emília Horváthová's *Cigáni po prichode do Europy* (The Passage of Gypsies throughout Europe)," *Journal of the Gypsy Lore Society*, Third Series, Vol. 43, Nos. 1–2 (January–April 1964), p. 69; László Makkai, "Transformation into a Western-type State, 1196–1301," in *A History of Hungary* ed. Peter F. Sugar, Péter Hanák, and Tibor Frank (Bloomington: Indiana University Press, 1990), pp. 26–27; György Balázs and Károly Szelényi, *The Magyars: The Birth of a European Nation* (Budapest: Corvina, 1989), pp. 62, 80–81, describes the battle of Muhi in some detail; David M. Crowe, "The *Liuli* (Gypsies) of Central Asia, *AACAR Bulletin*, Vol. 6, No. 1 (Spring 1993), p. 2.

4. Angus Fraser, *The Gypsies* (Oxford: Blackwell, 1992), p. 60; Makkai, "Transformation into a Western-type State," p. 30.

5. "Cigáni," *Enciklopedia Slovenska*, Vol. I (Bratislava: Veda, 1977–1982), p. 320; Pál Engel, "The Age of the Angevines, 1301–1382," in Sugar, Hanák, and Frank, eds., *History of Hungary*, pp. 48–49; Willy Guy, "Ways of Looking at Roms: The Case of Czechoslovakia," in *Gypsies, Tinkers and Other Travellers* ed. Farnham Rehfisch (New York: Academic Press, 1975), p. 208; Dr. Eva Davidova, "The Gypsies in Czechoslovakia. Part I: Main Characteristics and Brief Historical Development," translated by D.E. Guy, *Journal of the Gypsy Lore Society*, Third Series, Vol. 69, Nos. 3–4 (July–October 1970), p. 88.

6. Horváthová, *Cigáni na Slovensku*, p. 36.

7. Davidova, "Gypsies in Czechoslovakia," I, p. 88. Davidova places Roźmberk (Hungarian Rózyhegy) in Bohemia, though it is possible she meant Ruzomberok, which lies at the foot of the High Tatras in Slovakia.

8. Ibid.; Guy, "Ways of Looking at Roms," pp. 205–206; Fraser, *The Gypsies*, pp. 63, 75–76; Horváthová, *Cigáni na Slovensku*, pp. 37–38.

9. János Bak, "The Late Medieval Period, 1382–1526," in Sugar, Hanák, and Frank, eds. *History of Hungary*, p. 79; Ferenc Szakály, "The Early Ottoman Period, Including Royal Hungary, 1526–1606," in Sugar, Hanák, and Frank, eds., *History of Hungary*, p. 84; Fraser, *The Gypsies*, p. 111; R. W. Seton-Watson, *A History of the Czechs and Slovaks* (Hamden, CT: Archon Books, 1965), p. 86; Guy, "Ways of Looking at Roms," p. 208; Davidova, "Gypsies in Czechoslovakia," I, p. 89; Horváthová, *Cigáni na Slovensku*, pp. 99–100.

10. Guy, "Ways of Looking at Roms," p. 208; Davidova, "Gypsies in Czechoslovakia," I, p. 89; Kann and David, *Peoples of the Eastern Habsburg Lands*, pp. 72–73; Szakály, "The Early Ottoman Period," pp. 84–85.

11. Victor S. Mamatey, *Rise of the Habsburg Empire, 1526–1815* (New York: Holt, Rinehart and Winston, 1971), pp. 32–33; Stanford Shaw, *History of the Ottoman Empire and Modern Turkey*, Volume I; *Empire of the Gazis: The Rise and Decline of the Ottoman Empire, 1280–1808* (Cambridge: Cambridge University Press, 1976), pp. 101–102; Fraser, *The Gypsies*, p. 156.

12. Fraser, *The Gypsies*, p. 112; Joseph Kalvoda, "The Gypsies of Czechoslovakia," in *The Gypsies of Eastern Europe* ed. David M. Crowe and John Kolsti (Armonk, NY: M.E. Sharpe, Inc., 1991), p. 94; Davidova, "Gypsies in Czechoslovakia," I, p. 89; Guy, "Ways of Looking at Roms," p. 206; "Cigáni," *Enciklopedia Slovenska*, I, p. 321.

13. Guy, "Ways of Looking at Roms," p. 206; Davidova, "Gypsies in Czechoslovakia," I, pp. 89–90; Horváthová, *Cigáni na Slovensku*, pp. 58–59.

14. Mamatey, *Rise of the Habsburg Empire*, pp. 49–50; Seton-Watson, *History of the Czechs and Slovaks*, pp. 107–108.

15. Mamatey, *Rise of the Habsburg Empire*, pp. 51–53, 116; Seton-Watson, *History of the Czechs and Slovaks*, pp. 109–118; Monroe, *Bohemia and the Čechs*, pp. 109–114; Kann and David, *Peoples of the Eastern Habsburg Lands*, pp. 103–105.

16. Peter F. Sugar, "The Principality of Transylvania," in Sugar, Hanák, and Frank, eds., *History of Hungary*, pp. 132–134.

17. Kann and David, *Peoples of the Eastern Habsburg Lands*, p. 117; Guy, "Ways of Looking at Roms," pp. 206–209; Davidova, "Gypsies in Czechoslovakia," I, pp. 89–90; Horváthová, *Cigáni na Slovensku*, p. 60.

18. Mamatey, *Rise of the Habsburg Empire*, pp. 69–78.

19. O. Van Kappen, "A Prague Edict against Gypsies (1710)," *Journal of the Gypsy Lore Society*, Third Series, Vol. 42, Nos. 3–4 (July–October 1963), pp. 118–119; Horváthová, *Cigáni na Slovensku*, p. 60.

20. Kappen, "Prague Edict against the Gypsies," pp. 119–121; Guy, "Ways of Looking at Roms," p. 207; Horváthová, *Cigáni na Slovensku*, pp. 60–61; for more on the Gypsy warning signs in Germany, see Richard Andree, "Old Warning-Placards for Gypsies," *Journal of the Gypsy Lore Society*, New Series, Vol. 5, No. 3 (1911–12), pp. 202–204.

21. Horst Haselsteiner, "Cooperation and Confrontation between Rulers and the Noble Estates, 1711–1790," in Sugar, Hanák, and Frank, eds., *History of Hungary*, pp. 138–141; Mamatey, *Rise of the Habsburg Empire*, pp. 90–91, 94–95; Horváthová, *Cigáni na Slovensku*, pp. 113–114.

22. Seton-Watson, *History of the Czechs and Slovaks*, pp. 142–143; Mamatey, *Rise of the Habsburg Empire*, pp. 104–106; Horváthová, *Cigáni na Slovensku*, pp. 61, 113; Davidova, "Gypsies in Czechoslovakia," I, p. 90.

23. Fraser, *The Gypsies*, pp. 157–158, 195; Davidova, "Gypsies in Czechoslovakia," I, p. 90; Guy, "Ways of Looking at Roms," p. 209; Horváthová, *Cigáni na Slovensku*, p. 114.

24. David M. Crowe, "The Gypsies in Hungary," in Crowe and Kolsti, eds., *Gypsies of Eastern Europe*, p. 117; Fraser, *The Gypsies*, pp. 158–159; Davidova, "Gypsies in Czechoslovakia," I, p. 90; Horváthová, *Cigáni na Slovensku*, pp. 118–125; Guy, "Ways of Looking at Roms," p. 207.

25. Fraser, *The Gypsies*, pp. 193–194; Ian Hancock, *The Pariah Syndrome* (Ann Arbor, MI: Karoma Publishers, 1987), p. 51; Horváthová, *Cigáni na Slovensku*, pp. 135–136; Crowe, "Gypsies in Hungary," pp. 117–118.

26. Fraser, *The Gypsies*, p. 159; Horváthová, *Cigáni na Slovensku*, pp. 125–136; Guy, "Ways of Looking at Roms," p. 207.

27. Horváthová, *Cigáni na Slovensku*, p. 134; J. H. Schwicker, *Die Zigeuner in Ungarn und Siebenbürgen* (Wein und Teschen: Verlag von Karl Brochasta, 1883), p. 63.

28. Kann and David, *Peoples of the Eastern Habsburg Lands*, pp. 193, 247; Mamatey, *Rise of the Habsburg Empire*, p. 133.

29. Mamatey, *Rise of the Habsburg Empire*, pp. 131, 138; C. A. Macartney, *The Habsburg Empire, 1790–1918* (London: Weidenfeld and Nicolson, 1968), pp. 132–133.

30. Kann and David, *Peoples of the Eastern Habsburg Lands*, pp. 194–197, 248–249.

31. Seton-Watson, *History of the Czechs and Slovaks*, pp. 187–188; Éva Somogyi, "The Age of Neoabsolutism," in Sugar, Hanák, and Frank, eds. *History of Hungary*, pp. 236–238.

32. Macartney, *The Habsburg Empire*, p. 441; Horváthová, *Cigáni na Slovensku*, pp. 136–137, 142; "Cigáni," *Enciklopedia Slovenska*, p. 321; Czech now became one of the ten major languages in the empire and was promoted as the official language of the Slovaks. German remained the "language of the Monarchy" and, with Magyar and Czech, became the dominant languages of the Slovak regions of Hungary. Kann and David, *Peoples of the Eastern Habsburg Lands*, pp. 376–377; Macartney, *The Habsburg Empire*, pp. 441, 457.

33. Tibor Frank, "Hungary and the Dual Monarchy, 1867–1890," in Sugar, Hanák, and Frank, eds., *History of Hungary*, pp. 254–255; Kann and David, *Peoples of the*

Eastern Habsburg Lands, pp. 380–381; Anna I. Duirchova, "Glimpse of the Rom: Excursions in Slovakia," *Journal of the Gypsy Lore Society,* Third Series, Vol. 50, Nos. 1–2 (January–April 1971), p. 35.

34. Schwicker, *Die Zigeuner in Ungarn und Siebenbürgen,* pp. 76–80; Horváthová, *Cigáni na Slovensku,* pp. 61–64, 137–138, 148; Guy, "Ways of Looking at Roms," p. 207.
35. Horváthová, *Cigáni na Slovensku,* pp. 138–142.
36. By 1910, 61.8 percent of the population of Slovakia worked the land, while 20.3 percent were involved in industry and trade. Figures for the Czech lands were 40.0 and 34.2 percent respectively. Slovak "per capita industrial production, and percentrage population employed in indusry represented respectively about one-half and one-third of the European average." Kann and David, *Peoples of the Eastern Habsburg Lands,* p. 389.
37. Davidova, "Gypsies in Czechoslovakia," I, p. 91.
38. Fraser, *The Gypsies,* pp. 252–253.
39. Seton-Watson, *History of the Czechs and Slovaks,* pp. 187–288; regional deaths within the Austro-Hungarian Empire showed 26.7 percent of these deaths of those from Moravian-Slovak areas, 23.7 percent from purely Slovak areas, and 22.5 percent from "Purely Czech" regions. Macartney, *The Habsburg Empire,* pp. 812–813 n. 2; Austria–Hungary counted 1.2 million to 1.25 million dead and 5.77 million to 5.82 million wounded during World War I. David Crowe, *World War I and Europe in Crisis, 1914–1935* (Piscataway, NJ: Research and Education Association, 1990), p. 40; Géza Jeszensky, "Hungary through World War I and the End of the Dual Monarchy," in Sugar, Hanák, and Frank, eds., *History of Hungary,* p. 292; Barbara Jelavich, *The Habsburg Empire in European Affairs, 1814–1918* (Chicago: Rand McNally, 1969), p. 168.
40. Horváthová, *Cigáni na Slovensku,* pp. 147–148.
41. Hans Kohn, *The Habsburg Empire, 1804–1918* (New York: Van Nostrand Reinhold Company, 1961), p. 100.
42. Kann and David, *Peoples of the Eastern Habsburg Lands,* pp. 323–325, 391–392; Victor S. Mamatey, "The Establishment of the Republic," in Victor S. Mamatey and Radomír Luža, eds., *A History of the Czechoslovak Republic, 1918–1948* (Princeton, NJ: Princeton University Press, 1973), p. 26.
43. Vaclav L. Beneš, "Czechoslovak Democracy and Its Problems, 1918–1920," in Mamatey and Luža, *History of the Czechoslovak Republic,* pp. 46, 49; Guy, "Ways of Looking at Roms," p. 211.
44. Malbone W. Graham, Jr., *New Governments of Central Europe* (New York: Henry Holt, 1926), pp. 295–296; Beneš, "Czechoslovak Democracy and Its Problems," p. 96; Milena Hübschmannová, "Co je tzv. [tak zvana] cikánská otázka?" (What is the So-called Gypsy Problem?), *Sociologick y časopis* (Sociologial Journal), No. 2 (1970), p. 112.
45. Vladimir Srb, "Cigáni v Československu (Gypsies in Czechoslovakia)," *Demografié,* Vol. 11, No. 3 (1969), p. 194; Vladimir Srb and J. Job, "Nekteré demografické, ekonomické a kulturné charakteristiky romskéno obyvatelstva v ČSSR 1970 (Some Demographic, Economic, and Cultural Characteristics of the Romany Population in the CSSR in 1970)," *Demografié,* Vol. 16, No. 2 (1974), p. 179; Horváthová, *Cigáni na Slovensku,* pp. 156–157, 160–161. Horváthová says that there were 28,593 Rom in the 1931 census [1930], with 26,956 in Slovakia; "Schwierigkeiten mit den Zigeunern in der Tschechoslowakei," *Osteuropa,* Vol. 11, No. 6 (June 1971), p. A123; Davidova, "Gypsies in Czechoslovakia," I, p. 94.
46. Beneš, "Czechoslovak Democracy and Its Problems," p. 40. Beneš calls the December 1, 1930, census the 1931 census.
47. Davidova, "Gypsies in Czechoslovakia," I, pp. 92–93; Guy, "Ways of Looking at Roms," p. 211; Jiří Lípa, "The Fate of Gypsies in Czechoslovakia under Nazi

Domination," in *A Mosaic of Victims: Non–Jews Persecuted and Murdered by the Nazis*, ed. Michael Berenbaum, (New York: New York University Press, 1990), pp. 208–209. (this one-dimensional article is based exclusively on Ctibor Nečas's *Nad osudem českých a slovenských Cikánů ův letech 1939–1945* [The Fate of the Czech and Slovak Gypsies, 1939–1945] [Brno: Univerzita J.E. Purkyne, 1981]); Horváthová, *Cigáni na Slovensku*, pp. 161–163.

48. Guy, "Ways of Looking at Roms," pp. 211–212; Davidova, "Gypsies in Czechoslovakia," I, pp. 92–93.
49. Davidova, "Gypsies in Czechoslovakia," pp. 93–94; Guy, "Ways of Looking at Roms," p. 212; Horváthová, *Cigáni na Slovensku*, pp. 165–166, 168.
50. Victor S. Mamatey, "Development of Czechoslovak Democracy," in Mamatey and Luža, *History of the Czechoslovak Republic*, p. 143.
51. "In a Gypsy School," translated by Stuart E. Mann, *Journal of the Gypsy Lore Society*, Third Series, Vol. 13, No. 3 (1934), pp. 117–118; Horváthová, *Cigáni na Slovensku*, p. 168; Užhorod was occupied by the Soviet Union at the end of World War II and made part of Ukraine in 1945. It is now the city of Užhgorod, Ukraine; Josef Kalvoda and David Crowe, "National Minorities in Czechoslovakia, 1919–1980," in *Eastern European National Minorities, 1919–1980: A Handbook*, ed. Stephen M. Horak (Littleton, CO: Libraries Unlimited, Inc., 1985), p. 123.
52. "In a Gypsy School," pp. 118–119.
53. Horváthová, *Cigáni na Slovensku*, p. 168.
54. Czechoslovakia also lost the small but important region of Tešin (Polish Trans-Olza) to Poland on October 2, 1938. Only 35 percent of the population in Tešin was Polish. Theodor Prochazka, "The Second Republic, 1938–1939," in Mamatey and Luža, *History of the Czechoslovak Republic*, pp. 258–261; Anna M. Cienciala, *Poland and the Western Powers, 1938–1939* (London: Routledge & Kegan Paul, 1968), pp. 142–143.
55. Kalvoda and Crowe, "National Minorities in Czechoslovakia," pp. 122–123; see also David M. Crowe, *The Baltic States and the Great Powers: Foreign Relations, 1938–1940* (Boulder, CO: Westview Press, 1993), pp. 50–51, for details about the move into Czechoslovakia and its relationship to other Nazi schemes at the time; Prochazka, "The Second Republic," pp. 261, 268–269; Jörg K. Hoensch, "The Slovak Republic, 1939–1945," in Mamatey and Luža, *History of the Czechoslovak Republic*, pp. 275–276.
56. Nečas, *Nad osudem*, pp. 24, 28, 71; Donald Kenrick and Grattan Puxon, *The Destiny of Europe's Gypsies* (New York: Basic Books, 1972), pp. 135, 183–184; Guy, "Ways of Looking at Roms," pp. 212–213; David J. Kostelancik, "The Gypsies of Czechoslovakia: Political and Ideological Considerations in the Development of Policy," *Studies in Comparative Communism*, Vol. 22, No. 4 (Winter 1989), p. 309; Horváthová, *Cigáni na Slovensku*, p. 170.
57. Lípa, "Fate of Gypsies in Czechoslovakia," pp. 212–213; Kenrick and Puxon, *Destiny of Europe's Gypsies*, p. 131; the shipment of Czech Rom to Léty took place evenly over the 16 month period in question, while shipments to Hodonín rose dramatically in the spring of 1941. Nečas, *Nad osudem*, p. 31.
58. Kenrick and Puxon, *Destiny of Europe's Gypsies*, pp. 131–132; Nečas, *Nad osudem*, p. 32, says the date for this decree was March 9, 1942; Leni Yahil, *The Holocaust: The Fate of European Jewry* (New York: Oxford University Press, 1987), pp. 299–300; Gotthold Rhode and Johannes Gutenberg, "The Protectorate of Bohemia and Moravia, 1939–1945," in Mamatey and Luža, *History of the Czechoslovak Republic*, p. 320; Heydrich replaced Neurath on September 27, 1941, because Hitler felt the former chancellor had been too lenient toward the Jews and others. Heydrich was assassinated by agents of the London-based Czech government-in-exile in Prague on May 27, 1942. Yahil, *The Holocaust*, p. 297; Edourd Calic, *Reinhard Heydrich* (New York: Military Heritage Press, 1985), pp. 253–254.

59. Kenrick and Puxon, *Destiny of Europe's Gypsies*, p. 133; Lípa, "Fate of Gypsies in Czechoslovakia," pp. 213–214; there were three separate camps in the Auschwitz (Oświęcim) area. The first was known to the SS as Auschwitz I, while the camp in nearby Birkenau Woods was known as Auschwitz II—Birkenau. A third camp, Auschwitz III, was an industrial center. Birkenau was the site of the extermination camp. Yahil, *The Holocaust*, pp. 364–365; Rudolf Höss, *Death Dealer: The Memoirs of the SS Kommandant at Auschwitz*, ed. Steven Paskuly, translated by Andrew Pollinger (Buffalo, NY: Prometheus Books, 1992), p. 34.

60. Benno Müller-Hill, *Murderous Science: Elimination by Scientific Selection of Jews, Gypsies, and Others, Germany, 1933–1945*, translated by George R. Fraser (Oxford: Oxford University Press, 1988), p. 17.

61. Fraser, *The Gypsies*, p. 265; Franciszek Piper, *Auschwitz: How Many Perished Jews, Poles, Gypsies* (Krakow: Poligrafia ITS, 1991), p. 51; Lípa, "Fate of Gypsies in Czechoslovakia," p. 214; Nečas, *Nad osudem*, pp. 62–63; Appendix II in Höss's memoirs states that 21,667 Gypsies had been shipped to Birkenau from February 26, 1943 to July 21, 1944. Of this number, 2,991 were sent to other camps, while "over 15,000 had died in Birkenau by August 1, 1944." Höss, *Death Dealer*, pp. 362–363.

62. Höss, *Death Dealer*, pp. 136–138; Kazimierz Smoleń, *Auschwitz 1940–1945* (Oświęcimiu: Państwowe Muzeum w Oświęcimiu, 1969), pp. 21–22; Fraser, *The Gypsies*, p. 266.

63. Kenrick and Puxon, *Destiny of Europe's Gypsies*, pp. 135, 183; Fraser, *The Gypsies*, p. 267; Horváthová, *Cigáni na Slovensku*, p. 170; Kostelancik, "Gypsies of Czechoslovakia," p. 309.

64. Kenrick and Puxon, *Destiny of Europe's Gypsies*, pp. 134–135; the transport of March 11, 1943, held 642 Rom. Nečas, *Nad osudem*, p. 63; Dr. Josef Mengele performed ghastly medical experiments on inmates at the Auschwitz complex. Shmuel Krakowski, "Mengele, Josef," in *Encyclopedia of the Holocaust*, Vol. 3, ed. Israel Gutman, (New York: Macmillan, 1990), pp. 971–972. Elisabeth Koch is possibly a reference to Ilse Koch, the wife of Buchenwald commandant Karl Otto Koch, who gained deadly notoriety as the "witch" or "bitch" of Buchenwald because of her "extreme cruelty to prisoners," her nymphomania, and human skin collection. Ilse Koch was never at Auschwitz. Shmuel Spector, "Koch, Karl Otto," in Gutman, ed., *Encyclopedia of the Holocaust*, Vol. 2, pp. 809–810.

65. Hoensch, "The Slovak Republic, 1939–1945," pp. 278–279, 284–286; Lípa, "Fate of Gypsies in Czechoslovakia," pp. 209–210; Nečas, *Nad osudem*, p. 70.

66. Lípa, "Fate of Gypsies in Czechoslovakia," p. 210; Gypsy and Jewish service regulations were included in legislation of January 18, 1940, and February 29, 1940. Nečas, *Nad osudem*, pp. 82–129, devotes a great deal of time to the little-known history of the Gypsy labor units (*pracovni utvary*) from 1941 to 1944. He provides detailed Gypsy inmate statistics for the camps at Bystré nad Topl'ou, Dubnica nad Váhom, Ilava, and Revuca; Kenrick and Puxon, *Destiny of Europe's Gypsies*, p. 136.

67. Lípa, "Fate of Gypsies in Czechoslovakia," p. 211; Nečas, *Nad osudem*, pp. 74–75, 130.

68. Kenrick and Puxon, *Destiny of Europe's Gypsies*, p. 136; Horváthová, *Cigáni na Slovensku*, p. 171.

69. Kenrick and Puxon, *Destiny of Europe's Gypsies*, p. 137; Horváthová, *Cigáni na Slovensku*, p. 171; the train regulations were issued on June 13, 1944, while the other mandates appeared on June 19–21, 1944. Nečas, *Nad osudem*, pp. 130–132.

70. Kenrick and Puxon, *Destiny of Europe's Gypsies*, pp. 137–138; Hoensch, "The Slovak Republic, 1939–1945" pp. 293–295; Anna Josko, "The Slovak Resistance Movement," in Mamatey and Luža, *History of the Czechoslovak Republic*, pp. 375–380, 382–383.

71. Kenrick and Puxon, *Destiny of Europe's Gypsies*, pp. 137–138; authorities later found a mass grave at Kremniče, which was occupied by the Germans from November 5,

1944, to January 12, 1945. It contained 3,723 bodies, some of them Gypsies. Nečas, *Nad osudem*, pp. 138–141.

72. Lípa, "Fate of Gypsies in Czechoslovakia," pp. 211–213; Nečas, *Nad osudem*, pp. 111–112, 134–137; Kenrick and Puxon, *Destiny of Europe's Gypsies*, p. 138; Horváthová, *Cigáni na Slovensku*, p. 173 n. 34; Kostelancik, "The Gypsies of Czechoslovakia," p. 309. The Gypsies were not Slovakia's only victims after the Slovak National Insurrection. Estimates are that from August 1944 until April 1945 "7,500 soldiers and 2,500 partisans were killed and 3,723 civilians were murdered and buried in mass graves; 900 were burned in lime kilns; 30,000 people were deported to German concentration camps; 60 communities were completely destroyed by fires and 142 were partially wiped out"; Josko, "Slovak Resistance Movement," p. 383.

73. Radomir Luža, "Czechoslovakia between Democracy and Communism, 1945–1948," in Mamatey and Luža, *History of the Czechoslovak Republic*, pp. 390–398; Radimor Luža, *The Transfer of the Sudeten Germans: A Study of Czech-German Relations, 1933–1962* (New York: New York University Press, 1964), pp. 286–287. Czech officials shipped 1,334,856 Germans to the American Zone in Germany during this period and 636,482 to the Soviet Zone. Another 30,000 Germans left Czechoslovakia over the next two years.

74. Kostelancik, "The Gypsies of Czechoslovakia," pp. 309–310; Guy, "Ways of Looking at Roms," p. 213; Tomáš Grulich and Tomáš Haišman, "Institucionální zájem o cikánské obyvatelstvo v Československu v letech 1945–1958 (Institutional Interest in the Solution of the Gypsy Question in Czechoslovakia, 1945–1958)," *Česky Lid*, Vol. 73, No. 2 (1986), p. 73.

75. Kostelancik, "The Gypsies of Czechoslovakia," pp. 310–311; Vladimir Srb, "Cigáni v Československu," p. 194; Zdenek Suda, *The Czechoslovak Socialist Republic* (Baltimore, MD: The Johns Hopkins University Press, 1969), pp. 32–36; Luža, "Czechoslovakia between Democracy and Communism," pp. 412–415.

76. Kostelancik, "The Gypsies of Czechoslovakia," pp. 310–311; Grulich and Haišman, "Institucionální zájem o cikánske," p. 74.

77. Kostelancik, "The Gypsies of Czechoslovakia," pp. 311, 320; Kalvoda, "Gypsies of Czechoslovakia," p. 93.

78. Otto Ulč, "Communist National Minority Policy: The Case of the Gypsies in Czechoslovakia," *Soviet Studies*, Vol. 20, No. 4 (April 1969), pp. 422–424; "Minorities in Eastern Europe," *East Europe*, Vol. 8, No. 3 (March 1959), pp. 13–14.

79. "Minorities in Eastern Europe," p. 14; Kostelancik, "The Gypsies of Czechoslovakia," p. 311, improperly places the date for the passage of Law No. 74 as November 17, 1958; Grulich and Haišman, "Institucionální zájem o cikánske," pp. 77–78; Guy, "Ways of Looking at Roms," pp. 214–215. Guy estimates the number of "registered 'nomads'" at 20,000–27,000; Ulč, "Communist National Minority Policy," pp. 424–426, says officials estimated that the semi–nomadic Rom were the largest group among the Gypsies.

80. Kostelancik, "The Gypsies of Czechoslovakia," p. 426; Kalvoda, "Gypsies of Czechoslovakia," pp. 98–99.

81. Kostelancik, "The Gypsies of Czechoslovakia," pp. 312–313; Ulč, "Communist National Minority Policy," pp. 430–431. Of the 56,000 Rom in eastern Slovakia, only 2.2 percent had an adequate water supply; Guy, "Ways of Looking at Roms," pp. 219–222.

82. Ulč, "Communist National Minority Policy," pp. 432–433; Kostelancik, "The Gypsies of Czechoslovakia," pp. 312–314; Guy, "Ways of Looking at Roms," pp. 219–220; Hübschmannová, "Co je zv. cikánská otázka?" p. 115 n.19.

83. Otto Ulč, "Czechoslovakia," in *Communism in Eastern Europe*, Second Edition, ed. Teresa Rakowska-Harmstone (Bloomington: Indiana University Press, 1984), pp. 121–123; William Shawcross, *Dubcek* (New York: Touchstone Books/Simon & Schuster, Inc., 1990), pp. 114–119.

84. Srb, "Cigáni v Československu," p. 194; Kostelancik, "The Gypsies of Czechoslovakia," pp. 317–318; Dr. Eva Davidova, "The Gypsies in Czechoslovakia, Part II: Post-War Developments," *Journal of the Gypsy Lore Society,* Third Series, Vol. 1, Nos. 1–2 (January–April 1971), pp. 53–54; Guy, "Ways of Looking at Roms," pp. 220–221, 223, n. 44; Grattan Puxon, "Gypsies: Blacks of Eastern Europe," *The Nation,* April 17, 1976, pp. 461–462; Hübschmannová, "Co je tak zv. cikánská otázka," pp. 105, 112 n. 16, 113–114, 116 n. 23, 117–118; Kalvoda, "Gypsies of Czechoslovakia," pp. 101–103; Otto Ulč, "Gypsies in Czechoslovakia: A Case of Unfinished Integration," *Eastern European Politics and Societies,* Vol. 2, No. 2 (Spring 1988), pp. 310–312.

85. Vladimir Srb, "Demograficky profil československych Romu (Demographic Profile of the Czechoslovakian Rom)," *Česky Lid,* Vol. 72 (1985), p. 139; Vladimir Srb, "K integraci cikánskeho obyvatelstva v ČSSR (Integration of the Gypsy Population in Czechoslovakia)," *Demografié,* Vol. 21, No. 4 (1979), p. 323; Srb and Job, "Nekteré demografické," p. 173; Kostelancik, "The Gypsies of Czechoslovakia," p. 106; Paul S. Shoup, *The East European and Soviet Data Handbook* (New York: Columbia University Press, 1981), pp. 42, 48; Chris Cook and John Stevenson, *The Longman Handbook of Modern European History, 1763–1985* (London: Longman, 1987), pp. 216, 218.

86. Rachael Tritt, Jeri Laber, and Lois Whitman, *Struggling for Ethnic Identity: Czechoslovakia's Endangered Gypsies* (New York: Human Rights Watch, 1992), pp. 19, 139–144.

87. Ibid., pp. 20, 24, 26–27; Ulč, "Gypsies in Czechoslovakia," pp. 314–315.

88. Srb, "Demograficky profil československych Romu," pp. 139–140. There were 88,507 Gypsies in the Czech Republic in 1980 and 199,853 in Slovakia; Ulč, "Gypsies in Czechoslovakia," pp. 315–316; Kalvoda, "Gypsies of Czechoslovakia," pp. 108–109.

89. Kostelancik, "The Gypsies of Czechoslovakia," pp. 313–315. In 1980, 59 percent of the Gypsies in Slovakia lived in the lowest classification for housing, Class IV.

90. Kindergarten attendance rates in eastern Slovakia, where 53 percent of Slovakia's Rom lived in 1980, rose from 10 percent to 66 percent between 1970 and 1980. Ulč, "Gypsies in Czechoslovakia," pp. 319–320.

91. Kostelancik, "The Gypsies of Czechoslovakia," pp. 313–315; Ulč, "Gypsies in Czechoslovakia," pp. 322–323.

92. Ulč, "Gypsies in Czechoslovakia," pp. 322 n.36, 326.

93. Ibid., pp. 323–328.

94. Kalvoda, "Gypsies in Czechoslovakia," p. 106.

95. J. F. Brown, *Surge to Freedom: The End of Communist Rule in Eastern Europe* (Durham, NC: Duke University Press, 1991), pp. 150, 152, 164, 170; Tony R. Judt, "Metamorphosis: The Democratic Revolution in Czechoslovakia," in *Eastern Europe in Revolution,* ed. Ivo Banac (Ithaca, NY: Cornell University Press, 1992), pp. 96–100; Bernard Wheaton and Zdeněk Kavan, *The Velvet Revolution; Czechoslovakia, 1988–1991* (Boulder, CO: Westview Press, 1992), pp. 39–47. Ironically, the large crowd of students had gathered to commemorate similar brutality toward one of their own, Jan Opletal, fifty years earlier at the hands of the Nazis; Zdeněk Suda, "Czechoslovakia," in *Yearbook on International Communist Affairs; 1990,* ed. Richard F. Staar and Margit N. Grigory (Stanford: Hoover Institution Press, 1990), p. 327; Theodore Draper, "A New History of the Velvet Revolution," *The New York Review of Books,* January 14, 1993, pp. 14–18.

96. Otto Ulč, "Integration of the Gypsies in Czechoslovakia," *Ethnic Groups,* Vol. 9, No. 2 (1991), pp. 112–113; in 1986, Ščuka produced the "musical drama *Amaro Drom* (Our Road) only the second play in Romanes ever to be staged in Czechoslovakia." Grattan Puxon, *Roma: Europe's Gypsies* (London: Minority Rights Group, 1987), p. 11.

97. Radio Free Europe/Radio Liberty, "Ethnic Minorities and Foreigners," *Radio Free Europe Research,* Vol. 14, No. 39 (September 22, 1989), pp. 33, 36–37; Ulč,

"Integration of the Gypsies in Czechoslovakia," pp. 113–114; Czechoslovakia's population was 15,658,079, in July 1989 and 15,683,234 a year later, an increase of 25,155. Suda, "Czechoslovakia," p. 319, and Carol Skalnik Leff, "Czechoslovakia," in *1991 Yearbook on International Communist Affairs*, ed. Richard F. Staar and Margit N. Grigory (Stanford, CA: Hoover Institution Press, 1991), p. 269.

98. Jan Orbman, "Crime Rate Among the Young," *Radio Free Europe Research*, Vol. 12, No. 32 (August 14, 1987), p. 18; Martina Nevesky, "The Gypsy Problem," *Radio Free Europe Research*, Vol. 14, No. 31 (August 4, 1989), p. 40; Jan Orbman, "Minorities Not a Major Issue Yet," *Report on Eastern Europe*, Vol. 2, No. 50 (December 13, 1991), p. 11; Wheaton and Kavan, *The Velvet Revolution*, p. 147; Jiri Pehe, "Crime Rises in Czechoslovakia," *RFE/RL Research Report*, Vol. 1, No. 14 (April 3, 1992), p. 58; Kalvoda, "Gypsies of Czechoslovakia," p. 112, claims the Rom were responsible for 15.6 percent of all crimes in the Czech Republic.

99. Jiri Pehe, "Racial Violence Increasing," *Report on Eastern Europe*, Vol. 1, No. 20 (May 18, 1990), pp. 15, 18; David Binder, "European Gypsies Issue Call for Human Rights at Meeting," *The New York Times*, May 5, 1993, p. 6; Tritt, *Struggling for Ethnic Identity*, pp. 13–14.

100. Jiri Pehe, "Law on Romanies Causes Uproar in Czech Republic," *RFE/RL Research Report*, Vol. 2, No. 7 (February 12, 1993), pp. 18–22.

101. Times Mirror (Los Angeles), *The Pulse of Europe: A Survey of Political and Social Values and Attitudes* (Washington, DC: Times-Mirror Center for People & the Press, 1992), pp. 184–185; Freedom House and The American Jewish Committee, *Democracy, Economic Reform and Western Assistance in Czechoslovakia, Hungary and Poland: A Comparative Public Opinion Survey* (New York: Freedom House and the American Jewish Committee, 1991), pp. 63–65; "Iron in the Soul," *The Economist*, March 12, 1994, pp. 55–56; Jane Perlez, "A New Slovak Government Pledges Moderation," *The New York Times*, March 17, 1994, p. A6; Peter Maas, "Half a Century after Hitler, Gypsies Face New Fight to Exist," *The Washington Post*, August 13, 1993, p. A29; "Reported Racist Remarks Makes Slovakians Angry," Greensboro *News & Record*, September 7, 1993, p. A5; "His Struggle," *The Economist*, September 18–24, 1993, p. 56.

102. Henry Kamm, "In Slovak Gypsy Ghetto, Hovels and Plea for Jobs," *The New York Times*, November 28, 1993, p. A4; Monica Nemcokov, "Don't Blame Slovakia for Gypsy Problem," *The New York Times*, December 15, 1993, p. A14.

103. Henry Kamm, "Gypsies and the Czechs: Poverty, Not a Welcome," *The New York Times*, December 8, 1993, p. A7; Henry Kamm, "Havel Sees Hatred, Gypsies as a Litmus Test for Czechs," *The New York Times*, December 10, 1993, p. A4.

CHAPTER 3

1. Emília Horváthová, *Cigáni na Slovensku* (Bratislava: Vydatel'stvo Slovenskej Akademie Vied, 1964), p. 33.

2. "Cigáni," *Encyclopedia Slovensku*, Vol. I (Bratislava: Veda, 1977-82), p. 320; Willy Guy, "Ways of Looking at Roms: The Case of Czechoslovakia," in *Gypsies, Tinkers and Other Travellers*, ed. Farnham Rehfisch (New York: Academic Press, 1975), p. 208; Dr. Eva Davidova, "The Gypsies in Czechoslovakia. Part I: Main Characteristics and Brief Historical Development," translated by D. E. Guy, *Journal of the Gypsy Lore Society*, Third Series, Vol. 69, Nos. 3–4 (July–October 1970), p. 88; Angus Fraser, *The Gypsies* ·(Oxford: Blackwell, 1992), pp. 47–50; László Makkai, "Transformation into a Western–Type State, 1196–1301," in *A History of Hungary*, ed. Peter Sugar, Péter Hanák, and Tibor Frank (Bloomington: Indiana University Press, 1990), p. 30.

3. Tatomir Vukanović, *Romi (Tsigani) u Jugoslaviji* (Gypsies in Yugoslavia) (Vranje: Nova Jugoslavija, 1983), p. 23; Milenko Filipović, "Visočki Cigani," *Etnološka*

314 A HISTORY OF THE GYPSIES OF EASTERN EUROPE AND RUSSIA

Biblioteka, Vol. 16 (Zagreb: Etnografski musej u Zagreb, 1932), p. 3; George C. Soulis, "The Gypsies in the Byzantine Empire and the Balkans in the Late Middle Ages," *Dumbarton Oaks Papers,* Vol. 15 (1961), p. 161; Willy A. Bachich, "Maritime History of the Eastern Adriatic," in *Croatia: Land, People, Culture,* ed. Francis H. Eterovich and Christopher Spalatin, Vol. II (Toronto: University of Toronto Press, 1970), p. 127; Lázlo Makkai, "The Foundation of the Hungarian Christian State, 950–1196," in Sugar, Hanák, and Frank, *History of Hungary,* p. 19; György Balázs and Karoly Szelenyi, *The Magyars: The Birth of a European Nation* (Budapest: Corvina, 1989), p. 37; Fred Singleton, *A Short History of the Yugoslav Peoples* (Cambridge: Cambridge University Press, 1989), p. 29; Fraser, *The Gypsies,* pp. 60–61; Jószef Vekerdi, "Earliest Arrival Evidence on Gypsies in Hungary," *Journal of the Gypsy Lore Society,* Fourth Series, Vol. 1, No. 2 (1976), pp. 170-171; Miklos Tomka, "Die Zigeuner in der Ungarischen Gesellschaft (The Gypsies in Hungarian Society)," *East European Quarterly,* Vol. 4, No. 1 (March 1970), p. 3; László Siklós, "The Gypsies," *The New Hungarian Quarterly,* Vol. 11, No. 40 (1970), p. 150; Sigismund became Holy Roman Emperor in 1410 and King of Bohemia in 1420. Denis Sinor, *History of Hungary* (Westport, CT: Greenwood Press, 1976), pp. 60-103, passim; Rena C. Gropper, *Gypsies in the City: Cultural Patterns and Survival* (Princeton, NJ: The Darwin Press, 1975), pp. 7-8; Davidova, "The Gypsies in Czechoslovakia," I, p. 88.

4. Fraser, *The Gypsies,* pp. 61, 109–111; János Bak, "The Late Medieval Period, 1382–1526," in Sugar, Hanák, and Frank, *History of Hungary,* pp. 76–77, 79; István Hoóz, "Census Relative to Gipsy Population in the 18th and 19th Centuries," in *A Magyarországban Cigányösszeirás Eredményei: 1893 januar 31-én végrehajtott* (Results of the Gypsy Census in Hungary: 31 January 1893) (Budapest: Az Athenaeum R. Tásulat Könyvnyomdáa, 1893), pp. 19, 21 n. 1. Hoóz mistakenly claims that "the bishop Sigismund of Pécs had 25 tabernacles of gipsies in 1396, under the magistracy of Tamás Bolgár;" Will Durant, *The Renaissance: A History of Civilization in Italy from 1304–1576 A.D.* (New York: Simon and Schuster, 1953), pp. 365–367; though elected Hungary's monarch by the majority of nobles in 1526 upon the death of Louis II after Mohács, a minority continued to support Ferdinand I, the King of Bohemia. Ferdinand I invaded Hungary in 1527 and drove Zápolyai into Poland. The Ottoman ruler, Suleiman I, recognized Zápolyai as king in early 1528 and helped him drive Ferdinand into western and northern Hungary. Ferenc Szakály, "The Early Ottoman Period, Including Royal Hungary, 1526–1606," in Sugar, Hanák, and Frank, *History of Hungary,* pp. 83–84; Fraser, *The Gypsies,* p. 111; R. W. Seton-Watson, *A History of the Czechs and Slovaks* (Hamden, CT: Archon Books, 1965), p. 86; Guy, "Ways of Looking at Roms," p. 208; Davidova, "The Gypsies in Czechoslovakia," I, p. 89; Horváthová, *Cigáni na Slovensku,* pp. 99–100.

5. Fraser, *The Gypsies,* p. 110.

6. Ibid., pp. 110–111; Ferenc Szakály, "The Early Ottoman Period," in Sugar, Hanák, and Frank, eds. *History of Hungary,* pp. 83–86; Hoóz, "Census Relative to Gipsy Population," p. 21 n. 2.

7. Victor S. Mamatey, *Rise of the Habsburg Empire, 1526–1815* (New York: Holt, Rinehart and Winston, 1971), pp. 32–33; Stanford Shaw, *History of the Ottoman Empire and Modern Turkey,* Vol. I: *Empire of the Gazis: The Rise and Decline of the Ottoman Empire, 1280–1808* (Cambridge: Cambridge University Press, 1976), pp. 101–102; Fraser, *The Gypsies,* pp. 111, 156.

8. Fraser, *The Gypsies,* p. 111.

9. Guy, "Ways of Looking at Roms," p. 208; Davidova, "The Gypsies in Czechoslovakia," I, p. 89; Robert A. Kann and Zdeněk David, *The Peoples of the Eastern Habsburg Lands, 1526–1918,* (Seattle, WA: University of Washington Press, 1984), pp. 72–73; Szakály, "The Early Ottoman Period," pp. 84–85; Mamatey, *Rise of the Habsburg Empire,* pp. 32–33; Shaw, *Empire of the Gazis,* pp. 101–102; Fraser, *The Gypsies,* pp. 111, 156.

10. Fraser, *The Gypsies*, pp. 156–157; Hoóz, "Census Relative to Gipsy Population," p. 21 n. 1.
11. Kann and David, *Peoples of the Eastern Habsburg Lands*, p. 117; Guy, "Ways of Looking at Roms," pp. 206–209; Davidova, "The Gypsies in Czechoslovakia," I, pp. 89–90; Horváthová, *Cigáni na Slovensku*, p. 60; Hoóz, "Census Relative to Gipsy Population," p. 19.
12. Mamatey, *Rise of the Habsburg Empire*, pp. 69–78; O. van Kappen, "A Prague Edict against Gypsies (1710)," *Journal of the Gypsy Lore Society*, Third Series, Vol. 42, Nos. 3–4 (July–October 1963), pp. 118–121; Horváthová, *Cigáni na Slovensku*, pp. 60–61; Guy, "Ways of Looking at Roms," p. 207.
13. Hoóz, "Census Relative to Gipsy Population," p. 19; Horst Haselsteiner, "Cooperation and Confrontation between Rulers and the Noble Estates, 1711–1790," in Sugar, Hanák, and Frank, *History of Hungary*, pp. 138–141; Mamatey, *Rise of the Habsburg Empire*, pp. 90–91, 94–95; Horváthová, *Cigáni na Slovensku*, pp. 113–114.
14. Fraser, *The Gypsies*, p. 157.
15. Seton-Watson, *History of the Czechs and Slovaks*, pp. 142–143; Mamatey, *Rise of the Habsburg Empire*, pp. 104–106; Horváthová, *Cigáni na Slovensku*, pp. 61, 113; Davidova, "The Gypsies in Czechoslovakia," I, p. 90.
16. Fraser, *The Gypsies*, pp. 157–158, 195; Davidova, "The Gypsies in Czechoslovakia," I, p. 90; Guy, "Ways of Looking at Roms," p. 209; Horváthová, *Cigáni na Slovensku*, p. 114.
17. David M. Crowe, "The Roma (Gypsies) of Hungary through the Kádár Era," *Nationalities Papers*, Vol. 19, No. 3 (Winter 1991), pp. 297, 307 n. 2; Fraser, *The Gypsies*, p. 158; Davidova, "The Gypsies in Czechoslovakia," I, p. 90; Horváthová, *Cigáni na Slovensku*, pp. 118–119; Donald Kenrick and Grattan Puxon, *The Destiny of Europe's Gypsies* (New York: Basic Books, 1972), pp. 50–51.
18. Haselsteiner, "Cooperation and Confrontation between Rulers and the Noble Estates," pp. 152–153; Kann and David, *Peoples of the Eastern Habsburgs Lands*, p. 247; Fraser, *The Gypsies*, pp. 158–159; Hoóz, "Census Relative to Gipsy Population," p. 19.
19. Fraser, *The Gypsies*, p. 159; Guy, "Ways of Looking at Roms," p. 207; Horváthová, *Cigáni na Slovensku*, pp. 118–125.
20. Fraser, *The Gypsies*, pp. 191–192.
21. Ibid., pp. 192, 195. Gypsies in this part of Hungary were divided, caste-wise, along sedentary and nomadic lines. Nomadic Rom felt superior to their sedentary cousins.
22. Ibid., pp. 192–193, 195–197.
23. Mamatey, *Rise of the Habsburg Empire*, pp. 131–132, 134–135. Joseph II also "freed the Jews from most of the civil disabilities under which they had suffered" and allowed them to settle throughout the empire.
24. Fraser, *The Gypsies*, pp. 195–196; Ian Hancock, *The Pariah Syndrome* (Ann Arbor, MI: Karoma Publishers, 1987), p. 51; Horváthová, *Cigáni na Slovensku*, pp. 135–136; Crowe, "Roma of Hungary," p. 297; Konrad Bercovici, *Gypsies: Their Life, Lore, and Legends* (New York: Greenwich House, 1983), pp. 92–93; Jean-Paul Clébert, *The Gypsies*, translated by Charles Duff (New York: E.P. Dutton, 1963), p. 73.
25. Horváthová, *Cigáni na Slovensku*, pp. 125–136; Guy, "Ways of Looking at Roms," p. 207.
26. J. H. Schwicker, *Die Zigeuner in Ungarn und Siebenbürgen* (Wien und Teschen: Verlag von Karl Brochasta, 1883), pp. 63, 66–70; Hoóz, "Census Relative to Gipsy Population," p. 19; Horváthová, *Cigáni na Slovensku*, p. 134; Fraser, *The Gypsies*, p. 183; Tomka, "Die Zigeuner," p. 4; C. A. Macartney, *The Habsburg Empire, 1789–1918* (London: Weidenfeld and Nicolson, 1968), p. 81.
27. Guy, "Ways of Looking at Roms," pp. 209–210; Fraser, *The Gypsies*, pp. 159–160.
28. Mamatey, *Rise of the Habsburg Empire*, pp. 131, 138; Macartney, *The Habsburg Empire*, pp. 132–133.
29. Tomka, "Die Zigeuner," p. 4; Hoóz, "Census Relative to Gipsy Population," p. 19.

30. Alan Walker, *Franz Liszt*, Volume I: *The Virtuoso Years, 1811–1847* (New York: Alfred A. Knopf, 1983), p. 319; Fraser, *The Gypsies*, pp. 201–203; Geoffrey Hindley, "Hungarian Music to the Age of Liszt," in *The Larousse Encyclopedia of Music*, ed. Geoffrey Hindley (New York: Crescent Books, 1986), p. 320; Franz Liszt, *The Gipsy in Music*, Vol. II (London: William Reeves Bookseller Limited, 1926), pp. 341–343.

31. Walker, *Franz Liszt*, I, pp. 338–339.

32. Liszt, *Gipsy in Music*, II, pp. 271–276. Geoffrey Hindley says that Liszt was particularly moved by the reception accorded him by the Rom in his hometown, Raiding, upon his return in 1840. Hindley, "Hungarian Music to the Age of Liszt," p. 319.

33. Alan Walker, *Franz Liszt*, Vol. II: *The Weimar Years, 1848–1861* (New York: Alfred A. Knopf, 1989), pp. 380–390; Bela Bartók, *The Hungarian Folk Song*, edited by Benjamin Suchoff, translated by M. D. Calvocoressi (Albany: State University of New York Press, 1981), p. 99.

34. "Hungary in the Age of Bartók," in *The Larousse Encyclopedia of Music*, ed. Geoffrey Hindley (New York: Crescent Books, 1986), p. 414; Walker, *Franz Liszt*, I, p. 341; Fraser, *The Gypsies*, p. 249; Walker, *Franz Liszt*, II, pp. 389–390.

35. George Barany, "The Age of Royal Absolutism, 1790–1848," in Sugar, Hanák, and Frank, eds., *History of Hungary*, pp. 174–208 passim.

36. István Deák, "The Revolution and the War of Independence, 1848–1849," in Sugar, Hanák, and Frank, eds., *History of Hungary*, pp. 209–211.

37. Barany, "Age of Royal Absolutism," pp. 200, 204.

38. Deák, "Revolution and the War of Independence," pp. 214–217.

39. Fraser, *The Gypsies*, p. 203; Deák, "Revolution and the War of Independence," pp. 231–232.

40. Éva Somogyi, "The Age of Neoabsolutism, 1849–1867," in Sugar, Hanák, and Frank, eds., *History of Hungary*, p. 236; Deák, "Revolution and War of Independence," p. 209.

41. Somogyi, "Age of Neoabsolutism," pp. 236–239.

42. Ibid., pp. 236–237, 241–242.

43. Ibid., pp. 236–246; Hans Kohn, *The Habsburg Empire, 1804–1918* (New York: Van Nostrand Reinhold Company, 1961), p. 41.

44. Somogyi, "Age of Neoabsolutism," pp. 246–251; Tibor Frank, "Hungary and the Dual Monarchy, 1867–1890," in Sugar, Hanák, and Frank, eds., *History of Hungary*, p. 252.

45. Frank, "Hungary and the Dual Monarchy," pp. 254–255.

46. Fraser, *The Gypsies*, pp. 193, 211–212, 248–249.

47. Hoóz, "Census Relative to Gipsy Population," p. 20. Hoóz confusingly mentions Elek Fényes's analysis of the 1851 census, which indicated a total Rom population of 93,600, then breaks it down as "in Transylvania 60,000, in Hungary 121,000, in the Serbia Voivodeship 12,000," for a total population of 193,000. Presumably he meant there were only 21,000 Gypsies in Hungary. Tomka, "Die Zigeuner," p. 4; Schwicker, *Die Zigeuner*, pp. 75–82; István Hoóz, "The 1893 Year Gipsy Census and Its Results," in *A Magyarországban Cigányösszeirás Eredményei*, pp. 26–27.

48. Hoóz, "The 1893 Year Gipsy Census," pp. 24–27; Tomka, "Die Zigeuner," pp. 4–5.

49. Hoóz, "The 1893 Year Gipsy Census," pp. 26–27; Tomka, "Die Zigeuner," p. 5.

50. Hoóz, "The 1893 Year Gipsy Census," pp. 27–28; Géza Jeszenszky, "Hungary through World War I and the End of the Dual Monarchy," in Sugar, Hanák, and Frank, eds., *History of Hungary*, p. 274.

51. Jeszenszky, "Hungary through World War I," pp. 269–270, 274–275; Jörg K. Hoensch, *A History of Modern Hungary, 1867–1986*, translated by Kim Traynor (London: Longman Group, 1988), pp. 35, 73–76; Andrew C. Janos, *The Politics of Backwardness in Hungary, 1825–1945* (Princeton, NJ: Princeton University Press, 1982), p. 117; Joseph Rothschild, *East Central Europe between the Two World Wars* (Seattle: University of Washington Press, 1990), p. 153. Historic Hungary had a 1910 population of 18,264,533, while Croatia-Slavonia had 2,621,954 inhabitants.

52. Tomka, "Die Zigeuner," pp. 6–7; Kenrick and Puxon, *Destiny of Europe's Gypsies*, p. 56.
53. Jeszenszky, "Hungary through World War I," pp. 291–293; David M. Crowe, *World War I and Europe in Crisis, 1914–1935* (Piscataway, NJ: Research and Education Association, 1990), pp. 40–41, 46; C. A. Macartney, *A History of Hungary, 1929–1945*, Part I (New York: Frederick A. Praeger, Inc., 1956), p. 4; Tibor Hadjú and Zsuzsa L. Nagy, "Revolution, Counterrevolution, Consolidation," in Sugar, Hanák, and Frank, eds., *History of Hungary*, p. 314.
54. Martin L. Kovacs and David M. Crowe, "National Minorities in Hungary, 1919–1980," in *Eastern European National Minorities, 1919–1980: A Handbook*, ed. Stephen M. Horak (Littleton, CO: Libraries Unlimited, Inc., 1985), pp. 164–165. There were about 550,000 Germans left in Hungary in 1920; J. C. Paikert, "Hungary's National Minority Policies, 1920–1945," *The American Slavic and East European Review*, Vol. 12, No. 2 (1953), pp. 202–203, 207–208, 218.
55. Paikert, "Hungary's National Minority Policies," pp. 214, 217; Tomka, "Die Zigeuner," p. 7; Crowe, "Roma of Hungary," p. 298; Janos, *Politics of Backwardness*, p. 330.
56. Mária Ormos, "The Early Interwar Years, 1921–1938," in Sugar, Hanák, and Frank, eds., *History of Hungary*, pp. 329–332; Hungary was officially a monarchy without a king, something World War I's victors insisted on in the creation of a new Hungary. Hajdú and Nagy, "Revolution, Counterrevolution, Consolidation," pp. 312–313.
57. Ormos, "The Early Interwar Years," pp. 331–335; Janos, *Politics of Backwardness*, p. 289.
58. Ormos, "The Early Interwar Years," pp. 337–338; Janos, *Politics of Backwardness*, p. 289; Hoensch, *History of Modern Hungary*, pp. 137–139; Rothschild, *East Central Europe*, p. 178; Tomka, "Die Zigeuner," p. 7; Kovacs and Crowe, "National Minorities in Hungary," p. 167; Randolph L. Braham, *A Magyar Holocaust* (The Holocaust in Hungary), Vol. 1 (Budapest: Gondolat, 1988), pp. 106–107.
59. Hoensch, *History of Modern Hungary*, pp. 139–143, 148–149; Ctibor Nečas, *Nad osudem českých a slovenských Cikánů v letech 1939–1945* (Brno: Univerzita J.E. Purkyne, 1981), pp. 24, 28; Kenrick and Puxon, *Destiny of Europe's Gypsies*, p. 183; Kovacs and Crowe, "National Minorities in Hungary," pp. 165, 167; Braham, *A Magyar Holocaust*, pp. 111–115.
60. Hoensch, *History of Modern Hungary*, pp. 149–151; Janos, *Politics of Backwardness*, pp. 301–302; Kenrick and Puxon, *Destiny of Europe's Gypsies*, p. 124.
61. Rothschild, *East Central Europe*, p. 195; László Kövágó, *Nemzetiségek a mai Magyar-Országon* (Nationalities in Today's Hungary) (Budapest: Kossuth, 1981), p. 9.
62. The First Jewish Law of 1938 had reduced by 20 percent the number of Jews in the professions and the country's economic life, while the Second Jewish Law the following year placed further economic and professional restrictions on the Jews. Kovacs and Crowe, "National Minorities in Hungary," p. 167; Hoensch, *History of Modern Hungary*, p. 154; Macartney, *History of Hungary*, Part 2, p. 15.
63. Joseph B. Schechtman, "The Gypsy Problem," *Midstream*, Vol. 12, No. 9 (November 1966), pp. 56–57.
64. Hoensch, *History of Modern Hungary*, pp. 153–156; Kovacs and Crowe, "National Minorities in Hungary," pp. 167–168; Randolph L. Braham, *The Politics of Genocide: The Holocaust in Hungary*, Vol. 1 (New York: Columbia University Press, 1981), pp. 405–411.
65. State Museum of Auschwitz-Birkenau and the Documentary and Cultural Centre of German Sintis and Roms, *Memorial Book: The Gypsies at Auschwitz-Birkenau*, Vols. 1–2 (München: K. G. Saur, 1993), pp. 3, 942–944, 960–972, 1469–1471; Kenrick and Puxon, *Destiny of Europe's Gypsies*, p. 227 n. 5, err when they note that there were Hungarian Gypsies among numbers 3944–4141. Furthermore, all of the Rom assigned these latter numbers were male, not female, as they assert, and arrived at the Gypsy Camp on March 17–18, 1943, not March 16.

66. Kenrick and Puxon, *Destiny of Europe's Gypsies*, pp. 125, 227 n. 10; Crowe, "Roma of Hungary," p. 299; Hoensch, *History of Modern Hungary*, pp. 155–158; John Bierman, *Righteous Gentile* (New York: Bantam Books, 1983), p. 117; Lévai Jenö, *Raoul Wallenberg* (Budapest: Magyar Téka, 1948), passim; Leni Yahil, *The Holocaust: The Fate of European Jewry* (New York: Oxford University Press, 1990), pp. 642–648.

67. Hoensch, *History of Modern Hungary*, pp. 161–177 passim; Bennett Kovrig, *Communism in Hungary from Kun to Kádár* (Stanford, CA: Hoover Institution Press, 1979), pp. 71, 133, 144, 162; Crowe, "Roma of Hungary," p. 299; Paul S. Shoup, *The East European and Soviet Data Handbook* (New York: Columbia University Press, 1981), p. 137; Tomka, "Die Zigeuner," p. 8; László Siklós, "The Gypsies," *The New Hungarian Quarterly*, Vol. 11, No. 40 (1970), p. 151.

68. Kovacs and Crowe, "National Minorities in Hungary," pp. 168–171; Nigel Swain, *Hungary: The Rise and Fall of Feasible Socialism* (London: Verso, 1992), pp. 189–190.

69. Crowe, "Roma of Hungary," p. 299.

70. "Minorities in Eastern Europe," *East Europe*, Vol. 8, No. 3 (March 1959), p. 14; Shoup, *East European and Soviet Data Handbook*, p. 137; Siklós, p. 151; Tomka, "Die Zigeuner," pp. 10–13.

71. Mihály Hajdu, "Gypsies 1980," *Hungarian Digest*, No. 6 (1980), p. 33.

72. Hajdu, "Gypsies 1980," p. 33; Tamás Ervin and Révész Tamás, *Búcsú a cigányteleptöl* (Farewell to the Gypsy Quarter) (Budapest: Kossuth Könyvkiadó, 1977), p. 16; Grattan Puxon, *Rom: Europe's Gypsies* (London: Minority Rights Group, 1973), p. 16; "Minorities in Eastern Europe," p. 14; "Discrimination," *East Europe*, Vol. 8, No. 12 (December 1959), p. 11.

73. Siklós, "The Gypsies," pp. 151, 153–154; Hajdu, "Gypsies 1980," p. 33; Puxon, *Rom* (1973), p. 16; Swain, *Hungary*, p. 202.

74. Hajdu, "Gypsies 1980," pp. 31–32; Grattan Puxon, *Roma: Europe's Gypsies* (London: Minority Rights Group, 1975), pp. 12–13.

75. Hajdu, "Gypsies 1980," pp. 31–32.

76. László Rózsa, "Gypsies and Public Opinion," *The New Hungarian Quarterly*, Vol. 20, No. 73 (Spring 1979), p. 126; Grattan Puxon, *Rom: Europe's Gypsies* (London: Minority Rights Group, 1987), p. 10; Eva Lengyel, "The Gypsy Problem Continues to Confront Society," *Radio Free Europe Research*, Hungary No. 6 (April 22, 1983), p. 17.

77. Puxon, *Roma* (1973), p. 16; Hajdu, "Gypsies 1980," p. 31.

78. William O. McCagg, "Gypsy Life in Socialist Hungary and Czechoslovakia," *Nationalities Papers*, Vol. 19, No. 3 (Winter 1991), p. 323.

79. Swain, *Hungary*, p. 204; Siklós, "The Gypsies," p. 158.

80. Hajdu, "Gypsies 1980," pp. 30–31; Marg Csapo, "Preschool Special Education in Hungary," *Early Child Development and Care*, Vol. 14, Nos. 3–4 (March 1984), p. 252; Siklós, "The Gypsies," p. 159; Zita Réger, "Bilingual Gypsy Children in Hungary: Explorations in 'Natural' Second-Language Acquisitions at an Early Age," *International Journal of the Sociology of Language*, No. 19 (1979), p. 60; Lengyel, "Gypsy Problem Continues to Confront Society," p. 17.

81. Rózsa, "Gypsies and Public Opinion," pp. 126, 128; Lengyel, "Gypsy Problem Continues to Confront Society," pp. 17–18.

82. Edith Markos, "The Fast-Growing Gypsy Minority and Its Problems," *Radio Free Europe Research*, Hungary No. 5 (June 15, 1987), p. 14; Swain, *Hungary*, pp. 196–197.

83. "The Employment of Gypsies," *Radio Free Europe Research*, Hungary No. 19 (August 8, 1978), p. 6.

84. Lengyel, "Gypsy Problem Continues to Confront Society," pp. 16–17.

85. Edith Markos, "Dim Prospects for Improving the Plight of the Gypsies," *Radio Free Europe Research*, Hungary No. 10 (September 4, 1985), pp. 13–14.

86. Lengyel, "Gypsy Problem Continues to Confront Society," pp. 14–15.
87. "Gypsies in Eastern Europe and the Soviet Union," *Radio Free Europe Research Report,* RAD Background Report No. 72 (April 12, 1978), p. 4.
88. Shoup, *East European and Soviet Data Handbook,* p. 137; Réger, "Bilingual Gypsy Children in Hungary," p. 80 n. 1; Hajdu, "Gypsies 1980," p. 30; "Hungary's Gypsies," *Radio Free Europe Research,* Hungary, No. 9 (April 12, 1978), p. 6. According to Zoltan D. Barany in "Hungary's Gypsies," *Report on Eastern Europe* (July 20, 1990), p. 26, Hungary's Roma population was conservatively estimated to number between 380,000 and 400,000 in 1990, but more likely to be in the 700,000 to 800,000 range.
89. Bennet Kovrig, "Hungary," in *Yearbook on International Communist Affairs, 1987,* ed., Richard F. Staar and Margit N. Grigory (Stanford, CA: Hoover Institution Press, 1987), pp. 303–304.
90. Puxon, *Rom* (1975), p. 12; "Greater Solicitude for Ethnic Minorities," *Radio Free Europe Research,* Hungary No. 10 (April 19, 1978), pp. 6–7; "Congress of Ethnic Minorities," *Radio Free Europe Research,* Hungary No. 30 (December 4, 1978), pp. 8–9. *Magyar Hirek* estimated that 3.2–3.6 million Hungarians lived just outside of Hungary's borders in 1969; "Additional Census for Minorities to Encourage Ethnic Consciousness," *Radio Free Europe Research,* Hungary No. 11 (July 3, 1980), p. 15; Laszlo Ribansky, "Nationalities in Hungary: Few in Number but Pampered," *Radio Free Europe Research,* RAD Background Report No. 259 (October 28, 1980), pp. 2–4.
91. Markos, "Dim Prospects for Improving the Plight of the Gypsies," pp. 12–13.
92. Ibid.
93. Ibid., p. 13.
94. Lengyel, "Gypsy Problem Continues to Confront Society," pp. 16, 18; Markos, "Dim Prospects for Improving the Plight of the Gypsies," pp. 11–12; Puxon, *Rom* (1975), p. 12; Puxon, *Rom* (1987), p. 10; Fraser, *The Gypsies,* p. 277; Grattan Puxon, "Gypsies: Blacks of Eastern Europe," *The Nation* (April 17, 1976), p. 463; Crowe, "Roma of Hungary," pp. 303–304.
95. Markos, "Dim Prospects for Improving the Plight of the Gypsies," p. 14; J. F. Brown, *Surge to Freedom: The End of Communist Rule in Eastern Europe* (Durham, NC: Duke University Press, 1991), p. 105.
96. Markos, "Dim Prospects for Improving the Plight of the Gypsies," p. 15.
97. Markos, "The Fast-Growing Gypsy Minority and Its Problems," pp. 13–14. In 1989, *Magyar Nemzet* (Hungarian Nation) reported that Roma were now responsible for 52 percent of all crimes in Hungary, while *Heti Világgazdasag* claimed that 60–70 percent of the country's 16,000 prison inmates were Roma. Barany, "Hungary's Gypsies," pp. 27, 31.
98. Gale Stokes, *The Walls Came Tumbling Down: The Collapse of Communism in Eastern Europe* (New York: Oxford University Press, 1993), p. 96; Miklós K. Radváyi, "Hungary," in *Yearbook on International Communist Affairs, 1990,* ed. Richard F. Staar and Margit N. Grigory (Stanford, CA: Hoover Institution Press, 1990), pp. 346–351.
99. Barany, "Hungary's Gypsies," p. 29.
100. Ibid.
101. Ibid.; see Charles Jókay, "Hungary," in *1991 Yearbook on International Communist Affairs,* ed. Richard Staar and Margit N. Grigory (Stanford, CA: Hoover Institution Press, 1991), p. 309, for complete results of both rounds of elections in Hungary on March 25 and April 8, 1990.
102. László Bruszt and David Stark, "Remaking the Political Field in Hungary: From the Politics of Confrontation to the Politics of Competition," in *Eastern Europe in Revolution,* ed. Ivo Banac, (Ithaca, NY: Cornell University Press, 1992), pp. 50–51; Barany, "Hungary's Gypsies," pp. 29–30; the AFD won 21.93 percent of the vote in the March 25 elections, while the HDF garnered 24.7 percent. In the April 8 elections, the HDF won 164 seats in Hungary's national legislature, while the AFD got 93 seats. Jókay, "Hungary," p. 309.

103. Judith Ingram, "Hungary's Gypsy Women: Scapegoats in a New Democracy," *Ms,* September/October 1991, p. 17; János Kenedi, "Why Is the Gypsy the Scapegoat and Not the Jew?" *East European Reporter,* Vol. 2, No. 1 (Spring 1986), p. 14; Paul Hockenos, *Free to Hate: The Rise of the Right in Post-Communist Eastern Europe* (New York: Routledge, 1993), p. 156; *Times-Mirror* (Los Angeles), *The Pulse of Europe: A Survey of Political and Social Values and Attitudes* (Washington, DC: *Times-Mirror* Center for the People & the Press, 1992), p. 184; Freedom House and the American Jewish Committee, *Democracy, Economic Reform and Western Assistance in Czechoslovakia, Hungary and Poland: A Comparative Public Opinion Survey* (New York: Freedom House and the American Jewish Committee, 1991), pp. 62–65.

104. Edith Oltay, "Crime Rate Rising Sharply," *Report on Eastern Europe* (August 30, 1991), p. 32.

105. "The Next Great Trek of the Gypsies," *World Press Review,* Vol. 37, No. 11 (November 1990), p. 44; Edith Oltay, "Poverty on the Rise," *Report on Eastern Europe* (January 25, 1991), p. 14; Edith Oltay put Gypsy unemployment figures at 70 percent in mid–1993, and national unemployment rates at 13 percent, in her "Hungary Passes Law on Minority Rights," *RFE/RL Research Report* (August 20, 1993), p. 58; Henry Kamm, "Gypsies in a Hungarian City Suffering from the Economic Change," *The New York Times,* November 7, 1993, p. A9; according to Edith Oltay, many of Hungary's "street prostitutes are Gypsies from poor families, and a substantial number are under eighteen." Edith Oltay, "Prostitution Thriving in Hungary," *RFE/RL Research Report* (May 28, 1993), p. 40.

106. Gábor Vajda, "Gypsies Face a Crisis of Confidence," *Budapest Week,* Vol. 3, No. 27 (September 9–15, 1993), p. 5.

107. Judith Pataki, "Increasing Intolerance of Foreigners," *RFE/RL Research Report* (May 8, 1992), pp. 34–35; Judith Pataki, "Hungary Copes with Refugee Influx," *RFE/RL Research Report* (April 30, 1993), pp. 35–36.

108. Judith Pataki, "Dramatic Surge in Racist Attacks Prompt Foreign Students to Leave Hungarian Universities," *The Chronicle of Higher Education,* April 15, 1992, p. A48; though some prominent members of Csurka's party distanced themselves from his comments, which also included comments on "Jewish and foreign influence over Hungarian affairs," this was not his first prejudicial foray. The popular writer and former communist opposition leader had a track record of anti-Semitic allusions in earlier radio broadcasts and in the newsletter he edited, *Hungarian Forum.* Though the HDF officially condemned anti-Semitism, it had allowed Csurka to play on these sentiments among "some of its members and supporters in order to gain votes" in the 1990 elections. "Hungarian Attack Sets Off a Storm," *The New York Times,* September 20, 1992, p. 8; Hockenos, *Free to Hate,* pp. 154–155; Swain, *Hungary,* pp. 17, 29; Craig R. Whitney, "East Europe's Frustration Finds Target: Immigrants," *The New York Times,* November 13, 1992, p. A4; Judith Ingram, "Boys Impatient for 'Great Hungary' to Take Wing," *The New York Times,* January 15, 1993, p. A4; Edith Oltay, "Criminal Proceedings against Hungarian Fascist Party," *RFE/RL Daily Report* (February 3, 1994), n.p.; "Gipsies March against Rise in Racist Attacks," *The European* July 15–18, 1993, p. 14.

109. Alfred A. Reisch, "First Law on Minorities Drafted," *Report on Eastern Europe* (December 13, 1991), pp. 16–17; Vajda, "Gypsies Face a Crisis of Confidence," p. 5.

110. Oltay, "Hungary Passes Law on Minority Rights," pp. 57–60; "Gipsies March Against Rise in Racist Attacks," p. 14.

CHAPTER 4

1. Georges Castellan, *A History of the Romanians,* translated by Nicholas Bradley (Boulder, CO: East European Monographs, 1989), pp. 28–35; Pál Engel, "The Age of

the Angevines, 1301–1382," in *A History of Hungary*, ed. Peter F. Sugar, Péter Hanák, and Tibor Frank (Bloomington: Indiana University Press, 1990), p. 40; Norman Davies, *God's Playground: A History of Poland*, Vol. 1: *The Origins to 1795* (New York: Columbia University Press, 1982), pp. 108–109; R. W. Seton-Watson, *A History of the Roumanians* (Cambridge: Cambridge University Press, 1934), pp. 24–29; Peter F. Sugar, *Southeastern Europe under Ottoman Rule, 1354–1804* (Seattle: University of Washington Press, 1977), p. 115; Sam Beck, "The Origins of Gypsy Slavery in Romania," *Dialectical Anthropology*, Vol. 14, No. 1 (1989), pp. 55–56; George C. Soulis, "The Gypsies in the Byzantine Empire and the Balkans in the Late Middle Ages," *Dumbarton Oaks Papers*, Vol. 15 (1961), p. 162.

2. Angus Fraser, *The Gypsies* (Oxford: Blackwell, 1992), p. 58; P. N. Panaitescu, "The Gypsies in Wallachia and Moldavia: A Chapter of Economic History," *Journal of the Gypsy Lore Society*, Third Series, Vol. 20, No. 2 (April 1941), pp. 64–67; Beck, "Origins of Gypsy Slavery," pp. 54–55; Halil İnalcik, "Servile Labor in the Ottoman Empire," in *The Mutual Effects of the Islamic and Judeo-Christian Worlds: The East European Pattern*, ed. Abraham Ascher, Tibor Halasi-Kun, and Béla Király (Brooklyn, NY: Brooklyn College Press, 1979), p. 37; Soulis, "Gypsies in the Byzantine Empire," p. 162; Castellan, *History of the Romanians*, pp. 32–33.

3. Beck, "Origins of Gypsy Slavery," p. 56; Ian Hancock, *The Pariah Syndrome* (Ann Arbor, MI: Karoma Publishers, 1987), p. 22; Castellan, *History of the Romanians*, pp. 38–39; Seton-Watson, *History of the Roumanians*, p. 44.

4. Sugar, *Southeastern Europe under Ottoman Rule*, pp. 115, 121, 126–127; Panaitescu, "Gypsies in Wallachia and Moldavia," p. 67; Stanford Shaw, *History of the Ottoman Empire and Modern Turkey*, Vol. 1: *Empire of the Gazis: The Rise and Decline of the Ottoman Empire, 1280–1808* (Cambridge: Cambridge University Press, 1976), pp. 59, 73, 122, 155–157.

5. Hancock, *Pariah Syndrome*, pp. 16–17.

6. Ibid. p. 22; M. Gaster, "Mixed Marriages," *Journal of the Gypsy Lore Society*, Third Series, Vol. 13, No. 4 (1934), p. 226; M. Gaster, "Rumanian Gypsies in 1560," *Journal of the Gypsy Lore Society*, Third Series, Vol. 12, No. 1 (1933), p. 59; İnalcik, "Servile Labor in the Ottoman Empire," pp. 36, 38. Wallachian slaves were an important commodity in the Ottoman slave trade in the fifteenth century.

7. Seton-Watson, *History of the Roumanians*, p. 80; Hancock, *Pariah Syndrome*, p. 23.

8. Sugar, *Southeastern Europe under Ottoman Rule*, pp. 134–137; Seton-Watson, *History of the Roumanians*, pp. 126–127, 133–134.

9. M. Gaster, "Two Rumanian Documents Concerning Gypsies," *Journal of the Gypsy Lore Society*, Third Series, Vol. 9, No. 4 (1930), pp. 179–180; Seton-Watson, *History of the Roumanians*, pp. 141–142; Sugar, *Southeastern Europe under Ottoman Rule*, p. 137; Castellan, *History of the Romanians*, p. 88; Ifor L. Evans, *The Agrarian Revolution in Roumania* (Cambridge: Cambridge University Press, 1924), pp. 21–23, 51; Hancock, *Pariah Syndrome*, p. 24; Panaitescu, "Gypsies in Wallachia and Moldavia," p. 68 n. 1.

10. Hancock, *Pariah Syndrome*, p. 25; Gaster, "Two Rumanian Documents," pp. 181–182.

11. Panaitescu, "Gypsies in Wallachia and Moldavia," pp. 69–70 n. 2; Gaster, "Two Rumanian Documents," pp. 181–182.

12. Barbara Jelavich, *History of the Balkans*; Vol. 1, *Eighteenth and Nineteenth Centuries* (Cambridge: Cambridge University Press, 1983), pp. 204–214; Seton-Watson, *History of the Roumanians*, pp. 158, 160–161, 164; William Wilkinson, *An Account of the Principalities of Wallachia and Moldavia* (New York: Arno Press & The New York Times, 1971), pp. 155, 173–175; Hancock, *Pariah Syndrome*, p. 30.

13. Hancock, *Pariah Syndrome*, p. 30; W. Bruce Lincoln, *Nicholas I: Emperor and Autocrat of All the Russias* (Bloomington: Indiana University Press, 1978), pp. 187–190; Seton-Watson, *History of the Roumanians*, pp. 207–210; Alex. Russell,

"Classification and Numbers of Wallachian Gypsies in 1837," *Journal of the Gypsy Lore Society*, New Series, Vol. 6, No. 2 (1912–13), p. 150; Demetrius Dvoichenko Markov, "General Count Pavel D. Kisselev and the Organic Regulation in the Danubian Principalities," *Balkan Studies*, Vol. 31, No. 2 (1990), pp. 287–292.

14. Hancock, *Pariah Syndrome*, pp. 27–29. The 1818 Wallachian Penal Code declared, "Gypsies are born slaves. . . . Anyone born of a mother who is a slave, is also a slave. . . . Any owner has the right to sell or give away his slaves. . . . Any Gypsy without an owner is the property of the Prince."

15. Ibid., pp. 31–32, 34; Fraser, *The Gypsies*, p. 224.

16. Hancock, *Pariah Syndrome*, pp. 32, 34, says 5,582 Gypsy families were emancipated by Ghica, while Fraser, *The Gypsies*, p. 224, says the number was 4,000 families; Wilkinson, *Account of the Principalities*, pp. 168–169; Tihomir R. Gjorgjević, "Rumanian Gypsies in Serbia," *Journal of the Gypsy Lore Society*, Third Series, Vol. 8, No. 1 (1929), p. 12; Russell, "Classification and Number of Wallachian Gypsies," p. 150; Seton-Watson, *History of the Roumanians*, pp. 214–217; David Mitrany also used the figure of 150,000 Gypsy *robi* in his *The Land & the Peasant in Rumania* (London: Humphrey Milford, 1930), p. 50 n.1.

17. Hancock, *Pariah Syndrome*, p. 34; Fraser, *The Gypsies*, pp. 224–225; Seton Watson, *History of the Roumanians*, pp. 212–214; Castellan, *History of the Romanians*, p. 122.

18. Lincoln, *Nicholas I*, pp. 191–194; Nicholas Riasanovsky, *Nicholas I and Official Nationality in Russia, 1825–1855* (Berkeley: University of California Press, 1969), pp. 209–210.

19. Castellan, *History of the Romanians*, p. 123.

20. Ibid., pp. 123–124; Andrei Oţetea, *A Concise History of Romania* (London: Robert Hale, 1985), p. 330; Gjorgjević, "Rumanian Gypsies in Serbia," p. 15.

21. Seton-Watson, *History of the Roumanians*, pp. 225–227; Castellan, *History of the Romanians*, p. 124; Oţetea, *Concise History of Romania*, pp. 331–333; Lincoln, *Nicholas I*, pp. 312–313.

22. Seton-Watson, *History of the Roumanians*, pp. 227–229; Castellan, *History of the Romanians*, p. 124; Oţetea, *Concise History of Romania*, pp. 331–333.

23. Castellan, *History of the Romanians*, pp. 128–133; István Deák, "The Revolution of 1848–49 in Transylvania and the Polarization of National Destinies," in *Transylvania: The Roots of Ethnic Conflict*, ed. John F. Cadzow, Andrew Ludanyi, and Louis J. Elteto (Kent, OH: Kent State University Press, 1983), pp. 121–122. There were 1.2 million Romanians, 830,000 Hungarians, 200,000 Saxons, and other minorities in Transylvania in 1848; Éva Somogyi, "The Age of Neoabsolutism, 1849–1867," in Sugar, Hanák, and Frank, *History of Hungary*, pp. 236–237; Andrew C. Janos, *The Politics of Backwardness in Hungary, 1825–1945* (Princeton, NJ: Princeton University Press, 1982), pp. 84, 87–89; Lincoln, *Nicholas I*, pp. 313–314; Fraser, *The Gypsies*, pp. 225–226.

24. Seton-Watson, *History of the Roumanians*, p. 229; M. Gaster, "Bill of Sale of Gypsy Slaves in Moldavia, 1851," *Journal of the Gypsy Lore Society*, Third Series, Volume 2, No. 2 (1923), pp. 68–81.

25. Castellan, *History of the Romanians*, pp. 124–125; Gaster, "Bill of Sale of Gypsy Slaves," p. 69.

26. Lincoln, *Nicholas I*, pp. 330–339; Seton-Watson, *History of the Roumanians*, pp. 230–231; Castellan, *History of the Romanians*, p. 125; Oţetea, *Concise History of Romania*, p. 343.

27. Castellan, *History of the Romanians*, p. 125; Oţetea, *Concise History of Romania*, p. 343; Seton-Watson, *History of the Roumanians*, pp. 234–235.

28. Seton-Watson, *History of the Roumanians*, pp. 227–229; Hancock, *Pariah Syndrome*, p. 35; Gjorgjević, "Rumanian Gypsies in Serbia," p. 15; Fraser, *The Gypsies*, p. 226.

29. Castellan, *History of the Romanians*, p. 126; Panaitescu, "Gypsies in Wallachia and Moldavia," pp. 71–72 n. 3; Seton-Watson, *History of the Roumanians*, pp. 262–263; Oţetea, *Concise History of Romania*, p. 348.

30. Castellan, *History of the Romanians*, pp. 126–127, 133–134.
31. Ibid., pp. 133–135; Seton-Watson, *History of the Roumanians*, pp. 305–310; according to Konrad Bercovici in his *Gypsies: Their Life, Lore, and Legends* (New York: Greenwich House, 1983), p. 62, Cuza "was of Gypsy origin." Consequently, he treated Gypsy criminals, particularly the fiercely independent Laieşi, somewhat differently than non-Gypsies. Cuza said that the penalty for a non-Rom horse thief should be five years, while a Laieşi should only be imprisoned for three months for the same crime, since he could not survive any longer in confinement.
32. Hancock, *Pariah Syndrome*, pp. 42–44.
33. Ibid., p. 35.
34. Ibid., pp. 37–44; Fraser, *The Gypsies*, pp. 226–238.
35. Hancock, *Pariah Syndrome*, pp. 37–38; Bercovici, *Gypsies*, pp. 57–58; J.W. Ozanne, *Three Years in Roumania* (London: Chapman & Hall, 1878), pp. 47, 57–66; Gjorgjević, "Rumanian Gypsies in Serbia," p. 13.
36. Gjorgjević, "Rumanian Gypsies in Serbia," pp. 9–15.
37. Ibid., pp. 10–11; Ozanne, *Three Years in Roumania*, pp. 65–66.
38. Charles Boner, *Transylvania: Its Products and People* (London: Longmans, Green, Reader, and Dyer, 1865), pp. 348–353; T.W. Thompson, "Gypsies in the Mezöség of Transylvania," *Journal of the Gypsy Lore Society*, New Series, Vol. 8, No. 3 (1914–1915), pp. 194–195.
39. Boner, *Transylvania*, pp. 424–428; T.W. Thompson, "Gypsy Prisoners at Szamos Ujvár, Transylvania," *Journal of the Gypsy Lore Society*, New Series, Vol. 8, No. 3 (1914–1915), pp. 195–196.
40. Gjorgjević, "Rumanian Gypsies in Serbia," pp. 13–14.
41. Castellan, *History of the Romanians*, pp. 136–142; Seton-Watson, *History of the Roumanians*, pp. 367–369.
42. William John Haley, "The Gypsy Conference at Bucharest," *Journal of the Gypsy Lore Society*, Third Series, Vol. 13, No. 4 (1934), p. 184; Castellan, *History of the Romanians*, pp. 141–143; Chris Cook and John Stevenson, *The Longman Handbook of Modern European History, 1763–1985* (London: Longman, 1987), p. 220; Seton-Watson, *History of the Roumanians*, pp. 385–389; Oţetea, *Concise History of Romania*, p. 403.
43. Seton-Watson, *History of the Roumanians*, p. 387; Hancock, *Pariah Syndrome*, p. 45.
44. Castellan, *History of the Romanians*, pp. 153–157; David M. Crowe, *World War I and Europe in Crisis, 1914–1935* (Piscataway, NJ: Research and Education Association, 1990), p. 12; Oţetea, *Concise History of Romania*, pp. 414–417.
45. Castellan, *History of the Romanians*, pp. 157–158; Oţetea, *Concise History of Romania*, pp. 418–421.
46. Castellan, *History of the Romanians*, pp. 158–166; Oţetea, *Concise History of Romania*, pp. 421–430.
47. Elemér Illyés, *National Minorities in Romania: Change in Transylvania* (Boulder, CO: East European Monographs, 1982), pp. 33–35; Joseph S. Roucek, *Contemporary Roumania and Her Problems* (Stanford, CA: Stanford University Press, 1932), pp. 186–187.
48. Castellan, *History of the Romanians*, pp. 176–180; Illyés, *National Minorities in Romania*, pp. 86–89; Joseph Rothschild, *East Central Europe between the Two World Wars* (Seattle: University of Washington Press, 1990), pp. 288–290.
49. Rothschild, *East Central Europe*, pp. 288–289.
50. Ibid., pp. 290–291; Mitrany, *Land & Peasant in Rumania*, p. 225.
51. T. Oakes Hirst, "Bukovina Gypsies in 1922," *Journal of the Gypsy Lore Society*, Third Series, Vol. 24, Nos. 1–2 (January–April 1945), p. 61.
52. Bercovici, *Gypsies*, pp. 56–74.
53. David M. Crowe, "The Gypsy Historical Experience in Romania," in *The Gypsies of Eastern Europe*, ed. David M. Crowe and John Kolsti (Armonk, NY: M.E. Sharpe,

Inc., 1991), p. 69; Haley, "The Gypsy Conference at Bucharest," pp. 182–187; Ian Hancock, "The East European Roots of Romani Nationalism," in Crowe and Kolsti, eds., *Gypsies of Eastern Europe,* pp. 140–141; Donald Kenrick and Grattan Puxon, *The Destiny of Europe's Gypsies* (New York: Basic Books, 1972), p. 205; Bercovici, *Gypsies,* p. 56.

54. Haley, "The Gypsy Conference at Bucharest," pp. 186–187.

55. Ibid., pp. 184, 187; Kenrick and Puxon, *Destiny of Europe's Gypsies,* p. 205; Crowe, "Gypsy Historical Experience in Romania," pp. 69–70; F.G. Ackerley, "The Voice of the Gypsies," *Journal of the Gypsy Lore Society,* Third Series, Vol. 21, Nos. 1–2 (January–April 1942), pp. 71–72; Hancock, "East European Roots of Romani Nationalism," pp. 140–141; Dan Ionescu, "The Gypsies Organize," *Report on Eastern Europe* (June 29, 1990), p. 42.

56. Ionescu, "The Gypsies Organize," p. 42; Helsinki Watch, *Destroying Ethnic Identity: The Persecution of the Gypsies in Romania* (New York: Human Rights Watch, 1991), p. 11; George Potra, *Contribuţiuni la Istoricul iganilor din România* (Contributions to the History of the Gypsies in Romania) (Bucureşti: Fundaţia Regele Carol I, 1939), pp. 121–122; F. G. Ackerley, "George Potra's *Contribuţiuni la Istoricul Tiganilor din România,*" *Journal of the Gypsy Lore Society,* Third Series, Vol. 21, Nos. 1–2 (January–April 1942), p. 68.

57. Rothschild, *East Central Europe,* pp. 296–306. King Ferdinand I died in 1927, and a regency was set up to rule for Michael.

58. Ibid., pp. 285, 307–309; Hugh Seton-Watson, *Eastern Europe between the Wars* (Boulder, CO: Westview Press, 1986), pp. 75, 205–207.

59. Rothschild, *East Central Europe,* pp. 309–315; Castellan, *History of the Romanians,* pp. 200–204.

60. Bessarabia had been put in the Soviet sphere of influence in the secret Nazi-Soviet accord of August 23, 1939. Stalin, who had just occupied the Baltic states, integrated Bessarabia and northern Bukovina into the Moldavian SSR. Max Beloff, *The Foreign Policy of Soviet Russia, 1929–1941,* Vol. II (London: Oxford University Press, 1966), pp. 331–333; David M. Crowe, *The Baltic States and the Great Powers: Foreign Relations, 1938–1940* (Boulder, CO: Westview Press, 1993), pp. 174–175; Rothschild, *East Central Europe,* pp. 315–317; Castellan, *History of the Romanians,* p. 207.

61. Castellan, *History of the Romanians,* pp. 208–210; Rothschild, *East Central Europe,* pp. 316–317; Jean Ancel, "The 'Christian' Regimes of Romania and the Jews, 1940–1942," *Holocaust and Genocide Studies,* Vol. 7, No. 1 (Spring 1993), pp. 15, 18. Romania's first wartime anti-Semitic legislation had been adopted on September 9, 1940 but was shelved by Antonescu after Jewish leaders reminded him of his promise that his government would be "based on faith and justice, on law, order and humanity." Joseph B. Schechtman, "The Transnistria Reservation," *YIVO Annual of Jewish Social Science,* Vol. 8 (1953), pp. 178–179; Julius B. Fisher, "How Many Jews Died in Transnistria?" *Jewish Social Studies,* Vol. 20, No. 2 (April 1958), p. 97; Kenrick and Puxon, *Destiny of Europe's Gypsies,* pp. 129–130.

62. Rothschild, *East Central Europe,* pp. 316–317; Castellan, *History of the Romanians,* pp. 207–210; Kenrick and Puxon, *Destiny of Europe's Gypsies,* pp. 128–129; Jean-Paul Clébert, *The Gypsies,* translated by Charles Duff (New York: E. P. Dutton, 1963), p. 209; it is peculiar to note that the Bucharest press "reported that 25,000 Jews were deported to Transnistria in the middle of October 1942," a figure identical to the number of Roma shipped to the "reservation." Schechtman, "The Transnistria Reservation," p. 181 [178–196]; Dalia Ofer, "The Holocaust in Transnistria: A Special Case of Genocide," in ed. Lucjan Dobroszycki and Jeffrey S. Gurock *The Holocaust in the Soviet Union* (Armonk, NY: M.E. Sharpe, 1993), pp. 133–136, 143. The three major waves of Jewish deportations to Transnistria took place between the fall of 1941

and the spring of 1942, the summer of 1942 through the spring of 1943, and from the summer of 1943 to March 1944; I. C. Butnaru, *The Silent Holocaust: Romania and Its Jews* (New York: Greenwood Press, 1992), pp. 112–162 passim.

63. Kenrick and Puxon, *Destiny of Europe's Gypsies*, p. 129.
64. Bohdan Krawchenko, *Social Change and National Consciousness in Twentieth-Century Ukraine* (New York: St. Martin's Press, 1985), pp. 161–162; Kenrick and Puxon, *Destiny of Europe's Gypsies*, p. 129; there were approximately 125,000 ethnic Germans in Transnistria. Schechtman, "The Transnistria Reservation," pp. 178–179.
65. Kenrick and Puxon, *Destiny of Europe's Gypsies*, pp. 129–130.
66. Helsinki Watch, *Destroying Ethnic Identity* (Romania), pp. 106–107.
67. Joseph B. Schechtman, "The Gypsy Problem," *Midstream*, Vol. XII, No. 9 (November 1966), pp. 56–57.
68. Helsinki Watch, *Destroying Ethnic Identity* (Romania), pp. 14–15; Kenrick and Puxon, *Destiny of Europe's Gypsies*, p. 130.
69. Kenrick and Puxon, *Destiny of Europe's Gypsies*, pp. 129–130; Castellan, *History of the Romanians*, p. 210.
70. Castellan, *History of the Romanians*, pp. 210–223.
71. Ibid., pp. 223–224; Walter M. Bacon, Jr., "Romania," in *Communism in Eastern Europe*, 2nd edition, ed. Teresa Rakowska-Harmstone (Bloomington: Indiana University Press, 1984), pp. 167–168; Sam Beck, "Ethnicity, Class, and Public Policy: Tiganii/Gypsies in Socialist Romania," in *Papers for the V Congress of Southeast European Studies*, ed. Kot K. Shangriladze and Erica W. Townsend (Belgrad, September 1984) (Columbus, OH: Slavica Publishers, 1984), pp. 27–28.
72. Bacon, "Romania," p. 168; Illyés, *National Minorities in Romania*, pp. 107, 111, 113, 115–116; Trond Gilberg, *Nationalism and Communism in Romania: The Rise and Fall of Ceausescu's Personal Dictatorship* (Boulder, CO: Westview Press, 1990), p. 170.
73. Illyés, *National Minorities in Romania*, p. 35; Fred S. Pisky, "The People," in *Romania*, ed. Stephen Fischer-Galati (New York: Frederick A. Praeger, 1957), pp. 54, 56.
74. Helsinki Watch, *Destroying Ethnic Identity* (Romania), pp. 17–18; Illyés, *National Minorities in Romania*, p. 118; Beck, "Ethnicity, Class, and Public Policy," pp. 26–27.
75. Trond Gilberg, *Modernization in Romania since World War II* (New York: Praeger Publishers, 1975), pp. 216, 223, 225–227; Trond Gilberg, "Ethnic Minorities in Romania under Socialism," *East European Quarterly*, Vol. 7, No. 4 (January 1974), pp. 445, 447, 456, 459–463.
76. Gilberg, "Ethnic Minorities in Romania," pp. 439, 441, 464; Gilberg, *Modernization in Romania*, pp. 216, 223–225; Paul S. Shoup, *The East European and Soviet Data Handbook* (New York: Columbia University Press, 1981), p. 139.
77. Gilberg, "Ethnic Minorities in Romania," pp. 439, 441, 464; Gilberg, *Modernization in Romania*, p. 225.
78. Gilberg, *Modernization in Romania*, pp. 226–227, 230; Michael Shafir, *Romania: Politics, Economics and Society* (London: Frances Pinter, 1985), p. 109.
79. Gilberg, *Modernization in Romania*, pp. 213–214. It is interesting to compare Gilberg's complimentary views of Ceausescu's minorities policy in the above study with his analysis 15 years later in his *Nationalism and Communism in Romania*, pp. 173–179; Robert R. King, *History of the Romanian Communist Party* (Stanford, CA: Hoover Institution Press, 1980), pp. 131–134.
80. Helsinki Watch, *Destroying Ethnic Identity* (Romania), pp. 18–19, 109–110; Zoltan D. Barany, "Democratic Changes Bring Mixed Blessings for Gypsies," *RFE/RL Research Report* (May 15, 1992), p. 43; Grattan Puxon, *Rom: Europe's Gypsies* (London: Minority Rights Group, 1973), pp. 16–17, 23; Grattan Puxon, *Rom: Europe's Gypsies* (London: Minority Rights Group, 1975), p. 17, estimated that Romania's Gypsy population had grown to 661,500 by 1975; Michael Shafir, "Preliminary Results of the 1992 Romanian Census," *RFE/RL Research Report*

(July 24, 1992), p. 65; "Gypsies in Eastern Europe and the Soviet Union," *Radio Free Europe Research*, RAD Background Report No. 72 (April 12, 1978), p. 5.

81. Helsinki Watch, *Destroying Ethnic Identity* (Romania), pp. 108–109.
82. Ibid., pp. 109–111; Gilberg, *Nationalism and Communism in Romania*, p. 166.
83. Ibid., pp. 111–113.
84. Ibid., pp. 113–114.
85. Ibid., pp. 114–115.
86. Ibid., pp. 115–116.
87. Ibid., p. 22; Gilberg, *Nationalism and Communism in Romania*, pp. 176–177.
88. Helsinki Watch, *Destroying Ethnic Identity* (Romania), pp. 22–23; Gilberg, *Nationalism and Communism in Romania*, pp. 237–239; according to Grattan Puxon in his *Roma: Europe's Gypsies* (London: Minority Rights Group, 1987), pp. 10–11, 10% of Romania's Gypsies were "on the road at any one time;" Brian Hall, *Stealing from a Deep Place: Travels in Southeastern Europe* (New York: Farrar, Straus, Giroux, 1990), pp. 32–34.
89. Nestor Ratesh, *Romania: The Entangled Revolution* (New York: Praeger Publishers, 1991), pp. 7, 21–43; Ion Pacepa, *Red Horizons* (Washington, D.C.: Regnery Gateway, 1990), pp. 427–437. These pages contain the transcripts of the Ceauşescus' "trial."
90. Andrei Codrescu, *The Hole in the Flag* (New York: Avon Books, 1991), p. 37; Gale Stokes, *The Walls Came Tumbling Down: The Collapse of Communism in Eastern Europe* (New York: Oxford University Press, 1993), pp. 162–166; Katherine Vedery and Gail Kligman, "Romania after Ceauşescu: Post-Communist Communism?" in *Eastern Europe in Revolution*, ed. Ivo Banac (Ithaca, NY: Cornell University Press, 1992), pp. 118–119.
91. Stokes, *Walls Came Tumbling Down*, p. 172; Ratesh, *Romania*, pp. 49–52; Robert R. King," "Romania," in *1991 Yearbook on International Communist Affairs*, ed. Richard F. Staar and Margit N. Grigory (Stanford, CA: Hoover Institution Press, 1991), pp. 333–335; John Kifner, "A Country is Haunted," *The New York Times*, February 20, 1990, p. A6.
92. Celestine Bohlen, "Rumania's Rulers Agree to Share Power," *The New York Times*, February 2, 1990, p. A9; John Kifner, "Fighting Abates in Transylvania but Not the Anger," *The New York Times*, March 27, 1990, p. A7; Celestine Bohlen, "In Transylvania, the Battle for the Past Continues," *The New York Times*, March 18, 1990, p. A13; George Schöpflin and Hugh Poulton, *Romania's Ethnic Hungarians* (London: Minority Rights Group, 1990), p. 21; Ionescu, "The Gypsies Organize," p. 41; "Gypsy Kings," *The Economist*, May 15, 1993, p. 62; in 1993, the colorful Cioaba had himself named Emperor of All the Gypsies, an event disputed by his competitor, Emperor Iulian I of All the Gypsies. However, according to Dan Ionescu, Cioaba's power was "somewhat limited," and he was "'a king in theory' rather than in practice." Regardless, he played the role well, and evidently had enriched himself in the process. "Gypsy Throne Has Two Competitors, *Winston-Salem Journal*, August 10, 1993, p. 2; Codrescu, *Hole in the Flag*, p. 216; one journalist said Cioaba drove "a Mercedes, lives with an extended family in a large home in the city of Sibiu, and is quick to flash a smile with his gold-capped teeth." Matthew C. Vita, "The Gypsies: Threatened Again in Europe," *Austin American-Statesman*, December 1, 1991, p. C5.
93. Dan Ionescu, "The Ethnic Minorities," *Radio Free Europe Research*, Romania No. 3 (April 22, 1987), p. 19; Patricia Howard, "National Minorities in Eastern Europe," *Radio Free Europe Research*, RAD Background Report No. 156 (September 9, 1987), p. 6; Puxon, *Roma* (1987), p. 13; André Liebich, "Minorities in Eastern Europe: Obstacles to a Reliable Count," *RFE/RL Research Report*, Vol. 1, No. 20 (May 15, 1992), p. 38; Dan Ionescu, "Romania's First Post Communist Census," *RFE/RL Research Report* (March 13, 1992), pp. 58–59; in 1990, the Minority Rights Group calculated there were 2 million Hungarians in Romania, primarily in Transylvania,

plus 750,000 Gypsies, and 210,000 Germans. Schöpflin and Poulton, *Romania's Ethnic Hungarians*, pp. 5–6; Vladimir V. Kusin, "The Ethnic Factor," *Report on Eastern Europe*, (November 9, 1990), p. 35.

94. Ionescu, "The Gypsies Organize," pp. 39, 41.

95. Ionescu, "The Gypsies Organize," p. 42; Jackie Nesbitt, *Fourth World Romani Congress, Serock, Warsaw, Poland, 8th–12th April 1990* (Essex County: Essex County Council; Education Department, 1990), pp. 10, 14. Cioaba lost his seat on the World Romani Congress's Praesidium to Octavia Stoica primarily because of "Romanian national politics;" T. A. Acton, "After the Fourth World Romani Congress: Romani Encyclopaedists Set to Work," unpublished manuscript, n. d., pp. 2–3; Helsinki Watch, *Destroying Ethnic Identity* (Romania), p. 90.

96. Ionescu, "The Gypsies Organize," p. 42.

97. Ibid., p. 41.

98. Ibid., p. 40; Helsinki Watch, *Since the Revolution: Human Rights in Romania* (New York: Human Rights Watch, 1991), pp. 21–23; Helsinki Watch, *Destroying Ethnic Identity* (Romania), pp. 37–73 passim.

99. King, "Romania," in Starr and Grigory, *1991 Yearbook*, pp. 336–339; Helsinki Watch, *Destroying Ethnic Identity* (Romania), pp. 46–49, 88, 117–119; Sam Beck, "Violence Against Students in Bucharest Has Broad Implications for the Future," *The Chronicle of Higher Education*, September 5, 1990, p. B4.

100. Dan Ionescu, "Violence Against Gypsies Escalates," *Report on Eastern Europe* (June 21, 1991), p. 23; Helsinki Watch, *Destroying Ethnic Identity* (Romania), p. 82.

101. Dan Ionescu, "The Exodus," *Report on Eastern Europe* (October 26, 1990), pp. 25, 28; Dan Ionescu, "Recent Emigration Figures," *Report on Eastern Europe* (February 15, 1991) p. 22; Barbara Marshall, "German Migration Policies," in *Developments in German Politics*, ed. Gordon Smith, William E. Paterson, Peter H. Merkle, and Stephen Padgett (Durham, NC: Duke University Press, 1992), p. 247; unofficial German unification was in full swing between November 9, 1989, when the Berlin Wall was fully opened, and October 3, 1990, when the German Democratic Republic ceased to exist. William E. Paterson and Gordon Smith, "German Unity," in Smith, Paterson, Merkle, and Padgett, eds., *Developments in German Politics*, p. 9; J. F. Brown, *Surge to Freedom: The End of Communist Rule in Eastern Europe* (Durham, NC: Duke University Press, 1991), p. 147; Marc Fisher, "Germany's Gypsy Question," *The Washington Post*, November 1, 1992, pp. F1, F5, F7; Ferdinand Protzman, "Germany Fears the Spread of Anti-Foreign Violence," *The New York Times*, August 28, 1992, p. A6; Ferdinand Protzman, "In Rostock, Asylum-Seekers Lived in Powder Keg," *The New York Times*, September 3, 1992, p. A6; Marc Fisher, "Bonn, Bucharest Cement Accord to Repatriate Romanian Gypsies," *The Washington Post*, September 25, 1992, pp. A27, A30; Jack Kelley, "Gypsy Stereotypes Fuel Germany's Hatred," *USA Today*, November 25, 1992, p. 8A; "Romanian Gypsies are Skeptical About Germany's Financial Help," *The New York Times*, September 26, 1992, p. 3; Stephen Kinzer, "Germany Cracks Down; Gypsies Come First," *The New York Times*, September 27, 1992, p. E5; "Gypsies in Germany Face Crisis," *Chicago Tribune*, October 4, 1992, p. 18; Ferdinand Protzman, "Germany Attacks Rise as Foreigners Become Scapegoat," *The New York Times*, November 2, 1992, pp. A1, A4; Stephen Kinzer, "Germans in Accord on a Law to Limit Seekers of Asylum," *The New York Times*, December 8, 1992, pp. A1, A6.

102. Kelley, "Gypsy Stereotypes Fuel Germany's Hatred," p. 8A; "Gypsies in Germany Face Crisis," p. 18; "Romanian Gypsies are Skeptical," p. 3; many Gypsies failed to receive land allotments under the Land Law of February 1991 because they were not adequately informed of the "complicated application process" before the deadline for applications. Helsinki Watch, *Destroying Ethnic Identity* (Romania), pp. 84–85.

103. Ceaușescu took these measures, which also included harsh strictures against divorce, to deal with "a potential labour shortage." Special "vigilante squads" promoted the

program in the workplace, and women were forced to undergo periodic exams to determine if they were using any form of birth control. Shafir, *Romania,* p. 127, and Gilberg, *Nationalism and Communism in Romania,* p. 66; "Iliescu Signs Adoption Law," *Report on Eastern Europe* (July 26, 1991), p. 54; James Nachtwey, "Romania's Lost Children," *The New York Times Magazine,* June 24, 1990, pp. 28–33; "Rise in Deaths Under Romania's Abortion Ban," *News & Record* (Greensboro, NC), October 5, 1992, p. A4; Howard Alstein, "Rescuing Romania's Orphans," *The New York Times,* November 28, 1992, p. A13; Kathleen Hunt, "The Romanian Baby Bazaar," *The New York Times Magazine,* March 24, 1991, pp. 23–29, 38, 53; David J. and Sheila Rothman, "The New Romania," *The New York Review of Books,* September 23, 1993, p. 56.

104. Helsinki Watch, *Destroying Ethnic Identity* (Romania), pp. 93, 120; Barany, "Democratic Changes Bring Mixed Blessings for Gypsies," p. 45; Henry Kamm, "In New Eastern Europe, An Old Anti-Gypsy Bias," *The New York Times,* November 17, 1993, p. A6; part of Iliescu's problem centered around "a closely divided Parliament," which depended "on extreme nationalist parties for his government's survival." One of the most virulent anti-Gypsy parties, the Greater Romania Party, and the widely popular weekly *Romania Mare* consistently made attacks against Gypsies, which the latter blamed for "the country's economic and social malaise." Celestine Bohlen, "Where the Fires of Hatred Are Easily Stoked," *The New York Times,* August 4, 1991, p. E3; Michael Shafir, "The Greater Romania Party," *Report on Eastern Europe* (November 15, 1991), p. 25; Michael Shafir, "Promises and Reality," *Report on Eastern Europe* (January 14, 1991), p. 36; Michael Shafir, "Schopflinian Reality and Romanian Realism," *Report on Eastern Europe* (February 15, 1991), p. 37; Michael Shafir, "Growing Political Extremism in Romania," *RFE/RL Research Report* (April 2, 1993), pp. 18–25; Michael Shafir and Dan Ionescu, "The Minorities in 1991: Mutual Distrust, Social Problems, and Disillusion," *Report on Eastern Europe* (December 13, 1991), p. 27.

CHAPTER 5

1. David M. Crowe, "The Liuli (Gypsies) of Central Asia," *AACAR Bulletin,* Vol. 6, No. 1 (Spring 1993), p. 2; Kh. Kh. Nazarov, "Contemporary Ethnic Developments of the Central Asian Gypsies (Liuli)," *Soviet Anthropology and Archaeology,* Vol. 21, No. 3 (Winter 1982–83), pp. 4–6. This article originally appeared in *Etnicheskie protsessy i natsional'nykh grupp srednei Azii i Kazakhstana* (Ethnic Processes and Nationality Groups in Central Asia and Kazakhstan), ed. R. Sh. Dzharyglasinova and L. S. Tolstova (Moskva: Izdatel'stvo "Nauka," 1980), pp. 167–185; A. L. Balsham, *The Wonder That Was India* (New York: Grove Press, 1959), pp. 512–513; Angus Fraser, *The Gypsies* (Oxford: Blackwell, 1992), p. 35; Romila Thapar, *A History of India,* Vol. 1 (Harmondsworth: Penguin Books, 1974), pp. 229–232, 280; "Sredneaziatskie tsygane (Central Asian Gypsies)," in *Narody sredy Azii i Kazakhstana* (The People of Central Asia and Kazakhstan), ed. S.P. Tolstova, T.A. Zhdanko. S.M. Abramzona, and N.A. Kislyakova, Vol. 2 (Moskva: Izdatel'stvo akademii nauk SSSR, 1963), p. 598; Rene Grousset, *The Empire of the Steppes,* translated by Naomi Walford (New Brunswick, NJ: Rutgers University Press, 1907), pp. 443–446; A.V. German, *Bibliografiya o tsyganakh* (A Gypsy Bibliography) (Moskva: Tsentrizday, 1930), p. 10.
2. Volodymyr Kubijovyč and R. Senkus, "Gypsies," in *Encyclopedia of Ukraine,* ed. Volodymyr Kubijovyc, Vol. 2 (Toronto: University of Toronto Press, 1984), p. 106; T. V. Venttsel', "Tsygane," in E. M. Zhukov, *Sovetskaya istoricheskaya entsiklopediya,* Vol. 15 (Moskva: Izdatel'stvo "Sovetskaya entsiklopediya," 1961), p. 789; L. N. Cherenkov, "Nekotorye problemy etnografiocheskogo izucheniya tsygan SSSR" (Some Problems with the Ethnographic Study of Gypsies in the USSR), in *Malye i dispersnye etnicheskie*

gruppy v evropeiskoi chasti SSSR (geografiya rasseleniya i kul'turnye traditsii) (Small and Dispersed Ethnic Groups in the European Part of the USSR [Geographic Settling and Cultural Traditions]), ed. I.I. Krupnik (Moskva: Moskovskii filial Geograficheskogo obshchestva SSSR, 1985), p. 6; Jerzy Ficowski, *The Gypsies in Poland: History and Customs*, translated by Eileen Healey (Warsaw: Interpress, 1991), pp. 12–14; Jerzy Ficowski, *Cyganie na Polskich Drogach* (Gypsies on the Polish Road) (Kraków: Wydownictwo Literackie, 1985), pp. 21–31; Paul Ariste, "Gypsy Studies," *Journal of the Gypsy Lore Society*, Third Series, Vol. 43, Nos. 1–2 (January–April 1964), p. 59.

3. Cherenkov, "Nekotorye problemy etnograficheskogo izucheniya tsygan SSSR," p. 7; A. P. Barannikov, *The Ukrainian and South Russian Gypsy Dialects* (Leningrad: Academy of Sciences of the USSR, 1934), p. 8.

4. Ian Hancock, "Gypsy History in Germany and Neighboring Lands," in *The Gypsies of Eastern Europe*, ed. David M. Crowe and John Kolsti (Armonk, NY: M.E. Sharpe, Inc., 1991), pp. 11–12; Ficowski, *Gypsies in Poland*, p. 15.

5. Ficowski, *The Gypsies in Poland*, pp. 15–16, 19–20, 33–34; Ficowski, *Cyganie na Polskich Drogach*, pp. 32–39, 52.

6. Paul Ariste, "The Latvian Legend of May Rose," *Journal of the Gypsy Lore Society*, Third Series, Vol. 40, Nos. 3–4 (July–October 1961), pp. 101–102; Ya. S. Grosula, *Istoriya Moldavskoi SSR* (History of the Moldavian SSR) (Kishinev: "Shtiintsa," 1982), p. 99; N. G. Demeter and L. N. Cherenkov, "Tsygane v Moskve," in *Etnicheskie gruppy v gorodakh evropeiskoi chasti SSSR* (Ethnic Groups in the Cities of the European Part of the USSR), ed. I. I. Krupnik (Moskva: Moskovskii filial Geograficheskogo obshchestva SSSR, 1987), p. 40; E. O. Winstedt, "A Gypsy Traitor," *Journal of the Gypsy Lore Society*, Third Series, Vol. 22, Nos. 1–2 (January–April 1943), p. 63. Winstedt errs when he places the capture of Azov on June 3, 1696. See, for example, Richard H. Warner, "Azov Campaign of 1695–1696," in *The Modern Encyclopedia of Russian and Soviet History*, ed. Joseph L. Wieczynski, Vol. 2 (Gulf Breeze, Fl: Academic International Press, 1976), p. 215; W. R. Halliday, "A Russian Gypsy Renegade," *Journal of the Gypsy Lore Society*, Third Series, Vol. 2, No. 3 (1923), p. 96.

7. Barannikov, *Ukrainian and South Russian Gypsy Dialects*, pp. 8–9.

8. Demeter and Cherenkov, "Tsygane v Moskve," p. 40; Theodore Shabad, *Geography of the USSR: A Regional Survey* (New York: Columbia University Press, 1951), pp. 268–269. Tobolsk remained the governmental center of western Siberia until 1824.

9. German, *Bibliografiya o tsyganakh*, p. 11; Reimer Gronemeyer, *Zigeuner in Osteuropa: Eine Bibliographie zu den Ländern Polen, Tschechoslowakei und Ungarn (Mit einen Anhang über ältere Sowjetische Literatur* (Gypsies in East Europe: A Bibliography on Poland, Czechoslovakia and Hungary [with an Appendix on Older Soviet Literature]) (München: K. G. Saur, 1983), p. 237. Gronemeyer cites in some detail P. Keppen's *Chronologicheski Ukazatel' materialov dlja istorii inorodcev Evropejskoj Rossii* (Chronological Index of Material for the History of Foreigners in European Russia) (St. Petersburg, 1861), in pp. 236–240; Demeter and Cherenkov, "Tsygane v Moskve," p. 40; M. S. Anderson, *Peter the Great* (London: Thames and Hudson Ltd., 1978), p. 128.

10. Cherenkov, "Nekotorye problemy etnograficheskogo izucheniya tsygan SSSR," pp. 8–9; V.I. Naulko, "The Present Ethnic Composition of the Population of the Ukrainian SSR," *Soviet Sociology*, Vol. 3, No. 1 (Summer 1964), p. 20.

11. Barannikov, *Ukrainian and South Russian Gypsy Dialect*, p. 9.

12. German, *Bibliografiya o tsyganakh*, p. 26; Gronemeyer, *Zigeuner in Osteuropa*, p. 237; Marie Seton, "The Evolution of the Gypsy Theatre in the U.S.S.R.," *Journal of the Gypsy Lore Society*, Third Series, Vol. 14, No. 2 (1935), p. 65.

13. Barannikov, *Ukrainian and South Russian Gypsy Dialects*, pp. 10, 39; German, *Bibliografiya o tsyganakh*, p. 26; Isabel de Madariaga, *Russia in the Age of Catherine the Great* (London: Weidenfeld and Nicolson, 1981), pp. 66, 72, 208.

14. I. Rom-Lebedev, *Ot tsyganskogo khoro k teatru "Romen"* (From Gypsy Choirs to the Theatre "Romen") (Moskva: "Iskusstvo," 1990), p. 45; Vladimir Bobri, "Gypsies and Gypsy Choruses of Old Russia," *Journal of the Gypsy Lore Society,* Third Series, Vol. 40, Nos. 3–4 (July–October 1961), p. 117; Fraser, *The Gypsies,* p. 205; Vladimir Morosan, *Choral Performance in Pre-Revolutionary Russia* (Ann Arbor, MI: UMI Research Press, 1986), p. 65; Alfred E. Hamill, "Gypsies In and About Russian Literature," *Journal of the Gypsy Lore Society,* Third Series, Vol. 22, Nos. 1–2 (January–April 1943), p. 58.

15. Konrad Bercovici, *Gypsies: Their Life, Lore, and Legends* (New York: Greenwich House, 1983), pp. 205–206.

16. Madariaga, *Russia in the Age of Catherine the Great,* pp. 93, 100–101, 313; Vasili Klyuchevsky,. *Peter the Great* (New York: Vintage Books, 1958), p. 117.

17. Gronemeyer, *Zigeuner in Osteuropa,* p. 237; German, *Bibliografiya o tsyganakh,* p. 26; for a look at Browne's long rule over Livonia and Estonia, see David M. Crowe, "Riga," in Wieczynski, ed. *The Modern Encyclopediya of Russian and Soviet History* (1990), Vol. 52, pp. 111–113.

18. German, *Bibliografiya o tsyganakh,* p. 26; Gronemeyer, *Zigeuner in Osteuropa,* p. 237; Madariaga, *Russia in the Age of Catherine the Great,* pp. 40, 57.

19. Barannikov, *Ukrainian and South Russian Gypsy Dialects,* p. 10; Madariaga, *Russia in the Age of Catherine the Great,* pp. 347, 359, 364–367.

20. W. R. Halliday, "Russian Gypsies," *Journal of the Gypsy Lore Society,* Third Series, Vol. 4, No. 3 (1925), p. 143.

21. Elsie M. Hall, "Gentile Cruelty to Gypsies," *Journal of the Gypsy Lore Society,* Third Series, Vol. 11, No. 2 (1932), p. 49; Madariaga, *Russia in the Age of Catherine the Great,* p. 450.

22. German, *Bibliografiya o tsyganakh,* p. 27; Gronemeyer, *Zigeuner in Osteuropa,* p. 237; Ficowski, *Gypsies of Poland,* pp. 20–21; Ficowski, *Cyganie na Polskich Drogach,* pp. 50–54.

23. German, *Bibliografiya o tsyganakh,* p. 27; Gronemeyer, *Zigeuner in Osteuropa,* p. 237; Arthur Thesleff, "Report on the Gypsy Problem," *Journal of the Gypsy Lore Society,* New Series, Vol. 5, No. 2 (1911–12), p. 94; Roderick E. McGrew, "The Politics of Absolutism: Paul I and the Bank of Assistance for the Nobility," in *Paul I: A Reassessment of His Life and Reign,* ed. Hugh Ragsdale (Pittsburgh, PA: University Center for International Studies, University of Pittsburgh, 1979), p. 104.

24. German, *Bibliografiya o tsyganakh,* p. 27; Alexander I weakened the traditional powers of the Senate during this period, and created ministries to replace Peter the Great's colleges to create a more efficient administration. Kochubei was a prominent member of Alexander I's "Unofficial Committee" set up to consider governmental and other reforms during the first years of his reign. Allen McConnell, *Tsar Alexander I: Paternalistic Reformer* (New York: Thomas Y. Crowell Company, 1970), pp. 38–41; Elmo E. Roach, "Kochubei, Viktor Pavlovich," in Wieczynski, ed., *The Modern Encyclopedia of Russian and Soviet History* (1980), Vol. 17, pp. 91–92.

25. German, *Bibliografiya o tsyganakh,* pp. 27–28; actually, there are Greater and Lesser Uzen rivers that flow out of the Saratov oblast into Kazakstan. L. V. Andreeva, et al., *Malyi atlas SSSR* (Small Atlas of the USSR) (Moskva: Glavnoe Upravlenie Geodezii i Kartografii pri Sovete Ministrov SSSR, 1978), pp. 38–39; Shabad, *Geography of the USSR,* p. 195.

26. German, *Bibliografiya o tsyganakh,* p. 28; Thesleff, "Report on the Gypsy Problem," p. 95.

27. German, *Bibliografiya o tsyganakh,* p. 28; Alan Palmer, *Alexander I: Tsar of War and Peace* (New York: Harper & Row, 1974), pp. 175, 364.

28. George F. Jewsbury, "Bessarabia, Russian Relations With," in Wieczynski, ed., *The Modern Encyclodpedia of Russian and Soviet History* (1977), Vol. 4 (Gulf Breeze, FL: Academic International Press, 1977), pp. 84–85.

29. Jewsbury, "Bessarabia," p. 85; German, *Bibliografiya o tsyganakh,* pp. 28–29.
30. Ficowski, *Gypsies in Poland,* pp. 24–25; Ficowski, *Cyganie na Polskich Drogach,* pp. 62–66.
31. German, *Bibliografiya o tsyganakh,* pp. 28–29.
32. Ibid., p. 29; W. Bruce Lincoln, *Nicholas I: Emperor and Autocrat of All the Russias* (Bloomington: Indiana University Press, 1978), pp. 193–194; Henry H. Hirschbiel, "Kiselev, Pavel Dmitrievich," in Wieczynski, ed., *The Modern Encyclopedia of Russian and Soviet History* (1980), Vol. 17, p. 43.
33. German, *Bibliografiya o tsyganakh,* pp. 239–240.
34. John Shelton Curtiss, *Russia's Crimean War* (Durham, NC: Duke University Press, 1979), pp. 470–471, 501–502, 530–533; W. E. Mosse, *Alexander II and the Modernization of Russia* (New York: Collier Books, 1962), pp. 32, 41, 67; William H. Hill, "Alexander II," in Wieczynski, ed., *The Modern Encyclopedia of Russian and Soviet History* (1976), Vol. 1, p. 136; Richard Pipes, *Russia Under the Old Regime* (New York: Charles Scribners Sons, 1974), pp. 165–166.
35. Ficowski, *Gypsies in Poland,* pp. 26–33; Alexander Gieysztor, Stefan Kieniewicz, Emanuel Rostworowski, Janusz Tazbir, and Henryk Wereszycki, *History of Poland,* 2nd edition (Warszawa: PWN — Polish Scientific Publishers, 1979), pp. 350, 364. Napoleon I had abolished serfdom in the smaller Duchy of Warsaw in 1807, a fact reaffirmed by Alexander I in the Polish constitution drawn up at the Congress of Vienna in 1815; Fraser, *The Gypsies,* p. 229; Norman Davies, *God's Playground: A History of Poland,* Vol. 2 (New York: Columbia University Press, 1982), pp. 187–188, 351–365. To counter promises made by local Polish rulers during the January Uprising, the tsar granted "the peasants full freehold of the land they worked" and compensated the nobility with state bonds. These efforts did little to improve the lot of Poland's rural masses; "Red Roses on the Snow," *Sputnik,* No. 10 (October 1981), p. 65.
36. E. A. Druts and A. N. Gessler, "Fok'lor russikh Tsygan," in Krupnik, ed., *Malye i dispersnye etnicheskie,* pp. 118–119; Bobri, "Gypsies and Gypsy Choruses of Old Russia," pp. 118–119; Morosan, *Choral Performance in Pre-Revolutionary Russia,* pp. 64–66; Nicholas Riasanovsky, *Nicholas I and Official Nationality in Russia, 1825–1855* (Berkeley: University of California Press, 1969), p. 21. Liszt first visited Russia in 1842, where he rebuked Tsar Nicholas I for speaking while he played. In 1843, Liszt expressed sympathy for Polish nationalists in front of the tsar, whom he came to detest. Alan Walker, *Franz Liszt,* Vol. 1; *The Virtuoso Years, 1811–1847* (New York: Alfred A. Knopf, 1983), pp. 288–289 n. 9, 374–380; Franz Liszt, *The Gipsy in Music,* translated by Edwin Evans (London: William Reeves Bookseller Limited, 1926), pp. 149, 155.
37. Joel Janicki, "Gypsies," in *The Modern Encyclopedia of Russian and Soviet Literature,* Vol. 9, ed. George J. Gutsche (Gulf Breeze, FL: Academic International Press, 1989), p. 187.
38. Demeter and Cherenkov, "Tsygane v Moskve," p. 40; Henri Troyat, *Pushkin,* translated by Nancy Amphoux (New York: Minerva Press, 1975), pp. 5–6, 631; Leksa Manush, "The Problem of the Folk Music of the Gypsies (Sources of Gypsy Music in Europe)," *Soviet Anthropology and Archeology,* Vol. 25, No. 3 (Winter 1986–87), p. 17; Alaina Lemon, "Roma (Gypsies) in the Soviet Union and the Moscow Theatre 'Romen,'" *Nationalities Papers,* Vol. 19, No. 3 (Winter 1991), p. 365.
39. Bobri, "Gypsies and Gypsy Choruses of Old Russia," pp. 115–118; Rom-Lebedev, *Ot tsyganskogo khora,* pp. 46, 49.
40. Bobri, "Gypsies and Gypsy Choruses of Old Russia," pp. 117–120.
41. Bertha Malnik, "The Moscow Gypsy Theatre, 1957–8," *Journal of the Gypsy Lore Society,* Third Series, Vol. 38, Nos. 3–4 (July–October 1959), p. 83; Richard Anthony Leonard, *A History of Russian Music* (New York: Minerva Press, 1968), p. 35.

42. Bobri, "Gypsies and Gypsy Choruses of Old Russia," pp. 116–117; Rom-Lebedev, *Ot tsyganskogo khora,* pp. 50–52; D. S. Mirsky, *A History of Russian Literature,* ed. Francis J. Whitfield (New York: Vintage Books, 1958), pp. 295–296. Markevich was a "reactionary" novelist of the 1860s and 1870s who struck out at the "Polish intrigue and nihilism" prominent during the era of the January Uprising in Poland.

43. Troyat, *Pushkin,* pp. 264–267; Mirsky, *History of Russian Literature,* pp. 92–93; McConnell, *Tsar Alexander I,* pp. 196–197; Hamill, "Gypsies In and About Russian Literature," p. 58; "The Gypsies," in Alexander Pushkin, *Selected Works,* translated by Irina Zheleznova, Vol. 1; *Poetry,* (Moscow: Progress Publishers, 1974), pp. 65, 82.

44. Manush, "Problem of the Folk Music of the Gypsies," p. 17; Janicki, "Gypsies," p. 188; Mirsky, *History of Russian Literature,* pp. 105, 232, 361; Troyat, *Pushkin,* pp. 82–83, 264–267; Hamill, "Gypsies In and About Russian Literature," p. 58; Henri Troyat, *Tolstoy* (New York: Dell, 1969), pp. 346, 352–353, 364, 421–422; Thomas E. Berry, "Aputkin, Aleksei Nikolaevich (1840–93)," in *Handbook of Russian Literature,* ed. Victor Terras (New Haven, CT: Yale University Press, 1985), p. 25.

45. Troyat, *Tolstoy,* pp. 82–83.

46. Ibid., pp. 85–86, 162–164.

47. Mirsky, *History of Russian Literature,* pp. 216–218; Preeti Sahgal, "Aleksandr Blok and Appolon Grigor'ev: A Synthesized View of Life and Art," Ph.D diss. University of Virginia, 1983, p. 186; Dmitri Obolensky, *The Penguin Book of Russian Verse* (Baltimore, MD: Penguin Books, 1967), p. 214; Rom-Lebedev, *Ot tsyganskogo khora,* pp. 63–64.

48. Janicki, "Gypsies," pp. 188–189; Sahgal, "Aleksandr Blok and Appolon Grigor'ev," pp. 184–187; Yu. Lotman and Z. Mints, 'Chelovek prorody' v Russkoi literature XIX veka i 'tysganskaya tema' u Bloka (The "Nature of Man" in 19th-century Russian Literature and the "Gypsy Theme" in Blok), in *Blokovskii sbornik: Trudy nauchnoi konferentsii, posvyacheshennoi izuchenyu zhizni i tvorchestva A.A. Bloka, Mai 1962* (A Blok Collection: Works from a Scholarly Conference Devoted to the Study of the Life and Creations of A. A. Blok, May 1962), ed., Z. G. Mints and L. A. Aboldyeva (Tartu: Tartuskii gosudarstvennyi universitet, 1964), pp. 103–110, 112–114, 117–118. Blok was also affected by Pushkin and Tolstoi's Gypsy themes.

49. Janicki, "Gypsies," p. 188; Richard Gregg, "Tyutchev, Fyodor Ivanovich," in Terras, *Handbook of Russian Literature,* p. 492.

50. Rom-Lebedev, *Ot tsyganskogo khora,* pp. 54, 57–59; Bobri, "Gypsies and Gypsy Choruses of Old Russia," p. 119; Avrahm Yarmolinsky, *Turgenev: The Man, His Art and His Age* (New York: The Orion Press, 1959), pp. 105, 358; Mirsky, *History of Russian Literature,* p. 199; Jan Kochanowski, "Maskir Romende (Among Gypsies): The Views of a Latvian Gypsy," *Journal of the Gypsy Lore Society,* Third Series, Vol. 44, Nos. 3–4 (July–October 1965), p. 138.

51. E. H. Carr, *Dostoevsky, 1821–1881* (London: George Allen & Unwin, Ltd., 1962), p. 237.

52. Leonard, *History of Russian Music,* pp. 228–229.

53. Bobri, "Gypsies and Gypsy Choruses of Old Russia," pp. 114–115.

54. Geroid Tanquary Robinson, *Rural Russia under the Old Regime* (Berkeley: University of California Press, 1969), p. 63; German, *Bibliografiya o tsyganakh,* pp. 11–12, 33–34; Rom urban figures were more than twice the average for the general Russian population living in towns and cities between 1796 and 1897. Approximately 3.6 percent (1.3 million) of Russia's population lived in cities and towns in 1796, compared to 12.6 percent (16.3 million) in 1897. Nicholas V. Riasanovsky, "The Problem of the Peasant," in *The Peasant in Nineteenth Century Russia,* ed. Wayne S. Vucinich, (Stanford, CA: Stanford University Press, 1968), p. 263.

55. German, *Bibliografiya o tsyganakh,* p. 12; Henry Bauer, Andreas Kappeler, and Bridgette Roth, eds., *Die Nationalitäten des Russichen Reiches in der Volkszählung von 1897* (The Nationalities in the Russian Census of 1897), Vol. A (Stuttgart: Franz

Steiner Verlag, 1991), p. 199; Bauer, Kappeler, and Roth, *Die Nationalitäten des Russiches Reiches*, Vol. B, pp. 144, 212–469 passim. This detailed analysis of the 1897 census breaks down respondents by choice of native language and then by occupation, education, age, and region; N. N. Agarwal, *Soviet Nationalities Policy* (Agra: Sri Ram Mehra & Co., 1969), pp. 16–18; Riasanovsky, "The Problem of the Peasant," p. 263; Robinson, *Rural Russia under the Old Regime*, pp. 288–289 n. 1; Thesleff, "Report on the Gypsy Problem," pp. 90, 94; Thesleff, "Report on the Gypsy Problem," *Journal of the Gypsy Lore Society*, New Series, Vol. 5, No. 3 (1911–12), p. 218; "Gypsies," in *Encyclopedia Litaunica*, ed. Simas Suziedelis and Raphael Sealey, Vol. 2 (Boston: Encyclopedia Lituanica, 1972), p. 408.

56. Robinson, *Rural Russia under the Old Regime*, pp. 94–97, 288–289 n. 1; Riasanovsky, "The Problem of the Peasant," p. 263; Richard G. Robinson, Jr., *Famine in Russia, 1891–1892* (New York: Columbia University Press, 1975), pp. 170–171, 188–189; one example of the repressive nature of the regime of Alexander III was its restrictive, and sometimes violent, policies toward the Jews. The architect of these "reforms," Konstantin P. Pobedonostsev, the chief adviser to Alexander III and Nicholas II, felt "that the Russian government ought to repress and isolate the Jews." Anti-Gypsy sentiments often mirrored anti-Semitic feelings. Salo W. Baron, *The Russian Jew under Tsars and Soviets* (New York: Schocken Books, 1987), pp. 44–52; Robert F. Byrnes, *Pobedonostsev: His Life and Thought* (Bloomington: Indiana University Press, 1968), pp. 206–207.

57. Donald Kenrick and Grattan Puxon, *The Destiny of Europe's Gypsies*, p. 146; German, *Bibliografiya o tsyganakh*, p. 50; A. P. Barannikov, "W. I. Philonenko: 'The Crimean Gypsies,'" *Journal of the Gypsy Lore Society*, Third Series, Vol. 10, No. 2 (1931), pp. 144–145.

58. Devey Fearon de l'Hoste Ranking, "The Gypsies of Central Russia: Introduction," *Journal of the Gypsy Lore Society*, New Series, Vol. 4, No. 3 (January 1911), pp. 196, 198–199; Devey Fearon de l'Hoste Ranking, "The Gypsies of Central Russia: The Gypsies of Kisilefka," *Journal of the Gypsy Lore Society*, New Series, Vol. 4, No. 4 (April 1911), pp. 245–247, 251–255. The third part of this article is Devey Fearon de l'Hoste Ranking, "The Gypsies of Central Russia: Manners and Customs," *Journal of the Gypsy Lore Society*, New Series, Vol. 6, No. 2 (1912–13), pp. 90–110; Thesleff, "Report on the Gypsy Problem," p. 95.

59. Hancock, "Gypsy History in Germany," p. 14; Fraser, *The Gypsies*, p. 251; Cherenkov, "Nekotorye problemy etnograficheskogo izucheniya tsygan SSSR," pp. 7–9.

60. Rom-Lebedev, *Ot tsyganskogo khora*, pp. 55–57; William Ferguson, "Russian Gypsy Singers," *Journal of the Gypsy Lore Society*, Third Series, Vol. 12, No. 2 (1933), p. 108; Ludmilla Kafanova, "Gypsy Theatre Romen," *Sputnik*, No. 9 (September 1972), p. 92; "Red Roses on the Snow," pp. 62–63.

61. German, *Bibliografiya o tsyganakh*, pp. 6–8, 25–37, 47, 52–53, 57–63; Ranking, "Gypsies of Central Russia," pp. 195–196; Bernard J. Gilliat-Smith, "The Dialect of the Gypsies of Northern Russia," *Journal of the Gypsy Lore Society*, Third Series, Vol. 15, No. 2 (1932), pp. 71–72; K. P. Patkanoff, "Some Words on the Dialects of the Trans-Caucasian Gypsies—Boša and Karači," *Journal of the Gypsy Lore Society*, New Series, Vol. 1, No. 3 (January 1908), pp. 229–257. This is an abbreviated translation of his 1887 work.

62. David M. Crowe, *World War I and Europe in Crisis, 1914–1935* (Piscataway, NJ: Research and Education Association, 1990), pp. 18–29, 67–70.

63. Lemon, "Roma (Gypsies) in the Soviet Union," p. 367.

64. Graham Smith, "Nationalities Policy from Lenin to Gorbachev," in *The Nationalities Question in the Soviet Union*, ed. Graham Smith (New York: Longman, 1990), p. 6; Hugh Seton-Watson, "Russian Nationalities in Historical Perspective," in *The Last*

334   A HISTORY OF THE GYPSIES OF EASTERN EUROPE AND RUSSIA

Empire: Nationality and the Soviet Future, ed. Robert Conquest (Stanford, CA: Hoover Institution Press, 1986), p. 24.

65. David Crowe, N. G. Demeter, and Alaina Lemon, "Gypsies," in *Encyclopedia of World Cultures*, ed. Paul Friedrich and Norma Diamond, Vol. VI: *Russia and Eurasia/China* (Boston: G. K. Hall, 1994), pp. 145–148; "Stop Persecution of Gypsies," *Women and Revolution*, No. 38 (Winter 1990–91), p. 7; the Central Executive Committee (CEC) "assumed most of the executive and legislative powers of the Congress of Soviets," the Soviet Union's "supreme authority." In reality, the CEC "merely rubber-stamped decisions made by the ruling Party officials." David M. Crowe, "Central Executive Committee of the USSR," in Wieczynski, ed. *The Modern Encyclopedia of Russian and Soviet History* (1978), Vol. 6, pp. 171–172.

66. T. V. Ventsel', "Tsygane," in *Sovetskaya istoricheskaya entsiklopediya*, Vol. 15 (Moskva: Izdatel'stvo "Sovetskaya Entsiklopediya," 1961), p. 790.

67. Ilya Gitlits, "Gipsies in the USSR," *Sputnik*, No. 9 (September 1972), p. 103; Barannikov, *Ukrainian and South Russian Gypsy Dialects*, p. 7; Maurice Hindus, *Red Bread: Collectivization in a Russian Village* (Bloomington: Indiana University Press, 1988), pp. 323–324; Bercovici, *Gypsies*, p. 195; I. P. Tsameryan, *Teoreticheskie problemy obrazovaniya i razvitiya sovetskogo mnogonatsional'nogo gosudarstva* (Theoretical Problems on Education and Development of the Many Nationalities of the Soviet State) (Moskva: Izdatel'stvo "Nauka," 1973), p. 162; Frank Lorimer, *The Population of the Soviet Union: History and Prospects* (Geneva: League of Nations, 1946), pp. 55, 57. Lorimer lists the official 1926 Roma population in the Soviet Union as 61,234. The Soviet Union had a total population of 147,027,915, in 1926; *Narodnoe khozyaistvo SSSR, 1922–1982* (National Economy of the USSR, 1922–1982) (Moskva: "Finansy i Statistika," 1982), p. 33; there were 13,600 Gypsies in the Ukrainian Soviet Socialist Republic in 1926, with 2,500 of them in cities. There were 1,300 Gypsies in the Crimea, and 6,800 Roma in the northern Caucasus. Kubijovyč and Senkus, "Gypsies," p. 106.

68. Crowe, Demeter, and Lemon, "Gypsies," pp. 145–148; Fraser, *The Gypsies*, pp. 275–276.

69. Crowe, Demeter, and Lemon, "Gypsies," pp. 145–148; German, *Bibliografiya o tsyganakh*, pp. 9–10, 69–71. Other prominent leaders in the new Gypsy union were N. Pankov, N. Dudarova, D. Polyakov, and its secretary, I. Lebed; Demeter and Cherenkov, "Tsygane v Moskve," p. 44; Barannikov, *Ukrainian and South Russian Gypsy Dialects*, p. 28; Lemon, "Roma (Gypsies) in the Soviet Union" pp. 362, 366. Lemon strongly disagreed with Barannikov's assertions about Gypsy urban culture and their musical heritage and felt "there is much that is special to Romani culture."

70. E. Glyn Lewis, *Multilingualism in the Soviet Union: Aspects of Language Policy and Its Implementation* (The Hague: Mouton, 1972), pp. 132–134; Lorimer, *Population of the Soviet Union*, p. 57.

71. Lemon, "Roma (Gypsies) in the Soviet Union," p. 362; V. de Gila-Kochanowski, "N. A. Pankov," *Journal of the Gypsy Lore Society*, Third Series, Vol. 38, Nos. 3–4 (July–October 1959), pp. 159–160. Pankov helped Sergievskii and Barannikov with their *Tsygansko-russkii slovar* (1938) and was elected to the Union of Soviet Writers in 1944; Seton, "Evolution of the Gypsy Theatre," p. 71; German references 253 items on Gypsy subjects between 1926 and 1930, compared to 439 items between 1780 and 1925. *Bibliografiya o tsyganakh*, pp. 1–128 passim; Barannikov, *Ukrainian and South Russian Gypsy Dialects*, pp. 28–29; Gilliat-Smith, "The Dialect of the Gypsies of Northern Russia," p. 72; R. S. Demeter and P. S. Demeter, *Tsygansko-russkii i Tsyganskii slovar': Kelderarskii dialekt* (Gypsy-Russian and Russian-Gypsy Dictionary: Kalderash Dialect) (Moskva: "Russkii Yazyk," 1990), p. 8.

72. Lemon, "Roma (Gypsies) in the Soviet Union," p. 361; Rom-Lebedev, *Ot tsyganskogo khora*, pp. 163–164; Kafanova, "Gypsy Theatre Romen," p. 95; A. P. Barannikov, "On the Russian Gypsy Singers of Today," *Journal of the Gypsy Lore Society*, Third Series, Vol. 11, Nos. 3–4 (1932), pp. 189–190.

73. Barannikov, "On the Russian Gypsy Singers," pp. 189–191.
74. Ibid., pp. 191–192.
75. Crowe, "Liuli (Gypsies) of Central Asia," p. 3; Lemon, "Roma (Gypsies) in the Soviet Union," pp. 360–361; Barannikov, "On the Russian Gypsy Singers," pp. 191–192; Rom-Lebedev, *Ot tsyganskogo khora,* pp. 165–169; Demeter and Cherenkov, "Tsygane v Moskve," pp. 44–45; Larry E. Holmes, "Lunarcharshii, Anatolii Vasil'evich," in Wieczynski, ed., *The Modern Encyclopedia of Russian and Soviet History* (1981), Vol. 20, pp. 192–193.
76. Seton, "Evolution of the Gypsy Theatre," pp. 66–68; Benjamin Pinkus, *The Jews of the Soviet Union* (Cambridge: Cambridge University Press, 1989), pp. 121–123; Kafanova, "Gypsy Theatre Romen," p. 96.
77. "Red Roses on the Snow," pp. 63–64; Seton, "Evolution of the Gypsy Theatre," pp. 68–71; Janicki, "Gypsies," pp. 187–188; Lemon, "Roma (Gypsies) in the Soviet Union," pp. 363–364; Kafanova, "Gypsy Theatre Romen," p. 92; Rom-Lebedev, *Ot tsyganskogo khora,* pp. 178–179.
78. Crowe, *World War I and Europe in Crisis,* pp. 92–95; David M. Crowe, "Anti-Semitism and Anti-Jewish Policy in the Soviet Union and Russia, 1917–1992," Unpublished manuscript (1992), p. 4; Stalin blamed peasant resistance on the *kulaks,* rich, middle class peasants, and made them villains in the war against peasant opponents to his collectivization schemes. One member of the Gypsy Song and Dance Ensemble in Bryansk, Nikolai Volshaninov, told a Soviet journalist in the late 1960s that as head "of one of the first Gypsy collective farms in the country," he was involved "in the life-and-death struggle . . . against the kulaks." During the class war, "Volshaninov's four brothers-in-law were all killed by kulak bullets." Mark Barinov, "How Real are Those Gypsies," *Sputnik,* No. 6 (1967), p. 208; Lemon, "Roma (Gypsies) in the Soviet Union," p. 363.
79. Crowe, Demeter, and Lemon, "Gypsies," pp. 145–148; Crowe, "Liuli (Gypsies) of Central Asia," p. 3.
80. David M. Crowe, *The Baltic States and the Great Powers: Foreign Relations, 1938–1940* (Boulder, CO: Westview Press, 1993), pp. 77–81, 150–175; Bohdan B. Budurowycz, *Polish-Soviet Relations, 1932–1939* (New York: Columbia University Press, 1963), pp. 186–187. Soviet forces occupied an area of 196,000 square miles in Poland; prior to the fall of 1938, when Poland acquired a small portion of Czechoslovakian Silesia (Teschen, Ciesyzn, or Tešin), Poland consisted territorially of 388,634 square kilometers. The 1931 census showed a total Polish population of 31,915,779. Joseph Rothschild, *East Central Europe between the Two World Wars* (Seattle: University of Washington Press, 1990), pp. 35–36.
81. Kenrick and Puxon, *Destiny of Europe's Gypsies,* pp. 183–184; Ficowski, *Gypsies in Poland,* p. 36; Vanya Kochanowski, "Some Notes on the Gypsies of Latvia," *Journal of the Gypsy Lore Society,* Third Series, Vol. 25, No. 3 (July 1946), p. 34, says of the 5,000 Latvian Gypsies, 3,000 to 3,5000 were Cigny, or Latvian Gypsies, who lived in Kurzeme, Vidzeme, or Zemgale, while the rest of the country's Roma were Haladytxa, or Polish-Russian Gypsies, who lived in Latgale and part of Zemgale; V. I. Koslov, "Processes of Ethnic Change and Population Dynamics among the Peoples of the USSR," *Soviet Anthropology and Archeology,* Vol. 26, No. 3 (Winter 1987–88), p. 51; Gerhard Simon, *Nationalismus und Nationalitätenpolitik in der Sowjetunion* (Baden-Baden: Nomas Verlagsgesellschaft, 1986), p. 424.
82. Kochanowski, "Some Notes on the Gypsies of Latvia," p. 113; Crowe, *Baltic States and the Great Powers,* pp. 163–178.
83. The Einsatzgruppen, "the mobile arms of the German extermination machinery," were formed before the German invasion of Poland in 1939, where they "initiated a massive terror campaign against Jews and the Polish intelligentsia and upper classes that claimed tens of thousands of victims." Yitzhak Arad, Shmuel Krakowski, and

Shmuel Spector, eds., *The Einsatzgruppen Reports* (New York: Holocaust Library and Yad Vashem, 1989), ii–vii; Zvi Gitelman, "Soviet Reactions to the Holocaust, 1945–1991," in *The Holocaust in the Soviet Union,* ed. Lucjan Dobroszycki and Jeffrey S. Gurock (Armonk, NY: M.E. Sharpe, 1993), pp. 4–6; Kenrick and Puxon, *Destiny of Europe's Gypsies,* p. 143; Louis L. Snyder, *Encyclopedia of the Third Reich* (New York: Paragon House, 1989), pp. 81–82, 317, 321, 324; Christopher R. Browning, *Ordinary Men: Reserve Police Battalion 101 and the Final Solution* (New York: HarperCollins, 1992), pp. 9–10.

84. The Karaites were a small "nonrabbinic" group of Jews in the Crimea, Lithuania, and Ukraine that claimed to be "a separate ethnoreligious group." The Germans accepted them as "Germanic Goths who had adopted a distinct form of Judaism as a religion, and the Crimean Tatar tongue as a language." As a result, they did not suffer the fate of the Krymchaks, "the indigenous Jewish community of the Crimean peninsular, whose native tongue [was] Judeao-Crimean Tatar." The Krymchaks were "almost entirely exterminated by the Nazis." Michael Zand, "Notes on the Culture of the Non-Ashkenazic Jewish Communities under Soviet Rule," in *Jewish Culture and Identity in the Soviet Union,* ed. Yaacov Ro'i and Avi Beker (New York: New York University Press, 1991), pp. 378–380; Ronald Wixman, *The Peoples of the USSR: An Ethnographic Handbook* (Armonk, NY: M.E. Sharpe, Inc., 1988), pp. 94, 114; Arad, Krakowski, and Spector, eds., *Einsatzgruppen Reports,* pp. 153, 158, 198, 256, 267, 273, 284, 309, 318, 325–326, 344; Einsatzgruppen reports of the execution of 824 Roma in Simferopol by mid-December 1941 counters the popular myth about the execution of 800 of the city's Gypsies on Christmas Eve, 1941. Kenrick and Puxon, *Destiny of Europe's Gypsies,* pp. 145–146; Hancock, "Gypsy History in Germany," p. 19.

85. Matthew Cooper, *The Nazi War against Soviet Partisans, 1941–1944* (New York: Stein and Day, 1979), pp. 59–64, 93–94, 176–178; Alexander Werth, *Russia at War, 1941–1945* (New York: E. P. Dutton, 1964), pp. 710–717; Arad, Krakowski, and Spector, eds., *Einsatzgruppen Reports,* p. 370; Kenrick and Puxon, *Destiny of Europe's Gypsies,* pp. 144, 147–148; Edgar M. Howell, *The Soviet Partisan Movement, 1941–1944* (Washington: Department of the Army, 1956), pp. 59, 97, 116–122; Charles V.P. von Luttichau, "Some Observations on Guerilla Warfare in Russia during World War II," unpublished manuscript, n.d., pp. 21–22, 33, n. 31.

86. Gitelman, "Soviet Reactions to the Holocaust," pp. 6–8; William Korey, "A Monument over Babi Yar," in Dobroszycki and Gurock, eds., *Holocaust in the Soviet Union,* pp. 62–64. The killings were done by Sonderkommando 4a of Einsatzgruppe C, aided by order Police Battalion No. 9; Rabbi Abraham Cooper, Adaire Klein, and Avra Shapiro, *Babi Yar, 1941–1991* (Los Angeles: Simon Wiesenthal Center, 1991), pp. 9–16, 51–52; Anatoly Kuznetzov, *Babi Yar: A Documentary Novel* (New York: Dell, 1969), pp. i, 100; Browning, *Ordinary Men,* p. 18.

87. Kenrick and Puxon, *Destiny of Europe's Gypsies,* pp. 128–129, 146; David Crowe, "The Gypsy Historical Experience in Romania,." in Crowe and Kolsti, eds., *Gypsies of Eastern Europe,* p. 70; Browning, *Ordinary Men,* p. 42.

88. Kenrick and Puxon, *Destiny of Europe's Gypsies,* pp. 148–149; Gabriel Tyrnauer, *Gypsies and the Holocaust: A Bibliography and Introductory Essay* (Montreal: Montreal Institute for Genocide Studies, 1991), xiii–xiv; Gerald Reitlinger, *The SS: Alibi of a Nation* (New York: Da Capo Press, 1989), p. 186, n. 1; Benno Müller-Hill, *Murderous Science: Elimination by Scientific Selection of Jews, Gypsies, and Others, Germany, 1933–1945,* translated by George R. Fraser (Oxford: Oxford University Press, 1988), p. 59.

89. Kenrick and Puxon, *Destiny of Europe's Gypsies,* pp. 89–90, 148; Michael Burleigh and Wolfgang Wipperman, *The Racial State: Germany, 1933–1945* (Cambridge: Cambridge University Press, 1991), p. 125; Snyder, *Encyclopedia of the Third Reich,* p. 36; Robert Wistrich, *Who's Who in Nazi Germany* (New York: Bonanza Books, 1984), pp. 22–25.

90. Kenrick and Puxon, *Destiny of Europe's Gypsies*, pp. 148–149.
91. Ibid., *Destiny of Europe's Gypsies*, pp. 148–150, 183–184; Crowe, Demeter, and Lemon, "Gypsies," pp. 145–148; State Museum of Auschwitz-Birkenau and the Documentary and Cultural Centre of German Sintis and Roms, *Memorial Book: The Gypsies at Auschwitz-Birkenau*, Vols. I–II (München: K. G. Saur, 1993), pp. 3, 1469–1471; Kochanowski, "Notes on the Gypsies of Latvia," pp. 115–116; Paul Ariste, "Concerning the Baltic Gypsies and Their Dialects," *Journal of the Gypsy Lore Society*, Third Series, Vol. 43, Nos. 1–2 (January–April 1964), p. 59; Dora Yates, "*Mustlastest*," *Journal of the Gypsy Lore Society*, Third Series, Vol. 38, Nos., 3–4 (July–October 1959), p. 150; Ficowski, *Gypsies in Poland*, p. 49; Jerzy Ficowski, "The Polish Gypsies of To-Day," *Journal of the Gypsy Lore Society*, Third Series, Vol. 29, Nos. 3–4 (July–October 1950), p. 95; Jerzy Ficowski, "The Gypsy in the Polish People's Republic," *Journal of the Gypsy Lore Society*, Third Series, Vol. 35, Nos. 1–2 (January–April 1956), p. 29. There were about 5,000–6,000 Roma in Poland by the end of World War II, a figure that rose to 30,000 by 1949. Poland was the first Soviet-bloc country that begin "to try to integrate nomadic Rom voluntarily" in 1952. Since this effort proved ineffective in halting Gypsy nomadism, authorities implemented a crash program against nomadism in 1964. Poland's Roma population rose steadily over the years and reached 70,000 (0.19 percent of the population) in 1986. Over the next six years, the country's Gypsy population declined to 15,000 as large numbers of Roma fled to Germany. Poles told this author in the summer of 1992 that the country had no Gypsies and that those who were in the country were not Polish. These sentiments reflected the strong public dislike of the Gypsies that exploded in violent outbursts against the prosperous Gypsy community in Mlawa on June 26, 1991. In a poll taken by Freedom House and the American Jewish Committee in the early 1990s, 72 percent of the Polish respondents said they preferred not to have any Roma living near them, sentiments shared by Polish students in a poll taken by the Sociological Research Department of the Institute for Scientific Policy and Higher Education in 1991. Grattan Puxon, *Roma: Europe's Gypsies* (London: Minority Rights Group, 1987), pp. 9–10, 13; Ficowski, *Gypsies in Poland*, p. 52; David McQuaid, "The Growing Assertiveness of Minorities," *RFE/RL Report on Eastern Europe* (December 13, 1991), p. 23; "Poles Vent their Economic Rage on Gypsies," *The New York Times*, July 25, 1991, p. A5; Freedom House and the American Jewish Committee, *Democracy, Economic Reform and Western Assistance in Czechoslovakia, Hungary and Poland: A Comparative Public Opinion Survey* (New York: Freedom House and The American Jewish Committee, 1991), pp. 63–65; Barbara Wilska-Duszynska, "Poles and Strangers: Student Attitudes towards National Minorities," translated by PNB, *Nowa Europa*, No. 106 (July 2, 1992), pp. 8–12, David M. Crowe, "Personal Interviews," Warsaw, Cracow, and Zamocz, Poland, July 8–13, 1992.
92. Werth, *Russia at War*, p. 251; Stanislav Radzinsky, "A Stirring Play at the Moscow Gypsy Theatre," *Journal of the Gypsy Lore Society*, Third Series, Vol. 24, Nos. 3–4 (July–October 1945), pp. 120–121; "Moscow's Gypsy Theatre," *Journal of the Gypsy Lore Society*, Third Series, Vol. 26, Nos. 3–4 (July–October 1947), p. 173; Sergei Bogomazov, "Moscow Gypsy Artists in Wartime," *Journal of the Gypsy Lore Society*, Third Series, Vol. 24, Nos. 1–2 (January–April 1945), pp. 60–61; Kafanova, "Gypsy Theatre Romen," p. 94.
93. David M. Crowe, "Joseph Stalin, 1879–1953," in *Research Guide to European Historical Biography*, ed. James A. Moncure, Vol. 4 (Washington, DC: Beacham Publishing, Inc., 1992), pp. 1783, 1787; Crowe, "Anti-Semitism and Anti-Jewish Policy in the Soviet Union," pp. 5–9; Crowe, Demeter, and Lemon, "Gypsies," pp. 145–148.
94. David M. Crowe, "Nikita Khrushchev, 1894–1971," in Moncure, ed. *Research Guide to European Historical Biography*, Vol. 2, p. 1066.

95. Crowe, Demeter, and Lemon, "Gypsies," pp. 145–148; T. V. Ventsel', "Gypsies," in *Great Soviet Encyclopedia,* Vol. 28 (New York: Macmillan, 1978), p. 437; "Tsygane," in *Sovetskaya istoricheskaya entsiklopediya,* Vol. 15, p. 790; Lemon, "Roma (Gypsies) in the Soviet Union," pp. 369–370 n. 7.

96. Basil Ivan Rákóczi, "An Artist's Visit to the Gypsies of Southern France and to the U.S.S.R.," *Journal of the Gypsy Lore Society,* Third Series, Vol. 40, Nos. 3–4 (July–October 1961), pp. 125–126; Malnick, "Moscow Gypsy Theatre," p. 84; Crowe, Demeter, and Lemon, "Gypsies," pp. 145–148.

97. Fraser, *The Gypsies,* pp. 271–272; Cherenkov, "Nekotorye problemy etnograficheskogo izucheniya tsygan SSSR," pp. 6–7; I. M. Andronikova, "Evolution of the Dwellings of the Russian Gypsies," *Soviet Anthropology and Archeology,* Vol. 11, No. 1 (Summer 1972), p. 24; Nikolai Cherkhasin, "Gipsy Drovers on the Trail," *Sputnik,* No. 9 (September 1972), pp. 100–103.

98. Bernard Comrie, *The Languages of the Soviet Union* (Cambridge: Cambridge University Press, 1981), p. 157; Wixman, *Peoples of the USSR,* p. 77; Simon, *Nationalismus und Nationalitätenpolitik in der Sowjetunion,* pp. 436, 442; Arkadii A. Isupov, *Natsional'nyi sostavnaseleniya SSSR (po itogam perepisi 1959 g.)* (Composition of the Population of the USSR [Based on the 1959 Census]) (Moskva: Izdatel'stvo "Statistika," 1961), p. 16; Goskomstat SSSR, *Natsional'nyi sostav naseleniya SSSR po dannym vsesoyuznoi naseleniya 1989 g.* (Composition of the Population of the USSR According to Data from the All-Union Population Census of 1989) (Moskva: "Finansy i Statistika," 1991), pp. 11–12. This document has census data on Gypsies for the 1959, 1979, and 1989 censuses; George Brunner, "Die Rechtslage der Minderheiten nach sowjetsischem Verfassungsrecht (The Legal Status of Minorities in Soviet Constitutional Law)," in *Die Minderheiten in der Sowjetunion und das Volkerrecht* (Minorities in the Soviet Union and International Law), ed. George Brunner and Allan Kagedan (Köln: Markus Verlag, 1988), p. 53; Lewis, *Multilingualism in the Soviet Union,* p. 22, 133; Kozlov, "Processes of Ethnic Change," pp. 48–50, cites a 49.6 percent Gypsy population increase between 1939 and 1959. The national population increase was 9.5 percent during the same period. O. A. Gantskaia and L. N. Terent'eva, "Ethnographic Studies of Ethnic Processes in the Baltic Area," *Soviet Anthropology and Archeology,* Vol. 6, No. 3 (Winter 1967–68), p. 25; Ann Sheehy, "Language Affiliation Data from the Census of 1979," *The All-Union Census of 1979 in the USSR* (Munich: Radio Liberty Research Bulletin, 1980), pp. 6–10; Nicholas Dima, *Bessarabia and Bukovina: The Soviet-Romanian Territorial Dispute* (Boulder/New York: East European Monographs and Columbia University Press, 1982), p. 76; Yu. D. Desheriev and I. F. Protchenko, *Razvitie yazykov narodov SSSR v sovetskuyu epokhy* (The Development of the Languages of the People of the USSR in the Soviet Epoch) (Moskva: Izdatel'stvo "Prosvetsenie," 1968), p. 19, states that there were 22,515 Rom in Ukraine at this time; Kubijovyč and Senkus, "Gypsies," p. 106, say there were 28,000 Rom in Ukraine in 1959; Naulko, "Present Ethnic Composition of the Population of the Ukrainian SSR," p. 22, shows a Ukrainian Gypsy population of 23,000 in 1959; "Sredneaziatskie tsygane," in *Narody srednei Azii i Kazakstana,* ed. S.P. Tolstova, T.A. Zhdanov, S. M. Abramzova, and N. A. Kislyakova, Vol. 2, p. 597.

99. Crowe, Demeter, and Lemon, "Gypsies," pp. 145–148; Crowe, "Liuli of Central Asia," pp. 3–4; Harald Haarmann, *Spracherhaltung und Sprachwechsel als Probleme der interlingualen Soziolinguistik: Studien zur Gruppenmehrsprachigkeit der zigeuner in der Sowjetunion* (Linguistic Preservation and Change as Problems of Interlingual Sociolinguistics: Studies in Group Multilingualism of Gypsies in the Soviet Union) (Hamburg: Helmut Buske Verlag, 1979), pp. 16–17, 20, 22, 60; 89.2 percent of Moldavian Gypsies chose Romani as their primary language, a substantial increase over 1959 figures, when 71.2 percent chose Romani as their native tongue. Iu. V. Arutiunian with L. A. Tul'tseva, "Common Sociopsychological Features and Some Ethnic Features

of Cultural Life," in "A Preliminary Ethosociological Study of Way of Life (On Data of the Moldavian SSR)," ed. Iu. V. Arutiunian, L.M. Drobizheva, and V.S. Zelenchuk, eds., *Soviet Sociology*, Vol. 21, No. 4 (Spring 1983), pp. 72–75; these figures differ somewhat from those cited by Dima in *Bessarabia and Bukovina*, p. 103, who says that 79.1 percent of the Gypsies in Moldavia chose Romani as their native tongue in 1979; "Gypsies in Eastern Europe and the Soviet Union," *Radio Free Europe Research Report*, RAD Background Report No. 72 (April 12, 1978), p. 6; Grattan Puxon estimated the Soviet Gypsy population to be 414,000 in 1970; *Rom: Europe's Gypsies* (London: Minority Rights Group, 1973), pp. 14–15, 23; "Census Data on Changes in Nationality Composition," Joint Publication Research Service (UPA–90–072) (September 28, 1990), p. 71; Sheehy, "Language Affiliation Data," p. 10.

100. Gitlits, "Gipsies in the USSR," p. 103; Grattan Puxon, *Rom: Europe's Gypsies* (London: Minority Rights Group, 1975), p. 12; L. N. Cherenkov, "Tsyganskaya literatura (Gypsy Literature)," in *Literaturnyi entsiklopedicheskii slovar'* (Literary Encyclopedia) ed. V. M. Kozhevnikova and P. A. Nikolaeva (Moskva: "Sovetskaya entsiklopediya," 1987), p. 492; Crowe, "Liuli of Central Asia," p. 3; Rom-Lebedev, *Ot tsyganskogo khora*," pp. 206–207, 225, 227; Kafanova, "Gypsy Theatre Romen," pp. 94, 96; Janicki, "Gypsies," p. 189; Valentin Sazhin, "Attitudes towards Gypsies in Ukraine (1989)," translated by Tanya E. Mairs, *Nationalities Papers*, Vol. 19, No. 3 (Winter 1991), p. 341; Valery Blinov, "Vladimir Semyonovich Vysotsky," in Terras, ed., *Handbook of Russian Literature*, p. 516; Manush, "Problem of the Folk Music of the Gypsies," p. 20, 31, nn. 24, 25; Leksa Manush, "Folk'lor latyshskikh tsygan (osnovnye zhanay i tematika) (The Folklore, Latvian Gypsies [Primary Knowledge and Themes])," *Sovetskaya Etnografiya*, No. 3 (Mai–Iyun' 1981), pp. 115–116.

101. Tsentral'noe Statisticheskoe Upravlenie SSSR (Central Statistical Administration of the USSR), *Naselenie SSSR: Po dannym Vsesoyuznoi perepisi neseleniya 1979 goda* (Population of the USSR: According to Data from the All-Union Population Census of 1979) (Moskva: Izdatel'stvo politicheskoi literatury, 1980), pp. 25, 27; Goskomstat SSSR, *Natsional'nyi sostav naseleniya SSSR, 1989,* pp. 11–12, 15–16; "Census Data on Changes in Nationality Composition," p. 71; Grattan Puxon, *Roma: Europe's Gypsies* (London: Minority Rights Group, 1980), p. 19; Sheehy, "Language Affiliation Data," p. 10; Brunner and Kagedan, eds., *Die Minderheiten in der Sowjetunion*, pp. 47, 53; Georg Brunner and Boris Meissner, *Nationalitäten Probleme in der Sowjetunion und Osteuropa* (Köln: Markus Verlag, 1982), p. 206; Kubijovyč and Senkus, "Gypsies," p. 106; Crowe, "Liuli of Central Asia," p. 4; Nazarov, "Contemporary Ethnic Development of the Central Asian Gypsies (Liuli)," pp. 3, 4, 8; Alexandre Bennigsen and S. Enders Wimbush, *Muslims of the Soviet Empire: A Guide* (Bloomington: Indiana University Press, 1986), pp. 2–3, 124.

102. Alexander Sydorenko, "Mikhail Gorbachev," in Moncure, ed., *European Historical Biography*, Vol. 2, p. 814; Daniel C. Diller, ed., *The Soviet Union*, 3rd ed. (Washington, DC: Congressional Quarterly, 1990), pp. 1–2, 132–133.

103. Nebojša Bato Tomašević and Rajko Djurić, *Gypsies of the World* (New York: Henry Holt, 1988), p. 214; Jackie Nesbitt, *Fourth World Romani Congress: Serock, Warsaw, Poland, 8th–12th April 1990* (Essex County: Essex County Council, Education Department, 1990), pp. 1, 10–11, 14–15. Nadezda Yemetz, a Rom delegate from Latvia, insisted that she represented Latvian Gypsies and thus did not consider herself part of the Soviet delegation. T. A. Acton, "After the Fourth World Romani Congress Romani Encyclopaedists Set to Work," unpublished manuscript, n.d., pp. 1,3; Dr. T. A. Acton, "Gypsies Heard in Europe," *The Guardian*, June 22, 1990, pp. 55–56; though this was the first time that Soviet Gypsy delegates had been allowed to attend a World Romani Congress, six Soviet Roma had taken part in a conference in Moscow in 1965 that brought together "scholars of the languages of India, Pakistan, Ceylon, and Nepal." Gitlits, "Gipsies in the USSR," p. 103.

104. Rom-Lebedev, *Ot tsyganskogo khora*, pp. 240–241; R. S. Demeter and P. S. Demeter, *Obraztsy Fol'klora Tsygan-Kelderarei* (Moskva: Glavnaya Redaksiya Vostochnoi Literatury, 1981), pp. 1–264 passim; Goskomstat SSSR, *Natsional'nyi sostav naseleniya SSSR, 1989*, pp. 5–6, 11–12, 15–16, 22–23; Puxon, *Roma* (1987), p. 17; "Census Data on Changes in Nationality Composition," pp. 67, 71; George Demeter said in his report to the World Romani Congress in 1990 that "there are five to six thousand Kalderash Roma and more than a hundred thousand other Gypsies" in the Soviet Union at that time. Given the figures from the census the year before, it can only be presumed that someone misquoted his remarks. Nesbitt, *Fourth World Romani Congress*, p. 11.

105. "Nationality Composition of Urban Population by Republics," Joint Publication Research Service (UPA–90–066) (December 4, 1990), pp. 12, 16, 19, 22.

106. Valentin Shzhin, "Attitudes towards Gypsies in Ukraine (1980)," *Nationalities Papers*, Vol. 19, No. 3 (Fall 1991), p. 340; *Times-Mirror* (Los Angeles), *The Pulse of Europe: A Survey of Political and Social Values and Attitudes* (Washington, DC: *Times-Mirror* Center for the People & the Press, 1991), pp. 228–229.

107. "Every Man a Tsar," *The New Yorker*, December 27, 1993, p. 8; Vladimir Zhirinovsky, "Growing Up Extremist: Zhirinovsky on His Life as Loser, Lover, and Leader," *The Washington Post*, December 19, 1993, p. C4. Zhirinovsky got 5.8 million votes in the 1991 elections; "Line Blurs between Fascists, Patriots," *News & Record* (Greensboro, NC), May 6, 1993, p. A12; "Moscow Police Deny Racism in Crackdown," *News & Record* (Greensboro, NC), October 15, 1993, p. A11; Lucian Perkins, "Faces of a Nation," *The Washington Post Magazine*, December 12, 1993, p. 27; Elizabeth Teague, "Zhirinovsky's Regional Policy," *RFE/RL Daily Report*, No. 7 (December 21, 1993), n.p.; Kjell Engelbrekt, "Bulgaria Expels Zhirinovsky," *RFE/RL Daily Report*, No. 1 (December 29, 1993), n.p.; Michael Shafir, "Romanian Reaction to Zhirinovsky," *RFE/RL Daily Report*, No. 1 (December 30, 1993), n.p.; "What is Russia for Free Press," *The Economist*, January 8, 1994, p. 55; Zhirinovsky, whose father was Jewish, has been attacked as a creature of the former KGB. On January 24, 1994, Dmitir Vasiliev, the head of the wildly anti-Semitic Pamyat organization, criticized Zhirinovsky for hiding his Jewish roots and besmirching "the idea of Russian national rebirth." Fred Hiatt, "Gorbachev Tied to Zhirinovsky?" *The Washington Post*, January 14, 1994, p. A27; Vera Tolz, *RFE/RL Daily Report*, No. 1 (January 25, 1994), n.p.; for an excellent, more in-depth look at Zhirinovsky, the LDP, Pamyat, and other right wing movements in Russia, see Walter Laqueur's *Black Hundred: The Rise of the Extreme Right in Russia* (New York: Harper Collins, 1993), pp. 204–221, 254–259.

CHAPTER 6

1. Tatomir Vukanović, *Romi (Tsigani) u Jugoslaviji* (Gypsies in Yugoslavia) (Vranje: Nova Jugoslavija, 1983), p. 22; Nebojša Bato Tomašević and Rajko Djurić, *Gypsies of the World* (New York: Henry Holt, 1988), p. 155; George C. Soulis, "The Gypsies in the Byzantine Empire and the Balkans in the Late Middle Ages," *Dumbarton Oaks Papers*, Vol. 15 (1961), p. 160; Angus Fraser, *The Gypsies* (Oxford: Blackwell, 1992), pp. 47–48; Konrad Bercovici, *Gypsies: Their Life, Lore, and Legends* (New York: Greenwich House, 1983), p. 36; Raymond Pearson, *National Minorities in Eastern Europe, 1848–1945* (London: Macmillan, 1983), p. 37. Some Albanian Gypsy folk traditions also trace the origins of the Gypsies to Egyptian slaves in Spain who displeased the king and were forced to flee to Albania. Margaret Hasluck, "The Gypsies of Albania," *Journal of the Gypsy Lore Society*, Third Series, Vol. 17, No. 2 (April 1938), pp. 49–50.

2. Tihomir Gjorgjević, "Vrste Tsigana u Srbiji" (The Types of Gypsies in Serbia), in *Nas narodni Zhivot*, Vol. 2 (Belgrade: Prosveta, 1984), pp. 297–298; Tihomir Gjorgjević, "Tsigani kao nosioci kulture" (Gypsies as Carriers of Culture) in *Nas narodni Zhivot*,

Vol. 3 (Belgrade: Prosveta, 1984), p. 13; Tihomir R. Gjorgjević, "Von den Zigeunem in Serbien," *Journal of the Gypsy Lore Society*, New Series, Vol. 1, No. 3 (January 1908), p. 222.

3. Leo Weiner, "Ismailites," *Journal of the Gypsy Lore Society*, New Series, Vol. 4, No. 2 (October 1910), pp. 94–95; Andrew Arjeh Marchbin, "A Critical History of the Origin and Migration of the Gypsies," Ph.D. diss., University of Pittsburgh, 1939, pp. 61–62; Fraser, *The Gypsies*, p. 57; Soulis, "The Gypsies in the Byzantine Empire," p. 161.

4. Djurdjica Petrović, "Tsigani u srednjovekovnom Dubrovniku," in *Zbornik filozofskoq fakulteta*, ed. Milutin Garashanin, Kniga XIII–1 (Belgrade: Naučno Delo, 1976), pp. 124–125; Soulis, "The Gypsies in the Byzantine Empire," p. 161; Vukanović, *Romi u Jugoslaviji*, p. 23.

5. Vukanović, *Romi u Jugoslaviji*, p. 23; Milenko Filipović, "Višocki Cigani," *Etnološka Biblioteka*, Vol. 16 (Zagreb: Etnografski musej u Zagreb, 1932), p. 3; Soulis, "The Gypsies in the Byzantine Empire," p. 161. In 1102, Croatia became part of the medieval Hungarian empire through the joining of the two thrones. From the Croatian perspective, a Croatian-Hungarian union now came into existence, which Hungarian scholars view as "a close constitutional bond...which survived for more than eight hundred years." Others see the relationship as "often troubled." Willy A. Bachich, "Maritime History of the Eastern Adriatic," in *Croatia: Land, People, Culture*, ed. Francis H. Eterovich and Christopher Spalatin, Vol. 2 (Toronto: University of Toronto Press, 1970), p. 127; László Makkai, "The Foundation of the Hungarian Christian State, 950–1196," in *A History of Hungary*, ed. Peter F. Sugar, Péter Hanák, and Tibor Frank (Bloomington: Indiana University Press, 1990), p. 19; György Balázs and Károly Szelényi, *The Magyars: The Birth of a European Nation* (Budapest: Corvina, 1989), p. 37; Fred Singleton, *A Short History of the Yugoslav Peoples* (Cambridge: Cambridge University Press, 1989), p. 29; Fraser, *The Gypsies*, pp. 60–61.

6. Singleton, *History of the Yugoslav Peoples*, pp. 25–26, 46–47; Donald Kenrick and Grattan Puxon, *The Destiny of Europe's Gypsies* (New York: Basic Books, Inc., 1972), p. 29; H. C. Darby, "Serbia," in *A Short History of Yugoslavia: From Early Times to 1966*, ed. Stephen Clissold (Cambridge: Cambridge University Press, 1968), p. 103; H. C. Darby, "Bosnia and Hercegovina," in Clissold, ed., *Short History of Yugoslavia*, pp. 62–63; Peter F. Sugar, *Southeastern Europe under Ottoman Rule, 1354–1804* (Seattle: University of Washington Press, 1977), p. 21. The "Kosovo Epic," long a stimulus for Serbian national pretensions, added to the myth of Kosovo as the "Serbian Jerusalem," the "ancient heartland of the Serbian kingdom." Pedro Ramet, "Kosovo and the Limits of Yugoslav Socialist Patriotism," *Canadian Review of Studies in Nationalism*, Vol. 16, Nos. 1–2 (1989), p. 228; Soulis, "The Gypsies in the Byzantine Empire," p. 161; Stanford Shaw, *History of the Ottoman Empire and Modern Turkey*, Vol. 1; *Empire of the Gazis: The Rise and Decline of the Ottoman Empire, 1280–1808* (Cambridge: Cambridge University Press, 1976), pp. 18–22; John Kolsti, "Albanian Gypsies: The Silent Survivors," in *The Gypsies of Eastern Europe*, ed. David M. Crowe and John Kolsti (Armonk, NY: M. E. Sharpe, Inc., 1991), p. 51.

7. Bachich, "Maritime History in the Eastern Adriatic," pp. 131–132; Petrović, "Tsigani u srednjovekovnom Dubrovniku," pp. 124–126, 128–132, 143–145, 156–158; Vukanović, *Romi u Jugoslaviji*, pp. 24–25; T. P. Vukanović, "Musical Culture among the Gypsies of Yugoslavia," *Journal of the Gypsy Lore Society*, Third Series, Vol. 41, Nos. 1–2 (January–April 1962), p. 43.

8. Sugar, *Southeastern Europe under Ottoman Rule*, pp. 44–45, 74–75, 273; Milenko S. Filipović, *Among the People: Native Yugoslav Ethnography (Selected Writing of Milenko S. Filipović)*, ed. E. A. Hammel, Robert S. Ehrich, Radmila Fabrijanić-Filipović, Joel M. Halpern, and Albert B. Lord (Ann Arbor, MI: Michigan Slavic Publications, 1982), p. 253; Robert Donia and William G. Lockwood, "The Bosnian Muslims: Class, Ethnicity, and Political Behavior in a European State," in *Muslim-*

Christian Conflicts: Economic, Political, and Social Origins, ed. Suad Joseph and Barbara L. K. Pillsbury (Boulder, CO: Westview Press, 1978), p. 188.

9. Margaret Hasluck, "Firman of A. H. 1013–14 (A.D. 1604–05) Regarding Gypsies in the Western Balkans," *Journal of the Gypsy Lore Society,* Third Series, Vol. 27, Nos. 1–2 (January–April 1848), pp. 1–4, 5 n. 12–16, 6 n. 24, 9; Vukanović, *Romi u Jugoslaviji,* pp. 50–51; Fraser, *The Gypsies,* pp. 175–176; Shaw, *Empire of the Gazis,* pp. 120, 150; George C. Soulis, "A Note on the Taxation of the Balkan Gypsies in the Seventeenth Century," *Journal of the Gypsy Lore Society,* Third Series, Vol. 38, Nos. 3–4 (July–October 1959), p. 156, n. 1.

10. Kenrick and Puxon, *Destiny of Europe's Gypsies,* pp. 50, 55; Fraser, *The Gypsies,* p. 177; Rade Uhlik, "Gypsy Folk-Tales," *Journal of the Gypsy Lore Society,* Third Series, Vol. 37, Nos. 1–2 (January–April 1958), p. 5; Alexander Petrović, "Contributions to the Study of the Serbian Gypsies: Marriage," *Journal of the Gypsy Lore Society,* Third Series, Vol. 15, No. 3 (1936), p. 91; Bernard J. Gilliat-Smith, "The Dialect of the Gypsies of Serbo-Croatia," *Journal of the Gypsy Lore Society,* Third Series, Vol. 27, Nos. 3–4 (July–October 1948), p. 142; Bernard J. Gilliat-Smith, "Review of Rade Uhlik, *Iz ciganske Onomastile,*" *Journal of the Gypsy Lore Society,* Third Series, Vol. 36, Nos. 3–4 (July–October 1957), p. 137; Tihomir R. Gjorgjević, "Rumanian Gypsies in Serbia," *Journal of the Gypsy Lore Society,* Third Series, Vol. 8, No. 1 (1929), p. 10. The Serbian for spoonmaker is *Kašikari*; David M. Crowe, "The Gypsy Historical Experience in Romania," in Crowe and Kolsti, eds., *The Gypsies of Eastern Europe,* pp. 62–63.

11. "Gypsies of Eastern Europe, 1673," *Journal of the Gypsy Lore Society,* New Series, Vol. 1, No. 2 (October 1907), pp. 186–187; T. P. Vukanović, "The Position of Women among Gypsies in the Kosovo-Metohija Region," *Journal of the Gypsy Lore Society,* Third Series, Vol. 40, Nos. 3–4 (July–October 1961), p. 82; Kenrick and Puxon, *Destiny of Europe's Gypsies,* p. 19.

12. Hasluck, "Firman of A. H. 1013–14," Appendix, pp. 10–12; Soulis, "A Note on the Taxation of the Balkan Gypsies," pp. 154–156.

13. Filipović, "Visočki Cigani," pp. 3–4.

14. Gjorgjević, "Rumanian Gypsies in Serbia," p. 17; Darby, "Serbia," p. 109; Sugar, *Southeastern Europe under Ottoman Rule,* pp. 199–200, 222; the new Greek Phanariot rulers of Wallachia and Moldavia saw 77 changes in rulers from 1714 to 1821. R. W. Seton-Watson, *A History of the Roumanians* (Cambridge: Cambridge University Press, 1934), p. 127; Crowe, "The Gypsy Historical Experience in Romania," p. 64.

15. Victor S. Mamatey, *Rise of the Habsburg Empire, 1526–1815* (New York: Holt, Rinehart and Winston, 1971), pp. 82–85, 100; Darby, "Serbia," pp. 109–110; H. C. Darby, "Croatia," in Clissold, ed., *Short History of Yugoslavia,* p. 35; C. A. Macartney, *The Hapsburg Empire, 1789–1918* (London: Weidenfeld and Nicolson, 1968), p. 9; Robert A. Kann and Zdeněk V. David, *The Peoples of the Eastern Habsburg Lands, 1526–1918* (Seattle: University of Washington Press, 1984), pp. 181–182, 280.

16. Vukanović, *Romi u Jugoslaviji,* pp. 63–64; Stanko Guldescu, "Croatian Political History, 1526–1918," in Eterovich and Spalatin, ed. *Croatia,* pp. 30–31; David M. Crowe, "The Gypsies in Hungary," in Crowe and Kolsti, eds., *Gypsies of Eastern Europe,* p. 117; Mamatey, *Rise of the Habsburg Empire,* pp. 129–131, 133–134. Though Joseph II's efforts to integrate Hungary totally into the Austrian Empire robbed Croatia of its "autonomy," his Serfdom Patent of 1781 and his new penal code of 1787 affected the status of Roma throughout his imperial domains.

17. Vukanović, *Romi u Jugoslaviji,* p. 63; T. P. Vukanović, "The Gypsy Population in Yugoslavia," *Journal of the Gypsy Lore Society,* Third Series, Vol. 42, Nos. 1–2 (January–April 1963), p. 12; Crowe, "The Gypsies in Hungary," p. 117; Mamatey, *Rise of the Habsburg Empire,* pp. 137–138.

18. Crowe, "The Gypsies in Hungary," p. 117; Fraser, *The Gypsies,* p. 183, mistranslates Schwicker's reference to "Croatia-Slavonia" as Slovenia. See J. H. Schwicker, *Die*

Zigeuner in Ungarn und Siebenbürgen (Wien und Teschen: Verlag von Karl Brochaster, 1883), pp. 62–67; Miklos Tomka, "Die Zigeuner in der Ungarischen Gesellschaft," *East European Quarterly*, Vol. 4, No. 1 (March 1970), p. 4; Macartney, *The Habsburg Empire*, p. 81; Mamatey, *Rise of the Habsburg Empire*, pp. 95–96, n. 24.

19. Mamatey, *Rise of the Habsburg Empire*, pp. 137–139. Leopold II, faced with the threat of Prussian-Turkish and Polish-Russian alliances, as well as the prospect of insurrection in Hungary, made peace with Istanbul as part of his effort "to defuse the explosion."

20. Shaw, *Empire of the Gazis*, pp. 266–268; Singleton, *History of the Yugoslav Peoples*, p. 76.

21. Alexander Petrović, "Contribution to the Study of the Serbian Gypsies: 'Bijeli' or White Gypsies," *Journal of the Gypsy Lore Society*, Third Series, Vol. 19, No. 3 (July 1940), pp. 89–90, 92. The Gypsies settled in the villages of Šabac, Loznica, Krupanj, and Ljubovija, among others.

22. Singleton, *History of the Yugoslav Peoples*, pp. 75–79; as many as 150 Serbian leaders were killed by the Janissaries. Barbara Jelavich, *History of the Balkans*; Vol. 1, *Eighteenth and Nineteenth Centuries* (Cambridge: Cambridge University Press, 1983), pp. 193–199.

23. Jelavich, *History of the Balkans*, I. pp. 199–202; the Treaty of Bucharest was concluded on May 12, 1812, and ended the Russo-Turkish War of 1806–1812. A. D. Fadeev, "Bucharest, Treaty of 1812," in *The Modern Encyclopedia of Russian and Soviet History*, ed. Joseph L. Wieczynski, Vol. 5 (Gulf Breeze, FL: Academic International Press, 1977), pp. 214–215.

24. Kann and David, *Peoples of the Eastern Habsburg Lands*, pp. 282–283; T. P. Vukanović, "Part Taken by Gypsies in the Peasant Rebellion in Srem (Syrmium) in 1807," *Journal of the Gypsy Lore Society*, Third Series, Vol. 48, Nos 1–2 (January–April 1969), pp. 77–78; Tican is possibly derived from the Serbian for "Gypsy," *Ciganin*.

25. Singleton, *History of the Yugoslav Peoples*, p. 82.

26. Ibid., pp. 82–84; Stanford J. Shaw and Ezel Kural Shaw, *History of the Ottoman Empire and Modern Turkey*, Vol. 2, *Reform, Revolution, and Republic: The Rise of Modern Turkey, 1808–1975* (Cambridge: Cambridge University Press, 1977), pp. 14–15; Jelavich, *History of the Balkans*, I, pp. 202–203; Darby, "Serbia," pp. 116–118.

27. Kolsti, "Albanian Gypsies," p. 51; Petrović, "'Bijeli' or White Gypsies," p. 90; Alexander Petrović, "Contributions to the Study of the Serbian Gypsies: Feast Days," *Journal of the Gypsy Lore Society*, Third Series, Vol. 16, No. 3 (1937), p. 111.

28. Vukanović, "The Gypsy Population in Yugoslavia," p. 13.

29. Ibid.; Vukanović, "Musical Culture among the Gypsies of Yugoslavia," p. 43; Gjorgjević, "Rumanian Gypsies in Serbia," pp. 18–19.

30. Gjorgjević, "Rumanian Gypsies in Serbia," pp. 17–18; Andrew McFarlane, "Conjectural Ancestry of the Rudari," *Journal of the Gypsy Lore Society*, Third Series, Vol. 30, Nos. 3–4 (July–October 1951), pp. 153–154.

31. Vukanović, "The Gypsy Population in Yugoslavia," pp. 12–13. In this article, Vukanović said there were only 79 Rom living in Belgrade in 1854; Vukanović, *Romi u Jugoslaviji*, pp. 71, 75; Vanek Šiftar, *Cigáni: Minulost v Sedanjosti* (Murska Sobota: Pomurska Zaloźba, 1970), p. 18.

32. Tihomir R. Gjorgjević, "Two Bible Stories in the Tradition of Serbian Gypsies," *Journal of the Gypsy Lore Society*, Third Series, Vol. 13, No. 1 (1934), p. 33; Kann and David, *Peoples of the Eastern Habsburg Lands*, pp. 425–427.

33. Erasmus Sanneus, "Serbian Gypsy Bear-Leaders about 1851," *Journal of the Gypsy Lore Society*, Third Series, Vol. 14, No. 3 (1935), pp. 203–204.

34. Ibid., pp. 204–205; Tomašević and Djurič, *Gypsies of the World*, p. 156.

35. E. O. Winstedt, "Rudari in Germany," *Journal of the Gypsy Lore Society*, Third Series, Vol. 34, Nos. 1–2 (January–April 1955), p. 76; Fraser, *The Gypsies*, pp. 223, 226, 228, 236; Tihomir P. Vukanović, "Gypsy Bear-Leaders in the Balkan Peninsular," *Journal of the Gypsy Lore Society*, Third Series, Vol. 38, Nos. 3–4 (July–October 1959), p. 111; Tomašević and Djurič, *Gypsies of the World*, p. 156.
36. Ian Hancock, *The Pariah Syndrome* (Ann Arbor, MI: Karoma Publishers, 1987), p. 118.
37. Vukanović, "Gypsy Population in Yugoslavia," p. 12; Singleton, *History of the Yugoslav Peoples*, pp. 94–95; Jelavich, *History of the Balkans*, I, pp. 244–246. The concept of a Greater Serbia, based upon a Serbian document, the *Nacertanije* of 1844, was to consist of the *pashalik* of Belgrade and surrounding areas, plus "Bosnia, Hercegovina...the Kosovo region, Montenegro, the Vojvodina, and northern Albania"; Gjorgjević, *Nas Narodni Zhivot*, Vol. 2, p. 42.
38. Jelavich, *History of the Balkans*, I, pp. 350–360. The population of Bosnia and Hercegovina was "about 43 percent Orthodox or Serb and 22 percent Catholic or Croat"; Darby, "Bosnia and Hercegovina," pp. 67–69; H. C. Darby, "Montenegro," in Clissold, ed., *Short History of Yugoslavia*, pp. 82–83. Montenegro's population, estimated to be about 120,000 in 1840, was about half Muslim; Shaw, *Reform, Revolution, and Republic*, pp. 165–166, 178–184, 187–192. The humiliating Serbian defeat in the summer of 1876 prompted the Serb ruler, Prince Miloš Obrenović, desperately to offer the sultan a desperate pledge of loyalty and a promise to allow Turkey to "occupy four main forts in the country," among other things. The Pan-Slavist Russian head of the Serb army, General Mikhail G. Cherniaev, convinced Prince Miloš to reject these terms after they had been reworked by the Western powers. Cherniaev then unwisely reinitiated his offensive against the sultan; David Mackenzie, "Cherniaev, Mikhail Grigor'evich," in Wieczynski, ed., *The Modern Encyclopedia of Russian and Soviet History* (1978), Vol. 6, p. 239; Mihailo D. Stojanović, *The Great Powers and the Balkans, 1875–1878* (Cambridge: Cambridge University Press, 1968), pp. 275–276, 278–280.
39. E. O. Winstedt, "Gypsy Civilization," *Journal of the Gypsy Lore Society*, New Series, Vol. 2, No. 1 (July 1908), p. 92; Gjorgjević, *Nas narodni Zhivot*, Vol. 2, p. 344, Vol. 3, pp. 43, 122–123; Kenrick and Puxon, *Destiny of Europe's Gypsies*, p. 50; Petrović, "Feast Days," p. 111.
40. Vukanović, "Gypsy Population in Yugoslavia," pp. 12–15.
41. Gjorgjević, "Von den Zigeunern in Serbien," pp. 219–221; Gjorgjević, "Rumanian Gypsies in Serbia," p. 8.
42. Šiftar, *Cigani*, pp. 63–64; Pavla Štrukelj, *Romi na Slovenskem* (Gypsies in Slovenia) (Ljubljana: Cankarjeva Založba v Ljubljani, 1980), p. 57; Schwicker, *Die Zigeuner in Ungarn und Siebenbürgen*, pp. 75, 80; H. C. Darby, "Slovenia," in Clissold, ed., *Short History of Yugoslavia*, pp. 21–22.
43. Tihomir R. Gjorgjević, "Die Zigeuner in Vlasenicäer Bezirke in Bosnien," *Journal of the Gypsy Lore Society*, New Series, Vol. 1, No. 2 (October 1907), pp. 146–147; Macedonius, *Stalin and the Macedonian Question* (St. Louis, MO: Pearlstone, 1948), p. 69; H. C. Darby, "Macedonia," in Clissold, ed., *Short History of Yugoslavia*, p. 135.
44. Darby, "Serbia," pp. 130–133; Barbara Jelavich, *History of the Balkans*, Vol. 2, *Twentieth Century* (Cambridge: Cambridge University Press, 1983), pp. 97–100; Singleton, *History of the Yugoslav Peoples*, pp. 112–114. Serbia's population increased from 2.9 million to 4.4 million as a result of acquisitions made after the Second Balkan War.
45. Ivo Banac, *The National Question in Yugoslavia: Origins, History, Politics* (Ithaca, NY: Cornell University Press, 1988), pp. 295–296.
46. David M. Crowe, *World War I and Europe in Crisis: 1914–1935* (Piscataway, NJ: Research and Education Association, 1990), pp. 3–6.
47. Singleton, *History of the Yugoslav Peoples*, pp. 119–124; Crowe, *World War I and Europe in Crisis*, pp. 9–10.

48. Viktor Lebzelter, "Contribution to the Anthropology of Serbian Gypsies," *Journal of the Gypsy Lore Society*, Third Series, Vol. 3, No. 4 (1924), p. 184; Vukanović, "Gypsy Bear-Leaders in the Balkan Peninsular," p. 123; Alexander Petrović, "The Beginning of Menstruation among the Gypsies of Rogatica," *Journal of the Gypsy Lore Society*, Third Series, Vol. 14, No. 3 (1935), p. 156; Margaret Hasluck, "The Gypsies of Albania," *Journal of the Gypsy Lore Society*, Third Series, Vol. 17, No. 4 (October 1938), p. 110; Vukanović, "Musical Culture among the Gypsies of Yugoslavia," pp. 45–46.

49. Petrović, "'Bijeli' or White Gypsies," p. 94. The feast day of Bibi was the most important holiday for Serbian Rom; Gypsies "appear high on the casualty lists of both world wars." Pearson, *National Minorities in Eastern Europe*, p. 204.

50. Singleton, *History of the Yugoslav Peoples*, pp. 124–130, 133; H.C. Darby and R.W. Seton-Watson, "The Formation of the Yugoslav State," in Clissold, ed., *Short History of Yugoslavia*, pp. 162–166. There were over 5.5 million Orthodox Christians in the new southern Slav kingdom, 4.7 million Roman Catholics, 1.3 million Muslims, almost 230,000 Protestants, and smaller numbers of Uniate Christians, Jews, and others; Fred Singleton, *Twentieth Century Yugoslavia* (New York: Columbia University Press, 1976), pp. 66–68; Vukanović, *Romi u Jugoslaviji*, p. 121; 1918 estimates for the Gypsy population in greater Macedonia were 43,100, only 270 less than 1912 figures. Macedonius, *Stalin and the Macedonian Question*, pp. 69–70.

51. Vojislav Stanovčić, "History and Status of Ethnic Conflicts," in *Yugoslavia: A Fractured Federalism*, ed. Dennison Rusinow (Washington, DC: The Wilson Center Press, 1988), p. 25; Singleton, *History of the Yugoslav Peoples*, pp. 135–144, 149–150.

52. Malbone W. Graham, Jr., *New Governments of Central Europe* (New York: Henry Holt, 1926), pp. 376–379.

53. Gjorgjević, *Nas narodni Zhivot*, p. 173; Petrovic, "'Bijeli' or White Gypsies," p. 94; Vukanović, "Musical Culture Among the Gypsies of Yugoslavia," p. 57; Singleton, *History of the Yugoslav Peoples*, pp. 149–150, 154; R. W. Seton-Watson and R. G. D. Laffan, "Yugoslavia Between the Wars," in Clissold, ed., *Short History of Yugoslavia*, pp. 174–176; Jelavich, *History of the Balkans*, Vol. 2, p. 200. For a detailed analysis of White Gypsy life in the Bosnian village of Visoko just north of Sarajevo during this period, see Milenko S. Filipović, *Visocki Cigani* (Zagreb: Etnološka Biblioteka, 1932), pp. 1–19 passim.

54. Petrović, "Marriage," p. 118; Petrović, "Feast Days," pp. 124–125, 134; Vukanović, *Romi u Jugoslaviji*, p. 275.

55. Kolsti, "Albanian Gypsies," p. 52; Banac, *National Question in Yugoslavia*, p. 298.

56. Kenrick and Puxon, *Destiny of Europe's Gypsies*, p. 55; Kolsti, "Albanian Gypsies," pp. 52–53; Joseph Swire, *King Zog's Albania* (New York: Liverith, 1937), pp. 195–196.

57. Swire, *King Zog's Albania*, pp. 195–196; Hasluck, "The Gypsies of Albania," pp. 50, 57–58; Edith Durham, *High Albania* (Boston: Beacon Press, 1987), pp. 251–252.

58. Klaus-Detlev Grothusen, *Jugoslawien* (Göttingen: Vandenhoeck & Ruprecht, 1954), pp. 16, 373–375, Tables 4 and 5; Jure Petričević, *Nacionalnost Stanovništva Jugoslavije* (Brugg: Verlag Adria, 1983), p. 29.

59. Singleton, *History of the Yugoslav Peoples*, pp. 160–163; Joseph Rothschild, *East Central Europe between the Two World Wars* (Seattle: University of Washington Press, 1990), p. 246.

60. Seton-Watson and Laffan, "Yugoslavia Between the Wars," pp. 178, 189–200. King Alexander had created nine *banovinas* and the Prefecture of Belgrade in 1929 when he renamed the country Yugoslavia.

61. N. B. Jopson, "Romano Lil (Tsiganske Novine)," *Journal of the Gypsy Lore Society*, Third Series, Vol. 15, No. 2 (1936), pp. 86–89; Petrovic, "Feast Days," p. 33; Grattan Puxon, *Roma: Europe's Gypsies* (London: Minority Rights Group, 1987), p. 12.

62. Rebecca West, *Black Lamb and Grey Falcon: A Journey through Yugoslavia* (New York: Penguin Books, 1982), pp. 66–67.

63. West, *Black Lamb and Grey Falcon*, pp. 308, 657, 659–660, 823–824; Seton-Watson and Laffan, "Yugoslavia Between the Wars," p. 198; the 1921 and 1931 censuses showed that 31.2 percent of the population in Macedonia was Muslim, most of them listed as Turks and Albanians. These percentages also held true for the 1940 census, which showed a total Yugoslav Macedonian population of 1,071,426. George B. Zotiades, *The Macedonian Controversy* (Thessaloniki: Society for Macedonian Studies, 1954), p. 21; Grattan Puxon called the gunpowder Gypsies *Top-hane* in his "Rom in Macedonia." (The Turkish word referred to Gypsy "gun- and powder-makers serving the Ottoman garrison" before 1912.) "Working in conditions of servitude," they got a "'payment' in the form of small allowances of beans and flour for the dirty and dangerous labour of making gunpowder." They lived in Topana, the "old Gypsy quarter of Skopje," which in 1951 Puxon said "was a ramshackle collection of blue-washed cottages and shacks housing some 16,000 Roma." Most of Topana's Rom were Arlija Gypsies, subdivided into Baručia (gunpowder makers), Topanca (Topana-born), Oristivaca (from Priština) and several others. The community also had "Džambasa (dealers, especially horse-dealers) . . . and the Kovaca (blacksmiths)." Gratton Puxon, "Roma in Macedonia," *Journal of the Gypsy Lore Society*, Fourth Series, Vol. 1, No. 2 (1976), p. 128.

64. Singleton, *History of the Yugoslav Peoples*, pp. 172–175; Stephen Clissold, "Occupation and Resistance," in Clissold, ed., *Short History of Yugoslavia*, pp. 200–211; Jelavich, *History of the Balkans*, Vol. 2, p. 201; Rothschild, *East Central Europe*, p. 246.

65. Dennis Reinhartz, "Damnation of the Outsider: The Gypsies of Croatia and Serbia in the Balkan Holocaust, 1941–1945," in Crowe and Kolsti, eds., *Gypsies of Eastern Europe*, pp. 84–88; Kenrick and Puxon, *Destiny of Europe's Gypsies*, pp. 109–112, 183; Edmund Paris, *Genocide in Satellite Croatia, 1941–1945*, translated by Lois Perkins (Chicago: The American Institute for Balkan Affairs, 1961), pp. 62, 211; Clissold, "Occupation and Resistance," pp. 209–210; at the same time that the Ustaša sought to eliminate Croatia's Roma, it also adopted a three-pronged assault on the NDH's 2 million Serbs, who made up almost one-third of Croatia's 6.5 million people. One-third were to be murdered, one-third deported, and one-third converted to Roman Catholicism. Though figures vary widely, conservative estimates indicate that 350,000 Serbs died at Croatian hands between 1941 and 1944, while the Serbs claim that 750,000 were butchered. About 80 percent of Croatia's 18,000 Jews died during this period. The NDH's 700,000–750,000 Muslims, primarily in Bosnia and Hercegovina, were dealt with in mixed fashion. Singleton, *Twentieth Century Yugoslavia*, pp. 86–88; Paris, *Genocide in Satellite Croatia*, p. 217; Toussaint Hocevar and David Crowe, "National Minorities in Yugoslavia, 1919–1980," in *Eastern European National Minorities, 1919–1980: A Handbook*, ed. Stephan M. Horak (Littleton, CO: Libraries Unlimited, Inc., 1985), p. 239; Raul Hilberg, *The Destruction of the European Jews*, Vol. 2 (New York: Holmes & Meier, 1985), p. 718; Jelavich, *History of the Balkans*, Vol. 2, pp. 263–264.

66. Kenrick and Puxon, *Destiny of Europe's Gypsies*, pp. 111–119; Reinhartz, "Damnation of the Outsider," pp. 88–89; Hilberg, *Destruction of the European Jews*, Vol. 2, pp. 683, 692. The regulations on the Gypsies were included in a much broader decree on the Jews; Christopher R. Browning, *Fateful Months: Essays on the Emergence of the Final Solution*, revised edition (New York: Holmes & Meier, 1991), pp. 7, 69–71, 80–81. Commandants at Semlin were members of the SS; Vukanović, *Romi u Jugoslaviji*, p. 121.

67. Štrukelj, *Romi na Slovenskem*, pp. 61, 97–98; Crowe, "The Gypsies in Hungary," p. 119; Robert L. Koehl, *RKFDV: German Resettlement and Population Policy, 1939–1945* (Cambridge, MA: Harvard University Press, 1957), p. 129; Singleton, *History of the Yugoslav Peoples*, pp. 175–176; Clissold, "Occupation and Resistance," pp. 209–210.

68. Kolsti, "Albanian Gypsies," pp. 53–57; Kenrick and Puxon, *Destiny of Europe's Gypsies*, pp. 119–123; Jelavich, *History of the Balkans*, Vol. 2, pp. 273–275.

69. Singleton, *Twentieth Century Yugoslavia*, p. 86.

70. Jan F. Triska, ed., *Constitutions of the Communist Party-States* (Stanford, CA: The Hoover Institution on War, Revolution and Peace, 1968), pp. 456–458; Frits W. Hondius, *Yugoslav Community of Nations* (The Hague: Mouton, 1968), pp. 182–183; Alan J. Whitehorn, "Yugoslav Constitutional Developments: An Expression of Growing Nationality Rights and Powers (1945–1972)," *East European Quarterly*, Vol. 9, No. 3 (Fall 1975), pp. 346–347.

71. Pearson, *National Minorities in Eastern Europe*, p. 202.

72. Puxon, *Rom: Europe's Gypsies* (London: Minority Rights Group, 1973), p. 18; Martine Tassy, "La poésie des Roms de Macedoine," *Études Tsiganes*, No. 4 (1991), pp. 21–22.

73. Shoup, *East European and Soviet Data Handbook*, p. 144, note b; Šiftar, *Cigani*, p. 71; *Enciklopedija Jugoslavije*, Vol. 2 (Zagreb: Izdanje i naklada leksikografskog zavoda FNJR, 1955–1971), p. 376; Vukanović, "Gypsy Population in Yugoslavia," pp. 16–22; Vukanović says the total Rom population in 1948 was 72,693, Vukanović, *Romi u Jugoslaviji*, pp. 123–129; other authors also give slightly different demographic figures. Paul Shoup, for example, says there were 72,736 Roma in Yugoslavia in 1948 in *Communism and the Yugoslav National Question* (New York: Columbia University Press, 1968), p. 266, while Werner Markert indicates a Gypsy population of 72,671 in *Jugoslawien* (Köln: Böhlau-Verlag, 1954), p. 16.

74. Vukanović, "Gypsy Population in Yugoslavia," pp. 23–26; Vukanović, *Romi u Jugoslaviji*, pp. 129–132; Štrukelj, *Romi na Slovenskem*, pp. 61, 97–98, 318. The Prekmurje region of Slovenia had a Gypsy population of 1,187 in 1953, and the Dolenjsken region 422; Shoup, *East European and Soviet Data Handbook*, pp. 143–144, 156–157; Shoup, *Communism and the Yugoslav National Question*, p. 267; Hondius, *Yugoslav Community of Nations*, p. 23.

75. M. George Zaninovich, *The Development of Socialist Yugoslavia* (Baltimore, MD: The Johns Hopkins University Press, 1968), pp. 44, 73–78, 82, 88, 100–101; Jelavich, *History of the Balkans*, Vol. 2, pp. 388, 392; the 1958 program of the 8th congress of the renamed Communist Party, the League of Communists of Yugoslavia, emphasized the rights of minorities with the context of Yugoslav national unity. *Yugoslavia's Way: The Program of the League of the Communists of Yugoslavia*, translated by Stopyan Pribechevich (New York: All Nations Press, 1958), pp. 194–195.

76. Zaninovich, *Development of Socialist Yugoslavia*, pp. 110–112; Puxon, "Roma in Macedonia," p. 128; Grattan Puxon, *Rom: Europe's Gypsies* (London: Minority Rights Group, 1975), p. 15; Vukanović, "Musical Culture among the Gypsies of Yugoslavia," p. 49; "Hanka: A Gypsy Film in Yugoslavia," *Journal of the Gypsy Lore Society*, Third Series, Vol. 35, Nos. 3–4 (July–October 1956), pp. 180–181.

77. Vukanović, *Romi u Jugoslaviji*, pp. 131–132; Petričević, *Nacionalnost Stanovnistva Jugoslavije*, pp. 51–52; Georgeoff and Crowe, "National Minorities in Yugoslavia," pp. 227–229; Shoup, *East European and Soviet Data Handbook*, p. 143; Kenrick and Puxon, *Destiny of Europe's Gypsies*, p. 208; Peter R. Prifti, *Socialist Albania since 1644: Domestic and Foreign Developments* (Cambridge, MA: The MIT Press, 1978), pp. 2, 240–241; Ramadan Marmullarku, *Albania and the Albanians*, translated by Margot and Bosko Miloslavjević (New York: Archon Books, 1975), p. 159.

78. Seventy-eight nations provided relief aid to Macedonia. The Russians built a factory "for prefabricating homes," and the British sent prefab housing. Bart Macdowell, *Gypsies: Wanderers of the World* (Washington, DC: National Geographic Society, 1970), p. 120; Elsie Ivancich Dunin, "Dance Change in the Context of the Gypsy St. George's Day, Skopje, Yugoslavia, 1967–1977," *Papers from the Fourth and Fifth Annual Meetings, Gypsy Lore Society, North American Chapter*, ed. Joanne Grumet (New York: Gypsy

Lore Society, North American Chapter, 1985), pp. 110, 112; Tomašević and Djurič, *Gypsies of the World*, p. 156; Puxon, "Roma in Macedonia," pp. 128–129; Puxon, *Roma* (1987), p. 12; Tassy, "La poésie des Roms de Macedoine," p. 21.

79. Sabrina P. Ramet, *Nationalism and Federalism in Yugoslavia, 1962–1991*, 2nd ed. (Bloomington: Indiana University Press, 1992), pp. 84, 86–93; Singelton, *History of the Yugoslav Peoples*, pp. 244–250; Whitehorn, "Yugoslav Constitutional Developments," pp. 349–352; Fraser, *The Gypsies*, pp. 272–273; the majority of Skopje's Rom call themselves "'Turski Cigani,' a synonym for Moslem rather than as being Turkish." Dunin, "Dance Change in the Context of the Gypsy St. George's Day," p. 110; William G. Lockwood, "East European Gypsies in Western Europe: The Social and Cultural Adaptation of the Xoraxané," *Nomadic Peoples*, Nos. 21–22 (December 1986), pp. 63–64; some Xoraxané maintained a "two-fold environments" lifestyle divided between Yugoslavia and Italy. Leonardo Piasere, "In Search of New Niches: The Productive Organization of the Peripatetic Xoraxané in Italy," in *The Other Nomads: Peripatetic Minorities in Cross-Cultural Perspective*, ed. Arpana Rao (Köln: Böhlau Verlag, 1987), pp. 111–113; there were "8,000 foreign-born Gypsies" in Germany in 1970, "including many migrant workers from Yugoslavia." Kenrick and Puxon, *Destiny of Europe's Gypsies*, p. 192.

80. Singleton, *History of the Yugoslav Peoples*, pp. 259–264; Ramet, *Nationalism and Federalism in Yugoslavia*, pp. 66, 73–74; David Mackenzie, "The Background: Yugoslavia since 1964," in *Nationalism in the USSR and Eastern Europe in the Era of Brezhnev and Kosygin*, ed. George W. Simmonds (Detroit, MI: The University of Detroit Press, 1977), p. 454; during this period, the government rigidly applied "republican and ethnic keys" in giving out jobs "in all federal departments," which enhanced opportunities in the "smaller republics and nationalities." Dennis Rusinow, "Nationalities Policy and the 'National Question,'" in *Yugoslavia in the 1980s*, ed. Pedro Ramet (Boulder, CO: Westview Press, 1985), pp. 136–137; though the Serbs only made up 39.7 percent of the population in 1971, they made up 60.5 percent of the army's officer corps and 46 percent of its generals. Bogdan Denis Denitch, *The Legitimation of a Revolution: The Yugoslav Case* (New Haven, CT: Yale University Press, 1976), p. 114.

81. Prifti, *Socialist Albania since 1944*, pp. 240–241; Tirvo Indjic, *Affirmative Action: The Yugoslav Case* (New York: The Rockefeller Foundation, 1984), p. 211; Grattan Puxon, *Rom* (1973), p. 23; "Probleme mit Jugoslawiens Zigeunern," *Osteuropa* Heft 4 (April 1978), p. A249; "Zigeuner zwischen Albanern und Serbien," *Osteuropa*, Heft 6 (June 1972), p. A197.

82. "Probleme mit Jugoslawiens Zigeunern," p. A251; Puxon, "Roma in Macedonia," p. 130; Puxon, *Rom* (1973), p. 19.

83. Puxon, *Rom* (1973), p. 18; Dunin, "Dance Change in the Context of the Gypsy St. George's Day," p. 114; Grattan Puxon, *Roma: Europe's Gypsies* (London: Minority Rights Group, 1980), p. 18; Hugh Poulton, *The Balkans: Minorities and States in Conflict* (London: Minority Rights Group, 1991), p. 89; Indjic, *Affirmative Action*, p. 215; Tassy, "La poésie des Roms de Macedoine," p. 25; Tetovo had been the center of ethnic unrest in the late 1960s. Stephen E. Palmer, Jr. and Robert R. King, *Yugoslav Communism and the Macedonian Question* (New York: Archon Books, 1971), pp. 181–182; officially, there were 6 Romany "cultural-artistic societies" out of 1,743 in Yugoslavia in 1975–1976. Milutin Dedić, "Cultural-Artistic Amateurism," *Yugoslav Survey*, Vol. 22, No. 2 (May 1981), p. 136; Kenrick and Puxon, *Destiny of Europe's Gypsies*, pp. 211–212.

84. Indjic, *Affirmative Action*, p. 212; Puxon, *Roma* (1987), p. 12.

85. Indjic, *Affirmative Action*, pp. 214–215; Balic served as head of the World Romani Congress from 1981–1990. Jackie Nesbitt, *Fourth World Romani Congress: Serock, Warsaw, Poland, 8th–12th April 1990* (Essex County: Essex County Council Education Department, 1990), p. 1.

86. Poulton, *The Balkans*, pp. 87–88.

87. Ramet, *Nationalism and Federalism in Yugoslavia*, p. 196; Poulton, *The Balkans*, p. 90; the number of Albanians in the republic, now 19.8 percent of the population, grew from 279,871 in 1971 to 377,726 a decade later. Seventy-five percent of Kosovo's population in 1981 was Albanian. Montenegro's Roma population was 1,471 in 1981. Petričević, *Nacionalnost stanovništva Jugoslavije*, pp. 87, 95, 127, 137, 146, 165, 173.

88. Ruza Petrović, "The National Composition of the Population," *Yugoslav Survey*, Vol. 24, No. 3 (August 1983), pp. 26–27; Petričević, *Nacionalnost stanovnistva Jugoslavije*, p. 72. While Yugoslavia's population grew by almost 2 million between 1971 and 1981, some of the dominant groups, such as the Serbs and the Croats, experienced slight population declines. The Hungarians, Turks, Slovaks, Romanians, and Bulgars also saw a drop in numbers, while the Albanians, the Muslims, the Macedonians, and the Montenegrans enjoyed increases; Poulton, *The Balkans*, p. 87; "Zur Lage der Zigeuner in Kroatien und Slowenien," *Osteuropa*, Heft 7 (July 1983), p. A377; Puxon, *Roma* (1980), p. 19; Indjic, *Affirmative Action*, p. 220, n. 7.

89. Ramet, *Nationalism and Federalism in Yugoslavia*, pp. 214–221; Dusan Nečak, "A Chronology of the Decay of Tito's Yugoslavia, 1980–1991," *Nationalities Papers*, Vol. 21, No. 1 (Spring 1993), pp. 177–179.

90. Indjic, *Affirmative Action*, pp. 212–213.

91. Puxon, *Roma* (1980), p. 18; Puxon, *Roma* (1987), p. 12.

92. Indjic, *Affirmative Action*, pp. 212–213; in 1980, Kosovo had the highest unemployment rate in Yugoslavia. Sabrina Ramet viewed its economic future as "increasingly hopeless." Ramet, *Nationalism and Federalism in Yugoslavia*, pp. 139–140, 160; Peter Prifti, "Kosova's Economy: Problems and Prospects," in *Studies on Kosova*, ed. Arshi Pipa and Sami Repishti (Boulder, CO: East European Monographs, 1984), pp. 142–143; Ian Hancock, "Gypsy History in Germany and Neighboring Lands: A Chronology Leading to the Holocaust and Beyond," in Crowe and Kolsti, eds., *Gypsies of Eastern Europe*, p. 22.

93. Ramet, *Nationalism and Federalism in Yugoslavia*, pp. 239, 243, 248; Nečak, "Chronology of the Decay," pp. 180–183; Poulton, *The Balkans*, pp. 90–91.

94. Project on Ethnic Relations, *The Romanies in Central and Eastern Europe: Illusions and Reality* (Princeton, NJ: Project on Ethnic Relations, 1992), p. 8; Zoltan D. Barany, "Democratic Changes Bring Mixed Blessings for Gypsies," *RFE/RL Research Report*, Vol. 1, No. 20 (May 15, 1992), p. 44; Poulton, *The Balkans*, pp. 87–90.

95. Poulton, *The Balkans*, p. 91; Chuck Sudetic, "Pharoahs in Their Past? So the Yugoslavs Say," *The New York Times*, November 21, 1990, p. A4.

96. Nečak, "A Chronology of the Decay," p. 183; Misha Glenny, *The Fall of Yugoslavia: The Third Balkan War* (London: Penguin Books, Ltd., 1992), pp. 143, 162–164, 167–168; Helsinki Watch, *War Crimes in Bosnia-Hercegovina* (New York: Human Rights Watch, 1992), pp. 7–8, 24–25; the almost indistinguishable population of Bosnia-Hercegovina was 43.7 percent Muslims, 31.3 percent Serbs, and 17.3 percent Croats. Robert M. Hayden, "The Partition of Bosnia-Hercegovina, 1990–1993," *RFE/RL Research Report*, Vol. 2, No. 22 (May 28, 1993), pp. 2, 6–14; Patrick Moore, "Chronology of Events," *RFE/RL Research Report*, Vol. 1, No. 50 (December 18, 1992), pp. 34–35; "A Glimmer in Bosnia," *The Economist*, March 5, 1994, p. 51; Nancy Benac, "U.S. Prods Serbs to Link Peace Chain," *News & Record* (Greensboro, NC), March 19, 1994, p. A1.

97. Patrick Moore, "The Minorities' Plight Amid Civil War," *Report on Eastern Europe* (December 13, 1991), p. 32.

98. "Refugees Keep Out," *The Economist*, September 19, 1992, p. 66; Iva Dominis and Ivo Bicanic, "Refugees and Displaced Persons in the Former Yugoslavia," *RFE/RL Research Report*, Vol. 2, No. 3 (January 15, 1993), pp. 1–2. Estimates on the number of refugees from the battle zones in Yugoslavia ranged from 1.428 million in late

1992 to 2.75 million; David Dyker and Vesna Bojicic, "The Impact of Sanctions on the Serbian Economy," *RFE/RL Research Report*, Vol. 2, No. 21 (May 21,1993), pp. 50–54.

99. Hugh Poulton, "The Roma in Macedonia: A Balkan Success Story," *RFE/RL Research Report*, Vol. 2, No. 19 (May 7, 1993), pp. 42–45. In the April 1991 Macedonian census, there were officially 55,575 Gypsies in the country, far below Roma estimates of 200,000; Hugh Poulton, "The Republic of Macedonia after UN Recognition," *RFE/RL Research Report*, Vol. 2, No. 23 (June 4, 1993), pp. 22–23; Duncan M. Perry, "Politics in the Republic of Macedonia: Issues and Parties," *RFE\RL Research Report*, Vol. 2, No. 23 (June 4, 1993), pp. 31, 37.

CHAPTER 7

1. John Kolsti, "Albanian Gypsies: The Silent Survivors," in David Crowe and John Kolsti, eds., *The Gypsies of Eastern Europe* (Armonk, NY: M. E. Sharpe, 1991), p. 51.
2. Margaret Hasluck, "The Gypsies of Albania," *Journal of the Gypsy Lore Society*, Vol. 17, No. 2 (April 1938), pp. 49–50.
3. Marcel Courthiades, "Social and Historical Profile of the Rromanis in Albania," Unpublished Manuscript (1998), p. 1.
4. Margaret Hasluck, "Firman of A.H. 1013–14 (A.D. 1604–05) regarding Gypsies in the Western Balkans," *Journal of the Gypsy Lore Society*, Vol. 27, Nos. 1–2 (January-April 1848), pp. 1–4, 5 n12–16, 6 n24, 9; Tatomir Vukanovic, *Romi (Tsigani) u Jugoslaviji* (Vranje: Nova Jugoslavija, 1983), pp. 50–51; Angus Fraser, *The Gypsies* (Oxford: Blackwell, 1992), pp. 175–176; Stanford Shaw, *History of the Ottoman Empire and Modern Turkey*, Volume I: *Empire of the Gazis: The Rise and Decline of the Ottoman Empire, 1280–1808* (Cambridge: Cambridge University Press, 1976), pp. 120, 150; George C. Soulis, "A Note on the Taxation of the Balkan Gypsies in the Seventeenth Century," *Journal of the Gypsy Lore Society*, Vol. 38, Nos. 3–4 (July-October 1959), p. 156, n1.
5. Courthiades, "Social and Historical Profile of the Rromanis in Albania," p. 1.
6. Hasluk, "Firman of A. H. 1013–14," pp. 10–11.
7. Kolsti, "Albanian Gypsies," p. 52.
8. Ibid., p. 53.
9. Joseph Swire, *King Zog's Albania* (New York: Liveright Publishing Company, 1937), p. 196.
10. Hasluck, "Gypsies of Albania," I, p. 50.
11. Ibid., pp. 50–51; Courthiades, "Social and Historical Profile of the Rromanis in Albania," p. 2.
12. Courthiades, "Social and Historical Profile of the Rromanis in Albania," pp. 5–6.
13. European Roma Rights Center, *No Record of the Case: Roma in Albania* (Budapest: European Roma Rights Center, 1997), p. 12.
14. Courthiades, "Social and Historical Profile of the Rromanis in Albania," p. 13.
15. Hasluck, "Gypsies of Albania," pp. 108–112.
16. Miranda Vickers and James Pettifer, *Albania: From Anarchy to a Balkan Identity* (New York: New York University Press, 1997), pp. 4, 216–230; 40 percent of the work force was unemployed in 1991.
17. Fabian Schmidt, "From Anarchy to an Uncertain Stability," in Peter Rutland, *The Challenge of Integration: Annual Survey of Eastern Europe and the Former Soviet Union, 1997* (Armonk, NJ: M. E. Sharpe, 1998), pp. 237–239.
18. Central Intelligence Agency, *The World Factbook (2006)*, https://www.cia.gov/cia/publications/factbook/geos/al.html, p. 3 [accessed July 31, 2006].

19. "Albania," *The World Factbook (2006)*, p. 8; Janusz Bugajski, *Ethnic Politics in Eastern Europe: A Guide to Nationality Policies, Organizations, and Parties* (Armonk, NY: M. E. Sharpe, 1995), p. 268; Vickers and Pettifer, *Albania*, p. 186; Courthiades, "Social and Historical Profile of the Rromanis in Albania," p. 1; Albania's 1997 population was 3.25 million. Schmidt, "From Anarchy to an Uncertain Stability," p. 236; Alphia Abdikeeva, *Roma Poverty and the Roma National Strategies: The Cases of Albania, Greece and Serbia* (London: Minority Rights Group International, 2005), p. 3.

20. Open Society Foundation, "Monitoring the National Roma Strategy," p. 2, http://www.soros.al/English/news/roma2.htm, [accessed August 1, 2006].

21. Abdikeeva, "Roma Poverty," p. 4; "Albania," *The World Fact Book (2006)*, pp. 1–2, 8; p. 3.

22. "Monitoring the National Roma Strategy,: p. 2; *The World Fact Book*, p. 5.

23. Maria Koinova, "Roma of Albania," *Minorities in Southeast Europe* (Budapest: Center for Documentation and Information on Minorities in Europe—Southeast Europe, 2000), p. 16.

24. Ibid., pp. 2–3.

25. Minority Rights Group International, *Gender and Minority Issues in Albania* (London: Minority Rights Group International, 2003), p. 5; Amaro Drom, *"Innocent Smiles": Trafficking in Persons Report in the Albanian Roma Community* (Tirane: Amaro Drom and Minority Rights Group International, 2005), pp. 9–10.

26. *"Innocent Smiles,"* p. 12.

27. Abdikeeva, "Roma Poverty," p. 5.

28. Ibid., p. 5.

29. Open Society Foundation Soros, "Monitoring the National Roma Strategy," pp. 1–3, http://www.soros.al/English/news/roma2.htm, [accessed August 1, 2006].

30. Ibid., pp. 3–4.

31. Ibid., pp. 4–5.

32. Robert M. Hayden, "The Partition of Bosnia-Hercegovina, 1990–1993," *RFE/RL Research Report*, Vol. 2, No. 22 (May 28, 1993), pp. 2, 6–14; American Committee to Save Bosnia, "Convoy Bosnia—A Summary of the Crisis in Bosnia," (1993), p. 1; Jeremy Druker, "Present but Unaccounted for," *Transitions*, Vol. 4, No. 4 (September 1997), p. 23; Judith Latham, "Roma in the Former Yugoslavia," *Nationalities Papers*, Vol. 27, No. 2 (June 1999), p. 213; European Roma Rights Center, *The Non-constituents: Rights Deprivation of Roma in Post-genocide Bosnia and Herzegovina* (Budapest: European Roma Rights Center, 2004), pp. 11, 20; Roger Thurow, "Another Country," *The Wall Street Journal* (August 24, 1999), p. A1.

33. European Roma Rights Center, *The Non-constituents*, p. 20.

34. Latham, "Roma in the Former Yugoslavia," p. 215.

35. Ibid., pp. 216–217; Thurow, "Another Country," pp. A1, A6.

36. Committee of Ministers, Council of Europe, "Fact-finding Mission to Bosnia and Herzxegovina on the Situation of the Roma/Gypsies (May 16–21, 1996)," p. 2, http:www.coe.int/T/DG3/RomaTravellers/documentation/fieldvisits/missionbih_en.asp, [accessed August 16, 2006].

37. Human Rights Watch, *Hopes Betrayed: Trafficking of Women and Girls to Post-conflict Bosnia and Herzegovina for Forced Prostitution* (New York: Human Rights Watch, 2002), pp. 15–20.

38. Central Intelligence Agency, "Bosnia and Herzegovina," *The World Factbook (2006)*, p. 9, https://www.cia.gov/cia/publications/factbook/geos/bk.html, [accessed August 8, 2006); Department for International Development, "Bosnia-Herzegovina," p. 1, http://www.dfid.gov.uk/countries/europe/bosniaherzegovina.asp, [accessed August 8, 2006]. Open Society Institute, "Roma in Bosnia and Herzegovina," *Joint Women's Roma Initiative*, p. 1, http:www.romawomensinitiatives.org, [accessed August 8, 2006]; UNICEF, "Bosnia and Herzegovina," p. 5, http://www.unicef.org/infobycountry/ bosniaherzegovina_statistics.html, [accessed August 8, 2006].

39. European Roma Rights Center, *The Non-constituents*, p. 204.

40. Ibid., p. 205.
41. European Roma Rights Centre, "Roma Recognized by New Minority Rights Law in Bosnia and Herzegovina," p. 1, http://www.errc.org.cikk.php?cikk'1096&archiv'1, [accessed August 8, 2006].
42. European Roma Rights Center, *The Non-constituents*, pp. 206–207.
43. United Nations, International Convention on the Elimination of All Forms of Racial Discrimination, "Bosnia and Herzegovina," CERD/C/464/Add. 1 (May 20, 2005), p. 27.
44. United Nations, International Committee on the Elimination of All Forms of Racial Discrimination, "Bosnia and Herzegovina," CERD/C/SR.1735 (March 1, 2006), pp. 6–8.
45. European Roma Rights Center, "Summary of Pressing Concerns: Bosnia and Herzegovina," July 3, 2006, pp. 1–3.
46. Project on Ethnic Relations, *The Roma in Bulgaria: Collaborative Efforts between Local Authorities and Nongovernmental Organizations* (Princeton: Project on Ethnic Relations, 1998), p. 1.
47. Bugajski, *Ethnic Politics in Eastern Europe*, pp. 250–251; United States Department of State, *Bulgaria Country Report on Human Rights Practices for 1998* (Washington, DC: Bureau of Democracy, Human Rights, and Labor, 1999), p. 8.
48. Department of State, *Bulgaria Country Report, 1998*, pp. 2–3, 13–15; Human Rights Watch, *World Report: Bulgaria* (1999), p. 1; Human Rights Watch, *Human Rights Developments: Bulgaria* (1999), pp. 1–2; the problems of police and court mistreatment of the Roma was first reported in Human Rights Watch's *Children of Bulgaria: Police Violence and Arbitrary Confinement* (New York: Human Rights Watch, 1996).
49. European Union, "Commission: Bulgaria's and Romania's accession possible in 2007, if preparation efforts are intensified," May 16, 2006, IP/06/634, pp. 1–2; European Union, "Key Findings of the May 2006 monitoring reports on Bulgaria and Romania," May 16, 2006, MEMO/06/201, pp. 1–2.
50. Rumyan Russinov, "The Bulgarian Framework Programme for Equal Integration of Roma: participation in the policy-making process." European Roma Rights Centre, 2006, pp. 1–7, http://www.errc.org/cikk.php?cikk'1729&archiv'1, [accessed August 21, 2006].
51. Ibid., pp. 2–8.
52. Council of Europe, "Third report on Bulgaria," June 27, 2003, p. 2, http:www.coe.int/t/e/human_rights/ecri/1-ecri/2-country-by-country_approach/bulgaria/B, [accessed August 24, 2006].
53. Bulgarian Helsinki Committee, *Annual Report of the Bulgarian Helsinki Committee* (Sofia: Bulgarian Helsinki committee, 2005), pp. 2–3.
54. European Roma Rights Center, *Profession: Prisoner (Roma Detention in Bulgaria)* (Budapest: European Roma Rights Center, 1997), p. 7.
55. *Case of Nachova and Others v. Bulgaria*, Applications nos. 43577/98 and 43579/98. Judgement, Strasbourg, July 6, 2005, pp. 1–42; "European Court of Human Rights Confirms Racial Discrimination in Landmark Bulgarian Case," *Open Justice Society Initiative*, July 7, 2005, pp. 1–2.
56. Project on Ethnic Relations, *The Roma in Bulgaria: Collaborative Efforts between Local Authorities and Nongovernmental Organizations* (Princeton: Project on Ethnic Relations, 1998), p. 8; European Roma Rights Centre, "Roma-Police Seminars in Bulgaria," *Notebook* (2003), pp. 1–3, http:www.errc.org/cikk.php?cikk'507&archiv'1 [accessed August 21, 2006].
57. Margarita Ilieva, "The Bulgarian Draft Anti-discrimination Law; an Opportunity to Make Good on the Constitutional Promise of Equality in a Post-communist Society," *Notebook* (2003), pp. 1–6, http://www.errc.org/cikk.php?cikk'1444&archiv'1 [accessed August 21, 2006].
58. European Roma Rights Center, "Five Roma rights Victories under New Bulgarian Equality Law," September 30, 2004, p. 2, http://www.errc.org/cikk.php?cikk'2022&archiv'1, [accessed August 21, 2006].

59. Central Intelligence Agency, "Bulgaria," *The World Factbook* (2006), p. 5, https://www. cia.gov/cia/publications/factbook/geos/bu.html, [accessed August 24, 2006]; Ilona Tomova, *The Gypsies in the Transition Period* (Sofia: International Center for Minority Studies and Intercultural Relations, 1995), p. 60; Jennifer Tanaka, "Parallel worlds: Romani and non-Romani schools in Bulgaria," *Notebook* (2003), p. 1, http://www. errc.org/cikk.php?cikk'1045&archiv'1 [accessed August 21, 2006].
60. Tomova, *The Gypsies in the Transition Period*, p. 58.
61. Khristo Kyuchukov, "Projects in Romani Education: Bulgaria," *Meet the ERRC* (2003), pp. 1–2, http://www.errc.org/cikk.php?cikk'57&archiv'1 [accessed August 21, 2006].
62. Deyan Kolev, "Roma Folklore Classes in Bulgarian Schools: Preparing the Ground for the Desegregation of Romani Education," *Research and Policy* (2003), pp. 1–3, 5, http:ww.errc.org/cikk.php?cikk'1854&archiv'1 [accessed August 21, 2006].
63. "Bulgarian Ministry of Education and Science Issues Landmark 'Instruction for the Integration of Minority Children and Pupils,' " *Snapshots from Around Europe* (2003), p. 1, http://www.errc.org/cikk.php?cikk'1627&archiv'1 [accessed August 21, 2006].
64. Donka Panayotova, "Successful Romani School Desegregation; The Vidin Case," *Notebook* (2003), pp. 1–5, http://www.errc.org/cikk.php?cikk'1630&archiv'1 [accessed August 21, 2006].
65. European Roma Rights Center, "Desegregation Court Victory," February 28, 2006, pp. 1–2, http://www.errc.org/cikk.php?cikk'2411&archiv'1 [accessed August 21, 2006].
66. Council of Europe, "European Social Charter (revised), 3.V.1996, p. 12, http://conventions. coe.int/treaty/en/Treaties/Html/163.htm [accessed August 30, 2006]; "Bulgarian Authorities Urged to Halt Forced Evictions of Roma," p. 1, http://www.errc.org/ cikk.php?cikk'2606&archiv'1 [accessed August 21, 2006].
67. Andrei Iliev, "Participation of Bulgarian Roma in the 2001 General Elections and Prospects for Political Representation," *Notebook* (2003), pp. 1–3, http://www.errc.org/ cikk.php?cikk'1232&archiv'1 [accessed August 21, 2006].
68. "Increased Romani Participation Fuels Anti-Romani Racism in Bulgarian Local Elections," *Snapshots from Around Europe* (2003), p. 1, http://www.errc.org/cikk.php? cikk'1231&archiv'1 [accessed August 21, 2006]; Rumyan Russinov, "Romani Politics as a Profession," *Meet the ERRC* (2003), pp. 1–2, http:www.errc.org/cikk.php?cikk'1992 &archiv'1 [accessed August 21, 2006].
69. *National Programme for Roma* (Zagreb: National Program for Roma, 2004), pp. 1–2.
70. Ana Bogdanović, "The Croatian National Programme for the Roma: An Example of Gender Inequality?" (August 2005), *Eumap.org*, pp. 1–3.
71. European Roma Rights Center, *Shadow Report of the European Roma Rights Center on the Republic of Croatia's Combined Second and Third Periodic Reports to the Committee on Elimination of Discrimination against Women* (Budapest: European Roma Rights Center, 2005), pp. 1–2.
72. United Nations Committee on the Rights of the Child, *Concluding Observations of the Committee on the Rights of the Child: CROATIA* (Geneva: United Nations, 2004), pp. 1–14.
73. Jasminka Dedić, "The Erasure: Administrative Ethnic Cleansing in Slovenia," *Notebook* (2003), p. 1, http://www.errc.org/cikk.php?cikk'1109 [accessed October 19, 2006]; Tatjana Perić, "Insufficient: Government Programmes for Roma in Slovenia," *Roma Rights* (2001), pp. 1–2; Council of Europe, *Second Report on Slovenia* (Geneva: Council of Europe, 2003), p. 10.
74. Council of Europe, *Comments on the Follow-up Report on Slovenia (2003–2005) by the Council of Europe Commissioner for Human Rights* (Brussels: Council of Europe, 2006), pp. 4–5; "Roma in Slovenia Threatened with Segregation at School," *Snapshots from around Europe* (2005), p. 1, http://www.errc.org/cikk.php?cikk'2342&archiv'1 [accessed October 19, 2006].

75. Jiri Pehe, "'Law on Romanies Causes Uproar in Czech Republic," *RFE/RL Research Report*, Vol. 2, No. 7 (February 12, 1993), pp. 18–22; Henry Kamm, "In Slovak Gypsy Ghetto, Hovels and Plea for Jobs," *New York Times* (November 28, 1993), p. A4; Monica Nemcokov, "Don't Blame Slovakia for Gypsy Problem," *New York Times*, (December 15, 1993), p. A14; Central Intelligence Agency, *The World Factbook (2006)*, p. 3. https://www.cia.gov/cia/publications/factbook/geos/ez.html [accessed September 12, 2006].

76. Rom News Network, "The Association of Czechoslovak Roma in Canada (1998)," p. 1, http://www.romnews.com/community/modules.php?op'modload&name'Sections&file in [accessed September 12, 2006]; "The Long, Hot Czech Summer," *Notebook* (2007), pp. 1–5. http://www.errc.org/cikk.php?cikk'1538&archiv'1 [accessed September 1, 2006].

77. Rom News Network, "The Association of Czechoslovak Roma in Canada," p. 1; "The Long, Hot Czech Summer," pp. 1–5.

78. Stanislav Penc and Jan Urban, "Czech Republic: Extremist Acts Galvanize Roma Population," *Transitions*, Vol. 5, No. 7 (July 1998), p. 39.

79. "Police Abuse of Roma in Písek, Czech Republic," *Snapshots from Around Europe* (1997), p. 1, http://www.errc.org/cikk.php?cikk'26&archiv'1 [accessed September 1, 2006].

80. "Abuse of Roma by Officials in the Czech Republic," *Snapshots from Around Europe* (1999), p. 1, http://www.errc.org/cikk.php?cikk'568&archiv'1 [accessed September 1, 2006].

81. European Roma Rights Center, *A Special Remedy: Roma and Schools for the Mentally Handicapped in the Czech Republic* (Budapest: European Roma Rights Center, 1999), p. 10.

82. David M. Crowe, "Roma in Eastern Europe: The Wall in the Czech Republic," in ed., Meghan Appel, O'Meara *History behind the Headlines: The Origins of Conflicts Worldwide*, (New York: The Gale Group, 2000), pp. 214–224.

83. Ibid., pp. 214, 221; Arie Farnam, "White Residents Nostalgic about Usti Wall," *The Prague Post* (May 3, 2000), p. 1 http://www.praguepost.cz/news050300d.html.

84. *Roma Rights*, No. 2, 2004, p. 49.

85. "Challenging Coercive Sterilisations of Romani Women in the Czech Republic (2005)," p. 2, http://www.errc.org/cikk.php?cikk'2228&archiv'1, [accessed September 1, 2006]

86. "UN Committee against Torture Urges the Czech Republic to Investigate Alleged Coercive Sterilisation of Romani Women," *Advocacy* (2004), pp. 1–2, http://www.errc.org/cikk.php?cikk'1988&archiv'1 [accessed September 1, 2006]; "Response of the Czech Government Commissioner for Human rights to ERRC Action on Coercive Sterlilisations of Romani Women in the Czech Republic," *Advocacy* (2004), pp. 1–3, http://www.errc.org/cikk.php?cikk'2072&archiv'1 [accessed September 1, 2006]; "Coercive Sterilisations in the Czech Republic" (September 16, 2004), pp. 1–3, http://www.errc.org/cikk.php?cikk'2014&archiv'1 [accessed September 1, 2006]; Claude Cahn, "Breakthrough: Challenging Coercive Sterilisations of Romani Women in the Czech Republic," *Advocacy* (2004), pp. 1–6, http://www.errc.org/cikk. php?cikk'2071&archiv'1 [accessed September 1, 2006]; "Challenging Coercive Sterilisations of Romani Women in the Czech Republic, pp. 1–8; "Czech Public Defender of Rights," pp. 1–4, http://www.ochrance.cz/en/ombudsman/obecne.php [accessed September 12, 2006].

87. "First Civil Complaint Filed regarding Coercive Sterilisations of Romani Women," *Snapshots from Around Europe* (2005), p. 1, http://www.errc.org/cikk.php?cikk' 2309&archiv'1 [accessed September 1, 2006]; "First Court Victory in Central Europe on Coercive Sterilisation of Romani Women," *News Roundup: Snapshots from Around the World* (2006), pp. 1–2, http://www.errc.org/cikk.php?cikk'2475&archiv'1 [accessed

September 1, 2006]; *Závěrečné stanovisko veřejného ochránce práv ve věci sterilizací prováděných v rozporu s právem a návrhy opatření k nápravě* (Praha: Veřejny Ochránce Práv Ombudsman, 2005), pp. 71–73.

88. European Roma Rights Centre, League of Human Rights, and Gender Studies, *Shadow Report to the Committee on the Elimination of All Forms of Discrimination against Women for the Czech Republic* (Prague and Budapest: European Roma rights Centre, League of Human Rights, and Gender Studies, 2006), pp. 18–19.

89. Laura Laubeová, "The Fiction of Ethnic Homogeneity: Minorities in the Czech Republic," in Maria A. Biro and Petra Kovacs, eds., *Diversity in Action: Local Public Management of Multi-Ethnic Communities in Central and Eastern Europe* (Budapest: Central European Press, 2001), p. 142.

90. European Commission against Racism and Intolerance, *Third Report on the Czech Republic* (Brussels: Council of Europe, 2004), p. 15.

91. Ibid., pp. 15–27.

92. European Commission against Racism and Intolerance, *Third Report on Slovakia* (Brussels: Council of Europe, 2004), pp. 8–16; Michal Vašečka, "The Roma," in Grigorij Mesežnikov, Michal Ivantyšyn, and Tom Nicholson, eds. *Slovakia, 1998–1999: A Global Report on the State of Society*, (Bratislava: Institute for Public Affairs, 1999), p. 395; Boris Vaňo, *The Demographic Characteristics of Roma Population in Slovakia*, trans. František Bernadič (Bratislava: Institute of Informatics and Statistics, Demographic Research Centre, 2001), p. 13; Boris Vaňo, *Projection of Roma Population in Slovakia until 2025*, trans. František Bernadič (Bratislava: Institute of Informatics and Statistics, 2002), p. 6.

93. "Non-exhaustive List of Anti-Romani and Other Harmful Statements by Members of the Parties of the Slovak Governing Coalition," (2006), p. 1, http://www.errc.org.cikk. php?cikk'2609&archiv'1 [accessed September 6, 2006].

94. David Z. Scheffel, *Svinia in Black and White: Slovak Roma and Their Neighbors* (Peterborough, ON: Broadview Press, 2005), pp. 28–29.

95. Ibid., p. 29.

96. European Roma Rights Center, *Time of the Skinheads: Denial and Exclusion of Roma in Slovakia* (Budapest: European Roma Rights Center, 1997), p. 23.

97. Ina Zoon, *On the Margins: Slovakia* (New York: Open Society Institute, 2001), p. 22; Central Intelligence Agency, *The World Factbook (2006)*, pp. 7–8, https://www.cia.gov/cia/publications/factbook/geos/lo.html [accessed September 13, 2006].

98. Zoon, *On the Margins*, p. 23.

99. "Winter without Heating or Hot Water for Roma in Luna IX," *Snapshots from Around Europe* (2006), p. 1, http://www.errc.org/cikk.php?cikk'2580&archiv'1 [accessed September 6, 2006].

100. European Monitoring Centre on Racism and Xenophobia, *Breaking the Barriers— Romani Women and Access to Public Health Care* (Luxembourg: Office for Official Publications of the European Communities, 2003), p. 12.

101. Vašečka, "The Roma," p. 413; "Slovakia's Unloved Ones," *The Economist* (March 4, 2000), p. 51.

102. Zoon, *On the Margins*, pp. 50, 52.

103. "Extreme Rights Deprivation among Roma in Slovakia Leads to Unrest," *Snapshots from Around Europe* (2004), p. 1, http://www.errc.org.cikk.php?cikk'1884&archiv'1 [accessed September 6, 2006].

104. United States Congress, *Romani Human Rights in Europe*. Hearing before the Commission on Security and Cooperation in Europe, 104th Congress, Second Session, July 21, 1998 (Washington, DC: U.S. Government Printing Office, 1998), p. 22.

105. Claude Cahn, "Smoke and Mirrors: Roma and Minority Policy in Hungary," *Notebook*, pp. 1–4, http://www.errc.org/cikk.php?cikk'1255&archiv'1 [accessed September 6, 2006].

106. Project on Ethnic Relations, *The Roma in Hungary: Government Policies, Minority Expectations, and the International Community* (Princeton: Project on Ethnic Relations, 2000), p. 9; Éva Orsós, "My Central European family," *Meet the ERRC*, pp. 1–3, http://www.errc.org/cikk.php?cikk'1010&archiv'1 [accessed September 6, 2006].

107. Eva Sobotka, "Hungary: Council of Europe Delegation Alarmed by Treatment of Roma in Hungary," *Central European Review*, Vol. 3, No. 4 (January 29, 2001), pp. 3–4, http://www.ce-review.org/01/4/romanews4.html [accessed September 21, 2006].

108. Office of the High Commissioner for Human Rights, "Concluding Observations of the Committee for the Elimination of Racial Discrimination: Hungary. 01/11/2002," pp 1–3. http://www.unhchr.ch/tbs/doc/nsf/(Symbol)/A.57.18,paras.367–390.En? Opendocument [accessed September 23, 2006]; "ERRC Action as Hungary Goes before the United Nations Committee on the Elimination of Racial Discrimination, *Advocacy* (2002), pp. 1–3, http://www.errc.org/cikk.php?cikk'161&archiv'1 [accessed September 6, 2006].

109. "Reports on Public Attitudes about Roma in Hungary," *Snapshots from Around Europe*, p. 1, http://www.errc.org/cikk/php?cikk'1803&archiv'1 [accessed September 6, 2006].

110. "Hate Speech by Mayor in Hungary," *Snapshots from Around Hungary*, p. 1, http://www/errc.org/cikk.php?cikk'864&archiv'1 [accessed September 6, 2006]; "Racist Lessons in Hungary," *Snapshots from Around Europe*," p. 1, http://www.Errc.org/cikk.php?cikk'684&archiv'1 [accessed September 6, 2006]; "Racist Hungarian Textbook Removed from Curriculum," *Snapshots from Around Europe*, p. 1, http://www.errc.org/cikk.php?cikk'1009&archiv'1 [accessed September 6, 2006].

111. Knudsen, "Online Gypsy-Killing Game Controversy," *RomNews Network Community*, p. 1, http://www.romnews.com/community/modules.php?op'modload&name'News& file'arctic [accessed September 24, 2006]; "Prominent Roma Raise Voices against Hostility against Roma in Hungary," *Budapest Week* (July 27, 2005), p. 1, http://www.budapestweek.com/newsites/headlines/headlines04.html [accessed September 24, 2006].

112. "Prominent Roma Raise Voices against Hostility against Roma in Hungary," p. 1.

113. *European Roma Rights Center Shadow Report to the United Nations Committee on the Rights of the Child* (Budapest: European Roma Rights Centre, 2005), pp. 2–3, 21.

114. "Prominent Roma Raise Voices against Hostility against Roma in Hungary," p. 1.

115. Robert E. Koulish, "Attitudes towards Roma Minority Rights in Hungary: A Case of Ethnic Doxa, and the Contested Legitimization of Roma Inferiority," *Nationalities Papers*, Vo. 31, No. 3 (September 2003), p. 328; this source estimates the Roma population in Hungary to be between 500,000 and 800,000.

116. Noel Malcolm, *Kosovo: A Short History* (New York: HarperCollins, 1999), p. 209; European Roma Rights Center, *Roma Rights*, No. 2 (1999), p. 1; Shani Rafati, "Invisible Roma in Kosovo," Unpublished Manuscript (1999), p. 1; Kosovo's Ministry of Public Services Says the Roma Make Up 1.7 percent of the Population. Insttitucionet e Përkohshme Vetëqeverisëse, *Kosovo and Its Population: A Brief Description* (Prishtina: Ministry of Public Services, 2003), p. 4.

117. Malcolm, *Kosovo*, p. 206.

118. Ibid., pp. 207–208.

119. Ibid., p. 208; Crowe, *History of the Gypsies*, p. 222.

120. UNHCR, "Background Paper on Refugees and Asylum Seekers from Kosovo" (February 1996), p. 4.

121. Malcolm, Kosovo, pp. 334–337.

122. UNHCR, "Background Paper," p. 5.

123. Tim Judah, *The Serbs: History, Myth & the Destruction of Yugoslavia* (New Haven: Yale University Press, 1997), p. 29.

124. Crowe, *History of the Gypsies of Eastern Europe*, pp. 230–231; Malcolm, *Kosovo*, pp. 344–346.

125. Carlotta Gall, "Kosovo War over, Gypsies Find Themselves Alone." *The New York Times* (July 11, 1999), p. 6; there is also some evidence that the Serbs made a similar alliance with ethnic Turks in Kosovo. Steven Erlanger, "As NATO Pours In, Fearful Serbs Pour Out," *The New York Times* (June 14, 1999), p. A11.

126. Claude Cahn and Tatjana Peric, "Roma and the Kosovo Conflict," *Roma Rights*, No. 2, 1999, p. 1.

127. Gall, "Kosovo War Over," p. 6.

128. Ibid., p. 6.

129. Ibid., p. 6; a number of press accounts support Makolli's claim that the Serb's forced the Roma to work as grave diggers. Peter Finn, "Pollashka's List," *The Washington Post* (June 20, 1999), p. A22; David J. Lynch, "Hidden Children Return to Find Slain Families, Friends," *USA Today* (June 16, 1999), p. 7A; Ian fisher with David Rohde, "Return to Many Villages Is Visit to 'Crime Scenes.'" *The New York Times* (June 17, 1999), p. A19; some Albanian Kosovars thought the Roma were paid by the Serbs for their work. Ellen Knickmeyer, "Villagers Describe More Massacres; Serb Withdrawal Allows Verification," *The Charlotte Observer* (June 16, 1999), p. 15A.

130. Rromani Baxt, "The Situation of the Rroma in Cossivia," August 1998, pp. 3–4.

131. Ibid., pp. 3–4.

132. Cahn and Peric, "Roma and the Kosovo Conflict," pp. 2–3.

133. Ibid., p. 3; Carlotta Gall, "Kosovo Rebels Said to Allow Violence against Serbs," *The New York Times* (August 3, 1999), p. A5.

134. Ian Fisher, "Germans Plan Curfew as Crime Rises in a City," *The New York Times* (June 28, 1999), p. A8; David Rohde, "Kosovar Attack on Gypsies Reveals Desire for Revenge," *The New York Times* (June 7, 1999), p. A12; Carlotta Gall, "Albanians Loot and Burn, Aiming Wrath at Gypsies," *The New York Times* (June 24, 1999), p. A14; Tamara Jones, "Relief Convoy: A Cynical Humanitarian and the Kosovo Refugees," *The Washington Post Magazine* (July 4, 1999), pp. 21, 24; Human Rights Watch, *Failure to Protect: Anti-minority Violence in Kosovo* (New York: Human Rights Watch, 2004), pp. 26–30.

135. "Declaration of the Rromani Union concerning the Recent Events in Kosovo" (April 18, 1999), p. 2.

136. Press Statement, European Roma Rights Center, Budapest, "Human Rights Project Sofia" (June 23, 1999), pp. 3–6; letter of Commission on Security and Cooperation in Europe to Secretary of State Madeline Albright, July 15, 1999, pp. 1–2; Erika Schlager to David Crowe, September 13, 1999.

137. Steven Erlanger, "After Slow Start, U. N. Asserts Role in Running Kosovo," *The New York Times* (August 11, 1999), pp. A1, A10; by the end of August 1999, the United Nations High Commissioner for Refugees estimated that there were 173,000 Kosovar Roma and Serbs in Serbia, though only 133,737 were officially registered as such. Steven Erlanger, "Serbs Driven from Kosovo Live Crowded and in Want," *The New York Times* (September 2, 1999), p. A3; Dr. Bernard Kouchner, the UN's administrator for Kosovo, told the UN Security Council on September 11, 1999, that Kosovo had a population of 1.4 million Albanians, 97,000 Serbs, and 73,000 individuals from other ethnic groups, including Roma. *RFE/RL Newsline*, Vol. 3, No. 178, Part II, September 13, 1999.

138. *Roma Rights*, no. 1, 2002, p. 104.

139. *Roma Rights*, no. 2, 2002, p. 52.

140. *Roma Rights*, no. 1, 2004, pp. 83–88.

141. *Roma Rights*, no. 2, 2004, p. 57.

142. "Members of European Parliament Hear Testimonies of Rights Abuse of Roma in Kosova," (2005), pp. 1–2. http://www.errc.org/cikk.php?cikk'2272&archiv'1 [accessed September 4, 2006].

143. "Romani Families Remain in Toxic Camps in Kosovo," *Snapshots from Around Europe* (2005), p. 1, http://www.erroc.org/cikk.php?cikk'2330&archiv'1 [accessed September 4, 2006]; Olivia Ward, "Poisoned Children," *Toronto Star* (November 13, 2005), p. A12.

144. Ibid., p. A12; "ERRC/ENAR/ERO Joint Statement: Roma Rights in Kosovo (September 19, 2005)," p. 1, http://www.errc.org/cikk.php?cikk'2386&archiv'1 [accessed September 4, 2006].
145. Latham, "Roma of the Former Yugoslavia," p. 218; Poulton, *The Balkans*, p. 90.
146. European Roma Rights Center, *A Pleasant Fiction*, p. 8.
147. Latham, "Roma of the Former Yugoslavia," p. 219; European Roma Rights Center, *A Pleasant Fiction*, pp. 7–8, 33–34; United Nations Development Programme, *Faces of Poverty, Faces of Hope: Vulnerability Profiles for Decade of Roma Inclusion Countries* (Bratislava: United Nations Development Programme, 2005), p. 43.
148. European Roma Rights Center, *A Pleasant Fiction*, pp. 17–23; Latham, "Roma of the Former Yugoslavia," p. 219; Jonathan Fox, "Roma (Gypsies) Macedonia," Unpublished Manuscript (December 12, 1995), p. 2.
149. European Roma Rights Center, *A Pleasant Fiction*, p. 49; Latham, "Roma in the Former Yugoslavia," p. 219. Roma economist Šemci Šajnov says that Roma unemployment rates at this time were about 80 percent; Nadir Redzepi and Aleksandra Bojadzieva, *Policies for Improvement of the Employment of Roma in Macedonia* (London: Minority Rights Group International, 2005), p. 1.
150. Ibid., pp. 1–4.
151. European Roma Rights Center, *A Pleasant Fiction*, pp. 47, 64–70.
152. Ibid., p. 73.
153. Ibid., pp. 87–90; Lambert, "Roma of the Former Yugoslavia," p. 219.
154. Ibid., pp. 89–90; Fox, "Roma (Gypsies) Macedonia," p. 2; Latham, "Roma in the Former Yugoslavia," p. 219; Hugh Poulton, "The Roma in Macedonia: A Balkan Success Story," *RFE/RL Research Report*, Vol. 2, No. 19 (May 7, 1993), pp. 42–45; Hugh Poulton, "The Republic of Macedonia after UN Recognition," *RFE/RL Research Report*, Vol. 2, No. 23 (June 4, 1993), pp. 22–23; Duncan M. Perry, "Politics in the Republic of Macedonia: Issues and Parties," *RFE\RL Research Report*, Vol. 2, No. 23 (June 4, 1993), pp. 31, 37.
155. Macedonian Center for International Cooperation, *Applied Education for Young Roma* (Skopje: Macedonian Center for International Cooperation, 2005), pp. 1–4; Operation Dayswork, DanChurchAid, MCIC, *Challenging the Past: Education for Young Roma* (Copenhagen: Dansk Erhvervstryk, 2004), pp. 1–10; United States Agency for International Development, *US AID from the American People: Macedonia* (Washington, DC: United States Agency for International Development, 2005), p. 1.
156. Shayna Plaut and Azibija Memedova, "Blank Face, Private Strength: Romani Identity as Represented in the Public and Private Sphere," in Azbija Memedova, Shayna Plaut, Andrea Boscoboinik, and Christian Giordano, eds. *Roma's Identities in Southeastern Europe: Macedonia* (Rom: Ethnobarometer, 2005), p. 32; European Roma Rights Centre and National Roma Centrum, *Written Comments of the European Roma Rights Centre and the National Roma Centrum concerning the Former Yugoslav Republic of Macedonia* (Budapest: European Roma Rights Centre, 2006), p. 2.
157. Andrzej Mirga, "Addressing the Challenges of Romani Children's Education in Poland—Past and Current Trends and Possible Solutions," p. 3, http://www.per-usa.org/PolandRomaeducation.doc [accessed October 18, 2006]; Central Intelligence Agency, *The World Factbook* (2006), p. 4, https://www.cia.gov/cia/publications/ factbook/geos/pl.html [accessed October 21, 2006].
158. European Roma Rights Center, *The Limits of Solidarity: Roma in Poland after 1989* (Budapest: European Roma Rights Center, 2002), p. 28; Mirga, "Addressing the Challenges of Romani Children," pp. 3–4.
159. Mirga, "Addressing the Challenges of Romani Children," pp. 4–5.
160. Ibid., p. 5.

161. Tomasz Kamusella, "Poland's Minorities in the Transition from Soviet-Dominated Ethnic Nation-State to Democratic Civic Nation-State," p. 24, http:www.univie.ac.at/spacesofidentity/_Vol_3_4/_HTML/kamusella.html [accessed October 22, 2006].

162. Dr. Sławomir Łodziński, *The Protection of National Minorities in Poland* (September 1999), p. 17, http://www.mineres.lv/reports/poland/poland_NGO.htm [accessed October 19, 2006]; Council of Europe, *Third Report on Poland* (Geneva: Council of Europe, 2005), pp. 25–26.

163. Mirga, "Addressing the Challenges of Romani Children," pp. 8, 12–13.

164. Ministry of Interior and Administration, *Programme for the Roma Community in Poland* (Warsaw: Ministry of Interior and Administration, 2004), p. 2.

165. Central Intelligence Agency, *The World Factbook (2006)*, pp. 3, 5, https://www.cia.gov/cia/publications/factbook/geos/ro.html [accessed October 3, 2006].

166. Council of Europe, *Third Report on Romania* (Brussels: Council of Europe, 2006), p. 17; Open Society Institute, *Monitoring Local Implementation of the Government Strategy for the Improvement of the Condition of Roma* (Budapest: Open Society Institute, 2004), p. 10.

167. Ibid., p. 20.

168. *Case of Moldovan and Others v. Romania*, Applications nos. 41138/98 and 64320/01, July 5, 2005, pp. 1–8, http://cmiskp.echr.coe.int/tkp197/viewhbkm.asp?sessionId'3244661&skin'hudoc-en&acti [accessed September 20, 2005].

169. Laura Surdu and Mihai Surdu, *Broadening the Agenda: The Status of Romani Women in Romania* (New York: Open Society Institute, 2006), pp. 5, 9.

170. Ibid., p. 5.

171. Ibid., pp. 31–41.

172. Ibid., pp. 43–52.

173. Ibid., pp. 53–58.

174. Ibid., pp. 59–64.

175. Ibid., pp. 65–67; "Plan to segregate Roma in Romania," *Snapshots from Around Europe* (2001), p. 1, http://www.errc.org/cikk.php?cikk'655&archiv'1 [accessed September 6, 2006]; "Attempted Ghettoization of Roma in Romanian Town," *Snapshots from Around Europe* (2001), p. 1, http://www.errc.org/cikk.php?cikk'1727&archiv'1 [accessed September 6, 2006].

176. "Roma Expelled from Romanian Capital," *Snapshots from Around Europe* (2002), p. 1, http://www.errc.org/cikk.php?cikk'931&archiv'1 [accessed September 6, 2006]; "Evictions of Roma in Romania," *Snapshots from Around Europe* (2002), pp. 1–2, http://www.errc.org/cikk.php?cikk'1623&archiv'1 [accessed September 6, 2006]; "Roma Forcibly Evicted by Romanian Officials," *Snapshots from Around Europe* (2003), p. 1, http://www.errc.org/cikk.php?cikk'1315&archiv'1 [accessed September 6, 2006]; "Romanian Mayor Announces Intention to Evict Romani Families," *Snapshots from Around Europe* (2004), p. 1, http://www.errc.org/cikk.php?cikk'2103&archiv'1 [accessed September 6, 2006]; "Roma Houses Destroyed in Romanian Town of Seica Mare," *News Roundup: Snapshots from Around the World* (2006), p. 1, http:www//errc.org/cikk.php?cikk'2493&archiv'1 [accessed September 6, 2006].

177. Surdu and Surdu, *Broadening the Agenda*, pp. 69–71; Critsti Mihalache, "Obstacles to the Participation of Roma in Elections in Romania," *Notebook* (2004), pp. 1–2, http://www.errc.org/cikk.php?cikk'1364&archiv'1 [accessed September 6, 2006].

178. Commission on Security and Cooperation in Europe, *The Romani Minority in Russia* (Washington, DC: Commission on Security and Cooperation in Europe, 2006), p. 3; European Commission against Racism and Intolerance, *Third Report on the Russian Federation* (Brussels: Council of Europe, 2006), p. 14; International Federation for Human Rights, *The Roma of Russia: the Subject of Multiple Forms of Discrimination*

(Paris: International Federation for Human Rights, 2004), p. 30; European Roma Rights Center, *Violations of Roma Rights in the Russian Federation* (Budapest: European Roma Rights Center, 2004), p. 2.

179. European Roma Rights Centre, *In Search of Happy Gypsies: Persecution of Pariah Minorities in Russia* (Budapest: European Roma Rights Centre, 2005), p. 3.
180. *The Roma of Russia*, pp. 6–7.
181. *The Romani Minority in Russia*, pp. 22–23, 54–60.
182. *The Roma of Russia*, p. 8; *Third Report on the Russian Federation*, p. 15; *The Romani Minority in Russia*, pp. 19–20, 22.
183. *In Search of Happy Gypsies*, pp. 160–161.
184. Ibid., p. 161.
185. *Third Report on the Russian Federation*, p. 15; *In Search of Happy Gypsies*, p. 203.
186. Aleksandra Mitrović and Gradimir Zajić, "Social Position of the Roma in Serbia," in Centre for Anti-war Action, *The Roma in Serbia*, trans. Srdan Vujica, Ljiljana Bajić, and Pavle Perenčević (Belgrade: Institute for Criminological and Sociological Research, 1998), p. 19; "European Roma Rights Center Press Release to European Council" (September 23, 2002), p. 3n1, http://www.errc.org/cikk.php?cikk'271&archiv'1 [accessed September 11, 2006].
187. Mitrović and Zajić, "Social Position of the Roma in Serbia," p. 45; Dragoljub Acković, *Roma in Serbia: Introducing Romany Language and Culture into Primary Schools* (London: Minority Rights Group, n.d.), pp. 1–3; Central Intelligence Agency, "Serbia," *The World Factbook (2006)*, p. 4, http:www.cia.gov/cia/publications/factbook/geos/rb.html [accessed September 7, 2006]; UN Office of the High commissioner for Human Rights and European Roma Rights Center, *Memorandum: The Protection of Roma Rights in Serbia and Montenegro* (Geneva: The United Nations, 2003), p. 27; "Romani Pupils Face Verbal and Physical Assault at School in Serbia and Montenegro," *Snapshots from Around Europe* (2003), pp. 1–2, http://www.errc.org/cikk.php?cikk'1122&archiv'1 [accessed September 11, 2006].
188. Refika Mustafic, "Opre Roma!" pp. 1–2, http://www.errc.org/cikk.php?cikk'1242&archiv'1 [accessed September 11, 2006].
189. Ibid., p. 2.
190. United Nations Committee against Torture, "Yugoslavia Violated Treaty in 1995 Danilograd (Montenegro)," pp. 1–14, http://groups.yahoo.com/group/balkanhr/message/4952, [accessed October 10, 2006]; "ERRC/HLC Letter to Montenegrin Prime Minister" (May 8, 2003), http://www.errc.org/cikk.php?cikk'311&archiv'1 [accessed September 11, 2006]; "Montenegrin Government Agrees to Pay 985,000 Euros in Compensation to Pogrom Victims (July 4, 2003), p. 1, http://www.errc.org/cikk.php?cikk'330&archiv'1 [accessed September 11, 2006]; "985,000 Euro Compensation for Romani Victims of 1995 Pogrom in Serbia and Montenegro," *Snapshots from Around Europe* (2003), p. 1, http://www.errc.org/cikk.php?cikk'1121&archiv'1 [accessed September 11, 2006].
191. Serguei Chabanov, "Skinhead Violence Targeting Roma in Yugoslavia," *Notebook*, pp. 1–9, http://www.errc.org/cikk.php?cikk'1816&archiv'1 [accessed September 11, 2006]; "Book Published in Memory of Romani Victim of Racially-Motivated Killing in Yugoslavia," *Snapshots from Around Europe*, p. 1; http://www.errc.org/cikk.php? cikk'506&archiv'1 [accessed September 11, 2006]; "UN Torture Committee Again Rules against Police Abuse of Roma in Serbia and Montenegro" (December 12, 2005), pp. 1–2, http://www.errc.org/cikk. php?cikk'2578&archiv'1; "UN Torture Committee Instructs Government to Investigate Police Abuse of Roma," *Snapshots from Around Europe* (2005), p. 1, http://www.errc.org/cikk.php?cikk'2578&archiv'1 [accessed September 11, 2006].
192. World Organization against Torture, *State Violence in Serbia and Montenegro: An Alternative Report to the United Nations Human Rights Committee* (Geneva: World Organisation against Torture, 2004), pp. 11–12.

193. European Roma Rights Center, *The Misery of Law: The Rights of Roma in the Transcarpathian Region of Ukraine* (Budapest: European Roma Rights Center, 1997), p. 10.
194. Matt Hagengruber, "Roma Realities and Possibilities," *The Christian Science Monitor* (August 2, 2005), p. 2, http://www.csmonitor.com/2005/0802/p09s01-woeu.htm [accessed October 24, 2006].
195. Roma Women's Initiatives, "Roma Women Conference in Kiev, Ukraine" (June 19, 2003), p. 1, http://www.romawomensinitiatives.org/resources1.asp?ID'49& kategorija'4&podkategor [accessed October 24, 2006].
196. European Roma Rights Center, *Written Comments of the European Roma Rights Centre concerning Ukraine for Consideration by the Untied Nations Committee on the Elimination of Racial Discrimination* (Budapest: European Roma Rights Center, 2006), p. 40.
197. Ibid., pp. 40–41.
198. Ibid., p. 5.
199. Dženo Association, "Roma Situation in Ukraine" (September 25, 2006), pp. 1–7, http://www.dzeno.cz/?id'11533 [accessed October 24, 2006].

B·I·B·L·I·O·G·R·A·P·H·Y

ARTICLES

"Abuse of Roma by Officials in the Czech Republic." *Snapshots from Around Europe* (1999), 1 page. http://www.errc.org/cikk.php?cikk=568&archiv=1.

Ackerley, F.G. "George Potra's *Contributiuni la Istoricul Tiganilor din Romania.*" *Journal of the Gypsy Lore Society*. Third Series. Vol. XXI, Nos. 1–2 (January-April 1942), pp. 68–71.

———. "Romani-Esi." *Journal of the Gypsy Lore Society*. Third Series. Vol. XXVII, Nos. 3–4 (July-October 1948), pp. 157–158.

———. "The Voice of the Gypsies." *Journal of the Gypsy Lore Society*. Third Series. Vol. XXI, Nos. 1–2 (January-April 1942), pp. 71–72.

Acton, T.A. "After the Fourth World Romani Congress Encyclopaedists Set to Work." Unpublished Report, n.d., pp. 1–5.

"Additional Census for Minorities to Encourage Ethnic Consciousness." *Radio Free Europe Research*. Hungary No. 11 (3 July 1980), pp. 14–15.

American Committee to Save Bosnia. "Convoy Bosnia—a Summary of the Crisis in Bosnia" (1993), pp. 1–2.

Ancel, Jean. "The 'Christian' Regimes of Romania and the Jews, 1940–1942." *Holocaust and Genocide Studies*. Vol. 7 No. 1 (Spring 1993), pp. 14–29.

Andree, Richard. "Old Warning-Placards for Gypsies." *Journal of the Gypsy Lore Society*. New Series. Vol. V, No. 3 (1911–12), pp. 202–204.

Andronikova, I.M. "Evolution of the Dwellings of the Russian Gypsies." *Soviet Anthropology and Archeology*. Vol. IX, No. 1 (Summer 1972), pp. 3–28.

Ariste, Paul. "Concerning the Baltic Gypsies and Their Dialects." *Journal of the Gypsy Lore Society*. Third Series. Vol. XLIII, Nos. 1–2 (January-April 1964), pp. 58–61.

———. "Gypsy Studies." *Journal of the Gypsy Lore Society*. Third Series. Vol. XLIII, Nos. 1–2 (January-April 1964), pp. 56–61.

———. "The Latvian Legend of May Rose." *Journal of the Gypsy Lore Society*. Third Series. Vol. XL, Nos. 3–4 (July-October 1961), pp. 100–105.

Arutiunian, Iu. V., L.M. Drobizheva, and V.S. Zelenchuk, eds. "A Preliminary Ethnosociological Study of Way of Life (On Data of the Moldavian SSR)." *Soviet Sociology*. Vol. XXI, No. 4 (Spring 1983), pp. 45–112.

"Attempted ghettoization of Roma in Romanian town," *Snapshots from around Europe* (2001), 1 page, http://www.errc.org/cikk.php?cikk=1727&archiv=1.

Baest, Torsten F. "Bulgaria's War at Home: The People's Republic and Its Turkish Minority (1944–1985)." *Across Frontiers* (Winter 1985), pp. 18–26.

Barannikov, A.P. "On the Russian Gypsy Singers of Today." *Journal of the Gypsy Lore Society*. Third Series. Vol. XI, Nos. 3–4 (1932), pp. 187–192.

———. "W.I. Philonenko: 'The Crimean Gypsies.'" *Journal of the Gypsy Lore Society*. Third Series. Vol. X, No. 2 (1931), pp. 144–146.

Barany, Zoltan D. "Democratic Changes Bring Mixed Blessings for Gypsies." *RFE\RL Research Report* (15 May 1992), pp. 40–47.

———. "Hungary's Gypsies." *Report on Eastern Europe* (July 20, 1990), pp. 26–31.

Barinov, Mark. "How Real are Those Gypsies." *Sputnik*, No. 6 (1967), pp. 206–211.

Beck, Sam. "The Origins of Gypsy Slavery in Romania." *Dialectical Anthropology*. Vol. 14, No. 1 (1989), pp. 53–61.

Bobri, Vladimir. "Gypsies and Gypsy Choruses of Old Russia." *Journal of the Gypsy Lore Society*. Third Series. Vol. XL, Nos. 3–4 (July-October 1961), pp. 112–120.

Bogdanović, Ana. "The Croatian National Programme for the Roma: An Example of Gender Inequality?" (August 2005), *Eumap.org*, pp. 1–3.

Bogomazov, Sergei. "Moscow Gypsy Artists in Wartime." *Journal of the Gypsy Lore Society*. Third Series. Vol. XXIV, Nos. 1–2 (January-April 1945), pp. 60–61.

"Book published in memory of Romani victim of racially-motivated killing in Yugoslavia." *Snapshots from around Europe*, 1 pag, http://www.errc.org/cikk.php?cikk=506&archiv=1.

"Bulgarian Authorities urged to Halt Forced Evictions of Roma." 1 page, http://www.errc.org/cikk.php?cikk=2606&archiv=1.

"Bulgarian Ministry of Education and Science Issues Landmark 'Instruction for the Integration of Minority Children and Pupils.'" *Snapshots from around Europe* (2003), p. 1, http://www.errc.org/cikk.php?cikk=1627&archiv=1.

Cahn, Claude. "Breakthrough: Challenging Coercive Sterilisations of Romani Women in the Czech Republic." *Advocacy* (2004), pp. 1–6, http://www.errc.org/cikk.php?cikk=2071&archiv=1.

———. "Smoke and mirrors: Roma and minority policy in Hungary." *Notebook*, pp. 1–4. http://www.errc.org/cikk.php?cikk=1255&archiv=1.

Case of Moldovan and Others v. Romania, Applications nos. 41138/98 and 64320/01, 5 July 2005, pp. 1–8, http://cmiskp.echr.coe.int/tkp197/viewhbkm.asp?sessionId=3244661&skin=hudoc-en&acti.

"Census Data on Changes in Nationality Composition." JPRS-UPA-90–072 (28 December 1990), pp. 64–71.

Chabanov, Serguei. "Skinhead violence targeting Roma in Yugoslavia," *Notebook*, pp. 1–9, http://www.errc.org/cikk.php?cikk=1816&archiv=1.

"Challenging Coercive Sterilisations of Romani Women in the Czech Republic (2005)." pp. 1–2. http://www.errc.org/cikk.php?cikk=2228&archiv=1.

Cherkashin, Nikolai. "Gipsy Drovers on the Trail." *Sputnik*, No. 9 (September 1972), pp. 100–103.

"Congress of Ethnic Minorities." *Radio Free Europe Research*. Hungary No. 30 (4 December 1978), pp. 8–9.

Council of Europe. "European Social Charter (revised), 3.V.1996, pp. 1–12. http://conventions.coe.int/treaty/en/Treaties/Html/163.htm.

Courthiades, Marcel. "Social and Historical Profile of the Rromanis in Albania." Unpublished manuscript (1998), pp. 1–7.

Crowe, David M. "Anti-Semitism and Anti-Jewish Policy in the Soviet Union and Russia, 1917–1992." Unpublished manuscript (1992), pp. 1–21.

———. "The Liuli (Gypsies) of Central Asia." *AACAR Bulletin*. Vol. VI, No. 1 (Spring 1993), pp. 1–6.

———. "The Roma (Gypsies) of Hungary through the Kádár Era." *Nationalities Papers*. Vol. XIX, No. 3 (Winter 1991), pp. 297–311.

Csapo, Marg. "Preschool Special Education in Hungary." *Early Child Development and Care*. Vol. 14, Nos. 3–4 (March 1984), pp. 251–268.

Davidova, Dr. Eva. "The Gypsies in Czechoslovakia. Part I: Main Characteristics and Brief Historical Development," translated by D.E. Guy. *Journal of the Gypsy Lore Society*. Third Series. Vol. LXIX, Nos. 3–4 (July-October 1970), pp. 84–97.

———. "The Gypsies in Czechoslovakia. Part II: Post-War Developments." *Journal of the Gypsy Lore Society*. Third Series. Vol. I, Nos. 1–2 (January-April 1971), pp. 39–54.

"Declaration of the Rromani Union Concerning the Recent Events in Kosovo." April 18,1999, pp. 1–2.

Dedic, Milutin. "Cultural-Artistic Amateurism." *Yugoslav Survey*. Vol. XXII, No. 2 (May 1981), pp. 121–140.

Dedić, Jasminka. "The Erasure: Administrative Ethnic Cleansing in Slovenia," *Notebook* (2003), pp. 1–2. http://www.errc.org/cikk.php?cikk=1109.

Department for International Development. "Bosnia-Herzegovina," http://www.dfid.gov.uk/countries/europe/bosniaherzegovina.asp, pp. 1–2.

"Discrimination." *East Europe*. Vol. 8, No. 12 (December 1959), pp. 3–18.

Dominis, Iva and Ivo Bicanic. "Refugees and Displaced Persons in the Former Yugoslavia." *RFE\RL Research Report* (15 January 1993), pp. 1–4.

Druker, Jeremy. "Present but Unaccounted for," *Transitions*, Vol. 4, No. 4 (September 1997), p. 23

Duirchova, Anna I. "Glimpse of the Rom: Excursions in Slovakia." *Journal of the Gypsy Lore Society*. Third Series. Vol. L, Nos. 1–2 (January-April 1971), pp. 24–40.

Dyker, David and Vesna Bojicic. "The Impact of Sanctions on the Serbian Economy." *RFE\RL Research Report* (21 May 1993), pp. 50–54.
Dženo Association. "Roma Situation in Ukraine." September 25, 2006, pp. 1–7, http://www.dzeno.cz/?id=11533.
"The Employment of Gypsies." *Radio Free Europe Research*. Hungary No. 19 (8 August 1978), pp. 5–8.
Engelbrekt, Kjell. "Bulgaria Expels Zhirinovsky." *RFE/RL Daily Report*. No. 1 (29 December 1993), n.p.
Erlanger, Steven. "After Slow Start, U. N. Asserts Role in Running Kosovo." *The New York Times*. August 11, 1999, pp. A1, A10
————. "As NATO Pours In, Fearful Serbs Pour Out." *The New York Times*. June 14, 1999, p. A11.
————. "Serbs Driven from Kosovo Live Crowded and In Want." *The New York Times*. September 2, 1999, p. A3.
"ERRC Action as Hungary Goes Before the United Nations Committee on the Elimination of Racial Discrimination." *Advocacy* (2002), pp. 1–3, http://www.errc.org/cikk.php?cikk=161&archiv=1.
"ERRC/ENAR/ERO Joint Statement: Roma Rights in Kosovo (September 19, 2005)." p. 1, http://www.errc.org/cikk.php?cikk=2386&archiv=1.
"ERRC/HLC Letter to Montenegrin Prime Minister," (May 8, 2003), http://www.errc.org/cikk.php?cikk=311&archiv=1.
"Ethnic Minorities and Foreigners." *Radio Free Europe Research* (22 September 1989), pp. 33–37.
"European Court of Human Rights Confirms Racial Discrimination in Landmark Bulgarian Case." *Open Justice Society Initiative*, 7 July 2005, pp. 1–2.
European Roma Rights Center. "Desegregation Court Victory," February 28, 2006, pp. 1–2. http://www.errc.org/cikk.php?cikk=2411&archiv=1.
————. "Five Roma rights Victories under New Bulgarian Equality Law," September 30, 2004, p. 2. http://www.errc.org/cikk.php?cikk=2022&archiv=1.
————. "Human Rights Project Sofia." June 23, 1999, pp. 1–6.
"European Roma Rights Center Press Release to European Council," September 23, 2002, p. 1–3, http://www.errc.org/cikk.php?cikk=271&archiv=1.
European Roma Rights Center. *Roma Rights*, No. 2 (1999), 1 page.
————. "Summary of Pressing Concerns: Bosnia and Herzegovina." 3 July 2006, pp. 1–3.
European Roma Rights Centre, "Roma-police seminars in Bulgaria." *Notebook* (2003), pp. 1–3, http:www.errc.org/cikk.php?cikk=507&archiv=1.
————. "Roma Recognized by New Minority Rights Law in Bosnia and Herzegovina," http://www.errc.org/cikk.php?cikk=1096&archiv=1, 1 page.
European Union. "Commission: Bulgaria's and Romania's accession possible in 2007, if preparation efforts are intensified." 16 May 2006, IP/06/634, pp. 1–2.
————. "Key Findings of the May 2006 monitoring reports on Bulgaria and Romania." 16 May 2006, MEMO/06/201, pp. 1–2.
"Evictions of Roma in Romania," *Snapshots from around Europe* (2002), pp. 1–2, http://www.errc.org/cikk.php?cikk=1623&archiv=1.
"Extreme Rights Deprivation among Roma in Slovakia Leads to Unrest." *Snapshots from around Europe* (2004), 1 page, http://www.errc.org.cikk.php?cikk=1884&archiv=1.
Farnam, Arie. "White Residents Nostalgic about Soft Wall." *The Prague Post*, May 3, 2000, p. 1. http://www.praguepost.cz/news050300d.html.
Ferguson, William. "Russian Gypsy Singers." *Journal of the Gypsy Lore Society*. Third Series. Vol. XII, No. 2 (1933), p. 108.
Ficowski, Jerzy. "The Gypsy in the Polish People's Republic." *Journal of the Gypsy Lore Society*. Third Series. Vol. XXXV, Nos. 1–2 (January-April 1956), pp. 28–38.
————. "The Polish Gypsies of To-Day." *Journal of the Gypsy Lore Society*. Third Series. Vol. XXIX, Nos. 3–4 (July-October 1950), pp. 92–102.
Filipovic, Milenko. "Visocki Cigani." *Etnoloska Biblioteka*. Vol. 16 (1932), pp. 1–20.
Finn, Peter. "Pollashka's List." *The Washington Post*. June 20, 1999, p. A22.
"First Civil Complaint Filed Regarding Coercive Sterilisations of Romani Women." *Snapshots from Around Europe* (2005), 1 page, http://www.errc.org/cikk.php?cikk=2309&archiv=1.
"First Court Victory in Central Europe on Coercive Sterilisation of Romani Women." *News Roundup: Snapshots from Around the World* (2006), pp. 1–2, http://www.errc.org/cikk.php?cikk=2475&archiv=1.

Fisher, Ian. "Germans Plan Curfew as Crime Rises in a City." *The New York Times*. June 28,1999, p. A8.
Fisher, Ian with David Rohde. "Return to Many Villages is Visit to 'Crime Scenes.' " *The New York Times*. June 17, 1999, p. A19.
Fisher, Julius B. "How Many Jews Died in Transnistria?" *Jewish Social Studies*. Vol. XX, No. 2 (April 1958), pp. 95–101.
Gall, Carlotta. "Albanians Loot and Burn, Aiming Wrath at Gypsies." *The New York Times*. June 24, 1999, p. A14.
———. "Kosovo Rebels Said to Allow Violence Against Serbs." *The New York Times*. August 3, 1999, p. A5.
———. "Kosovo War Over, Gypsies Find Themselves Alone." *The New York Times*. July 11, 1999, p. 6
Gantskaia, O.A. and L.N. Terent'eva. "Ethnographic Studies of Ethnic Processes in the Baltic Area." *Soviet Anthropology and Archeology*. Vol. VI, No. 3 (Winter 1967–68), pp. 23–38.
Gaster, Dr. M. "Bill of Sale of Gypsy Slaves in Moldavia, 1851." *Journal of the Gypsy Lore Society*. Third Series. Volume II, No. 2 (1923), pp. 68–81.
———. "Rumanian Gypsies in 1560." *Journal of the Gypsy Lore Society*. Third Series. Vol. XII, No. 1 (1933), p. 59.
———. "Two Rumanian Documents Concerning Gypsies." *Journal of the Gypsy Lore Society*. Third Series. Vol. IX, No. 4 (1930), pp. 179–180.
Gila-Kochanowski, V. de. "N.A. Pankov." *Journal of the Gypsy Lore Society*. Third Series. Vol. XXXVIII, Nos. 3–4 (July-October 1959), pp. 159–160.
Gilberg, Trond. "Ethnic Minorities in Romania under Socialism." *East European Quarterly*. Vol. VII, No. 4 (January 1974), pp. 435–464.
Gilliat-Smith, Bernard J. "The Dialect of the Gypsies of Northern Russia." *Journal of the Gypsy Lore Society*. Third Series. Vol. XV, No. 2 (1932), pp. 71–88.
———. "The Dialect of the Gypsies of Serbo-Croatia." *Journal of the Gypsy Lore Society*. Third Series. Vol. XXVII, Nos. 3–4 (July-October 1948), pp. 142–143.
———. "Endani 'Relatives.' " *Journal of the Gypsy Lore Society*. Third Series. Vol. XXXVII, Nos. 3–4 (July-October 1958), p. 156.
———. "The Dialect of the Drindaris." *Journal of the Gypsy Lore Society*. New Series. Vol. VII, No. 4 (1913–14), pp. 260–298.
———. "The Gypsies in Bulgaria (1948)." *Journal of the Gypsy Lore Society*. Third Series. Vol. XXVII, Nos. 3–4 (July-October 1948), pp. 156–157.
———. "Review of Rade Uhlik, *Iz ciganske Onomastile*." *Journal of the Gypsy Lore Society*. Third Series. Vol. XXXVI, Nos. 3–4 (July-October 1957), pp. 133–139.
Gitlits, Ilya. "Gipsies in the USSR." *Sputnik*, No. 9 (September 1972), p. 103.
Gjorgjevic, Tihomir R. "Rumanian Gypsies in Serbia." *Journal of the Gypsy Lore Society*. Third Series. Vol. VIII, No. 1 (1929), pp. 7–25.
———. "Two Bible Stories in the Tradition of Serbian Gypsies." *Journal of the Gypsy Lore Society*. Third Series. Vol. XIII, No. 1 (1934), pp. 26–37.
———. "Die Zigeuner in Vlasenicaer Bezirke in Bosnien." *Journal of the Gypsy Lore Society*. New Series. Vol. I, No. 2 (October 1907), pp. 146–149.
———. "Von den Zigeunern in Serbien." *Journal of the Gypsy Lore Society*. New Series. Vol. I, No. 3 (January 1908), pp. 219–227.
"Greater Solicitude for Ethnic Minorities." *Radio Free Europe Research*. Hungary No. 10 (19 April 1978), pp. 6–10.
Grulich, Tomas and Tomas Haisman. "Institucionální zájem o cikánske obyvatelstvo v Ceskoslovensku v letech 1945–1958." *Cesky Lid*, Vol. 73, No. 2 (1986), pp. 72–85.
"Gypsies in Eastern Europe and the Soviet Union." *Radio Free Europe Research Report*. RAD Background Report No. 72 (12 April 1978), pp. 1–7.
"Gypsies of Eastern Europe, 1673." *Journal of the Gypsy Lore Society*. New Series. Vol. I, No. 2 (October 1907), pp. 186–187.
"The Gypsies." *East Europe*. Vol. 14, No. 10 (October 1965), pp. 20–25.
Hagengruber, Matt. "Roma Realities and Possibilities," *The Christian Science Monitor* (August 2, 2005), p. 2, http://www.csmonitor.com/2005/0802/p09s01-woeu.htm.
Hajdu, Mihály. "Gypsies 1980." *Hungarian Digest*. No. 6 (1980), pp. 28–34.
Haley, William John. "The Gypsy Conference at Bucharest." *Journal of the Gypsy Lore Society*. Third Series. Vol. XIII, No. 4 (1934), pp. 182–190.
Hall, Elsie M. "Gentile Cruelty to Gypsies." *Journal of the Gypsy Lore Society*. Third Series. Vol. XI, No. 2 (1932), pp. 49–71.

Halliday, W.R. "A Russian Gypsy Renegade." *Journal of the Gypsy Lore Society*. Third Series. Vol. II, No. 3 (1923), p. 96.

Hamill, Alfred E. "Gypsies in and About Russian Literature." *Journal of the Gypsy Lore Society*. Third Series. Vol. XXII, Nos. 1–2 (January-April 1943), pp. 57–58.

Hancock, Ian. "The Romani Diaspora." *The World and I* (March 1989), pp. 613–623.

"Hanka: A Gypsy Film in Yugoslavia." *Journal of the Gypsy Lore Society*. Third Series. Vol. XXXV, No. 3–4 (July-October 1956), pp. 180–181.

Hasluck, Margaret. "Firman of A.H. 1013–14 (A.D. 1604–05) Regarding Gypsies in the Western Balkans." *Journal of the Gypsy Lore Society*. Third Series. Vol. XXVII, Nos. 1–2 (January-April 1948), pp. 1–12.

———. "The Gypsies of Albania." *Journal of the Gypsy Lore Society*. Third Series. Vol. XVII, No. 2 (April 1938), pp. 49–61.

———. "The Gypsies of Albania." *Journal of the Gypsy Lore Society*. Third Series. Vol. XVII, Jubilee Number (1938), pp. 18–31.

———. "The Gypsies of Albania." *Journal of the Gypsy Lore Society*. Third Series. Vol. XVII, No. 4 (October 1938), pp. 108–122.

"Hate speech by mayor in Hungary." *Snapshots from around Hungary*, 1 page, http://www/errc, org/cikk.php?cikk=864&archiv=1.

Hayden, Robert M. "The Partititon of Bosnia and Hercegovina, 1990–1993." *RFE/RL Research Report* (28 May 1993), pp. 1–14.

Hirst, T. Oakes. "Bukovina Gypsies in 1922." *Journal of the Gypsy Lore Society*. Third Series. Vol. XXIV, Nos. 1–2 (January-April 1945), pp. 61–62.

Hoppe, Hans-Joachim. "Bulgarian Nationalities Policy in Occupied Thrace and Aegean Macedonia." *Nationalities Papers*. Vol. XIV, Nos. 1–2 (Spring-Fall 1986), pp. 89–100.

Howard, Patricia. "National Minorities in Eastern Europe." *Radio Free Europe Research*. RAD Background Report No. 156 (9 September 1987), pp. 1–8.

Hübschmannova, Milena. "Co je tzv. cikánska otázka?" *Sociologick y casopsis*, No. 2 (1970), pp. 105–120.

"Hungary's Gypsies." *Radio Free Europe Research Report*. Hungary No. 9 (12 April 1978), pp. 5–7.

Ilchev, Ivan and Duncan Perry. "Bulgarian Ethnic Groups: Politics and Perceptions." *RFE\RL Research Report* (19 March 1993), pp. 35–41.

"Iliescu Signs Adoption Law." *Report on Eastern Europe* (July 26, 1991), p. 54.

Iliev, Andrei. "Participation of Bulgarian Roma in the 2001 general elections and prospects for political representation." *Notebook* (2003), pp. 1–3. http://www.errc.org/cikk.php? cikk=1232&archiv=1.

Ilieva, Margarita. "The Bulgarian Draft Anti-Discrimination Law; An Opportunity to Make Good on the Constitutional Promise of Equality in a Post-Communist Society." *Notebook* (2003), pp. 1–6. http://www.errc.org/cikk.php?cikk=1444&archiv=1.

"In a Gypsy School," translated by Stuart E. Mann. *Journal of the Gypsy Lore Society*. Third Series. Vol. XIII, No. 3 (1934), pp. 117–119.

"Increased Romani Participation Fuels Anti-Romani Racism in Bulgarian Local Elections." *Snapshots from around Europe* (2003), 1 page. http://www.errc.org/cikk.php?cikk=1231 &archiv=1.

Ingram, Judith. "Hungary's Gypsy Women: Scapegoats in a New Democracy." *Ms* (September/ October 1991), pp. 17–19.

Ionescu, Dan. "The Ethnic Minorities." *Radio Free Europe Research*. Romania No. 3 (22 April 1987), pp. 17–21.

———. "The Exodus." *Report on Eastern Europe* (October 26, 1990), pp. 25–31.

———. "The Gypsies Organize." *Report on Eastern Europe* (June 29, 1990) pp. 39–44.

———. "Recent Emigration Figures." *Report on Eastern Europe* (February 15, 1991), pp. 21–24.

———. "Romania's First Post Communist Census." *RFE/RL Research Report* (13 March 1992), pp. 57–61.

———. "Violence against Gypsies Escalates." *Report on Eastern Europe* (June 21, 1991), pp. 23–26.

Jones, Tamara. "Relief Convoy: A Cynical Humanitarian and the Kosovo Refugees." *The Washington Post Magazine*. July 4, 1999, pp. 21, 24.

Jopson, N.B. "Romano Lil (Tiganske Novine)." *Journal of the Gypsy Lore Society*. Third Series. Vol. XV, No. 2 (1936), pp. 86–91.

Kafanova, Ludmilla. "Gypsy Theatre Romen." *Sputnik*. No. 9 (September 1972), pp. 91–99.

Kamm, Henry. "In Slovak Gypsy Ghetto, Hovels and Plea for Jobs." *The New York Times*, November 28, 1993, p. A4.

Kamusella, Tomasz. "Poland's Minorities in the Transition from Soviet-Dominated Ethnic Nation-State to Democratic Civic Nation-State," pp. 1–24, http:www.univie.ac.at/spacesofidentity/ _Vol_3_4/_HTML/kamusella.html.

Kappen, O. van. "A Prague Edict against Gypsies (1710)." *Journal of the Gypsy Lore Society*. Third Series. Vol. XLII, Nos. 3–4 (July-October 1963), pp. 117–121.

Kenedi, János. "Why is the Gypsy the Scapegoat and Not the Jew?" *East European Reporter*. Vol. 2, No. 1 (Spring 1986), pp. 11–14.

Kenrick, Donald S. "Notes on the Gypsies in Bulgaria." *Journal of the Gypsy Lore Society*. Third Series. Vol. XLV, Nos. 3–4 (July-October 1966), pp. 77–84.

———. "The Gypsies of Bulgaria Before and After 10th of November." Paper Delivered before the 1991 Annual Meeting of the Gypsy Lore Society, pp. 1–8.

———. "The World Romani Congress—April 1971." *Journal of the Gypsy Lore Society*. Third Series. Vol. L, Nos. 3–4 (July-October 1971), pp. 101–108.

Knickmeyer, Ellen. "Villagers Describe More Massacres; Serb Withdrawal Allows Verification." *The Charlotte Observer*. June 16, 1999, p. 15A.

Knudsen. "Online Gypsy-Killing Game Controversy." *RomNews Network Community*. 1 page, http://www.romnews.com/community/modules.php?op=modload&name=News&file= arctic.

Kochanowski, Dr. Jan. "Maskir Romende (Among Gypsies): The Views of a Latvian Gypsy." *Journal of the Gypsy Lore Society*. Third Series. Vol. XLIV, Nos. 3–4 (July-October 1965), pp. 137–140.

Kochanowski, Vanya. "Some Notes on the Gypsies of Latvia." *Journal of the Gypsy Lore Society*. Third Series. Vol. XXV, No. 3 (July 1946), pp. 34–38.

Kolev, Deyan. "Roma Folklore Classes in Bulgarian Schools: Preparing the Ground for the Desegregation of Romani Education," *Research and Policy* (2003), pp. 1–5. http:www. errc.org/cikk.php?cikk=1854&archiv=1.

Koslov, V.I. "Changes in the Ethnic Composition of Rumania and Bulgaria." *Soviet Sociology*. Vol. III, No. 2 (Fall 1964), pp. 26–38.

———. "Processes of Ethnic Change and Population Dymanics among the Peoples of the USSR." *Soviet Anthropology and Archeology*. Vol. XXVI, No. 3 (Winter 1987–88), pp. 46–60.

Kostelancik, David J. "The Gypsies of Czechoslovakia: Political and Ideological Considerations in the Development of Policy." *Studies in Comparative Communism*. Vol. XXII, No. 4 (Winter 1989), pp. 307–321.

Kostov, Kiril. "Virkhu proizkhoda na tsiganite i tekniya ezik." *Bulgarski ezik*. Vol. VII, No. 4 (1957), pp. 344–349.

Koulish, Robert E. "Attitudes towards Roma Minority Rights in Hungary: A Case of Ethnic Doxa, and the Contested Legitimization of Roma Inferiority." *Nationalities Papers*, Vol. 31, No. 3 (September 2003), pp. 327–345.

Kusin, Vladimir V. "The Ethnic Factor." *Report on Eastern Europe* (November 9, 1990), pp. 34–39.

Kyuchukov, Khristo. "Projects in Romani Education: Bulgaria." *Meet the ERRC* (2003), pp. 1–2. http://www.errc.org/cikk.php?cikk=578&archiv=1.

Latham, Judith."Roma in the Former Yugoslavia," *Nationalities Papers*, Vol. 27, No. 2 (June 1999), pp. 205–226.

Lebzelter, Dr. Viktor. "Contribution to the Anthropology of Serbian Gypsies." *Journal of the Gypsy Lore Society*. Third Series. Vol. III, No. 4 (1924), p. 184.

Lemon, Alaina. "Roma (Gypsies) in the Soviet Union and the Moscow Theatr 'Roman.' " *Nationalities Papers*. Vol. XIX, No. 3 (Winter 1991), pp. 359–372.

Lengyel, Eva. "The Gypsy Problem Continues to Confront Society." *Radio Free Europe Research*. Hungary No. 6 (22 April 1983), pp. 14–18.

Liebich, André. "Minorities in Eastern Europe: Obstacles to a Reliable Count." *RFE/RL Research Report* (15 May 1992), pp. 32–39.

Lockwood, William G. "East European Gypsies in Western Europe: The Social and Cultural Adaptation of the Xoraxane." *Nomadic Peoples*. No. 21/22 (December 1986), pp. 63–70.

Lynch, David J. "Hidden Children Return to Find Slain Families, Friends." *USA Today*. June 16, 1999, p. 7A.

Macfie, R.A. Scott. "Bulgarian Gypsies." *Journal of the Gypsy Lore Society*. Vol. III, No. 4 (1924), pp. 188–190.

Malnick, Dr. Bertha. "The Moscow Gypsy Theatre, 1957–8." *Journal of the Gypsy Lore Society*. Third Series. Vol. XXXVIII, Nos. 3–4 (July-October 1959), pp. 81–85.

Mann. S.E. "Emília Horváthová's *Cigáni po prichode do Europy* (The Passage of Gypsies throughout Europe)." *Journal of the Gypsy Lore Society*. Third Series. Vol. XLIII, Nos. 1–2 (January-April 1964), pp. 68–71.

Manush, Leksa. "Fol'klor latyshskikh tsygan (osnovnye zhanay i tematika)." *Sovetskaya Etnografiya*. No. 3 (Mai-Iyun' 1981), pp. 113–123.

————. "The Problem of the Folk Music of the Gypsies (Sources of Gypsy Music in Europe)." *Soviet Anthropology and Archeology*. Vol. XXV, No. 3 (Winter 1986–87), pp. 17–34.

Marinov, Vasil. "Nablyudeniya vurkhy bita na tsigani v Bulgariya." *Izvestiya na etnografiskiya institut i muzei*. Kniga V. Sofiya: Isdatelstvo na Bulgarskata akademiya na naukite, 1962, pp. 227–275.

Markos, Edith. "Dim Prospects for Improving the Plight of the Gypsies." *Radio Free Europe Research*. Hungary No. 10 (4 September 1985), pp. 11–15.

————. "The Fast-Growing Gypsy Minority and Its Problems." *Radio Free Europe Research*. Hungary No. 5 (15 June 1987), pp. 13–16.

Markov, Demetrius Dvoichenko. "General Count Pavel D. Kisselev and the Organic Regulation in the Danubian Principalities." *Balkan Studies*. Vol. 31, No. 2 (1990), pp. 283–294.

Marushiakova, Elena. "Ethnic Identity among Gypsy Groups in Bulgaria." *Journal of the Gypsy Lore Society*. Series 5. Vol. 2, No. 2 (August 1992), pp. 95–115.

McCagg, William O. "Gypsy Life in Socialist Hungary and Czechoslovakia." *Nationalities Papers*. Vol. XIX, No. 3 (Winter 1991), pp. 313–336.

McFarlane, Andrew. "Conjectural Ancestry of the Rudari." *Journal of the Gypsy Lore Society*. Third Series. Vol. XXX, Nos. 3–4 (July-October 1951), pp. 153–154.

McQuaid, David. "The Growing Assertiveness of Minorities." *RFE/RL Report on Eastern Europe* (December 13, 1991), pp. 19–23.

"Members of European Parliament Hear Testimonies of Rights Abuse of Roma in Kosova." (2005), pp. 1–2. http://www.errc.org/cikk.php?cikk=2272&archiv=1.

Mihalache, Cristi. "Obstacles to the Participation of Roma in Elections in Romania," *Notebook* (2004), pp. 1–2, http://www.errc.org/cikk.php?cikk=1364&archiv=1.

Milton, Sybil. "The Context of the Holocaust." *German Studies Review*. Vol. XIII, No. 2 (May 1990), pp. 269–283.

"Minorities in Eastern Europe." *East Europe*. Vol. 8, No. 3 (March 1959), pp. 3–14.

"Minorities in Eastern Europe—II." *East Europe*. Vol. 8, No. 4 (April 1959), pp. 3–11.

"Minorities in Eastern Europe: Obstacles to a Reliable Count." *RFE/RL Research Report* (15 May 1992), pp. 32–39.

Mirga, Andrzej. "Addressing the Challenges of Romani Children's Education in Poland—Past and Current Trends and Possible Solutions." pp. 1–7, http://www.per-usa.org/PolandRomaeducation.doc.

Moore, Patrick. "Chronology of Events." *RFE/RL Research Report* (18 December 1992), pp. 32–37.

————. "The Minorities' Plight amid Civil War." *Report on Eastern Europe* (December 13, 1991), pp. 29–32.

"Montenegrin Government Agrees to Pay 985,000 Euros in Compensation to Pogrom Victims (July 4, 2003), 1 page, http://www.errc.org/cikk.php?cikk=330&archiv=1.

"Moscow's Gypsy Theatre." *Journal of the Gypsy Lore Society*. Third Series. Vol. XXVI, Nos. 3–4 (July-October 1947), p. 173.

Mustafic, Refika. "Opre Roma!" pp. 1–2, http://www.errc.org/cikk.php?cikk=1242&archiv=1.

"Nationality Composition of Urban Population by Republics." JPRS-UPA-90–066 (4 December 1990), pp. 12–22.

Naulko, V.I. "The Present Ethnic Composition of the Population of the Ukrainian SSR." *Soviet Sociology*. Vol. III, No. 1 (Summer 1964), pp. 12–23.

Nazarov, Kh.Kh. "Contemporary Ethnic Developments of the Central Asian Gypsies (Liuli)." *Soviet Anthropology and Archeology*. Vol. XXI, No. 3 (Winter 1982–83), pp. 3–28.

Necak, Dusan. "A Chronology of the Decay of Tito's Yugoslavia, 1980–1991." *Nationalities Papers*. Vol. XXI, No. 1 (Spring 1993), pp. 173–181.

Nemcokov, Monica. "Don't Blame Slovakia for Gypsy Problem." *The New York Times*. December 15, 1993, p. A14.

Nevesky, Martina. "The Gypsy Problem." *Radio Free Europe Research* (4 August 1989), pp. 37–43.

"985,000 Euro Compensation for Romani Victims of 1995 Pogrom in Serbia and Montenegro," *Snapshots from around Europe* (2003), 1 page, http://www.errc.org/cikk.php?cikk=1121&archiv=1.

"Non-Exhaustive List of Anti-Romani and Other Harmful Statements by Members of the Parties of the Slovak Governing Coalition." (2006), p. 1, http://www.errc.org.cikk.php?cikk= 2609&archiv=1.

Office of the High Commissioner for Human Rights. "Concluding observations of the Committee fo the Elimination of Racial Discrimination: Hungary. 01/11/2002," pp 1–3. http://www.unhchr.ch/tbs/doc/nsf/(Symbol)/A.57.18,paras.367–390.En?Opendocument.

Oltay, Edith. "Crime Rate Rising Sharply." Report on Eastern Europe (August 30, 1991), pp. 32–35.

———. "Criminal Proceedings against Hungarian Fascist Party." RFE/RL Daily Report (3 February 1994), n.p.

———. "Hungary Passes Law on Minority Rights." RFE/RL Research Report (20 August 1993), pp. 57–61.

———. "Poverty on the Rise." Report on Eastern Europe (January 25, 1991), pp. 13–16.

———. "Prostitution Thriving in Hungary." RFE/RL Research Report (28 May 1993), pp. 40–42.

Open Society Foundation, "Monitoring the National Roma Strategy," http://www.soros.al/ English/news/roma2.htm, pp 1–2.

Orbman, Jan. "Crime Rate among the Young." Radio Free Europe Research (14 August 1987), pp. 17–20.

———. "Minorities Not a Major Issue Yet." Report on Eastern Europe (December 13, 1991), pp. 9–13.

Orsós, Éva. "My Central European family." Meet the ERRC, pp. 1–3, http://www.errc.org/cikk. php?cikk=1010&archiv=1.

Paikert, J.C. "Hungary's National Minority Policies, 1920–1945." The American Slavic and East European Review. Vol. XII, No. 2 (1953), pp. 201–218.

Panaitescu, P.N. "The Gypsies in Wallachia and Moldavia: A Chapter of Economic History." Journal of the Gypsy Lore Society. Third Series. Vol. XX, No. 2 (April 1941), pp. 58–72.

Panayotova, Donka. "Successful Romani School Desegregation; The Vidin Case." Notebook (2003), pp. 1–5, http://www.errc.org/cikk.php?cikk=1630&archiv=1.

Pataki, Judith. "Hungary Copes with Refugee Influx." RFE/RL Research Report (30 April 1993), pp. 35–38.

———. "Increasing Intolerance of Foreigners." RFE/RL Research Report (8 May 1992), pp. 34–38.

Patkanoff, K.P. "Some Words on the Dialects of the Trans-Causcasian Gypsies—Bosa and Karaci." Journal of the Gypsy Lore Society. New Series. Vol. I, No. 3 (January 1908), pp. 229–257.

Pehe, Jiri. "Crime Rises in Czechoslovakia." RFE/RL Research Report (3 April 1992), pp. 55–59.

———. "Law on Romanies Causes Uproar in Czech Republic." RFE/RL Research Report (12 February 1993), pp. 18–22.

———. "Racial Violence Increasing." Report on Eastern Europe (May 18, 1990), pp. 14–18.

Pekelsky, Vladimir. "Die Zigeunerfrage in den ost-und sudosteuropa staaten." Osteuropa, Heft 9 (September 1970), pp. 616–620.

Penc, Stanislav and Jan Urban. "Czech Republic: Extremist Acts Galvanize Roma Population." Transitions. Vol. 5, No. 7 (July 1998), p. 39.

Peri, Tatjana. "Insufficient: Government programmes for Roma in Slovenia," Roma Rights (2001), pp. 1–2.

Perry, Duncan M. "Bulgaria: A New Constitution and Free Elections." RFE/RL Research Report (3 January 1992), pp. 78–83.

"Plan to segregate Roma in Romania," Snapshots from around Europe (2001), 1 page, http://www.errc.org/cikk.php?cikk=655&archiv=1.

———. "Politics in the Republic of Macedonia: Issues and Parties." RFE/RL Research Report (4 June 1993), pp. 31–37.

Petrovic, Alexander. "The Beginning of Menstruation among the Gypsies of Rogatica." Journal of the Gypsy Lore Society. Third Series. Vol. XIV, No. 3 (1935), pp. 156–159.

———. "Contributions to the Study of the Serbian Gypsies: Marriage." Journal of the Gypsy Lore Society. Third Series. Vol. XV, No. 3 (1936), pp. 107–126.

———. "Contributions to the Study of the Serbian Gypsies: Feast Days." Journal of the Gypsy Lore Society. Third Series. Vol. XVI, No. 3 (1937), pp. 111–137.

Petrovic, Ruza. "The National Composition of the Population." Yugoslav Survey. Vol. XXIV, No. 3 (August 1983), pp. 21–34.

'Petrulengro.' "Report on the Gypsy Tribes of North-East Bulgaria." Journal of the Gypsy Lore Society. New Series. Vol. IX, No. 1 (1915–16), pp. 1–54.

———. "Report on the Gypsy Tribes of North-East Bulgaria." Journal of the Gypsy Lore Society. New Series. Vol. IX, No. 2 (1915–16), pp. 65–110.

"Police Abuse of Roma in Písek, Czech Republic." Snapshots from Around Europe (1997). 1 page. http://www.errc.org/cikk.php?cikk=26&archiv=1.

Popov, Vesselin. "The Gypsies and Traditional Bulgarian Culture." *Journal of the Gypsy Lore Society.*
    Series 5. Vol. 3, No. 1 (February 1993), pp. 21–33.
Poulton, Hugh. "The Republic of Macedonia after UN Recognition." *RFE/ RL Research Report*
    (4 June 1993), pp. 22–30.
———. "The Roma in Macedonia: A Balkan Success Story." *RFE/RL Research Report* (7 May 1993),
    pp. 42–45.
"Probleme mit Jugoslawiens Zigeunern." *Osteuropa,* Heft 4 (April 1978), pp. A247-A251.
"Prominent Roma raise voices against hostility against Roma in Hungary." *Budapest Week* (July 27,
    2005). 1 page, http://www.budapestweek.com/newsites/headlines/headlines04.html.
Puxon, Grattan. "Gypsies: Blacks of Eastern Europe." *The Nation.* No. 222 (17 April 1976),
    pp. 460–464.
———. "Roma in Macedonia." *Journal of the Gypsy Lore Society.* Fourth Series. Vol., No. 2 (1958),
    pp. 128–132.
"Racist Hungarian textbook removed from curriculum." *Snapshots from around Europe.* 1 page,
    http://www.errc.org/cikk.php?cikk=1009&archiv=1.
"Racist lessons in Hungary." *Snapshots from around Europe.* 1 page, http://www.errc.org/
    cikk.php?cikk=684&archiv=1.
Radzinsky, Stanislav. "A Stirring Play at the Moscow Gypsy Theatre." *Journal of the Gypsy Lore
    Society.* Third Series. Vol. XXIV, Nos. 3–4 (July-October 1945), pp. 120–121.
Rafati, Shani. "Invisible Roma in Kosovo." Unpublished manuscript (1999), pp. 1–3.
Rakówczi, Basil Ivan. "An Artist's Visit to the Gypsies of Southern France and to the U.S.S.R." *Journal
    of the Gypsy Lore Society.* Third Series. Vol. XL, Nos. 3–4 (July-October 1961), pp. 116–127.
Ramet, Pedro. "Kosovo and the Limits of Yugoslav Socialist Patriotism." *Canadian Review of Studies
    in Nationalism.* Vol. XVI, Nos. 1–2 (1989), pp. 227–250.
Ranking, Devey Fearon de l'Hoste. "The Gypsies of Central Russia: Introduction." *Journal of the
    Gypsy Lore Society.* New Series. Vol. IV, No. 3 (January 1911), pp. 195–217.
———. "The Gypsies of Central Russia: The Gypsies of Kisilefka." *Journal of the Gypsy Lore
    Society.* New Series. Vol. IV, No. 4 (April 1911), pp. 245–258.
———. "The Gypsies of Central Russia: Manners and Customs." *Journal of the Gypsy Lore Society.*
    New Series. Vol. VI, No. 2 (1912–13), pp. 90–110.
"Red Roses on the Snow." *Sputnik.* No. 10 (October 1981), pp. 58–65.
Réger, Zita. "Bilingual Gypsy Children in Hungary: Explorations in 'Natural' Second-Language
    Acquisitions at an Early Age." *International Journal of the Sociology of Language,* No. 19
    (1979), pp. 59–82.
Reisch, Alfred A. "First Law on Minorities Drafted." *Report on Eastern Europe* (December 13, 1991),
    pp. 14–18.
"Reports on public attitudes about Roma in Hungary." *Snapshots from around Europe,* 1 page,
    http://www.errc.org/cikk/php?cikk=1803&archiv=1.
"Response of the Czech Government Commissioner for Human rights to ERRC Action on Coercive
    Sterilisations of Romani Women in the Czech Republic." *Advocacy* (2004), pp. 1–3,
    http://www.errc.org/cikk.php?cikk=2072&archivp>=1.
RFE/RL Newsline. Vol. 3, No. 178, Part II. September 13, 1999.
Ribansky, Laszlo. "Nationalities in Hungary: Few in Number but Pampered." *Radio Free Europe
    Research.* RAD Background Report No. 259 (28 October 1980), pp. 2–4.
Rohde, David. "Kosovar Attack on Gypsies Reveals Desire for Revenge." *The New York Times.* June
    7, 1999, p. A12.
"Roma Forcibly Evicted by Romanian Officials," *Snapshots from around Europe* (2003), 1 page,
    http://www.errc.org/cikk.php?cikk=1315&archiv=1.
Rom News Network. "The Association of Czechoslovak Roma in Canada (1998)," 1 page, http://
    www.romnews.com/community/modules.php?op=modload&name=Sections&file=in.
"Roma Expelled from Romanian Capital," *Snapshots from around Europe* (2002), 1 page,
    http://www.errc.org/cikk.php?cikk=931&archiv=1.
"Roma Houses Destroyed in Romanian Town of Seica Mare," *News Roundup: Snapshots from around
    the World* (2006), 1 page, http:www//errc.org/cikk.php?cikk=2493&archiv=1.
"Roma in Slovenia Threatened with Segregation at School." *Snapshots from around Europe* (2005), 1
    page, http://www.errc.org/cikk.php?cikk=2342&archiv=1.
"Romani Families Remain in Toxic Camps in Kosovo." *Snapshots from around Europe* (2005), 1 page,
    http://www.erroc.org/cikk.php?cikk=2330&archiv=1.
"Romani Pupils Face Verbal and Physical Assault at School in Serbia and Montenegro," *Snapshots
    from around Europe* (2003), pp. 1–2, http://www.errc.org/cikk.php?cikk=1122&archiv=1.

"Romanian Mayor Announces Intention to Evict Romani Families," *Snapshots from around Europe* (2004), 1 page, http://www.errc.org/cikk.php?cikk=2103&archiv=1.

Romanov, Manush. "Chants rom de Bulgarie." *Études Tsiganes*. No. 1 (1991), pp. 32–38.

Roma Women's Initiatives. "Roma Women Conference in Kiev, Ukraine," June 19, 2003, 1 page, http://www.romawomensinitiatives.org/resources1.asp?ID=49&kategorija=4&podkategor

Rromani Baxt. "The Situation of the Rroma in Cossivia." August 1998, pp. 1–4.

Rózsa, László. "Gypsies and Public Opinion." *The New Hungarian Quarterly*. Vol. XX, No. 73 (Spring 1979), pp. 126–130.

Russell, Alex. "Classiciation and Number of Wallachian Gypsies in 1837." *Journal of the Gypsy Lore Society*. New Series. Vol. VI, No. 2 (1912–13), p. 150.

Russinov, Rumyan. "The Bulgarian Framework Programme for Equal Integration of Roma: participation in the policy-making process." European Roma Rights Centre, 2006, http://www.errc.org/cikk.php?cikk=1729&archiv=1, pp. 1–7.

Russinov, Rumyan. "Romani Politics as a Profession," *Meet the ERRC* (2003), pp. 1–2. http:www.errc.org/cikk.php?cikk=1992&archiv=1.

Sanneus, Erasmus. "Serbian Gypsy Bear-Leaders about 1851." *Journal of the Gypsy Lore Society*. Third Series. Vol. XIV, No. 3 (1935), pp. 203–205.

Sazhin, Valentin. "Attitudes towards Gypsies in Ukraine (1989)," translated by Tanya E. Mairs. *Nationalities Papers*. Vol. XIX, No. 3 (Winter 1991), pp. 337–357.

Schechtman, Joseph B. "The Gypsy Problem." *Midstream*. Vol. XII, No. 9 (November 1966), pp. 52–60.

———. "The Transnistria Reservation." *YIVO Annual of Jewish Social Science*. Vol. VIII (1953), pp. 178–196.

Scheitanow, N. "A Contribution to the Dialect of the Sofia Gypsies." *Journal of the Gypsy Lore Society*. Third Series. Vol. XIII, No. 3 (1934), pp. 159–172.

"Schwierigkeiten mit den Zigeunern in der Tscheshoslowakei." *Osteuropa*. Vol. 11, No. 6 (June 1971), pp. A122-A126.

Seton, Marie. "The Evolution of the Gypsy Theatre in the U.S.S.R." *Journal of the Gypsy Lore Society*. Third Series. Vol. XIV, No. 2 (1935), pp. 64–72.

Shafir, Michael. "The Greater Romania Party." *Report on Eastern Europe* (November 15, 1991), pp. 25–30.

———. "Growing Political Extremism in Romania." *RFE/RL Research Report* (2 April 1993), pp. 18–25.

———. "Preliminary Results of the 1992 Romanian Census." *RFE/RL Research Report* (24 July 1992), pp. 62–68.

———. "Promises and Reality." *Report on Eastern Europe* (January 14, 1991), pp. 32–37.

———. "Romanian Reaction to Zhirinovsky." *RFE/RL Daily Report*. No. 1 (30 December 1993), n.p.

———. "Schopflinian Reality and Romanian Realism." *Report on Eastern Europe* (February 15, 1991), pp. 32–40.

Shafir, Michael and Dan Ionescu. "The Minorities in 1991: Mutual Distrust, Social Problems, and Disillusion." *Report on Eastern Europe* (December 13, 1991), pp. 24–28.

Sheehy, Ann. "Language Affiliation Data from the Census of 1979." *The All-Union Census of 1979 in the USSR*. Munich: Radio Liberty Research Bulletin, 1980, pp. 1–14.

Siklós, László. "The Gypsies." *The New Hungarian Quarterly*. Vol. XI, No. 40 (1970), pp. 150–162.

Soulis, George C. "The Gypsies in the Byzantine Empire and the Balkans in the Late Middle Ages." *Dumbarton Oaks Papers*. Vol. 15 (1961), pp. 143–165.

———. "A Note on the Taxation of the Balkan Gypsies in the Seventeenth Century." *Journal of the Gypsy Lore Society*. Third Series. Vol XXXVIII, Nos. 1–2 (January-April 1959), pp. 154–156.

Silverman, Carol. "Bulgarian Gypsies: Adaptation in a Socialist Context." *Nomadic Peoples*. Nos. 21–22 (December 1986), pp. 51–62.

———. "Tsiganes musique et politiques en Bulgare." *Études Tsiganes*. No. 4 (1988), pp. 14–20.

Sobotka, Eva. "Hungary: Council of Europe Delegation alarmed by treatment of Roma in Hungary," *Central European Review*. Vol. 3, No. 4 (29 January 2001), pp. 1–4, http://www.ce-review.org/01/4/romanews4.html.

Spolu International Foundation. "Albania," pp. 1–2. http://www.spolu.nl/m5a_albania.html.

Srb, Vladimir. "Cikani v Ceskoslovensku." *Demografie*. Vol. 11, No. 3 (1969), pp. 193–195.

———. "Demograficky profil ceskoslovenskych Romu." *Cesky Lid*. Vol. 72 (1985), pp. 139–148.

———. "K integraci cikánskeho obyvatelstva v CSSR." *Demografié*. Vol. XXI, No. 4 (1979), pp. 321–324.

Srb, Vladimir and J. Job. "Nekteré demografické, ekonomické a kulturné charakteristiky romského obyvatelstva v CSSR 1970." *Demografié*. Vol. XVI, No. 2 (1974), pp. 172–183.

"Stop Persecution of Gypsies." *Women and Revolution*. No. 38 (Winter 1990–91), pp. 1–7.

Tanaka, Jennifer. "Parallel worlds: Romani and non-Romani schools in Bulgaria." *Notebook* (2003), p. 1, http://www.errc.org/cikk.php?cikk=1045&archiv=1.

Tassay, Martine. "La poésie des Roms de Macedoine." *Études Tsiganes*. No. 4 (1991), pp. 20–29.

Teague, Elizabeth. "Zhirinovsky's Regional Policy." *RFE/RL Daily Report*. No. 7 (21 December 1993), n.p.

Thesleff, Arthur. "Report on the Gypsy Problem." *Journal of the Gypsy Lore Society*. New Series. Vol. V, No. 3 (1911–12), pp. 218–269.

Thompson, T.W. "Gypsies in the Mezöség of Transylvania." *Journal of the Gypsy Lore Society*. New Series. Vol. VIII, No. 3 (1914–1915), pp. 194–195.

———. "Gypsy Prisoners at Szamos Ujvár, Transylvania." *Journal of the Gypsy Lore Society*. New Series. Vol. VIII, No. 3 (1914–1915), pp. 195–196.

Thurow, Roger. "Another Country." *The Wall Street Journal* (August 24, 1999), p. A1.

Tomka, Miklos. "Die Zigeuner in der Ungarischen Gesellschaft." *East European Quarterly*. Vol. IV, No. 1 (March 1970), pp. 2–24.

Troxel, Luan. "Bulgaria's Gypsies: Numerically Strong, Politically Weak." *RFE/RL Research Report* (6 March 1992), pp. 58–61.

Uhlik, Rade. "Gypsy Folk-Tales." *Journal of the Gypsy Lore Society*. Third Series. Vol. XXXVII, Nos. 1–2 (January-April 1958), pp. 4–12.

Ulc, Otto. "Communist National Minority Policy: The Case of the Gypsies in Czechoslovakia." *Soviet Studies*. Vol. XX, No. 4 (April 1969), pp. 421–443.

———. "Gypsies in Czechoslovakia: A Case of Unfinished Integration." *Eastern European Politics and Societies*. Vol. 2, No. 2 (Spring 1988), pp. 306–332.

———. "Integration of the Gypsies in Czechoslovakia." *Ethnic Groups*. Vol. 9, No. 2 (1991), pp. 107–117.

"UN Torture Committee Again Rules Against Police Abuse of Roma in Serbia and Montenegro." (December 12, 2005), pp. 1–2, http://www.errc.org/cikk.php?cikk=2578&archiv=1.

United Nations Committee against Torture. "Yugoslasvia Villated Treaty in 1995 Danilovgrad (Montenegro)," pp. 1–14, http://groups.yahoo.com/group/balkanhr/message/4952.

"UN Committee against Torture Urges the Czech Republic to Investigate Alleged Coercive Sterilisation of Romani Women." *Advocacy* (2004), pp. 1–2, http://www.errc.org/cikk.php?cikk=1988&archiv=1.

UNHCR. "Background Paper on Refugees and Asylum Seekers from Kosovo." February 1996, pp. 1–4.

UNICEF. "Bosnia and Herzegovina," http://www.unicef.org/infobycountry/bosniaherzegovina_statistics.html, pp. 1–5,

"UN Torture Committee Instructs Government to Investigate Police Abuse of Roma." *Snapshots from around Europe* (2005), 1 page, http://www.errc.org/cikk.php?cikk=2578&archiv=1.

Vajda, Gábor. "Gypsies Face a Crisis of Confidence." *Budapest Week*. Vol. III, No. 27 (September 9–15, 1993), p. 5.

Vekerdi, József. "Earliest Arrival Evidence on Gypsies in Hungary." *Journal of the Gypsy Lore Society*. Fourth Series. Vol. I, No. 2 (1976), pp. 170–172.

Vukanovic, Tihomir P. "Gypsy Bear-Leaders in the Balkan Peninsular." *Journal of the Gypsy Lore Society*. Third Series. Vol. XXXVIII, Nos. 3–4 (July-October 1959), pp. 106–127.

———. "The Gypsy Population in Yugoslavia." *Journal of the Gypsy Lore Society*. Third Series. Vol. XLII, Nos. 1–2 (January-April 1963), pp. 10–27.

———. "Musical Culture among the Gypsies of Yugoslavia." *Journal of the Gypsy Lore Society*. Third Series. Vol. LXI, Nos. 1–2 (January-April 1962), pp. 41–61.

———. "Part Taken by Gypsies in the Peasant Rebellion in Srem (Syrium) in 1807." *Journal of the Gypsy Lore Society*. Third Series. Vol. XLVIII, Nos. 1–2 (January- April 1969), pp. 77–79.

———. "The Position of Women among Gypsies in the Kosovo-Metohija Region." *Journal of the Gypsy Lore Society*. Third Series. Vol. XL, Nos. 3–4 (July-October 1961), pp. 81–100.

Ward, Olivia. "Poisoned Children." *Toronto Star*, November 13, 2005, p. A12.

Weiner, Leo. "Ismailites." *Journal of the Gypsy Lore Society*. New Series. Vol. IV, No. 2 (October 1910), pp. 83–100.

Whitehorn, Alan J. "Yugoslav Constitutional Developments: An Expression of Growing Nationality Rights and Powers (1945–1972)." *East European Quarterly*. Vol. IX, No. 3 (Fall 1975), pp. 345–368.

Wilska-Duszynska, Barbara. "Poles and Strangers: Student Attitudes towards National Minorities." Translated by PNB. *Nowa Europa*. No. 106 (2 July 1992), pp. 8–12.

Winstedt, E.O. "Gypsy Civilization." *Journal of the Gypsy Lore Society*. New Series. Vol. II, No. 1 (July 1908), pp. 91–93.

Winstedt, E.O. "A Gypsy Traitor." *Journal of the Gypsy Lore Society*. Third Series. Vol. XXII, Nos. 1–2 (January-April 1943), p. 63.
————. "Rudari in Germany." *Journal of the Gypsy Lore Society*. Third Series. Vol. XXXIV, Nos. 1–2 (January-April 1955), pp. 76–78.
"Winter without Heating or Hot Water for Roma in Luna IX." *Snapshots from around Europe* (2006), 1 page, http://www.errc.org/cikk.php?cikk=2580&archiv=1.
Yates, Dora. "*Muslastest*." *Journal of the Gypsy Lore Society*. Third Series. Vol. XXXVIII, Nos. 3–4 (July-October 1959), pp. 150–151.
"Zigeuner zwischen Albanern und Serbien." *Osteuropa*. Heft 6 (June 1972), pp. A197-A198.
"Zur Lage der Zigeuner in Kroatien und Slowenien." *Osteuropa*. Heft 7 (July 1983), pp. A375-A378.

BOOKS

Abdikeeva, Alphia. *Roma Poverty and the Roma National Strategies: The Cases of Albania, Greece and Serbia* (London: Minority Rights Group International, 2005).
Acković, Dragoljub. *Roma in Serbia: Introducing Romany Language and Culture into Primary Schools*. London: Minority Rights Group, n.d.
Agarwal, N.N. *Soviet Nationality*. Agra: Sri Ram Mehra & Co., 1969.
A Magyarországban Czigáyösszeirás Eredményei: 1893 januar 31-én végrehajtott. Budapest: Az Athenaeum R. Tásulat Könyvnyomdáa, 1893.
Anderson, M.S. *Peter the Great*. London: Thames and Hudson Ltd., 1978.
Andreeva, L.V., et al. *Malyi atlas SSSR*. Moskva: Glavnoe Upravlenie Geodezii i Kartografii pri Sovete Ministrov SSSR, 1978.
Arad, Yitzhak, Shmuel Krakowski, and Shmuel Spector, eds. *The Einsatzgruppen Reports*. New York: Holocaust Library and Yad Vashem, 1989.
Ascher, Abraham, Tibor Halasi-Kun, and Béla K. Király, eds., *The Mutual Effects of the Islamic and Judeo-Christian Worlds: The East European Pattern*. Brooklyn: Brooklyn College Press, 1979.
Balás, György and Károly Szeléyni. *The Magyars: The Birth of a European Nation*. Budapest: Corvina, 1989.
Balsham, A.L. *The Wonder that Was India*. New York: Grove Press, Inc., 1959.
Banac, Ivo., ed. *East Europe in Revolution*. Ithaca: Cornell University Press, 1992.
————. *The National Question in Yugoslavia: Origins, History, Politics*. Ithaca: Cornell University Press, 1988.
Barannikov, A.P. *The Ukrainian and South Russian Gypsy Dialects*. Leningrad: Academy of Sciences of the USSR, 1934.
Baron, Salo W. *The Russian Jew under Tsars and Soviets*. New York: Schocken Books, 1987.
Bartók, Bela. *The Hungarian Folk Song*. Edited by Benjamin Suchoff, translated by M.D. Calvocoressi. Albany: State University of New York Press, 1981.
Bennigsen, Alexandre and Enders Wimbush. *Muslims of the Soviet Empire: A Guide*. Bloomington: Indiana University Press, 1986.
Bercovici, Konrad. *Gypsies: Their Life, Lore, and Legends*. New York: Greenwich House, 1983.
Berenbaum, Michael. *A Mosaic of Victims: Non-Jews Persecuted and Murdered by the Nazis*. New York: New York University Press, 1990.
Bierman, John. *Righteous Gentile*. New York: Bantam Books, 1983.
Biro, Maria A. and Petra Kovacs, editors. *Diversity in Action: Local Public Management of Multi-Ethnic Communities in Central and Eastern Europe*. Budapest: Central European Press, 2001.
Braham, Randolph L. *A Magyar Holocaust*. 2 Vols. Budapest: Gondolat, 1988.
————. *The Politics of Genocide: The Holocaust in Hungary*. 2 Vols. New York: Columbia University Press, 1981.
Brown, J.F. *Bulgaria under Communist Rule*. New York: Praeger Publishers, 1970.
————. *Surge to Freedom*. Durham: Duke University Press, 1991.
Browning, Christopher R. *Fateful Months: Essays on the Emergence of the Final Solution*. Revised Edition. New York: Holmes & Meier, 1991.
————. *Ordinary Men: Reserve Police Battalion 101 and the Final Solution*. New York: Harper Collins Publishers, Inc., 1992.
Brunner, Georg and Allan Kagedan. *Die Minderheiten in der Sowjetunion und das Volkerrecht*. Markus Verlag Köln, 1988.

BIBLIOGRAPHY

375

Brunner, Georg and Boris Meissner. *Nationalitäten Probleme in der Sowjetunion und Osteuropa.* Markus Verlag Köln, 1982.

Budurowycz, Bohdan B. *Polish-Soviet Relations, 1932–1939.* New York: Columbia University Press, 1963.

Bugajski, Janusz. *Ethnic Politics in Eastern Europe: A Guide to Nationality Policies, Organizations, and Parties.* Armonk, NY: M. E. Sharpe, 1995.

Bulgarian Helsinki Committee. *Annual Report of the Bulgarian Helsinki Committee.* Sofia: Bulgarian Helsinki Committee, 2005.

Burleigh, Michael and Wolfgang Wippermann. *The Racial State: Germany, 1933–1945.* Cambridge: Cambridge University Press, 1991.

Byrnes, Robert F. *Pobedonostsev: His Life and Thought.* Bloomington: Indiana University Press, 1968.

Calic, Edourd. *Reinhard Heydrich.* New York: Military Heritage Press, 1985.

Carr, E.H. *Doestoevsky, 1821–1881.* London: George Allen & Unwin Ltd., 1962.

Case of Nachova and Others v. Bulgaria, Applications nos. 43577/98 and 43579/98. Judgement. Strasbourg, 6 July 2005.

Center for Documentation and Information on Minorities in Europe. *Minorities in Southeast Europe.* Budapest: Center for Documentation and Information on Minorities in Europe—Southeast Europe, 2000.

Central Intelligence Agency, *The World Factbook (2006),* https://www.cia.gov/cia/publications/factbook/geos/al.html.

Centre for Anti-War Action. *The Roma in Serbia.* Translated by Srdan Vujica, Ljiljana Bajić, and Pavle Perenčević. Belgrade: Institute for Criminological and Sociological Research, 1998.

Chary, Frederick B. *The Bulgarian Jews and the Final Solution, 1940–1944.* Pittsburgh: University of Pittsburgh Press, 1972.

Cherenkov, L.N., ed. *Tsygansko-russkii i Tsyganskii slovar': Kelderarskii dialekt.* Moskva: "Russkii Yazyk," 1990.

Cienciala, Anna M. *Poland and the Western Powers, 1938–1939.* London: Routledge & Kegan Paul, 1968.

Clébert, Jean-Paul. *The Gypsies.* Translated by Charles Duff. New York: E.P. Dutton, 1963.

Clissold, Stephen, ed. *A Short History of Yugoslavia: From Early Times to 1966.* Cambridge: Cambridge University Press, 1968.

Clogg, Richard, ed. *Balkan Society in the Age of Greek Independence.* Totowa: Barnes & Noble Books, 1981.

Coles, Paul. *The Ottoman Impact on Europe.* London: Harcourt, Brace & World, Inc., 1968.

Commission on Security and Cooperation in Europe, *The Romani Minority in Russia* Washington, D.C.: Commission on Security and Cooperation in Europe, 2006.

Committee of Ministers, Council of Europe, *Fact-finding Mission to Bosnia and Herzegovina on the Situation of the Roma/Gypsies (16–21 May 1996).* http:www.coe.int/T/DG3/RomaTravellers/documentation/fieldvisits/missionbih_en.asp.

Comrie, Bernard. *The Languages of the Soviet Union.* Cambridge: Cambridge University Press, 1981.

Conquest, Robert, ed. *The Last Empire: Nationality and the Soviet Future.* Stanford: Hoover Institution Press, 1986.

Cook, Chris and John Stevenson. The Longman Handbook of Modern European History, 1763–1985. London: Longman, 1987.

Cooper, Rabbi Abraham, Adaire Klein, and Avra Shapiro. *Babi Yar, 1941–1991.* Los Angeles: Simon Wiesenthal Center, 1991.

Cooper, Matthew. *The Nazi War against Soviet Partisans, 1941–1944.* New York: Stein and Day, 1979.

Council of Europe. *Comments on the Follow-up Report on Slovenia (2003–2005) by the Council of Europe Commissioner for Human Rights.* Brussels: Council of Europe, 2006.

———. *Second Report on Slovenia.* Brussels: Council of Europe, 2003.

———. *Third Report on Bulgaria.* Brussels: Council of Europe, 2003.

———. *Third Report on Poland.* Brussels: Council of Europe, 2005.

———. *Third Report on Romania.* Brussels: Council of Europe, 2006.

Crampton, R.J. *Short History of Modern Bulgaria.* Cambridge: Cambridge University Press, 1989.

Crowe, David M. *The Baltic States and the Great Powers: Foreign Relations, 1938–1940.* Boulder: Westview Press, 1993.

———. *World War I and Europe in Crisis: 1914–1935.* Piscataway: Research and Education Association, 1990.

Crowe, David M. and John Kolsti, eds. *The Gypsies of Eastern Europe.* Armonk: M.E. Sharpe, Inc., 1991.
Curtiss, John Shelton. *Russia's Crimean War.* Durham: Duke University Press, 1979.
Davies, Norman. *God's Playground: A History of Poland.* 2 Volumes. New York: Columbia University Press, 1982.
Dellin, L.A.D., ed. *Bulgaria.* New York: Frederick A. Praeger, 1957.
Demeter, R.S. and P.S. Demeter. *Obraztsy Fol'klora Tsygan-Kelderarei.* Moskva: Glavnaya Redaktsiya Vostochnoi Literatury, 1981.
Denitch, Bogdan Denis. *The Legitimation of a Revolution: The Yugoslav Case.* New Haven: Yale University Press, 1976.
Desheriev, Yu. D. and I.F. Protchenko. *Razvitie yazykov narodov SSSR v sovetskuyu epokhy.* Moskva: Izdatel'stvo "Prosvetsenie," 1968.
Diller, Daniel C., ed. *The Soviet Union.* Third Edition. Washington, D.C.: Congressional Quarterly, 1990.
Dima, Nicholas. *Bessarabia and Bukovina: The Soviet-Romanian Territorial Dispute.* Boulder/New York: East European Monographs and Columbia University Press, 1982.
Dobroszycki, Lucjan and Jeffrey S. Gurock, eds. *The Holocaust in the Soviet Union.* Armonk: M.E. Sharpe, 1993.
Durant, Will. *The Renaissance: A History of Civilization in Italy from 1304–1576 A.D.* New York: Simon and Schuster, 1953.
Durham, Edith. *High Albania.* Boston: Beacon Press, 1987.
Dzharyglasinova, R. Sh. and L.S. Tolstova, eds. *Etnicheskie protsessy i natsional'nykh grupp srednei Azii i Kazakhstana.* Moskva: Izdatel'stvo "Nauka," 1980.
Encyclopedia Slovensku. Bratislava: Veda, 1977–82.
Enciklopedija Jugoslavije. Zagreb: Izdanje i naklada leksikografskog zavoda FNJR, 1956.
Ervin, Tamás and Révész Tamás. *Búcsú a cigányteleptöl.* Budapest: Kossuth Könyvkiadó, 1977.
Eterovich, Francis H. and Christopher Spalatin, eds. *Croatia: Land, People, Culture.* 2 Volumes. Toronto: University of Toronto Press, 1970.
European Commission against Racism and Intolerance. *Third Report on the Czech Republic.* Brussels: Council of Europe, 2004.
———. *Third Report on the Russian Federation.* Brussels: Council of Europe, 2006.
———. *Third Report on Slovakia.* Brussels: Council of Europe, 2004.
European Monitoring Centre on Racism and Xenophobia. *Breaking the Barriers—Romani Women and Access to Public Health Care.* Luxembourg: Office for Official Publications of the European Communities, 2003.
European Roma Rights Center. *The Limits of Solidarity: Roma in Poland after 1989.* Budapest: European Roma Rights Center, 2002.
———. *The Misery of Law: The Rights of Roma in the Transcarpathian Region of Ukraine.* Budapest: European Roma Rights Center, 1997.
European Roma Rights Center. *A Special Remedy: Roma and Schools for the Mentally Handicapped in the Czech Republic.* Budapest: European Roma Rights Center, 1999.
———. *The Non-Constituents: Rights Deprivation of Roma in Post-Genocide Bosnia and Herzegovina.* Budapest: European Roma Rights Center, 2004.
———. *Profession: Prisoner (Roma Detention in Bulgaria).* Budapest: European Roma Rights Center, 1997.
———. *Shadow Report of the European Roma Rights Center on the Republic of Croatia's Combined Second and Third Periodic Reports to the Committee on Elimination of Discrimination against Women.* Budapest: European Roma Rights Center, 2005.
———. *Time of the Skinheads: Denial and Exclusion of Roma in Slovakia.* Budapest: European Roma Rights Center, 1997.
———. *Violations of Roma Rights in the Russian Federation.* Budapest: European Roma Rights Center, 2004.
———. *Written Comments of the European Roma Rights Centre Concerning Ukraine for Consideration by the Untied Nations Committee on the Elimination of Racial Discrimination.* Budapest: European Roma Rights Center, 2006.
European Roma Rights Center Shadow Report to the United Nations Committee on the Rights of the Child. Budapest: European Roma Rights Centre, 2005.
European Roma Rights Centre. *In Search of Happy Gypsies: Persecution of Pariah Minorities in Russia.* Budapest: European Roma Rights Centre, 2005.

―――. League of Human Rights, and Gender Studies. *Shadow Report to the Committee on the Elimination of All Forms of Discrimination against Women for the Czech Republic*. Prague and Budapest: European Roma rights Centre, League of Human Rights, and Gender Studies, 2006.

European Roma Rights Centre and National Roma Centrum. *Written Comments of the European Roma Rights Centre and the National Roma Centrum Concerning the Former Yugoslav Republic of Macedonia*. Budapest: European Roma Rights Centre, 2006.

Feffer, John. *Shock Waves: Eastern Europe after the Revolutions*. Boston: South End Press, 1992.

Ficowski, Jerzy. *Cyganie na Polskich Drogach*. Kraków: Wydownictwo Literackie, 1985.

―――. *The Gypsies of Poland: History and Customs*, Translated by Eileen Healey. Warsaw: Interpress, 1991.

Fox, Jonathan. "Roma (Gypsies) Macedonia." Unpublished manuscript (December 12, 1995), pp. 1–2.

Framework Program for Equal Integration of Roma in Bulgarian Society. http://www.ncedi. government.bg/en/RPRIRBGO-Englsih.htm, pp. 1–2.

Fraser, Angus. *The Gypsies*. Oxford: Blackwell Publishers, 1992.

Freedom House and The American Jewish Committee. *Democracy. Economic Reform and Western Assistance in Czechoslovakia, Hungary and Poland: A Comparative Public Opinion Survey*. New York: Freedom House and The American Jewish Committee, 1991.

Friedrich, Paul and Norma Diamond, eds. *Encyclopedia of World Cultures*, Vol. IV: *Russia and Eurasia/China*. Boston: G.K. Hall & Co., 1994.

Garashanin, Milutin, ed. *Zbornik filozofskog fakulteta*. Kniga XIII-1. Belgrade: Nau no Delo, 1976.

Genov, G.P. *Bulgaria and the Treaty of Neuilly*. Sofia: Hrist G. Danov & Co., 1935.

German, A.V. *Bibliografiya o tsyganakh*. Moskva: Tsentrizday, 1930.

Gieysztor, Alexander, Stefan Kieniewicz, Emanuel Rostworowski, Janusz Tazbir, and Henryk Wereszycki. *History of Poland*. 2nd Edition. Warszawa: PWN—Polish Scientific Publishers, 1979.

Gjorgjevic, Tihomir. *Nas narodni Zhivot*. 3 Vols. Belgrade: Prosveta, 1984.

Glenny, Misha. *The Fall of Yugoslavia: The Third Balkan War*. London: Penguin Books, Ltd., 1992.

Goskomstat SSSR. *Natsional'nyi sostav naseleniya SSSR po dannym vsesoyuznoi naseleniya 1989 g.* Moskva: "Finansy i Statistika," 1991.

Graham, Malbone W., Jr. *New Governments of Central Europe*. New York: Henry Holt and Company, 1926.

Great Soviet Encyclopedia. New York: Macmillan, 1973.

Gronemeyer, Reimer. *Zigeuner in Osteuropa: Eine Bibliographie zu den Ländern Polen, Tschechoslowakei und Ungarn (Mit einen Anhang über ältere Sowjetische Literatur)*. München: K.G. Saur, 1983.

Gronemeyer, Reimer and Georgia A. Rakelmann, *Die Zigeuner: Reisende in Europa: Roma, Sinti, Manouches, Gitanos, Gypsies, Kalderash, Vlach und andere*. Köln: Dumont Buchverlag, 1988.

Gropper, Rena C. *Gypsies in the City: Cultural Patterns and Survival*. Princeton: The Darwin Press, 1975.

Grothusen, Klaus-Detlev. *Jugoslawien*. Vandenhoeck & Ruprecht in Göttingen, 1954.

―――, ed. *Südosteuropa-Handbuch: Bulgarien*. Band VI. Vandenhoeck & Ruprecht in Göttingen, 1990.

Groueff, Stephane. *Crown of Thorns: The Reign of King Boris III of Bulgaria, 1918–1943*. Lanham: Madison Books, 1987.

Grosula, Ya.S. *Istoriya Moldavskoi SSR*. Kishinev: "Shtiintsa," 1982.

Grousset, Rene. *The Empire of the Steppes*. Translated by Naomi Walford. New Brunswick: Rutgers University Press, 1970.

Grumet, Joanne. ed. *Papers from the Fourth and Fifth Annual Meetings, Gypsy Lore Society, North American Chapter*. New York: Gypsy Lore Society, North American Chapter, 1985.

Gutman, Israel, ed. *Encyclopedia of the Holocaust*. 4 Volumes. New York: Macmillan Publishing Company, 1990.

Gutsche, George J., ed. *The Modern Encyclopedia of Russian and Soviet Literature*. Gulf Breeze, Fl: Academic International Press, 1989-present.

Haarmann, Harald. *Spracherhaltung und Sprachwechsel als Probleme der interlingualen Soziolinguistik: Studien zur Gruppenmehrsprachigkeit der Zigeuner in der Sowjetunion*. Hamburg: Helmut Buske Verlag, 1979.

Hammel, E.A., Robert S. Erich, Ramila Fabrijanic-Filipovic, Joel M. Halperin, and Albert B. Lord, eds. *Among the People: Native Yugoslav Ethnography (Selected Writing of Milenko S. Filipovic)*. Ann Arbor: Michigan Slavic Publications, 1982.

Hancock, Ian. *The Pariah Syndrome*. Ann Arbor: Karoma Publishers, Inc., 1987.

Helsinki Watch. *Destroying Ethnic Identity: The Gypsies of Bulgaria*. New York: Human Rights Watch, 1991.
———. *War Crimes in Bosnia-Hercegovina*. New York: Human Rights Watch, 1992.
Hilberg, Raul. *The Destruction of the European Jews*. 3 Volumes. New York: Holmes & Meier, 1985.
Hindley, Geoffrey, ed. *The Larousse Encyclopedia of Music*. New York: Crescent Books, 1986.
Hindus, Maurice. *Red Bread: Collectivization in a Russian Village*. Bloomington: Indiana University Press, 1988.
Hockenos, Paul. *Free to Hate: The Rise of the Right in Post-Communist Eastern Europe*. New York: Routledge, 1993.
Hoensch, Jörg K. *A History of Modern Hungary, 1867–1986*. Translated by Kim Traynor. London: Longman Group UK Limited, 1988.
Hondius, Frits W. *Yugoslav Community of Nations*. The Hague: Mouton, 1968.
Horak, Stephen M., ed. *Eastern European National Minorities, 1919–1980: A Handbook*. Littleton: Libraries Unlimited, Inc.,1985.
Horváthová, Emília. *Cigáni na Slovensku*. Bratislava: Vytadel'stvo Slovenskej Akademie Vied, 1964.
Höss, Rudolf. *Death Dealer: The Memoirs of the SS Kommandant at Auschwitz*. Edited by Steven Paskuly, translated by Andrew Pollinger. Buffalo: Prometheus Books, 1992.
Howell, Edgar M. *The Soviet Partisan Movement, 1941–1944*. Washington, D.C.: Department of the Army, 1956.
Human Rights Watch. *Children of Bulgaria: Police Violence and Arbitrary Confinement*. New York: Human Rights Watch, 1996.
———. *Failure to Protect: Anti-Minority Violence in Kosovo*. New York: Human Rights Watch, 2004.
———. *Hopes Betrayed: Trafficking of Women and Girls into Post-Conflict Bosnia and Herzegovina for Forced Prostitution* (New York: Human Rights Watch, 2002).
———. *World Report: Bulgaria*. New York: Human Rights Watch, 1999.
Hundley, Geoffrey, ed. *The Larousse Encyclopedia of Music*. New York: Crescent Books, 1971.
Indjic, Tirvo. *Affirmative Action: The Yugoslav Case*. New York: The Rockefeller Foundation, 1984.
Insttitucionet e Përkohshme Vetëqeverisëse. *Kosovo and Its Population: A Brief Description*. Prishtina: Ministry of Public Services, 2003.
International Federation for Human Rights, *The Roma of Russia: The Subject of Multiple Forms of Discrimination*. Paris: International Federation for Human Rights, 2004.
Isaev, M.I. *Sto tridtsat' ravnopravnykh*. Moscow: Izdatel'stvo "Nauka," 1970.
Isupov, Arkadii A. *Natsional'nyi sostav naseleniya SSSR (po itogam perepisi 1959 g.)*. Moskva: Izdatel'stvo "Statistika," 1961.
Janos, Andrew C. *The Politics of Backwardness in Hungary, 1825–1945*. Princeton: Princeton University Press, 1982.
Jelavich, Barbara. *The Habsburg Empire in European Affairs, 1814–1918*. Chicago: Rand McNally & Company, 1969.
———. *History of the Balkans*. Vol. I: *Eighteenth and Nineteen Centuries*. Cambridge: Cambridge University Press, 1989.
———. *History of the Balkans*. Vol. II: *Twentieth Century*. Cambridge: Cambridge University Press, 1988.
Johnson, Stowers. *Gay Bulgaria*. London: Robert Hale Limited, 1964.
Joseph, Suad and Barbara L.K. Pillsbury, eds. *Muslim-Christian Conflicts: Economic, Political, and Social Origins*. Boulder: Westview Press, 1978.
Judah, Tim. *The Serbs: History, Myth & the Destruction of Yugoslavia*. New Haven: Yale University Press, 1997.
Kann, Robert A. and Zdenek V. David. *The Peoples of the Eastern Habsburg Lands, 1526–1918*. Seattle: University of Washington Press, 1984.
Karpat, K.H. *The Turks of Bulgaria: Their History, Culture and Political Fate of a Minority*. Istanbul: The Isis Press, 1990.
Kenrick, Donald and Grattan Puxon. *The Destiny of Europe's Gypsies*. New York: Basic Books, 1972.
Keppen, P. *Chronologiceski Ukazatel' materialov dlja istorii inorodcev Evropeskoj Rossii*. St. Petersburg, 1861.
Kinross, Lord. *The Ottoman Centuries: The Rise and Fall of the Turkish Empire*. New York: Morrow Quill Paperbacks, 1977.
Kirk, Dudley. *Europe's Population in the Interwar Years*. Geneva: League of Nations, 1946.
Klein, George and Milan J. Reban, eds. *The Politics of Ethnicity in Eastern Europe*. Boulder/ New York: East European Monographs and Columbia University Press, 1981.

Klyuchevsky, Vasili. *Peter the Great.* New York: Vintage Books, 1958.
Koehl, Robert L. *RKFDV: German Resettlement and Population Policy, 1939–1945.* Cambridge: Harvard University Press, 1957.
Kohn, Hans. *The Habsburg Empire, 1804–1918.* New York: Van Nostrand Reinhold Company, 1961.
Kövágó, László. *Nemzetiségek a mai Magyar-Országon.* Budapest: Kossuth,1981.
Kovrig, Bennett. *Communism in Hungary from Kun to Kádár.* Stanford: Hoover Institution Press, 1979.
Kozhevnikova, V.M. and P.A. Nikolaeva, eds. *Literaturnyi entsiklopedicheskii slovar'.* Moskva: "Sovetskaya entsiklopediya," 1987.
Krupnik, I.I., ed. *Etnicheskie gruppy v gorodakh evropeiskoi chasti SSSR.* Moskva: Moskovskii filial Geographicheskogo obshchestva SSSR, 1987.
————., ed. *Malye i dispersnye etnicheskie gruppy v evropeiskoi chasti SSSR (Geografiya rasselenyi i kul'turnye traditsii).* Moskva: Moskovskii filial Geografischeskogo obshchestva SSSR, 1985.
Kubijovyc, Volodymyr, ed. *Encyclopedia of the Ukraine.* Toronto: University of Toronto Press, 1984.
Kuznetsov, Anatloy. *Babi Yar: A Documentary Novel.* Dell Publishing Co., Inc., 1969.
Ladas, Stephen P. *The Exchange of Minorities: Bulgaria, Greece and Turkey.* New York: The Macmillan Company, 1932.
Leonard, Richard Anthony. *A History of Russian Music.* New York: Minerva Press, 1968.
Lévai, Jenö. *Raoul Wallenberg.* Budapest: Magyar Téka, 1948.
Lewis, E. Glyn. *Multilingualism in the Soviet Union: Aspects of Language Policy and Its Implementation.* The Hague: Mouton, 1972.
Lincoln, W. Bruce. *Nicholas I: Emperor and Autocrat of All the Russias.* Bloomington: Indiana University Press, 1978.
Liégéois, Jean-Pierre. *Gypsies and Travellers.* Strasbourg: Council for Cultural Cooperation, 1987.
Liszt, Franz. *The Gipsy in Music.* 2 Volumes. London: William Reeves Bookseller Limited, 1926.
Łodziński, Dr. Sławomir. *The Protection of National Minorities in Poland* (September 1999). http://www.mineres.lv/reports/poland/poland_NGO.htm.
"The long, hot Czech summer." *Notebook* (2007), pp. 1–5. http://www.errc.org/cikk.php? cikk=1538&archiv=1.
Lorimer, Frank. *The Population of the Soviet Union: History and Prospects.* Geneva: League of Nations, 1946.
Los Angeles *Times Mirror. The Pulse of Europe: A Survey of Political and Social Values and Attitudes.* Washington: Times Mirror Center for The People & The Press, 1992).
Luttichau, Charles V.P. von. *Some Observations on Guerilla Warfare in Russia during World War II.* Unpublished manuscript, n.d.
Luza, Radomir. *The Transfer of the Sudeten Germans: A Study of Czech-German Relations, 1933–1962.* New York: New York University Press, 1964.
Macartney, C.A. *The Habsburg Empire, 1789–1918.* London: Weidenfeld & Nicolson, 1968.
————. *A History of Hungary, 1929–1945.* 2 Parts. New York: Frederick A. Praeger, Inc., 1956.
Macartney, C.A. and A.W. Palmer. *Independent Eastern Europe.* London: The Macmillan Company, Ltd., 1972.
Macdermott, Mercia. *A History of Bulgaria, 1393–1885.* New York: Frederick A. Praeger, Publisher, 1962.
Macedonian Center for International Cooperation. *Applied Education for Young Roma.* Skopje: Macedonian Center for International Cooperation, 2005.
Macedonius. *Stalin and the Macedonian Question.* St. Louis: The Pearlstone Publishing Company, 1948.
Madariaga, Isabel de. *Russia in the Age of Catherine the Great.* London: Weidenfeld and Nicolson, 1981.
Malcolm, Noel. *Kosovo: A Short History.* New York: HarperCollins, 1999.
Mamatey, Victor S. *Rise of the Habsburg Empire, 1526–1815.* New York: Holt, Rinehart and Winston, Inc., 1971.
Mamatey, Victor and Radomir Luza, eds. *A History of the Czechoslovak Republic, 1918–1948.* Princeton: Princeton University Press, 1973.
Marchbin, Andrew Arjeh. "A Critical History of the Origin and Migration of the Gypsies." Doctoral Dissertation. Pittsburgh: University of Pittsburgh, 1939.
Marmullarku, Ramadan. *Albania and the Albanians,* translated by Margot and Bosko Miloslavjevic. New York: Archon Books, 1975.
Mastny, Vojtech. ed., *Soviet/East European Survey, 1984–1986.* Durham: Duke University Press, 1986.

McConnell, Allen. *Tsar Alexander I: Paternalistic Reformer*. New York: Thomas Y. Crowell Company, 1970.
McDowell, Bart. *Gypsies: Wanderers of the World*. Washington: National Geographic Society, 1970.
Memedova, Azbija, Shayna Plaut, Andrea Boscoboinik, and Christian Giordano. Editors. *Roma's Identities in Southeastern Europe: Macedonia*. Rom: Ethnobarometer, 2005.
Meyer, Peter, Bernard D. Weinryb, Eugene Duschinsky, and Nicolas Sylvain, eds. *The Jews in Soviet Satellites*. Syracuse: Syracuse University Press, 1953.
Mesežnikov, Grigorij, Michal Ivantyšyn, and Tom Nicholson. Editors. *Slovakia, 1998–1999: A Global Report on the State of Society*. Bratislava: Institute for Public Affairs, 1999.
Ministere des Affaires Estrangeres et des Cultes. *La Vérité sur les accusations Contre la Bulgare*. Sofia: Imprimerie de l'etat, 1919.
Ministry of Foreign Affairs. *The Bulgarian Question and the Balkan States*. Sofia: State Printing Press, 1919.
Ministry of Interior and Administration, *Programme for the Roma Community in Poland*. Warsaw: Ministry of Interior and Administration, 2004.
Minority Rights Group. *Minorities in the Balkans*. London: Minority Rights Group, 1989.
———. *World Directory of Minorities*. Chicago: St. James Press, 1989.
Mints, Z.G. and L.A. Aboldyeva, eds. *Blokovskii sbornik: Trudy nauchnoi konferentsii, posvyashchennoi izuchenyu zhizni i tvorchestva A.A. Bloka, Mai 1962*. Tartu: Tartuskii gosudarstvennyi universitet, 1964.
Mirsky, D.S., edited by Francis J. Whitfield. *A History of Russian Literature*. New York: Vintage Books, 1958.
Moncure, James A., ed. *Research Guide to European Historical Biography*. 8 Volumes. Washington: Beacham Publishing, Inc., 1992.
Monroe, Will S. *Bohemia and the Cechs*. Boston: L.C. Page and Company, 1910.
Morosan, Vladimir. *Choral Performance in Pre-Revolutionary Russia*. Ann Arbor: UMI Research Press, 1986.
Mosse, W.E. *Alexander II and the Modernization of Russia*. New York: Collier Books, 1970.
Müller-Hill, Benno. *Murderous Science: Elimination by Scientific Selection of Jews, Gypsies, and Others: Germany, 1933–1945*. Translated by George R. Fraser. Oxford: Oxford University Press, 1988.
Narodnoe khozyaistvo SSSR, 1922–1982. Moskva: 'Finansy i Statistika,' 1982.
National Programme for Roma. Zagreb: National Program for Roma, 2004.
Necas, Ctibor. *Nad osudem ceskych a slovenskych Cikánu v letech 1939–1945*. Brno: Univerzita J.E. Purkyne, 1981.
Nesbitt, Jackie. *Fourth World Romani Congress: Serock, Warsaw, Poland, 8th–12th April 1990*. Essex Country: Essex County Council, Education Department, 1990.
Obolensky, Dmitri. *The Penguin Book of Russian Verse*. Baltimore: Penguin Books, 1967.
Office of the High Commissioner for Human Rights and European Roma Rights Center. *Memorandum: The Protection of Roma Rights in Serbia and Montenegro*. Geneva: The United Nations, 2003.
O'Meara, Meghan Appel, editor. *History Behind the Headlines: The Origins of Conflicts Worldwide* (New York: The Gale Group, 2000).
Open Society Institute. *Joint Women's Roma Initiative*, http:www.romawomensinitiatives.org.
———. *Monitoring Local Implementation of the Government Strategy for the Improvement of the Condition of Roma* (Budapest: Open Society Institute, 2004).
Operation Dayswork, DanChurchAid, MCIC. *Challenging the Past: Education for Young Roma*. Copenhagen: Dansk Erhvervstryk, 2004.
Palmer, Alan. *Alexander I: Tsar of War and Peace*. New York: Harper & Row, Publishers, 1974.
Palmer, Stephen E., Jr. and Robert R. King. *Yugoslav Communism and the Macedonian Question*. New York: Archon Books, 1971.
Paris, Edmund. *Genocide in Satellite Croatia, 1941–1945*. Translated by Lois Perkins. Chicago: The American Institute for Balkan Affairs, 1961.
Pearson, Raymond. *National Minorites in Eastern Europe, 1848–1945*. London: The Macmillan Press Ltd., 1983.
Petricevic, Jure. *Nacionalnost Stanovnista Jugoslavije*. Brugg: Verlag Adria, 1983.
Pinkus, Benjamin. *The Jews of the Soviet Union*. Cambridge: Cambridge University Press, 1989.
Pipa, Arshi and Sami Repishti. Editors. *Studies on Kosova*. Boulder: East European Monographs, 1984.
Piper, Franciszek. *Auschwitz: How Many Perished Jews, Poles, Gypsies . . .* Krakow: Poligrafia ITS, 1991.

Poulton, Hugh. *The Balkans: Minorities and States in Conflict*. London: Minority Rights Group, Ltd., 1991.
————. *Minorities in the Balkans*. London: Minority Rights Group, 1989.
Prifti, Peter R. *Socialist Albania since 1644: Domestic and Foreign Developments*. Cambridge: The MIT Press, 1978.
Project on Ethnic Relations. *The Roma in Bulgaria: Collaborative Efforts between Local Authorities and Nongovernmental Organizations*. Princeton: Project on Ethnic Relations, 1998.
————. *The Roma in Hungary: Government Policies, Minority Expectations, and the International Community*. Princeton: Project on Ethnic Relations, 2000.
————. *The Romanies in Central and Eastern Europe: Illusions and Reality*. Princeton: Project on Ethnic Relations, 1992.
Pushkin, Alexander. *Selected Works*, Volume One: *Poetry*. Translated by Irina Zheleznova. Moscow: Progress Publishers, 1974.
Puxon, Grattan. *Rom: Europe's Gypsies*. London: Minority Rights Group,1973.
————. *Rom: Europe's Gypsies*. London: Minority Rights Group, 1975.
————. *Roma: Europe's Gypsies*. London: Minority Rights Group, 1980.
————. *Roma: Europe's Gypsies*. London: Minority Rights Group, 1987.
Ragsdale, Hugh, ed. *Paul I: A Reassessment of His Life and Reign*. Pittsburgh: University Center for International Studies, University of Pittsburgh, 1979.
Rakowski-Harmstone, Teresa, ed. *Communism in Eastern Europe*. Second Edition. Bloomington: Indiana University Press, 1984.
Ramet, Pedro, ed. *Yugoslavia in the 1980s*. Boulder: Westview Press, 1985.
Ramet, Sabrina P. *Nationalism and Federalism in Yugoslavia, 1962–1991*. Second Edition. Bloomington: Indiana University Press, 1992.
Rao, Arpana. *The Other Nomads: Peripatetic Minorities in Cross-Cultural Perspective*. Köln: Bohlau Verlag, 1987.
Redzepi, Nadir and Aleksandra Bojadzieva. *Policies for Improvement of the Employment of Roma in Macedonia*. London: Minority Rights Group International, 2005.
Rehfisch, Farham, ed. *Gypsies, Tinkers and Other Travellers*. New York: Academic Press, 1975.
Reitlinger, Gerald. *The SS: Alibi of a Nation*. New York: Da Capo Press, 1989.
Riasanovsky, Nicholas. *Nicholas I and Official Nationality in Russia, 1825–1855*. Berkeley: University of California Press, 1969.
Robinson, Geroid Tanquary. *Rural Russia under the Old Regime*. Berkeley: University of California Press, 1969.
Robinson, Richard G. Jr. *Famine in Russia, 1891–1892*. New York: Columbia University Press, 1975.
Rogger, Hans. *Russia in the Age of Modernisation and Revolution, 1881–1917*. London: Longman Group Limited, 1983.
Roi, Yaacov and Avi Beker. *Jewish Culture and Identity in the Soviet Union*. New York: New York University Press, 1991.
Rom-Lebedev, I. *Ot Tsyganskogo khora k teatru 'Romen'*. Moskva: "Iskusstvo," 1990.
Rothschild, Joseph. *East Central Europe between the Two World Wars*. Seattle: University of Washington Press, 1990.
Rusinow, Dennison. *Yugoslavia: A Fractured Federalism*. Washington: The Wilson Center Press, 1988.
Rutland, Peter. *The Challenge of Integration: Annual Survey of Eastern Europe and the Former Soviet Union, 1997*. Armonk, NJ: M. E. Sharpe, 1998.
Saab, Ann Pottinger. *Reluctant Icon: Gladstone, Bulgaria, and the Working Class, 1856–1878*. Cambridge: Harvard University Press, 1991.
Sahgal, Preeti. "Aleksandr Blok and Appolon Grigor'ev: A Synthesized View of Life and Art." Doctoral Dissertation. Charlottesville: University of Virginia, 1983.
Schechtman, Joseph B. *Postwar Population Transfers in Europe, 1945–1955*. Philadelphia: University of Pennyslvania Press, 1962.
Scheffel, David Z. *Svinia in Black and White: Slovak Roma and their Neighbors*. Peterborough, ON: Broadview Press, 2005.
Schwicker, Dr. J.H. *Die Zigeuner in Ungarn und Siebenbürgen*. Wien und Teschen: Verlag von Karl Brochasta, 1883.
Seton-Watson, R.W. *A History of the Czechs and Slovaks*. Hamden: Archon Books, 1965.
————. *A History of the Roumanians*. Cambridge: Cambridge University Press, 1934.
————. *The Russian Empire, 1801–1917*. Oxford: Oxford University Press, 1967.
Shabad, Theodore. *Geography of the USSR: A Regional Survey*. New York: Columbia University Press, 1951.

Shashi, Dr. S.S. *Roma: The Gypsy World*. Delhi: Sundeep Prekashan, 1990.
Shaw, Stanford. *History of the Ottoman Empire and Modern Turkey*. Volume I. *Empire of the Gazis: The Rise and Decline of the Ottoman Empire, 1280–1808*. Cambridge: Cambridge University Press, 1976.
Shaw, Stanford J. and Ezel Kural Shaw. *History of the Ottoman Empire and Modern Turkey*. Volume II. *Reform, Revolution, and Republic: The Rise of Modern Turkey, 1808–1975*. Cambridge: Cambridge University Press, 1977.
Shawcross, William. *Dubcek*. New York: Touchstone Books/Simon & Schuster, Inc., 1990.
Shoup, Paul. *Communism and the Yugoslav National Question*. New York: Columbia University Press, 1968.
———. *The East European and Soviet Data Handbook*. New York: Columbia University Press, 1981.
Siftar, Dr. Vanek. *Cigani: Minulost v Sedanjosti*. Murska Sobota: Pomurska Zalozba, 1970.
Simmonds, George W., ed. *Nationalism in the USSR & Eastern Europe in the Era of Brezhnev & Kosygin*. Detroit: The University of Detroit Press, 1977.
Simon, Gerhard. *Nationalismus und Nationalitäten in der Sowjetunion*. Baden-Baden: Nomas Verlagsgesellschaft, 1986.
Simons, William B., ed. *The Constitutions of the Communist World*. Alphen aan den Rijn: Sijthoff & Noordhoff, 1980.
Simsir, Bilal N., ed. *The Turks of Bulgaria in International Fora Documents*. 2 Volumes. Ankara: Turkish Historical Society Printing House, 1990.
Singleton, Fred. *A Short History of the Yugoslav Peoples*. Cambridge: Cambridge University Press, 1989.
———. *Twentieth Century Yugoslavia*. New York: Columbia University Press, 1976.
Sinor, Denis. *History of Hungary*. Westport: Greenwood Press, 1976.
Smith, Graham, ed. *The Nationalities Question in the Soviet Union*. New York: Longman, 1990.
Smolen, Kazimierz. *Auschwitz 1940–1945*. Oswiecimiu: Panstwowe Muzeum w Oswiecimiu, 1969.
Snyder, Louis L. *Encyclopedia of the Third Reich*. New York: Paragon House, 1989.
Sovetskaya istoricheskaya entsiklopediya. Moskva: Izdatel'stvo "Sovetskaya entsiklopediya," 1961.
Spolu International Foundation, *Annual Report 2005*. Utrecht: Spolu International Foundation, 2006.
Staar, Richard and Margit N. Grigory. Editors. *1991 Yearbook on International Communist Affairs*. Stanford: Hoover Institution Press, 1991.
———. Editors. *Yearbook on International Communist Affairs, 1987*. Stanford: Hoover Institution Press, 1987.
———. Editors. *Yearbook on International Communist Affairs, 1990*. Stanford: Hoover Institution Press, 1990.
St. Clair, S.G.B. and Charles A. Brophy. *A Residence in Bulgaria: Or Notes on the Resources and Administration of Turkey*. London: John Murray, 1869.
State Museum of Auschwitz-Birkenau and the Documentary and Cultural Centre of German Sintis and Roms. *Memorial Book: The Gypsies at Auschwitz-Birkenau*. 2 Volumes. München: K.G. Saur, 1993.
Stojanovic, Mihailo D. *The Great Powers and the Balkans, 1875–1878*. Cambridge: Cambridge University Press, 1968.
Stokes, Gale. *The Walls Came Tumbling Down: The Collapse of Communism in Eastern Europe*. New York: Oxford University Press, 1993.
Strukelj, Pavla. *Romi na Slovenskem*. Ljubljana: Cankarjeva Zalozba v Ljubljani, 1980.
Suda, Zdenek. *The Czechoslovak Socialist Republic*. Baltimore: The Johns Hopkins Press, 1969.
Sugar, Peter F. *Southeastern Europe under Ottoman Rule, 1354–1804*. Seattle: University of Washington Press, 1977.
Sugar, Peter F. Péter Hanák, and Tibor Frank. *A History of Hungary*. Bloomington: Indiana University Press, 1990.
Sumner, B.H. *Russia and the Balkans, 1870–1880*. Hamden: Archon Books, 1962.
Surdu, Laura and Mihai Surdu. *Broadening the Agenda: The Status of Romani Women in Romania*. New York: Open Society Institute, 2006.
Suziedelis, Simas and Raphael Sealey, eds. *Encyclopedia Lituanica*. Boston: Encyclopedia Lituanica, 1972.
Swain, Nigel. *Hungary: The Rise and Fall of Feasible Socialism*. London: Verso, 1992.
Swire, Joseph. *King Zog's Albania*. New York: Liverith Publishing Corporation, 1937.
Terras, Victor, ed. *Handbook of Russian Literature*. New Haven: Yale University Press, 1985.
Thapar, Romila. *A History of India*. 2 Volumes. Harmondsworth: Penguin Books, 1974.

BIBLIOGRAPHY 383

Tolstova, S.P., T.A. Zhdanko, S.M. Abramzona, and N.A. Kislyakova. *Narody sredy Azii I Kazakhstana.* 2 volumes. Moskva: Izdatel'stvo akademii nauk SSSR, 1963.
Tomasevic, Nebojsa Bato and Rajko Djuric. *Gypsies of the World.* New York: Henry Holt and Company, 1988.
Tomova, Ilona. *The Gypsies in the Transition Period.* Sofia: International Center for Minority Studies and Intercultural Relations, 1995.
Triska, Jan. F. ed. *Constitutions of the Communist Party-States.* Stanford: The Hoover Institution on War, Revolution and Peace, 1968.
Tritt, Rachael, Jeri Laber, and Lois Whitman. *Struggling for Ethnic Identity: Czechoslovakia's Endangered Gypsies.* New York: Human Rights Watch, 1992.
Troyat, Henri. *Pushkin.* Translated by Nancy Amphoux. New York: Minerva Press, 1975.
———. *Tolstoy.* New York: Dell Publishing Co., Inc., 1969.
Tsameryan, I.P. *Teoreticheskie problemy obrazovaniya i razvitiya sovetskogo mnogonatsional'nogo gosudarstvo.* Moskva: Izdatel'stvo "Nauka," 1973.
Tsentral'noe Statisticheskoe Upravlenie SSSR. *Naselenie SSSR: Po dannym Vsesoyuznoi perepisi neseleniya 1979 goda.* Moskva: Izdatel'stvo politicheskoi literatury, 1980.
Tyrnauer, Gabriel. *Gypsies and the Holocaust: A Bibliography and Introductory Essay.* Montreal: Montreal Institute for Genocide Studies, 1991.
United Nations Committee on the Rights of the Child. *Concluding Observations of the Committee on the Rights of the Child: CROATIA.* Geneva: United Nations, 2004.
United Nations Development Programme. *Faces of Poverty, Faces of Hope: Vulnerability Profiles for Decade of Roma Inclusion Countries.* Bratislava: United Nations Development Programme, 2005.
United Nations. International Convention on the Elimination of All Forms of Racial Discrimination. *Bosnia and Herzegovina.* CERD/C/464/Add. 1 May 20, 2005.
———. International Committee on the Elimination of All Forms of Racial Discrimination. *Bosnia and Herzegovina.* CERD/C/SR.1735.
United States Agency for International Development. *US AID from the American People: Macedonia.* Washington, D.C.: United States Agency for International Development, 2005.
United States Congress. *Romani Human Rights in Europe.* Hearing before the Commission on Security and Cooperation in Europe, 104th Congress, Second Session, July 21, 1998. Washington: U.S. Government Printing Office, 1998.
United States Department of State. *Bulgaria Country Report on Human Rights Practices for 1998.* Washington, D.C.: Bureau of Democracy, Human Rights, and Labor, 1999.
United States Holocaust Memorial Museum. *Fifty Years Ago: Revolt Amid the Darkness.* Washington: United States Holocaust Memorial Museum, 1993.
Vaňo, Boris. *Projection of Roma Population in Slovakia until 2025.* Translated by František Bernadi. Bratislava: Institute of Informatics and Statistics, 2002.
———. *The Demographic Characteristics of Roma Population in Slovakia.* Translated by František Bernadič. Bratislava: Institute of Informatics and Statistics, Demographic Research Centre, 2001.
Vickers, Robert H. *History of Bohemia.* Chicago: Charles Sergel Company, 1894.
Vickers, Miranda and James Pettifer, *Albania: From Anarchy to a Balkan Identity.* New York: New York University Press, 1997.
Vucinich, Wayne S., ed. *The Peasant in Nineteenth Century Russia.* Stanford: Stanford University Press, 1968.
Vukanovic, Tatomir. *Romi (Tsigani) u Jugoslaviji.* Vranje: Nova Jugoslavija, 1983.
Walker, Alan. *Franz Liszt.* Volume I: *The Virtuoso Years, 1811–1847.* New York: Alfred A. Knopf, 1983.
———. *Franz Liszt.* Volume II: *The Weimar Years, 1848–1861.* New York: Alfred A. Knopf, 1989.
Weinberg, Gerhard L. *Germany and the Soviet Union, 1939–1941.* Leiden: E.J. Brill, 1972.
Werth, Alexander. *Russia at War, 1941–1945.* New York: E.P. Dutton & Company, Inc., 1964.
West, Rebecca. *Black Lamb and Grey Falcon: A Journey through Yugoslavia.* New York: Penguin Books, 1982.
Wheaton, Bernard and Zdenek Kavan. *The Velvet Revolution: Czechoslovakia, 1988–1991.* Boulder: Westview Press, 1992.
Wieczynski, Joseph L. Editor. *The Modern Encyclopedia of Russian and Soviet History.* Gulf Breeze: Academic International Press, 1976-present.
Wistrich, Robert. *Who's Who in Nazi Germany.* New York: Bonanza Books, 1984.

Wixman, Robert. *The Peoples of the USSR: An Ethnographic Handbook.* Armonk: M.E. Sharpe, Inc., 1988.
World Organization Against Torture. *State Violence in Serbia and Montenegro: An Alternative Report to the United Nations Human Rights Committee.* Geneva: World Organisation Against Torture, 2004.
Yahil, Leni. *The Holocaust: The Fate of European Jewry.* New York: Oxford University Press, 1990.
Yarmolinsky, Avrahm. *Turgenev: The Man, His Art and His Age.* New York: The Orion Press, 1959.
Yugoslavia's Way: The Program of the League of the Communists of Yugoslavia. Translated by Stopyan Pribechevich. New York: All Nations Press, 1958.
Zaninovich, M. George. *The Development of Socialist Yugoslavia.* Baltimore: The Johns Hopkins University Press, 1968.
Závěrečné stanovisko veřejného ochránce práv ve věci sterilizací prováděných v rozporu s právem a návrhy opatření k nápravě. Praha: Veřejny Ochránce Práv Ombudsman, 2005.
Zoon, Ina. *On the Margins: Slovakia.* New York: Open Society Institute, 2001.
Zotiades, George B. *The Macedonian Controversy.* Thessaloniki: Society for Macedonian Studies, 1954.

CORRESPONDENCE

Commission on Security and Cooperation in Europe to Secretary of State Madeline Albright, July 15, 1999, 2 pages.
Schlager, Erika to David Crowe, September 13,1999.

NEWSPAPERS AND MAGAZINES

Austin American Statesman
Chicago Tribune
The Chronicle of Higher Education
The Economist
The European
Greensboro *News & Record*
The Guardian
Los Angeles *Times Mirror*
The New York Times
The New Yorker
The New York Review of Books
USA Today
The Washington Post
The Washington Post Magazine
Winston-Salem Journal
World Press Review

I·N·D·E·X